The Grey House
Homeland
Security
Directory

2008

Fifth Edition

The Grey House Homeland Security Directory

Federal Agencies, State Agencies, Products & Services and Information Resources

Grey House Publishing

MILLERTON, NY 12546

PUBLISHER:	Leslie Mackenzie
EDITOR:	Richard Gottlieb
EDITORIAL DIRECTOR:	Laura Mars-Proietti
PRODUCTION MANAGER:	Karen Stevens
PRODUCTION ASSISTANTS:	Anthony delVecchio; Sarah Miles; Jael Powell; Erica Schneider; Bobbie-Jo Scutt
COMPOSITION:	David Garoogian
MARKETING DIRECTOR:	Jessica Moody

Grey House Publishing, Inc.
185 Millerton Road
Millerton, NY 12546
518.789.8700
FAX 518.789.0545
www.greyhouse.com
e-mail: books @greyhouse.com

First edition published 2004
Printed in the USA

The Grey House homeland security directory : federal agencies, state agencies, products & services and information resources. – 5th ed. (2008)-
    1,022 p. 27.5 cm.
    Annual
    Includes index.
1. Civil defense--United States--Directories. 2. National security--United States--Directories. I. Title: Homeland security directory.

UA927 .G74
363.3'5—dc21
ISBN: 978-1-59237-196-9 softcover

Table of Contents

Introduction

Department of Homeland Security Organizational Charts

SECTION FOUR: INDUSTRY RESOURCES

SECTION FIVE: INDEXES

Introduction

This is the fifth edition of *The Grey House Homeland Security Directory*. Six years after the 9/11 terrorist attack and the creation of The Department of Homeland Security, the national threat level is Elevated, and High for all domestic and international flights. Fighting the War on Terror – from our troops in Iraq, to local DHS funding, to screening bags at a baseball game – continues to be not only controversial, but often downright divisive among public and private leaders, as well as next-door neighbors.

The Department of Homeland Security continues to reorganize for maximum efficiency. Following this Introduction you'll find 25 up-to-the-minute Organizational Charts from DHS, designed to "increase its ability to prepare, prevent, and respond to terrorist attacks and other emergencies . . . and to better integrate the Department and give Department employees better tools to accomplish their mission." Changes include:

- Improving national response and recovery efforts by focusing FEMA on its core functions of response and recovery;
- Integration of the Federal Air Marshal Service into the Transportation Security Administration for broader aviation security efforts;
- Merging Legislative and Intergovernmental Affairs to better share homeland security information with members of Congress and state and local officials;
- Assigning the Office of Security to the Management Directorate to better manage information systems, contractual activities, security accreditation, training and resources.

This new edition reflects these organizational changes, as well as hundreds of key personnel changes and the addition of 1,013 more companies that supply products and services for the homeland security industry.

CONTENT

This fifth edition of *The Grey House Homeland Security Directory* was prepared in the Grey House tradition of valuable resource directories. The carefully arranged sections, and current, detailed listings include 1,340 informative profiles of Federal and State agencies, 3,238 private company profiles, and 728 homeland security information resources. With 1,042 pages, a total of 5,306 listings and 13,975 key executives – 88 more pages, 1,095 more listings and 985 more executive names – it is once again the most comprehensive resource on homeland security available.

The research for this fifth edition of *The Grey House Homeland Security Directory* utilized Internet research, personal phone calls, fax and e-mail campaigns. We especially appreciate the State officials who took the time to answer our calls and respond to faxes, thus creating current, valuable State chapters.

ARRANGEMENT

Section One: Federal Agencies

This first section comprises 18 main chapters and 12 subchapters, including the Department of Homeland Security, its Directorates, and relevant branches of the Federal government. Refer to the Table of Contents for specific chapter arrangement. The headquarters is the first listing in each chapter, and is gray-shaded for quick recognition. Each of the 534 listings in this Federal section offers clear, concise descriptions as they relate to homeland security. All Federal listings have a list of key officials, many of them with a direct phone number and e-mail.

Section Two: State Agencies

The 806 listings in Section Two are arranged in alphabetical State chapters. The first listing in each state is the Main Homeland Security Office, and includes the Governor, Lieutenant Governor, Attorney General and the person most responsible for homeland security. As with the Federal officials, many State officials have a direct phone number and e-mail. Following the Main Homeland Security Office listing, each State chapter is comprised of agencies with homeland security responsibility. You will find Emergency Management and State Police, Emergency Services Agencies, the National Guard and a host of other agencies. The listings are arranged in alphabetical order, for easy access. Inconsistency still exists among States in regard to homeland security resources, resulting in a varying number of listings from State to State.

As State agencies continue to deal with changing responsibilities and variances in funding, this section provides comprehensive coverage of all those offices with responsibility for securing the homeland, before, during, or after a disaster. New to this edition, for example, are dozens of state contingency planning agencies.

Section Three: Manufacturers & Suppliers
This section begins with an alphabetical list of 753 (38 more than last edition) products and services represented by the 3,238 companies following the Product Listing. These private companies manufacture products and provide services of value to the homeland security industry, ranging from Access Control Locking Systems to Work Station Security Software.

The private sector continues to fine-tune its role in homeland security, as more companies offer more products and services in this demanding industry. We focused on companies involved in not only new technology such as biometrics, increasingly used for identification, fraud prevention, security, and consumer applications, but also improvements in existing technology such as telephony and access control.

These companies – 1,013 more than in the fourth edition -- are listed alphabetically by company name, and include address, phone, fax and web site. Each profile also includes a company description and a listing of the products and services it provides. Key executives' names often include direct phone numbers and e-mails. All companies profiled are carefully indexed by product or service.

Section Four: Industry Resources
This section of *The Grey House Homeland Security Directory* contains a variety of information resources from which you can do further research in the homeland security industry. You will find 728 resources (35 more than the last edition) that include Associations, Periodicals, Trade Shows & Seminars, Directories & Databases, and Web Sites. All resource listings include name, address, phone, fax, web site, description and key executives.

Section Five: Indexes
> **Entry Name Index** is an alphabetical list of all entries in the directory, with all State Agencies organized under their State.
>
> **Key Personnel Index** is an alphabetical list of all government officials and company executives whose responsibilities include an aspect of homeland security, with their affiliation.
>
> **Products & Services Index** lists alphabetically the 728 products and services in the homeland security industry, followed by the companies that offer that product or service.

We are pleased to offer this fifth edition of this comprehensive, completely revised resource of this changing industry. As the homeland security community continues to define itself, subsequent editions of *The Grey House Homeland Security Directory* will continue to be the premier reference directory on the subject.

Other Grey House directories in the Safety & Security field include *The Grey House Safety & Security Directory, The Grey House Transportation Security Directory & Handbook,* and *The Grey House Biometric Information Directory.*

As with many Grey House directories, *The Grey House Homeland Security Directory* is also available online, or as a customized database. Visit www.greyhouse.com for more information.

Praise for previous editions:
> "The Federal . . . section goes beyond . . . a compendium of contact information, though it does that extremely well. (It) **delivers a perspective of this complex organization that few could duplicate.** Every level . . . is described with a clarity and brevity that is refreshing.
>
> **"I was challenged to find (on the Internet) even a small percentage of the information provided . . . this is a must-have for anyone who is a preparedness service/product provider, or engaged in emergency response, business continuity and disaster recovery planning... I just can't find fault with this work."**

Edward Pearce, Associate Editor
Disaster Recovery Journal

FIND THE **TECHNOLOGY.**
BE THE **SOLUTION.**
SECURE OUR **FUTURE.**

★ **GOVSEC**™
THE GOVERNMENT SECURITY EXPO & CONFERENCE

A GOVSEC EVENT
US LAW ENFORCEMENT™
CONFERENCE & EXPOSITION

A GOVSEC EVENT
READY!™
THE EMERGENCY PREPAREDNESS AND
RESPONSE CONFERENCE & EXPOSITION

Whether your responsibility is government security, IT security or homeland security, your charge has never been more challenging than it is right now.

You need to secure your systems.
Assure continued operations.
Protect your infrastructure.
And do your job with fewer resources and higher expectations, where failure is not an option.

That's why you need to be at GovSec, U.S. Law and Ready! Conference and Exposition this year.

From an expo that's the **ONLY** full spectrum, 360-degree view of the latest products, tools and technology, to the industry's #1 rated learning event for homeland security and the must-attend networking events of the year... **you'll find everything you need to meet today's ever-challenging physical and IT security requirements at GovSec, U.S. Law and Ready! — America's Premier Homeland Security Event.**

REGISTER AT WWW.GOVSECINFO.COM
WITH **REGISTRATION CODE: GHPO8** FOR FREE EXPO REGISTRATION, PLUS EARLY-BIRD CONFERENCE RATES.

APRIL.23-24.2008
WASHINGTON CONVENTION CENTER
WASHINGTON, DC
WWW.GOVSECINFO.COM

FOR EVENT INFORMATION, CALL 800.687.7469 | **TO EXHIBIT,** CALL 800.687.7469 EXT.239

User Guide

Listings in *The Grey House Homeland Security Directory* are arranged as follows:

Federal Agencies are arranged in Federal Government Department chapters -- see Table of Contents for complete list. The first listing in each Federal chapter is the main office, or department headquarters, and is shaded in gray. Following the main listing, the entries are loosely grouped by certain criteria, often mission themes and jurisdiction. In the case of multi-layers, "children" are placed under "parents." For example, in the Department of Agriculture chapter, there is a listing for Food Safety & Inspection Service (FSIS), an agency under USDA. Following FSIS, are Office of Pubic Health & Science and Office of Food Service & Emergency Preparedness, both of which fall under FSIS.

State Agencies are arranged in State chapters – from Alabama to Wyoming. The first listing in each State chapter is the Main Homeland Security Office for that state. All Main Homeland Security listings include Governors, Lieutenant Governors, and Attorney Generals, as well as the person most responsible for homeland security who often holds another position within the state as well. Following the Main Homeland Security listing, the entries are alphabetical.

Companies are arranged alphabetically by company name. All company listings include contact information, company description as it relates to homeland security, and a list of the products and services the company provides.

Industry Resources are arranged by type of resource – Associations, Periodicals, Directories & Databases, Shows & Seminars, and then alphabetically by title.

Below is a sample listing illustrating each field of information that is included in a Federal or State listing. Each numbered item is described on the following page.

---

1 → **National Communication Systems**
Directorate of Information Analysis & Infrastructure Protection

2 → 3801 Nebraska Avenue NW
Washington, DC 20016

3 → 703-607-6100

4 → 703-607-4802

5 → info@ncs.gov

6 → www.ncs.gov

7 → The National Communication System's mission is to assist the President, the National Security Council, the Director of the Office of Science and Technology Policy and the Director of the Office of Management and Budget in the exercise of telecommunications functions and responsibilities. Duties include the coordination of the planning and provision of national security and emergency preparedness communications for the Federal government under all circumstances, including crisis or emergency, attack, recovery and reconstitution.

8 → **Major General Bruce M Lawlor**
Manager
Phone: 202-282-8000
Email: blawlor@ncs.gov

Brenton C Greene
Deputy Manager
Phone: 703-607-6100
Email: bgreene@ncs.gov

Fred Herr
Critical Infrastructure Protection Division
Phone: 703-607-6221
Email: fherr@ncs.gov

User Key

Each numbered item is a field of information that appears in a typical listing; see sample listing, opposite.

---

1. ➤ **Title:** Official name of Federal or State Agency. The second line will indicate the Government department it's under. The Federal listings that are shaded in gray indicate the main office, or headquarters.

2. ➤ **Address:** Physical location.

3. ➤ **Phone:** Main number of Agency.

4. ➤ **Fax:** Main fax number of Agency.

5. ➤ **E-mail:** Main e-mail address of Agency.

6. ➤ **Website:** Main website address of Agency. If it's a general site, links will lead you to the specific office or subdivision.

7. ➤ **Description:** Includes mission and its relevance to Homeland Security. Mission statements of many Government Agencies have been recently modified to specifically encompass homeland security responsibilities.

8. ➤ **Key Personnel:** Top Government officials located within the Agency. Most names include direct telephone numbers and e-mail addresses.

Note: The Company Listings in Section Three include the Products and Services that they provide, in addition to a company description. The Products & Services Index provides an easy way to find information on the specific product or services you are looking for. The company officials listed in the company profiles often include direct e-mails.

U.S. DEPARTMENT OF HOMELAND SECURITY

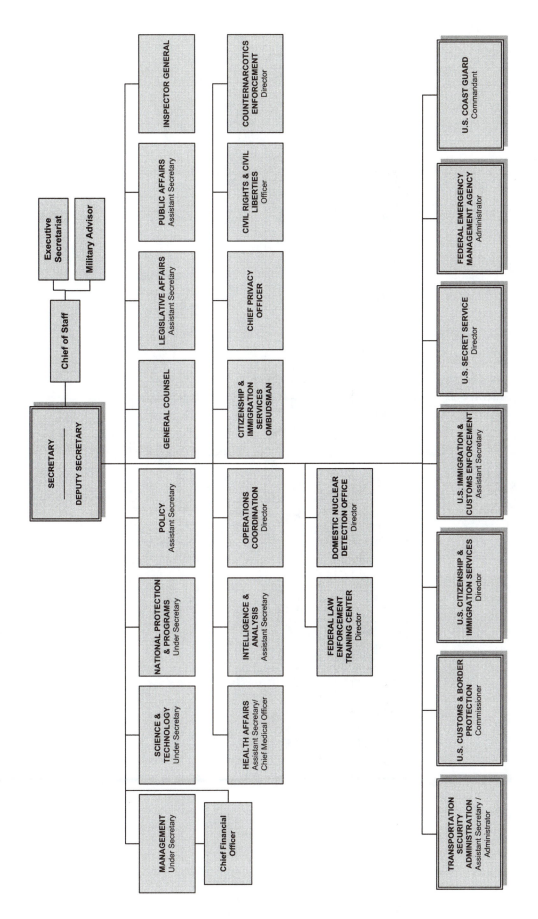

Approved 4/1/2007

TRANSPORTATION SECURITY ADMINISTRATION

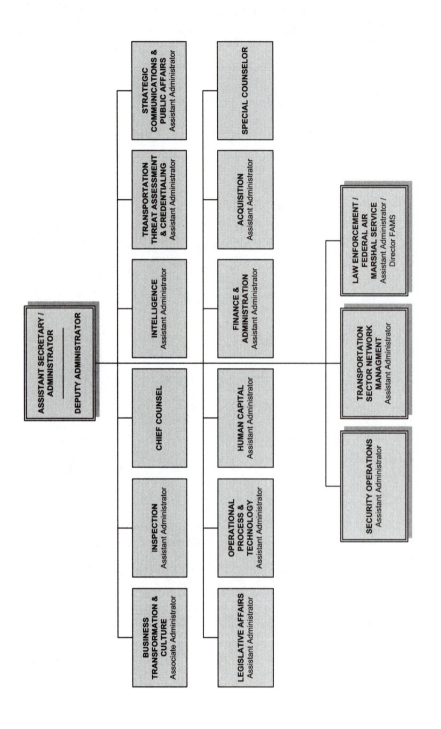

ASSISTANT SECRETARY / ADMINISTRATOR

DEPUTY ADMINISTRATOR

BUSINESS TRANSFORMATION & CULTURE
Associate Administrator

INSPECTION
Assistant Administrator

CHIEF COUNSEL

INTELLIGENCE
Assistant Administrator

TRANSPORTATION THREAT ASSESSMENT & CREDENTIALING
Assistant Administrator

STRATEGIC COMMUNICATIONS & PUBLIC AFFAIRS
Assistant Administrator

LEGISLATIVE AFFAIRS
Assistant Administrator

OPERATIONAL PROCESS & TECHNOLOGY
Assistant Administrator

HUMAN CAPITAL
Assistant Administrator

FINANCE & ADMINISTRATION
Assistant Administrator

ACQUISITION
Assistant Administrator

SPECIAL COUNSELOR

SECURITY OPERATIONS
Assistant Administrator

TRANSPORTATION SECTOR NETWORK MANAGMENT
Assistant Administrator

LAW ENFORCEMENT / FEDERAL AIR MARSHAL SERVICE
Assistant Administrator / Director FAMS

Approved 4/1/2007

U.S. Customs & Border Protection

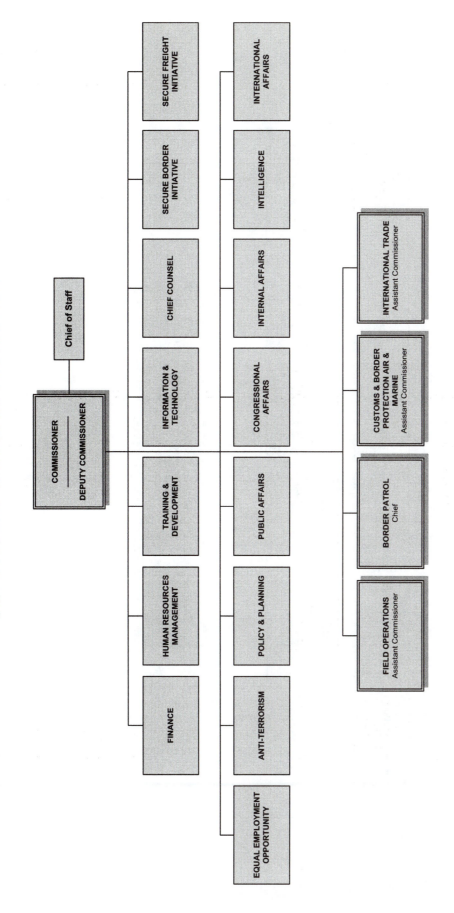

U.S. Citizenship & Immigration Services

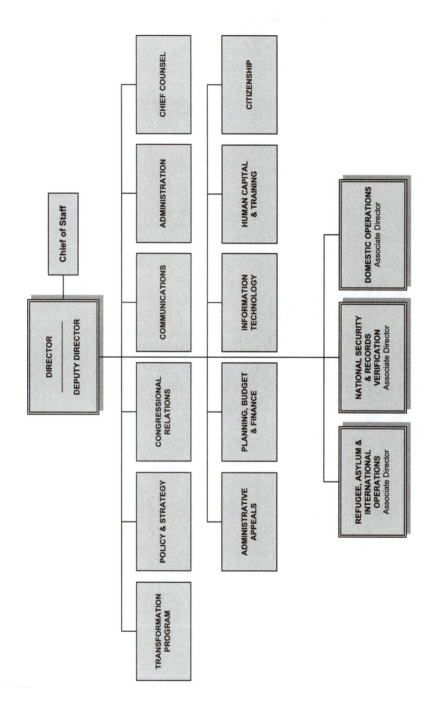

U.S. IMMIGRATION & CUSTOMS ENFORCEMENT

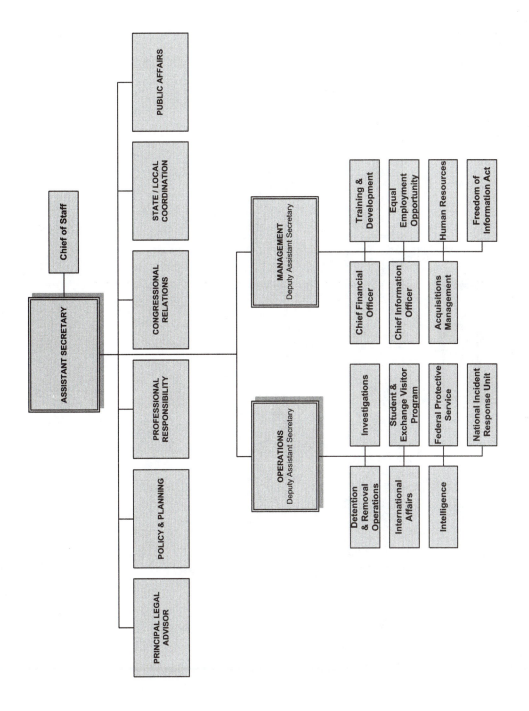

Approved 4/1/2007

U.S. SECRET SERVICE

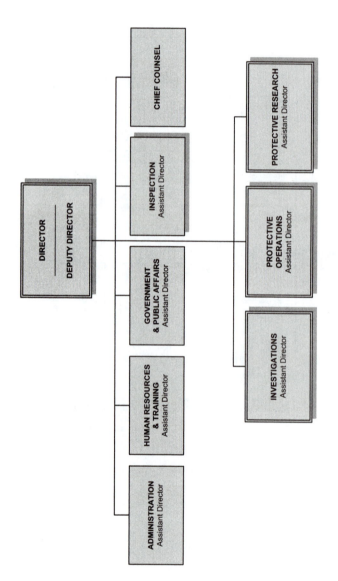

DIRECTOR
DEPUTY DIRECTOR

ADMINISTRATION
Assistant Director

HUMAN RESOURCES & TRAINING
Assistant Director

GOVERNMENT & PUBLIC AFFAIRS
Assistant Director

INSPECTION
Assistant Director

CHIEF COUNSEL

INVESTIGATIONS
Assistant Director

PROTECTIVE OPERATIONS
Assistant Director

PROTECTIVE RESEARCH
Assistant Director

Approved 4/1/2007

FEDERAL EMERGENCY MANAGEMENT AGENCY

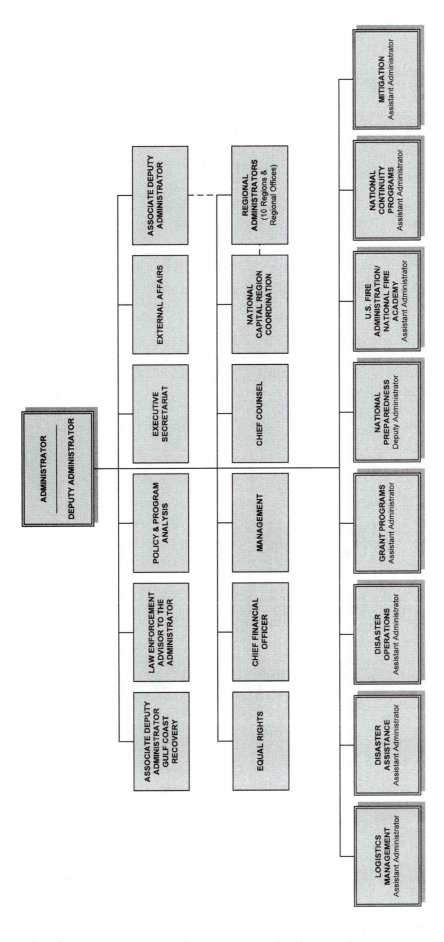

Approved 4/1/2007

U.S. COAST GUARD

```
                    ┌──────────────────────┐
                    │     COMMANDANT       │
                    │──────────────────────│
                    │   VICE COMMANDANT    │
                    └──────────────────────┘
                               │
                    ┌──────────────────────┐
                    │   CHIEF OF STAFF     │
                    └──────────────────────┘
```

- HUMAN RESOURCES
- INTELLIGENCE & CRIMINAL INVESTIGATIONS
- OPERATIONS
- ENGINEERING & LOGISTICS
- PLANS & POLICY
- COMMAND, CONTROL, COMMUNICATIONS, COMPUTERS & INFORMATION TECHNOLOGY
- RESOURCES
- ACQUISITION

PACIFIC AREA
Commander

- Districts
  - Mission Execution Units
- Maintenance & Logistics Command
  - Mission Support Units

ATLANTIC AREA
Commander

- Districts
  - Mission Execution Units
- Maintenance & Logistics Command
  - Mission Support Units

Approved 4/1/2007

OFFICE OF THE UNDER SECRETARY FOR MANAGEMENT

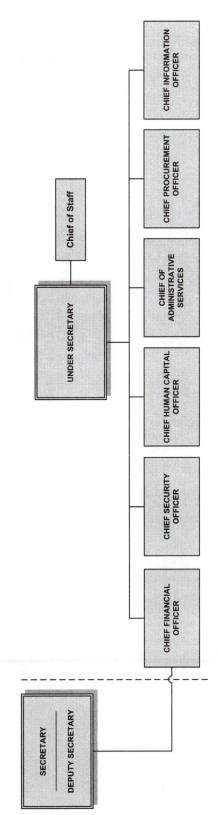

SECRETARY
DEPUTY SECRETARY

UNDER SECRETARY

Chief of Staff

CHIEF FINANCIAL OFFICER

CHIEF SECURITY OFFICER

CHIEF HUMAN CAPITAL OFFICER

CHIEF OF ADMINISTRATIVE SERVICES

CHIEF PROCUREMENT OFFICER

CHIEF INFORMATION OFFICER

Approved 4/1/2007

OFFICE OF THE UNDER SECRETARY FOR SCIENCE & TECHNOLOGY

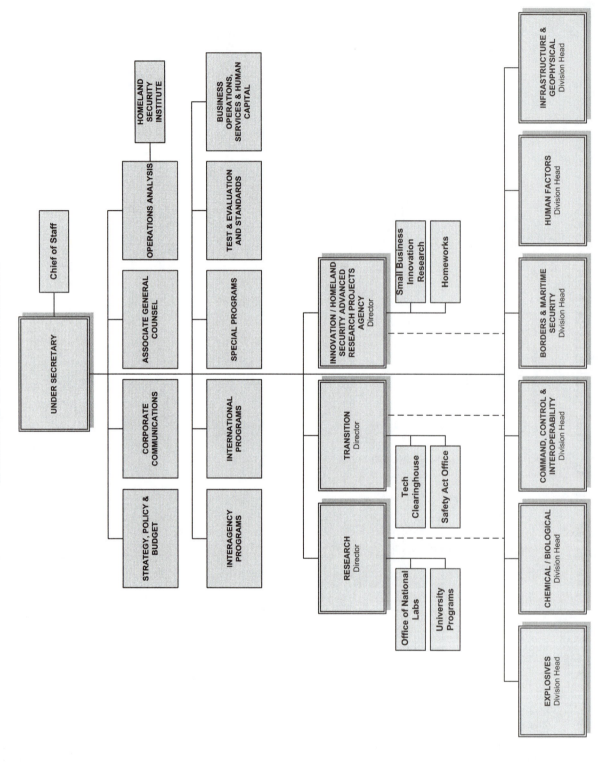

UNDER SECRETARY

Chief of Staff

STRATEGY, POLICY & BUDGET

CORPORATE COMMUNICATIONS

ASSOCIATE GENERAL COUNSEL

OPERATIONS ANALYSIS

HOMELAND SECURITY INSTITUTE

INTERAGENCY PROGRAMS

INTERNATIONAL PROGRAMS

SPECIAL PROGRAMS

TEST & EVALUATION AND STANDARDS

BUSINESS OPERATIONS, SERVICES & HUMAN CAPITAL

RESEARCH
Director

TRANSITION
Director

INNOVATION / HOMELAND SECURITY ADVANCED RESEARCH PROJECTS AGENCY
Director

Office of National Labs

University Programs

Tech Clearinghouse

Safety Act Office

Small Business Innovation Research

Homeworks

EXPLOSIVES
Division Head

CHEMICAL / BIOLOGICAL
Division Head

COMMAND, CONTROL & INTEROPERABILITY
Division Head

BORDERS & MARITIME SECURITY
Division Head

HUMAN FACTORS
Division Head

INFRASTRUCTURE & GEOPHYSICAL
Division Head

OFFICE OF THE UNDER SECRETARY FOR NATIONAL PROTECTION & PROGRAMS

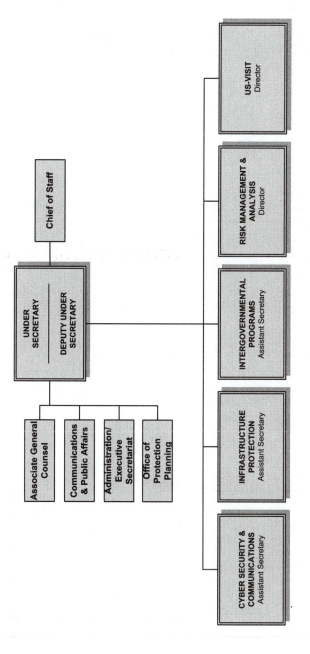

Chief of Staff

UNDER SECRETARY

DEPUTY UNDER SECRETARY

Associate General Counsel

Communications & Public Affairs

Administration/ Executive Secretariat

Office of Protection Planning

CYBER SECURITY & COMMUNICATIONS
Assistant Secretary

INFRASTRUCTURE PROTECTION
Assistant Secretary

INTERGOVERNMENTAL PROGRAMS
Assistant Secretary

RISK MANAGEMENT & ANALYSIS
Director

US-VISIT
Director

Approved 4/1/2007

OFFICE OF THE ASSISTANT SECRETARY FOR POLICY[1]

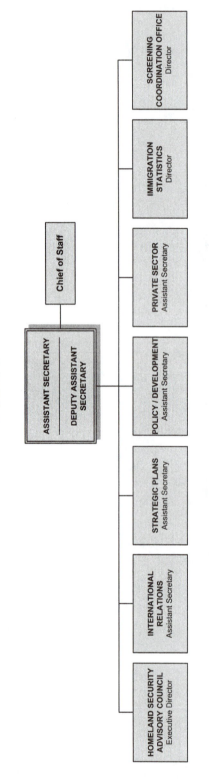

ASSISTANT SECRETARY

DEPUTY ASSISTANT SECRETARY

Chief of Staff

HOMELAND SECURITY ADVISORY COUNCIL
Executive Director

INTERNATIONAL RELATIONS
Assistant Secretary

STRATEGIC PLANS
Assistant Secretary

POLICY / DEVELOPMENT
Assistant Secretary

PRIVATE SECTOR
Assistant Secretary

IMMIGRATION STATISTICS
Director

SCREENING COORDINATION OFFICE
Director

1. The Administration has proposed legislation requesting authorization to title the head of this office as "Under Secretary for Policy."

Approved 4/1/2007

OFFICE OF THE GENERAL COUNSEL

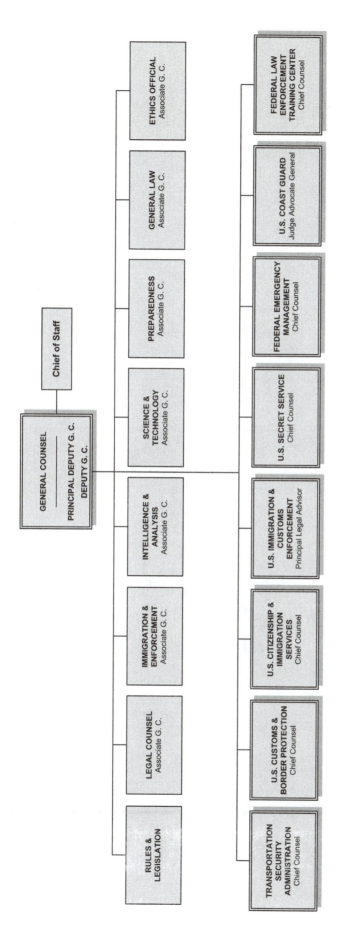

GENERAL COUNSEL
PRINCIPAL DEPUTY G. C.
DEPUTY G. C.

Chief of Staff

RULES & LEGISLATION

LEGAL COUNSEL
Associate G. C.

IMMIGRATION & ENFORCEMENT
Associate G. C.

INTELLIGENCE & ANALYSIS
Associate G. C.

SCIENCE & TECHNOLOGY
Associate G. C.

PREPAREDNESS
Associate G. C.

GENERAL LAW
Associate G. C.

ETHICS OFFICIAL
Associate G. C.

TRANSPORTATION SECURITY ADMINISTRATION
Chief Counsel

U.S. CUSTOMS & BORDER PROTECTION
Chief Counsel

U.S. CITIZENSHIP & IMMIGRATION SERVICES
Chief Counsel

U.S. IMMIGRATION & CUSTOMS ENFORCEMENT
Principal Legal Advisor

U.S. SECRET SERVICE
Chief Counsel

FEDERAL EMERGENCY MANAGEMENT
Chief Counsel

U.S. COAST GUARD
Judge Advocate General

FEDERAL LAW ENFORCEMENT TRAINING CENTER
Chief Counsel

Approved 4/1/2007

OFFICE OF THE ASSISTANT SECRETARY FOR LEGISLATIVE AFFAIRS

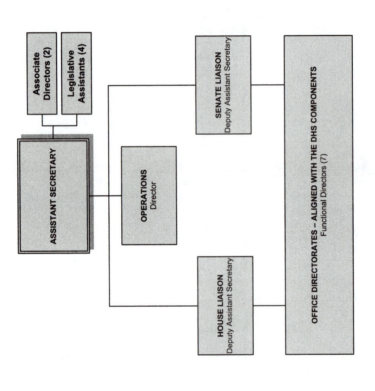

ASSISTANT SECRETARY

Associate Directors (2)

Legislative Assistants (4)

OPERATIONS
Director

HOUSE LIAISON
Deputy Assistant Secretary

SENATE LIAISON
Deputy Assistant Secretary

OFFICE DIRECTORATES – ALIGNED WITH THE DHS COMPONENTS
Functional Directors (7)

Approved 4/1/2007

OFFICE OF THE ASSISTANT SECRETARY FOR PUBLIC AFFAIRS

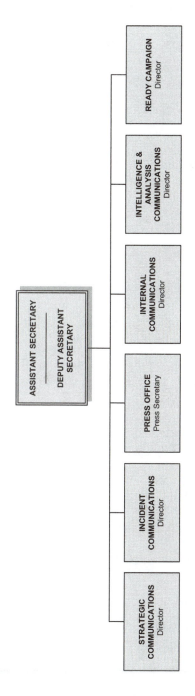

ASSISTANT SECRETARY

DEPUTY ASSISTANT SECRETARY

STRATEGIC COMMUNICATIONS
Director

INCIDENT COMMUNICATIONS
Director

PRESS OFFICE
Press Secretary

INTERNAL COMMUNICATIONS
Director

INTELLIGENCE & ANALYSIS COMMUNICATIONS
Director

READY CAMPAIGN
Director

Approved 4/1/2007

OFFICE OF THE INSPECTOR GENERAL

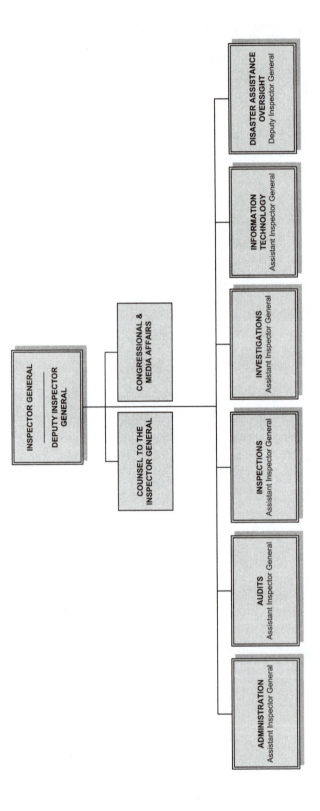

INSPECTOR GENERAL
DEPUTY INSPECTOR GENERAL

COUNSEL TO THE INSPECTOR GENERAL

CONGRESSIONAL & MEDIA AFFAIRS

ADMINISTRATION
Assistant Inspector General

AUDITS
Assistant Inspector General

INSPECTIONS
Assistant Inspector General

INVESTIGATIONS
Assistant Inspector General

INFORMATION TECHNOLOGY
Assistant Inspector General

DISASTER ASSISTANCE OVERSIGHT
Deputy Inspector General

Approved 4/1/2007

OFFICE OF THE ASSISTANT SECRETARY FOR HEALTH AFFAIRS

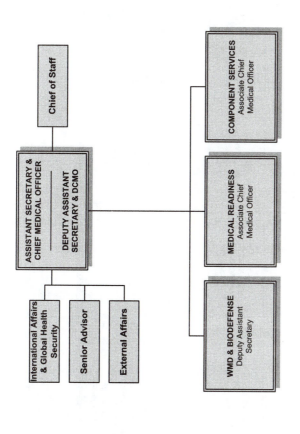

Chief of Staff

ASSISTANT SECRETARY & CHIEF MEDICAL OFFICER

DEPUTY ASSISTANT SECRETARY & DCMO

International Affairs & Global Health Security

Senior Advisor

External Affairs

WMD & BIODEFENSE
Deputy Assistant Secretary

MEDICAL READINESS
Associate Chief Medical Officer

COMPONENT SERVICES
Associate Chief Medical Officer

OFFICE OF THE ASSISTANT SECRETARY FOR INTELLIGENCE & ANALYSIS

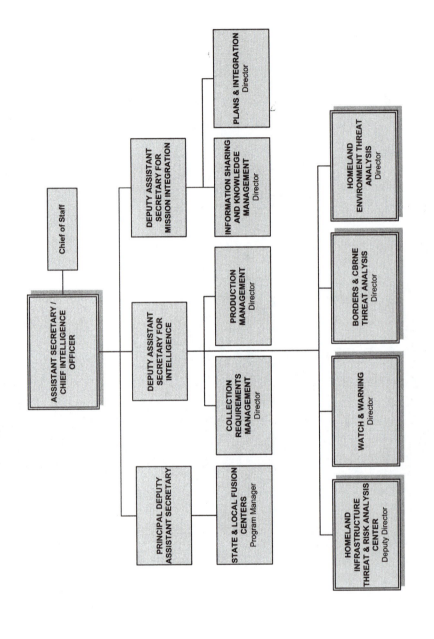

OFFICE OF THE DIRECTOR OF OPERATIONS COORDINATION

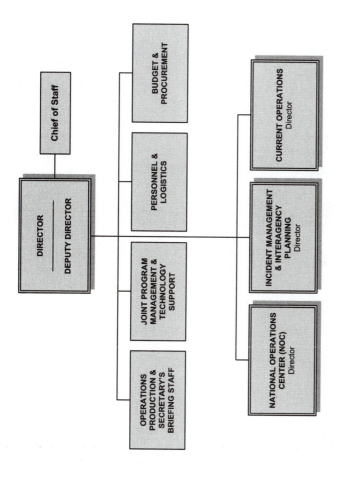

Chief of Staff

DIRECTOR
DEPUTY DIRECTOR

OPERATIONS PRODUCTION & SECRETARY'S BRIEFING STAFF

JOINT PROGRAM MANAGEMENT & TECHNOLOGY SUPPORT

PERSONNEL & LOGISTICS

BUDGET & PROCUREMENT

NATIONAL OPERATIONS CENTER (NOC)
Director

INCIDENT MANAGEMENT & INTERAGENCY PLANNING
Director

CURRENT OPERATIONS
Director

OFFICE OF THE CITIZENSHIP AND IMMIGRATION SERVICES

OMBUDSMAN

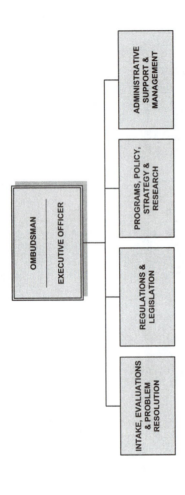

OMBUDSMAN

EXECUTIVE OFFICER

INTAKE, EVALUATIONS & PROBLEM RESOLUTION

REGULATIONS & LEGISLATION

PROGRAMS, POLICY, STRATEGY & RESEARCH

ADMINISTRATIVE SUPPORT & MANAGEMENT

Approved 4/1/2007

OFFICE OF THE CHIEF PRIVACY OFFICER

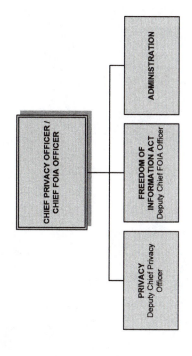

CHIEF PRIVACY OFFICER / CHIEF FOIA OFFICER

PRIVACY
Deputy Chief Privacy Officer

FREEDOM OF INFORMATION ACT
Deputy Chief FOIA Officer

ADMINISTRATION

Approved 4/1/2007

CIVIL RIGHTS & CIVIL LIBERTIES

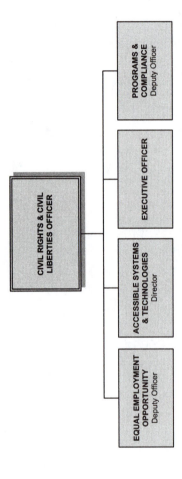

CIVIL RIGHTS & CIVIL LIBERTIES OFFICER

EQUAL EMPLOYMENT OPPORTUNITY
Deputy Officer

ACCESSIBLE SYSTEMS & TECHNOLOGIES
Director

EXECUTIVE OFFICER

PROGRAMS & COMPLIANCE
Deputy Officer

Approved 4/1/2007

COUNTERNARCOTICS ENFORCEMENT

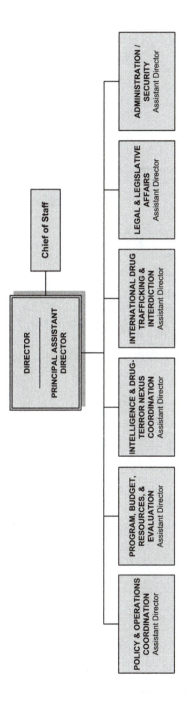

DIRECTOR

PRINCIPAL ASSISTANT DIRECTOR

Chief of Staff

POLICY & OPERATIONS COORDINATION
Assistant Director

PROGRAM, BUDGET, RESOURCES, & EVALUATION
Assistant Director

INTELLIGENCE & DRUG-TERROR NEXUS COORDINATION
Assistant Director

INTERNATIONAL DRUG TRAFFICKING & INTERDICTION
Assistant Director

LEGAL & LEGISLATIVE AFFAIRS
Assistant Director

ADMINISTRATION / SECURITY
Assistant Director

Approved 4/1/2007

FEDERAL LAW ENFORCEMENT TRAINING CENTER

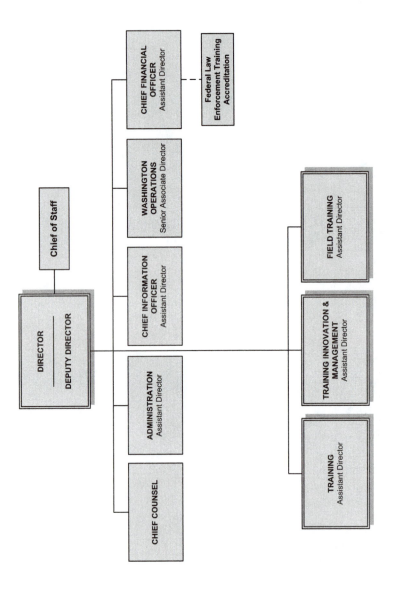

Approved 4/1/2007

OFFICE OF THE DIRECTOR OF
DOMESTIC NUCLEAR DETECTION OFFICE

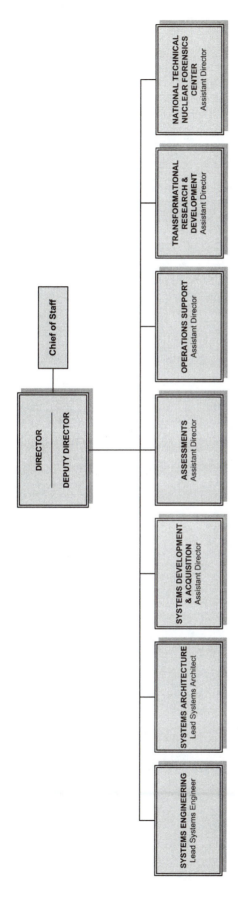

DIRECTOR

DEPUTY DIRECTOR

Chief of Staff

SYSTEMS ENGINEERING
Lead Systems Engineer

SYSTEMS ARCHITECTURE
Lead Systems Architect

SYSTEMS DEVELOPMENT
& ACQUISITION
Assistant Director

ASSESSMENTS
Assistant Director

OPERATIONS SUPPORT
Assistant Director

TRANSFORMATIONAL
RESEARCH &
DEVELOPMENT
Assistant Director

NATIONAL TECHNICAL
NUCLEAR FORENSICS
CENTER
Assistant Director

FEDERAL

Department of Homeland Security

Department of Homeland Security

Headquarters
US Department of Homeland Security
Washington, DC 20528
Phone: 202-282-8000
Phone: 202-282-8010
URL: www.dhs.gov

Description: The Department of Homeland Security (DHS) was established to provide a unified core for the vast and complex national network of the more than 87,000 organizations and institutions at the federal, state, and local levels involved in the effort to secure the nation. The comprehensive national strategy seeks to develop a complementary system that connects all levels of government without duplicating effort. Strategic goals include: awareness—identify and understand threats and vulnerabilities; prevention—detect, deter and mitigate these threats; protection—safeguard people, critical infrastructure, property and the economy from acts of terrorism, natural disasters and other emergencies; response—lead, manage, and coordinate response to such emergencies; recovery—lead efforts to restore and rebuild; service—facilitate lawful trade, travel and immigration; and organizational excellence.

Michael Chertoff
Secretary
Phone: 202-282-8000
e-mail: michael.chertoff@dhs.gov

Michael P Jackson
Deputy Secretary
Phone: 202-282-8000

Paul A Schneider
Under Secretary Management
Phone: 202-205-4613

Robert D Jamison
Acting Under Secretary National Protection & Programs

Jay M Cohen
Under Secretary Science & Technology
Phone: 202-254-5606

Gus P Coldebella
Acting General Counsel

Stewart A Baker
Assistant Secretary for Policy

Charles E Allen
Assistant Secretary for Intelligence & Analysis

W Ralph Basham
Commissioner US Customs and Border Protection

Mark J Sullivan
Director US Secret Service

Admiral Thad W Allen
Commandant US Coast Guard

Julie L Myers
Assistant Secretary US Immigration and Customs Enforcement (ICE)

R David Paulison
Administrator FEMA (Federal Emergency Management Agency)

Kip Hawley
Assistant Secretary/ Administrator Transportation Security Administration (TSA)

Emilio T Gonzalez
Director US Citizenship and Immigration Services

Chad Sweet
Chief of Staff
Phone: 202-282-8256

Richard L Skinner
Inspector General
Phone: 202-254-4100
e-mail: rick.skinner@dhs.gov

Daniel W Sutherland
Officer for Civil Rights and Civil Liberties
Phone: 202-401-1474

Connie L Patrick
Director Federal Law Enforcement Training Center

RAdm Daniel B Lloyd
Military Advisor

Dr Jeffrey W Runge
Acting Assistant Secretary/Chief Medical Officer for Health Affairs

Roger T Rufe Jr
Director Operations Coordination

Vayl Oxford
Director Domestic Nuclear Detection Office

J Edward Fox
Assistant Secretary for Public Affairs
Phone: 202-282-8010

Hugo Teufel III
Chief Privacy Officer

Donald H Kent Jr
Assistant Secretary for Legislative Affairs

Prakash I Khatri
Ombudsman Citizenship & Immigration Services
e-mail: cisombudsman@dhs.gov

Donald E Powell
Federal Coordinator of Gulf Coast Rebuilding

Gregory Garcia
Assistant Secretary for Cyber Security & Communications

Alfonso Martinez-Fonts
Assistant Secretary for Private Sector Office

Robert B Stephan
Assistant Secretary for Infrastructure Protection

Richard C Barth PhD
Assistant Secretary for Policy Development

Eric Fagerholm
Acting Assistant Secretary for Strategic Plans

Anne P Petera
Assistant Secretary for Intergovernmental Programs

Uttam Dhillon
Director Office of Counternarcotics Enforcement

David L Norquist
Chief Financial Officer

Donald G Bathurst
Chief of Administrative Services Officer

Marta Brito Perez
Chief Human Capital Officer

Scott Charbo
Chief Information Officer

Elaine C Duke
Chief Procurement Officer

Jerry Williams
Acting Chief Security Officer

William H Webster
Chair Homeland Security Advisory Council

Policy Directorate
DHS
US Department of Homeland Security
Washington, DC 20528
Phone: 202-282-8000
URL: www.dhs.gov/xabout/structure/editorial_0871.shtm

Description: The Policy Directorate develops and integrates department-wide policies, programs and planning in order to better coordinate the Department's prevention, protection, response and recovery missions.

Stewart A Baker
Assistant Secretary for Policy

Eric Fagerholm
Acting Assistant Secretary Strategic Plans

Richard C Barth PhD
Assistant Secretary Policy Development

Alfonso Martinez-Fonts
Assistant Secretary Private Sector

Phone: 202-282-8484
e-mail: private.sector@dhs.gov

Michael Hoefer
Director Immigration Statistics
Phone: 202-786-9900
e-mail: immigrationstatistics@dhs.gov

Kathleen I Kraninger
Director Screening Coordination Office

Office of Health Affairs
DHS
US Department of Homeland Security
Washington, DC 20528
Phone: 202-254-6479
URL: www.dhs.gov/xabout/structure/editorial_0880.shtm

Description: The Office of Health Affairs (OHA) contributes to domestic health and the security of the nation, working in full collaboration with other DHS components and federal partners. The responsibilities carried out and overseen by this office do not replace any other programs within DHS but rather enhances these other programs in planning for and responding to the consequences of catastrophic incidents. The three divisions of the OHA are: Weapons of Mass Destruction & Biodefense; Medical Readiness; and Component Services.

Jeffrey W Runge MD
Acting Assistant Secretary/Chief Medical Officer

Dr Donald Noah
Deputy Assistant Secretary WMD& Biodefense

Dr Til Jolly
Associate Chief Medical Officer-Medical Readiness

Dr William Lang
Associate Chief Medical Officer-Component Services

Office of Intelligence & Analysis
DHS
US Department of Homeland Security
Washington, DC 20528
Phone: 202-282-8353

Description: The Assistant Secretary is responsible for coordinating with the Intelligence Community and providing guidance on homeland security specific issues. The Office uses information and intelligence from multiple sources to identify and assess current and future threats to the US.

Charles E Allen
Assistant Secretary/Chief Intelligence Officer
Phone: 202-282-8353

Jack Tomarchio
Principal Deputy Assistant Secretary
Phone: 202-282-8000

Office of Operations Coordination
DHS
US Department of Homeland Security
Washington, DC 20528
URL: www.dhs.gov/xabout/structure/editorial_0797.shtm

Description: The Office is responsible for monitoring the security of the US on a daily basis and coordinating activities within DHS, with governors, Homeland Security Advisors, law enforcement partners and critical infrastructure operators in all 50 states and major urban areas. The main two "halves" of the office are the intelligence side and the law enforcement side. The National Operations Center provides 24/7/365 real-time situational awareness and monitoring of the nation, incidents and activities in conjunction with the Office of Intelligence and Analysis.

Roger T Rufe Jr
Director

Federal Law Enforcement Training Center (FLETC)
DHS
1131 Chapel Crossing Road
Glynco, GA 31524
Phone: 912-267-2100
Fax: 912-267-2071
URL: www.fletc.gov

Description: The Federal Law Enforcement Training Center serves as an interagency law enforcement training organization for more than 80 federal agencies with personnel located throughout the United States and its territories. The Center also provides services to state, local, and international law enforcement agencies and, as space permits, other Federal agencies with related law enforcement missions.

Connie L Patrick
Director
Phone: 912-267-2070

Kenneth Keene
Deputy Director
Phone: 912-267-2070

Peggy D Dixon
Public Affairs Office
Phone: 912-267-2447

Domestic Nuclear Detection Office (DNDO)
DHS
US Department of Homeland Security
Washington, DC 20528
Phone: 202-282-8000
e-mail: dndoinfo@dhs.gov

Description: The Domestic Nuclear Detection Office is part of the national effort to protect the nation from radiological and nuclear threats. It is jointly staffed and has seven offices each responsible for managing these functional areas: Operations Support; Assessments; Transformational Research & Development; Systems Engineering; Systems Architect; Systems Developmental Acquisition; and National Technical Nuclear Forensics Center.

Vayl Oxford
Director

Michael Carter
Deputy Director

Office for Civil Rights and Civil Liberties
DHS
US Department of Homeland Security
Washington, DC 20528
Mailing Address: MS 0800
Phone: 202-401-1474
Phone: 866-644-8360

Fax: 202-401-4708
URL: www.dhs.gov/xabout/structure/editorial_0371.shtm
e-mail: civil.liberties@dhs.gov

Description: The Office for Civil Rights and Civil Liberties is designed to protect civil rights and liberties and to support homeland security by providing the Department of Homeland Security with consistent legal and policy advice on the full range of civil rights and liberties issues the Department will face, and by serving as an information and communication channel for the public regarding all aspects of these issues.

Daniel W Sutherland
Officer for Civil Rights and Civil Liberties
Phone: 202-401-1474

Interagency Coordinating Council on Emergency Preparedness & Individuals with Disabilities
Office for Civil Rights and Civil Liberties
Washington, DC 20528
Phone: 202-282-8000
URL: www.dhs.gov/xpreresp/committees/editorial_0591.shtm
e-mail: disability.preparedness@dhs.gov

Description: Established to ensure that the federal government appropriately supports safety and security for individuals with disabilities in disaster situations. The council will consider the unique needs of agency employees with disabilities in their emergency preparedness planning; consider these needs and encourage the provision of appropriate technical assistance; and facilitate cooperation among federal, state, local and tribal governments and private organizations in the implementation of emergency preparedness plans.

Office of Inspector General
DHS
US Department of Homeland Security
Washington, DC 20528
Phone: 202-254-4100
Phone: 800-323-8603
URL: www.dhs.gov/xoig/
e-mail: dhsoighotline@dhs.gov

Description: The Office of Inspector General (OIG) serves as an independent and objective inspection, audit, and investigative body to promote effectiveness, efficiency, and economy in the Department of Homeland Security's programs and operations, and to prevent and detect fraud, abuse, mismanagement, and waste in such programs and operations. Congress enacted the Inspector General Act of 1978, as amended, to ensure integrity and efficiency in government. The Homeland Security Act of 2002, as amended, established an Office of Inspector General in the Department of Homeland Security. The Inspector General is appointed by the President and subject to Senate confirmation. The OIG is to examine, evaluate and, where necessary, critique these operations and activities, recommending ways for the Department to carry out its responsibilities in the most effective, efficient, and economical manner possible.

Richard L Skinner
Inspector General
Phone: 202-254-4100
e-mail: richard.skinner@dhs.gov

James L Taylor
Principal Deputy Inspector General
Phone: 202-254-4100

Matthew Jadacki
Deputy Inspector General Disaster Assistance Oversight

Edward F Cincinnati
Assistant Inspector General Administration
Phone: 202-254-4100
e-mail: ed.cincinnati@dhs.gov

David Zavada
Assistant Inspector General Audits
Phone: 202-254-4100

Frank Deffer
Assistant Inspector General Information Technology
Phone: 202-254-4100
e-mail: frank.deffer@dhs.gov

Carlton I Mann
Assistant Inspector General Inspections
Phone: 202-254-4100
e-mail: robert.ashbaugh@dhs.gov

Elizabeth M Redman
Assistant Inspector General Investigations
Phone: 202-254-4100
e-mail: lisa.redman@dhs.gov

Tamara Faulkner
Congressional Affairs Liaison & Media/Public Outreach
Phone: 202-254-4100
e-mail: tamara.faukner@dhs.gov

Richard N Reback
General Counsel
Phone: 202-254-4100
e-mail: richard.reback@dhs.gov

Office of Citizenship & Immigration Services Ombudsman
DHS
US Department of Homeland Security
Washington, DC 20528
Mailing Address: MS 1225
URL: www.dhs.gov/cisombudsman
e-mail: cisombudsman@dhs.gov

Description: The CIS Ombudsman provides recommendations for resolving individual and employer problems with USCIS in order to ensure national security and the integrity of the legal immigration system. The Ombudsman strives to increase efficiency in administering citizenship and immigration services and improve customer service. The Ombudsman works in close connection with the CIS Director and reports directly to the Deputy Director for Homeland Security.

Prakash I Khatri
CIS Ombudsman

Office of Legislative Affairs
DHS
US Department of Homeland Security
Washington, DC 20528
Mailing Address: MS 0150
Phone: 202-447-5890
Fax: 202-447-5437
URL: www.dhs.gov/xabout/structure/editorial_0574.shtm

Description: The Office serves as the primary liaison to members of Congress and their staffs, the White House and Executive Branch and other federal agencies, providing timely information about homeland security and national security issues. It enhances the department's ability to prevent, protect against and respond to threats and hazards against the nation.

Donald H Kent Jr
Assistant Secretary

Homeland Security Advisory Council
Policy Directorate
US Department of Homeland Security
Washington, DC 20528
Phone: 202-447-3135
Fax: 202-282-9207
URL: www.dhs.gov/xinfoshare/committees/editorial_0331.shtm
e-mail: HSAC@dhs.gov

Description: The Homeland Security Advisory Council (HSAC) provides advice and recommendations to the Secretary on matters related to homeland security. The council is comprised of leaders from state and local government, first responder communities, the private sector and academia.

William H Webster
Chair
Phone: 202-447-3135

James R Schlesinger
Vice Chair
Phone: 202-447-3135

Doug Hoelscher
Executive Director
Phone: 202-447-3135

Jared L Cohon
Chair - Academe, Policy & Research Senior Advisory Committee
Phone: 202-447-3135

Richard A Andrews
Chair - Emergency Responder Senior Advisory Committee
Phone: 202-447-3135

Herbert D Kelleher
Chair - Private Sector Senior Advisory Committee
Phone: 202-447-3135

Jared L Cohon
Chair - Secure Borders & Open Doors Advisory Committee
Phone: 202-447-3135

National Infrastucture Advisory Council
DHS
US Department of Homeland Security
Washington, DC 20528
Mailing Address: MS 8530
Phone: 703-235-5352
Fax: 703-235-5887
URL: www.dhs.gov/xprevprot/committees/editorial_0353.shtm
e-mail: NIAC.Niac@dhs.gov

Description: The council was formerly known as the President's Critical Infrastructure Protection Board. It provides the President, through the Secretary of Homeland Security with advice on the security of the critical infrastructure sectors and their information systems. The council is composed of a maximum of 30 members, appointed by the President from private industry, academia, and state and local government.

Erle A Nye
Chair

Critical Infrastructure Partnership Advisory Council
DHS
US Department of Homeland Security
Washington, DC 20528
URL: www.dhs.gov/xprevprot/committees/editorial_0843.shtm

Description: Established to facilitate effective coordination between federal infrastructure protection programs with the infrastructure protection activities of the private sector and of state, local, territorial and tribal governments. Membership is made up of members of existing Sector Coordinating Councils (SCCs) and representatives from existing Government Coordinating Councils (GCCs).

Protected Critical Infrastructure Information (PCII) Program
DHS
US Department of Homeland Security
Washington, DC 20528
Phone: 202-360-3023
Phone: 202-282-8000
URL: www.dhs.gov/pcii
e-mail: pcii-info@dhs.gov

Description: The Protected Critical Infrastructure Information (PCII) Program is designed to encourage private industry to share sensitive security-related business information with the federal government. PCII is used in pursuit of a more secure homeland, focusing primarily on analyzing and securing critical infrastructure and protected systems, developing risk assessments and identifying vulnerabilities and assisting with recovery. The PCII Program was established pursuant to the Critical Infrastructure Information Act of 2002 (CII Act). It creates a new framework that enables members of the private sector to voluntarily submit sensitive information regarding the nation's critical infrastructure to homeland security with the assurance that the information, if it satisfies the requirements of the CII Act will be protected from public disclosure.

Office of the Federal Coordinator for Gulf Coast Rebuilding
DHS
US Department of Homeland Security
Washington, DC 20528
Phone: 202-282-8000

Description: The Office was created in November of 2005 by Executive Order 13390 as part of a long-term plan for rebuilding the region devastated by Hurricanes Katrina, Rita and Wilma. It Coordinates federal efforts and helps state and local officials reach consensus on their vision for the region.

Donald E Powell
Federal Coordinator

Office of Counternarcotics Enforcement
DHS
US Department of Homeland Security
Washington, DC 20528
Phone: 202-282-8000

Description: The director of the Office of Counternarcotics Enforcement serves as the primary policy advisor to the Secretary for department-wide counternarcotics issues and coordinates efforts to monitor and combat connections between illegal drug trafficking and terrorism.

Uttam Dhillon
Director

Office of Public Affairs
DHS
US Department of Homeland Security
Washington, DC 20528
Phone: 202-282-8010
Fax: 202-282-8403
URL: www.dhs.gov

J Edward Fox
Assistant Secretary Public Affairs

Russ Knocke
Press Secretary

FEDERAL

Department of Homeland Security
Transportation Security Administration

Transportation Security Administration (TSA)
Headquarters
601 S 12th Street
Arlington, VA 22202-4220
Phone: 571-227-2829
Phone: 866-289-9673
URL: www.tsa.gov

Description: The Transportation Security Administration prevents terrorist attacks and protects the US transportation networks through a strategy of layered security. Over 43,000 security officers, air marshals, directors, inspectors, and managers are the frontline of defense, to ensure safe travel. While the TSA's primary mission remains to protect air passengers and crew, Federal Air Marshals have an ever expanding role in homeland security and work closely with other law enforcement agencies.

Kip Hawley
Administrator/Assistant Secretary TSA

Gale Rossides
Acting Deputy Administrator/Associate Administrator Business Transformation & Culture

Dana A Brown
Director FAMS/Assistant Administrator Law Enforcement

John P Sammon
Assistant Administrator TSNM

Morris McGowan
Assistant Administrator Security Operations

Francine Kerner
Chief Counsel
e-mail: francie.kerner@dhs.gov

William W Gaches
Assistant Administrator Intelligence & Analysis

K David Holmes Jr
Assistant Administrator Inspection

Stephanie Rowe
Assistant Administrator Transportation Threat Assessment & Credentialing

Ellen Howe
Assistant Administrator Strategic Communications & Public Affairs

Jeff Sural
Assistant Administrator Legislative Affairs

Mike Golden
Assistant Administrator Operational Process & Technology/CIO/CTO

Richard Whitford
Assistant Administrator Human Capital

David Nicholson
Assistant Administrator Finance & Administration/CFO

Richard Gunderson
Assistant Administrator Acquisition

Kimberly Walton
Acting Special Counselor
Phone: 571-227-1917

Office of Law Enforcement-Federal Air Marshal Service
Transportation Security Administration (TSA)
601 S 12th Street
Arlington, VA 22202-4220

Description: The Office of Law Enforcement directs all TSA law enforcement activities and related critical incident management functions. The Federal Air Marshal Service has a vital mission within DHS; to deter, detect, and defeat hostile acts that target US air carriers, airports, passengers and crews, as well as security priorities beyond air service. Other law enforcement programs include: Federal Flight Deck Officer Program, Armed Security Officer Program, Crew Member Self-Defense Training Program, and TSA National Explosives Detection Canine Team Program. There are 21 field offices strategically located near airports throughout the nation, hundreds of law enforcement assistant directors directly located at airports, and Federal Air Marshals at each of the 56 FBI offices.

Dana A Brown
Assistant Administrator/Director Federal Air Marshal Service

Office of Transportation Sector Network Management (TSNM)
Transportation Security Administration (TSA)
601 S 12th Street
Arlington, VA 22202-4220
URL: www.tsa.gov/what_we_do/tsnm/index.shtm

Description: The TSNM leads the unified national effort to protect and secure the nation's intermodal transportation systems. It ensures the safe movement of passengers and promotes the free flow of commerce through a strategy that includes threat and operator security status assessment, closing gaps in security standards, and enhancement of security systems. There are ten divisions: Commercial Airlines; Commericial Airports; Air Cargo; Freight Rail; Highway & Motor Carriers; Maritime; Mass Transit; International; Pipelines; and General Aviation.

John P Sammon
Assistant Administrator

David Bernier
General Manager Commercial Airlines

Charlotte Bryan
General Manager Commercial Airports

Edward Kelly
General Manager Air Cargo

Gil Kovar
General Manager Freight Rail

Dirk Ahle
General Manager General Aviation

William Arrington
General Manager Highway & Motor Carriers

Richard Stein
General Manager International

Captain James Clarkson
General Manager Maritime

Paul Lennon
General Manager Mass Transit

Jack Fox
General Manager Pipelines

Office of Security Operations
Transportation Security Administration (TSA)
601 S 12th Street
Arlington, VA 22202-4220
URL: www.tsa.gov

Morris McGowan
Assistant Administrator

Mel J Carraway
General Manager Field Operations

FEDERAL

Department of Homeland Security
Customs & Border Protection

US Customs & Border Protection (CBP)
Headquarters
1300 Pennsylvania Avenue NW
Washington, DC 20229
Phone: 202-344-2001
Phone: 202-354-1000
Fax: 202-344-1380
URL: www.cbp.gov

Description: US Customs & Border Protection (CBP) is the unified border agency within DHS. CBP combined the inspectional workforces and broad border authorities of US Customs, US Immigration, APHIS (Animal Plant Health Inspection Service), and the entire US Border Patrol. There are more than 41,000 employees managing, controling and protecting the nation's borders. Their priority is to prevent terrorists and terrorist weapons from entering the country, while also facilitating the flow of legitimate trade and travel. CBP uses the latest in technology and multiple strategies to accomplish it's goal.

W Ralph Basham
Commissioner
Phone: 202-927-2001

Deborah J Spero
Deputy Commissioner
Phone: 202-927-1010
e-mail: deborah.j.spero@dhs.gov

Steven A Atkiss
Chief of Staff
Phone: 202-927-2001

Alfonso Robles
Chief Counsel
Phone: 202-344-2990
e-mail: alfonso.robles@dhs.gov

Franklin C Jones
Special Assistant Equal Employment Opportunity
Phone: 202-344-1610
e-mail: franklin.c.jones@dhs.gov

Will Houston
Director Office of Policy & Planning
Phone: 202-344-2700

L Thomas Bortmes
Director of Intelligence
Phone: 202-344-1150

Thomas L Bush
Acting Director Office of Anti-Terrorism

Jayson P Ahern
Assistant Commissioner Field Operations
Phone: 202-344-1620

David V Aguilar
Assistant Commissioner Border Patrol
Phone: 202-344-2050

Michael C Kostelnik
Assistant Commissioner CBP Air & Marine
Phone: 202-344-3950

Thomas J Walter
Assistant Commissioner Training & Development
Phone: 202-344-1130

Michael C Mullen
Assistant Commissioner International Affairs & Trade Relations
Phone: 202-344-3000

James F Tomsheck
Assistant Commissioner Internal Affairs
Phone: 202-344-1800

William A Anthony
Acting Assistant Commissioner Public Affairs
Phone: 202-344-1770

Daniel Baldwin
Assistant Commissioner International Trade
Phone: 202-863-6000

Thaddeus M Bingel
Assistant Commissioner Congressional Affairs
Phone: 202-344-1760

Ken Ritchhart
Acting Assistant Commissioner Information & Technology/CIO
Phone: 202-344-1680

Office of Anti-Terrorism
US Customs & Border Protection (CBP)
1300 Pennsylvania Ave NW
Washington, DC 20229

Description: The Office serves as the principal advisor to the Commissioner and other senior officials on CBP anti-terrorism programs. It monitors, coordinates, recommends, assesses and participates in the development of all policy, programs, training and matters relating to terrorism to ensure that the agency is maximizing its efforts in relation within the federal law enforcement community and homeland security structure.

Office of International Trade
US Customs & Border Protection (CBP)
1300 Pennsylvania Ave NW
Washington, DC 20229
Phone: 202-863-6000

Description: The Office of International Trade directs the nation's trade policy and national trade program functions of CBP and provides uniformity and clarity for the strategy to facilitate legitimate trade. It ensures the CBP's ability to protect the American economy from unfare trade practices and illicit commercial enterprises.

Daniel Baldwin
Assistant Commissioner

Office of Border Patrol
US Customs & Border Protection (CBP)
1300 Pennsylvania Avenue NW
Room 6.5E
Washington, DC 20229
Phone: 202-344-2050
Fax: 202-344-3140
URL: www.cbp.gov/xp/border_security/border_patrol

Description: Prevents terrorists and terrorist weapons, including weapons of mass destruction, from entering the 9,000 miles of land and coastal border of the US. The Chief of Border Patrol is the highest ranking Border Patrol Agent and directs more than 12,000 agents nationwide.

David V Aguilar
Chief
e-mail: david.aguilar@dhs.gov

Office of Air & Marine
US Customs & Border Protection (CBP)
1300 Pennsylvania Avenue NW
Room 6.3D
Washington, DC 20229
Phone: 202-344-3950
Fax: 202-344-3960
URL: www.cbp.gov/xp/cgov/border_security/air_marine/

Description: The office is responsible for protecting people and critical infrastructure by using an integrated and coordinated air and marine force to detect, interdict, and prevent acts of terrorism arising from unlawful movement of people, illegal drugs, and other contraband crossing the US borders. All marine and aviation assets, program and personnel were placed under the responsibilty of this office. Air resources: over 500 pilots and 250 aircrafts. Marine resources: over 200 vessels.

Michael C Kostelnik
Assistant Commissioner
Phone: 202-344-3950

David Lent
Chief of Staff
Phone: 202-344-1724

Jules Andersen
Mission Support Division
Phone: 202-353-4836
e-mail: jules.andersen@dhs.gov

Office of Intelligence
US Customs & Border Protection (CBP)
1300 Pennsylvania Avenue NW
Washington, DC 20229
Phone: 202-344-1150
Fax: 202-344-1738

Description: Produces timely, actionable, allsource intelligence in support of CBP's mission. The office reports directly to the Commissioner and also serves as the liaison to the Department of Homeland Security, the Intelligence Community and other federal law enforcement agencies.

L Thomas Bortmes
Executive Director
Phone: 202-344-1150

Carlos Cortez
International Intelligence Programs Division
Phone: 202-344-1727
e-mail: carlos.cortez@dhs.gov

Office of Field Operations
US Customs & Border Protection (CBP)
1300 Pennsylvania Avenue NW
Room 5.5C
Washington, DC 20229
Phone: 202-344-1620
Fax: 202-344-2777
URL: www.cbp.gov/xp/cgov/toolbox/contacts

Description: Twenty Field Operations Offices in the US provide centralized management oversight and operational assistance to ports of entry and preclearance offices. They ensure the dissemination and implementation of core CBP guidelines as well as other management functions.

Jayson P Ahern
Assistant Commissioner
Phone: 202-344-1620
e-mail: jayson.p.ahern@dhs.gov

Thomas S Winkowski
Acting Deputy Assistant Commissioner
Phone: 202-344-1600

Robert M Jacksta
Executive Director Travel Security & Facilitation
Phone: 202-344-1220
e-mail: robert.m.jacksta@dhs.gov

Jennifer Sava
Executive Director Operations
Phone: 202-344-1850

Richard Balaban
Executive Director Mission Support
Phone: 202-344-1270

Jeffrey Grode
Executive Director Agricultural Program Liaison
Phone: 202-344-3298

Paul Morris
Executive Director Admissability Requirements & Migration Control (ARMC)
Phone: 202-344-1438

Al Gina
Executive Director Container Security Initiative (CSI)
Phone: 202-344-3040

Atlanta Field Operations Office
1699 Phoenix Parkway
Suite 400
College Park, GA 30349

Phone: 678-284-5900
Fax: 678-284-5932

Description: Provides guidance to regional ports and ensures the dissemination and implementation of core CBP guidelines and other management functions. The Atlanta Field Operations Office has authority over the following ports of entry: Atlanta, GA; Brunswick, GA; Charleston, SC; Charleston, WV; Charlotte, NC; Columbia, SC; Front Royal, VA; Georgetown, SC; Greenville - Spartanburg, Greer, SC; Morehead City - Beaufort, NC; Myrtle Beach International Airport, Myrtle Beach, SC; Newport News, VA; New River Valley Airport, Dublin, VA; Norfolk, VA; Raleigh - Durham, Morrisville, NC; Richmond - Petersburg, VA; Savannah, GA; Wilmington, NC; and Winston - Salem, Greensboro, NC.

Robert C Gomez
Director
e-mail: robert.gomez@dhs.gov

Zachary Mann
Special Agent/Press Officer
Phone: 305-219-0628
e-mail: zachary.mann@dhs.gov

Baltimore Field Operations Office
103 South Gay Street
Suite 715
Baltimore, MD 21202
Phone: 410-962-6200
Fax: 410-962-2423

Description: Provides guidance to regional ports and ensures the dissemination and implementation of core CBP guidelines and other management functions. The Baltimore Field Operations Office has authority over the following ports of entry: Baltimore, MD; Harrisburg, Middletown PA; Philadelphia, PA; Pittsburgh, PA; Washington-Dulles, Sterling, VA; and Wilmington, New Castle, DE.

Michael Lovejoy
Director
Phone: 410-962-6200

Eric Blum
Acting Director Port Security Media Division
Phone: 202-344-1770

Michael Friel
Director Border Security Media Division
Phone: 202-344-1770

Boston Field Operations Office
10 Causeway Street
Room 801
Boston, MA 02222
Phone: 617-565-6208
Fax: 617-565-6277

Description: Provides guidance to regional ports and ensures the dissemination and implementation of core CBP guidelines and other management functions. The Boston Field Operations Office has authority over the following ports of entry: Bangor, ME; Bar Harbor, ME; Bath (Portland), ME; Beecher Falls, VT; Belfast, ME; Boston, MA; Bridgeport, CT; Bridgewater, ME; Burlington International Airport, South Burlington, VT; Calais, ME; Derby Line, VT; Eastport, ME; Fall River (New Bedford), MA; Fort Fairfield, ME; Fort Kent, ME; Gloucester (Beverly),

MA; Hartford, CT; Highgate Springs, VT; Houlton, ME; Jackman, ME; Jonesport (Calais), ME; Lawrence (Gloucester), Beverly, MA; Limestone, ME; Logan Airport (East Boston), MA; Madawaska, ME; Manchester (User Fee Airport), NH; New Bedford, MA; New Haven, CT; New London (Hartford), CT; Newport, RI; Norton, VT; Plymouth (New Bedford), MA; Portland, ME; Portsmouth, NH; Providence, RI; Richford, VT; Rockland (Belfast), ME; Salem (Gloucester), MA; Springfield, MA; St. Albans, VT; Van Buren, ME; Vanceboro, ME; and Worcester, MA.

Steven J Farquharson
Director
e-mail: steven.j.farquharson@dhs.gov

Nancy Gilcoine
Assistant Director Immigration Policy
Phone: 617-565-6215
e-mail: nancy.gilcoine@dhs.gov

Theodore Woo
Public Affairs Officer
Phone: 617-565-6331

Buffalo Field Operations Office
4455 Genesee Street
Buffalo, NY 14225
Phone: 716-626-0400
Fax: 716-626-7627

Description: Provides guidance to regional ports and ensures the dissemination and implementation of core CBP guidelines and other management functions. The Buffalo Field Operations Office has authority over the following ports of entry: Albany; Alexandria Bay; Binghamton (Johnson City); Buffalo; Champlain; Massena (Rooseveltown); Ogdensburg; Rochester; Syracuse; and Trout River (Constable) all in the state of New York.

James Engelman
Director

Kevin Corsaro
Public Affairs Liaison
Phone: 716-626-0400

Chicago Field Operations Office
610 S Canal Street
Room 900
Chicago, IL 60607
Phone: 312-983-9100
Fax: 312-886-4921

Description: Provides guidance to regional ports and ensures the dissemination and implementation of core CBP guidelines and other management functions. The Chicago Field Operations Office has authority over the following ports of entry: Ashtabula/Conneaut, OH; Chicago (Rosemont), IL; Cincinnati, OH-Lawrenceburg (Erlanger, KY) ; Cleveland (Middleburg Heights), OH; Columbus (Groveport), OH; Davenport, IA-Moline and Rock Island, Moline, IL; Dayton (Vandalia), OH; Decatur, IL; Des Moines, IA; Duluth, MN & Superior, WI; Erie, PA; Fort Wayne (Yoder), IN; Green Bay, WI; Indianapolis, IN; Kansas City, MO; Lexington, KY; Louisville (Mascoutah Newport, IL), KY; Milwaukee, WI; Minneapolis, MN; Omaha, NE; Owensboro, KY-Evansville, IN; Peoria (Bartonville), IL; Racine, WI; Rochester, MN; Rockford, IL; Sioux Falls, SD; Spirit of St. Louis Airport, Chesterfield, MO; Springfield, MO; St. Louis,

MO; Toledo - Sandusky, OH; Waukegan, IL; West Chicago, IL; Wheeling, IL; Wichita, KS; Wilmington, OH.

David J Murphy
Director

Cherise Miles
Press Officer
Phone: 312-983-5344
e-mail: cherise.miles@dhs.gov

Detroit Field Operations Office
613 Abbott Street
Suite 300
Detroit, MI 48226
Phone: 313-226-2955
Fax: 313-226-3035

Description: Provides guidance to regional ports and ensures the dissemination and implementation of core CBP guidelines and other management functions. The Detroit Field Operations Office has authority over the following ports of entry: Battle Creek; Detroit; Detroit Metropolitan Airport; Grand Rapids; Port Huron; Saginaw/Bay City/Flint (Freeland); and Sault Sainte Marie, all in the state of Michigan.

Gurdit Dhillon
Director

Ron Smith
Press Officer
Phone: 312-983-5344

El Paso Field Operations Office
9400 Viscount Boulevard
Suite 104
El Paso, TX 79925-7030
Phone: 915-633-7300
Fax: 915-633-7392

Description: Provides guidance to regional ports and ensures the dissemination and implementation of core CBP guidelines and other management functions. The El Paso Field Operations Office has authority over the following ports of entry: Albuquerque, NM; Columbus, NM; El Paso, TX; Fabens, TX; Presidio, TX; and Santa Teresa, NM.

Luis Garcia
Director

Roger Maier Sr
Press Officer
Phone: 915-633-7300
e-mail: roger.maier@dhs.gov

Houston Field Operations Office
2323 S Shepherd
Suite 1200
Houston, TX 77019
Phone: 713-387-7200
Fax: 713-387-7202

Description: Provides guidance to regional ports and ensures the dissemination and implementation of core CBP guidelines and other management functions. The Houston Field Operations Office has authority over the following ports of entry: Addison Airport, Addison, TX; Alliance Airport, Fort Worth, TX; Amarillo, TX; Austin, TX; Corpus Christi, TX; Dallas/Ft. Worth, Irving, TX; Freeport, TX; Houston, TX; Lubbock, TX; McKinney, TX; Midland, TX; Oklahoma City, OK; Port Arthur, TX; Port Lavaca - Point Comfort, Corpus Christi, TX; Sabine, TX; San Antonio, TX; Sugarland, TX; and Tulsa, OK.

Jeffrey Baldwin
Director

Laredo Field Operations Office
109 Shiloh Drive
Suite 300
Laredo, TX 78045
Phone: 956-753-1700
Fax: 956-753-1754

Description: Provides guidance to regional ports and ensures the dissemination and implementation of core CBP guidelines and other management functions. The Laredo Field Operations Office has authority over the following ports of entry: Brownsville/Los Indios; Del Rio/Amistad Dam; Eagle Pass; Hidalgo/Pharr; Laredo; Progreso; Rio Grande City/Los Ebanos; and Roma/Falcon Dam, all in the state of Texas.

Leticia Moran
Director
Phone: 956-753-1700

Richard Pauza
Press Officer
Phone: 956-753-1749
e-mail: richard.j.pauza@dhs.gov

Los Angeles Field Operations Office
1 World Trade Center
Suite 705
Long Beach, CA 90831
Phone: 562-980-3100
Fax: 562-980-3107

Description: Provides guidance to regional ports and ensures the dissemination and implementation of core CBP guidelines and other management functions. The Los Angeles Field Operations Office has authority over the following ports of entry: Las Vegas, NV; Los Angeles/Long Beach Seaport, CA; Los Angeles International Airport-Cargo Operations, Los Angeles, CA; Ontario Airport, CA; Palm Springs, CA; Port Hueneme, CA; and Victorville (S California Logistics Airport), CA.

Kevin Weeks
Director

Michael Fleming
Press Officer
Phone: 562-980-3110
e-mail: michael.fleming@dhs.gov

Miami Field Operations Office
909 SE 1st Avenue
Suite 980
Miami, FL 33131
Phone: 305-810-5120
Fax: 305-810-5143

Description: Provides guidance to regional ports and ensures the dissemination and implementation of core CBP guidelines and other management functions. The Miami Field Operations Office has authority over the following ports of entry: Key West; Miami International Airport; Miami Seaport; Port Everglades, Fort

Lauderdale; and West Palm Beach, Riviera Beach all in the state of Florida.

Harold E Woodward
Director

Zachary Mann
Special Agent/Press Officer
Phone: 305-219-0628
e-mail: zachary.mann@dhs.gov

New Orleans Field Operations Office

1515 Poydras Street
Suite 880
New Orleans, LA 70112
Phone: 504-670-2404
Fax: 504-670-2286

Description: Provides guidance to regional ports and ensures the dissemination and implementation of core CBP guidelines and other management functions. The New Orleans Field Operations Office has authority over the following ports of entry: Baton Rouge, LA; Birmingham, AL; Chattanooga, TN; Gramercy, LA; Gulfport, MS; Huntsville, AL; Knoxville, TN; Lake Charles, LA; Little Rock - North Little Rock, AR; Memphis, TN; Mobile (including Theodore), AL; Morgan City, LA; Nashville, TN; New Orleans (includes Belle Chasse, Concession), LA; Pascagoula, MS; Shreveport - Bossier City, LA; Tri-City User Fee Airport, Blountville, TN; and Vicksburg, Flowood, MS.

Robert Gomez
Acting Director
Phone: 504-670-2404

Virginia Dabbs
Press Officer
Phone: 504-670-2140
e-mail: virginia.dabbs@dhs.gov

New York Field Operations Office

One Penn Plaza
11th Floor
New York, NY 10119-0035
Phone: 646-733-3100
Fax: 646-733-3245

Description: Provides guidance to regional ports and ensures the dissemination and implementation of core CBP guidelines and other management functions. The New York Field Operations Office has authority over the following ports of entry: John F. Kennedy International Airport, Jamaica, NY; Morristown Airport, Morristown, NJ; New York/Newark, NJ; and Perth Amboy, NJ.

Susan T Mitchell
Director
Phone: 646-733-3100

Janet Rapaport
Press Officer
Phone: 212-514-8324
e-mail: janet.rapaport@dhs.gov

Lucille Cirillo
OFO Public Affairs Liaison
Phone: 646-733-2810

Portland Field Operations Office

8337 NE Alderwood Road
Room 200
Portland, OR 97220
Mailing Address: PO Box 55700, 97238-5700
Phone: 503-326-7625
Fax: 503-326-7629

Description: Provides guidance to regional ports and ensures the dissemination and implementation of core CBP guidelines and other management functions. The Portland Field Operations Office has authority over the following ports of entry: Alcan, AK; Anchorage, AK; Astoria, OR; Boise, ID; Centennial Airport, Englewood, CO; Coos Bay, OR; Dalton Cache, AK; Denver, CO; Eagle County Regional Airport, Gypsum, CO; Fairbanks, AK; Jefferson County Airport, Broomfield, CO; Juneau, AK; Ketchikan, AK; Kodiak, Anchorage, AK; Longview, WA; Newport, OR; Portland, OR; Sitka, AK; Skagway, AK; Valdez, AK; and Wrangell, AK.

Nat Aycox
Director
Phone: 415-744-1530
e-mail: nat.aycox@dhs.gov

Roxanne Hercules
Public Affairs Liaison
Phone: 415-744-1530

San Diego Field Operations Office

610 W Ash Street
Suite 1200
San Diego, CA 92101
Phone: 619-652-9966
Fax: 619-557-5394

Description: Provides guidance to regional ports and ensures the dissemination and implementation of core CBP guidelines and other management functions. The San Diego Field Operations Office has authority over the following ports of entry: Andrade, Winterhaven, CA; Calexico East, Calexico, CA; Calexico West, Calexico, CA; Otay Mesa, San Diego, CA; San Diego, CA; San Ysidro, CA; and Tecate, CA.

Adele Fasano
Director

Vincent Bond
Press Officer
Phone: 619-744-5224
e-mail: vincent.bond@dhs.gov

San Francisco Field Operations Office

33 New Montgomery Street
16th Floor
San Francisco, CA 94105
Phone: 415-744-1530
Fax: 415-744-7005

Description: Provides guidance to regional ports and ensures the dissemination and implementation of core CBP guidelines and other management functions. The San Francisco Field Operations Office authority over the following ports of entry: Eureka, CA; Fresno, CA; Hilo, HI; Honolulu, HI; Honolulu International Airport, HI; Kahului, HI; Kona, Kailua-Kona, HI; Monterey, CA; Nawiliwili - Port Allen, Lihue, HI; Reno, NV; Sacramento,

CA; Salt Lake City, UT; San Francisco, CA; San Francisco International Airport, CA; and San Jose International Airport, CA.

Nat Aycox
Director
Phone: 415-744-1530
e-mail: nat.aycox@dhs.gov

Roxanne Hercules
Public Affairs Liaison
Phone: 415-744-1530

San Juan Field Operations Office
#1 La Puntilla Street
Office Room 203
San Juan, 00901
Puerto Rico
Phone: 787-729-6950
Fax: 787-729-6978

Description: Provides guidance to regional ports and ensures the dissemination and implementation of core CBP guidelines and other management functions. The San Juan Field Operations Office has authority over the following ports of entry: Aguadilla, PR; Charlotte Amalie, VI (Area Port of St. Thomas); Cruz Bay (St. John), VI; Fajardo, Puerto Real, PR; Luis Munoz Marin International Airport, Isla Verde, PR; Mayaguez, PR; Ponce, PR; San Juan, PR (Area Port); and St. Croix, Fredericksted, VI.

Marcelino Borges
Director

Virginia Dabbs
Press Officer
Phone: 504-670-2140
e-mail: virginia.dabbs@dhs.gov

Seattle Field Operations Office
1000 Second Avenue
Suite 2200
Seattle, WA 98104-1049
Phone: 206-553-6944
Fax: 206-553-1401

Description: Provides guidance to regional ports and ensures the dissemination and implementation of core CBP guidelines and other management functions. The Seattle Field Operations Office has authority over the following ports of entry: Ambrose, ND; Antler, ND; Baudette, MN; Blaine, WA; Butte Airport, MT; Carbury, Souris, ND; Del Bonita, Cut Bank, MT; Dunseith, ND; Eastport, ID; Fargo - Hector International Airport, ND; Fortuna, ND; Grand Forks, ND; Grand Portage, MN; Great Falls, MT; Hannah, ND; Hansboro, ND; International Falls, MN; Kalispell Airport, MT; Lancaster, MN; Maida, ND; Morgan, Loring, MT; Neche, ND; Noonan, ND; Northgate, Flaxton, ND; Noyes, MN; Opheim, MT; Oroville Area Port, WA; Pembina, ND; Piegan, Babb, MT; Pinecreek, Roseau, MN; Portal, ND; Porthill, ID; Raymond Area Port, MT; Roosville, Eureka, MT; Roseau, MN; Saint John, ND; Sarles, ND; Scobey, MT; Seattle, WA; Sherwood, ND; Sumas, WA; Sweetgrass Area Port, MT; Tacoma, WA; Turner, MT; Walhalla, ND; Warroad, MN; Westhope, ND; Whitetail, MT; Whitlash, MT; and Wild Horse, MT; Williston-Sloulin Field International Airport, ND; Willowcreek Havre, MT.

Robert Klee
Director

Mike Milne
Press Officer
Phone: 206-553-6944

Tampa Field Operations Office
1624 East Seventh Avenue
Suite 300
Tampa, FL 33605
Phone: 813-228-2381
Fax: 813-225-7110

Description: Provides guidance to regional ports and ensures the dissemination and implementation of core CBP guidelines and other management functions. The Tampa Field Operations Office has authority over the following ports of entry: Area Port of Jacksonville; Area Port of Orlando; Area Port of Tampa; Cape Canaveral; Daytona Beach; Fernandina Beach; Fort Myers; Melbourne; Panama City; Pensacola; Port Manatee; Sanford; Sarasota; and St. Petersburg, all in the state of Florida.

Denise Crawford
Director
e-mail: denise.crawford@dhs.gov

Zachary Mann
Special Agent/Press Officer
Phone: 305-219-0628
e-mail: zachary.mann@dhs.gov

Tucson Field Operations Office
4740 N Oracle Road
Suite 310
Tucson, AZ 85705
Phone: 520-407-2300
Fax: 520-407-2350

Description: Provides guidance to regional ports and ensures the dissemination and implementation of core CBNP guidelines and other management functions. The Arizona Field Operations Office has authority over the following ports of entry: Douglas; Lukeville; Naco; Nogales; Phoenix; San Luis; Sasabe; Scottsdale Airport; Tucson; and Williams Gateway Airport, all within the state of Arizona.

Donna DeLaTorre
Director

Brian Levin
Public Affairs Liaison
Phone: 520-407-2319

FEDERAL

Department of Homeland Security
Citizenship & Immigration Services

US Citizenship & Immigration Services (CIS)
Headquarters
20 Massachusetts Avenue NW
Washington, DC 20529
Phone: 202-272-1000
Phone: 202-272-1200
Fax: 202-272-8118
URL: www.uscis.gov

Description: US Citizenship and Immigration Services is comprised of fifteen thousand federal employees and contractors working in approximately 250 headquarters and field offices. It is responsible for the administration of immigration and naturalization adjudication functions and establishing immigration services policies and priorities. The Department of Homeland Security (DHS) has administered the nation's immigration laws since March 1, 2003 when the Immigration and Naturalization Service (INS) became part of DHS. Through US Citizenship and Immigration Services (USCIS), DHS continues the tradition of welcoming immigrants into the country by administering services such as immigrant and nonimmigrant sponsorship; adjustment of status; work authorization and other permits; naturalization of qualified applicants for US citizenship; and asylum or refugee processing. The proposed FY 2008 budget for this department is $2.6 billion.

Dr Emilio T Gonzalez
Director
Phone: 202-272-1000

Jonathan Scharfen
Deputy Director
Phone: 202-272-8000

Tom Paar
Chief of Staff
Phone: 202-272-1400

Alfonso Aguilar
Chief Citizenship Office
Phone: 202-272-1310

Carlos Iturregui
Chief Office of Policy & Strategy

Jose Montero
Counselor to the Director/Chief Communications Officer

Lynden Melmed
Chief Counsel

Michael Aytes
Associate Director Domestic Operations Directorate

Lori Scialabba
Associate Director Refugee, Asylum & International

Operations Directorate
Phone: 202-272-1663

Daniel Renaud
Chief Transformation Program

Sarah Taylor
Chief Office of Congressional Relations

Jeffrey Conklin
Chief Information Officer
Phone: 202-272-1700

Janis Sposato
Chief Human Capital Officer

Rendell Jones
Chief Financial Officer

Domestic Operations Directorate
US Citizenship & Immigration Services
20 Massachusetts Avenue NW
Washington, DC 20529
Phone: 202-272-1710
Fax: 202-272-1718

Michael Aytes
Associate Director
Phone: 202-272-1710

Donald Neufeld
Field Operations Office
Phone: 202-272-1001

Deborah A Rogers
Information & Customer Service Office
Phone: 202-272-1915

Pearl Chang
Program & Regulation Development Office
Phone: 202-272-8436

Refugee, Asylum and International Operations Directorate
US Citizenship & Immigration Services
20 Massachusetts Avenue NW
Washington, DC 20529
Phone: 202-272-1663
Fax: 202-272-1564

Lori Scialabba
Associate Director

Joseph E Langlois
Asylum
Phone: 202-305-2663
e-mail: joseph.langlois@dhs.gov

Office of Policy and Strategy
US Citizenship & Immigration Services
20 Massachusetts Avenue NW
Washington, DC 20529
Phone: 202-272-1470
Fax: 202-272-1480

Carlos Iturregui
Chief

David R Howell
Deputy Chief

Lisa Roney
Evaluation & Research Division

Richard A Sloan
Regulations Division
Phone: 202-272-8377
e-mail: richard.sloan@dhs.gov

Michael Biggs
Policy Division
Phone: 202-272-1470
e-mail: michael.biggs@dhs.gov

Office of Administration
US Citizenship & Immigration Services
20 Massachusetts Avenue NW
Washington, DC 20529
Phone: 202-272-1570
Fax: 202-272-1553

Nancy Gulliams
Chief Administrative Officer
Phone: 202-272-1570

Renee Downs
Deputy Chief Administrative Officer
Phone: 202-272-1570

Gina V Barrett
Facilities Management Division
Phone: 202-272-1600

Office of Public Affairs & Communications
US Citizenship & Immigration Services
20 Massachusetts Avenue NW
Washington, DC 20529
Phone: 202-272-1200
Fax: 202-272-1322

Description: Provides accurate, timely, immigration-related information in order for the news media and the public to be well informed about DHS immigration-related bureaus, missions, capabilities and activities.

Jose Montero
Director/Chief Communications Officer

Mariela Melero
Deputy Director

Maureen Lenihan
Internal Communications Division

Angelica M Alfonso
Director Strategic Communications

National Benefits Center
US Citizenship & Immigration Services
PO Box 648005
Lee's Summit, MO 64064
Phone: 800-375-5283
URL: uscis.gov/graphics/fieldoffices/nbc/

Description: The National Benefits Center was originally established to handle the mail, file, data entry, and adjudication of most applications for immigration services and benefits. The center has six divisions, which are: Adjudications, Records, Fraud Detection, Customer Relations, Administration, and Information Technology.

Robert Cowan
Director

Jack Bennett
Deputy Director

California Service Center
US Citizenship & Immigration Services
PO Box 30111
Laguna Nigel, CA 92607-0111
Phone: 949-389-3000
Phone: 800-375-5283

Description: Service Centers were established to handle the mail, file, data entry, and adjudication of most applications for immigration services and benefits. The California Service Center accepts and processes certain applications and petitions from people residing in the following jurisdictions: California, Nevada, Arizona, Hawaii, and the Territory of Guam.

Christina Poulos
Director
Phone: 949-389-3000

Gerald McMahon
Deputy Director

Nebraska Service Center
US Citizenship & Immigration Services
PO Box 87565
Lincoln, NE 68501-7565
Phone: 800-375-3676
URL: www.uscis.gov/graphics/fieldoffices/nebraska/index.htm

Description: Service Centers were established to handle the mail, file, data entry, and adjudication of most applications for immigration services and benefits. The Nebraska Service Center accepts and processes applications and petitions from people residing in the following states: Alaska, Arizona, California, Colorado, Hawaii, Idaho, Illinois, Indiana, Iowa, Kansas, Michigan, Minnesota, Missouri, Montana, Nebraska, Nevada, North Dakota, Ohio, Oregon, South Dakota, Utah, Washington, Wisconsin, Wyoming and the Territory of Guam.

Gerard Heinauer
Director

Gregory W Christian
Deputy Director

Texas Service Center
US Citizenship & Immigration Services
PO Box 851182
Mesquite, TX 75185-1182

Phone: 214-381-1423
Phone: 800-375-5283
Fax: 214-767-7405
URL: www.uscis.gov/graphics/fieldoffices/texas/index.htm

Description: Services centers were established to handle the mail, file, data entry, and adjudication of most applications for immigrations services and benefits. The Texas Service Center accepts and processes certain applications and petitions from individuals residing in the following states: Alabama, Arkansas, Connecticut, Delaware, Florida, Georgia, Kentucky, Louisiana, Maine, Maryland, Massachusetts, Mississippi, New Hampshire, New Jersey, New Mexico, New York, North Carolina, Oklahoma, Pennsylvania, Puerto Rico, Rhode Island, South Carolina, Tennessee, Texas, Virginia, Virgin Islands, Vermont, Washington DC, and West Virginia.

Evelyn Upchurch
Director

Vermont Service Center
US Citizenship & Immigration Services
75 Lower Weldon Street
Saint Albans, VT 05479-9400
Phone: 802-527-3192
Phone: 800-375-5283
URL: www.uscis.gov/graphics/fieldoffices/vermont/index.htm

Description: Service Centers were established to handle the mail, file, data entry, and adjudication of most applications for immigration services and benefits. The Vermont Service Center accepts and processes certain applications and petitions from people residing in the following states: Connecticut, Delaware, Maine, Maryland, Massachusetts, New Hampshire, New Jersey, New York, Pennsylvania, Puerto Rico, Rhode Island, Vermont, Virginia, US Virgin Islands, West Virginia, and the District of Columbia.

Paul Novak
Director
Phone: 802-527-3192

Sandra Bushey
Deputy Director

Arlington Asylum Office
US Citizenship & Immigration Services
1525 Wilson Boulevard
3rd Floor
Arlington, VA 22209
Phone: 703-235-4100

Description: The Asylum Office in Arlington has jurisdiction over the following in the state of Pennsylvania: Allegheny, Armstrong, Beaver, Bedford, Blair, Bradford, Butler, Cambria, Clarion, Clearfield, Crawford, Elk, Erie, Fayette, Forest, Greene, Indiana, Jefferson, Lawrence, McKean, Mercer, Somerset, Venango, Warren, Washington, and Westmoreland. The Asylum Office in Arlington also has jurisdiction over the District of Columbia, the western portion of the state of Pennsylvania, and the states of Maryland, Virginia, West Virginia, North Carolina, Georgia, Alabama, and South Carolina.

Marla J Belvedere
Asylum Office Director

John Kramar
Deputy Director

Chicago Asylum Office
US Citizenship & Immigration Services
401 South LaSalle Street
8th Floor
Chicago, IL 60605
Phone: 312-353-9607
Fax: 312-886-0204

Description: The Asylum Office in Chicago has jurisdiction over the states of Illinois, Indiana, Michigan, Wisconsin, Minnesota, North Dakota, South Dakota, Kansas, Missouri, Ohio, Iowa, Nebraska, Montana, Idaho, and Kentucky.

Kenneth Madsen
Asylum Office Director

Houston Asylum Office
US Citizenship & Immigration Services
16630 Imperial Valley Drive
Suite 200
Houston, TX 77060
Mailing Address: PO Box 670626, 77267
Phone: 281-774-4830

Description: The Asylum office of Houston has jurisdiction over the states of Louisiana, Arkansas, Mississippi, Tennessee, Texas, Oklahoma, New Mexico, Colorado, Utah, and Wyoming.

Marie Hummert
Asylum Office Director
Phone: 281-774-4830

Richard Rhodie
Community Relations Coordinator
Phone: 281-774-4830

Los Angeles Asylum Office
US Citizenship & Immigration Services
1585 S Manchester Avenue
Anaheim, CA 92802
Phone: 714-808-8000

Description: The mission of the U.S. Asylum Program is to implement asylum laws in a way that is fair, timely, and consistent with international humanitarian principles and our domestic tradition of providing refuge for the oppressed. The Asylum Office in Los Angeles has jurisdiction over the states of Arizona and Hawaii, the Territory of Guam, the following counties in the state of California: Los Angeles, Orange, Riverside, San Bernardino, San Luis Obispo, Santa Barbara, Ventura, Imperial, and San Diego, and the southern portion of the state of Nevada currently within the jurisdiction of the Las Vegas Sub Office.

George S Mihalko
Acting Asylum Office Director
Phone: 714-808-8207

Miami Asylum Office
US Citizenship & Immigration Services
99 SE 5th Street
3rd Floor
Miami, FL 33131-2501
Phone: 305-960-5600
Fax: 305-530-6071

Description: The mission of the US Asylum Program is to implement asylum laws in a way that is fair, timely and consistent with international humanitarian principles and our domestic tradition of providing refuge for the oppressed. The Asylum Office in Miami has jurisdiction over the state of Florida, the Commonwealth of Puerto Rico, and the US Virgin Islands.

Erich J Cauller
Asylum Office Director
e-mail: erich.cauller@dhs.gov

Erin Fatica
Deputy Director
e-mail: erin.fatica@dhs.gov

New York Asylum Office
US Citizenship & Immigration Services
One Cross Island Plaza
3rd Floor
Rosedale, NY 11422
Phone: 718-723-5954
Fax: 718-723-1121

Description: The Asylum Office in New York has jurisdiction over the state of New York excluding the jurisdiction of the Albany Sub Office, the Buffalo District Office, and the boroughs of Manhattan and the Bronx.

Patricia Jackson
Asylum Office Director

Mick Dedukaj
Deputy Director

Newark Asylum Office
US Citizenship & Immigration Services
1200 Wall Street West
4th Floor
Lyndhurst, NJ 07071-3614
Phone: 201-531-0555
Fax: 201-531-1877

Description: The Newark Asylum Office in Lyndhurst, New Jersey, has jurisdiction over the states of Connecticut, Delaware, Maine, Massachusetts, New Hampshire, New Jersey, Rhode Island, and Vermont. The Newark Asylum Office also has jurisdiction over the following counties in the state of New York: Albany, Allegany, Bronx, Broome, Cattaraugus, Cayuga, Chautauqua, Chemung, Chenango, Clinton, Columbia, Cortland, Delaware, Erie, Essex, Franklin, Fulton, Genesse, Greene, Hamilton, Herkimer, Jefferson, Lewis, Livingston, Madison, Monroe, Montgomery, New York (Manhattan), Niagara, Oneida, Onondaga, Ontario, Orleans, Oswego, Otsego, Rensselaer, Saint Lawrence, Saratoga, Schenectady, Schoharie, Schuyler, Seneca, Steuben, Tioga, Tompkins, Warren, Washington, Wayne, Wyoming and Yates. The Newark Asylum Office also has jurisdiction over the following counties in Pennsylvania: Adams, Berks, Bucks, Cameron, Carbon, Centre, Chester, Clinton, Columbia, Cumberland, Dauphin, Delaware, Franklin, Fulton, Huntingdon, Juniata, Lackawanna, Lancaster, Lebanon, Lehigh, Luzerne, Lycoming, Mifflin, Monroe, Montgomery, Montour, Northampton, Northumberland, Perry, Philadelphia, Pike, Potter, Schuylkill, Snyder, Sullivan, Susquehanna, Tioga, Union, Wayne, Wyoming and York.

Susan Raufer
Asylum Office Director

Aster Zeleke
Deputy Director

San Francisco Asylum Office
US Citizenship & Immigration Services
75 Hawthorne Street
#303S
San Francisco, CA 94105-3920
Phone: 415-293-1234

Description: The Asylum Office in San Francisco has jurisdiction over the following counties in the State of California: Alameda, Alpine, Amador, Butte, Calaveras, Colusa, Contra Costa, Del Norte, El Dorado, Fresno, Glenn, Humboldt, Inyo, Kern, Kings, Lake, Lassen, Madera, Marin, Mariposa, Mendocino, Merced, Modoc, Mono, Monterey, Napa, Nevada, Placer, Plumas, Sacramento, San Benito, San Francisco, San Jaoquin, San Mateo, Santa Clara, Santa Cruz, Shasta, Sierra, Siskiyou, Solano, Sonoma, Stanislaus, Sutter, Tehama, Trinity, Tulare, Tuolumne, Yolo, and Yuba. The Asylum Office in San Francisco also has jurisdiction over the portion of Nevada currently under the jursdiction of the Reno Sub Office, and the states of Oregon, Washington, and Alaska.

Emilia Bardina
Asylum Office Director
Phone: 415-293-1204

Carlton Yue
Deputy Director

Anchorage District Office
US Citizenship & Immigration Services
620 East 10th Avenue
Suite 102
Anchorage, AK 99501
Phone: 800-375-5283

Description: District Offices are where most immigration field staff are located. District Offices are responsible for enforcing immigration laws in that jurisdiction. Certain applications are filed directly with District Offices, many kinds of interviews are conducted at these Offices, and immigration staff are available to answer questions, provide forms, etc.

Bernadette Nocerino-Doody
District Director
Phone: 907-271-4064

Atlanta District Office
US Citizenship & Immigration Services
Martin Luther King Jr Federal Building
77 Forsyth Street SW
Atlanta, GA 30303
Phone: 800-375-5283

Description: District Offices are where most immigration field staff are located. District Offices are responsible for enforcing immigration laws in that jurisdiction. Certain applications are filed directly with District Offices, many kinds of interviews are conducted at these Offices, and immigration staff are available to answer questions, provide forms, etc.

Rosemary L Melville
District Director
Phone: 404-331-0253

Baltimore District Office
US Citizenship & Immigration Services
Fallon Federal Building

31 Hopkins Plaza
Baltimore, MD 21201-2829
Phone: 800-375-5283

Description: District Offices are where most immigration field staff are located. District Offices are responsible for enforcing immigration laws in that jurisdiction. Certain applications are filed directly with District Offices, many kinds of interviews are conducted at these Offices, and immigration staff are available to answer questions, provide forms, etc.

Richard Caterisano
District Director
Phone: 410-962-2008

Boston District Office
US Citizenship & Immigration Services
John F Kennedy Federal Building
Government Center
Boston, MA 02203
Phone: 800-375-5283

Description: District Offices are where most immigration field staff are located. District Offices are responsible for enforcing immigration laws in that jurisdiction. Certain applications are filed directly with District Offices, many kinds of interviews are conducted at these Offices, and immigration staff are available to answer questions, provide forms, etc.

Denis Riordan
District Director
Phone: 617-565-4215

Buffalo District Office
US Citizenship & Immigration Services
Federal Center
130 Delaware Avenue
Buffalo, NY 14202-2404
Phone: 800-375-5283

Description: District Offices are where most immigration field staff are located. District Offices are responsible for enforcing immigration laws in that jurisdiction. Certain applications are filed directly with District Offices, many kinds of interviews are conducted at these Offices, and immigration staff are available to answer questions, provide forms, etc.

M Francis Holmes
District Director
Phone: 716-551-4741

Chicago District Office
US Citizenship & Immigration Services
101 West Congress Parkway
Chicago, IL 60604
Phone: 312-239-5900

Description: District Offices are where most immigration field staff are located. District Offices are responsible for enforcing immigration laws in that jurisdiction. Certain applications are filed directly with District Offices, many kinds of interviews are conducted at these Offices, and immigration staff are available to answer questions, provide forms, etc.

Ruth A Dorochoff
District Director
Phone: 312-385-1904

Cleveland District Office
US Citizenship & Immigration Services
AJC Federal Building
1240 East Ninth Street, Room 501
Cleveland, OH 44199-2085
Phone: 216-535-0530
Phone: 800-375-5283

Description: District Offices are where most immigration field staff are located. District Offices are responsible for enforcing immigration laws in that jurisdiction. Certain applications are filed directly with District Offices, many kinds of interviews are conducted at these Offices, and immigration staff are available to answer questions, provide forms, etc.

Mark B Hansen
District Director
Phone: 216-535-0350

Dallas District Office
US Citizenship & Immigration Services
8101 N Stemmons Freeway
Dallas, TX 75247
Phone: 800-375-5283

Description: District Offices are where most immigration field staff are located. District Offices are responsible for enforcing immigration laws in that jurisdiction. Certain applications are filed directly with District Offices, many kinds of interviews are conducted at these Offices, and immigration staff are available to answer questions, provide forms, etc.

Angela Barrows
District Director
Phone: 214-905-5724

Detroit District Office
US Citizenship & Immigration Services
333 Mount Elliot
Detroit, MI 48207-4385
Phone: 313-259-5354
Phone: 800-375-5283

Description: District Offices are where most immigration field staff are located. District Offices are responsible for enforcing immigration laws in that jurisdiction. Certain applications are filed directly with District Offices, many kinds of interviews are conducted at these Offices, and immigration staff are available to answer questions, provide forms, etc.

Maria Chavez
Acting District Director
Phone: 313-568-6000

El Paso District Office
US Citizenship & Immigration Services
1545 Hawkins Boulevard
Suite 167
El Paso, TX 79925
Phone: 800-375-5283

Description: District Offices are where most immigration field staff are located. District Offices are responsible for enforcing immigration laws in that jurisdiction. Certain applications are filed directly with District Offices, many kinds of interviews are conducted at these Offices, and immigration staff are available to answer questions, provide forms, etc.

Raymond Adams
District Director
Phone: 915-225-1750

Harlingen District Office
US Citizenship & Immigration Services
1717 Zoy Street
Harlingen, TX 78552
Phone: 800-375-5283

Description: District Offices are where most immigration field staff are located. District Offices are responsible for enforcing immigration laws in that jurisdiction. Certain applications are filed directly with District Offices, many kinds of interviews are conducted at these Offices, and immigration staff are available to answer questions, provide forms, etc.

Alfonso R De Leon
District Director
Phone: 956-389-7565

Honolulu District Office
US Citizenship & Immigration Services
595 Ala Moana Boulevard
Honolulu, HI 96813
Phone: 800-375-5283

Description: District Offices are where most immigration field staff are located. District Offices are responsible for enforcing immigration laws in that jurisdiction. Certain applications are filed directly with District Offices, many kinds of interviews are conducted at these Offices, and immigration staff are available to answer questions, provide forms, etc.

David Gulick
District Director
Phone: 808-532-3748

Houston District Office
US Citizenship & Immigration Services
126 Northpoint Drive
Houston, TX 77060
Phone: 800-375-5283

Description: District Offices are where most immigration field staff are located. District Offices are responsible for enforcing immigration laws in that jurisdiction. Certain applications are filed directly with District Offices, many kinds of interviews are conducted at these Offices, and immigration staff are available to answer questions, provide forms, etc.

Sharon A Hudson
District Director
Phone: 281-774-4610

Kansas City District Office
US Citizenship & Immigration Services
9747 Northwest Conant Avenue
Kansas City, MO 64153
Phone: 800-375-5283

Description: District Offices are where most immigration field staff are located. District Offices are responsible for enforcing immigration laws in that jurisdiction. Certain applications are filed directly with District Offices, many kinds of interviews are conducted at these Offices, and immigration staff are available to answer questions, provide forms, etc.

Michael Jaromin
District Director
Phone: 816-891-0684

Los Angeles District Office
US Citizenship & Immigration Services
300 North Los Angeles Street
Room 1001
Los Angeles, CA 90012-3336
Phone: 800-375-5283

Description: District Offices are where most immigration field staff are located. District Offices are responsible for enforcing immigration laws in that jurisdiction. Certain applications are filed directly with District Offices, many kinds of interviews are conducted at these Offices, and immigration staff are available to answer questions, provide forms, etc.

Jane Arellano
District Director
Phone: 213-830-4940

Miami District Office
US Citizenship & Immigration Services
7880 Biscayne Boulevard
Miami, FL 33138
Phone: 800-375-5283

Description: District Offices are where most immigration field staff are located. District Offices are responsible for enforcing immigration laws in that jurisdiction. Certain applications are filed directly with District Offices, many kinds of interviews are conducted at these Offices, and immigration staff are available to answer questions, provide forms, etc.

Jack Bulger
District Director
Phone: 305-762-3515

New Orleans District Office
US Citizenship & Immigration Services
2424 Edenborn Avenue
Metairie, LA 70001
Phone: 800-375-5283

Description: District Offices are where most immigration field staff are located. District Offices are responsible for enforcing immigration laws in that jurisdiction. Certain applications are filed directly with District Offices, many kinds of interviews are conducted at these Offices, and immigration staff are available to answer questions, provide forms, etc.

M Stella Jarina
District Director
Phone: 504-599-7950

New York City District Office
US Citizenship & Immigration Services
Jacob Javits Federal Building
26 Federal Plaza
New York, NY 10278
Phone: 800-375-5283

Description: District Offices are where most immigration field staff are located. District Offices are responsible for enforcing immigration laws in that jurisdiction. Certain applications are filed directly with District Offices, many kinds of interviews are

.

conducted at these Offices, and immigration staff are available to answer questions, provide forms, etc.

Andrea Quarantillo
District Director
Phone: 212-264-3972

Newark District Office
US Citizenship & Immigration Services
Peter Rodino Jr Federal Building
970 Broad Street
Newark, NJ 07102-2506
Phone: 800-375-5283

Description: District Offices are where most immigration field staff are located. District Offices are responsible for enforcing immigration laws in that jurisdiction. Certain applications are filed directly with District Offices, many kinds of interviews are conducted at these Offices, and immigration staff are available to answer questions, provide forms, etc.

John Thompson
District Director
Phone: 973-645-4421

Philadelphia District Office
US Citizenship & Immigration Services
1600 Callowhill Street
Philadelphia, PA 19130
Phone: 800-375-5283

Description: District Offices are where most immigration field staff are located. District Offices are responsible for enforcing immigration laws in that jurisdiction. Certain applications are filed directly with District Offices, many kinds of interviews are conducted at these Offices, and immigration staff are available to answer questions, provide forms, etc.

Donald Monica
District Director
Phone: 215-656-7156

Phoenix District Office
US Citizenship & Immigration Services
2035 North Central Avenue
Phoenix, AZ 85004
Phone: 800-375-5283

Description: District Offices are where most immigration field staff are located. District Offices are responsible for enforcing immigration laws in that jurisdiction. Certain applications are filed directly with District Offices, many kinds of interviews are conducted at these Offices, and immigration staff are available to answer questions, provide forms, etc.

Robert J Okin
District Director
Phone: 602-514-7799

Portland, Maine District Office
US Citizenship & Immigration Services
176 Gannett Drive
South Portland, ME 04106
Phone: 800-375-5283

Description: District Offices are where most immigration field staff are located. District Offices are responsible for enforcing immigration laws in that jurisdiction. Certain applications are

filed directly with District Offices, many kinds of interviews are conducted at these Offices, and immigration staff are available to answer questions, provide forms, etc.

Rodolfo Lara
District Director
Phone: 207-780-3624

San Antonio District Office
US Citizenship & Immigration Services
8940 Fourwinds Drive
San Antonio, TX 78239
Phone: 800-375-5283

Description: District Offices are where most immigration field staff are located. District Offices are responsible for enforcing immigration laws in that jurisdiction. Certain applications are filed directly with District Offices, many kinds of interviews are conducted at these Offices, and immigration staff are available to answer questions, provide forms, etc.

Kenneth Pasquarell
District Director
Phone: 210-967-7073

San Diego District Office
US Citizenship & Immigration Services
880 Front Street
Suite 1234
San Diego, CA 92101
Phone: 800-375-5283

Description: District Offices are where most immigration field staff are located. District Offices are responsible for enforcing immigration laws in that jurisdiction. Certain applications are filed directly with District Offices, many kinds of interviews are conducted at these Offices, and immigration staff are available to answer questions, provide forms, etc.

Debra A Rogers
District Director
Phone: 619-557-3484

San Francisco District Office
US Citizenship & Immigration Services
630 Sansome Street
San Francisco, CA 94111
Phone: 800-375-5283

Description: District Offices are where most immigration field staff are located. District Offices are responsible for enforcing immigration laws in that jurisdiction. Certain applications are filed directly with District Offices, many kinds of interviews are conducted at these Offices, and immigration staff are available to answer questions, provide forms, etc.

Rosemary Melville
District Director
Phone: 415-844-5200

San Juan District Office
US Citizenship & Immigration Services
San Patrico Office Center
7 Tabonuco Street, Suite 100
Guaynabo, 00968
Puerto Rico
Mailing Address: PO Box 365068

Phone: 800-375-5283

Description: District Offices are where most immigration field staff are located. District Offices are responsible for enforcing immigration laws in that jurisdiction. Certain applications are filed directly with District Offices, many kinds of interviews are conducted at these Offices, and immigration staff are available to answer questions, provide forms, etc.

Enid Stulz
Acting District Director
Phone: 787-706-2346

St. Paul District Office
US Citizenship & Immigration Services
2901 Metro Drive
Suite 100
Bloomington, MN 55425
Phone: 800-375-5283

Description: District Offices are where most immigration field staff are located. District Offices are responsible for enforcing immigration laws in that jurisdiction. Certain applications are filed directly with District Offices, many kinds of interviews are conducted at these Offices, and immigration staff are available to answer questions, provide forms, etc.

Denise Frazier
District Director
Phone: 952-853-2920

Washington District Office
US Citizenship & Immigration Services
2675 Prosperity Avenue
Fairfax, VA 22031
Phone: 800-375-5283

Description: District Offices are where most immigration field staff are located. District Offices are responsible for enforcing immigration laws in that jurisdiction. Certain applications are filed directly with District Offices, many kinds of interviews are conducted at these Offices, and immigration staff are available to answer questions, provide forms, etc.

Greg Christian
District Director
Phone: 703-285-6030

FEDERAL

Department of Homeland Security
Immigration & Customs Enforcement

US Immigration & Customs Enforcement (ICE)
Headquarters
425 I Street NW
Washington, DC 20536
URL: www.ice.gov
e-mail: ice.publicaffairs@dhs.gov

Description: Immigration and Customs Enforcement was established in March of 2003 and is the largest investigative branch of the DHS. It is responsible for eliminating vulnerabilities in the nation's borders, and enforcing economic, infrastructure and transportation security. The organization is composed of four law enforcement divisions and several support divisions. These divisions combine to form a new investigative approach with new resources to provide unparalleled investigation, interdiction and security services to the public and the law enforcement partners in federal and local sectors.

Julie L Myers
Assistant Secretary

John P Clark
Deputy Assistant Secretary Operations

Theresa Bertucci
Deputy Assistant Secretary Management

Nick Smith
Chief of Staff

Gary W Schenkel
Director Federal Protective Service

Judy Rogers
Acting Director Office of Congressional Relations

John P Torres
Director Office of Detention & Removal Operations

Michael J Vanacore
Director Office of International Affairs

Marcy Forman
Director Office of Investigations

Jamie Zuieback
Acting Director Office of Public Affairs

Susan Cullen
Director Office of Policy & Planning

Charles N DeVita
Director Office of Training & Development

Traci A Lembke
Director Office of Professional Responsibility

Deborah Lewis
Director Office of Equal Employment Opportunity

Alex S Keenan
Chief Financial Officer

William J Howard
Principal Legal Advisor

Luke McCormack
Chief Information Officer

Christine M Greco
Chief Human Capital Officer

Cyber Crimes Center (C3)
US Immigration & Customs Enforcement
11320 Random Hills Road
Suite 400
Fairfax, VA 22030
Phone: 703-293-8005
Phone: 800-973-2867
Fax: 703-293-9127
URL: www.ice.gov/about/cybercrimes/index.htm
e-mail: cybercrimescenter@dhs.gov

Description: Investigates domestic and international criminal activity occuring on or facilitated by the Internet. It brings together the Child Exploitation Section, the Computer Forensics Section and the Cyber Crimes Section into one facility.

Federal Protective Service
US Immigration & Customs Enforcement
Washington, DC 20536
Phone: 202-690-9632
URL: www.ice.gov

Description: The Federal Protective Service (FPS) is charged with providing the vast federal communities the necessary levels of protection to safeguard the employees and visitors to the more than 8,800 federal agencies nationwide. Its work focuses on the interior security of the nation and the reduction of crimes and potential threats to federal facilities throughout the nation. Uniformed officers and special agents respond to calls for assistance, conduct investigations and assist in occupant emergency planning.

Gary W Schenkel
Director

Law Enforcement Support Center (LESC)
US Immigration & Customs Enforcement
188 Harvest Lane
Williston, VT 05495
Phone: 802-872-6050
URL: www.ice.gov/partners/lesc/

Description: Established in 1994, the support center is the critical point of contact for the national law enforcement community, providing timely, accurate information and assistance to officers and investigators at the local, state and federal levels. The LESC operates year round and provides identification and immigration status on individuals who have been arrested or are under investigation.

J Scott Blackman
Unit Chief

Office of Congressional Relations
US Immigration & Customs Enforcement
Washington, DC 20536

Description: The office represents ICE's core values and DHS objectives through federal Congressional liaison activities. They effectively accomplish this by promoting Congressional awareness of ICE operations, national and local programs, policies and initiatives.

Judy Rogers
Acting Director

Office of Detention & Removal Operations
US Immigration & Customs Enforcement
801 I Street NW
Suite 900
Washington, DC 20536
Phone: 202-305-2734

Description: The Office is responsible for promoting public safety and national security by ensuring the departure of all removable aliens from the US through the fair enforcement of immigration laws.

John P Torres
Director

Office of Intelligence
US Immigration & Customs Enforcement
Washington, DC 20536

Description: The office is responsible for collecting, analyzing and sharing strategic and tactical intelligence data for use by ICE and DHS.

Susan E Lane
Acting Director

Office of International Affairs
US Immigration & Customs Enforcement
425 I Street NW
Attn: 800 N Capitol, 3rd Fl
Washington, DC 20536
Phone: 202-732-0350

Description: The office interacts with the international community on behalf of ICE through investigations of immigration and customs violations, management of the Visa Security Program and the International Visitor's Program, representation with international organizations, conducting international training and guiding repatriation efforts.

Office of Investigations
US Immigration & Customs Enforcement
Washington, DC 20536

Description: The Office uses its legal authority to investigate issues such as immigration crime, human smuggling, narcotics, weapons smuggling, cyber crime and export enforcement issues. Special agents conduct investigations aimed at protecting critical infrastructure industries that are vulnerable to attack or exploitation.

Marcy Forman
Director

Small Business Program
US Immigration & Customs Enforcement
ICE Office of Procurement
24000 Avila Road, Room 5020
Laguna Niguel, CA 92607
URL: www.ice.gov/partners/procurement_contacts.htm

Description: The ICE Small Business Program allows for increased participation and practicable opportunities in ICE acquisitions to small disadvantaged, women-owned small business, small business, veteran-owned small business, service-disabled veteran-owned small business, and HUBZone small business concerns.

Alan Barclay
Contact
Phone: 949-425-7023
e-mail: alan.barclay@dhs.gov

FEDERAL

Department of Homeland Security
Secret Service

United States Secret Service
Headquarters
950 H Street NW
Washington, DC 20223-0001
Phone: 202-406-5700
Fax: 202-406-5246
URL: www.secretservice.gov/index.shtml

Description: The United States Secret Service is a crucial component of the Department of Homeland Security, with the dual mission of protection and criminal investigations. The Secret Service protects the President, government leaders and their families. Since its inception it has been involved in protecting the integrity of the nation's financial systems. Over the years, the agency's jurisdiction has expanded and among other things, provides protection for National Special Security Events (NSSE), when designated as such by the Secretary of the Department of Homeland Security. In addition, the Secret Service's National Threat Assessment Center (NTAC) responds to the increasing public concern about targeted, violent attacks throughout the country. NTAC advises law enforcement and other professionals and organizations who are responsible for investigating and preventing targeted violence. NTAC also develops and provides guidance and training to federal, state and local law enforcement personnel with the goal of preventing targeted violence.

Mark Sullivan
Director
Phone: 202-406-5700

Brian Nagel
Deputy Director

John J Kelleher
Chief Counsel
Phone: 202-406-5771

Don B Personette
Deputy Chief Counsel
Phone: 202-406-5771

Connie Brannon
Equal Employment Opportunity Director
Phone: 202-406-6550

Secret Service Office of Homeland Security
United States Secret Service
950 H Street NW
Washington, DC 20223-0001
Phone: 202-406-9010
Fax: 202-406-5246
URL: www.secretservice.gov

Description: The Secret Service Office of Homeland Security is mandated by statue and executive order to carry out two signifi-

cant missions: protection and criminal investigations. The Secret Service protects the President and Vice President, their families, heads of state, and other designated individuals, investigates threats against these protectees, protects the White House, Vice President's Residence, Foreign Missions, and other buildings within Washington DC, and plans and implements security designs for designated National Special Security Events.

Paul D Irving
Assistant Director
Phone: 202-406-9610

Elaine Heinlein
Homeland Security Advisor
Phone: 202-406-9610

National Threat Assessment Center (NTAC)
United States Secret Service
950 H Street NW
Washington, DC 20223-0001
Phone: 202-406-5708
URL: www.secretservice.gov/ntac.shtml
e-mail: ntac@secretservice.gov

Description: The National Threat Assessment Center (NTAC) was created to provide leadership and guidance to the emerging field of threat assessment. NTAC offers timely, realistic, useful, and effective advice to law enforcement and other professionals and organizations with responsibilities to investigate and/or prevent targeted violence. The NTAC also develops and provides threat assessment training and research associated with public official, stalking/domestic, workplace, and school-based violence.

Office of Administration
United States Secret Service
950 H Street NW
Washington, DC 20223-0001
Phone: 202-406-5780
Fax: 202-406-5006
URL: www.secretservice.gov

Paul Irving
Assistant Director
Phone: 202-406-5780

Jeffrey Eisenbeiser
Deputy Assistant Director
Phone: 202-406-5780

David Iacovetti
Administrative Operations Branch
Phone: 202-406-5825

Dale Burkett
Financial Management Division
Phone: 202-406-5619

William Aumand
Protective Operations & Administration Acquisition Branch
Phone: 202-406-6940

Tom Campbell
Training & Investigation Acquisition Branch
Phone: 202-406-6940

Office of Investigations
United States Secret Service
950 H Street NW
Washington, DC 20223-0001
Phone: 202-406-5716
Fax: 202-406-5052
URL: www.secretservice.gov

Description: Safeguards the payment and financial systems of the United States through the investigation of crimes that involve computer and telecommunications fraud, false identification documents, money laundering, and financial institution fraud. Its proactive approach includes these divisions: Criminal Investigations, Forensic Services, and Investigative Support.

Michael Stenger
Assistant Director
Phone: 202-406-5716

Michael Merritt
Deputy Assistant Director

Lisa Risley
Deputy Assistant Director

Derek Verdeyen
Deputy Assistant Director

AT Smith
Deputy Assistant Director

Craig Magaw
Criminal Investigative Division
Phone: 202-406-9330

Lee Fields
Forensic Services Division
Phone: 202-406-5926

Douglas Burke
Investigative Support Division
Phone: 202-406-5773

Office of Inspection
United States Secret Service
950 H Street NW
Washington, DC 20223-0001
Phone: 202-406-5766
Fax: 202-406-5624
URL: www.secretservice.gov

Uniformed Division
United States Secret Service
950 H Street NW
Suite 3700
Washington, DC 20223-0001
Phone: 202-406-6667

URL: www.secretservice.gov/ud.shtml

Curtis B Eldridge Jr
Chief
Phone: 202-406-6667

Jeffrey Banocy
Assistant Chief
Phone: 202-406-6667

Gary S Coffey
Foreign Missions Branch
Phone: 202-634-2555

Kevin Simpson
Naval Observatory Branch
Phone: 202-575-1157

Office of Protective Operations
United States Secret Service
950 H Street NW
Washington, DC 20223-0001
Phone: 202-406-5721
Fax: 202-406-5897
URL: www.secretservice.gov/protection_works.shtml

Timothy J Koerner
Assistant Director
Phone: 202-406-5721

Thomas Grupski
Inspections Division
Phone: 202-406-5721

Tracy Gast
Special Services Division
Phone: 202-406-0001

Office of Protective Research
United States Secret Service
950 H Street NW
Washington, DC 20223-0001
Phone: 202-406-5725
Fax: 202-406-6480
URL: www.secretservice.gov/protective_reseach.shtml

Office of Government & Public Affairs
United States Secret Service
950 H Street NW
Washington, DC 20223-0001
Phone: 202-406-5708
Fax: 202-406-9069
URL: www.secretservice.gov

Thomas Grupski
Assistant Director
Phone: 202-406-5708

John R Sullivan
Deputy Assistant Director Congressional Affairs Program
Phone: 202-406-5676

Eric Zahren
Public Affairs Program Special-Agent-in-Charge
Phone: 202-406-5708

Office of Human Resources & Training
United States Secret Service
950 H Street NW

Suite 8600
Washington, DC 20223-0001
Phone: 202-406-6500
Fax: 202-406-6501
URL: www.secretservice.gov

Julie Pierson
Assistant Director
Phone: 202-406-6500

Margaret Mannix
Deputy Assistant Director
Phone: 202-406-6500

Donato Coyer
Deputy Assistant Director
Phone: 202-406-6500

Keith Hill
Deputy Assistant Director
Phone: 202-406-6500

Secret Service Procurement Division
United States Secret Service
950 H Street NW
Washington, DC 20223-0001
Phone: 202-406-6940
Fax: 202-406-6940
URL: www.secretservice.gov/procurement.shtml

Jeff Rosenfield
Chief
Phone: 202-406-6940

Kelly Curtin
Deputy Chief

FEDERAL

Department of Homeland Security
Federal Emergency Management Agency

Federal Emergency Management Agency (FEMA)
Headquarters
500 C Street SW
Washington, DC 20472
Phone: 202-566-1600
Phone: 800-621-3362
Fax: 202-646-3930
URL: www.fema.gov
e-mail: opa@fema.gov

Description: The Federal Emergency Management Agency (FEMA) takes the lead in the effort to prepare the nation for all hazards and effectively manage federal response and recovery efforts following any national incident. FEMA also initiates proactive mitigation activities, trains first responders and manages the National Flood Insurance Program. The agency often partners with 27 federal agencies, the American Red Cross and state and local emergency management agencies. FEMA employs more than 2,600 full time employees and has on standby nearly 4,000 disaster assistance employees. With the signing of the Post-Katrina Emergency Reform Act, by the President in 2006, functions of the Preparedness Directorate (now National Protection & Programs Directorate) were transferred to FEMA. The following were transferred to the responsibility of FEMA: The Office of National Capital Region Coordination; The Radiological Emergency Preparedness Program (REPP); The Chemical Stockpile Emergency Preparedness Division (CEPP); The United States Fire Administration (USFA); and The Office of Grants & Training. (Some of these will undergo name changes and different programs will be broken up under separate directorates.)

R David Paulison
Administrator
Phone: 202-646-3900

Harvey E Johnson Jr
Deputy Administrator/COO
Phone: 202-646-3900

Gil H Jamieson
Associate Deputy Administrator Gulf Coast Recovery
Phone: 202-646-4090

Robert Shea
Associate Deputy Administrator
Phone: 202-646-3900

Corey Gruber
Deputy Administrator National Preparedness Directorate

Diedre Lee
Director Management & Chief Acquisition Officer

Tony Cira
Chief Information Officer

Glenn Cannon
Assistant Administrator Disaster Operations
Phone: 202-646-3577

Carlos J Castillo
Assistant Administrator Disaster Assistance
Phone: 202-646-4546

David I Maurstad
Assistant Administrator Mitigation
Phone: 202-646-2781

William Smith
Assistant Administrator Logistics Management Directorate

Charles L Hopkins III
Assistant Administrator National Continuity Programs Directorate
Phone: 202-646-4145

Albert H Fluman
Director NIMS National Integration Center

Cortez Lawrence
Superintendent Emergency Management Institute

Marko Bourne
Director Policy & Programs Analysis

John P Philbin PhD
Director Office of External Affairs

David A Trissell
Chief Counsel

Christopher T Geldart
Director National Capital Region Coordination

Nathaniel Fogg
Counselor to the Administrator & Deputy Administrator

Elizabeth Edge
Executive Secretariat
Phone: 202-646-3675

Pauline Campbell
Director Office of Equal Rights

Margaret A Young
Chief Financial Officer

Disaster Assistance Directorate
FEMA
500 C Street SW
Washington, DC 20472
Phone: 202-646-4546
Fax: 202-646-2730

27

Description: The mission of the Disaster Assistance Directorate is to ensure that individuals and communities affected by disasters are able to return to normal functions with minimal suffering and disruption of services. The following programs are administered: Individual Assistance; Public Assistance; Federal Coordinating Officer Program; and the National Response Plan Emergency Support Functions #14.

Carlos J Castillo
Assistant Administrator
Phone: 202-646-4546

Disaster Operations Directorate
FEMA
500 C Street SW
Washington, DC 20472
Phone: 202-646-3577
Fax: 202-646-4060

Description: The Directorate is responsible for coordinating the development and execution of interagency plans, policies and procedures for response operations in Presidential disaster and emergency declarations and other Incidents of National Significance.

Glenn Cannon
Assistant Administrator
Phone: 202-646-3577

Bob Powers
Acting Deputy Assistant Administrator
Phone: 202-646-3866

Mitigation Directorate
FEMA
500 C Street SW
Washington, DC 20472
Phone: 202-646-2781

Description: Manages a range of programs designed to reduce future losses to homes, schools, businesses, critical facilities and public buildings from natural disasters. It also manages the National Flood Insurance Program (NFIP).

David I Maurstad
Assistant Administrator
Phone: 202-646-2781

National Continuity Programs Directorate
FEMA
500 C Street SW
Washington, DC 20472
Phone: 202-646-4145
Fax: 202-646-4137
URL: www.fema.gov/about/offices/onsc

Description: National Continuity Programs (formerly the Office of National Security Coordination (ONSC)) represents FEMA and DHS as the Federal Executive Branch Lead Agent, to coordinate and ensure continuity of national essential functions and minimize the disruption of essential operations. The Office is responsible for policy, test, training and exercises of activities involving continuity of operations, continuity of government, and contingency programs as well as management of the Mount Weather Emergency Operations Center in support of a wide variety of FEMA and DHS functions.

Charles L Hopkins III
Assistant Administrator
Phone: 202-646-4145

Ann Buckingham
Deputy Assistant Administrator
Phone: 202-646-4145

Rex Wamsley
Contnuity of Operations Division Director
Phone: 202-646-2897
e-mail: rex.wamsley@dhs.gov

Steven Borth
Federal Coordination Branch Chief
Phone: 202-646-4329

Donna Royce
Operations Division Director
Phone: 202-646-3994

Kevin G Briggs
Readiness Division Director
Phone: 202-646-4166
e-mail: kevin.briggs@dhs.gov

National Preparedness Directorate
FEMA
500 C Street SW
Washington, DC 20472

Description: A new directorate created to strengthen FEMA's capabilities.

Corey Gruber
Acting Deputy Administrator

NIMS National Integration Center (NIC)
FEMA
500 C Street SW
Washington, DC 20472
Phone: 202-646-3850
URL: www.fema.gov/emergency/nims
e-mail: nims-integration-center@dhs.gov

Description: NIMS was developed to meet the needs of responders from different jurisdictions in emergency situations including acts of terrorism. Practices include a unified approach to incident management; standard command and management structures; and emphasis on preparedness, mutual aid and resource management.

Albert H Fluman
Director NIMS Integration Training Center
Phone: 202-646-4605

Carol Cameron
Deputy Director
Phone: 202-646-4554

Juanita Harris
Strategic Resource Management Branch Chief
Phone: 202-646-3158

James Mullikin
System Evaluation & Compliance Branch Chief
Phone: 202-646-4692

Kyle Blackman
Resource Planning & Coordination Branch Chief
Phone: 202-646-4676

Tracey Haynes
Resource & Development Standards & Technology Branch Chief
Phone: 202-646-3264

Paul Ganem
Training & Exercises Branch Chief
Phone: 202-646-3879

Office of National Capitol Region Coordination
National Preparedness Directorate
Washington, DC 20528
Phone: 202-282-8000

Description: Oversees and coordinates federal programs in relationship with the National Capitol Region to ensure adequate information sharing, planning, training and execution of domestic preparedness activities.

Christopher T Geldart
Director

US Fire Administration
FEMA
16825 S Seton Avenue
Emmitsburg, MD 21727
Phone: 301-447-1000
Fax: 301-447-1346
URL: www.usfa.dhs.gov

Description: Reduces life and economic losses due to fire and related emergencies through leadership, advocacy, coordination and support. The Administration is an entity of FEMA and serves the nation independently but in coordination with other federal agencies, fire protection and emergency service communities.

Gregory Cade
Assistant Administrator
Phone: 301-447-1018

Denis Onieal
National Fire Academy Superintendent
Phone: 301-447-1117

Alex Furr
National Fire Data Center Division Director
Phone: 301-447-1353

Cortez Lawrence
National Fire Programs Division Director
Phone: 301-447-1147

Ronald Face
Support Services Division Director
Phone: 301-447-1223

FEMA Region I: Serving CT, MA, ME, NH, RI, VT
99 High Street
6th Floor
Boston, MA 02110
Phone: 617-956-7506
Phone: 877-336-2734
Fax: 617-956-7519

Arthur W Cleaves
Regional Administrator
Phone: 617-956-7506

Kenneth L Horak
Deputy Regional Administrator
Phone: 617-956-7506
e-mail: kenneth.horak@dhs.gov

John Carleton
National Preparedness Division Director
Phone: 617-956-7567

Jeanne Gallagher
Response & Recovery Division Director

Paul Ford
Emergency Analyst

Nicole Andrews
Tribal Contact
Phone: 617-304-2432
e-mail: nicole.andrews@dhs.gov

Marty Bahamonde
Media Contact
Phone: 617-956-7547
e-mail: marty.bahamonde@dhs.gov

FEMA Region II: Serving NY, NJ, PR, USVI
26 Federal Plaza
Suite 1337
New York, NY 10278
Phone: 212-680-3600
Fax: 212-680-3681

Steve Kempf
Regional Administrator
Phone: 212-680-3609

Joseph F Picciano
Deputy Regional Administrator
Phone: 212-680-3609
e-mail: joe.picciano@dhs.gov

Sean Waters
Emergency Analyst
Phone: 212-680-3605

Mike Beeman
National Preparedness Division Director

Mike Pena
Response & Recovery Division Director
Phone: 212-680-3680

Kristina Simpson
External Affairs Information Desk
Phone: 212-680-8516
e-mail: kristina.simpson1@dhs.gov

FEMA Region III: Serving DC, DE, MD, PA, WV, VA
One Independence Mall
615 Chestnut Street, 6th Floor
Philadelphia, PA 19106-4404
Phone: 215-931-5604
Fax: 215-931-5621

Jonathan Sarubbi
Regional Administrator
Phone: 215-931-5604

Patricia G Arcuri
Deputy Regional Administrator
Phone: 215-931-5604
e-mail: patricia.arcuri@dhs.gov

Robert P Welch
National Preparedness Division Director
Phone: 215-931-5540

Thomas Majusiak
Response & Recovery Division Director

Niki Edwards
Media Contact
Phone: 215-931-5614
e-mail: niki.edwards1@dhs.gov

FEMA Region IV: Serving AL, FL, GA, TN, KY, NC, SC, MS
3003 Chamblee-Tucker Road
Atlanta, GA 30341
Phone: 770-220-5200
Fax: 770-220-5230

Major Phillip May
Regional Administrator
Phone: 770-220-5224

Mary Lynne Miller
Deputy Regional Administrator
Phone: 770-220-5224
e-mail: mary-lynne.miller@dhs.gov

Kevin Kelkenberg
National Preparedness Division Director
Phone: 770-220-5454

Paul Fay
Response & Recovery Division Director

Steve Denham
Emergency Analyst

Mary Hudak
Media Contact
Phone: 770-220-5226
e-mail: mary.hudak@dhs.gov

FEMA Region V: Serving IL, IN, MI, MN, OH, WI
536 S Clark Street
6th Floor
Chicago, IL 60605
Phone: 312-408-5500
Fax: 312-408-5234

Edward G Buikema
Regional Administrator
Phone: 312-408-5501

Janet M Odeshoo
Deputy Regional Administrator
Phone: 312-408-5504
e-mail: janet.odeshoo@dhs.gov

James Duncan
National Preparedness Division Director
Phone: 312-408-5550

David A Skarosi
Response & Recovery Division Director
Phone: 312-408-5506

Jean Baker
Media Contact
Phone: 312-408-5515
e-mail: jean.baker@dhs.gov

FEMA Region VI: Serving AR, LA, NM, OK, TX
800 N Loop 288
Federal Regional Center
Denton, TX 76209-3698
Phone: 940-898-5399
Fax: 940-898-5325

William E Peterson
Regional Administrator
Phone: 940-898-5104

Gary Jones
Deputy Regional Administrator
Phone: 940-898-5104
e-mail: gary.jones@dhs.gov

Frank A Pagano
Federal Insurance & Mitigation Director

Robert Hendrix
National Preparedness Division Director
Phone: 940-898-5346

Tony Robinson
Response & Recovery Division Director

Reba Kestler
Tribal Contact
Phone: 940-898-5213
e-mail: reba.kestler@dhs.gov

David Passey
Media Contact
Phone: 940-898-5287
e-mail: david.passey@dhs.gov

FEMA Region VII: Serving IA, KS, MO, NE
9221 Ward Parkway
Suite 300
Kansas City, MO 64114-3372
Phone: 816-283-7063
Fax: 816-283-7582

Richard G Hainje
Regional Administrator
Phone: 816-283-7054
e-mail: richard.hainje@dhs.gov

Arthur Freeman
Deputy Regional Administrator
Phone: 816-283-7062
e-mail: arthur.freeman@dhs.gov

James Nelson
Tribal Contact-Kansas City, MO
Phone: 816-283-7020
e-mail: james.nelson@dhs.gov

Pam Franke
Tribal Contact-NE, IA, MO, KS
Phone: 816-283-7008
e-mail: pam.franke@dhs.gov

Brian Bowman
Media Contact
Phone: 816-283-7080
e-mail: brian.bowman@dhs.gov

FEMA Region VIII: Serving CO, MT, ND, SD, UT, WY

Denver Federal Ctr, Building 710
Box 25267
Denver, CO 80225-0267
Phone: 303-235-4800
Fax: 303-235-4976

Robert L Flowers
Regional Administrator
Phone: 303-235-4812

Scott J Logan
Tribal Contact
Phone: 303-235-4864
e-mail: scott.logan@dhs.gov

Marijo Camrud
Program Specialist
e-mail: marijo.camrud@dhs.gov

FEMA Region IX: Serving AZ, CA, Guam, HI, NV, CNMI, RMI, FSM, American Samoa

1111 Broadway
Suite 1200
Oakland, CA 94607-4052
Phone: 510-627-7100
Fax: 510-627-7112

Nancy Ward
Regional Administrator
Phone: 510-627-7100

Karen Armes
Deputy Regional Administrator
Phone: 510-627-7100
e-mail: karen.armes@dhs.gov

Kevin J Clark
Emergency Analyst
Phone: 510-627-7102

Farley Howell
National Preparedness Division

Robert Fenton
Response & Recovery Division

Kim Walz
Public Affairs Officer
Phone: 510-627-7006
e-mail: kim.walz@dhs.gov

FEMA Region X: Serving AK, ID, OR, WA

130 228th Street SW
Federal Regional Center
Bothell, WA 98021-8627
Phone: 425-487-4600

Fax: 425-487-4622

Susan Reinertson
Regional Administrator
Phone: 425-487-4604

Kathleen Cox
Tribal Contact-Alaska & Idaho
Phone: 425-487-4765

Andrew Hendrickson
Tribal Contact-Washington & Oregon
Phone: 425-487-4784

Michael Howard
Public Affairs Officer
Phone: 425-487-4610
e-mail: mike.howard@dhs.gov

FEMA Caribbean Area Division

159 Calle Chardon
New San Juan Office Bldg, 6th Floor
Hato Rey, 00918
Puerto Rico
Mailing Address: PO Box 70105, San Juan PR, 00936
Phone: 787-296-3514
Phone: 787-729-7624

Alejandro De LaCampa
Division Director
Phone: 787-296-3514

FEMA Pacific Area Division

Building T-112, Stop 120
Fort Shafter
Honolulu, HI 96858-5000
Phone: 808-851-7900
Fax: 808-851-7927

Woodrow Goins
Division Director
Phone: 808-851-7900

Meredith Schigetani
Tribal Contact

FEDERAL

Department of Homeland Security
Coast Guard

US Coast Guard
Headquarters
2100 Second Street SW
Washington, DC 20593
Phone: 202-372-4411
Phone: 202-372-4600
Fax: 202-372-4960
URL: www.uscg.mil; homeport.uscg.mil
e-mail: Locator@comdt.uscg.mil

Description: The United States Coast Guard (USCG) is a multi-mission, military and maritime first responder. It protects the public, the environment, and US economic and security interests in any maritime region, including international waters, the nation's coastlines, ports and inland waterways. Although it is the smallest of the seven uniformed services of the US, the USCG plays a broad and important role in homeland security, law enforcement, search and rescue, and marine environmental pollution response. Crews react to a wide variety of maritime disasters, such as bridge and waterway accidents. The Coast Guard's specially trained National Strike Force teams, based in different parts of the country, act quickly to clean up oil and hazardous materials spills, and provide assistance during natural disasters, working closely with the EPA, FEMA, and state and local agencies. The Commandant of the Coast Guard reports directly to the Secretary of Homeland Security. Upon declaration of war or when the President so directs, the Coast Guard would operate as an element of the Department of Defense.

Admiral Thad W Allen
Commandant
Phone: 202-372-4411

Vice Admiral Vivien S Crea
Vice Commandant
Phone: 202-372-4422

Barbara Gitschier
Chief Executive Secretariat
Phone: 202-372-4402

Vice Admiral Robert J Papp Jr
Chief of Staff
Phone: 202-372-4546

Commander Melissa Bert
Special Assistant
Phone: 202-372-4403

Commander Brendan McPherson
Press Secretary
Phone: 202-372-4407

Joseph N Ingolia
Chief Administrative Law Judge
Phone: 202-372-4440

Charles W Bowen
Master Chief Petty Officer
Phone: 202-372-4433

Captain William F Cuddy Jr
Chaplain
Phone: 202-372-4435

Coast Guard Research & Development Center
US Coast Guard
1082 Shennecossett Road
Groton, CT 06340-6048
Phone: 860-441-2600
Fax: 860-441-2792
URL: www.rdc.uscg.gov

Description: The Coast Guard Research and Development Center is the sole facility within the Coast Guard for performing research, development, test and evaluation in support of its mission. This center combines expertise in business practices with knowledge of existing and emerging science and technology, especially as they relate to homeland security of the Untited States.

Captain Thomas Jones
Commanding Officer
Phone: 860-441-2600
e-mail: thomas.w.jones@uscg.mil

Donald F Cundy
Technical Director
Phone: 860-441-2615
e-mail: don.f.cundy@uscg.mil

Operations
US Coast Guard
2100 Second Street SW
Washington, DC 20593
Phone: 202-372-2000
URL: www.uscg.mil

Rear Admiral David Pekoske
Assistant Commandant
Phone: 202-372-2000

Intelligence & Criminal Investigations
US Coast Guard
2100 Second Street SW
Room 3316
Washington, DC 20593
Phone: 202-372-2700
URL: www.uscg.mil; homeport.uscg.mil

Description: Muli-faceted programs which support the full range of Coast Guard missions, including ports, waterways, coastal security, and national defense.

James F Sloan
Assistant Commandant
Phone: 202-372-2700

Rob Irvin
Counterintelligence
Phone: 202-372-2711

Jack Cornett
Coast Guard Investigative Service
Phone: 202-493-6600

Captain Patrick Nemeth
Intelligence Coordination Center

Richard Harding
Intelligence Systems & Security Division
Phone: 202-372-2745

Prevention
US Coast Guard
2100 Second Street SW
Washington, DC 20593
Phone: 202-372-1001
URL: www.uscg.mil

Anthony Regalbuto
Technical Advisor Inspection & Compliance
Phone: 202-372-1018
e-mail: anthony.regalbuto@uscg.mil

Jeffery G Lantz
Director National & International Standards
Phone: 202-372-1351

Response Operations
US Coast Guard
2100 Second Street SW
Washington, DC 20593
Phone: 202-372-2010
URL: www.uscg.mil/hq/g-m/nmc/response/

Rear Admiral Wayne E Justice
Assistant Commandant
Phone: 202-372-2010

National Strike Force
US Coast Guard
National Strike Force Coordination Center
1461 North Road Street
Elizabeth City, NC 27909
Phone: 252-331-6000
Fax: 252-331-6012
URL: www.uscg.mil/hq/nsfweb/NSF/

Description: The National Strike Force (NSF) provides highly trained and experienced personnel and specialized equipment to Coast Guard and other federal agencies to facilitate preparedness for and response to hazardous substance pollution incidents to protect public health and the environment. The NSF minimizes the adverse impact from such hazardous materials releases as well as weapons of mass destruction (WMD) incidents and is thus a vital component of the homeland security mission. The National Strike Force Coordination Center provides support and

standardization guidance to the Atlantic, Gulf and Pacific Strike Teams.

Captain Roderick E Walker
Commander

International Affairs Staff
US Coast Guard
2100 Second Street SW
Room 4420
Washington, DC 20593
Phone: 202-372-4453
Fax: 202-372-4965
URL: www.uscg.mil/international
e-mail: intl@comdt.uscg.mil

Katherine E Johnson
Director/Foreign Policy Advisor
Phone: 202-372-4450

Captain Charley Diaz
Deputy Director
Phone: 202-372-4452

David Zimmerman
Regional Branch Chief
Phone: 202-372-4460

Commander Christopher M Smith
International Organizations, Planning & External Coordination
Phone: 202-372-4470
e-mail: csmith@comdt.uscg.mil

Donna Sukkar
Resource Management Branch Chief
Phone: 202-372-4480
e-mail: dsukkar@comdt.uscg.mil

Governmental and Public Affairs
US Coast Guard
2100 Second Street SW
Room 3416
Washington, DC 20593
Phone: 202-372-4620
Fax: 202-372-4900
URL: www.uscg.mil/news/cgnews.html

Rear Admiral Mary E Landry
Assistant Commandant Governmental & Public Affairs
Phone: 372-460-5530

Captain James Howe
Chief Congressional & Governmental Affairs
Phone: 202-245-0520

Captain James McPherson
Chief Public Affairs
Phone: 202-372-4620

Jordan St John
Chief Community Relations
Phone: 202-372-4640

Coast Guard Small Business Program
Office of Procurement Management
2100 Second Street SW
Room 5222
Washington, DC 20593-0001

Phone: 202-475-3222

Description: The Coast Guard Small Business Program maintains key information for small and disadvantaged businesses interested in contracting with the United States Coast Guard and the Department of Homeland Security.

Phyllis Miriashtiani
Manager
e-mail: phyllis.e.miriashtiani@uscg.mil

Atlantic Area
US Coast Guard
Portsmouth, VA
URL: www.uscg.mil/lantarea/

VAdm D Brian Peterman
Commander

Captain Steven H Ratti
Chief of Staff

Pacific Area
US Coast Guard
Alameda, CA
Phone: 510-437-3522
Fax: 510-437-3774
URL: www.uscg.mil/pacarea/

VAdm Charles D Wurster
Commander
Phone: 510-437-3522

Captain Daniel A Neptun
Chief of Staff
Phone: 510-437-3522

MCPO Kevin Isherwood
Command Master Chief

FEDERAL

Department of Homeland Security
Management Directorate

Management Directorate
Headquarters
US Department of Homeland Security
Washington, DC 20528
Phone: 202-447-3400
Fax: 202-447-3713
URL: www.dhs.gov/xabout/structure/editorial_0096.shtm

Description: The Management Directorate is responsible for ensuring that all Department of Homeland Security's more than 170,000 employees have clear responsibilities and means of communication with other personnel and management. In addition, this Directorate is responsible for budget; appropriations; expenditure of funds; accounting and finance; information technology systems; facilities, property, equipment and other material resources; identification and tracking of performance measurements relating to the responsibilities of DHS.

Paul A Schneider
Under Secretary
Phone: 202-447-3400

Donald G Bathurst
Chief Administrative Services Officer

David L Norquist
Chief Financial Officer
Phone: 202-447-5751

Marta Brito Perez
Chief Human Capital Officer
Phone: 202-357-8200

Scott Charbo
Chief Information Officer
Phone: 202-447-0700

Elaine C Duke
Chief Procurement Officer
Phone: 202-447-5300

Jerry Williams
Acting Chief Security Officer

Office of Administrative Services
Management Directorate
US Department of Homeland Security
Washington, DC 20528
Phone: 202-282-8288

Donald Bathurst
Chief Administrative Officer
e-mail: donald.bathurst@dhs.gov

Lee Salet
Executive Assistant to CAO

Phone: 202-282-8288
e-mail: lee.salet@dhs.gov

Office of the Chief Financial Officer
Management Directorate
7th & D Streets SW
Washington, DC 20528
Phone: 202-447-5751

David Norquist
Chief Financial Officer
Phone: 202-447-5751
e-mail: david.nordquist@dhs.gov

Mary Ann Woodson
Deputy CFO
Phone: 202-447-5751

Kate Valentine
Chief of Staff
Phone: 202-447-5173

Jennifer Barber
Executive Assistant to CFO
Phone: 202-447-5171

Deborah Schilling
Budget Division
Phone: 202-447-5155

John McNamara
Financial Management Division
e-mail: john.mcnamara@dhs.gov

Stacey Marcott
Program Analysis & Evaluation Division

Office of Human Capital
Management Directorate
1201 New York Avenue NW
13th Floor
Washington, DC 20528
Phone: 202-357-8200
Fax: 202-357-8259

Marta Brito Perez
Chief Human Capital Officer
Phone: 202-357-8200

Jackie Mayi
Executive Assistant to CHCO
Phone: 202-357-8200

Eugene Sexton
Human Capital Management Division
Phone: 202-357-8200

Shawn Flinn
Human Resource Policy & Programs Division
Phone: 202-357-8200

Office of Information Technology
Management Directorate
US Department of Homeland Security
Washington, DC 20528
Phone: 202-447-0700

Scott Charbo
Chief Information Officer
Phone: 202-447-0700
e-mail: scott.charbo@dhs.gov

Robert West
Chief Information Security Officer/Director
e-mail: robert.west@dhs.gov

Alan Shelton
Infrastructure Management Office
e-mail: alan.shelton@dhs.gov

Office of Procurement
Management Directorate
US Department of Homeland Security
Washington, DC 20528
Phone: 202-447-5300

Description: The Office of Procurement is responsible for the business management duties, including acquisition of products and services.

Elaine C Duke
Chief Procurement Officer
Phone: 202-447-5300

Mui Erkun
Ombudsman for Procurement
Phone: 202-447-5300
e-mail: mui.erkun@dhs.gov

Janice McCollim
Executive Assistant to CPO
Phone: 202-447-3109

David Childs
Competitive Sourcing & Privatization Division
Phone: 202-447-5266
e-mail: david.childs@dhs.gov

Van Pace
Grants Management Division
Phone: 202-447-5269
e-mail: van.pace@dhs.gov

Kevin Boshears
Small & Disadvantaged Business Utilization Office
Phone: 202-447-5555
e-mail: kevin.boshears@dhs.gov

Office of Small & Disadvantaged Business Utilization (OSDBU)
Office of Procurement
245 Murray Lane, Bldg 410, Room 3124-A
Washington, DC 20528
Phone: 202-447-5555
Fax: 202-772-9730
URL: www.dhs.gov/xopbiz/smallbusiness/

e-mail: openforbusiness@dhs.gov

Description: The Office of Small and Disadvantaged Business Utilization ensures that all legislative specified categories of small businesses in prime contracts and subcontracts are effectively utilized to the maximum extent possible. The Office also assures that small and disadvantaged businesses are given ample opportunities within the Department of Homeland Security.

Kevin Boshears
Director
Phone: 202-447-5555
e-mail: kevin.boshears@dhs.gov

Dan Sturdivant
Assistant to Director for Outreach/Veteran-Owned SBA
Phone: 202-447-5289
e-mail: dan.sturdivant@dhs.gov

Mary Ellen Dorsey
Small Business Advocate
Phone: 202-447-5288
e-mail: maryellen.dorsey@dhs.gov

Joe Capuano
Small Business Advocate
Phone: 202-447-5287
e-mail: joe.capuano@dhs.gov

Kyle Groome
Subcontracting Compliance Program Manager
Phone: 202-447-5281
e-mail: kyle.groome@dhs.gov

Wendy Hill
SBA/Women-Owned Business
Phone: 202-447-5286
e-mail: wendy.hill@dhs.gov

Angela Williams
Mentor-Protege Program Manager
Phone: 202-447-5280
e-mail: angela.williams1@dhs.gov

Bernard Durham
SBA Procurement Center Representative
Phone: 202-447-5283
e-mail: bernard.durham@hq.dhs.gov

Office of Security
Management Directorate
US Department of Homeland Security
Washington, DC 20528
URL: www.dhs.gov/xabout/structure/editorial_0635.shtm

Description: The Office of Security protects and safeguards DHS personnel, property, facilities and information through the following measures: develops, implements and oversees security policies, programs and standards; delivers security awareness training and education to department personnel; and provides security support to DHS component agencies.

FEDERAL

Department of Homeland Security
Science & Technology Directorate

Science & Technology Directorate
Headquarters
US Department of Homeland Security
Washington, DC 20528
Phone: 202-282-8000
Phone: 202-282-8010
Fax: 202-282-8404
URL: www.dhs.gov/xabout/structure/editorial_0530.shtm

Description: The Science and Technology Directorate (S&T) is the primary research and development arm of DHS. In partnership with the private sector, national laboratories, universities, and other domestic and foreign government agencies, it helps push innovation and drive development and the use of high technology in support of homeland security. The Directorate is putting emphasis on enabling Border Patrol agents, airport baggage-screeners, Federal Air Marshals, Coast Guardmen, and other emergency responders to accomplish their mission in securing the nation. There are six primary divisions that address critical homeland security needs. They are the Explosives Division; Chemical and Biological Division; Border and Maritime Security Division; Command, Control & Interoperability Division; Human Factors Division; and Infrastructure/Geophysical Division.

Jay M Cohen
Under Secretary
Phone: 202-254-5606

Richard Williams
Chief Financial Officer

Office of Interoperability & Compatibility/SAFECOM
Science & Technology Directorate
PO Box 57243
Washington, DC 20037
Phone: 866-969-7233
URL: www.safecomprogram.gov/SAFECOM/
e-mail: safecom@dhs.gov

Description: The Safecom Program serves as the umbrella program within the federal government to help local, state, tribal and federal public safety agencies improve public safety response through more efficient and effective interoperable wireless communications.

Dr David G Boyd
Director

Homeland Security Science & Technology Advisory Committee (HSSTAC)
Science & Technology Directorate
US Department of Homeland Security

Washington, DC 20528
Mailing Address: Room 10-115
Phone: 202-254-5041
Fax: 202-254-6177
URL: www.dhs.gov/xres/committees/gc_1163242152895.shtm

Description: The advisory committee serves as a source of independent, scientific and technical planning advice for the Under Secretary for Science and Technology.

Homeland Security Institute
Science & Technology Directorate
2900 South Quincy Street
Suite 800
Arlington, VA 22206
Phone: 703-416-2000
URL: www.homelandsecurity.org

Description: The Homeland Security Institute is DHS's first Federally Funded Research & Development Center and is part of the S&T's activities and programs. It was established pursuant to Section 312 of the Homeland Security Act of 2002. It delivers independent, objective analyses and advises in core areas important in the support of policy development, decision-making and evaluation of new ideas.

Ruth David PhD
President/CEO

Philip Anderson PhD
VP & Institute Director

Robert Tuohy
Deputy Director Operations

George Thompson
Deputy Director Programs

Robert August
Deputy Director Systems

John Markey PhD
Deputy Director Threats

Plum Island Animal Disease Center
Science & Technology Directorate
PO Box 848
Greenport
Orient Point, NY 11944
Phone: 631-323-3200
Phone: 631-323-3207
Fax: 631-323-3295

Description: The Plum Island Animal Disease Center, formerly under the United States Department of Agriculture, conducts the research and diagnosis necessary to protect the nation's animal industries and exports from catastrophic economic losses caused by foreign animal disease agents accidentally or deliberately introduced into the United States. DHS is responsible for the safety and security of the facility.

Luis L Rodriguez
Research Leader
Phone: 631-323-3364
e-mail: luis.rodriguez@ars.usda.gov

Environmental Measurements Laboratory
Science & Technology Directorate
201 Varick St
5th Floor
New York, NY 10014
Phone: 212-620-3619
Phone: 212-254-5664
Fax: 212-620-3651
URL: www.eml.st.dhs.gov

Description: The Environmental Measurements Laboratory (EML) is a government-owned and operated laboratory which seeks to improve the understanding of current and future threats through research, development, testing and evaluation. As part of its Radiological Emergency Management System (REMS), EML has installed a monitoring platform on its roof in NYC supporting a suite of instruments to provide vital information in the event of a release of radioactive or other hazardous materials due to a terrorist attack. This platform serves as an operational test bed for newly developed radiation sensor systems that can be used by local first responders and to transition equipment from the test phase to operational field trials.

Adam R Hutter
Acting Director
Phone: 212-620-3619
e-mail: adam.hutter@dhs.gov

Christopher Kelly
Office of Public Affairs
Phone: 202-254-5664
e-mail: christopher.kelly1@dhs.gov

FEDERAL

Department of Homeland Security
National Protection & Programs Directorate

National Protection & Programs Directorate
Headquarters
US Department of Homeland Security
Washington, DC 20528
Phone: 202-282-8000
URL: www.dhs.gov/xabout/structure/editorial_0794.shtm

Description: The National Protection & Programs Directorate works to advance DHS's risk-reduction mission. Reducing risk requires an integrated approach that encompasses both physical and virtual threats and their associated human elements. The Post-Katrina Emergency Reform Act transferred much of National Preparedness programs to FEMA, but excluded certain elements; thus the Preparedness Directorate was reorganized and renamed the National Protection & Programs Directorate.

Robert D Jamison
Acting Under Secretary

Office of Cyber Security & Communications
National Protection & Programs Directorate
US Department of Homeland Security
Washington, DC 20528
Phone: 202-282-8000

Description: The Office strives to assure the security, resiliency and reliability of the nation's cyber and communications infrastructure in collaboration with public and private sectors, including international partners. Programs include the National Communications System (NCS) and the National Cyber Security Division.

Gregory T Garcia
Assistant Secretary

National Communications System
Office of Cyber Security & Communications
US Department of Homeland Security
Washington, DC 20528
Phone: 703-235-5516
Phone: 202-282-8000
URL: www.ncs.gov
e-mail: ncsweb1@dhs.gov

Description: The National Communication System's (NCS) mission is to assist the President, the National Security Council, the Director of the Office of Science and Technology Policy and the Director of the Office of Management and Budget in the exercise of telecommunications functions and responsibilities. Duties include the coordination of the planning and provision of national security and emergency preparedness communications for the federal government under all circumstances, including crisis or emergency, attack, recovery and reconstitution.

Robert D Jamison
Manager

Gregory T Garcia
Deputy Manager

Sallie MacDonald
Director

Thomas J Falvey
Deputy Director/Chief of Staff/Customer Service Division

Jeff Glick
Critical Infrastructure Protection Division Chief

James G Bittner Jr
Plans & Resources Division Chief

Gary D Amato
Technology & Programs Division Chief

Brian Carney
National Coordinating Center (NCC) Manager

National Cyber Security Division
Office of Cyber Security & Communications
US Department of Homeland Security
Washington, DC 20528
Phone: 202-282-8000
URL: www.dhs.gov/xabout/structure/editorial_0839.shtm

Description: The National Cyber Security Division seeks to protect the critical cyber infrastructure 24 hours a day, 7 days a week. It works collaboratively with public, private and international entities to secure cyberspace and America's cyber assets.

Office of Infrastructure Protection
National Protection & Programs Directorate
US Department of Homeland Security
Washington, DC 20528
Phone: 202-282-8000

Description: The Office of Infrastructure Protection (OIP) allows DHS to increase the nation's level of preparedness and the ability to respond and recover quickly in the event of an attack, natural disaster or other emergency. The OIP communicates threats, vulnerabilities, incidents, potential protective measures, and best practices to enhance protection, response, mitigation and restoration activities, nationally and internationally.

Robert B Stephan
Assistant Secretary

Office of Intergovernmental Programs
National Protection & Programs Directorate
US Department of Homeland Security

Washington, DC 20528
Phone: 202-282-8000

Description: Promotes an integrated national approach to homeland security by ensuring, coordinating and advancing federal interaction with state, local, tribal and territorial governments.

Anne P Petera
Assistant Secretary

Office of Risk Management & Analysis
National Protection & Programs Directorate
US Department of Homeland Security
Washington, DC 20528
Phone: 202-282-8000

Description: The Office serves as the DHS Executive Agent for national-level risk management and analysis of homeland security risk. It will develop and embed a consistent standardized approach to risk and develop a coordinated approach to risk management for the department.

US-VISIT
National Protection & Programs Directorate
US Department of Homeland Security
Washington, DC 20528
Phone: 202-298-5200
Fax: 202-298-5201
URL:
www.dhs.gov/xtrvlsec/programs/content_multi_image_0006.shtm

Description: The US-VISIT Program is a top priority for DHS because it enhances the security of citizens and visitors; protects the privacy of visitors; ensures the integrity of the immigration system; and facilitates legitimate trade and travel. It is a part of a continuum of security measures that begins overseas and continues through a visitor's arrival in and departure from the US.

Robert Mocny
Director
Phone: 202-298-5200

PT Wright
Deputy Director/Mission Operations
Phone: 202-298-5200
e-mail: p.t.wright@dhs.gov

Manuel Rodriguez
Facilities & Engineering Office
Phone: 202-298-5200
e-mail: manny.rodriguez@dhs.gov

Scott Hastings
Information & Technology Management Office
Phone: 202-298-5200
e-mail: scott.hastings@dhs.gov

FEDERAL

Executive Office of the President

Executive Office of the President
1600 Pennsylvania Avenue NW
Washington, DC 20502
Phone: 202-456-1414
Phone: 202-456-1700
Fax: 202-456-2461
URL: www.whitehouse.gov/homeland

Description: In addition to the federal Department of Homeland Security, the President maintains a White House Office of Homeland Security to facilitate interagency cooperation against terrorism. Further, the President receives confidential advice from a Homeland Security Advisor to help the entire White House staff maintain a strong role in coordinating government-wide efforts to secure the homeland. With the creation of the Department of Homeland Security, the Homeland Security Council (similar to the National Security Council) came into existence. Chaired by the President, this council: assesses the objectives, commitments and risks of the United States in the interest of homeland security and makes resulting recommendations to the President; oversees and reviews homeland security policies of the federal government and makes recommendations to the President; and performs other functions that the President may direct. The President is responsible for proposing the budget for homeland security initiatives; this figure for FY 2008 totals $46.4 billion, which is a 8% increase over FY 2007.

George W Bush
President
Phone: 202-456-1414
e-mail: president@whitehouse.gov

Richard B Cheney
Vice President
Phone: 202-456-7549
e-mail: vice.president@whitehouse.gov

Edward P Lazear
Council of Economic Advisers Chairman

Steve Hadley
National Security Advisor
Phone: 202-456-1700

Frances Fragos Townsend
Homeland Security Council Director/Assistant to the President for Homeland Security & Counterterrorism

Rob Portman
Office of Management & Budget Director
Phone: 202-456-1700

John E Straub
Office of Administration Director

John Marburger
Office of Science & Technology Policy Director
Phone: 202-456-7116
e-mail: info@ostp.gov

John P Walters
Office of National Drug Control Policy Director

Stephen Friedman
President's Foreign Intelligence Advisory Board Chairman

Allan Hubbard
National Economic Council Director

Karl Zinsmeister
Domestic Policy Council Director

Jim Connaughton
Council on Environmental Quality Chairman

Jay Hein
Office of Faith-Based & Community Initiatives Director

Ambassador Susan C Schwab
Office of the US Trade Representative

RAdm Raymond A Spicer
White House Military Office Director/Deputy Assistant to the President

Carol E Dinkins
Privacy & Civil Liberties Oversight Board Chairwoman

National Counterterrorism Center
Washington, DC 20503
Mailing Address: Liberty Crossing Bldg, VA
URL: www.nctc.gov

Description: The National Counterterrorism Center is unique in that it serves as the primary organization for strategic operational planning for counterterrorism. It integrates and analyzes all intelligence pertaining to terrorism possessed or acquired by the US government (except that of domestic nature), serves as the central bank on terrorism information, and establishes the IT systems within and between other agencies.

VAdm John Scott Redd (Ret)
Director

Michael E Letter
Principal Deputy Director

National Security Council (NSC)
Executive Office of the President
1600 Pennsylvania Avenue NW
Washington, DC 20502
Phone: 202-456-9491

Fax: 202-456-9300
URL: www.whitehouse.gov/nsc

Description: The National Security Council is the President's principal forum for considering national security and foreign policy matters with his senior national security advisors and cabinet officials. Its function is to advise and assist the President on national security and foreign policies. The Council serves as the President's principal arm for coordinating these policies among various government agencies.

George W Bush
President/Chairman
Phone: 202-456-4141

Stephen J Hadley
Assistant to the President/National Security Advisor
Phone: 202-456-9491

Juan Carlos Zarate
Deputy National Security Advisor-Combating Terrorism
Phone: 202-456-9491
e-mail: juan.zarate@do.treas.gov

Elliott Abrams
Deputy National Security Advisor-Global Democracy Strategy
Phone: 202-456-9361

Richard B Cheney
Vice President/Member
Phone: 202-456-2326

Robert M Gates
Secretary of Defense/Member

Condoleezza Rice
Secretary of State/Member
Phone: 202-647-9572

Henry M Paulson Jr
Secretary of the Treasury/Member

President's Foreign Intelligence Advisory Board
Executive Office of the President
725 17th Street NW
Washington, DC 20503
Phone: 202-456-2352
Fax: 202-395-3403
URL: www.whitehouse.gov/pfiab/

Description: The President's Foreign Intelligence Advisory Board provides advice to the President concerning the quality and adequacy of intelligence collection, of analysis and estimates, of counterintelligence, and of other intelligence activities. The Advisory Board also advises the President on the legality of foreign intelligence activities.

Stephen Friedman
Chairman

Stephanie Osbourn
Executive Director

Darlene Connelly
Director/General Counsel

Office of Management & Budget
Executive Office of the President
725 17th Street NW
Washington, DC 20503

Phone: 202-395-3080
Phone: 202-395-4840
Fax: 202-395-3888
URL: www.whitehouse.gov/omb

Rob Portman
Director
Phone: 202-395-4840

Stephen McMillin
Deputy Director
Phone: 202-395-4742

Clay Johnson III
Deputy Director for Management
Phone: 202-456-7070

Austin Smythe
Executive Associate Director
Phone: 202-395-4844

Robert Lehman
Chief of Staff
Phone: 202-395-4561

National Security Programs Office
Office of Management & Budget
725 17th Street NW
Executive Office Building
Washington, DC 20503
Phone: 202-395-4657
Fax: 202-395-0345
URL: www.whitehouse.gov/omb

Robert Goldberg
International Affairs Division
Phone: 202-395-4770

Sara Horrigan
State Branch
Phone: 202-395-6124

J Michael Daniel
Command, Control, Communication & Intelligence Branch
Phone: 202-395-4802

Bryan Smith
Operations & Support Branch
Phone: 202-395-3671

Office of E-Government & Information Technology
Office of Management & Budget
725 17th Street NW
Executive Office Building
Washington, DC 20503
Phone: 202-395-1181
Fax: 202-395-3888
URL: www.whitehouse.gov/omb/egov/

Tim Young
Associate Administrator
Phone: 202-395-0379
e-mail: tkyoung@omb.eop.gov

Office of Federal Procurement Policy
Office of Management & Budget
725 17th Street NW
Executive Office Building

Washington, DC 20503
Phone: 202-395-5802
Fax: 202-395-3242
URL: www.whitehouse.gov/omb/procurement

Description: The Office plays a central role in shaping the policies and practices federal agencies use to acquire the goods and services needed to carry out their responsibilities. The federal government spends approximately $350 billion annually to meet mission needs.

Paul A Denett
Administrator
Phone: 202-395-5802

Robert A Burton
Deputy Administrator
Phone: 202-395-7808
e-mail: robert a. burton@omb.eop.gov

Mathew C Blum
Associate Administrator

Office of the Director of National Intelligence
ODNI
Washington, DC 20511
Phone: 202-201-1111
URL: www.odni.gov

Description: Ensures that the Intelligence Community works together as a team - military and civilian, abroad and at home, its budget is well-spent, and our community-wide analysis is objective, timely and relevant to the nation's needs. Four directorates comprise the ODNI, focusing on Management, Collection, Requirements and Analysis.

Michael McConnell
Director of National Intelligence
Phone: 202-201-1111

David Shedd
Deputy Director Policy, Plans & Requirements
Phone: 202-201-1111

Mary Margaret Graham
Deputy Director Collection
Phone: 202-201-1111

Dr Thomas Fingar
Deputy Director Analysis
Phone: 202-201-1111

Alden V Munson
Deputy Director Acquisition
Phone: 202-201-1111

Benjamin A Powell
General Counsel
Phone: 202-201-1111

Dale Meyerrose
Chief Information Officer
Phone: 202-201-1111

Central Intelligence Agency
Office of Public Affairs
Washington, DC 20505
Phone: 703-482-0623
Fax: 703-482-1739
URL: www.cia.gov

Description: The Central Intelligence Agency (CIA) collects, evaluates, and disseminates vital information on political, military, economic, scientific, and other developments abroad needed to safeguard national security. By Presidential appointment and consent of the Senate, the Director of the CIA heads the department and reports to the Director of National Intelligence. The CIA has four main components: the National Clandestine Service, the Directorate of Intelligence, the Directorate of Science & Technology, and the Directorate of Support. The Agency does the following: collects intelligence through human sources and by other appropriate means; correlates and evaluates intelligence related to national security and provides appropriate dissemination of such intelligence; and provides overall direction for and coordination of the collection of national intelligence outside the US through human sources by elements of the Intelligence Community authorized to undertake such collection. In coordination with other departments, it ensures that the most effective use is made of resources and that appropriate account is taken of the risks to the US and those involved in such collection; and performs other duties and functions related to intelligence affecting the national security as the President or the Director of National Intelligence may direct.

General Michael V Hayden
Director

Stephen R Kappes
Deputy Director

Michael J Morell
Associate Deputy Director

John A Kringen
Director, Directorate of Intelligence

Stephanie L O'Sullivan
Director, Directorate of Science & Technology

Scott White
Director, Directorate of Support

Carmen A Medina
Director, Center for the Study of Intelligence

John A Rizzo
General Counsel

Mark Mansfield
Director, Public Affairs Office
Phone: 703-482-0623

Paul Barry
Entertainment Industry Liaison

Office of the National Counterintelligence Executive
Office of the Director of National Intelligence
CS5, Room 300
Washington, DC 20505
Phone: 703-682-4500
Phone: 703-874-8058
Fax: 703-682-4510
URL: www.ncix.gov

Description: The Office develops, coordinates, and produces: an annual national counterintelligence strategy for the US government; annual foreign intelligence threat assessments and other analytic products; priorities for counterintelligence collection, investigations, and operations; counterintelligence budgets and evaluations; espionage damage assessments; and counterintelligence awareness, outreach and training standards policies.

Joel F Brenner
National Counterintelligence Executive
Phone: 703-874-8058

National Intelligence Council
Office of the Director of National Intelligence
Washington, DC 20502
Phone: 703-482-0623
Fax: 703-482-1739
URL: www.dni.gov/nic/

Description: The National Intelligence Council is the Intelligence Community's center for midterm and long-term strategic thinking within the US government, reporting to the Director of National Intelligence and providing the President and senior policymakers with analyses of foreign policy issues that have been reviewed and coordinated throughout the Intelligence Community.

Dr Thomas Fingar
Chairman

David Gordon
Vice Chairman

Craig R Gralley
Director Strategic Plans & Outreach

Mathew J Burrows
Director Analysis & Production Staff

Johnnie Carson
National Intelligence Officer for Africa

James J Shinn
National Intelligence Officer for East Asia

William A Anderson
National Intelligence Officer for Economics & Global Issues

Richard D Kauzlarich
National Intelligence Officer for Europe

John R Landry
National Intelligence Officer for Military Issues

Alan Pino
National Intelligence Officer for Near East

Fiona Hill
National Intelligence Officer for Russia & Eurasia

Lawrence K Gershwin
National Intelligence Officer for Science & Technology

Nancy J Powell
National Intelligence Officer for South Asia

Edward M Gistaro
National Intelligence Officer for Transnational Threats

Kenneth L Knight Jr
National Intelligence Officer for Warning

Vann H Van Diepen
National Intelligence Officer for Weapons of Mass Destruction/Proliferation

J Patrick Maher
National Intelligence Officer for Western Hemisphere

Intelligence Community
Office of the Director of National Intelligence
725 17th Street NW, NEOB
Washington, DC 20503
Phone: 202-456-1414
URL: www.intelligence.gov

Description: A federation of executive branch organizations that pursue intelligence activities necessary for the conduct of foreign relations and for ensuring the national security of the US. The members include: Air Force Intelligence, Army Intelligence, CIA, Defense Intelligence Agency, DHS, Energy Department, FBI, Marine Corps Intelligence, National Geospatial-Intelligence Agency, National Reconnaissance Office, Drug Enforcement Administration, National Security Agency, Navy Intelligence, State Department's Bureau of Intelligence & Research, Treasury Department and United States Coast Guard.

Office of Science & Technology Policy
Executive Office of the President
725 17th Street NW
Room 5228
Washington, DC 20502
Phone: 202-395-7116
Fax: 202-456-6021
URL: www.ostp.gov
e-mail: info@ostp.gov

Description: To serve as a source of scientific and technological analysis and judgement for the President with respect to major policies, plans, and programs of the federal Government. The office is authorized to lead an interagency effort to develop and implement sound science and technology policies and budgets and to work with the science and higher education communities, private sector, state and local government, and other nations toward this goal.

John H Marburger III PhD
Director
Phone: 202-456-7116

Diane Jones
Deputy Director Science Division
Phone: 202-456-6130

Dr Richard M Russell
Deputy Director Technology Division
Phone: 202-456-6046

Ted Wackler
Senior Director Homeland & National Security Division
Phone: 202-456-7116

Stan Sokul
Chief of Staff & General Counsel
Phone: 202-456-7116

Kristin Scuderi
Communications/Public Affairs
Phone: 202-456-7116

President's Council of Advisors on Science & Technology
Office of Science & Technology Policy
Executive Office of the President

725 17th Street NW
Washington, DC 20502
Phone: 202-456-6100
Fax: 202-456-6021
URL: www.ostp.gov/pcast/pcast.html

Description: Formed on September 30, 2001, the Council is responsible to enable the President to receive advice from the private sector and academic community on technology, scientific research priorities and math and science education.

John H Marburger III PhD
Director OSTP & Co-Chair PCAST

Floyd Kvamme
Co-Chair PCAST

Celia Merzbacher
Executive Director
Phone: 202-456-6108
e-mail: cmerzbacher@ostp.eop.gov

FEDERAL

Department of Agriculture

Department of Agriculture
Headquarters
1400 Independence Avenue SW
Room 200
Washington, DC 20250
Phone: 202-720-3631
Fax: 202-720-2166
URL: www.usda.gov

Description: The United States Department of Agriculture (USDA) provides leadership on food, agriculture, natural resources, rural development and related issues based on sound policy, the best available science, and efficient management. The Department's vision includes enhancing agricultural trade, protecting the nation's food supply, improving the nation's nutrition, and protecting and enhancing the national resource base and environment. As part of the Department's Strategic Plan, Strategic Goal 4 is: "Enhance protection and safety of the nation's agriculture and food supply." In the event of an agri-terror attack, the USDA, specifically its Animal and Plant Health Inspection Service, would partner with DHS to safeguard America's food and agricultural resources and provide crucial scientific and diagnostic expertise. Although DHS is now responsible for protecting America's borders, USDA will continue to determine what agricultural products can, or should not, come into the country. Through risk assesments, USDA continues to set agricultural policy that is then carried out by the DHS.

Michael O Johanns
Secretary of Agriculture
Phone: 202-720-3631

Charles F Conner
Deputy Secretary of Agriculture
Phone: 202-720-3631

Dale W Moore
Chief of Staff
Phone: 202-720-3631
e-mail: dale.moore@usda.gov

Michael E Neruda
Senior Advisor to the Secretary
Phone: 202-720-3631
e-mail: mike.neruda@usda.gov

Marc L Kesselman
General Counsel
Phone: 202-720-3351

Phyllis K Fong
Inspector General
Phone: 202-720-8001
e-mail: pkfong@oig.usda.gov

Charles R Christopherson Jr
Chief Financial Officer
Phone: 202-720-0727

Anthony Hulen
White House Liaison
Phone: 202-720-2406

Bruce Bundick
Executive Secretariat
Phone: 202-720-7100

Homeland Security
Department of Agriculture
1400 Independence Avenue SW
Room 216A
Washington, DC 20250
Phone: 202-720-7654
URL: www.usda.gov/homelandsecurity

Description: The Homeland Security website provides details on what steps are being taken by USDA to protect the Nation's food supply against natural and intentional disasters. It is important that producers, processors, transporters and USDA employees have a good understanding of homeland security issues and are properly trained. The Strategic Partnership Program Agroterrorism (SPPA) Initiative is one of the collaborations between DHS, the USDA, the FDA and the FBI to accomplish this.

Jeremy Stump
Senior Advisor International & Homeland Security Affairs
Phone: 202-720-7654

Office of Departmental Administration
Department of Agriculture
14th & Independence Avenue SW
Washington, DC 20250
Phone: 202-720-3291
Fax: 202-720-2191
URL: www.usda.gov/da

Description: USDA's central administrative management organization. Provides support to policy officials of the Department and overall direction and coordination for the administrative programs and services of the USDA. In addition, it manages the Headquarters Complex and provides direct customer service to Washington, DC employees.

Boyd K Rutherford
Assistant Secretary
Phone: 202-720-3291
e-mail: boyd.rutherford@usda.gov

Gilbert L Smith Jr
Deputy Assistant Secretary
Phone: 202-720-3291

Marc R Hillson
Chief Administrative Law Judge
Phone: 202-720-6383

Priscilla Carey
Director Operations
Phone: 202-720-3937
e-mail: priscilla.carey@usda.gov

W R Ashworth
Director Security Services
Phone: 202-720-9448
e-mail: russ.ashworth@usda.gov

Leslie Pozanek
Continuity of Operations Planning
Phone: 202-690-3493
e-mail: leslie.pozanek@usda.gov

Jim Redington
Chief Emergency Programs
Phone: 202-690-3191
e-mail: jim.redington@usda.gov

Office of Procurement & Property Management
Office of Departmental Administration
14th & Independence Avenue SW
Washington, DC 20250
Phone: 202-720-9448
Fax: 202-690-1209
URL: www.usda.gov/da/oppm.htm

Description: In addition to coordinating acquisitions and procurement, the office also coordinates USDA's disaster management and emergency planning response activities.

Glenn Haggstrom
Director
Phone: 202-720-9448
e-mail: glenn.haggstrom@usda.gov

Blake Velde
Hazardous Materials Management (Acting)
Phone: 202-205-0906
e-mail: blake.velde@usda.gov

Todd Repass
Procurement Policy Division
Phone: 202-720-6206
e-mail: todd.repass@usda.gov

Denise Hayes
Property Management Division
Phone: 202-720-7283
e-mail: denise.hayes@usda.gov

Michael McFarland
Procurement Operations
Phone: 202-690-0142
e-mail: michael.mcfarland@usda.gov

Office of Small & Disadvantaged Business Utilization
Office of Departmental Administration
1400 Independence Avenue SW

Room 1805 S
Washington, DC 20250
Phone: 202-720-7117
Phone: 877-996-7328
Fax: 202-720-3001
URL: www.usda.gov/osdbu

Description: Provides maximum opportunities for small businesses to participate in USDA contracting activities.

James E House
Director
Phone: 202-720-7117
e-mail: james.house@usda.gov

Joseph A Ware
Deputy Director
Phone: 202-690-3837
e-mail: joe.ware@usda.gov

Sherry Cohen
Women-Owned Business Program Analyst
Phone: 202-720-9839

Linda Epstein
Service Disabled Veteran-Owned Business Program Analyst
Phone: 202-720-6840
e-mail: linda.epstein@usda.gov

Barbara LaCour
Small Business Development
Phone: 202-720-7835
e-mail: barbara.lacour@usda.gov

Food Safety & Inspection Service (FSIS)
Department of Agriculture
1400 Independence Avenue SW
Room 331-E
Washington, DC 20250
Phone: 202-720-7025
Fax: 202-205-0158
URL: www.fsis.usda.gov

Description: Public health agency in the US Department of Agriculture responsible for ensuring that the nation's commercial supply of meat, poultry, and egg products is safe, wholesome, and correctly labeled and packaged.

David Goldman
Acting Administrator
Phone: 202-720-7025

Bryce Quick
Deputy Administrator
Phone: 202-720-7900

Danielle Schor
Chief of Staff
Phone: 202-720-6618

Dr F Edward Scarbrough
US Manager for CODEX
Phone: 202-205-7760
e-mail: ed.scarbrough@fsis.usda.gov

Terri Nintemann
Assistant Administrator, Public Affairs, Education & Outreach
Phone: 202-720-8217

Karen Stuck
Assistant Administrator, International Affairs
Phone: 202-720-3473

Kenneth Petersen
Assistant Administrator, Field Operations
Phone: 202-720-8803

Office of Food Defense & Emergency Response
Food Safety & Inspection Service (FSIS)
1400 Independence Avenue SW
Rm 3130 S
Washington, DC 20250
Phone: 202-720-5643
Fax: 202-690-5634
URL: www.fsis.usda.gov/About_FSIS/OFDER/

Description: Manages all homeland security activities within
FSIS. The office makes sure that scientists, policy makers, field
staff and management are prepared to prevent and respond to any
food security threat. The office also provides public education
and awareness on food safety.

Dr Carol Maczka
*Assistant Administrator Food Security & Emergency
Preparedness*
Phone: 202-720-5643
e-mail: carol.maczka@fsis.usda.gov

Dr Perfecto Santiago
Deputy Administrator
Phone: 202-205-0452

Mary K Cutshall
Director Biosurveillance & Emergency Response Staff
Phone: 202-690-6520

Dr Michelle Catlin
Acting Director, Scientific & Technical Support Staff
Phone: 202-690-6438

Office of Public Health Science
Food Safety & Inspection Service (FSIS)
1400 Independence Avenue SW
Room 341-E
Washington, DC 20250
Phone: 202-720-2644
Fax: 202-690-2980
URL: www.fsis.usda.gov/About_FSIS/OPHS/

Description: Provides expert scientific analysis, data, advice and
recommendations on all matters involving public health and science related to FSIS. The office works with the FDA in order to
detect and identify biological, chemical and radiological elements in food; conducts scientific tests to detect and prevent
foodborne illness outbreaks; monitors and evaluates public
health hazards associated with animal populations; and performs
risk assessments of biological/chemical hazards in meat, poultry
and egg products.

Dr David Goldman
Assistant Administrator
Phone: 202-720-2644

Loren Lange
Deputy Assistant Administrator
Phone: 202-205-0293

Dr Karen Hulebak
Chief Scientist
Phone: 202-205-0293
e-mail: karen.hulebak@fsis.usda.gov

Kristin G Holt
Centers for Disease Control Liaison
Phone: 404-639-3379
e-mail: kristin.holt@fsis.usda.gov

Janell Kause
Director Risk Assessment Division
Phone: 202-690-6346

Dr Bhabani Dey
*Acting Director Zoonotic Disease & Residue Surveillance
Division*
Phone: 202-690-2676

Dr Douglas Abbott
Director Food Emergency Response Network Division
Phone: 706-546-3587

Marketing & Regulatory Programs
Department of Agriculture
12th & Jefferson Drive SW
Whitten Federal Building, Room 228W
Washington, DC 20250
Phone: 202-720-4256
Fax: 202-720-5775
URL: www.aphis.usda.gov/mrp/

Description: Facilitates the domestic and international marketing of US agricultural products and ensures the health and care
of animals and plants. MRP agencies are active participants in
international and national standards setting, through international
organizations and federal-state cooperation. Three agencies operate under the MRP mission area: the Agricultural Marketing Service, the Animal and Plant Health Inspection Service (APHIS),
and the Grain Inspection, Packers and Stockyards Administration.

Bruce I Knight
Under Secretary
Phone: 202-720-4256

Chuck Lambert
Deputy Under Secretary
Phone: 202-720-7813

Agricultural Marketing Service
Marketing & Regulatory Programs
1400 Independence Ave SW
Room 3071
Washington, DC 20250
Phone: 202-720-4256

Lloyd C Day
Administrator
Phone: 202-720-5115
e-mail: lloyd.day@usda.gov

Kenneth C Clayton
Associate Administrator
Phone: 202-720-4276
e-mail: kenneth.clayton@usda.gov

Ellen King
Compliance & Analysis Programs

Phone: 202-720-6766
e-mail: ellen.king@usda.gov

Billy Cox
Public Affairs
Phone: 202-720-8998
e-mail: billy.cox@usda.gov

Animal & Plant Health Inspection Service (APHIS)
Marketing & Regulatory Programs
12th & Jefferson Drive SW
Room 312-E
Washington, DC 20250
Phone: 202-720-3668
Fax: 202-720-3054
URL: www.aphis.usda.gov
e-mail: aphis.web@aphis.usda.gov

Description: Responsible for protecting and promoting US agricultural health, carrying out wildlife damage management activities, regulating genetically engineered organisms, and administering the Animal Welfare Act. Its efforts in working with the USDA are integral to providing the nation with safe and affordable food. Because of its technical expertise and leadership, the scope of APHIS' protection function has expanded beyond pest and disease management to encompass responding to other countries' animal and plant health import requirements.

Ron DeHaven
Administrator
e-mail: ron.dehaven@aphis.usda.gov

Kevin Shea
Associate Administrator
e-mail: kevin.a.shea@aphis.usda.gov

Cindy Smith
Associate Administrator

Dan Sheesley
Deputy Administrator-International Services

Bethany Jones
Acting Deputy Administrator-Legislative & Public Affairs

William J Hudnall
Deputy Administrator-Marketing & Regulatory Programs Business Services

Michael Gregoire
Deputy Administrator-Policy & Program Development

Grain Inspection, Packers & Stockyards Administration (GIPSA)
Marketing & Regulatory Programs
1400 Independence Ave SW
Room 1094
Washington, DC 20250
Phone: 202-720-0219
URL: www.gipsa.usda.gov

Description: Facilitates the marketing of livestock, poultry, meat, cereals, oilseeds and related agricultural products and promotes fair and competitive trading practices for the overall benefit of consumers and American agriculture.

James E Link
Administrator

Phone: 202-720-0219
e-mail: james.e.link@usda.gov

David R Shipman
Deputy Administrator, Federal Grain Inspection Service
Phone: 202-720-9170
e-mail: david.r.shipman@usda.gov

Alan R Christian
Deputy Administrator, Packers & Stockyards Program
Phone: 202-720-7051
e-mail: alan.r.christian@usda.gov

Foreign Agricultural Service
Department of Agriculture
1400 Independence Avenue SW
Washington, DC 20250
Phone: 202-720-3935
Fax: 202-690-2159
URL: www.fas.usda.gov

Description: The Foreign Agricultural Service (FAS) is responsible for collecting, analyzing and disseminating information about global supply and demand, trade trends and market opportunities. Since it was established in 1953, world agricultural trade has changed significantly and the FAS is reviewing their functions and operations to see what can be done better to meet these challenges. The Office of Scientific and Technical Affairs addresses SPS measures and technical barriers to US food and agricultural trade. The Office of Negotiations & Agreements coordinates FAS's overall trade policy positions and leading USDA's efforts in multilateral, regional and bilateral trade negotiations.

Michael W Yost
Administrator
Phone: 202-720-3935
e-mail: michael.yost@fas.usda.gov

Constance C Jackson
Associate Administrator
Phone: 202-720-3935
e-mail: constance.jackson@fas.usda.gov

William L Brant II
Deputy Administrator-Office of Scientific & Technical Affairs
Phone: 202-720-2701
e-mail: william.brant@fas.usda.gov

Daryl Brehm
Director International Regulations & Standards Division
Phone: 202-690-0929
e-mail: daryl.brehm@fas.usda.gov

Robert Riemenschneider
Deputy Administrator-Office of Negotiations & Agreements
Phone: 202-720-6219
e-mail: robert.riemenschneider@usda.gov

David Mergen
Director Monitoring & Enforcement Division
Phone: 202-720-9519
e-mail: david.mergen@usda.gov

Maureen Quinn
Director Public Affairs Division
Phone: 202-720-3448
e-mail: maureen.quinn@usda.gov

Forest Service
Department of Agriculture
1400 Independence Ave SW
Washington, DC 20250
Phone: 202-205-8333
Phone: 202-205-1134
Fax: 202-205-0885
URL: www.fs.fed.us

Description: Sustains the health, diversity and productivity of the Nation's forests and grasslands to meet the needs of present and future generations. The Law Enforcement & Investigations office within the Forest Service protects people and natural resources and property within its jurisdiction, ensuring that prevention, investigation, enforcement and program management requirements are fully integrated.

Gail Kimbell
Chief
Phone: 202-205-1661
e-mail: akimbell@fs.fed.us

Sally Collins
Associate Chief
Phone: 202-205-1491
e-mail: sdcollins@fs.fed.us

Tim Decoster
Chief of Staff
Phone: 202-205-1661
e-mail: tdecoster@fs.fed.us

Joel Holtrop
Deputy Chief, National Fire System
Phone: 202-205-1523

Ann M Bartuska
Deputy Chief, Research & Development
Phone: 202-205-1665

Valdis E Mezainis
Director, International Programs
Phone: 202-273-4695
e-mail: vmezainis@fs.fed.us

John C Twiss
Director, Law Enforcement & Investigations
Phone: 703-605-4869
e-mail: jctwiss@fs.fed.us

Ann Melle
Assistant Director, Homeland Security
Phone: 703-605-4527

Larry Lesko
Coordinator, National Fire Plan
Phone: 202-205-1298

Stana Federighi
Director, Communications Office
Phone: 202-205-1470

Allison Stewart
National Press Officer
Phone: 202-205-0896

Office of Budget and Program Analysis
Department of Agriculture
1400 Independence Avenue SW
Washington, DC 20250

Phone: 202-720-3323
Fax: 202-720-6067
URL: www.obpa.usda.gov
e-mail: bca@obpa.usda.gov

Description: Provides centralized coordination and direction for the Department's budget, legislative and regulatory functions; analysis and evaluation in support of critical policy implementation; and develops and presents budget-related matters to Congress, the public and the news media.

W Scott Steele
Director
Phone: 202-720-3323

Michael Young
Associate Director
Phone: 202-720-5303

Dennis L Kaplan
Deputy Director Budget, Legislative & Regulatory Systems
Phone: 202-720-6667
e-mail: dlk@obpa.usda.gov

Chris Zehren
Deputy Director Program Analysis
Phone: 202-720-3396

Office of the Chief Information Officer
Department of Agriculture
1400 Independence Avenue SW
Room 414 W
Washington, DC 20250
Phone: 202-720-8833
Fax: 202-720-1031
URL: www.ocio.usda.gov

Description: Supervises and coordinates the design, acquisition, maintenance, use and disposal of information and Information Technology(IT) by USDA agencies.

Dave Combs
Chief Information Officer
Phone: 202-720-8833
e-mail: dave.combs@usda.gov

Jerry E Williams
Deputy Chief Information Officer
Phone: 202-720-8833
e-mail: jerry.williams@usda.gov

Lynn Allen
Associate CIO/Cyber Security
Phone: 202-690-0048

Chris S Niedermayer
Associate CIO/Information & Technology Management
Phone: 202-690-2118
e-mail: chris.niedermayer@usda.gov

Robert E Suda
Associate CIO/Integration & Operations
Phone: 202-720-5865

Kathleen A Rundle
National Information Technology Center
Phone: 816-926-6501
e-mail: kathleen.rundle@usda.gov

Communications Office
Department of Agriculture
12th & Jefferson Drive SW
Room 402-A
Washington, DC 20250
Phone: 202-720-4623
Fax: 202-720-5043

Description: Provides leadership, expertise, counsel and coordination for the development of communication and strategies which are vital to the overall function, awareness and acceptance of the US Department of Agriculture programs and policies, and serves as the principal USDA contact point for the dissemination of consistent, timely information.

Terri Teuber
Director
Phone: 202-720-4623
e-mail: terri.teuber@usda.gov

Nicol Andrews
Deputy Director
Phone: 202-720-4623
e-mail: nicol.andrews@usda.gov

Keith Williams
Press Secretary
Phone: 202-720-4623
e-mail: keith.williams@usda.gov

Corinne Hirsh
Deputy Press Secretary
Phone: 202-720-4623
e-mail: corinne.hirsh@usda.gov

Jim Brownlee
Comunications Coordinator-Natural Resources, Environment, Rural Development
Phone: 202-720-2091
e-mail: jim.brownlee@usda.gov

Wayne Baggett
Communications Coordinator-Research, Education, Economics, Farm & Foreign Agriculture
Phone: 202-720-2032
e-mail: wayne.baggett@usda.gov

Jerry Redding
Communications Coordinator-Food Safety Marketing & Regulatory Programs
Phone: 202-720-6959
e-mail: jerry.redding@usda.gov

Angela Harless
Communications Coordinator-Homeland Security
Phone: 202-720-6569
e-mail: angela.harless@usda.gov

Ron Hall
USDA News
Phone: 202-720-5747
e-mail: ron.hall@usda.gov

Phillip Shanholzer
Editor, AG News
Phone: 202-720-8138

FEDERAL

Department of Commerce

Department of Commerce
Headquarters
1401 Constitution Avenue NW
Washington, DC 20230
Phone: 202-482-2000
Phone: 202-482-2112
Fax: 202-482-4090
URL: www.doc.gov

Description: The United States Department of Commerce works closely with the Department of Homeland Security to protect America's economy. This relationship allows DHS to tap into science and technology strengths and expertise that the Department of Commerce provides in the security and technical standards arenas. Specifically, the Technology Administration's National Institute of Standards and Technology (NIST) researches programs for the detection of chemical, biological and other explosive threats. For American industry, NIST further assists in bringing homeland security technologies into the marketplace. The Department of Commerce promotes United States competitiveness in the global maketplace by strengthening and safeguarding the nation's economic information base, and providing effective management and stewardship of the nation's resources and assets to ensure sustainable economic opportunities.

Carlos M Gutierrez
Secretary
Phone: 202-482-2112
e-mail: cgutierrez@doc.gov

David A Sampson
Deputy Secretary
Phone: 202-482-8376

Claire Buchan
Chief of Staff
Phone: 202-482-4246

J V Schwan
Deputy Chief of Staff Policy
Phone: 202-482-4246

Nathaniel Wienecke
Assistant Secretary Legislative & Governmental Affairs
Phone: 202-482-5631

Otto J Wolff
Chief Financial Officer/Assistant Secretary Administration
Phone: 202-482-4951

Barry C West
Chief Information Officer
Phone: 202-482-4797

John J Sullivan
General Counsel
Phone: 202-482-4772

Johnnie E Frazier
Inspector General
Phone: 202-482-4661

Dan McCardell
Business Liaison Office
Phone: 202-482-1360

John Duncan
Policy & Strategic Planning Office
Phone: 202-482-4127

E Richard Mills
Public Affairs Office
Phone: 202-482-4883

Christy Simon
White House Liaison Office
Phone: 202-482-1684

Chris Israel
International IPR Enforcement Coordinator
Phone: 202-482-6200

National Institute of Standards & Technology (NIST)
Department of Commerce
100 Bureau Drive
MS 1070
Gaithersburg, MD 20899-1070
Phone: 301-975-6478
Phone: 301-975-2300
Fax: 301-869-8972
URL: www.nist.gov
e-mail: inquires@nist.gov

Description: Founded in 1901, NIST is a non-regulatory federal agency within the US Commerce Department's Technology Administration. NIST's mission is to promote innovation and industrial competitiveness for measurement, standards, and technology to enhance productivity, facilitate trade, and improve quality of life. NIST carries out its mission in four cooperative programs: NIST Laboratories — conducts research that advances the nation's technology infrastructure and is needed by US industry to continually improve products and services; Baldridge National Quality Program — promotes performance excellence among US manufacturers, service companies, educators, institutions and health care providers, conducts outreach programs and manages the annual Malcolm Baldridge National Quality Award; Hollings Manufacturing Extension Partnership — nationwide network of local centers offering technical and business assisitance to smaller manufacturers; Advanced Technology Program — accelerates the development of innovative technologies to broad national benefit by co-funding R&D partnerships with the private sector.

William A Jeffrey
Director
Phone: 301-975-2300
e-mail: director@nist.gov

James Turner
Deputy Director
Phone: 301-975-2300
e-mail: james.turner@nist.gov

Tom O'Brian
Boulder Laboratories
Phone: 303-497-5507

Dr Richard F Kayser
Materials Science & Engineering Laboratory
Phone: 301-975-5658
e-mail: richard.kayser@nist.gov

Marc Stanley
Advanced Technology Program
Phone: 800-287-3863
e-mail: atp@nist.gov

Roger Kilmer
Hollings Manufacturing Extension Partnership
Phone: 301-975-5020

Harry Hertz
Baldrige National Quality Program
Phone: 301-975-2036
e-mail: nqp@nist.gov

Willie May
Chemical Science & Technology Laboratory
Phone: 301-975-8300
e-mail: cstlinfo@nist.gov

Matthew Heyman
Chief of Staff
Phone: 301-975-2759
e-mail: matthew.heyman@nist.gov

Computer Security Division
NIST
100 Bureau Drive
MS 8930
Gaithersburg, MD 20899-8930
Phone: 301-975-8443
Fax: 301-948-1233
URL: www.csrc.nist.gov

Description: The Computer Security Division is one of the eight divisions within NIST's Information Technology laboratory. Its mission is to improve information systems security by: raising awareness of IT risks, vulnerability and protection requirements, particularly for new and emerging technologies; researching, studying, and advising agencies of IT vulnerabilities and devising techniques for the cost-effective security and privacy of sensitive federal systems; developing standards, metrics, tests and validation programs; and developing guidance to increase secure IT planning, implementation, management and operation.

Curtis Barker
Division Chief
Phone: 301-975-8443

William Burr
Security Technology Group Manager
Phone: 301-975-2914

Timothy Grance
Systems & Network Security Group Manager
Phone: 301-975-4242

Elizabeth Chew
Management & Assistance Group Manager
Phone: 301-975-8897

Ray Snouffer
Security Testing & Metrics Group Manager
Phone: 301-975-4436

Bureau of Industry & Security (BIS)
Department of Commerce
14th St & Constitution Avenue NW
Washington, DC 20230
Phone: 202-482-1455
Fax: 202-482-2387
URL: www.bis.doc.gov

Description: The mission of the Bureau of Industry and Security (BIS) is to advance US national security, foreign policy, and economic objectives by ensuring an effective export control and treaty compliance system and promoting continued US strategic technology leadership. BIS's activities include regulating the export of sensitive goods and technologies in an effective and efficient manner, enforcing export control, anti-boycott and public safety laws, cooperating with and assisting other countries on export control and strategic trade issues, assisting US industry to comply with international arms control agreements, monitoring the viability of the US defense industrial base, and ensuring that it is capable of satisfying US national and homeland security needs.

Mario Mancuso
Under Secretary
Phone: 202-482-1455
e-mail: mmancuso@bis.doc.gov

Mark Foulon
Deputy Under Secretary
Phone: 202-482-1427
e-mail: mfoulon@bis.doc.gov

Darryl W Jackson
Assistant Secretary Export Enforcement
Phone: 202-482-1561

Dawn Leaf
Chief Information Officer
Phone: 202-482-7884
e-mail: dleaf@bis.doc.gov

John T Masterson Jr
Chief Counsel
Phone: 202-482-5301
e-mail: ccis@bis.doc.gov

Erik Heilman
Director Congressional/Public Affairs
e-mail: eheilman@bis.doc.gov

Office of Export Enforcement (OEE)
BIS
14th St & Constitution Avenue NW
Washington, DC 20230
Phone: 202-482-1208
Fax: 202-482-5889
URL: www.bis.doc.gov/enforcement/

Description: Enforces export control and related public safety laws, with a focus on violations posing the most significant threats to US national and homeland security, foreign policy objectives and economic interests such as international terrorism, the proliferation of Weapons of Mass Destruction and their delivery systems, and unauthorized dual-use exports for military purposes. The Office investigates violations of the Export Administration Regulations, the Fastener Quality Act, the International Emergency Economic Powers Act; apprehends violators; and works with the BIS's Office of Chief Counsel and other officials.

Michael D Turner
Director, Export Enforcement
Phone: 202-482-1208

John Sonderman
Assistant Director, Operations
Phone: 202-482-1208

Tom Madigan
Assistant Director, Investigations
Phone: 202-482-4887

John McKenna
Special Agent-in-Charge, Boston, MA
Phone: 617-565-6030

Wendy Hauser
Special Agent-in-Charge, Chicago, IL
Phone: 312-353-6640

George Richardson
Special Agent-in-Charge, Dallas, TX
Phone: 214-767-9294

Earl Estrada
Special Agent-in-Charge, Los Angeles, CA
Phone: 949-251-9001

Michael Johnson
Special Agent-in-Charge, Miami, FL
Phone: 954-356-7540

Sidney M Simon
Special Agent-in-Charge, New York, NY
Phone: 718-370-0070

Julie Salcido
Special Agent-in-Charge, San Jose, CA
Phone: 408-291-4204

Rick L Shimon
Special Agent-in-Charge, Washington, DC
Phone: 703-487-9300

Office of Exporter Services (OES)
BIS
14th St & Constitution Avenue NW
Washington, DC 20230
Phone: 202-482-0436
Fax: 202-482-3322

URL: www.bis.doc.gov/About/ProgramOffices.htm

Description: Responsible for counseling exporters, conducting export control seminars, and drafting publishing changes to the Export Administration Regulations. It is also responsible for licensing and compliance actions relating to the special comprehensive license, and for administering the processing of license applications and commodity classifications.

Eileen M Albanese
Director
e-mail: ealbanes@bis.doc.gov

Michael Hoffman
Outreach & Educational Services Western Regional Office
Phone: 949-660-0144

Office of Enforcement Analysis (OEA)
BIS
14th St & Constitution Avenue NW
Washington, DC 20230
Phone: 202-482-4255
Fax: 202-482-0971
URL: www.bis.doc.gov/About/ProgramOffices.htm

Description: Assists the OEE field offices and BIS's export licensing offices by receiving and disseminating export control information on problem end-users and end-uses. The Office also makes licensing recommendations to BIS licensing officers based on intelligence information and input received from special agents in the field.

Thomas W Andrukonis
Director

Office of National Security and Technology Transfer Controls (NSTTC)
BIS
14th St & Constitution Avenue NW
Room 2626
Washington, DC 20230
Phone: 202-482-4196
Fax: 202-482-4094
URL: www.bis.doc.gov/About/ProgramOffices.htm

Description: Responsible for issues related to national security export and re-export controls. It implements multilateral export controls for national security reasons to comply with the Wassenaar Arrangement to control the spread of dual-use goods and related technologies. It is also responsible for US export control policy for high performance computers, encryption and administers the export licensing responsibilities for foreign nationals under the deemed export technology rule. It also administers the short supply provisions of the Export Administration Regulations. This office is responsible for policy actions, export licenses, commodity classifications, license determinations, and advisory opinions for affected commodities and is the focal point for commodity jurisdiction assessments.

Bernie Kritzer
Director
e-mail: bkritzer@bis.doc.gov

Office of International Programs (OIP)
BIS
14th St & Constitution Avenue NW
Washington, DC 20230

Phone: 202-482-8345
Fax: 202-501-8224
URL: www.bis.doc.gov/About/ProgramOffices.htm

Description: OIP leads BIS's international export control policy and program activities and controls it's export control initiatives, working with the Department of Commerce bureaus and other government agencies on various international cooperative endeavors with industries abroad. It assists the BIS's effort to help other countries develop or strengthen export controls and stop the proliferation of sensitive goods and technology to rogue states and terrorists. The office utilizes the technical expertise of the Chief Counsel and all parts of BIS.

Mi-Yong Kim
Director
Phone: 202-482-2538
e-mail: mkim@bis.doc.gov

EXBS Liaison Team
BIS-International Programs
14th St & Constitution Avenue NW
Room 4515
Washington, DC 20230
Phone: 202-482-8345
Fax: 202-501-8224
URL: www.bis.doc.gov/internationalprograms/index.htm

Description: Supports BIS mission to strengthen participating countries export control systems to keep biological, chemical and nuclear weapons and other sensitive materials out of the hands of terrorists and rogue states. This includes helping cooperating nations create the infrastructure that meets international standards which involves — building a legal framework, procedures, and requirements in order to regulate the transfers of sensitive items; enhancing enforcement capabilities to match this framework; and developing an approriate partnership between government and industry on export controls. The team works with the interagency to support the Department of State funded Export and Border Related Security (EXBS) Program.

Lara Howe
Export Policy Analyst
Phone: 202-482-4018
e-mail: lhowe@bis.doc.gov

Thomas Sefferly
Export Policy Analyst
Phone: 202-482-3405

Office of Antiboycott Compliance (OAC)
BIS
14th St & Constitution Avenue NW
Washington, DC 20230
Phone: 202-482-2381
Phone: 202-482-5914
Fax: 202-482-0913
URL: www.bis.doc.gov/antiboycottcompliance/

Description: Responsible for implementing the antiboycott provisions of the Export Administration Regulations. It performs three major functions: enforcing the regulations, assisting the public in antiboycott compliance, and compiling and analyzing information regarding international boycotts.

Ned Weant
Acting Director

Phone: 202-482-2381
e-mail: nweant@bis.doc.gov

Office of Nonproliferation & Treaty Compliance (NPTC)
BIS
14th St & Constitution Ave NW
Room 2093
Washington, DC 20230
Phone: 202-482-3825
Fax: 202-482-0751
URL: www.bis.doc.gov/About/ProgramOffices.htm

Description: Administers the Department's multilateral export control responsibilities and US foreign policy export controls. This Office is also responsible for the industrial compliance provisions of arms control and disarmament treaties, such as the Chemical Weapons Convention, and for representing US industry and security interests in deliberations, as in the Biological and Toxin Weapons Convention.

Joan Roberts
Acting Director
Phone: 202-482-0171
e-mail: jroberts@bis.doc.gov

Office of Strategic Industry & Economic Security (SIES)
BIS
14th St & Constitution Avenue NW
Washington, DC 20230
Phone: 202-482-4506
Fax: 202-482-5650
URL: www.bis.doc.gov/About/ProgramOffices.htm

Description: Responsible for implementing programs to ensure the US Defense industries can meet national security requirements, current and future.

Daniel Hill
Director Strategic Industries and Economic Security
Phone: 202-482-4506
e-mail: dhill@bis.doc.gov

Kevin Kurland
Director Office of Technology Evaluation
Phone: 202-482-4933
e-mail: kkurland@bis.doc.gov

Brad Botwin
Director Industrial Base Studies
Phone: 202-482-4060
e-mail: bbotwin@bis.doc.gov

Office of Business Liaison
Department of Commerce
1401 Constitution Avenue NW
Room 5062
Washington, DC 20230
Phone: 202-482-1360
Fax: 202-482-4054
URL: osec.doc.gov/obl

Description: Serves as the primary point for contact between the Department of Commerce and the business community, guiding individuals and businesses to the offices and policy experts best suited to respond to their needs.

Dan McCardell
Director
e-mail: dmccardell@doc.gov

Jennifer Andberg
Deputy Director
e-mail: jandberg@doc.gov

Robert Ollison
Deputy Director
Phone: 202-482-3943
e-mail: rollison@doc.gov

Office of Inspector General
Department of Commerce
1401 Constitution Avenue NW
Room 7898C
Washington, DC 20230
Phone: 202-482-4661
Fax: 202-482-0567
URL: www.oig.doc.gov
e-mail: oigweb@oig.doc.gov

Description: Promotes economy, efficiency and effectiveness; and detects and prevents fraud, waste, abuse and mismanagement in the Department's programs and operations. The Office provides timely, useful and reliable information and advice to Commerce officials, the Administration, Congress, and the public with the goal of improving the Department's management, operations and delivery of services to the public.

Johnnie E Frazier
Inspector General
Phone: 202-482-4661
e-mail: jfrazier@oig.doc.gov

Elizabeth Barlow
Deputy Inspector General
Phone: 202-482-3860
e-mail: ebarlow@oi.doc.gov

Jessica J Rickenbach
Assistant Inspector General Administration
Phone: 202-482-3052
e-mail: jrickenbach@oig.doc.gov

Jill A Gross
Assistant Inspector General Inspections & Program Evaluations
Phone: 202-482-2754
e-mail: jgross@oig.doc.gov

Edward L Blansitt
Assistant Inspector General Investigations
Phone: 202-482-3516
e-mail: eblansitt@oig.doc.gov

Judith J Gordon
Assistant Inspector General Systems Evaluation
Phone: 202-482-5643
e-mail: jgordon@oig.doc.gov

John Seeba
Assistant Inspector General Audits
Phone: 202-482-5910
e-mail: jseeba@oig.doc.gov

Office of the Chief Information Officer
Department of Commerce
1401 Constitution Avenue NW
Washington, DC 20230
Phone: 202-482-4797
Fax: 202-501-1180
URL: ocio.os.doc.gov

Description: Responsible for ensuring that the Department's programs make full and appropriate use of information technology. It supports the increased use of leading edge technology to enable the Department to carry out its mission better, with improved products and services at the lowest cost. High priority is accorded within the Office of Information Technology Security & Critical Infrastructure Protection to ensure the integrity of the Department's systems, data, products and services to ensure continuity of operations. The Office oversees the expenditure of approximately $1.5 billion each year for computer hardware, software, and services, and for networking and telecommunications and other Information Technology (IT).

Barry C West
Chief Information Officer
Phone: 202-482-4797
e-mail: bwest@doc.gov

John W McManus
Deputy CIO/CTO (Acting IT Security, Infrastructure & Technology Office)
Phone: 202-482-1888

Wayne Blackwood
Computer Services Office (Acting)
Phone: 703-487-4044
e-mail: wblackwood@doc.gov

Office of the General Counsel
Department of Commerce
14th St & Constitution Avenue NW
Room 5870
Washington, DC 20230
Phone: 202-482-4772
Fax: 202-482-0042
URL: www.ogc.doc.gov
e-mail: ogcexecutiveoffice@doc.gov

Description: The Office of the General Counsel has a diverse legal practice, based on the wide variety of issues in which the Department of Commerce is involved. They work with the BIS to enforce laws that control exports for reasons of national security, foreign policy and non-proliferation of Weapons of Mass Destruction, among other things. Commerce attorneys supervise the development of the Department's legislative and regulatory programs.

John J Sullivan
General Counsel
Phone: 202-482-4772

David K Bowsher
Deputy General Counsel
Phone: 202-482-4772
e-mail: dbowsher@doc.gov

Michael Levitt
Assistant General Counsel, Legislation & Regulations
Phone: 202-482-3151
e-mail: mlevitt@doc.gov

Joan Maginnis
Assistant General Counsel Finance & Litigation
Phone: 202-482-1328
e-mail: jmaginnis@doc.gov

Paulo Mendes
Executive Officer
Phone: 202-482-4994
e-mail: pmendes@doc.gov

Office of Small & Disadvantaged Business Utilization
Department of Commerce
14th St & Constitution Avenue NW
Room 6411
Washington, DC 20230
Phone: 202-482-1472
Fax: 202-482-0501
URL: www.osec.doc.gov/osdbu

Description: Responsible for advocating the use of small, small-disadvantaged, HUBZone, veteran-owned, 8(a), service disabled veteran-owned, and women-owned small businesses with the goal of fully integrating them into the US Department of Commerce's competitive base of contractors.

LaJuene Desmukes
Director
e-mail: Ldesmukes@doc.gov

Yvonne Vines
Business and Industry Specialist
e-mail: yvines@doc.gov

National Oceanic & Atmospheric Administration
Department of Commerce
14th St & Constitution Avenue NW
Room 6217
Washington, DC 20230
Phone: 202-482-6090
Phone: 202-482-3436
Fax: 202-408-3154
URL: www.noaa.gov

Description: Conducts research and gathers data about the global oceans, atmosphere, space, and sun, and applies this knowledge to science and service of all Americans. The Agency includes the National Environmental Satellite, Data and Information Services; National Marine Fisheries Service; National Ocean Service; National Weather Service; Oceanic and Atmospheric Research; Marine and Aviation Operations; and the NOAA Corps. It manages an annual budget of $4 billion.

VAdm Conrad C Lautenbacher Jr
Undersecretary/Administrator
Phone: 202-482-3436
e-mail: conrad.c.lautenbacher@noaa.gov

Scott Rayder
Chief of Staff
Phone: 202-482-0050
e-mail: scott.rayder@noaa.gov

John J Kelly
Deputy Under Secretary
Phone: 202-482-4569
e-mail: jack.kelly@noaa.gov

William Brennan
Deputy Assistant Secretary, International Affairs
Phone: 202-482-6196
e-mail: bill.brennan@noaa.gov

Richard W Spinrad
Assistant Administrator, Research
Phone: 301-713-2458
e-mail: richard.spinrad@noaa.gov

Jack Hayes
Director National Weather Service
Phone: 301-713-1632

Mary Kicza
Assistant Administrator Environment Satellite, Data & Information Service
Phone: 301-713-2010
e-mail: mary.kicza@noaa.gov

Jackie Dunnigan
Assistant Administrator National Ocean Service
Phone: 301-713-3074
e-mail: jack.dunnigan@noaa.gov

Paul Doremus
Assistant Administrator Program Planning & Intregration
Phone: 301-713-1622
e-mail: paul.n.doremus@noaa.gov

William Hogarth
Assistant Administrator National Marine Fisheries Service
Phone: 301-713-2239
e-mail: bill.hogarth@noaa.gov

Jane Luxton
General Counsel
Phone: 202-482-4627
e-mail: jane.luxton@noaa.gov

National Telecommunications & Information Administration (NTIA)
Department of Commerce
1401 Constitution Avenue NW
Washington, DC 20230
Phone: 202-482-1840
Fax: 202-501-0536
URL: www.ntia.doc.gov

Description: The President's principal adviser on telecommunications and information policy issues; frequently works with other Executive Branch agencies to develop and present the Administration's position on these issues. Since 1978 it has managed federal use of spectrum; administered infrastructure and public telecommunications facilities grants; and performed cutting-edge telecommunications research and engineering, including resolving technical telecommunications issues for the federal government and private sector. Telecommunications and information issues are dynamic, multi-disciplinary and complex. NTIA's expertise and advocacy enable the US to continue its lead in this area that is an integral part of American's competitiveness.

John M R Kneuer
Assistant Secretary Communications & Information
Phone: 202-482-1830

Kathy D Smith
Chief Counsel

Phone: 202-482-1816
e-mail: ksmith@ntia.doc.gov

Karl Nebbia
Associate Administrator Spectrum Management
Phone: 202-482-1850

Jane Coffin
Acting Associate Administrator International Affairs
Phone: 202-482-1087

Eric R Stark
Associate Administrator Policy Analysis & Development
Phone: 202-482-1880

Bernadette McGuire-Rivera
Associate Administrator Telecommunications & Information Applications
Phone: 202-482-5802

James V Wasilewski
Acting Director Congressional Affairs
Phone: 202-482-1551
e-mail: jwasilewski@ntia.doc.gov

Al Vincent
Director Institute for Telecommunication Sciences
Phone: 303-497-3500

Todd Sedmak
Director Communications
Phone: 202-482-0019

International Trade Administration
Department of Commerce
1401 Constitution Avenue NW
Washington, DC 20230
Phone: 202-482-2867
Phone: 800-872-8723
Fax: 202-482-4821
URL: trade.gov

Description: Headed by the Under Secretary for International Trade who oversees the operations of ITA's four units: The Commercial Service is the primary point of contact throughout the US and the world for help at every stage of the export process. Manufacturing and Services is the government's link to American industry. Market Access and Compliance keeps world markets open to products and aids in trade agreements with other countries. Import Administration impartially enforces trade laws, ensuring a level playing field in the domestic marketplace.

Franklin L Lavin
Under Secretary
Phone: 202-482-2867
e-mail: frank.lavin@mail.doc.gov

Michelle O'Neill
Deputy Under Secretary
Phone: 202-482-3917
e-mail: oneill_michelle@ita.doc.gov

David Bohigian
Market Access & Compliance
Phone: 202-482-3022
e-mail: bohigian_david@ita.doc.gov

Israel Hernandez
US & Foreign Commercial Service/Trade Promotion

Phone: 202-482-5777
e-mail: israel.hernandez@mail.doc.gov

David Spooner
Import Administration
Phone: 202-482-1780
e-mail: david_sponner@ita.doc.gov

Jamie P Estrada
Manufacturing & Services
Phone: 202-482-1872
e-mail: jamie.estrada@mail.doc.gov

FEDERAL

Department of Defense

Department of Defense
Headquarters
1000 Defense Pentagon
Washington, DC 20301-1000
Phone: 703-692-7100
Fax: 703-697-9080
URL: www.defenselink.mil

Description: The United States Department of Defense (DoD) closely coordinates homeland defense issues with the Department of Homeland Security. Rather than work as a lead agency in times of national threat, DoD operates primarily in support of other federal agencies, providing manpower as directed by the President. DoD contributes to homeland security through its military missions overseas, homeland defense (protection of US sovereignty, territory, domestic population, and critical defense infrastructure), and support to civil authorities. Missions carried out by the Department include domestic air defense, maritime intercept operations, and land-based defense of critical infrastructure and assets. DoD has supervisory responsibilities for all branches of the United States Armed Services (Army, Navy, Air Force, Marines and National Guard), most notably in their protection against anti-terrorism activities including destroying weapons of mass destruction. DoD has also established the US Northern Command, a unified force with responsibility for homeland defense.

Robert M Gates
Secretary
Phone: 703-692-7100

Gordon R England
Deputy Secretary
Phone: 703-692-7150

Kenneth J Krieg
Under Secretary Acquisition, Technology & Logistics

David S C Chu
Under Secretary Personnel & Readiness

Eric S Edelman
Under Secretary Policy

Tina Jonas
Under Secretary Comptroller

James R Clapper
Under Secretary Intelligence
Phone: 703-695-0971

William P Marriott
Executive Secretariat
Phone: 703-692-7120
e-mail: william.marriott@osd.pentagon.mil

William J Haynes II
General Counsel

Claude Kicklighter
Inspector General

J Dorrance Smith
Assistant Secretary for Public Affairs

Northern Command
Department of Defense
Peterson Air Force Base
250 Vandenberg St, Suite B016
Peterson AFB, CO 80914-3808
Phone: 719-554-6889
Phone: 719-556-7321
URL: www.northcom.mil
e-mail: northcompa@northcom.mil

Description: The Department of Defense established US Northern Command in 2002 to consolidate under a single unified command existing missions that were previously executed by other military organizations. The Command's primary mission includes: conducting operations to deter, prevent, defeat threats and aggression against the United States and its territories; as directed by the President or Secretary of Defense, provide military assistance, including consequence management operations. The Command plans, organizes and executes homeland defense missions, but has few permanently assigned forces. More than 1,200 civil service employees and uniformed personnel representing all service branches provide this essential unity of command from US Northern Command headquarters in Colorado Springs.

General Gene Renuart
Commander

Lt General William G Webster Jr
Deputy Commander

Major General Paul J Sullivan
Chief of Staff

Sgt Major Daniel R Wood
Command Sgt Major/Senior Enlisted Leader

Department of the Army
1500 Army Pentagon
Washington, DC 20310
Mailing Address: 101 Army Pentagon
Phone: 703-692-2000
URL: www.army.mil

Description: The army is one of the three military departments (Army, Navy, Air Force) that reports to the Department of Defense. It is composed of two distinct and equally important components: the active component and the reserve components

(Army reserve and Army National Guard). The Army's mission is to fight and win the nation's wars by providing prompt, sustained land dominance across a full range of military operations and spectrum of conflict in support of combatant commanders.

Pete M Geren
Acting Secretary

General George M Casey Jr
Chief of Staff

General Richard A Cody
Vice Chief of Staff

Sergeant Major Kenneth O Preston
Sergeant Major of the Army

Brig General Anthony A Cucolo III
Chief Public Affairs
Phone: 703-692-2000

Army Intelligence & Security Command (INSCOM)

Department of the Army
8825 Beulah Street
Fort Belvoir, VA 22060
Phone: 703-545-6700
Phone: 703-805-5001
URL: www.inscom.army.mil
e-mail: public.affairs@mi.army.mil

Description: INSCOM is a major Army command and intelligence organization that performs a variety of operations which includes: conduct and support relevant intelligence, security and information operations for Army, joint and combined forces; optimize national/theater/tactical partnerships; and exploit leading edge technology; and to meet the challenge of today, tomorrow and the 21st century. There are four brigades that tailor their support according to the appropriate needs. Current operational focus: the Global War On Terrorism and regional contingency operations.

Major General John DeFreitas III
Commanding General

Brig General Julie A Kraus
Deputy Commanding General

Sgt Major Maureen Johnson
Command Sergeant

J P Barham
Acting Public Affairs Officer

Department of the Navy

1000 Navy Pentagon
Washington, DC 20350-1000
URL: www.navy.mil

Description: The Department of the Navy has three principal components: the Navy Department, consisting of executive offices mostly in Washington DC; the operating forces, including the Marine Corps, the reserve components, and in time of war, the US Coast Guard (in peace a component of the Department Homeland Security); and the shore establishment.

Donald C Winter
Secretary

B J Penn
Assistant Secretary Installations & Environment

William A Navas Jr
Assistant Secretary Manpower & Reserve Affairs

Delores M Etter
Assistant Secretary Research, Development & Acquisition

Frank Jimenez
General Counsel

Admiral Michael G Mullen
Chief of Naval Operations

Master Chief Joe R Campa Jr
Master Chief Petty Officer

Office of Naval Intelligence

Department of Defense
4251 Suitland Rd
Washington, DC 20395
Phone: 301-669-3001
URL: www.nmic.navy.mi
e-mail: pao@nmic.navy.mil

Description: This Office has moved beyond their history to meet today's challenges. They have organized personnel, equipment, doctrine and training to better serve maritime customers - the joint war fighters, the Department of the Navy, and the maritime intelligence requirements of national agencies and departments. It supports joint operational commanders with a worldwide organization and an integrated workforce of active duty, reserve, officer and enlisted and civilian professionals. It brings military and civilian employees into a single command to provide one-stop shopping for national level maritime intelligence. Also hosts the Marine Corps Intelligence Activity and the Coast Guard Intelligence Coordination Center and the Naval Information Warfare Activity.

Captain Alexander Butterfield
Director
Phone: 301-669-3001

Gregory Spencer
Deputy Director
Phone: 301-669-3001

Department of the Navy Research, Development & Acquisition

Department of the Navy
1000 Navy Pentagon
Washington, DC 20350
Phone: 703-695-6950
Phone: 703-695-6315
Fax: 703-693-4618
URL: www.acquisition.navy.mil

Description: Mission: to provide weapons, systems and platforms for the men and women of the Navy/Marine Corps that support their missions and give them a technological edge over adversaries. The Assistant Secretary of the Navy for Research, Development & Acquisition serves as the Navy Acquisition Executive and has the authority for all acquisition functions programs and reports to Congress on these matters.

Dr Delores M Etter
Assistant Secretary RDA/Navy Acquistion Executive
Phone: 703-695-6315

John Thackrah
*Chief of Staff/Deputy Assistant Secretary Management &
Budget*
Phone: 703-697-4928

RAdm Kathleen Dussault
Deputy Assistant Secretary Acquisition Management
Phone: 703-614-9445

Allison Stiller
Deputy Assistant Secretary Ship Programs
Phone: 703-697-1710

William Balderson
Deputy Assistant Secretary Air Programs
Phone: 703-614-7794
e-mail: balderson.william@hq.navy.mil

Gary A Federici
Deputy Assistant Secretary C4I & Space
Phone: 703-614-6619

Anne Sandel
Deputy Assistant Secretary Integrated Warfare Systems
Phone: 703-614-8806

Roger Smith
Deputy Assistant Secretary Expiditionary Warfare Programs
Phone: 703-614-4794

RAdm Jeff Wieringa
Deputy Assistant Secretary International Programs
Phone: 703-601-9800

Dr Mike McGrath
Deputy Assistant Secretary RDT&E
Phone: 703-695-2204

Department of the Air Force
1670 Air Force Pentagon
Washington, DC 20330-1670
URL: www.af.mil

Michael W Wynne
Secretary

Dr Ronald M Sega
Under Secretary

General T Michael Moseley
Chief of Staff

Chief Master Sgt Rodney J McKinley
Chief Master Sergeant

Brig General William A Chambers
Director Communications

Mary L Walker
General Counsel

Brig General Michelle D Johnson
Public Affairs

Air Force National Security Emergency Preparedness (NSAP)
Department of Defense
1283 Anderson Way SW
Bldg 129
Ft McPherson, GA 30330
Phone: 800-366-0051

Fax: 404-464-4282
URL: www.1af.acc.af.mil/units/afnsep/
e-mail: afnsep@afnsep.af.mil

Description: The US Air Force National Security Emergency Preparedness directorate facilitates and coordinates USAF Defense Support to Civil Authorities for natural and man-made disasters and emergencies. It also advises and consults with the Office of the Secretary of Defense, combatant commands, and all levels of civil/military authorities on DSCA issues. It also provides Air Force leadership critical situational awareness to and from the field.

Michael Studdard
Operations
Phone: 404-464-4343

Marine Corps
Headquarters
2 Navy Annex (CMC)
Washington, DC 20380-1775
URL: www.hqmc.usmc.mil

Description: The U.S. Marine Corps maintains ready expeditionary forces, sea-based and integrated air-ground units for combat and contingency operations.

General James T Conway
Commandant

General Robert Magnus
Assistant Commandant

General James E Cartwright
Commander, US Strategic Command

Sgt Major Carlton W Kent
Sergeant Major

Lt General Richard Kramlich
Director Marine Corps Staff
Phone: 703-614-1128

BGen Richard M Lake
Director Intelligence

Robert D Hogue
General Counsel

Army National Guard
Department of Defense
1411 Jefferson Davis Highway
Arlington, VA 22204-1382
Phone: 703-607-7000
Phone: 703-607-3643
Fax: 703-607-3671
URL: www.arng.army.mil

Description: The Army National Guard is composed primarily of traditional Guardsmen - civilians who serve their country, state and community on a part-time basis. The National Guard has a unique dual mission that consists of both federal and state roles. For state missions, the governor can call the National Guard into action during local or statewide emergencies, such as storms, fires, or civil disturbances. Federal missions include Guard unit deployment to the Middle East for stabilization operations. See individual state listings in the State Agencies section.

Lt General Clyde A Vaughn
Director Army National Guard
Phone: 703-607-7000

BGen James W Nuttall
Deputy Director Army National Guard
Phone: 703-607-7060

Colonel Renwick Payne
Chief of Staff
Phone: 703-607-7578

Sgt Major John D Gipe
Command Sergeant Major
Phone: 703-607-7578

Air National Guard
Department of Defense
1411 Jefferson Davis Highway
Arlington, VA 22202
Phone: 703-607-2388
Fax: 703-607-3678
URL: www.ang.af.mil

Description: The Air National Guard has a unique dual mission that consists of both federal and state roles. Its mission is to: support national security objectives; protect life and property; preserve peace, order, and public safety; and participate in local, state, and national programs that add value to America. See individual state listings in the State Agencies section.

Lt General Craig R McKinley
Director Air National Guard
Phone: 703-607-2388

Office of Joint Chiefs of Staff
Department of Defense
9999 Joint Staff Pentagon
Washington, DC 20318-9999
Phone: 703-697-9121
Fax: 703-697-8758
URL: www.jcs.mil/

Description: The collective body of the JCS is headed by the Chairman, who sets the agenda and presides over meetings. Responsibilities as members take precedence over duties as the Chiefs of Military Services. The Chairman is the principal military adviser to the President, Secretary of Defense, and the National Security Council, however, all members are by law military advisers, and they may respond to a request or voluntarily submit, through the Chairman, advice or opinions to the President, Secretary of Defense, or NSC.

General Peter Pace
Chairman
Phone: 703-697-9121

Admiral Edmund P Giambastiani Jr
Vice-Chairman

General T Michael Moseley
Chief of Staff - Air Force

General George W Casey Jr
Chief of Staff - Army

Admiral Michael G Mullen
Chief Naval Operations

General James T Conway
Marine Corps Commandant

Lt General Walter L Sharp
Director of Joint Staff

Joint Forces Command (USJFCOM)
Department of Defense
1562 Mitscher Avenue
Suite 200
Norfolk, VA 23551
Phone: 757-836-6555
URL: www.jfcom.mil

Description: USJFCOM is one of the DoD's nine combatant commands and is comprised of active and reserve personnel from each branch of the armed forces, civil servants and contract employees. The commander oversees the Office's roles in innovation and experimentation, training, capabilities development and force provider as outlined in the Unified Command Plan.

AF General Lance L Smith
Commander/NATO Supreme Allied Commander Transformation

Army Lt General John R Wood
Deputy Commander

RAdm Miles B Wachendorf
Chief of Staff

Sgt Major Mark S Ripka
Command Sergeant Major

Joint Task Force Civil Support
Department of Defense
380 Fenwick Road
Building 96
Fort Monroe, VA 23651-1064
Phone: 757-788-6259
URL: www.jtfcs.northcom.mil

Description: Joint Task Force Civil Support plans and integrates DoD support to the designated Lead Federal Agency for domestic Chemical, Biological, Radiological, Nuclear and high yield Explosive (CBRNE) consequence management operations. When directed by Northern Command, the task force will deploy to the incident site, establish command and control of DoD forces and provide military assistance to civil authorities.

Major General Bruce E Davis
Commander

Colonel Randall W Holm
Deputy Commander

Raymond D James
Command Master Chief

Office of the Special Assistant Chemical & Biological Defense/Chemical Demilitarization Programs
Department of Defense
1000 Defense Pentagon
Washington, DC 20301
URL: www.acq.osd.mil/cp

Description: Leads, guides and integrates the chemical and biological defense programs to combat weapons of mass destruction.

Jean D Reed
Special Assistant

Colonel David G Jarrett
Deputy Special Assistant & Medical Director

Colonel Raymond L Naworol
Director, CBD Requirements & Operations Integration/Chief of Staff

Colonel Sandra B Wood
Director, CBRN Education & Training Integration

Office of the Inspector General
Department of Defense
400 Army Navy Drive
Suite 1000
Arlington, VA 22202-4704
Phone: 703-604-8300
Fax: 703-604-8310
URL: www.dodig.mil/

Description: The military Inspector General in America has traditionally served as an extension of the eyes, ears, and conscience of the Commander. Pursuant to the Inspector General Act of 1978, as amended, the Inspector General of the Department of Defense shall be principal advisor to the Secretary of Defense for matters relating to the prevention of fraud, waste, and abuse in the programs and operations of the Department. The law also requires the Inspector General to keep the Secretary of Defense and Congress fully and currently informed concerning fraud and other serious problems, abuses, and deficiences. In carrying out all of the other statutory duties, the Inspector General is obligated by law to give particular regard to the activities of the internal audit, inspection, and investigative units of the military departments with a view towards avoiding duplication and insuring effective coordination and cooperation.

Claude M Kicklighter
Inspector General
Phone: 703-604-8300

Thomas F Gimble
Principal Deputy Inspector General

John R Crane
Assistant Inspector General Communications & Congressional Liaison
Phone: 703-604-8324

Shelton R Young
Deputy Inspector General Intelligence

Richard T Race
Deputy Inspector General Investigations

Uldric L Fiore Jr
General Counsel

National Reconnaissance Office
Department of Defense
14675 Lee Road
Chantilly, VA 20151-1715
Phone: 703-808-1198
Fax: 703-808-1171

URL: www.nro.gov

Description: Designs, builds and operates the nation's reconnaissance satellites. NRO products, provided to an expanding list of customers like the CIA and the Department of Defense, can warn of potential trouble spots around the world, help plan military operations, and monitor the environment. As part of the Intelligence Community, the NRO plays a primary role in achieving information superiority for the United States. NRO is staffed by Department of Defense and CIA personnel and funded through the National Reconnaissance Program, part of the National Foreign Intelligence Program.

Dr Donald M Kerr
Director

Scott F Large
Principal Deputy Director

Major General John T Sheridan
Deputy Director

National Security Agency/Central Security Service
Department of Defense
NSA
Fort Meade, MD 20755
Phone: 301-688-6524
Fax: 301-688-6198
URL: www.nsa.gov
e-mail: nsapao@nsa.gov

Description: America's cryptologic organization. It coordinates, directs, and performs highly specialized activities to protect US government information systems and produce foreign signals intelligence information. A high technology organization, NSA is on the frontiers of communications and data processing. It is also one of the most important centers of foreign language analysis and research within the government.

Lt General Keith B Alexander
Director NSA/Chief CSS
Phone: 301-688-7111

John C Inglis
Deputy Director
Phone: 301-688-7333

Defense Intelligence Agency (DIA)
Department of Defense
7400 Defense Pentagon
Washington, DC 20301-7400
Phone: 703-695-0071
URL: www.dia.mil
e-mail: dia-pao@dia.mil

Description: This is a combat support agency and an important member of the US Intelligence Community. With over 11,000 military and civilian employees worldwide, DIA is a major producer and manager of foreign military intelligence. The Agency provides military intelligence to warfighters, defense policymakers and force planners, in the Department of Defense and the Intelligence Community, in support of US military planning and operations and weapon systems acquisition.

Lt General Michael Maples
Director
Phone: 703-695-7353

Leticia Long
Deputy Director
Phone: 703-697-5128

Defense Threat Reduction Agency (DTRA)
Department of Defense
8725 John J Kingman Road
MS 6201
Fort Belvoir, VA 22060-6201
Phone: 703-767-5870
Phone: 800-701-5096
Fax: 703-767-7857
URL: www.dtra.mil
e-mail: dtra.publicaffairs@dtra.mil

Description: The Defense Threat Reduction Agency safeguards the nation and it's interests from weapons of mass destruction (chemical, biological, radiological, nuclear and high yield explosives) by providing capabilities to reduce, eliminate, counter the threat and mitigate its effects. The Agency performs four essential functions to carry out its mission: combat support, technology development, threat control and threat reduction. DTRA work covers a broad spectrum of activities, including shaping the international environment to prevent the spread of weapons of mass destruction, responding to requirements to deter the use and reduce the impact of such weapons, and preparing for the future as WMD threats emerge and evolve.

Dr James A Tegnelia
Director
Phone: 703-767-4883

Major General Randal R Castro
Deputy Director

Security & Counterintelligence Directorate
Defense Threat Reduction Agency
8725 John J Kingman Road
Fort Belvior, VA 22060-6201
Mailing Address: MSC 6201
Phone: 703-767-5870
Phone: 703-767-4502
Fax: 703-767-4450
URL: www.dtra.mil/sc/

Description: The Security & Intelligence Directorate of DTRA aims to protect personnel, activities, information, facilities and cyberspace. It accomplishes it aim by maintaining awareness of all counterintelligence and force protection intelligence in support of agency missions, teams and conferences. It also manages the dissemination of intelligence products and identifies the agency's intelligence needs.

Threat Reduction Advisory Committee (TRAC)
Defense Threat Reduction Agency
8725 John J Kingman Road
Fort Belvior, VA 22060-6201
Mailing Address: MS 6201
Phone: 703-767-4759
URL: www.dtra.mil/ASCO/ab_asco_trac.cfm

Description: The TRAC advises and assists the Under Secretary of Defense (Acquisition, Technology & Logistics) on reduction of the threat to the US and its allies from chemical, biological, radiological, nuclear and high explosives. It identifies and considers emerging weapons of mass destruction threats, reviews counters to such threats and assesses the adequacy of DTRA and other programs' responses to national policy and emerging threats.

Colonel Rainer Stachowitz
Executive Director
e-mail: rainer.stachowitz@dtra.mil

Defense Advanced Research Projects Agency (DARPA)
Department of Defense
3701 N Fairfax Drive
Arlington, VA 22203-1714
Phone: 703-696-2400
Fax: 703-696-2209
URL: www.darpa.mil

Description: The Defense Advanced Research Projects Agency is the central research and development agency for the DoD. It develops imaginative, innovative and often high-risk research ideas offering a significant technological impact that will go well beyond the normal evolutionary developmental approaches to defense research. The Agency pursues these ideas from the demonstration of technical feasibility through the development of prototype systems.

Dr Anthony J Tether
Director
Phone: 703-696-2400

Robert F Leheny
Deputy Director
Phone: 703-696-2402

Ron Kurjanowicz
Chief of Staff
Phone: 703-696-2400

Christopher Earl
Special Assistant Technology
Phone: 571-218-4425
e-mail: chris.earl@darpa.mil

Richard McCormick Francis
Special Assistant Space

Paul Kozemchak
Special Assistant Intelligence Liaison
Phone: 703-696-7583

Kathy I MacDonald
Special Assistant Socom & Centcom

Norman Whitaker
Special Assistant Urban Challenge

Defense Sciences Office
Defense Advanced Research Projects Agency
3701 N Fairfax Drive
Arlington, VA 22203-1714
Phone: 571-218-4224
Fax: 571-218-4553
URL: www.darpa.mil/dso

Description: The Defense Sciences Office identifies and advances radically new technologies that promise to enhance national security and lead to revolutionary new military capabilities. It places no limit on the range of technical opportunities it pursues.

Dr Brett P Giroir
Director
Phone: 571-218-4224
e-mail: brett.giroir@darpa.mil

Barbara McQuiston
Deputy Director
Phone: 703-526-4759
e-mail: barbara.mcquiston@darpa.mil

Defense Security Service
Department of Defense
1340 Braddock Place
Alexandria, VA 22314
Phone: 703-325-5364
Fax: 703-325-7426
URL: www.dss.mil
e-mail: cpao@dss.mil

Description: Plays a crucial role in the national security community by conducting personnel security investigations and providing industrial security products and services, as well as offering comprehensive security eduction and training to the Department of Defense, military services and 23 other federal agencies.

Kathleen Watson
Director
Phone: 703-325-5364

Kevin Jones
Deputy Director Security Education, Training & Awareness/DSS Academy
Phone: 410-865-3253

Mary H Griggs
Deputy Director Industrial Security Program

Cynthia McGovern
Chief Information Officer
Phone: 703-325-9456

National Geospatial-Intelligence Agency
Department of Defense
4600 Sangamore Road
Bethesda, MD 20816-5003
Phone: 301-227-7300
Phone: 800-455-0899
Fax: 301-227-3696
URL: www.nga.mil
e-mail: queries1@nga.mil

Description: The National Geospatial-Intelligence Agency is a major combat support agency of the DoD and a member of the Intelligence Community. It provides timely, relevant, and accurate Geospatial Intelligence in support of national security objectives.

VAdm Robert B Murrett
Director
Phone: 301-227-7300

Lloyd B Rowland
Deputy Director
Phone: 301-227-7400

Mary M Irvin
Office of Geospatial Intelligence Management

Robert H Laurine
Chief Information Officer

Dawn R Eilenberger
Office of International Affairs & Policy

Katherine J Hall
Analysis & Production Directorate

Keith E Littlefield
Acquisition Directorate

Thomas J McCormick
Enterprise Operations Directorate

Peter M Makowsky
Source Operations & Management Directorate

Vonna W Heaton
InnoVision Directorate

Defense Procurement & Acquisition Policy
Department of Defense
3060 Defense Pentagon
Room 3E1044
Washington, DC 20301-3060
Phone: 703-695-7145
Fax: 703-693-1142
URL: www.acq.osd.mil/dpap
e-mail: dpap@osd.mil

Description: The Office of Defense Procurement and Acquisition Policy develops, promotes, and manages innovative department-wide policies for planning, pricing, awarding and administering contracts, business arrangements, and other transactions for supplies and services.

Shay Assad
Director
Phone: 703-695-7145

Office of Small Business Programs
Department of Defense
Crystal Gateway North
201 12th Street South, Ste 406
Arlington, VA 22202
Phone: 703-604-0157
Fax: 703-604-0025
URL: www.acq.osd.mil/osbp

Description: The Office of Small and Disadvantaged Business Utilization assures small and disadvantaged businesses opportunities within the Department of Defense and enables those involved in war efforts to gain access to small business efficiency, innovation and creativity.

Anthony R Martoccia
Director
Phone: 703-604-0157

FEDERAL

Department of Education

Department of Education
Headquarters
400 Maryland Avenue SW
Washington, DC 20202
Phone: 800-872-5327
Fax: 202-401-0689
URL: www.ed.gov

Description: The Department of Education works with the Department of Homeland Security and other federal agencies in ensuring that schools have complete, well-thought-out emergency plans that address traditional crises and emergencies such as fires, firearm incidents, and accidents, as well as biological, radiological, chemical and other terrorist activities. In furthering its commitment to the safety and security of all students, it developed a web site (www.ed.gov/admins/lead/safety/emergencyplan/index.html) to help schools and communities prepare and develop plans for responding to potential emergency situations, including natural disasters, violent incidents and terrorist acts. In addition to informational resources, the Department of Education also makes funds available to train personnel, parents and students in crisis response; coordinate with local emergency responders; purchase equipment; and coordinate with groups responsible for recovery initiatives, such as mental health personnel.

Margaret Mary Spellings
Secretary
Phone: 202-401-3000

Raymond Simon
Deputy Secretary
Phone: 202-401-0113
e-mail: ray.simon@ed.gov

Sara Martinez Tucker
Under Secretary
Phone: 202-401-8187

David L Dunn
Chief of Staff
Phone: 202-401-3000

Hudson La Force III
Senior Counselor to the Secretary
Phone: 202-260-7758
e-mail: hudson.la.force@ed.gov

Philip S Link
Executive Secretariat
Phone: 202-401-3067
e-mail: philip.link@ed.gov

JoAnn K Ryan
Executive Management Staff Director
Phone: 202-401-3082

Lauren Maddox
Assistant Secretary Office of Communications & Outreach
Phone: 202-401-0768

Michell Clark
Assistant Secretary Management Office
Phone: 202-260-7337
e-mail: michell.clark@ed.gov

Stephanie Monroe
Assistant Secretary Civil Rights Office
Phone: 202-245-6700

Timothy Magner
Office of Educational Technology Director
Phone: 202-401-1444
e-mail: tim.magner@ed.gov

Shayam Menon
Center for Faith-Based & Community Initiatives
Phone: 202-208-1724

Adam Chavarria
Executive Director, White House Initiative on Educational Excellence for Hispanic Americans
Phone: 202-401-7479
e-mail: adam.chavarria@ed.gov

Charles Greene
Executive Director, White House Initiative on Historically Black Colleges & Universities
Phone: 202-502-7511

Deborah Cavett
Executive Director, White House Initiative on Tribal Colleges & Universities
Phone: 202-219-7040

Office of Safe & Drug-Free Schools (OSDFS)
Department of Education
400 Maryland Avenue SW
Room 3E300
Washington, DC 20202-6450
Phone: 202-260-3954
Fax: 202-260-7767
URL: www.ed.gov/about/offices/list/osdfs
e-mail: osdfs.safeschl@ed.gov

Description: Administers, coordinates and recommends policy for improving quality and excellence of programs and activities that are designed to: provide financial assistance for drug and violence prevention activities; participate in the development of program policy related to prevention; participate in interagency committees, groups and partnerships related to prevention; participate with other federal agencies in the development of a national research agenda. Most recently the office held two Emergency Management for Schools Training sessions in 2007.

Deborah A Price
Assistant Deputy Secretary
Phone: 202-205-4169
e-mail: deborah.price@ed.gov

William Modzeleski
Associate Assistant Deputy Secretary
Phone: 202-260-3954
e-mail: bill.modzeleski@ed.gov

Charlotte Gillespie
Drug Violence Prevention-National Programs
Phone: 202-260-1862
e-mail: charlotte.gillespie@ed.gov

Paul Kesner
Drug Violence Prevention-State Programs
Phone: 202-205-8134
e-mail: paul.kesner@ed.gov

Robert Alexander
Director, Character, Civil & Correctional Education
Phone: 202-401-3354

Safe & Drug-Free Schools & Communities Advisory Committee
Department of Education
400 Maryland Avenue SW
Room 1E110
Washington, DC 20202
Phone: 202-205-4169
Fax: 202-205-5005
URL: www.ed.gov/about/bdscomm/list/sdfscac
e-mail: osdfsc@ed.gov

Description: The Committee was established to provide advice to the Secretary on federal, state and local programs designated to create safe and drug-free schools, and on issues related to crisis planning. It is comprised of federal agencies and private citizens who have high levels of expertise and experience in the areas of drug, alcohol and violence prevention, safe schools, mental health research and crisis planning.

Catherine Davis
Executive Director & DFO

Deborah A Price
Assistant Deputy Secretary Safe & Drug-Free Schools

William Modzeleski
Associate Assistant Deputy Secretary Safe & Drug-Free Schools

Office of Innovation & Improvement
Department of Education
400 Maryland Avenue SW
Washington, DC 20202
Phone: 202-205-4500
Fax: 202-401-4123
URL: www.ed.gov/about/offices/list/oii

Description: The Office of Innovation and Improvement is an entrepreneurial arm of the Department of Education. It makes strategic investments in promising education practices through grants to states, schools and community organizations. It also leads the movement for greater parental options and information

in education. This Office houses two dozen discretionary grant programs (ie: School Emergency Response and Crisis Management Plan) and coordinates the public school choice and supplemental educational services, provisions of No Child Left Behind Act. The Office is also responsible for aggressively disseminating information as a result of these grants to the education field. As part of this dissemination, the Office sponsors events, such as the Innovations in Education Exchange and other conferences and meetings, to communicate with the public.

Morgan Brown
Assistant Deputy Secretary
Phone: 202-205-4484

Margo Anderson
Associate Assistant Deputy Secretary
Phone: 202-205-0653

Virginia K Gentles
Associate Assistant Deputy Secretary

Edith Harvey
Director Improvement Programs
Phone: 202-260-1393

John Fiegel
Parental Options & Information
e-mail: john.fiegel@ed.gov

Sharon K Horn
Director Evaluation & Dissemination
Phone: 202-205-4956
e-mail: sharon.horn@ed.gov

Office of Communications & Outreach
Department of Education
400 Maryland Avenue SW
Washington, DC 20202
Phone: 202-401-0404
Phone: 800-872-5327
Fax: 202-401-8607
URL: www.ed.gov/about/offices/list/oco

Description: Leads the Department's communications and outreach efforts by overseeing press relations, publications, contacts with organizations, and communication with parents, students, educators, and citizens.

Lauren Maddox
Assistant Secretary
Phone: 202-401-0768

Norman Hall
Executive Officer
Phone: 202-401-0422
e-mail: norman.hall@ed.gov

Office of the Chief Information Officer
Department of Education
400 Maryland Avenue SW
Washington, DC 20202
Phone: 202-245-6400
Fax: 202-245-6621
URL: www.ed.gov/about/offices/list/ocio
e-mail: ocio@ed.gov

Description: Provides the technological solutions that enable the Department of Education to deliver world-class service to schools, students and their families. It advises and assists the

Secretary and other senior officials in acquiring information technology and managing information resources. The Chief Information Officer has the responsibility of establishing a management framework that leads the agency toward more efficient and effective operations.

Bill Vajda
Chief Information Officer
Phone: 202-245-6640
e-mail: bill.vajda@ed.gov

Office of the Inspector General
Department of Education
400 Maryland Avenue SW
Washington, DC 20202-1500
Phone: 202-245-6900
Fax: 202-245-6995
URL: www.ed.gov/about/offices/list/oig

Description: To promote the efficiency, effectiveness, and integrity of the Department's programs and operations. It conducts independent and objective audits, investigations, inspections, and other activities.

John P Higgins Jr
Inspector General
Phone: 202-245-6900
e-mail: john.higgins@ed.gov

Thomas L Sipes
Deputy Inspector General
Phone: 202-245-6900

Mary S Mitchelson
Counsel to the Inspector General
Phone: 202-245-6987
e-mail: mary.mitchelson@ed.gov

Tara Porter
Chief of Staff
Phone: 202-245-6588
e-mail: tara.porter@ed.gov

Michael E DeShields
Assistant Inspector General Investigations
Phone: 202-245-7058
e-mail: michael.deshields@ed.gov

Office of the General Counsel
Department of Education
400 Maryland Avenue SW
Washington, DC 20202
Phone: 202-401-6000
Fax: 202-205-2689
URL: www.ed.gov/about/offices/list/ogc

Description: The Office of the General Counsel is under the supervision of the General Counsel, who serves as principal adviser to the Secretary on all legal matters affecting Departmental programs and activities. The Office has three legal practice areas, each of which is headed by a Deputy General Counsel, and an operations management staff, headed by an Executive Officer.

Kent Talbert
General Counsel
Phone: 202-401-6000
e-mail: kent.talbert@ed.gov

Kent Talbert
General Counsel
Phone: 202-401-6000
e-mail: kent.talbert@ed.gov

Robert Wexler
Senior Counsel/Acting Chief of Staff
Phone: 202-401-6698
e-mail: rob.wexler@ed.gov

J Carolyn Adams
Operations Management Staff Executive Officer
Phone: 202-401-8340
e-mail: carolyn.adams@ed.gov

William Haubert
Business & Administrative Law Division
Phone: 202-401-6700
e-mail: william.haubert@ed.gov

Paul Riddle
Legislative Counsel Division
Phone: 202-401-6269
e-mail: paul.riddle@ed.gov

Susan E Craig
Educational Equity & Research Division
Phone: 202-401-8316

Stephen H Freid
Elementary, Secondary, Audit & Vocational Education Division
Phone: 202-401-8292

Susan A Winchell
Ethics Division (Acting)
Phone: 202-401-8309

Harold B Jenkins
Postsecondary Education Division
Phone: 202-401-8302

Elizabeth A M McFadden
Regulatory Services Division
Phone: 202-401-8300
e-mail: elizabeth.mcfadden@ed.gov

FEDERAL

Department of Energy

Department of Energy
Headquarters
1000 Independence Avenue SW
Washington, DC 20585-0001
Phone: 202-586-6210
Phone: 800-342-5363
Fax: 202-586-4403
URL: www.energy.gov

Description: The US Department of Energy's mission is to advance the national, economic and energy security of the nation. The Department has five stragtegic themes. Energy Security: promote energy security through reliable, affordable, and clean energy. Nuclear Security: ensure America's nuclear security. Scientific Discovery & Innovation: strengthen scientific discovery, economic competitiveness, and improve quality of life through innovations. Environmental Responsibility: protect the environment through responsible resolution of the legacy of nuclear weapons production. Management Excellence: enable the mission through sound management.

Dr Samuel W Bodman
Secretary
Phone: 202-586-6210
e-mail: the.secretary@hq.doe.gov

Jeffrey Clay Sell
Deputy Secretary/COO
Phone: 202-586-5500

Jeffrey Kupfer
Chief of Staff
Phone: 202-586-6210
e-mail: jeffrey.kupfer@hq.doe.gov

Dennis R Spurgeon
Acting Under Secretary of Energy
Phone: 202-586-7700

Dr Raymond L Orbach
Under Secretary for Science
Phone: 202-586-0505

William C Ostendorff
Acting Under Secretary for Nuclear Security/Administrator NNSA
Phone: 202-586-5555

James N Solit
Executive Secretariat
Phone: 202-586-5230

Karen A Harbert
Assistant Secretary for Policy & International Affairs
Phone: 202-586-8660

Jill L Sigal
Assistant Secretary for Congressional & Intergovernmental Affairs
Phone: 202-586-5450

Alexander A Kasner
Assistant Secretary for Energy Efficiency & Renewable Energy
Phone: 202-586-9220

Dennis R Spurgeon
Assistant Secretary for Nuclear Energy
Phone: 202-586-6630

James A Rispoli
Assistant Secretary for Environmental Management
Phone: 202-586-6850

Ingrid Kolb
Director Office of Management
Phone: 202-586-2550

Thomas N Pyke Jr
Chief Information Officer
Phone: 202-586-0166

David R Hill
General Counsel
Phone: 202-586-5281

Steve Isakowitz
Chief Financial Officer
Phone: 202-586-4171
e-mail: steve.isakowitz@hq.doe.gov

Gregory H Friedman
Inspector General
Phone: 202-586-4393

Anne W Kolton
Director Public Affairs
Phone: 202-586-4940
e-mail: anne.womack.kolton@hq.doe.gov

National Nuclear Security Administration
Department of Energy
1000 Independence Avenue SW
Washington, DC 20585
Phone: 202-586-7371
Phone: 202-586-5555
Fax: 202-586-3929
URL: www.nnsa.doe.gov

Description: The National Nuclear Security Administration enhances United States national security through the military application of nuclear science. It maintains and enhances the safety, security, reliability and performance of the United States nuclear weapons stockpile, including the ability to design, produce and test, in order to meet national security requirements; provides the United States Navy with safe, militarily effective nuclear propulsion; and responds to nuclear and radiological emergencies in the US and abroad.

William C Ostendorff
Acting Administrator/Principal Deputy Administrator
Phone: 202-586-5555

Admiral Kirkland H Donald
Deputy Administrator Naval Reactors Programs
Phone: 202-781-6174

Thomas P D'Agostino
Deputy Administrator Defense Programs
Phone: 202-586-7909
e-mail: thomas.dagostino@nnsa.doe.gov

William H Tobey
Deputy Administrator Office of Defense Nuclear Nonproliferation
Phone: 202-586-0645
e-mail: william.tobey@nnsa.doe.gov

William J Desmond
Associate Administrator Nuclear Security Program
Phone: 202-586-8900
e-mail: william.desmond@nnsa.doe.gov

Bruce Scott
Associate Administrator Infrastructure & Environment
Phone: 202-586-7349
e-mail: bruce.scott@nnsa.doe.gov

Joseph J Krol
Associate Administrator Emergency Operations
Phone: 202-586-9892
e-mail: joseph.krol@nnsa.doe.gov

Michael Kane
Associate Administrator Managment & Administration
Phone: 202-586-5753
e-mail: michael.kane@nnsa.doe.gov

William Barker
Chief of Staff
Phone: 202-586-5096
e-mail: william.barker@nnsa.doe.gov

David S Jonas
General Counsel
Phone: 202-586-5052

Catherine M Sheppard
Defense Nuclear Counterintelligence Chief
Phone: 202-586-9018

Steven Akoi
Office of the Deputy Under Secretary for Counterterrorism
Phone: 202-586-6063

Office of Defense Nuclear Nonproliferation
National Nuclear Security Administration
1000 Independence Avenue SW
Washington, DC 20585
Phone: 202-586-0645
Fax: 202-586-0862
URL: www.nnsa.doe.gov/na-20/

Description: The Office of Defense Nuclear Nonproliferation has as its mission to: detect, prevent, and reverse the proliferation of weapons of mass destruction, while mitigating the risks from nuclear operations. It accomplishes this by working closely with its international and regional partners and key federal agencies.

William H Tobey
Deputy Administrator
Phone: 202-586-0645
e-mail: william.tobey@nnsa.doe.gov

Kenneth E Baker
Principal Deputy Assistant Administrator
Phone: 202-586-0645
e-mail: ken.baker@nnsa.doe.gov

James M Turner
Nuclear Risk Reduction
Phone: 202-586-9466

Thelma J Cerveny
Nonproliferation Research & Development
Phone: 202-586-2400

Andrew J Bieniawski
Global Threat Reduction
Phone: 202-586-0775

David G Huizenga
International Material Protection & Cooperation
Phone: 202-586-0899

Adam Scheinman
Nonproliferation & International Security
Phone: 202-586-8525

Ken Chacey
Fissile Materials Disposition
Phone: 202-586-2695

Emergency Operations
National Nuclear Security Administration
1000 Independence Avenue SW
Washington, DC 20585
Phone: 202-586-9892
Fax: 202-586-3904
URL: www.nnsa.doe.gov/emergency.htm

Description: The Emergency Operations program administers and directs the emergency response capability programs of the Department of Energy and the National Nuclear Security Administration, ensuring the viability of the Department to respond to emergencies at their facilities and field sites, as well as to nuclear and radiological emergencies within the United States and abroad.

Joseph J Krol
Associate Administer for Emergency Operations
Phone: 202-586-9892
e-mail: joseph.krol@nnsa.doe.gov

James E Fairobent
Director, Emergency Management & Policy
Phone: 202-586-8759
e-mail: jim.fairobent@nnsa.doe.gov

Deborah A Wilber
Director, Emergency Response
Phone: 202-586-0592
e-mail: deborah.wilber@nnsa.doe.gov

Thomas M Black
Director, Emergency Management Implementation
Phone: 301-903-7314
e-mail: thomas.black@nnsa.doe.gov

Robert R Jordan
Director, Emergency Operations Support
Phone: 202-586-4941
e-mail: robert.jordan@nnsa.doe.gov

Office of Electricity Delivery & Energy Reliability
Department of Energy
1000 Independence Avenue SW
Washington, DC 20585
Phone: 202-586-1411
Fax: 202-586-1472
URL: www.oe.energy.gov

Description: The Office provides the following in support of and in coordination with DHS: manages the department's activities as they relate to critical infrastructure protection; conducts analysis of energy infrastructure vulnerabilities to physical disruptions and recommends preventative measures; and in accordance with the National Response Plan, conducts Emergency Support Function Twelve (energy) operations.

Kevin Kolevar
Director
Phone: 202-586-1411

Patricia Hoffman
Deputy Director Research & Development
Phone: 202-586-6074
e-mail: patricia.hoffman@hq.doe.gov

Marshall Whitenton
Deputy Director Permitting, Siting & Analysis
Phone: 202-586-9414
e-mail: mark.whitendon@hq.doe.gov

Alexis de Alvarez
Deputy Director Infrastructure Security & Energy Restoration
Phone: 202-586-1565
e-mail: alexis.deAlvarez@hq.doe.gov

Office of Nuclear Energy
Department of Energy
1000 Independence Avenue SW
Washington, DC 20585
Phone: 202-586-6630
Fax: 202-586-8353
URL: www.ne.doe.gov

Description: The Office of Nuclear Energy takes the lead in DOE investment in the development and exploration of advanced nuclear science and technology. Programs funded by the Office follow these two goals: maintain, enhance, and safeguard the nation's nuclear infrastructure capability to meet environmental and national security needs; and develop new nuclear generation technologies.

Dennis R Spurgeon
Assistant Secretary
Phone: 202-586-6630

Dennis M Miotla
Deputy Assistant Secretary Nuclear Power Deployment
Phone: 301-903-5338

W James Colsh
Director Human Capital & Business Services
Phone: 301-903-3796

Office of Intelligence & Counterintelligence
Department of Energy
1000 Independence Avenue SW
Washington, DC 20585
Phone: 202-586-2610
Fax: 202-586-8207
URL:
www.energy.gov/nationalsecurity/intelligence_counterterrorism.htm

Description: The Office of Intelligence and Counterintelligence ensures the security of critical programs (nuclear weapons, leading edge research and development projects) through the application of an effective and coordinated counterintelligence program. Activities are focused on protecting nuclear weapons secrets, but at the same time protecting other sensitive scientific endeavors in an effort to defeat terrorism.

Rolf Mowatt-Larssen
Director
Phone: 202-586-2610

Stanley Borgia
Deputy Director Office of Counterintelligence
Phone: 202-586-5901

Larry M Gresham
Deputy Director Office of Management
Phone: 202-586-2610

Alex Goodale
Deputy Director Office of Intelligence
Phone: 202-586-2085

Transportation Emergency Preparedness Program (TEPP)
Office of Environmental Management-Transportation
1000 Independence Avenue SW
Washington, DC 20585
Phone: 301-903-7284
Fax: 301-903-1431
URL: www.em.doe.gov/Transportation/TEPP_Home.aspx

Description: The DOE and its transportation activities have come under intense scrutiny, thus the Department has implemented this department-wide program to address preparedness issues for non-classified/non-weapons radioactive materials shipments. The TEPP integrates transportation emergency preparedness activities under a singular program for a standardized approach to transporting radioactive materials. There are eight regional coordinating offices, each with a designated TEPP Coordinator.

Dennis J Ashworth
Director Office of Transportation
Phone: 202-586-8548
e-mail: dennis.ashworth@hq.doe.gov

Ella McNeil
Headquarters Manager
Phone: 202-903-7284
e-mail: ella.mcneil@em.doe.gov

Office of the Chief Information Officer

Department of Energy
1000 Independence Avenue SW
Washington, DC 20585
Phone: 202-586-0166
Fax: 202-586-7966
URL: http://cio.energy.gov

Description: The mission is to advance the national, economic and energy security of the US; promote scientific and technological innovation in support of that mission; and ensure the environmental cleanup of the national nuclear weapons complex. The CIO provides advice and assistance to the Secretary of Energy and other senior managers to ensure that information resources are managed in a manner that implements the policies and procedures of legislation.

Thomas Pyke Jr
Chief Information Officer
Phone: 202-586-0166

Carl P Staton
Deputy Chief Information Officer
Phone: 202-586-0166

William G Lay
Associate CIO, IT Support Services
Phone: 202-586-7551
e-mail: bill.lay@hq.doe.gov

Theanne Gordon
Associate CIO, Planning, Architecture & E-Government
Phone: 202-586-9958
e-mail: theanne.gordon@hq.doe.gov

Harry Hixon
Associate CIO, Enterprise Operations
Phone: 301-903-2018
e-mail: harry.hixon@hq.doe.gov

Kevin R Cooke
Associate CIO, IT Corporate Management
Phone: 202-586-6566

William J Hunteman
Associate CIO, Cyber Security
Phone: 202-586-4775

Cyber Security

Office of the Chief Information Officer
1000 Independence Avenue SW
Washington, DC 20585
Phone: 202-586-4775
Phone: 202-586-0166
Fax: 202-586-7966
URL: http://cio.energy.gov/cybersecurity.htm

William J Hunteman
Associate CIO for Cyber Security
Phone: 202-586-4775

Anthony Z S Bailey
Acting Deputy Associate CIO
Phone: 202-586-8139

Roland M Lascola
Director Incident Management Division Director
Phone: 301-903-1417

Frederick A Catoe
Enterprise Services Division Director
Phone: 301-903-6453

Office of Health, Safety & Security

Department of Energy
1000 Independence Avenue SW
Washington, DC 20585
Phone: 301-903-3777
URL: www.hss.energy.gov

Description: The Office of Health, Safety & Security is the central organization within the Department of Energy responsible for health, safety, environment, and security; providing corporate-level leadership in coordinating and integrating these vital programs. The Chief Health, Safety & Security Officer advises the Deputy Secretary and Secretary on all matters related to health, safety and security complex wide.

Glenn Podonsky
Chief Health, Safety & Security Officer
Phone: 301-903-3777

Robert M Lingan
Office of Security Operations
Phone: 202-586-1461

John D Lazor
Office of Headquarters Security Operations
Phone: 202-586-6591

Jackie L Cowden
Office of Special Operations
Phone: 301-903-4291

Office of Procurement & Assistance Management

Department of Energy
950 L'Enfant Plaza
Room 7055
Washington, DC 20585
Mailing Address: 1000 Independenece Ave SW, 20585
Phone: 202-287-1310
Fax: 202-287-1305
URL: http://professionals.pr.doe.gov

Description: To ensure the development and implementation of Department of Energy (DOE) wide policies, procedures, programs, and management systems as they pertain to procurement and financial assistance, personal property management, maintenance management, and related activities to provide procurement services to headquarters.

Edward R Simpson
Director
Phone: 202-287-1310

Michael P Fischetti
Procurement & Assistance Policy
Phone: 202-287-1330

Edward R Simpson
Acting Contract Management/Resource Management Office
Phone: 202-287-1365
e-mail: edward.simpson@hq.doe.gov

John R Bashita
Director Headquarters Procurement Services
Phone: 202-287-1500

Office of Small & Disadvantaged Business Utilization

Department of Energy
1000 Independence Avenue SW
Room 5B148
Washington, DC 20585
Phone: 202-586-8383
Fax: 202-586-3075
URL: http://smallbusiness.doe.gov

Description: The DOE is committed to providing information to small business about contracting opportunities at both the prime and subcontract level. The Office of Small and Disadvantaged Business Utilization is the agency's focal point for these small businesses. It provides strategies for oversight of the development and execution of procurement policies and programs to ensure that an equitable portion of the total contracts and subcontracts for the Department of Energy's services and supplies are procured from small business concerns.

Theresa Alvillar-Speake
Director
Phone: 202-586-8383
e-mail: theresa.speake@hq.doe.gov

Adrienne Cisneros
Deputy Associate Director
Phone: 202-586-7951
e-mail: adrienne.cisernos@hq.doe.gov

Sterling Nichols
Program Manager, Business & Community Development
Phone: 202-586-8698
e-mail: sterling.nichols@hq.doe.gov

Brenda Degraffenreid
Senior Procurement Analyst
Phone: 202-586-4620
e-mail: brenda.degraffenreid@hq.doe.gov

Nickolas Demer
Procurement Analyst
Phone: 202-586-1614
e-mail: nickolas.demer@hq.doe.gov

FEDERAL

Department of Health & Human Services

Department of Health & Human Services
Headquarters
200 Independence Avenue SW
Washington, DC 20201
Phone: 202-619-0257
Phone: 877-696-6775
Fax: 202-690-7203
URL: www.hhs.gov

Description: The United States Department of Health and Human Services (HHS) is the lead federal agency addressing the medical and health consequences of all mass casualty events, whether terrorist-induced, accidental, or naturally occurring. In its homeland security role, HHS prepares communities for bioterrorism. It works with state and local groups to: enhance preparedness; develop and maintain response tools, such as the Strategic National Stockpile (see CDC); conduct research and development toward new vaccines, diagnostics and drugs; and partner with key organizations, such as the White House Office of Homeland Security, the Department of Homeland Security (DHS) and other academic and industrial groups. HHS and its Centers for Disease Control and Prevention also work with DHS to make medical and scientific decisions for the Select Agent Registration Program, enabling HHS to regulate the transfer of dangerous pathogens and toxins (Select Agents) from one facility to another. The President's budget included a request for more than $4 billion for biodefense activities at HHS to improve local and state public health systems, to expand existing biosurveillance efforts, and to fund research on medical counter-measures against potential bioterror agents.

Michael O Leavitt
Secretary
Phone: 202-690-7000
e-mail: mike.leavittVT@hhs.gov

Eric Hargan
Acting Deputy Secretary
Phone: 202-690-6133
e-mail: eric.hargan@hhs.gov

Richard McKeown
Chief of Staff
Phone: 202-690-8157

Ann C Agnew
Executive Secretariat
Phone: 202-690-5627
e-mail: ann.agnew@hhs.gov

Jack Kalavritinos
Director Intergovernmental Affairs
Phone: 202-690-6060
e-mail: jack.kalavritinos@hhs.gov

Charles E Johnson
Assistant Secretary Resources & Technology
Phone: 202-690-6396

Joe Ellis
Assistant Secretary Administration & Management
Phone: 202-690-7431
e-mail: joe.ellis@hhs.gov

Dr John Agwunobi
Assistant Secretary Health
Phone: 202-690-7694
e-mail: john.agwunobi@hhs.gov

Vince Ventimiglia
Assistant Secretary Legislation
Phone: 202-690-7627
e-mail: vince.ventimiglia@hhs.gov

Suzy Defrancis
Assistant Secretary Public Affairs
Phone: 202-690-7850
e-mail: suzy.defrancis@hhs.gov

RAdm W Craig Vanderwagen MD
Assistant Secretary Preparedness & Response
Phone: 202-205-2882
e-mail: william.vanderwagen@hhs.gov

Cecilia Sparks Ford
Department of Appeals Board, Chair
Phone: 202-565-0200
e-mail: cecilia.ford@hhs.gov

Winston Wilkinson
Director, Civil Rights Office
Phone: 202-619-0403
e-mail: winston.wilkinson@hhs.gov

William Steiger
Director, Global Health Affairs Office
Phone: 202-690-6174
e-mail: william.steiger@hhs.gov

Daniel R Levinson
Inspector General
Phone: 202-619-3148
e-mail: dan.levinson@oig.hhs.gov

Judge Perry Rhew
Chief Administrative Law Judge/Medicare Hearings & Appeals
Phone: 216-615-4000
e-mail: perry.rhew@hhs.gov

Robert M Kolodner MD
National Coordinator for Health Information Technology

Phone: 202-690-7151
e-mail: onchit.request@hhs.gov

Daniel Meron
General Counsel
Phone: 202-690-7741
e-mail: daniel.meron@hhs.gov

Office of the Assistant Secretary for Preparedness & Response
Department of Health & Human Services
200 Independence Avenue NW
Room 638G
Washington, DC 20201
Phone: 202-205-2882
Fax: 202-690-6512
URL: www.hhs.gov/aspr

Description: The Office of the Assistant Secretary for Preparedness & Response (ASRP) (formerly Office of Public Health Emergency Preparedness) serves as the Secretary's principal advisory staff on matters related to bioterrorism and public health emergencies. The Office also coordinates interagency activities between HHS, other federal departments/agencies/offices that are responsible for emergency preparedness and protection.

RAdm W Craig Vanderwagen MD
Assistant Secretary
Phone: 202-205-2882
e-mail: william.vanderwagen@hhs.gov

Gerald Parker
Principal Deputy Assistant Secretary
Phone: 202-205-2882
e-mail: gerald.parker@hhs.gov

Dr Stuart Nightingale
Deputy Assistant Secretary/Chief Medical Officer
Phone: 202-205-2882
e-mail: stuart.nightingale@hhs.gov

Dr Kevin Yeskey
Preparedness & Emergency Operations Office
Phone: 202-205-0872
e-mail: kevin.yeskey@hhs.gov

Carol D Linden PhD
Biomedical Advanced Research & Development Authority
Phone: 202-260-1200

Brian Kamoie JD, MPH
Policy & Strategic Planning Office
Phone: 202-205-4750
e-mail: brian.kamoie@hhs.gov

National Disaster Medical System (NDMS)
Office of the Assistant Secretary for Preparedness & Response
409 Third Street SW
Washington, DC 20024
Mailing Address: 330 Independence Ave SW, 20201
Phone: 800-872-6367
URL: www.ndms.dhhs.gov

Description: The National Disaster Medical System (NDMS) transitioned to HHS as of January 2007. Its overall purpose is to establish a single integrated national medical response capability for assisting state and local authorities in dealing with the medi-

cal impacts of major peacetime disasters and to provide support to the military and the Department of Veteran Affairs medical systems in caring for casualties evacuated back to the US from oversees armed conflicts. The components of NDMS consist of: medical response in the form of teams, supplies and equipment; patient movement from disaster areas to unaffected areas of the nation; and definitive medical care at participating hospitals in unaffected areas.

Jack Beall
Director
Phone: 202-205-7879
e-mail: jack.beall@hhs.gov

David Canton
Chief Medical Officer
Phone: 202-205-5391
e-mail: david.canton@hhs.gov

Ana Marie Balingit-Wines
Emergency Analyst
Phone: 202-205-8088
e-mail: anamarie.balingit-wines@hhs.gov

Meta Timmons
Veterinary Officer
e-mail: meta.timmons@hhs.gov

Food & Drug Administration
Department of Health & Human Services
5600 Fishers Lane
Parklawn Building
Rockville, MD 20857
Mailing Address: MC HF-1
Phone: 301-827-2410
Phone: 888-463-6332
Fax: 301-443-3100
URL: www.fda.gov

Description: The FDA is responsible for protecting the public health by assuring the safety, efficacy, and security of human and veterinary drugs, biological products, medical devices, the nation's food supply, cosmetics, and products that emit radiation. The FDA is also responsible for advancing the public health by helping to speed innovations that make medicines and foods more effective, safer, and more affordable; and helping the public get the accurate, science-based information they need to use medicines and foods to improve their health.

Andrew C von Eschenbach
Commissioner
Phone: 301-827-2410
e-mail: commissioner@oc.fds.gov

Janet Woodcock
Deputy Commissioner/Chief Medical Officer
Phone: 301-827-3310
e-mail: janet.woodcock@fda.hhs.gov

Randall Lutter
Acting Deputy Commissioner Policy
Phone: 301-827-3370
e-mail: randall.lutter@fda.hhs.gov

John R Dyer
Deputy Commissioner Operations/COO
Phone: 301-827-1166
e-mail: john.dyer@fda.hhs.gov

Murray M Lumpkin
Deputy Commissioner International/Special Programs
Phone: 301-827-5709
e-mail: murray.lumpkin@fda.hhs.gov

Ellen F Morrison
Crisis Management
Phone: 301-827-5660
e-mail: ellen.morrison@fda.hhs.gov

Norris E Alderson
Associate Commissioner Science & Health Coordination
Phone: 301-827-3340

Sheldon Bradshaw
Chief Counsel
Phone: 301-827-1137
e-mail: sheldon.bradshaw@fda.gov

Margaret O Glavin
Associate Commissioner Regulatory Affairs Office
Phone: 301-827-3101

Daniel G Schultz MD
Center for Devices & Radiological Health
Phone: 240-276-3939

Jesse L Goodman PhD
Center for Biologics Evaluation & Research
Phone: 301-827-0372

Robert E Brackett
Center for Food Safety & Applied Nutrition
Phone: 301-436-1600

William Slikker Jr PhD
National Center for Toxicology Research
Phone: 870-543-7516

Office of Crisis Management
FDA
5600 Fishers Lane
Parklawn Building
Washington, DC 20857
Phone: 301-827-5660
Fax: 301-827-3333
URL: www.fda.gov/oc/ocm/

Description: The Office of Crisis Management serves as the FDA's focal point for coordinating emergency and crisis response activities involving FDA regulated products or in situations when FDA regulated products need to be utilized or deployed. It coordinates intra and interagency activities related to crisis management, emergency preparedness and response, and security operations.

Ellen Morrison
Director
Phone: 301-827-5660
e-mail: ellen.morrison@fda.hhs.gov

Dorothy Miller
Emergency Operations
Phone: 301-827-5277
e-mail: dorothy.miller@fda.hhs.gov

Barry Smith
Security Operations
Phone: 301-827-7034
e-mail: barry.smith@fda.hhs.gov

Office of the Secretary's Regional Directors
Department of Health & Human Services
200 Independence Ave SW
Room 600E
Washington, DC 20201

Brian Golden
Regional Director - Region 1 Boston
Phone: 617-565-1500
e-mail: brian.golden@hhs.gov

Deborah Konopko
Regional Director - Region 2 New York
Phone: 212-264-4600
e-mail: deborah.konopko@hhs.gov

Gordon Woodrow
Regional Director - Region 3 Philadelphia
Phone: 215-861-4633
e-mail: gordon.woodrow@hhs.gov

Christopher Downing
Regional Director - Region 4 Atlanta
Phone: 404-562-7888
e-mail: chris.downing@hhs.gov

Maureen Lydon
Regional Director - Region 5 Chicago
Phone: 312-353-5160
e-mail: maureen.lydon@hhs.gov

Michael Garcia
Regional Director - Region 6 Dallas
Phone: 214-767-3301
e-mail: michael.garcia@hhs.gov

Fred Schuster
Regional Director - Region 7 Kansas City
Phone: 816-426-2821
e-mail: fred.schuster@hhs.gov

Joe Nunez
Regional Director - Region 8 Denver
Phone: 303-844-3372
e-mail: joe.nunez@hhs.gov

Thomas Lorentzen
Regional Director - Region 9 San Francisco
Phone: 415-437-8500
e-mail: thomas.lorentzen@hhs.gov

James Whitfield
Regional Director - Region 10 Seattle
Phone: 206-615-2010
e-mail: james.whitfield@hhs.gov

Regional Emergency Coordinator-I
Government Center
JFK Federal Building, Rm 2126
Boston, MA 02203
Phone: 617-565-1693
Fax: 617-565-1491

Description: Connecticut, Maine, Massachusetts, New Hampshire, Rhode Island, and Vermont.

Greg Banner
Phone: 617-565-1485
e-mail: gregory.banner@hhs.gov

Regional Emergency Coordinator-II

Jacob Javits Federal Building
26 Federal Plaza, 13th Fl
New York, NY 10278
Phone: 212-264-2802
Fax: 212-264-3424

Description: New Jersey, New York, Puerto Rico, and the Virgin Islands.

Andrew Flacks
Phone: 212-264-4494
e-mail: andrew.flacks@hhs.gov

Regional Emergency Coordinator-III

150 S Independence Mall West
Public Ledger Bldg, Ste 436
Philadelphia, PA 19106
Phone: 215-861-4635
Fax: 215-861-4625

Description: Delaware, District of Columbia, Maryland, Pennsylvania, Virginia, and West Virginia.

Harry Mayer
Phone: 215-861-4413
e-mail: harry.mayer@hhs.gov

Regional Emergency Coordinator-IV

Sam Nunn Atlanta Federal Center
61 Forsyth Street SW
Atlanta, GA 30303
Phone: 404-562-7911
Fax: 404-562-7899

Description: Alabama, Florida, Georgia, Kentucky, Mississippi, North Carolina, South Carolina, and Tennessee.

D Fletcher
Phone: 404-562-7911

Regional Emergency Coordinator-V

233 N Michigan Avenue
Suite 1300
Chicago, IL 60601
Phone: 312-353-4515
Fax: 312-353-7800

Description: Illinois, Indiana, Michigan, Minnesota, Ohio, and Wisconsin.

Carl Adrianopoli
Phone: 312-353-4515

Regional Emergency Coordinator-VI

1301 Young Street
Dallas, TX 75202
Phone: 214-767-3843
Fax: 212-767-3617

Description: Arkansas, Louisiana, New Mexico, Oklahoma, and Texas.

Jean Bennett
Phone: 214-767-3580
e-mail: jean.bennett@hhs.gov

Regional Emergency Coordinator-VII

Bolling Federal Building
601 E 12th Street
Kansas City, MO 64106
Phone: 816-426-2821

Description: Iowa, Kansas, Missouri, and Nebraska.

Jim Imholte
Phone: 816-426-2821
e-mail: jim.imholte@hhs.gov

Regional Emergency Coordinator- VIII

1961 Stout Street
Room 498
Denver, CO 80294-3538
Phone: 303-844-7855
Fax: 303-844-7250
URL: www.hhs.gov/region8

Description: Colorado, Montana, North Dakota, South Dakota, Utah and Wyoming.

Jim Imholte
Phone: 816-426-2821
e-mail: jim.imholte@hhs.gov

Regional Emergency Coordinator-IX

50 United Nations Plaza
FOB, Room 329
San Francisco, CA 94102
Phone: 415-437-8071
Fax: 415-437-8069

Description: Arizona, California, Hawaii, Nevada, American Samoa, Commonwealth of the Northern Mariana Islands, Federated States of Micronesia, Guam, Marshall Islands, and Republic of Palau.

Christopher Jones
Phone: 415-437-8386
e-mail: christopher.jones@hhs.gov

Regional Emergency Coordinator-X

2201 Sixth Avenue
Seattle, WA 98121
Mailing Address: MS RX-29
Phone: 206-615-2261
Fax: 206-615-2481

Description: Alaska, Idaho, Oregon and Washington.

Andrew Stevermer
Phone: 206-615-2266
e-mail: andrew.stevermer@hhs.gov

Small & Disadvantaged Business Utilization Office

Department of Health & Human Services
200 Independence Avenue SW
Room 360G, HHH Building
Washington, DC 20201
Phone: 202-690-7300
Fax: 202-260-4872
URL: www.hhs.gov/osdbu/

Description: The Office of Small and Disadvantaged Business Utilization (OSDBU) has organized its responsibilities, programs and activities under three lines of business: advocacy, outreach and unification of the business process. The OSDBU develops and implements appropriate outreach programs aimed at heightening the awareness of the small business community to the contracting opportunities available within the Department.

Debbie Ridgely
Director
Phone: 202-690-7300
e-mail: debbie.ridgely@hhs.gov

Arthuretta Martin
Deputy Director
Phone: 202-690-6845
e-mail: arthuretta.martin@hhs.gov

Clarence Randall
Senior Advisor
Phone: 202-205-9766
e-mail: clarence.randall@hhs.gov

Teneshia G Alston
SBA
Phone: 202-205-4919
e-mail: teneshia.alston@hhs.gov

Debra Peters
Procurement Analyst Service-Disabled Veteran Owned
Phone: 202-690-8457
e-mail: debra.peters@hhs.gov

FEDERAL

Department of Health & Human Services
Centers for Disease Control & Prevention

Centers for Disease Control & Prevention
Headquarters
1600 Clifton Road
Atlanta, GA 30333
Phone: 404-639-7000
Phone: 800-232-4636
Fax: 404-639-7111
URL: www.cdc.gov
e-mail: cdcinfo@cdc.gov

Description: The Centers for Disease Control and Prevention (CDC) is responsible for protecting the health and safety of the population — at home and abroad. CDC plays a critical role in protecting the public from widespread, deadly and mysterious illnesses and other health threats. Working under the Department of Health and Human Services, and with the Department of Homeland Security, CDC helps regulate the transfer of dangerous pathogens and toxins — commonly referred to as Select Agents.

Dr Julie L Gerberding
Director CDC/Administrator ATSDR
Phone: 404-639-7000
e-mail: jyg2@cdc.gov

Donald E Shriber JD
Associate Director CDC-Washington, DC Office
Phone: 202-690-8598
e-mail: dfs4@cdc.gov

William H Gimson
Chief Operating Officer
Phone: 404-639-7000
e-mail: whg1@cdc.gov

Stephanie Coursey-Bailey MD
Chief Public Health Practice
Phone: 404-639-4619
e-mail: smb0@cdc.gov

Lynn Austin PhD
Chief of Staff
Phone: 404-639-7663
e-mail: laa2@cdc.gov

Tanja Popvic MD
Chief Science Officer
Phone: 404-639-7000
e-mail: txp1@cdc.gov

Donna Garland
Director Office of Enterprise Communication
Phone: 404-639-7000

Bradley Perkins MD
Acting Director Office of Strategy & Innovation
Phone: 404-639-7000

James D Seligman
Chief Information Officer
Phone: 404-639-7601
e-mail: jds1@cdc.gov

Richard Besser MD
Coordinating Office for Terrorism Preparedness & Emergency Response
Phone: 404-639-7405

Coordinating Office of Terrorism Preparedness & Emergency Response (COTPER)
Centers for Disease Control & Prevention
1600 Clifton Road
Atlanta, GA 30333
Phone: 404-639-7405
Fax: 404-639-5073
URL: www.bt.cdc.gov

Description: The Office is responsible for all of CDC's public health emergency preparedness and emergency response activities. It has oversight of terrorism preparedness, response and protection for the nation from biological, chemical, radiological and naturally occuring emergencies.

Richard Besser MD
Director
Phone: 404-639-7405
e-mail: richard.besser@cdc.hhs.gov

Strategic National Stockpile (SNS)
Centers for Disease Control & Prevention
1600 Clifton Road
Atlanta, GA 30333
Phone: 404-639-3311
Phone: 800-232-4636
Fax: 404-639-1527
URL: www.bt.cdc.gov/stockpile/
e-mail: cdcinfo@cdc.gov

Description: A national repository of antibiotics, chemical antidotes, IV administration, antitoxins, airway maintenance supplies, life-support medications, and medical/surgical items. It is organized for flexible response and is designed to supplement and re-supply state and local public health agencies in the event of a national emergency. The SNS program works with governmental and non-governmental partners to upgrade the nation's public health capacity to respond to a national emergency. Critical to the success of this initiative is ensuring capacity is developed at federal, state, and local levels to receive, stage, and dispense SNS assets.

Coordinating Center for Infectious Diseases (CCID)
Centers for Disease Control & Prevention
1600 Clifton Road
Atlanta, GA 30333
Phone: 404-639-2100
Fax: 404-639-2170
URL: www.cdc.gov/about/organization/ccid.htm

Description: The reorganization of the Center was officially approved in 2007 to include the following programs: National Center for Immunization and Respiratory Diseases; National Center for Zoonotic, Vector-Borne and Enteric Diseases; National Center for HIV/AIDS, Viral Hepatitis, STD, and TB Prevention; and National Center for Preparedness, Detection and Control of Infectious Diseases.

Mitchell L Cohen
Director
Phone: 404-639-2100
e-mail: mitchell.cohen@cdc.hhs.gov

Anne Schuchat
Director National Center for Immunization & Respiratory Diseases
Phone: 404-639-8200
e-mail: anne.schuchat@cdc.hhs.gov

Lonnie J King DVM
Director National Center for Zoonotic, Vector-Borne & Enteric Diseases
Phone: 404-639-7380
e-mail: lonnie.king@cdc.hhs.gov

Kevin Fenton MD, PhD
Director National Center for HIV/AIDS, Viral Hepatitis, STD & TB Prevention
Phone: 404-639-8000
e-mail: kevin.fenton@cdc.hhs.gov

Rima Khabbaz MD
Director National Center for Preparedness, Detection & Control of Infectious Diseases
Phone: 404-639-3967
e-mail: rima.khabbaz@cdc.hhs.gov

Coordinating Center for Environmental Health & Injury Prevention (CCEHIP)
Centers for Disease Control & Prevention
1600 Clifton Road
Atlanta, GA 30333
Phone: 404-498-0008
Fax: 404-498-0083
URL: www.cdc.gov/about/organization/ccehip.htm

Description: The Center plans, directs, and coordinates national and global public health research, programs, and laboratory sciences that improve health and eliminate illness, disability, and death caused by injuries and environmental exposures. It includes the following programs: National Center for Environmental Health (NCEH-ATSDR) and National Center for Injury Prevention & Control (NCIPC). The ATSDR is a sister agency of the CDC under the Department of Health and Human Services, of which the CDC performs many of the administrative functions. The Director of the CDC also serves as the Administrator of the ATSDR.

Henry Falk MD
Director
Phone: 404-498-0008
e-mail: henry.falk@cdc.hhs.gov

Julie L Gerberding MD
Administrator ATSDR
Phone: 404-639-7000
e-mail: jyg2@cdc.gov

Ileana Arias PhD
Director National Center for Injury Prevention & Control
Phone: 770-488-4696
e-mail: ileana.arias@cdc.hhs.gov

National Center for Environmental Health/ATSDR
Coordinating Center for Environmental Health & Injury Prevention
1600 Clifton Road
Atlanta, GA 30333
Phone: 800-232-4636
URL: www.cdc.gov/nceh; www.atsdr.cdc.gov

Description: The NCEH-ATSDR provides national leadership in preventing and controlling disease and death resulting from interactions between people and the environment. Under congressional mandate the ATSDR is directed to perform functions that include public health assessments of waste sites, health consultations concerning specific hazardous substances, health surveillance and registries, response to emergency releases of hazardous substances, applied research in support of public health assessments, and education and training concerning hazardous substances.

Dr Howard Frumkin
Director
Phone: 404-498-0004
e-mail: howard.frumkin@cdc.hhs.gov

Dr Thomas H Sinks PhD
Deputy Director
Phone: 404-498-0004
e-mail: thomas.sinks@cdc.hhs.gov

Julie Fishman MPH
Associate Director Program Development
Phone: 404-498-0029
e-mail: julie.fishman@cdc.hhs.gov

Mark Bashor MD
Associate Director Science
Phone: 404-498-0068
e-mail: mark.bashor@cdc.hhs.gov

Mark Keim MD
Acting Associate Director Terrorism Preparedness & Emergency Response
Phone: 770-448-7345
e-mail: mark.keim@cdc.hhs.gov

Nabil Issa MS
Associate Director Information Systems
Phone: 770-448-7612
e-mail: nabil.issa@cdc.hhs.gov

Marilyn DiSirio
Associate Director Global Health

Phone: 404-498-0909
e-mail: marilyn.disirio@cdc.hhs.gov

Jana L Telfer
Associate Director Office of Communication
Phone: 404-498-0183
e-mail: jana.telfer@cdc.hhs.gov

Agency for Toxic Substances & Disease Registry (ATSDR)
National Center for Environmental Health/ATSDR
1600 Clifton Road
Atlanta, GA 30333
Phone: 800-232-4636
URL: www.atsdr.cdc.gov
e-mail: cdcinfo@cdc.gov

Description: ATSDR Divisions:

William Cibulas Jr PhD
Director Health Assessment & Consultation Division
Phone: 404-498-0007
e-mail: william.cibulas@cdc.hhs.gov

G David Williamson PhD
Director Health Studies Division
Phone: 404-488-1054
e-mail: david.williamson@cdc.hhs.gov

Tina Forrester PhD
Director Regional Operations Division
Phone: 404-498-0106
e-mail: tina.forrester@cdc.hhs.gov

Christopher DeRosa PhD
Director Toxicology & Environmental Medicine Division
Phone: 770-488-3301
e-mail: chistopher.derosa@cdc.hhs.gov

NCEH/National Center for Environmental Health
National Center for Environmental Health/ATSDR
1600 Clifton Road
Atlanta, GA 30333
URL: www.cdc.gov/nceh

Description: NCEH Divisions:

Sharunda Buchanan PhD
Director Emergency & Environmental Health Services Division
Phone: 770-488-7362
e-mail: sharunda.buchanan@cdc.hhs.gov

Michael A McGeehin PhD
Director Environmental Hazards & Health Effects Division
Phone: 770-488-3400
e-mail: michael.mcgeehin@cdc.hhs.gov

Eric Sampson PhD
Director Laboratory Sciences Division
Phone: 770-488-7950
e-mail: eric.sampson@cdc.hhs.gov

Coordinating Office for Global Health (COGH)
Centers for Disease Control & Prevention
1600 Clifton Road
Atlanta, GA 30333
Phone: 404-639-7420
Fax: 404-639-7490

URL: www.cdc.gov/about/organization/cogh.htm

Description: Provides leadership, coordination and support for CDC's global health activities with the goal of increasing global preparedness to prevent and control naturally-occuring and man-made threats to health. The Director of COGH is responsible for CDC's annual $900 million budget; global immunization and disease eradication activities; international training programs; and manages key strategies and partnerships with global ministries of health.

Stephen B Blount MD
Director
Phone: 404-639-7420
e-mail: stephen.blount@cdc.hhs.gov

Janna Brooks
Acting Chief Sustainable Management Development Program
Phone: 404-639-3270

Coordinating Center for Health Information & Service (CCHIS)
Centers for Disease Control & Prevention
1600 Clifton Road
Atlanta, GA 30333
Mailing Address: MS E33
URL: www.cdc.gov/about/organization/cchis.htm

Description: Assures that CDC provides high-quality information and programs in the most effective way to help people, families and communities protect their health and safety. The three programs listed below, along with the directors of each program make up the CCHIS.

Steven Solomon MD
Director
Phone: 404-498-0123
e-mail: steven.solomon@cdc.hhs.gov

Leslie Lenert PhD
Director National Center for Public Health Informatics
Phone: 404-498-2475

Jay Bernhardt
Director National Center for Health Marketing
e-mail: nchminfo@cdc.gov

Edward J Sondik PhD
Director National Center for Health Statistics
Phone: 800-232-4636
e-mail: nchsquery@cdc.gov

Coordinating Center for Health Promotion (CoCHP)
Centers for Disease Control & Prevention
1600 Clifton Road
Atlanta, GA 30333
Phone: 770-488-6540
Fax: 770-488-6448
URL: www.cdc.gov/about/organization/cchp.htm

Description: The Center plans, directs and coordinates a national program for the prevention of prematurity, mortality, morbidity and disability due to chronic disease, genomics and birth defects, among other things.

Kathleen E Toomey MD
Director
e-mail: kathleen.toomey@cdc.hhs.gov

Jose Cordero MD
Director National Center on Birth Defects & Developmental Disabilities
Phone: 770-488-5401
e-mail: jose.cordero@cdc.hhs.gov

Janet Collins PhD
Director National Center for Chronic Disease Prevention & Health Promotion
Phone: 770-498-3800
e-mail: janet.collins@cdc.hhs.gov

Muin Khoury MD
Director Office of Genomics & Disease Prevention
Phone: 770-488-8510
e-mail: muin.khoury@cdc.hhs.gov

National Institute for Occupational Safety & Health

Centers for Disease Control & Prevention
1600 Clifton Road
Atlanta, GA 30333
Phone: 404-498-2500
URL: www.cdc.gov/niosh

Description: The same Occupational Safety and Health Act of 1970 that created OSHA, also created NIOSH (National Institute for Occupational Safety & Health). It is the federal agency responsible for conducting research and making recommendations for the prevention of work-related injury and illness. It also has jursidiction over federal mine safety and health.

John Howard MD
Director
Phone: 202-245-0625

Diane D Porter
Deputy Director
Phone: 404-498-2500

Kelley Durst
Associate Director Planning & Performance
Phone: 404-498-2500

Kenneth F Martinez
Acting Associate Director Emergency Preparedness
Phone: 404-498-2535

Anita Schill PhD
Interim Associate Director Science
Phone: 404-498-2551

Allison Tanner
Associate Director Management
Phone: 404-498-2500

Epidemic Intelligence Service

Centers for Disease Control & Prevention
1600 Clifton Road
Atlanta, GA 30333
Mailing Address: MS E-92
Phone: 404-498-6110
URL: www.cdc.gov/eis/
e-mail: eisepo@cdc.gov

Description: The EIS was established in 1951 following the start of the Korean War as an early warning system against biological warfare and man-made epidemics. The program, composed of medical doctors, researchers, and scientists who serve in 2-year

assignments, today has expanded into a surveillance and response unit for all types of epidemics, including chronic disease and injuries. Over the past 50 years, officers have played pivotal roles in combating the root causes of major epidemics. The EIS played a key role in the global eradication of smallpox by sending officers to the farthest reaches of the world; restored public confidence in the first polio vaccine after a defective vaccine led to panic; and discovered how the AIDS virus was transmitted. More recently, officers have documented the obesity epidemic in the US, helped states reduce tobacco use, and studied whether disease outbreaks were a result of bioterrorism. Many of the nation's medical and public health leaders, including CDC directors and deans of the country's top schools of public health, are EIS alumni/ae.

Douglas Hamilton
Director

Epidemic Information Exchange

Centers for Disease Control & Prevention
1600 Clifton Road
Atlanta, GA 30333
URL: www.cdc.gov/epix
e-mail: epixhelp@cdc.gov

Description: The Center for Disease Control and Prevention's secure, web-based communications network that serves as a powerful communications exchange between CDC, state and local health departments, poison control centers, and other public health professionals.

Health Alert Network

Centers for Disease Control & Prevention
1600 Clifton Road
Atlanta, GA 30333
Phone: 800-311-3435
URL: www2a.cdc.gov/han
e-mail: healthalert@cdc.gov

Description: A nationwide, integrated information and communications system serving as a platform for distribution of health alerts, dissemination of prevention guidelines and other information, distance learning, national disease surveillance, and electronic laboratory reporting, as well as for CDC's bioterrorism and related initiatives to strengthen preparedness at the local and state levels. Currently the Health Alert Network (HAN) is a strong national program, providing vital health information and the infrastructure to support the dissemination of this information at the state and local levels and beyond.

FEDERAL

Department of the Interior

Department of the Interior
Headquarters
1849 C Street NW
Washington, DC 20240
Phone: 202-208-3100
Fax: 202-208-6956
URL: www.doi.gov
e-mail: webteam@ios.doi.gov

Description: The Department of the Interior (DOI) operates as America's conservation agency. DOI protects national landmarks and treasures, as well as energy and mineral resources. In response to the World Trade Center attacks in 2001, DOI established the Office of Law Enforcement, Security & Emergency Management to provide leadership, policy guidance and oversight to the Department's law enforcement, homeland security, emergency management and security programs related to the protection of classified and law-enforcement sensitive systems, procedures and information. The Department has been able to participate in homeland security in the following ways: provide additional police support in Washington DC and New York, upgrade security equipment and maintain adequate police force levels; increase protection for national assets, such as the Liberty Bell, Mount Rushmore and the USS Arizona; install security equipment upgrades at highly visible national monuments, including the Statue of Liberty, National Mall in Washington, Liberty Bell and Independence Hall in Philadelphia, Gateway Arch in St Louis, and other key sites in the National Park System; and repair Federal Hall, a national historic landmark damaged by the collapse of the World Trade Center. DOI manages 500 million acres of America's public lands, more than 2,400 operating facilities, and employs approximately 4,500 law enforcement officers.

Dirk Kempthorne
Secretary
Phone: 202-208-7351

Patricia Lynn Scarlett
Deputy Secretary
Phone: 202-208-3980
e-mail: lynn_scarlett@ios.doi.gov

David Bernhardt
Solicitor for the Interior
Phone: 202-208-4423
e-mail: david_bernhardt@ios.doi.gov

Earl Devaney
Inspector General
Phone: 202-208-5745
e-mail: earl_devaney@doioig.gov

C Stephen Allred
Assistant Secretary Land & Minerals Management

Phone: 202-208-6734
e-mail: stephen_allred@ios.doi.gov

Mark Limbaugh
Assistant Secretary Water & Science
Phone: 202-208-3186
e-mail: mark_limbaugh@ios.doi.gov

Carl J Artman
Assistant Secretary Indian Affairs
Phone: 202-208-7163
e-mail: carl_artman@ios.doi.gov

Mary A Bomar
Director National Park Service
Phone: 202-208-3818
e-mail: mary_bomar@nps.gov

Dale Hall
Director US Fish & Wildlife Service
Phone: 202-208-4717

Brent Wahlquist
Acting Director Office of Surface Mining
e-mail: bwahlqui@osmre.gov

Mark Myers
Director US Geological Survey
Phone: 703-648-7411
e-mail: mmyers@usgs.gov

Johnnie Burton
Director Minerals Management Service
Phone: 303-236-0330
e-mail: glen_burton@nbc.gov

Robert W Johnson
Commissioner Bureau of Reclamation
Phone: 202-513-0501

Ross Swimmer
Special Trustee for American Indians
Phone: 202-208-4866
e-mail: ross_swimmer@ios.doi.gov

W Hord Tipton
Chief Information Officer
Phone: 202-208-6194
e-mail: hord_tipton@ios.doi.gov

Tina Kreisher
Director Communications
Phone: 202-208-5256
e-mail: tina_kreisher@ios.doi.gov

Shane Wolfe
Press Secretary

Phone: 202-208-6416
e-mail: shane_wolfe@ios.doi.gov

Office of Law Enforcement, Security & Emergency Management (OLESEM)
Department of the Interior
1849 C Street NW
Washington, DC 20240
Mailing Address: Mailstop 7354-MIB
Phone: 202-208-6319
Fax: 202-219-1185
URL: www.doi.gov/watch_office/about_olesem/

Description: OLESEM serves as the central point of contact for the Department's law enforcement, intelligence gathering, emergency management, security policy and professional responsibility programs. The Office also represents the Department in high-level and interagency and intergovernmental committees and task forces that have been established to review homeland security and counter-terrorism issues.

Larry R Parkinson
Deputy Assistant Secretary
Phone: 202-208-5773

Kim A Thorsen
Director Law Enforcement & Security
Phone: 202-208-6319

Laurence Broun
Assistant Director Emergency Management Division
Phone: 202-208-3721

John Kmetz
Assistant Director Law Enforcement Division
Phone: 202-208-5903

Glenn F Smith
Assistant Director Security Division
Phone: 202-208-5836

Gary Van Horn
Assistant Director Information Sharing & Analysis Division
Phone: 202-208-6338

Salvatore Lauro
Assistant Director Professional Responsibility & Policy Compliance Division
Phone: 202-208-2977

Watch Office
OLESEM-Information Sharing & Analysis Division
1951 Constitution Ave NW
Washington, DC 20240
Mailing Address: MS 312-SIB
Phone: 202-208-4108
Phone: 877-246-1373
Fax: 202-208-3421
URL: watchoffice.doi.gov
e-mail: doi_watch_office@ios.doi.gov

Description: The Watch Office operates around the clock to provide timely reporting on critical information and serious incidents that impact the Department's responsibilities across the US. It effectively coordinates with the law enforcement, emergency management and security demands placed on the Department as a result of additional homeland security responsibilities and serves as a resource to all bureaus, offices and other cooperating agencies. The Watch Office distributes alerts, bulletins and advisories.

National Park Service
Department of the Interior
1849 C Street NW
Washington, DC 20240
Phone: 202-208-4621
Fax: 202-273-0896
URL: www.nps.gov

Description: The primary goals of the National Park Service (NPS) are to safeguard human life, safeguard the resources, and public and personal property. As the primary law enforcement and emergency operations entity in national parks, park rangers are regularly involved in all aspects of emergency operations including law enforcement, search & rescue, emergency medical services (of which 300 are trained as EMTs), wildland & structural fire, and responding to natural disasters.

Mary A Bomar
Director
Phone: 202-208-3818
e-mail: mary_bomar@nps.gov

Daniel Wenk
Deputy Director Operations
Phone: 202-208-3818
e-mail: dan_wenk@nps.gov

Cam Sholly
Chief of Staff
Phone: 202-513-7080
e-mail: cam_sholly@nps.gov

Christopher K Jarvi
Associate Director Partnership, Interpretation & Education, Volunteerism & Outdoor Recreation
Phone: 202-208-4829
e-mail: christopher_jarvi@nps.gov

Karen Taylor Goodrich
Associate Director Visitor & Resource Protection
Phone: 202-565-1020
e-mail: karen_taylor_goodrich@nps.gov

Michael Soukup
Associate Director Natural Resources, Stewardship & Science
Phone: 202-208-3884
e-mail: mike_soukup@nps.gov

Bill Shaddox
Acting Associate Director Park Planning, Facilities & Lands
Phone: 202-354-6943
e-mail: bill_shaddox@nps.gov

Jan Matthews
Associate Director Cultural Resources
Phone: 202-208-7625
e-mail: jan_matthews@nps.gov

David Barna
Chief Public Affairs Office
Phone: 202-208-6843
e-mail: david_barna@nps.gov

Stephen Morris
Chief International Affairs Office

Phone: 202-354-1803
e-mail: stephen_morris@nps.gov

John R Snyder
Acting Chief Information Officer
Phone: 202-354-1421
e-mail: john_r_snyder@nps.gov

Bruce Sheaffer
Comptroller
Phone: 202-208-4566
e-mail: bruce_sheaffer@nps.gov

United States Park Police
National Park Service
1100 Ohio Drive SW
Washington, DC 20242
Phone: 202-619-7350
Fax: 202-205-4861
URL: www.nps.gov/uspp/

Description: The United States Park Police provide law enforcement services to designated areas within the National Park Service (primarily DC, NYC, and San Francisco metro areas). The Force provides highly trained and professional police officers to prevent and detect criminal activity, conduct investigations, apprehend individuals suspected of committing offenses against federal, state and local laws, provide protection to the President of the United States and visiting dignitaries, and provide protective services to some of the most recognizable monuments and memorials worldwide.

Dwight E Pettiford
Chief Operations
Phone: 202-619-7350
e-mail: dwight_pettiford@nps.gov

David Stover
Deputy Chief Operations Commander
e-mail: david_stover@nps.gov

Major Robert Kass
Criminal Investigations Branch Commander
Phone: 202-610-8730

Major Robert Rule
Special Forces Branch Commander

Lt Thomas Neider
Support Services Branch Commander
Phone: 202-610-3505
e-mail: thomas_neider@nps.gov

Major Kevin Hay
Patrol Branch Commander

Sgt Robert LaChance
Public Information Office
Phone: 202-619-7163
e-mail: robert_lachance@nps.gov

Bureau of Reclamation
Department of the Interior
1849 C Street NW
Washington, DC 20240
Phone: 202-513-0501
Fax: 202-513-0309
URL: www.usbr.gov

Description: The Bureau of Reclamation manages, develops and protects water and related resources in an environmentally and economically sound manner in the interest of the American public. It is responsible for more than 500 dams, 348 reservoirs, and 58 hydroelectric powerplants. Because of its vital role in providing water, power, agricultural products, and recreational opportunities to the entire nation, the safety and security of Reclamation facilities and the people is of critical importance.

Robert W Johnson
Commissioner
Phone: 202-513-0501

Kerry Rae
Chief of Staff
Phone: 202-513-0327

Brenda Burman
Deputy Commissioner External & Intergovernmental Affairs
Phone: 202-513-7636

Larry Todd
Deputy Commissioner Administration & Budget

Dan DuBray
Chief Public Affairs
Phone: 202-513-0574

Michael J Ryan
Regional Director-Great Plains Region
Phone: 406-247-7600

Kirk C Rodgers
Regional Director-Mid Pacific Region
Phone: 916-978-5000

Bill McDonald
Regional Director-Pacific Northwest Region
Phone: 208-378-5012

Rick Gold
Regional Director-Upper Colorado Region
Phone: 801-524-3600

Security, Safety & Law Enforcement Office
Bureau of Reclamation
Denver Federal Center
PO Box 25007
Denver, CO 80225-0007
Phone: 303-445-3736
Fax: 303-445-6376
URL: www.usbr.gov/ssle/

Description: The Security, Safety and Law Enforcement (SSLE) Office is responsible for protecting the employees and facilities of the Bureau of Reclamation through the development and implementation of an integrated security, safety, and law enforcement program. It manages programs and projects related to security, safety and law enforcement, develops bureau-wide policies and guidelines for governing these programs, and provides the necessary oversight associated with these.

David Achterberg
Director
Phone: 303-445-3736

Kathy Norris
Program Management

Vincent Parolisi
Law Enforcement

Linda Rowley
Manager Safety & Health Services
Phone: 303-445-2695
e-mail: lrowley@do.usbr.gov

Bruce Muller
Dam Safety

Donald Taussig
Security Office

Office of Acquisition & Property Management
Department of the Interior
1849 C Street NW
Washington, DC 20240
Phone: 202-208-6352
Fax: 202-219-4244
URL: www.doi.gov/pam

Description: The Office of Acquisition and Property Management provides executive level leadership in the areas of acquisition and federal assistance (grants and cooperative agreements) as it relates to: real, museum and personal property; government furnished quarters; space management; energy efficiency, water conservation and renewable energy programs; motor vehicle fleet management; alternative fueled vehicles; integrated charge card program; and electronic commerce and related automated systems.

Debra Sonderman
Director
Phone: 202-208-6352
e-mail: ideas@ios.doi.gov

Melodee Stith
Associate Director Acquisition & Financial Assistance
Phone: 202-208-5830
e-mail: melodee_stith@ios.doi.gov

Michael Keegan
Associate Director Facilities & Property Management
Phone: 202-208-3347
e-mail: michael_keegan@ios.doi.gov

Linda Tribby
Quarters Program Manager
Phone: 202-513-0747
e-mail: linda_tribby@ios.doi.gov

Brian Biegler
Staff Curator
Phone: 202-208-4698
e-mail: brian.biegler@ios.doi.gov

Ronald C Wilson
Museum Program Curator
Phone: 202-208-3438
e-mail: ronald_c_wilson@ios.doi.gov

Mary Heying
Civil/Environmental Engineer
Phone: 202-208-4080
e-mail: mary_heying@ios.doi.gov

Office of Small & Disadvantaged Business Utilization
Department of the Interior
1849 C Street NW
Washington, DC 20240
Phone: 202-208-3493
Fax: 202-208-7444
URL: www.doi.gov/osdbu/

Description: The Office of Small and Disadvantaged Business Utilization works to: improve and increase the Department's performance in utilizing small, small disadvantaged, HUBZone, women-owned, and veteran-owned businesses as contractors and subcontractors. Currently, more than 49% of the $1.5 billion budget goes to small businesses.

Mark Oliver
Director
Phone: 202-208-3493

FEDERAL

Department of Justice

Department of Justice
Headquarters
950 Pennsylvania Avenue NW
Washington, DC 20530-0001
Phone: 202-514-2001
Fax: 202-307-6777
URL: www.usdoj.gov
e-mail: AskDOJ@usdoj.gov

Description: The Justice Department (DOJ) serves to enforce the law and defend the interests of the United States according to the law, and to ensure public safety against foreign and domestic threats. DOJ seeks not only to investigate and prosecute terrorist acts, but also to prevent them from happening. In 2006, the Department was reorganized to create the National Security Division and a new Assistant Attorney General for National Security was announced. The Division consolidates the Department's primary national security elements into one entity. It will improve coordination against terrorism within the Department, with the CIA, the DoD and other Intelligence Community agencies.

Alberto R Gonzales
Attorney General
Phone: 202-514-2001

Paul J McNulty
Deputy Attorney General
Phone: 202-514-2101

William W Mercer
Acting Associate Attorney General
Phone: 202-514-9500

Paul D Clement
Solicitor General
Phone: 202-514-2201
e-mail: paul.d.clement@usdoj.gov

Rachel L Brand
Assistant Attorney General Legal Policy
Phone: 202-514-4601

Tasia Scolinos
Director Public Affairs
Phone: 202-616-2777

Richard A Hertling
Acting Assistant Attorney General Legislative Affairs
Phone: 202-514-2141

Eric W Holland
Acting Director Intergovernmental & Public Liaison & Advisor to the Attorney General
Phone: 202-514-3465
e-mail: oipl@usdoj.gov

Kenneth L Wainstein
Assistant Attorney General National Security Division
Phone: 202-514-1057
e-mail: nsd.public@usdoj.gov

Glenn A Fine
Inspector General
Phone: 202-514-3435

Vance Hitch
Chief Information Officer
Phone: 202-514-0507

National Security Division
Department of Justice
950 Pennsylvania Avenue NW
Washington, DC 20530
Phone: 202-514-1057
Fax: 202-353-9836
URL: www.usdoj.gov/nsd
e-mail: nsd.public@usdoj.gov

Description: The National Security Division (NSD) carries out the Department of Justice's highest priority: combat terrorism and other threats to national security. The NSD consolidates the Department's primary national security elements which currently consists of the Office of Intelligence Policy & Review; the Counterterrorism and Counterespionage Sections (formerly part of the Criminal Division); and a new Law and Policy Office. This organization ensures greater coordination and unity of purpose between law enforcement agencies, attorneys, and the Intelligence Community.

Kenneth L Wainstein
Assistant Attorney General
Phone: 202-532-4607

Brett C Gerry
Deputy Assistant Attorney General Law & Policy Office
Phone: 202-514-1057

Michael J Mullaney
Counterterrorism Section Chief
Phone: 202-514-0849

John J Dion
Counterespionage Section Chief
Phone: 202-514-1187

Peggy Skelly-Nolen
Intelligence Policy & Review Office Counsel
Phone: 202-514-5600

Office of Justice Programs
Department of Justice
810 7th Street NW

Washington, DC 20531
Phone: 202-307-5933
Phone: 202-307-0703
Fax: 202-514-7805
URL: www.ojp.usdoj.gov

Description: Provides federal leadership and works to form partnerships with state and local government officials in developing the nation's capacity to prevent and control crime, improve the criminal and juvenile justice systems, increase knowledge about crime and related issues, and assist crime victims, rehabilitate neighborhoods, address gang violence, prison crowding and white-collar crime.

Regina B Schofield
Assistant Attorney General
Phone: 202-307-5933

Cybele K Daley
Deputy Assistant Attorney General External Affairs/Communications Officer
Phone: 202-307-5933

Beth McGarry
Deputy Assistant Attorney General Operations & Management
Phone: 202-307-5933

David W Hagy
Deputy Assistant Attorney General Policy Coordination/Director National Institute of Justice

Domingo S Herraiz
Director Bureau of Justice Assistance
Phone: 202-305-1367
e-mail: askbja@ojp.usdoj.gov

Jeffrey L Sedgwick
Director Bureau of Justice Statistics
Phone: 202-307-0765
e-mail: askbjs@usdoj.gov

Dennis Greenhouse
Community Capacity Development Officer
Phone: 202-616-1152
e-mail: dennis.greenhouse@usdoj.gov

J Robert Flores
Administrator Office of Juvenile Justice and Delinquency Prevention
Phone: 202-307-5911

John W Gillis
Director Office for Victims of Crime
Phone: 202-307-5983

Nicholas J Tzitzon
Chief of Staff

National Institute of Justice
Office of Justice Programs
810 7th Street NW
Washington, DC 20531
Phone: 202-307-2942
Fax: 202-307-6394
URL: www.ojp.usdoj.gov/nij

Description: The National Institute of Justice is the research, development and evaluation agency of the Department of Justice and is dedicated to researching crime control and justice issues. It provides objective, independent non-partisan, evidence-based

knowledge and tools to meet the challenges of crime and justice, particularly at the State and local levels. The Office of Research & Evaluation develops, conducts, directs and supervises research and evaluation activities across a wide variety of issues. The Office of Science & Technology manages technology research and technology assistance to state and local law enforcement and corrections agencies.

David W Hagy
Director
Phone: 202-307-2942

Timothy M Hagle
Chief of Staff
Phone: 202-305-1209

Jolene Hernon
Communications Division Chief
Phone: 202-307-1464

Thomas E Feucht
Deputy Director Research & Evaluation
Phone: 202-307-2949

Cindy Smith
International Center Chief
Phone: 202-353-2538

Marlene Beckman
Justice Systems Research Division Acting Chief
Phone: 202-616-3562

John Morgan
Deputy Director Science & Technology
Phone: 202-307-0645

Marc Caplan
Operational Technologies Division Chief
Phone: 202-307-2956

Susan Narveson
Investigative & Forensic Sciences Division Chief
Phone: 202-305-4884

Winifred Reed
Crime Control & Prevention Research Division Acting Chief
Phone: 202-307-2952

Executive Office for United States Attorneys
Department of Justice
950 Pennsylvania Avenue NW
Room 2242
Washington, DC 20530-0001
Phone: 202-514-2121
Fax: 202-616-2278
URL: www.usdoj.gov/usao/eousa/

Description: The Executive Office for United States Attorneys has as its mission to provide the States Attorneys with general executive assistance and direction, policy development, administrative management direction and oversight, operational support, coordination with other components of the Department and other federal agencies. These responsibilities include certain legal, budgetary, administrative, and personnel services, as well as legal education. Individual State Attorneys are listed in the State Agencies section that follows, under the Main Homeland Security Office listing. The 93 State Attorneys serve as the nation's principal litigators under the direction of the Attorney General.

Kenneth E Melson
Director
Phone: 202-514-2121

Steve Parent
Deputy Director
Phone: 202-514-2121

John Nowacki
Principal Deputy Director
Phone: 202-514-2121

Jay Macklin
Acting General Counsel
Phone: 202-514-4024

David Downs
COO/Acting Chief Information Officer
Phone: 202-616-6973

Tom Barns
Assistant Director Security Programs
Phone: 202-616-6640

United States Marshals Service
Department of Justice
Washington, DC 20530-1000
Phone: 202-307-9065
URL: www.usmarshals.gov
e-mail: us.marshals@usdoj.gov

Description: The United States Marshals Service with its 94 district offices is the nation's oldest and most versatile federal law enforcement agency. It has served the nation since 1789 through a variety of vital law enforcement activities including: protection of federal judicial officials; security, health and safety of government witnesses; fugitive investigations; housing pre-sentenced prisoners; managing and disposing of seized and forfeited property acquired by criminals through illegal activities; serving federal court criminal process; and special operations support.

John F Clark
Director
Phone: 202-307-9001

Robert Trono
Deputy Director
Phone: 202-307-9489

Gerald M Auerbach
General Counsel
Phone: 202-307-9054

Christopher Dudley
Chief of Staff
Phone: 202-307-9001

Lisa Dickinson
Equal Employment Opportunity
Phone: 202-307-9048

Edward Dolan
Comptroller & CFO
Phone: 202-307-9193

J McNulty
Executive Services Acting Assistant Director
Phone: 202-307-5140

A Roderick
Investigative Services Assistant Director
Phone: 202-307-9110

Robert J Finan
Judicial Services Assistant Director
Phone: 202-307-9500

S Jones
Prisoner Operations & Witness Security
Phone: 202-307-5100

J Ellis
Justice Prisoner & Alien Transportation System
Phone: 816-467-1900

Katherine Deoudes
Asset Forfeiture
Phone: 202-307-9009

M Kulstad
Public Affairs
Phone: 202-353-1469

Drug Enforcement Administration
Department of Justice
Drug Enforcement Agency
2401 Jefferson Davis Highway
Alexandria, VA 22301
Mailing Address: MS AES
Phone: 202-307-1000
Fax: 202-307-4778
URL: www.dea.gov

Description: The mission of the Drug Enforcement Administration (DEA) is to enforce the controlled substances laws and regulations of the United States and bring to the criminal and civil justice system of the United States, or any other competent jurisdiction, those organizations and principal members of organizations, involved in the growing, manufacture, or distribution of controlled substances appearing in or destined for illicit traffic in the United States. The DEA also recommends and supports non-enforcement programs aimed at reducing the availabilty of illicit controlled substances domestically and internationally.

Karen P Tandy
Administrator
Phone: 202-307-8000

Michele M Leonhart
Deputy Administrator
Phone: 202-307-7345

Michael A Braun
Assistant Administrator/Chief of Operations
Phone: 202-307-7340

Rogelio E Guevara
Chief Inspector

James D Craig
Assistant Administrator Operational Support
Phone: 202-307-4730

Frank M Kalder Jr
Chief Financial Officer
Phone: 202-307-7330

Wendy H Goggin
Chief Counsel
Phone: 202-307-7322

Cathie Kasch
Assistant Administrator Human Resources
Phone: 202-307-4680

Anthony P Placido
Assistant Administrator/Chief of Intelligence
Phone: 202-307-3607

Office of Acquisition Management
Drug Enforcement Administration
2401 Jefferson Davis Highway
Alexandria, VA 22301
Phone: 202-307-5074
URL: www.usdoj.gov/dea/acquisitions_contracts.html

Angel Perez
Section Chief
Phone: 202-307-5074

Barbara Joplin
Policy & Analysis Section Chief
Phone: 202-307-7808

Yolanda Tillman
Small Business Specialist
Phone: 202-307-7150

Bureau of Alcohol, Tobacco, Firearms & Explosives (ATF)
Department of Justice
650 Massachusetts Avenue NW
Washington, DC 20226
Phone: 202-927-8500
URL: www.atf.gov
e-mail: atfmail@atf.gov

Description: The Bureau of Alcohol, Tobacco, Firearms and Explosives (ATF) is dedicated to preventing terrorism, reducing violent crime, and protecting the nation through investigations and working directly and through partnerships. The ATF workforce performs the dual responsibility of enforcing federal criminal laws and regulating the firearms and explosives industries.

Michael J Sullivan
Acting Director
Phone: 202-927-8700

Ronnie A Carter
Deputy Director/COO
Phone: 202-927-8710

Tina Street
Chief of Staff
Phone: 202-927-8490

Lew Raden
Enforcement Programs & Services Assistant Director
Phone: 202-927-7940

Gergg Bailey
CIO/Science & Technology Office
Phone: 202-927-8390

Steve Rubenstein
Chief Counsel
Phone: 202-927-7772

Melanie Stinnett
Chief Financial Officer

William Hoover
Field Operations Office
Phone: 202-927-7970

Mark Logan
Training & Professional Development Office
Phone: 202-927-9380

Richard Chase
Professional Responsibility & Security Operations Office

W Larry Ford
Public & Governmental Affairs Office
Phone: 202-927-8500

US National Central Bureau of INTERPOL
Department of Justice
Department of Justice
Washington, DC 20530
Phone: 202-616-9000
Fax: 202-616-8400
URL: www.usdoj.gov/usncb

Description: The US National Central Bureau (USNCB) of INTERPOL facilitates international law enforcement cooperation as the United States representative with the International Criminal Police Organization (INTERPOL) on behalf of the Attorney General. Major functions of the Bureau include: to transmit information of criminal justice, humanitarian, or other law enforcement related nature between INTERPOL member countries and law enforcement agencies of the United States; coordinate and integrate information for international investigations; and respond to requests by law enforcement agencies when these are in agreement with the INTERPOL constitution.

Martin Renkiewicz
Director
Phone: 202-616-9700

Timothy A Williams
Deputy Director
Phone: 202-616-9700

Kevin R Smith
General Counsel
Phone: 202-616-7280

William Duda
Acting Assistant Director Interpol Operations & Command Center
Phone: 202-616-3459

Michael D Muth
Assistant Director US State & Local Liaison Division
Phone: 202-616-8272

Linda Winn
Assistant Director Drug Investigative Division
Phone: 202-616-3379

Timothy A Williams
Acting Assistant Director Terrorism & Violent Crime Division
Phone: 202-616-9700

Esteban Soto
Assistant Director Alien & Fugitive Division
Phone: 202-616-0310

Wai Man Leung
Assistant Director Economic Crimes Division
Phone: 202-616-9546

Herman Smith
Acting Assistant Director Administrative Services
Phone: 202-616-8215

Cristle Humes
Public Affairs Officer
Phone: 202-616-8006

National Drug Intelligence Center
Department of Justice
319 Washington Street
5th Floor
Johnstown, PA 15901-1624
Phone: 814-532-4601
Phone: 202-532-4040
Fax: 814-532-4690
URL: www.usdoj.gov/ndic
e-mail: ndic.contacts@usdoj.gov

Description: The mission of the National Drug Intelligence Center is to support intelligence community counterdrug efforts, and support national policymakers and law enforcement by producing timely strategic domestic drug intelligence assessments, focusing on the production, trafficking, and consumption trends and patterns of all illicit drugs inside United States' national borders and territories.

Irene S Hernandez
Acting Director
Phone: 814-532-4607

Thomas W Padden
Acting Deputy Director
Phone: 814-532-4984

Steven R Frank
Chief of Staff
Phone: 814-532-4728

Thomas W Padden
Acting General Counsel
Phone: 814-532-4984

Joseph E Donovan
Acting Assistant Director
Phone: 814-532-4630

David J Mrozowski
Intelligence Support Division Assistant Director
Phone: 814-532-4087

Bureau of Prisons
Department of Justice
320 First Street NW
Washington, DC 20534-0002
Phone: 202-307-3198
Phone: 202-307-3250
URL: www.bop.gov
e-mail: info@bop.gov

Description: The Bureau protects public safety by ensuring that federal offenders serve their sentences in safe, humane, cost-efficient and secure facilities. By means of a range of programs, the potential for future criminal activity, is reduced. The Bureau of Prisons is responsible for the custody and care of 193,000 federal offenders. About 85 percent of these inmates are confined in Bureau-operated correctional institutions or detention centers. The rest are confined through agreements with state and local government and through contracts with privately-operated community correction centers, detention centers, prisons, and juvenile facilities.

Harley G Lappin
Director
Phone: 202-307-3250

Bruce K Sasser
Administration Assistant Director
Phone: 202-307-3123

Joyce K Conley PhD
Correctional Programs Assistant Director
Phone: 202-307-3226

Newton E Kendig MD
Health Services Assistant Director
Phone: 202-307-3055

Whitney I Leblanc Jr
Human Resource Assistant Director
Phone: 202-307-3082

Paul M Laird
Industries, Education & Vocational Training Assistant Director
Phone: 202-308-3500

Thomas R Kane PhD
Information, Policy & Public Affairs Assistant Director
Phone: 202-514-6537

Morris Thigpen
National Institute of Corrections Director
Phone: 202-307-3106

Kathleen M Kenney
General Counsel/Assistant Director
Phone: 202-307-3062

Vanessa P Adams
Program Review Senior Deputy Assistant Director

Office of Small & Disadvantaged Business Utilization
Department of Justice
1331 Pennsylvania Avenue NW
National Place Building, Room 1010
Washington, DC 20530
Phone: 202-616-0521
Phone: 800-345-3712
Fax: 202-616-1717
URL: www.usdoj.gov/jmd/osdbu

Description: The Office of Small and Disadvantaged Business Utilization (OSDBU) works to improve and increase the Department of Justice's performance in utilizing small, small disadvantaged, small women-owned and veteran-owned businesses as contractors and subcontractors.

David Sutton
Director

FEDERAL

Department of Justice
Federal Bureau of Investigation

Federal Bureau of Investigation
Headquarters
935 Pennsylvania Avenue NW
Washington, DC 20535-0001
Phone: 202-324-3000
Phone: 202-324-3691
URL: www.fbi.gov

Description: The Federal Bureau of Investigation (FBI) is the principal investigative arm of the United States Department of Justice. Through its vast network of intelligence and law enforcement agents, the FBI works to neutralize terrorist cells and operatives in the United States and dismantle terror networks worldwide. The FBI has had a growing role in the Intelligence Community and the pace of operations have increased the need for special focus on longer-term, strategic efforts. Thus, there have been some structural changes to support these transformation efforts. The Bureau has created the position of the Associate Deputy Director and there are now five branches, each headed by an Executive Assistant Director. The FBI also supports other law enforcement and intelligence agencies. Because the FBI has both domestic intelligence and law enforcement capabilities, it is able to not only detect and investigate terrorist threats, but also to act on them through arrests and incarceration.

Robert S Mueller III
Director
Phone: 202-324-3444

John S Pistole
Deputy Director
Phone: 202-324-3444

Joseph L Ford
Associate Deputy Director

W Lee Rawls
Chief of Staff
Phone: 202-324-3444

Willie Hulon
Executive Assistant Director National Security Branch

Michael A Mason
Executive Assistant Director Criminal, Cyber, Response & Services Branch

Kerry E Haynes
Executive Assistant Director Science & Technology Branch

Zalmai Azmi
Chief Information Officer
Phone: 202-324-6165

Donald E Packham
Executive Assistant Director Human Resources Branch

John Miller
Public Affairs Office
Phone: 202-324-2727

Richard C Powers
Congressional Affairs Office

Valerie E Caproni
General Counsel
Phone: 202-324-6829

Candice M Will
Professional Responsibility Office
Phone: 202-324-8284

Sarah Zeigler
Ombudsman
Phone: 202-324-2156

National Security Branch (NSB)
FBI
935 Pennsylvania Avenue NW
Washington, DC 20535
Phone: 202-324-4885
Fax: 202-324-4705
URL: www.fbi.gov/hq/nsb/nsb.htm

Description: The National Security Branch is comprised of these four divisions: Counterterrorism; Counterintelligence; Directorate of Intelligence; and Weapons of Mass Destruction Directorate. The NSB positions the FBI to protect the US against weapons of mass destruction, terrorist attacks, foreign intelligence operations, and espionage by: integrating investigative and intelligence activities against current and emerging threats; providing useful and timely information and analysis to intelligence and law enforcement communities; and developing enabling capabilities consistent with applicable laws, the Attorney General and DNI guidance.

Willie Hulon
Executive Assistant Director
Phone: 202-324-4885

Philip Mudd
Associate Executive Assistant Director

Joseph Billy Jr
Counterterrorism Division

Timothy D Bereznay
Counterintelligence Division

Wayne M Murphy
Directorate of Intelligence

Dr Vahid Majidi
Weapons of Mass Destruction Directorate

Joint Terrorism Task Force (JTTF)
NSB - Counterterrorism Division
935 Pennsylvania Avenue NW
Washington, DC 20535
URL: www.fbi.gov/page2/dec04/jttf120114.htm

Description: The Joint Terrorism Task Forces are the nation's front line of defense on terrorism. Small groups of highly trained, locally based, investigators, analysts, linguists, SWAT experts, and other specialists from US law enforcement and intelligence agencies make up the task forces in 100 cities nationwide. There is at least one of these forces located in one of the 56 FBI field offices. The JTTFs coordinate their efforts through the inter-agency National Joint Terrorism Task Force located at the FBI headquarters in Washington, DC.

National Joint Terrorism Task Force
NSB - Counterterrorism Division
935 Pennsylvania Avenue NW
Washington, DC 20535
URL: www.fbi.gov

Description: The National Joint Terrorism Task Force was created in 2002 at the FBI's command center in Washington, DC Approximately 38 agencies are represented, spanning the fields of intelligence, public safety, and federal, state, and local law enforcement. The National Joint Terrorism Task Force collects terrorism information and intelligence and funnels it to the 100 Joint Terrorism Task Forces, various terrorism units within the FBI, and partner agencies.

Ken Love
Acting Chief

Criminal, Cyber, Response & Services Branch
FBI
935 Pennsylvania Avenue NW
Washington, DC 20535
URL: www.fbi.gov

Description: To ensure that the FBI maintains its high level of excellence in criminal investigations, the responsiblity for criminal and cyber investigations, coordination with law enforcement, international operations, and crisis response has been placed under one official. The Criminal, Cyber, Response & Services Branch is composed of the divisions listed below.

Michael A Mason
Executive Assistant Director

Kenneth W Kaiser
Criminal Investigative Division

James E Finch
Cyber Division
Phone: 202-324-2770

Michael J Wolf
Critical Incident Response Group
Phone: 202-324-3444

Thomas V Fuentes
International Operations Office

Louis F Quijas
Law Enforcement Coordination Office
Phone: 202-324-7126

Office of Law Enforcement Coordination (OLEC)
Criminal, Cyber, Response & Services Branch
935 Pennsylvania Avenue NW
Washington, DC 20535
Phone: 202-324-7126
Fax: 202-324-0920
URL: www.fbi.gov/hq/olec/olec.htm
e-mail: olec@leo.gov

Description: The Office of Law Enforcement Coordination was created within the Federal Bureau of Investigation to improve longstanding relationships with state, municipal, county, and tribal law enforcement on a national level. The FBI is committed to folding its law enforcement partners into the war on terror by sharing information more fully and coordinating more closely with local law enforcement. OLEC also serves as the FBI's primary liaison for the national law enforcement associations and responsible for liaison with DHS.

Louis F Quijas
Law Enforcement Coordination Officer
Phone: 202-324-7126

Science & Technology Branch
FBI
935 Pennsylvania Avenue NW
Washington, DC 20535
URL: www.fbi.gov/lawenforce.htm

Description: The Science & Technology Branch will ensure that the FBI continues to provide exceptional service to the law enforcement community and stays on top of technical innovation and developments in sciences to support investigative and intelligence-gathering activities.

Kerry E Haynes
Executive Assistant Director

Thomas E Bush III
Criminal Justice Information Services Division

Joseph A DiZinno
Laboratory Division

Marcus C Thomas
Operational Technology Division

Office of the Chief Information Officer
FBI
935 Pennsylvania Avenue NW
Washington, DC 20535
Phone: 202-324-6165
URL: www.fbi.gov/hq/ocio/ocio_home.htm

Description: As part of the restructuring of the Bureau, the Office of the Chief Information Officer has been more closely aligned with the components handling strategic planning, finance, security and facilities.

Zalmai Azmi
Chief Information Officer

Robert J Garrity Jr
Deputy Chief Information Officer/BPR Executive

Dean E Hall
Deputy Chief Information Officer

Jerome W Israel
Chief Technology Officer

John Martin Hope
IT Program Management

FBI Albany
200 McCarty Avenue
Albany, NY 12209
Phone: 518-465-7551
Fax: 518-431-7463
URL: http://albany.fbi.gov

John F Pikus
Special Agent in Charge

Richard J Licht
Asst Special Agent in Charge

Andrew W Vale
Asst Special Agent in Charge

FBI Albuquerque
4200 Luecking Park Avenue NE
Albuquerque, NM 87107
Phone: 505-889-1300
URL: http://albuquerque.fbi.gov

Thomas C McClenaghan
Special Agent in Charge

Scott O'Neal
Asst Special Agent in Charge

Robert M Evans
Asst Special Agent in Charge

FBI Anchorage
101 East Sixth Avenue
Anchorage, AK 99501-2524
Phone: 907-258-5322
Phone: 907-276-4441
URL: http://anchorage.fbi.gov
e-mail: anchoragefbi@ak.net

Toni Mari Fogle
Special Agent in Charge

David E Heller
Asst Special Agent in Charge

FBI Atlanta
2635 Century Parkway NE
Suite 400
Atlanta, GA 30345-3112
Phone: 404-679-9000
Fax: 404-679-6289
URL: http://atlanta.fbi.gov

Gregory Jones
Special Agent in Charge

Mark Giuliano
Asst Special Agent in Charge

FBI Baltimore
2600 Lord Baltimore Drive
Baltimore, MD 21244
Phone: 410-265-8080
Fax: 410-277-6677
URL: http://baltimore.fbi.gov

William D Chase
Special Agent in Charge

Frank E Goetz
Asst Special Agent in Charge

FBI Birmingham
1000 18th Street N
Birmingham, AL 35203-2396
Phone: 205-326-6166
Fax: 205-279-1590
URL: http://birmingham.fbi.gov
e-mail: birmingham@ic.fbi.gov

Carmen S Adams
Special Agent in Charge

Charles E Regan
Asst Special Agent in Charge

FBI Boston
One Center Plaza
Suite 600
Boston, MA 02108
Phone: 617-742-5533
Fax: 617-223-6327
URL: http://boston.fbi.gov

Warren T Bamford
Special Agent in Charge

Kevin Kline
Asst Special Agent in Charge

FBI Buffalo
One FBI Plaza
Buffalo, NY 14202-2698
Phone: 716-856-7800
Fax: 716-843-5288
URL: http://buffalo.fbi.gov
e-mail: buffalo@ic.fbi.gov

Laurie J Bennett
Special Agent in Charge

Karen L Ferguson
Asst Special Agent in Charge

FBI Charlotte
400 S Tryon Street, Suite 900
Wachovia Bldg
Charlotte, NC 28285-0001
Phone: 704-377-9200
URL: http://charlotte.fbi.gov
e-mail: charlotte.public@ic.fbi.gov

Nathan Gray Kendrick
Special Agent in Charge

Kenneth Moore
Asst Special Agent in Charge

Robert Clifford
Asst Special Agent in Charge

FBI Chicago
2111 W Roosevelt Road
Chicago, IL 60608

Phone: 312-421-6700
URL: http://chicago.fbi.gov

Robert D Grant
Special Agent in Charge

Arthur L Everett
Asst Special Agent in Charge

FBI Cincinnati
550 Main Street, Suite 9000
Cincinnati, OH 45202-8501
Phone: 513-421-4310
Fax: 513-562-5650
URL: http://cincinnati.fbi.gov
e-mail: cincinnati@fbi.gov

Timothy P Murphy
Special Agent in Charge

James H Robertson
Asst Special Agent in Charge

J Mark Batts
Asst Special Agent in Charge

FBI Cleveland
Federal Office Building
1501 Lakeside Avenue
Cleveland, OH 44114
Phone: 216-522-1400
Fax: 216-622-6717
URL: http://cleveland.fbi.gov
e-mail: cleveland.cv@ic.fbi.gov

C Frank Figliuzzi
Special Agent in Charge

Derek M Siegle
Asst Special Agent in Charge

FBI Columbia
151 Westpark Boulevard
Columbia, SC 29210-3857
Phone: 803-551-4200
URL: http://columbia.fbi.gov

Brian D Lamkin
Special Agent in Charge

FBI Dallas
One Justice Way
Dallas, TX 75220
Phone: 972-559-5000
URL: http://dallas.fbi.gov

Robert E Casey Jr
Special Agent in Charge

FBI Denver
Byron G Rogers FOB, Suite 1823
1961 Stout Street, 18th Floor
Denver, CO 80294-1823
Phone: 303-629-7171
URL: http://denver.fbi.gov

Richard C Powers
Special Agent in Charge

Cary B Nelson
Asst Special Agent in Charge

Joseph C Campbell
Asst Special Agent in Charge

FBI Detroit
477 Michigan Avenue
26th Floor PV
Detroit, MI 48226
Phone: 313-965-2323
URL: http://detroit.fbi.gov

Andrew G Arena
Special Agent in Charge

FBI El Paso
660 S Mesa Hills Drive
El Paso, TX 79912-5533
Phone: 915-832-5000
URL: http://elpaso.fbi.gov

Manuel E Mora
Special Agent in Charge

Kevin N August
Asst Special Agent in Charge-National Security Division

Joseph T Kinard
Asst Special Agent in Charge-Criminal Division

FBI Honolulu
Kalanianaole FOB, Room 4-230
300 Ala Moana Boulevard
Honolulu, HI 96850-0053
Mailing Address: PO Box 50164
Phone: 808-566-4300
URL: http://honolulu.fbi.gov
e-mail: honolulu@fbi.gov

Janet L Kamerman
Special Agent in Charge

Pamela J McCullough
Asst Special Agent in Charge

Robert Kauffman
Asst Special Agent in Charge

FBI Houston
2500 E TC Jester Boulevard
Suite 200
Houston, TX 77008-1300
Phone: 713-693-5000
URL: http://houston.fbi.gov
e-mail: houston@fbi.gov

Andrew Bland III
Special Agent in Charge

FBI Indianapolis
575 N Pennsylvania Street
FOB, Room 679
Indianapolis, IN 46204-1585
Phone: 317-639-3301
Fax: 317-321-6193
URL: http://indianapolis.fbi.gov

Keith L Lourdeau
Special Agent in Charge

James H Davis
Asst Special Agent in Charge

Danny L Barkley
Asst Special Agent in Charge

FBI Jackson
100 West Capitol Street
FOB, Suite 1553
Jackson, MS 39269-1601
Phone: 601-948-5000
URL: http://jackson.fbi.gov
e-mail: fbijn@leo.gov

Frederick T Brink
Special Agent in Charge

William W Jenkins
Asst Special Agent in Charge

Stephen F Gomez
Asst Special Agent in Charge

FBI Jacksonville
7820 Arlington Expressway
Suite 200
Jacksonville, FL 32211
Phone: 904-721-1211
URL: http://jacksonville.fbi.gov
e-mail: jacksonville@ic.fbi.gov

Michael J Folmar
Special Agent in Charge

FBI Kansas City
1300 Summit
Kansas City, MO 64105-1362
Phone: 816-512-8200
URL: http://kansascity.fbi.gov
e-mail: kansas.city@ic.fbi.gov

Monte C Strait
Special Agent in Charge

Thomas A Nunemaker
Asst Special Agent in Charge

FBI Knoxville
John J Duncan FOB, Suite 600
710 Locust Street
Knoxville, TN 37902-2537
Phone: 865-544-0751
URL: http://knoxville.fbi.gov
e-mail: knoxfbi@ko.gov

Richard L Lambert
Special Agent in Charge

Gary L Kidder
Media Relations Coordinator

FBI Las Vegas
John Lawrence Bailey Building
1787 West Lake Mead Blvd
Las Vegas, NV 89106-2135

Phone: 702-385-1281
URL: http://lasvegas.fbi.gov

Steven M Martinez
Special Agent in Charge

Mark I Doh
Asst Special Agent in Charge

William C Woerner
Asst Special Agent in Charge

FBI Little Rock
24 Shackleford W Boulevard
Little Rock, AK 72211-3755
Phone: 501-221-9100
Fax: 501-221-8509
URL: http://littlerock.fbi.gov
e-mail: little.rock@ic.fbi.gov

William Temple
Special Agent in Charge

FBI Los Angeles
11000 Wilshire Boulevard
FOB, Suite 1700
Los Angeles, CA 90024-3672
Phone: 310-477-6565
URL: http://losangeles.fbi.gov

J Stephen Tidwell
Assistant Director in Charge

Janice K Fedarcyk
Special Agent in Charge, Counterterrorism Division

Robert E Loosle
Special Agent in Charge, Criminal Division

Peter Brust
Special Agent in Charge, Counterintelligence/Cyber Division

FBI Louisville
600 Martin Luther King Jr Place
Room 500
Louisville, KY 40202-2231
Phone: 502-583-3941
Fax: 502-569-3869
URL: http://louisville.fbi.gov

Tracy A Reinhold
Special Agent in Charge

Larry R Willis
Asst Special Agent in Charge

David J Beyer
Media Coordinator

FBI Memphis
Eagle Crest Building
225 N Humphreys Boulevard, Suite 3000
Memphis, TN 38120-2107
Phone: 901-747-4300
URL: http://memphis.fbi.gov

My Harrison
Special Agent in Charge

FBI Milwaukee
330 East Kilbourn Avenue
Suite 600
Milwaukee, WI 53202-6627
Phone: 414-276-4684
Fax: 414-276-2400
URL: http://milwaukee.fbi.gov

Richard K Ruminski
Special Agent in Charge

James R McNally
Asst Special Agent in Charge

Monica Shipley
Public Affairs Coordinator

FBI Minneapolis
111 Washington Avenue S
Suite 1100
Minneapolis, MN 55401-2176
Phone: 612-376-3200
Fax: 612-376-3249
URL: http://minneapolis.fbi.gov
e-mail: minneapolis@ic.fbi.gov

Ralph S Boelter
Special Agent in Charge

Julio Quinones Jr
Asst Special Agent in Charge

Paul McCabe
Media Coordinator

FBI Mobile
200 N Royal Street
Mobile, AL 36602
Phone: 251-438-3674
Fax: 251-415-3235
URL: http://mobile.fbi.gov

Debra K Mack
Special Agent in Charge

Bill L Lewis
Asst Special Agent in Charge

FBI New Haven
600 State Street
New Haven, CT 06511-6505
Phone: 203-777-6311
Fax: 203-503-5098
URL: http://newhaven.fbi.gov
e-mail: fbinhct@leo.gov

Kimberly K Mertz
Special Agent in Charge

Alexis G Hatten
Asst Special Agent in Charge

Peter T Trahon
Asst Special Agent in Charge

FBI New Orleans
2901 Leon C Simon Boulevard
New Orleans, LA 70126
Phone: 504-816-3000

Fax: 504-816-3306
URL: http://neworleans.fbi.gov

James Bernazzani
Special Agent in Charge

Lewis M Chapman
Asst Special Agent in Charge

Michael Gant
Asst Special Agent in Charge

FBI New York
26 Federal Plaza
23rd Floor
New York, NY 10278-0004
Phone: 212-384-1000
URL: http://newyork.fbi.gov

Mark J Mershon
Assistant Director in Charge

FBI Newark
Claremont Tower
11 Centre Place
Newark, NJ 07102
Phone: 973-792-3000
Fax: 973-792-3035
URL: http://newark.fbi.gov

Pedro D Ruiz
Acting Special Agent in Charge

FBI Norfolk
150 Corporate Boulevard
Norfolk, VA 23502
Phone: 757-455-0100
Fax: 757-455-2647
URL: http://norfolk.fbi.gov
e-mail: norfolk@ic.fbi.gov

Cassandra M Chandler
Special Agent in Charge

FBI North Miami Beach
16320 NW Second Avenue
North Miami Beach, FL 33169-6508
Phone: 305-944-9101
URL: http://miami.fbi.gov
e-mail: miami@ic.fbi.gov

Jonathan Solomon
Special Agent in Charge

FBI Oklahoma City
3301 West Memorial Road
Oklahoma City, OK 73134
Phone: 405-290-7770
Fax: 405-290-3885
URL: http://oklahomacity.fbi.gov

Michael B Ward
Special Agent in Charge

Samuel J Macaluso
Asst Special Agent in Charge

Gregory R Melzer
Asst Special Agent in Charge

FBI Omaha
10755 Burt Street
Omaha, NE 68114-2000
Phone: 402-493-8688
URL: http://omaha.fbi.gov
e-mail: omaha@ic.fbi.gov

Paul C LaCotti
Special Agent in Charge

FBI Philadelphia
William J Green Jr FOB, 8th Floor
600 Arch Street
Philadelphia, PA 19106
Phone: 215-418-4000
URL: http://philadelphia.fbi.gov
e-mail: philadelphia@fbi.gov

J P Weis
Special Agent in Charge

Brian W Lynch
Asst Special Agent in Charge

FBI Phoenix
201 East Indianola Avenue
Suite 400
Phoenix, AZ 85012-2080
Phone: 602-279-5511
URL: http://phoenix.fbi.gov
e-mail: phoenix@ic.fbi.gov

John E Lewis
Special Agent in Charge

Stephen A Cocco
Asst Special Agent in Charge

FBI Pittsburgh
3311 East Carson Street
Pittsburgh, PA 15203
Phone: 412-432-4000
Fax: 412-432-4188
URL: http://pittsburgh.fbi.gov

Ray A Morrow
Special Agent in Charge

Robert C Rudge Jr
Asst Special Agent in Charge

Kevin P Deegan
Asst Special Agent in Charge

FBI Portland
Crown Plaza Building
1500 SW First Avenue, Suite 400
Portland, OR 97201-5828
Phone: 503-224-4181
Fax: 503-552-5400
URL: http://portland.fbi.gov
e-mail: portland@ic.fbi.gov

Robert J Jordan
Special Agent in Charge

Daniel R Nielsen
Asst Special Agent in Charge

Alan J Peters
Asst Special Agent in Charge

FBI Richmond
1970 E Parham Road
Richmond, VA 23228
Phone: 804-261-1044
URL: http://richmond.fbi.gov
e-mail: richmond@ic.fbi.gov

Charles J Cunningham
Special Agent in Charge

Robert E Gwaltney
Asst Special Agent in Charge

Clifford C Holly
Asst Special Agent in Charge

FBI Sacramento
4500 Orange Grove Ave
Sacramento, CA 95841-4205
Phone: 916-481-9110
Fax: 916-977-2300
URL: http://sacramento.fbi.gov

Drew S Parenti
Special Agent in Charge

Mark F Johnson
Asst Special Agent in Charge

David A Picard
Asst Special Agent in Charge

FBI Salt Lake City
257 Towers Building East
200 South, Suite 1200
Salt Lake City, UT 84111-2048
Phone: 801-579-1400
URL: http://saltlakecity.fbi.gov
e-mail: saltlakecity@ic.fbi.gov

Timothy J Fuhrman
Special Agent in Charge

FBI San Antonio
US Post Office Courthouse Bldg, Ste 200
615 East Houston Street
San Antonio, TX 78205-9998
Phone: 210-225-6741
URL: http://sanantonio.fbi.gov
e-mail: sa@fbi.gov

Ralph G Diaz
Special Agent in Charge

D True Brown
Asst Special Agent in Charge

FBI San Diego
Federal Office Building
9797 Aero Drive
San Diego, CA 92123-1800
Phone: 858-565-1255

Fax: 858-499-7991
URL: http://sandiego.fbi.gov
e-mail: san.diego@ic.fbi.gov

Daniel Dzwilewski
Special Agent in Charge

Stuart B Roberts
Asst Special Agent in Charge

FBI San Francisco
450 Golden Gate Avenue
13th Floor
San Francisco, CA 94102-9523
Phone: 415-553-7400
URL: http://sanfrancisco.fbi.gov

Charlotte B Thornton
Special Agent in Charge

FBI San Juan
150 Carlos Chardon Avenue
FOB, Suite 526, Hato Rey
San Juan, 00918-1716
Puerto Rico
Mailing Address: PO Box 366269, 00936-6269
Phone: 787-754-6000
URL: http://sanjuan.fbi.gov
e-mail: sanjuan@fbi.gov

Luis S Fraticelli
Special Agent in Charge

Jane Erickson
Asst Special Agent in Charge

FBI Seattle
1110 Third Avenue
Seattle, WA 98101-2904
Phone: 206-622-0460
URL: http://seattle.fbi.gov
e-mail: fbise@leo.gov

Laura M Laughlin
Special Agent in Charge

Steven R Fiddler
Asst Special Agent in Charge

FBI Springfield
900 E Linton Avenue
Springfield, IL 62703
Phone: 217-522-9675
URL: http://springfield.fbi.gov
e-mail: springfield@ic.fbi.gov

Weysan Dun
Special Agent in Charge

John H Stafford
Asst Special Agent in Charge

Janice Fields
Asst Special Agent in Charge

FBI St Louis
2222 Market Street
St. Louis, MO 63103

Phone: 314-231-4324
Fax: 314-589-2636
URL: http://stlouis.fbi.gov
e-mail: stlouis@ic.fbi.gov

Roland J Corvington
Special Agent in Charge

Thomas B Noble
Asst Special Agent in Charge

Peter Krusing
Media Relations Coordinator

FBI Tampa
5525 W Gray Street
Tampa, FL 33609
Phone: 813-253-1000
Fax: 813-253-1456
URL: http://tampa.fbi.gov
e-mail: tampa.division@ic.fbi.gov

David F Reign
Acting Special Agent in Charge

Kevin Ray Eaton
Asst Special Agent in Charge

Christopher W Davis
Asst Special Agent in Charge (Orlando)

FBI Washington
Washington Metropolitan Field Office
601 4th Street NW
Washington, DC 20535-0002
Phone: 202-278-2000
URL: http://washingtondc.fbi.gov
e-mail: washington.field@ic.fbi.gov

Joseph Persichini
Assistant Director in Charge

FEDERAL

Department of State

Department of State

Headquarters
2201 C Street NW
Washington, DC 20520
Phone: 202-647-4000
Phone: 202-647-5291
URL: www.state.gov

Description: The Department of State is the leading United States foreign affairs agency, and the Secretary of State is the President's principal foreign policy adviser. State exists to advise on and carry out the foreign policy of the President and the US objective to shape a freer, more secure and prosperous world. As the leader in foreign policy enactment, State works to bring together nations to discuss issues of international concern, including terrorism, nuclear smuggling and humanitarian crises. The Department's Counterterrorism Office coordinates all US government efforts to improve counterterrorism cooperation with foreign governments, as well as coordinating US government response to terrorist incidents in progress. The State Department's Arms Control and International Security division is involved in arms control, nonproliferation and disarmament issues. The Under Secretary of Arms Control and International Security is a member of the National Security Council and is responsible to provide policy direction on issues related to regional security and defense relations. State's Political Affairs division is responsible for integrating political, economic, and global, as well as security issues into bilateral relationships. It is responsible for coordinating the conduct of US foreign relations.

Condoleezza Rice
Secretary
Phone: 202-647-5291

John D Negroponte
Deputy Secretary
Phone: 202-647-8636

Brian Gunderson
Chief of Staff
Phone: 202-647-5548

Ruth E Elliott
Deputy Chief of Staff
Phone: 202-647-9572

Ambassador George M Staples
Director General Foreign Service
Phone: 202-647-9898

R Nicholas Burns
Under Secretary Political Affairs
Phone: 202-647-2471

Henrietta Holsman Fore
Under Secretary Management (Acting Director Foreign Assistance/USAID)
Phone: 202-647-1500

Frank C Urbancic
Counterterrorism Coordinator
Phone: 202-647-8949

Susan Burk
Deputy Coordinator Homeland Security
Phone: 202-647-7223

Paula J Dobriansky
Under Secretary for Democracy & Global Affairs/Coordinator
Phone: 202-647-6240

Karen P Hughes
Under Secretary Public Diplomacy & Public Affairs
Phone: 202-647-9199

Sean McCormack
Spokesman/Assistant Secretary for Public Affairs
Phone: 202-647-6607

Ambassador John V Hanford III
Ambassador-at-Large/International Religious Freedom
Phone: 202-647-1042

Ryan Crocker
US Embassy, Baghdad
e-mail: baghdadpressoffice@state.gov

Ambassador Clint Williamson
Ambassador-at-Large for War Crimes Issues
Phone: 202-647-5072

Eliot A Cohen
Counselor of the Department of State
Phone: 202-647-5529

Ambassador John Herbst
Reconstruction & Stabilization Coordinator
Phone: 202-663-0307

Office of the Coordinator for Counterterrorism

Department of State
2201 C Street NW
Room 2509
Washington, DC 20520
Phone: 202-647-8949
URL: www.state.gov/s/ct

Description: Coordinates and supports the development and implementation of all US Government policies and programs aimed at counterterrorism overseas.

Frank C Urbancic
Coordinator
Phone: 202-647-8949

Susan Burk
Deputy Coordinator Homeland Security
Phone: 202-647-7223

Gerald Feierstein
Deputy Coordinator Programs, Plans, Press & Public Diplomacy
Phone: 202-647-2183

Mark I Thompson
Deputy Coordinator Operations
Phone: 202-776-8359

Virginia Palmer
Deputy Coordinator Regional/Trans-Regional Affairs
Phone: 202-647-5810

Rhonda H Shore
Press & Public Affairs Advisor
Phone: 202-647-1845

Foreign Emergency Support Team (FEST)
Coordinator of Counterterrorism-Directorate of Operations
Washington, DC 20520
URL: www.state.gov/s/ct/about/c16664.htm

Description: The Foreign Emergency Support Team is the US Government's only interagency, on-call, short-notice team poised to respond to terrorist incidents worldwide. It is led and trained by the Operations Directorate of the Office of the Coordinator for Counterterrorism and assists US missions and host governments in responding quickly and effectively to terrorist attacks. FEST is able to leave within 4 hours of notification and has been deployed to over 20 countries since its inception in 1986.

Under Secretary for Arms Control & International Security Affairs
Department of State
2201 C Street NW
Room 7208
Washington, DC 20520
Phone: 202-647-1049
URL: www.state.gov/t

Description: The Under Secretary serves as the senior adviser to the President and the Secretary of State for Arms Control, Nonproliferation, and Disarmament. It leads the interagency policy process on nonproliferation and manages global US security policy, mainly in the areas on nonproliferation, arms control, regional security and defense relations, and arms transfers and security assistance. By delegation from the Secretary, the Under Secretary performs a range of functions under the Foreign Assistance Act, Arms Export Control Act, and related legislation.

Susan Koch
Senior Adviser
Phone: 202-647-0302

George Look
Executive Director International Security Advisory Board
Phone: 202-647-9501

Bureau of Political-Military Affairs
Under Secretary for Arms Control & International Security Affairs
2201 C Street NW
Washington, DC 20520
Phone: 202-647-9022
URL: www.state.gov/t/pm

Description: The principal link between the Departments of State and Defense. The Bureau of Political-Military Affairs provides policy direction in the areas of security assistance, military operations, military use of space, international security, post-conflict stabilization and defense strategy and trade. The Bureau plays a key role in the Global War on Terrorism by securing base access and overflight permission to support the deployment of military forces; promoting stability around the world by fostering effective defense relationships; managing humanitarian mine action programs around the world; and leading the Department of State efforts to promote critical infrastructure protection around the world.

Stephen Mull
Acting Assistant Secretary
Phone: 202-647-9023

Michael W Coulter
Deputy Assistant Secretary
Phone: 202-647-9023

Frank Ruggiero
Acting Deputy Assistant Secretary-Defense Trade Controls Directorate
Phone: 202-663-2861

Francisco Javier Gonzalez
Acting Director Regional Security & Arms Transfers Office
Phone: 202-647-9750

Kevin O'Keefe
Director Plans, Policy & Analysis Office
Phone: 202-647-7775

Brig Gen Lyn Sherlock
Director International Security Operations
Phone: 202-647-4059

Bill McGlynn
State Political Advisors (POLAD) Coordinator
Phone: 202-736-4776
e-mail: mcglynnwj@state.gov

David Pozorski
Special Advisor for State-Defense Exchanges
Phone: 202-647-0295
e-mail: pozorskiDR2@state.gov

Robert G Loftis
Senior Advisor for Security Negotiations/Agreements
Phone: 202-647-8325
e-mail: loftisRG@state.gov

Bureau of International Security & Nonproliferation
Under Secretary for Arms Control & International Security Affairs
2201 C Street NW
Washington, DC 20520
Phone: 202-647-9610
URL: www.state.gov/t/isn

Description: The Bureau of International Security & Nonpoliferation is responsible for a broad range of nonproliferation, counterproliferation and arms control functions. It leads the United States' efforts to prevent the spread of weapons of mass destruction (nuclear, chemical, and biological weapons) and their delivery systems. It works closely with the UN, the G-8 NATO, the OPCW and the IAEA and other organizations to reduce and eliminate the threat of weapons of mass destruction by terrorists.

John C Rood
Assistant Secretary
Phone: 202-647-9610

Patricia A McNerney
Principal Deputy Assistant Secretary for Counterproliferation
Phone: 202-647-6977

Donald A Mahley
Acting Deputy Assistant Secretary for Threat Reduction, Export Controls & Negotiations
Phone: 202-647-5999

Andrew Semmel
Acting Deputy Assistant Secretary for Nuclear Nonproliferation Policy & Negotiations
Phone: 202-647-5122

Thomas Lehrman
Acting Director Office of Weapons of Mass Destruction Terrorism
Phone: 202-647-8699

Paul Van Son
Director Office of Export Controls Cooperation
Phone: 202-647-0224

Pam Durham
Acting Director Office of Missile Threat Reduction
Phone: 202-647-4931

Christian J Kessler
Director Office of Conventional Arms Threat Reduction
Phone: 202-647-2718

Richard K Stratford
Director Office of Nuclear Energy, Safety & Security
Phone: 202-647-4061

Andrew Goodman
Director Office of Cooperative Threat Reduction
Phone: 202-736-7077

Robert Mikulak
Director Office of Chemical & Biological Weapons Threat Reduction
Phone: 202-647-5477

Under Secretary for Political Affairs
Department of State
2201 C Street NW
Room 7240
Washington, DC 20520
Phone: 202-647-2471
URL: www.state.gov/p

Description: Responsible for the Department's day-to-day activities, managing of overall regional and bilateral policy issues, integrating political, economic and security issues into the US'

bilateral relationships. There are six geographically defined and one functional bureau that report to the Under Secretary.

R Nicholas Burns
Under Secretary
Phone: 202-647-2471

Jendayi Elizabeth Frazer
Assistant Secretary Bureau of African Affairs
Phone: 202-647-2530

Christopher R Hill
Assistant Secretary Bureau of East Asian & Pacific Affairs
Phone: 202-647-9596

Daniel Fried
Assistant Secretary Bureau of European & Eurasian Affairs
Phone: 202-647-9626

C David Welch
Assistant Secretary Bureau of Near Eastern Affairs
Phone: 202-647-7209

Richard A Boucher
Assistant Secretary Bureau of South & Central Asian Affairs
Phone: 202-736-4325

Thomas A Shannon Jr
Assistant Secretary Bureau of Western Hemisphere Affairs
Phone: 202-647-5780

Kristen Silverberg
Assistant Secretary Bureau of International Organization Affairs
Phone: 202-647-9600

David Bame
Special Assistant
Phone: 202-647-4315

Bureau for International Narcotics & Law Enforcement Affairs
Under Secretary for Political Affairs
2201 C Street NW
Room 7333
Washington, DC 20520
Phone: 202-647-8464
URL: www.state.gov/p/inl

Description: The Bureau for International Narcotics and Law Enforcement Affairs advises the President, Secretary of State, other bureaus in the Department of State, and other departments and agencies within the United States government on the development of policies and programs to combat international narcotics and crime. Its programs aim to reduce the entry of illegal drugs into the US and minimize the impact of international crime on the US and its citizens. Counternarcotics and anticrime programs also complement the war on terrorism by promoting modernization of and supporting operations by foreign criminal justice systems and law enforcement agencies with the responsibility of counter-terrorism missions.

Anne W Patterson
Assistant Secretary
Phone: 202-647-8464

Thomas Schweich
Principal Deputy Assistant Secretary
Phone: 202-647-9822

Christy A McCampbell
Deputy Assistant Secretary
Phone: 202-647-0455

Charles Snyder
Acting Deputy Assistant Secretary for Civilian Police/Asia, Africa & Europe Programs
Phone: 202-647-8464

Elizabeth Verville
Deputy Assistant Secretary for Crime
Phone: 202-647-6642

Robert S Byrnes
Controller/Executive Director
Phone: 202-776-8750

James Kohler
Deputy Executive Director
Phone: 202-776-8526

Sharon Nell
Director Office of Aviation
Phone: 321-783-9821

Abelardo A Arias
Director Office of Americas Program
Phone: 202-647-9090

Robert Gifford
Director Office of Civilian Police & Rule of Law (CivPol Unit)
Phone: 202-647-0401

Steve Peterson
Director Office of Crime Programs
Phone: 202-312-9703

Charles Snyder
Director Office of Asia, Africa & Europe
Phone: 202-776-8746

Ron McMullen
Director Office of Afghanistan & Pakistan
Phone: 202-776-8877

Annie Pforzheimer
Director Policy, Planning & Coordination
Phone: 202-647-0396

Susan Pittman
Press & Public Affairs
Phone: 202-647-2842

Jeff White
Congressional Affairs
Phone: 202-647-0198

Bureau of Diplomatic Security
Department of State
Washington, DC 20522
Phone: 571-345-2502
URL: www.state.gov/m/ds

Description: Plays an essential role within the Department and has a broad scope of global responsibilities, with protection of people, information, and property as its top priority. It develops and implements effective security programs to safeguard all personnel who work in every US diplomatic mission around the world, all domestic State Department facilities, and assists foreign embassies and consulates in the United States with security for their missions and personnel. In this country, the Bureau pro-

tects the Secretary of State, the United States Ambassador to the United Nations, and foreign dignitaries below the head-of-state level who visit the United States.

Richard J Griffin
Assistant Secretary
Phone: 202-647-6290

Stephen J Mergens
Executive Director
Phone: 571-345-3816

Gregory B Starr
Principal Deputy Assistant Secretary/Director Diplomatic Security Service
Phone: 571-345-3815

Gregory B Starr
Deputy Assistant Secretary Diplomatic Security/Countermeasures
Phone: 571-345-3787

Pat Donovan
Assistant Director for Domestic Operations
Phone: 571-345-3836

Glen A Gershman
Director Domestic Facilities Protection
Phone: 202-647-0032

Stephen Brunette
Director Antiterrorism Assistance Program
Phone: 571-226-9631

David G Kidd
Director Investigations & Counterintelligence
Phone: 571-345-2945

Nace Crawford
Director Intelligence & Threat Analysis
Phone: 571-345-3936

David Benson
Director Training & Performance Support
Phone: 703-204-6205

Gary Gibson
Assistant Director International Programs
Phone: 571-345-3841

Raymond Bassi
Special Programs & Coordination
Phone: 571-345-2795

Office of Foreign Missions
Bureau of Diplomatic Security
3507 International Place NW
Washington, DC 20008-3025
Mailing Address: 3507 Int'l Place NW, DC 20522-3302
Phone: 202-647-3417
Fax: 202-647-0953
URL: www.state.gov/ofm
e-mail: ofminfo@state.gov

Description: Mandated by Congress, OFM (Office of Foreign Missions) provides legal foundation to facilitate secure and efficient operations of US missions abroad, and of foreign missions and international organizations in the US. In doing so, OFM serves the interests of the American public, the American diplomatic community abroad, and the foreign diplomatic community residing in the US to see that all diplomatic benefits, privileges, and immunities are properly exercised in accordance with federal and international laws.

Claude J Nebel
Deputy Assistant Secretary/OFM Deputy Director
Phone: 202-647-3417

John Sheely
Managing Director Operations
Phone: 202-647-3417

Laura M Ryan
Director Administration
Phone: 202-647-3199

Richard Massey
Director Travel, Property & Banking
Phone: 202-647-0325

Jacqueline D Robinson
Director Diplomatic Motor Vehicles & Accreditation
Phone: 202-895-3528

Terry V Davis
Acting Director Diplomatic Tax & Customs
Phone: 202-895-3540

Ron Mlotek
Legal Counsel
Phone: 202-895-3501

Michael Van Buskirk
Director Diplomatic Security Protective Liaison
Phone: 202-895-3608

Denise Duclon
Chicago Regional Director
Phone: 312-353-5762

Douglas S Dobson
Houston Regional Director
Phone: 713-272-2865

Alex Kirkpatrick
Los Angeles Regional Director
Phone: 310-235-6292

Dan M Cushman
Miami Regional Director
Phone: 305-442-4943

Donna J Winton
New York Regional Director
Phone: 212-826-4500

Steven Candy
San Francisco Acting Regional Director
Phone: 415-744-2910

Gladys Boluda
Protocol/Diplomatic Affairs Division
Phone: 202-647-1985

Office of Domestic Operations
Bureau of Diplomatic Security
1801 N Lynn Street
Arlington, VA 22209
Phone: 571-345-3836

Patrick Donovan
Assistant Director
Phone: 571-345-3836

Darwin Cadogan
Protection Office
Phone: 703-312-3322

Glen A Gershman
Domestic Facilities Protection Office
Phone: 202-647-0032

George Bailey
Security Support Division Chief
Phone: 202-663-1676

Bill Evans
Uniformed Operations Division Acting Chief
Phone: 202-647-0031

Office of Intelligence & Threat Analysis
Bureau of Diplomatic Security
1801 N Lynn Street
Room SA20
Arlington, VA 22209
Phone: 571-345-3936
URL: www.state.gov/m/ds/terrorism/c8584.htm

Description: The Office of Intelligence and Threat Analysis is the interface between the Department of State and the US Intelligence Community on all domestic and international terrorism matters. It researches, monitors and analyzes all source intelligence on terrorist activities and threats directed against Americans and US diplomatic and consular personnel and facilities overseas, in particular, threats against the Secretary of State, senior US officials, visiting foreign dignitaries, resident foreign diplomats, and foreign missions in the US for which the Department of State has a protective security responsibility.

Nace Crawford
Director
Phone: 571-345-3936

Office of Security Infrastructure
Bureau of Diplomatic Security
1801 N Lynn Street
Room SA20
Arlington, VA 22209
Phone: 571-345-3788

Donald Reid
Senior Coordinator
Phone: 571-345-3788

Mary Stone Holland
Director Computer Security
Phone: 571-345-2589

Cheryl Hess
Information Security Programs
Phone: 571-345-3080

James Onusko
Personnel Security & Suitability
Phone: 571-345-3219

Bureau of Intelligence & Research
Department of State
2201 C Street NW

Washington, DC 20520
Phone: 202-647-9177
URL: www.state.gov/s/inr

Description: The Bureau of Intelligence and Research (INR) draws on all-source intelligence, provides value-added independent analysis of events to Department policymakers, ensures that intelligence activities support foreign policy and national security purposes, and serves as the focal point in the Department for ensuring policy review of sensitive counterintelligence and law enforcement activities. The Office's primary mission is to harness intelligence to serve United States diplomacy. The Bureau also analyzes geographical and international boundary issues and is a member of the US Intelligence Community.

Randall M Fort
Assistant Secretary
Phone: 202-647-9177

John R Dinger
Principal Deputy Assistant Secretary
Phone: 202-647-7826

Paula Causey
Deputy for Intelligence Policy & Coordination
Phone: 202-647-7754

Stephen M Shaffer
Deputy for Media Analysis & Polling/Director Research Office
Phone: 202-203-7932

James Buchanan
Acting Deputy for Analysis & Information Management
Phone: 202-647-9633

Philip Harrick
Senior Advisor Security
Phone: 202-647-7536

Ed Kaska
Current Intelligence Staff
Phone: 202-647-6955

Linda L Donahue
Director Intelligence Coordination
Phone: 202-647-7679

Jon Gibney
Acting Director Intelligence Operations
Phone: 202-647-1153

Judson Barnes
Director Intelligence Resources
Phone: 202-647-4318

Debbie Glasberg
Acting Director Publications
Phone: 202-647-6069

Office of Small & Disadvantaged Business Utilization
Department of State
1701 N Ft Myers Drive
Arlington, VA 22219-2248
Mailing Address: A/SDBU DOState, SA6 Rm L500, DC 20522
Phone: 703-875-6822
Fax: 703-875-6825
URL: www.state.gov/m/a/sdbu

Description: Advocates US small business interests in the Department's acquisition process by providing to the small business community training and counseling about doing business with the Department; providing training and counseling to internal customers about contracting with small businesses; and assisting internal customers in identifying resources that result in increased opportunities for small businesses.

Gregory Mayberry
Director
Phone: 703-875-6823

Margaret Williams
Small Business Advocate
Phone: 703-875-6824

Willie Taylor
Veteran-Owned Business Representative
Phone: 703-875-4240
e-mail: taylorwl2@state.gov

Patricia B Culbreth
Women-Owned Business Representative
Phone: 703-875-6881
e-mail: culbrethpb@state.gov

Judith E Thomas
HUBZone Representative
Phone: 703-516-1953

Louis Pruitt
Overseas Building Operations Representative
Phone: 703-875-6586

Office of Procurement Executive
Department of State
1701 N Fort Myers Drive
Arlington, VA 22219
Phone: 703-516-1689
URL: www.statebuy.state.gov

Description: The Office of Procurement Executive assists overseas embassies and consulates in contracting for needed supplies, services, and construction. Although the contracts are normally signed by General Services Officers at the embassy or consulate, the Office provides guidance on contracting matters and assists in making solicitations available to US businesses.

Corey M Rinder
Procurement Executive Officer
Phone: 703-516-1689

Jan Visintainer
Competition Advocate/Ombudsman
Phone: 703-516-1693

Paulette White-Donnelly
Director Evaluation & Assistance Division
Phone: 703-516-1697
e-mail: donnellyPV@state.gov

Georgia K Hubert
Director Federal Assistance Division
Phone: 703-812-2526

Kimberly Triplett
Director Policy Division
Phone: 703-875-4079

FEDERAL

Department of Transportation

Department of Transportation
Headquarters
1200 New Jersey Ave SE
Washington, DC 20590
Phone: 202-366-4000
Phone: 866-377-8642
Fax: 202-366-7203
URL: www.dot.gov
e-mail: dot.comments@dot.gov

Description: The Department of Transportation (DOT) is responsible to ensure a fast, safe, efficient, accessible and convenient travel system. Recognizing that an efficient transportation system is vital not only to the movement of goods and services within our economy, but also to national defense issues, DOT plays a vital role in homeland security by keeping the transportation lines open in the event of an emergency, allowing rapid movement of personnel, equipment and supplies to effected areas. Jurisdiction of the administrations that make up the DOT include highway planning, development, and construction; motor carrier safety; urban mass transit; railroads; aviation; and the safety of waterways, ports, highways, and oil gas pipelines.

Mary E Peters
Secretary of Transportation

Robert Johnson
Chief of Staff

Brian Turmail
Assistant to the Secretary/Director Public Affairs
Phone: 202-366-4000

VAdm Thomas J Barrett
Acting Deputy Secretary & Administrator Pipeline & Hazardous Materials Safety Administration
Phone: 202-366-4433

Jeffrey N Shane
Undersecretary for Policy
Phone: 202-366-1815

Rosalind A Knapp
Acting General Counsel
Phone: 202-366-4702
e-mail: lindy.knapp@dot.gov

Tyler Duvall
Assistant Secretary for Transportation Policy
Phone: 202-366-0301

Andrew B Steinberg
Assistant Secretary for Aviation & International Affairs

Phyllis F Scheinberg
Assistant Secretary for Budget & Programs/CFO
Phone: 202-366-9191

Linda J Washington
Acting Assistant Secretary for Administration
Phone: 202-366-2332

Shane Karr
Assistant Secretary for Governmental Affairs
Phone: 202-366-4573
e-mail: shane.karr@dot.gov

Marion Blakey
Administrator Federal Aviation Administration
Phone: 202-267-3111

J Richard Capka
Administrator Federal Highway Administration
Phone: 202-366-0650

John H Hill
Administrator Federal Motor Carrier Safety Administration
Phone: 202-366-1927

Joseph H Boardman
Administrator Federal Railroad Administration
Phone: 202-493-6014

James S Simpson
Administrator Federal Transit Administration
Phone: 202-366-4040

Sean Connaughton
Maritime Administrator
Phone: 202-366-5823

Nicole Nason
Administrator National Highway Traffic Safety

Calvin L Scovel III
Inspector General
Phone: 202-366-1959

John A Bobo Jr
Acting Administrator Research & Innovative Technology Administration
Phone: 202-366-4180

Collister Johnson Jr
Administrator St Lawrence Seaway Development Corporation
Phone: 202-366-0091

Office of Inspector General
Department of Transportation
1200 New Jersey Ave SE
7th Floor
Washington, DC 20590
Phone: 202-366-1959
URL: www.oig.dot.gov
e-mail: oigpublicaffairs@iog.dot.gov

Description: Promotes effectiveness and heads off or stops, waste, fraud and abuse in the Department through audits and investigations.

Calvin L Scovel III
Inspector General
Phone: 202-366-1959

Todd J Zinser
Deputy Inspector General
Phone: 202-366-6767

Charles H Lee Jr
Assistant Inspector General for Investigations
Phone: 202-366-1967

Robin Hunt
Acting Assistant Inspector General for Aviation/Special Programs
Phone: 415-744-0420

Rebecca Batts
Assistant Inspector General for Surface/Maritime Programs
Phone: 202-366-5630

Office of Small & Disadvantaged Business Utilization
Department of Transportation
1200 New Jersey Ave SE
Washington, DC 20590
Phone: 202-366-1930
Phone: 800-532-1169
Fax: 202-366-7538
URL: www.osdbu.dot.gov

Description: The Office of Small and Disadvantaged Business Utilization assures the opportunity of small, disadvantaged and minority, women, and Service-Disabled Veteran-owned businesses to compete for inclusion in the Department of Transportation business.

Denise Rodriguez-Lopez
Director
Phone: 202-366-1930

Leonardo San Roman
Deputy Director
Phone: 202-366-1930

Gerardo Franco
Chief, Procurement Assistance Division
Phone: 202-366-1930
e-mail: jerry.franco@dot.gov

Arthur Jackson
Manager Regional Partnerships-Minority Business Center Division
Phone: 202-366-5344
e-mail: art.jackson@dot.gov

Nancy Strine
Chief, Financial Assistance Division
Phone: 202-366-5577
e-mail: nancy.strine@dot.gov

Patricia Hodge
Service Disabled Veteran & Women-Owned Business Advocate
Phone: 202-205-8992
e-mail: pat.hodge@dot.gov

Federal Aviation Administration
Department of Transportation
800 Independence Avenue SW
Washington, DC 20591
Phone: 202-267-3111
Phone: 866-835-5322
Fax: 202-267-5047
URL: www.faa.gov

Description: The Federal Aviation Administration is responsible for the safety of civilian aviation and aims to provide the safest, most efficient aerospace system in the world. First and foremost is the responsibility to issue and enforce regulations and standards related to the manufacture, operation, certification and maintenance of aircraft. It also is concerned with the rating and certification of airmen and airports and licenses commercial space and private sector launches.

Marion C Blakey
Administrator
Phone: 202-267-3111

Robert A Sturgell
Deputy Administrator
Phone: 202-267-8111
e-mail: robert.sturgell@faa.gov

Michael O'Malley
Chief of Staff
Phone: 202-267-7416

Ramesh K Punwani
Chief Financial Officer
Phone: 202-267-9105

David M Bowen
CIO & Assistant Administrator for Information Services
Phone: 202-493-4570

Lynne A Osmus
Assistant Administrator for Security & Hazardous Materials
Phone: 202-267-7211

Chris Rocheleau
Director Emergency Operations & Communications Office
Phone: 202-267-7211

James Filippatos
Assistant Administrator for International Aviation
Phone: 202-385-8900

Ruth Leverenz
Assistant Administrator Regions & Center Operations
Phone: 202-267-7369

Melanie A Alvord
Assistant Administrator for Communications
Phone: 202-267-3883

Daniel K Elwell
Assistant Administrator for Aviation Policy, Planning & Environment
Phone: 202-267-3927

Megan Rae Rosia
Assistant Administrator for Government & Industry Affairs
Phone: 202-267-3277

Ventris Gibson
Assistant Administrator for Human Resources Management
Phone: 202-267-3456

Kerry B Long
Chief Counsel
Phone: 202-267-3222

D Kirk Shaffer
Associate Administrator for Airports
Phone: 202-267-8738

David L Bennett
Director Airport Safety & Standards
Phone: 202-267-3053

Nicholas A Sabatini
Associate Administrator for Aviation Safety
Phone: 202-267-3131

Patricia Grace Smith
Associate Administrator for Commercial Space Transportation
Phone: 202-267-7793

Office of Aviation Safety
Federal Aviation Administration
800 Independence Avenue SW
Washington, DC 20591
Phone: 202-267-3131
URL: www.faa.gov/about/office_org/headquarters_offices/avs

Description: Responsible for the certification, production approval, and continued airworthiness of aircraft; certification of pilots, mechanics and others in safety-related positions; certification of all operational and maintenance enterprises in domestic civil aviation; developing regulations; civil flight operations; and oversight of approximately 7,500 US commercial airlines and air operators.

Nicholas A Sabatini
Associate Administrator
Phone: 202-267-3131

Margaret Gilligan
Deputy Associate Administrator
Phone: 202-267-7804

Vi Lipski
Director Quality & Integration
Phone: 202-493-5860

Stephen B Wallace
Director Accident Investigation
Phone: 202-267-9612

James J Ballough
Director Flight Standards Service
Phone: 202-267-8237

Anthony Ferrante
Director Air Traffic Safety Oversight Service
Phone: 202-267-5205

Office of Airport Safety & Standards
Federal Aviation Administration
800 Independence Avenue SW
Washington, DC 20591
Phone: 202-267-3053
Fax: 202-267-8821
URL:
www.faa.gov/about/office_org/headquarters_offices/arp/offices/a
as/

Description: The Office of Airport Safety and Standards has primary responsibility for all airport program matters related to airport safety, design, construction, maintenance, grant compliance and operations. It is comprised of three divisions-Engineering, Safety & Operations, and Compliance. The Safety & Operations division is responsible for the promotion of emergency operations, management planning and the direction of federal activities and their restoration after an attack or a natural disaster.

David L Bennett
Director
Phone: 202-267-3053
e-mail: david.bennet@faa.gov

James R White
Deputy Director
Phone: 202-267-7605
e-mail: james.white@faa.gov

Rick Marinelli
Airport Engineering Division Manager
Phone: 202-267-7669
e-mail: rick.marinelli@faa.gov

Ben Castellano
Airport Safety & Operations Division Manager
Phone: 202-267-3085
e-mail: ben.castellano@faa.gov

Charles Erhard
Airport Compliance Division Manager
Phone: 202-267-3085
e-mail: charles.erhard@faa.gov

Office of Security & Hazardous Materials
Federal Aviation Administration
800 Independence Avenue SW
Room 300E
Washington, DC 20591
Phone: 202-267-7211
Fax: 202-267-8496
URL: www.faa.gov/about/office_org/headquarters_offices/ash/

Description: To ensure and promote aviation safety and the integrity of the National Airspace System (NAS) and FAA employees and facilities from criminal and terrorist acts.

Lynne A Osmus
Assistant Administrator
Phone: 202-267-3111
e-mail: lynne.osmus@faa.gov

Claudio Manno
Deputy Assistant Administrator
Phone: 202-267-7211

William Wilkening Jr
Hazardous Materials Office
Phone: 202-267-7530
e-mail: william.wilkening@faa.gov

Chris Rocheleau
Emergency Operations & Communications
Phone: 202-267-7211

Thomas D Ryan
Operations Office
Phone: 202-267-7211

Bruce Herron
Internal Security & Investigations Office
Phone: 202-493-5405

Federal Highway Administration
Department of Transportation
1200 New Jersey Ave SE
Washington, DC 20590
Phone: 202-366-0660
Fax: 202-366-7239
URL: www.fhwa.dot.gov

Description: The mission is to keep America moving safely through proactive leadership, innovation, and excellence in service. It coordinates highway transportation programs in cooperation with states and other partners. The FHWA also manages a comprehensive research, development, and technology program.

J Richard Capka
Administrator
Phone: 202-366-0650

Frederick G Wright
Executive Director
Phone: 202-366-2242

Jeffrey F Paniati
Associate Administrator for Operations
Phone: 202-366-0408

Jeffrey Lindley
Associate Administrator for Safety
Phone: 202-366-2288

Elizabeth Alicandri
Director Safety Programs Office
Phone: 202-366-6409

Dennis C Judycki
Associate Administrator for Research, Development & Technology
Phone: 202-493-3999

Ian Grossman
Associate Administrator for Public Affairs
Phone: 202-493-3999

Mary B Phillips
Associate Administrator for Policy & Governmental Affairs
Phone: 202-366-0585

Gloria M Shepherd
Associate Administrator for Planning, Environment & Realty
Phone: 202-366-0116

James Ray
Chief Counsel
Phone: 202-366-0740

Albert T Park
Chief Financial Officer
Phone: 202-366-0622

Federal Motor Carrier Safety Administration
Department of Transportation
1200 New Jersey Ave SE
Washington, DC 20590
Phone: 202-366-9999
Phone: 800-832-5660
URL: www.fmcsa.dot.gov

Description: The Federal Motor Carrier Safety Administration activities contribute to ensuring safety in motor carrier operations through the following: development and enforcement of safety regulations; improving safety information systems and commercial motor vehicle technologies; strengthening equipment and operation standards; and increasing safety awareness. The Administration works with federal, state and local enforcement agencies, the motor carrier industry, labor safety interest groups and others.

John H Hill
Administrator
Phone: 202-366-1927

David H Hugel
Deputy Administrator
Phone: 202-366-1927

Rose A McMurray
Chief Safety Officer
Phone: 202-366-1927

Federal Railroad Administration
Department of Transportation
1120 Vermont Avenue NW
7th Floor
Washington, DC 20005
Phone: 202-493-6000
Fax: 202-493-6013
URL: www.fra.dot.gov

Description: The Federal Railroad Administration promotes and enforces rail safety regulations; administers railroad assistance programs; provides for the rehabilitation of NE Corridor rail passenger service; consolidates government support of rail transportation activities; and conducts research and development in support of improved railroad safety and national rail policy.

Joseph H Boardman
Administrator
Phone: 202-493-6014

Clifford C Eby
Deputy Administrator
Phone: 202-493-6015

S Mark Lindsey
Chief Counsel
Phone: 202-493-6052

Jo Strang
Associate Administrator for Safety
Phone: 202-493-6300

Mark E Yachmetz
Associate Administrator for Railroad Development
Phone: 202-493-6381

Steven W Kulm
Director Public Affairs
Phone: 202-493-6024
e-mail: steve.kulm@dot.gov

Office of Safety
Federal Railroad Administration
1120 Vermont Avenue NW
Washington, DC 20590
Mailing Address: MS 25
Phone: 202-493-6300

Phone: 202-493-6244
Fax: 202-493-6309
URL: www.fra.dot.gov/us/content/3
e-mail: correspondence@fra.dot.gov

Description: The Federal Railroad Administration Office of Safety plans, organizes, coordinates and administers railroad safety practices throughout the railroad industry and the States. It accomplishes this with more than 600 federal safety inspectors who operate out of eight regional offices nationally.

Jo Strang
Associate Administrator
Phone: 202-493-6300

Michael J Logue
Deputy Associate Administrator Safety Compliance & Program Implementation
Phone: 202-493-6308

Grady C Cothen Jr
Deputy Associate Administrator Safety Standards & Program Development
Phone: 202-493-6308

Edward W Pritchard
Safety Assurance & Compliance Office
Phone: 202-493-6244

William Schoonover
Hazardous Materials Division Director
Phone: 202-493-6244

John Leeds Jr
Safety Analysis Office
Phone: 202-493-6207

Federal Transit Administration
Department of Transportation
1200 New Jersey Ave SE
East Bldg 4/5th Floors
Washington, DC 20590
Phone: 202-366-4043
Phone: 866-377-8642
Fax: 202-366-9854
URL: www.fta.dot.gov

Description: The Federal Transit Administration assists in developing improved mass transportation systems for cities and communities nationwide. In providing financial, technical and planning assistance, the agency provides leadership and resources for safe and technologically advanced local transit systems while assisting in the development of local and regional traffic reduction.

James S Simpson
Administrator
Phone: 202-366-4040

Sherry E Little
Deputy Administrator
Phone: 202-366-4325

David B Horner
Chief Counsel

Wes Irvin
Associate Administrator Communications & Congressional Affairs Office
Phone: 202-366-4043

Susan Borinsky
Associate Administrator Planning & Environment

Barbara A Sisson
Associate Administrator Research, Demonstration & Innovation

Transit Safety & Security
Federal Transit Administration
1200 New Jersey Ave SE
Washington, DC 20590
Phone: 202-366-3526
URL: http://transit-safety.volpe.dot.gov

Description: The Transit Safety & Security program is part of a continuous effort to secure the nation's transit infrastructure. The implemented program by the FTA focuses on these three priorities: training all transit employees and supervisors; improving emergency preparedness; and increasing public awareness of security issues.

Michael Taborn
Director
Phone: 202-366-3526
e-mail: michael.taborn@dot.gov

Bridget Zamperini
Department of Homeland Security Coordinator
Phone: 202-366-0306
e-mail: bridget.zamperini@dot.gov

Anthony Tisdale
Emergency Coordinator-Emergency Management/Transit Security
Phone: 202-366-3949
e-mail: anthony.tisdale@dot.gov

Ken Lord
Emergency Coordinator-Emergency Management/Transit Security
Phone: 202-366-2836
e-mail: ken.lord@dot.gov

Gergory Brown
Emergency Coordinator-Emergency Management/Transit Security
Phone: 202-366-1622
e-mail: gregory.brown@dot.gov

Timothy Braxton
National Transit Database
Phone: 202-366-1646
e-mail: timothy.braxton@dot.gov

Carole Ferguson
Bus Safety & Security
Phone: 202-366-0219
e-mail: carole.ferguson@dot.gov

Richard Gerhart
Transit Security Management Team Leader
Phone: 202-366-8970
e-mail: richard.gerhart@dot.gov

Levern McElveen
Transit Safety Management Team Leader
Phone: 202-366-1651
e-mail: levern.mcelveen@dot.gov

Iyon Rosario
Child Safety, Operation Lifesaver, Light Rail, COOP
Phone: 202-366-2010
e-mail: iyon.rosario@dot.gov

Nancy Solkowski
Ferry Program, Information Sharing, National Resource Center, Transit Watch, Communications
Phone: 202-366-0124
e-mail: nancy.solkowski@dot.gov

Research and Innovative Technology Administration (RITA)
Department of Transportation
1200 New Jersey Ave SE
Washington, DC 20590
Phone: 202-366-4180
Fax: 202-366-3759
URL: www.rita.dot.gov

Description: Dedicated to the advancement of the Department of Tranportation priorities for innovation and research technologies that will improve the nation's mobility, promote economic growth, and ultimately deliver a better transportation system. The Administration fosters the exchange of ideas and information and is part university research lab and part Silicon Valley entrepreneurial company.

John Bobo
Deputy Administrator
Phone: 202-366-4180

Paul Feenstra
Governmental, International & Public Affairs Office
Phone: 202-366-4792

Dr Jan Brecht-Clark
Research, Development & Technology Office
Phone: 202-366-5447

Dr Curtis J Tompkins
Director Volpe National Transportation Systems Center
Phone: 617-494-2223

Frank Tupper
Director Transportation Safety Institute
Phone: 405-954-3153

Maritime Administration
Department of Transportation
1200 New Jersey Ave SE
West Bldg, 2nd Floor
Washington, DC 20590
Phone: 202-366-5823
Phone: 800-996-2723
Fax: 202-366-3889
URL: www.marad.dot.gov
e-mail: pao.marad@dot.gov

Description: The Maritime Administration strengthens the US maritime transportation system - including infrastructure, industry and labor - to meet the economic and security needs of the nation. MARAD promotes development and maintenance of an adequate, well-balanced, US merchant marine, sufficient to carry the nation's domestic waterborne commerce and a substantial portion of its waterborne foreign commerce, and capable of serving as a naval and military auxiliary in time of war or national emergency. The Administration also seeks to ensure that the

United States enjoys adequate shipbuilding and repair service, efficient ports, effective intermodal water and land transportation systems, and reserve shipping capacity in time of national emergency.

Sean T Connaughton
Administrator
Phone: 202-366-5823

Julie A Nelson
Deputy Administrator
Phone: 202-366-5823

Elizabeth Megginson
Chief Counsel
Phone: 202-366-5711

Gregory Hall
Director International Affairs Office
Phone: 202-366-5772

Shannon M Russell
Director Congressional & Public Affairs Office
Phone: 202-366-5807

Susan Clark
Media Relations/Public Affairs Officer
Phone: 202-366-5807

James Caponiti
Associate Administrator National Security Office
Phone: 202-366-5400

Office of National Security
Maritime Administration
1200 New Jersey Ave SE
West Bldg, 2nd Floor
Washington, DC 20590
Phone: 202-366-5400
Fax: 202-493-2180

Description: Administers MARAD's national security related programs that provide commercial and government-owned shipping capabilities in times of national emergency and to meet Department of Defense strategic sealift requirements.

James E Caponiti
Associate Administrator
Phone: 202-366-5400
e-mail: james.caponiti@dot.gov

William H Cahill
Ship Operations Office
Phone: 202-366-1875
e-mail: william.cahill@dot.gov

Thomas M P Christensen
National Security Plans Office/Emergency Preparedness
Phone: 202-366-5900
e-mail: thomas.christensen@dot.gov

Taylor E Jones II
Sealift Support Office
Phone: 202-366-2323
e-mail: sealift.marad@dot.gov

National Highway Traffic Safety Administration
Department of Transportation
1200 New Jersey Ave SE
West Bldg

Washington, DC 20590
Phone: 888-327-4236
URL: www.nhtsa.dot.gov

Description: Sets and enforces safety performance standards for motor vehicles and equipment, and through grants to state and local governments enables them to conduct effective local highway safety programs. The National Highway Traffic Safety Administration also investigates safety defects in motor vehicles, helps state and local communities reduce the threat of drunk drivers, and provides consumer information on motor vehicle safety topics.

Nicole Nason
Administrator

Pipeline & Hazardous Materials Safety Administration
1200 New Jersey Ave SE
East Bldg, 2nd Floor
Washington, DC 20590
Phone: 202-366-4433
Fax: 202-366-3666
URL: www.phmsa.dot.gov

Description: This safety administration provides the Department with a more focused research organization and separate operating administration for pipeline and hazardous materials transportation safety. It oversees the safety of the more than 800,000 daily shipments of hazardous materials in the US and the 64 percent of the nation's energy that is transported by pipelines. It is dedicated to working toward the elimination of transportation-related deaths and injuries in hazardous materials and pipeline transportation, and to promoting transportation solutions that enhance communities and protect the natural environment.

VAdm Thomas J Barrett
Administrator
Phone: 202-366-4433

Krista L Edwards
Deputy Administrator
Phone: 202-366-4433

Stacey Gerard
Assistant Administrator/Chief Safety Officer
Phone: 202-366-4433

David Kunz
Chief Counsel
Phone: 202-366-4400

Jeff Wiese
Acting Associate Administrator for Pipeline Safety
Phone: 202-366-4595

Dr Ted Wilke
Acting Associate Administrator for Hazardous Materials Safety
Phone: 202-366-0656

James E Wiggins
Associate Administrator for Governmental, International & Public Affairs
Phone: 202-366-4831
e-mail: publicaffairs@phmsa.dot.gov

Office of Pipeline Safety
Pipeline & Hazardous Materials Safety Administration
1200 New Jersey Ave SE

East Bldg, 2nd Floor
Washington, DC 20590
Phone: 202-366-4595
Fax: 202-366-4566
URL: http://ops.dot.gov

Description: Administers the Department's national regulatory program assuring the safe transportation of natural gas, petroleum and other hazardous materials by pipeline. The Office develops regulations and other risk management approaches to assure safety in design, construction, testing, operation, maintenance, and emergency response to pipeline facilities.

Jeff Wiese
Acting Associate Administrator
Phone: 202-366-4595
e-mail: jeff.wiese@dot.gov

William Gute
Deputy Associate Administrator
Phone: 202-366-4595
e-mail: william.gute@dot.gov

Rita Freeman-Kelly
Executive Director
Phone: 202-366-4595

Florence Hamn
Director Pipeline Safety Regulations
Phone: 202-366-3015

Richard Huriaux
Director Pipeline Safety National Standards
Phone: 202-366-4565

Tom Fortner
Director Pipeline Safety State Programs
Phone: 202-366-4564
e-mail: tom.fortner@dot.gov

Stan Kastansas
Director Pipeline Safety Enforcement & Program Performance
Phone: 202-366-3844

Joy Kadnar
Director Pipeline Safety Engineering & Emergency Support
Phone: 202-366-0568

Office of Hazardous Materials Safety
Pipeline & Hazardous Materials Safety Administration
1200 New Jersey Ave SE
East Bldg, 2nd Floor
Washington, DC 20590
Phone: 202-366-0656
Fax: 202-366-5713
URL: http://hazmat.dot.gov

Description: Responsible for putting into force and coordinating a national safety program for the transportation of hazardous materials by air, rail, highway and water. The functions of the Office of Hazardous Materials Safety can be consolidated into five categories: regulatory development, enforcement, training and information dissemination, domestic and international standards, and inter-agency cooperative activities.

Dr Ted Willke
Acting Associate Administrator
Phone: 202-366-0656
e-mail: ted.willke@dot.gov

Bob Richard
Deputy Associate Administrator
Phone: 202-366-0656

Edward T Mazzullo
Hazardous Materials Standards Office
Phone: 202-366-8553
e-mail: edward.mazzullo@dot.gov

Charles Hochman
Hazardous Materials Technology Office
Phone: 202-366-4545
e-mail: charles.hockman@dot.gov

Richard W Boyle
Radioactive Materials Branch
Phone: 202-366-4545
e-mail: richard.boyle@dot.gov

Delmer F Billings
Hazardous Materials Special Permits & Approvals Office
Phone: 202-366-4511
e-mail: delmer.billings@dot.gov

Ryan Posten
Hazardous Materials Enforcement Office
Phone: 202-366-4700

Douglas Smith
Enforcement Officer
Phone: 202-366-4700

David L Sargent
Hazardous Materials Initiatives & Training Office
Phone: 202-366-4900
e-mail: david.sargent@dot.gov

Duane Pfund
International Standards
Phone: 202-366-0656

Office of Hazardous Materials-Eastern Region
Pipeline & Hazardous Materials Safety Administration
820 Bear Tavern Road
Suite 306
West Trenton, NJ 08628
Phone: 609-989-2256
Fax: 609-989-2277
URL: www.phmsa.dot.gov/about/regions/eastern.html

Description: Area of coverage: Connecticut, Delaware, District of Columbia, Maine, Maryland, Massachusetts, New Hampshire, New Jersey, New York, Pennsylvania, Rhode Island, Vermont, Virginia, West Virginia.

Colleen Abbenhaus
Chief, Hazmat
Phone: 609-989-2256

Byron Coy
Acting Director, Pipeline
Phone: 609-989-2256

Anthony Murray
Transportation Specialist
Phone: 609-989-2181
e-mail: anthony.murray@dot.gov

Office of Hazardous Materials- Southern Region
Pipeline & Hazardous Materials Safety Administration
233 Peachtree Street NE
Suite 602
Atlanta, GA 30303
Phone: 404-832-1140
Fax: 404-832-1168
URL: www.phmsa.dot.gov/about/regions/southern.html

Description: Area of coverage: Alabama, Florida, Georgia, Mississippi, North Carolina, Puerto Rico, Tennessee, South Carolina.

John Heneghan
Chief, Hazmat
Phone: 404-832-1140

Linda Daugherty
Director, Pipeline
Phone: 404-832-1140

Tay Rucker
Transportation Specialist
Phone: 404-832-1145
e-mail: walter.rucker@dot.gov

Office of Hazardous Materials-Central Region
Pipeline & Hazardous Materials Safety Administration
2300 E Devon Avenue
Suite 478
Des Plaines, IL 60018-4696
Phone: 847-294-8580
Fax: 847-294-8590
URL: www.phmsa.dot.gov/about/regions/central.html

Description: Area of coverage: Illinois, Indiana, Iowa, Kentucky, Michigan, Minnesota, Missouri, Nebraska, North Dakota, Ohio, South Dakota, Wisconsin.

Kevin Boehne
Chief
Phone: 847-294-8580

Barbara J Waller
Transportation Specialist
Phone: 847-294-8589
e-mail: barbara.waller@dot.gov

Office of Hazardous Materials-Southwestern Region
Pipeline & Hazardous Materials Safety Administration
8701 S Gessner Road
Suite 1110
Houston, TX 77074
Phone: 713-272-2820
Fax: 713-272-2821
URL: www.phmsa.dot.gov/about/regions/southwestern.html

Description: Area of coverage: Arkansas, Colorado, Kansas, Louisiana, New Mexico, Oklahoma, Texas.

Billy C Hines
Chief, Hazmat
Phone: 713-272-2820

Rodrick M Seeley
Director, Pipeline
Phone: 713-272-2820

Aubrey Campbell
Transportation Specialist
Phone: 713-272-2822
e-mail: audrey.campbell@dot.gov

Office of Hazardous Materials-Western Region
Pipeline & Hazardous Materials Safety Administration
3401 Centrelake Drive
Suite 550B
Ontario, CA 91761
Phone: 909-937-3279
Fax: 909-390-5142
URL: www.phmsa.dot.gov/about/regions/western.html

Description: Area of coverage: Alaska, Arizona, California, Hawaii, Idaho, Montana, Nevada, Oregon, Utah, Washington, Wyoming.

Dan Derwey
Chief

Patricio Romero
Transportation Specialist
Phone: 909-937-3279
e-mail: pat.romero@dot.gov

St. Lawrence Seaway Development Corporation
Department of Transportation
1200 New Jersey Ave SE
Suite W32-300
Washington, DC 20590
Phone: 202-366-0091
Phone: 800-785-2779
Fax: 202-366-7147
URL: www.seaway.dot.gov
e-mail: research@sls.dot.gov

Description: The St. Lawrence Seaway Development Corporation (SLSDC) serves the maritime transportation industries by promoting and maintaining safe, reliable and efficient and environmentally responsible waterways for commercial and noncommercial vessels between the Great Lakes and the Atlantic Ocean. The SLSDC cooperates with the St. Lawrence Seaway Authority of Canada which has operational headquarters located in Massena, NY.

Collister Johnson Jr
Administrator
Phone: 202-366-0091

Craig H Middlebrook
Deputy Administrator
Phone: 202-366-0105

Anita K Blackman
Chief of Staff
Phone: 202-366-0091
e-mail: anita.k.blackman@sls.dot.gov

Kevin P O'Malley
Budget & Programs Office
Phone: 202-366-8982
e-mail: kevin.omalley@sls.dot.gov

Rebecca A McGill
Trade Development & Public Affairs Office
Phone: 202-366-5418
e-mail: rebecca.a.mcgill@sls.dot.gov

Sal Pisani
Associate Administrator-Operations Headquarters
Phone: 315-764-3209

Surface Transportation Board
395 East Street SW
Washington, DC 20423
Phone: 202-245-0245
URL: www.stb.dot.gov

Description: The Surface Transportation Board is decisionally independent from the DOT but affiliated with the Department administratively. It is responsible for the economic regulation of interstate surface transportation, primarily railroads, within the United States, and strives to ensure that competitive, efficient, and safe transportation services are provided to meet the needs of shippers, receivers, and consumers. The Board is also charged with promoting, where appropriate, substantive and procedural regulatory reform for the resolution of disputes.

Charles D Nottingham
Chairman
Phone: 202-245-0200

W Douglas Buttrey
Vice Chairman
Phone: 202-245-0220

Francis P Mulvey
Board Member
Phone: 202-245-0210

Leland L Gardner
Economics, Environmental Analysis & Administration Office
Phone: 202-245-0324

Melvin F Clemens Jr
Compliance & Consumer Assistance Office
Phone: 202-245-0278

Dan G King
Congressional & Public Services Office
Phone: 202-245-0230

Ellen D Hanson
General Counsel
Phone: 202-245-0260

David M Konschnik
Proceedings Office
Phone: 202-245-0350

Vernon A Williams
Secretary to the Board
Phone: 202-245-0335

FEDERAL

Department of the Treasury

Department of the Treasury
Headquarters
1500 Pennsylvania Avenue NW
Washington, DC 20220
Phone: 202-622-2000
Phone: 202-622-1100
Fax: 202-622-6415
URL: www.ustreas.gov

Description: The primary federal agency responsible for the economic and financial prosperity and security of the US, and thus responsible for a wide range of activities including advising the President on economic and financial issues, promoting the President's growth agenda, and enhancing corporate governance in financial institutions. Included in the Department are the following law enforcement bureaus: Internal Revenue Service-Criminal Investigations, Financial Crimes Enforcement Network, and Office of Foreign Assets Control. The Department oversees critical functions in enforcement, economic policy development, and international treaty negotiation. Treasury agents respond to and investigate bombings, arsons and shootings wherever they occur. They attack terrorist funding activities, and enforce economic sanctions on foreign terrorist organizations and countries that sponsor terrorism.

Henry M Paulson Jr
Secretary
Phone: 202-622-1100

Robert M Kimmitt
Deputy Secretary
Phone: 202-622-1080

James Wilkinson
Chief of Staff
Phone: 202-622-1906

Taiya Smith
Executive Secretary/Deputy Chief of Staff
Phone: 202-622-2000

Denise Dick
White House Liaison

Neel Kashkari
Senior Advisor to the Secretary

Robert Hoyt
General Counsel

Anna Escobedo Cabral
Treasurer
Phone: 202-622-0100

Clay Lowery
Under Secretary International Affairs (Acting)

Kevin I Fromer
Assistant Secretary Legislative Affairs

Wesley T Foster
Assistant Secretary for Management

Richard M Holcomb
Chief Financial Officer (Acting)

Edward Roback
Chief Information Officer (Acting)
Phone: 202-622-1200

Stuart Levey
Under Secretary Terrorism & Financial Intelligence
Phone: 202-622-8260

Eric Solomon
Assistant Secretary Tax Policy

Dennis Schindel
Inspector General (Acting)

J Russell George
Inspector General for Tax Administration
Phone: 202-622-6500

Michele Davis
Assistant Secretary Public Affairs/Director Policy Planning
Phone: 202-622-2960

Brookly McLaughlin
Deputy Assistant Secretary Public Affairs

Office of Terrorism & Financial Intelligence
Department of the Treasury
1500 Pennsylvania Avenue NW
Washington, DC 20220
Phone: 202-622-8260
Phone: 202-622-1466
Fax: 202-622-1914
URL: www.ustreas.gov/offices/enforcement/

Description: Marshals the Department of the Treasury's intelligence and enforcement functions with the aims of safeguarding the financial system against illicit use and combating rogue nations, terrorist facilitators, money launderers, drug kingpins, and other national security threats. Its bureaus and affiliates include: Office of Foreign Assets Control, Financial Crime Enforcement Network, Treasury Executive Office for Asset Forfeiture, and IRS-Criminal Investigation.

Stuart A Levey
Under Secretary
Phone: 202-622-8260

Patrick M O'Brien
Assistant Secretary Terrorist Financing

Janice B Gardner
Assistant Secretary Intelligence & Analysis
Phone: 202-622-1841

Daniel L Glaser
Deputy Assistant Secretary Terrorist Financing & Financial Crimes
Phone: 202-622-1466
e-mail: daniel.glaser@do.treas.gov

Kelly Wolslayer
Director Emergency Programs

Eric Hampl
Director Executive Office for Asset Forfeiture

Office of Foreign Assets Control
Office of Terrorism & Financial Intelligence
1500 Pennsylvania Avenue NW
Treasury Annex
Washington, DC 20220
Phone: 202-622-2500
Phone: 800-540-6322
Fax: 202-622-1657
URL: www.ustreas.gov/offices/enforcement/ofac/
e-mail: ofac_feedback@do.treas.gov

Description: The Office of Foreign Assets Control administers and enforces economic and trade sanctions based on United States foreign policy and national security goals against targeted foreign countries, terrorists, international narcotics traffickers, and those engaged in activities related to the proliferation of weapons of mass destruction. The Office acts under Presidential wartime and national emergency powers, as well as under authority granted by specific legislation, to impose controls on transactions and freeze foreign assets under United States jurisdiction. Many of the sanctions are based on United Nations and other international mandates, are multilateral in scope and involve close cooperation with allied governments.

Adam J Szubin
Director
Phone: 202-622-2500

Financial Crimes Enforcement Network
Department of the Treasury
PO Box 39
Vienna, VA 22183-0039
Phone: 703-905-3591
Fax: 703-905-3690
URL: www.fincen.gov
e-mail: webmaster@fincen.gov

Description: The mission of the Financial Crimes Enforcement Network is to safeguard the US financial system from the abuses of financial crime, including terrorist financing, money laundering, and other illicit activity. This is achieved through the support of law enforcement, intelligence, and regulatory agencies sharing and analysis of financial intelligence; networking people, ideas and information; administering the Bank Secrecy Act; and building global cooperation with counterpart financial intelligence units.

James H Freis Jr
Director

William F Baity
Deputy Director

Cynthia Clark
Deputy Chief Counsel
Phone: 703-905-3590

Patrick Conlon
Associate Director Analysis & Liaison Division

Diane K Wade
Associate Director Management Programs
Phone: 703-905-3770

Jack Cunniff
Associate Director Client Liaison & Services Division
Phone: 703-905-3586

Jamal El-Hindi
Associate Director Regulatory Policy & Programs Division

Office of Domestic Finance-Financial Institutions
Department of the Treasury
1500 Pennsylvania Avenue NW
Room 2326
Washington, DC 20220
Phone: 202-622-1703
Phone: 202-622-2610
Fax: 202-622-2027
URL: www.ustreas.gov/offices/domestic-finance/
e-mail: ofip@do.treas.gov

Description: The Office of Financial Institutions coordinates the Department's efforts regarding legislation and regulation of financial institutions, security markets and legislation that affects federal agencies that regulate or insure financial institutions. It coordinates the Department's efforts on ensuring the resiliency of the financial services sector in the wake of a terrorist attack. The Office supports the Under Secretary for Domestic Finance as Director of the Securities Investors Protection Corporation.

Robert K Steel
Under Secretary for Domestic Finance

Matthew Scogin
Senior Advisor to the Under Secretary

David Nason
Acting Assistant Secretary for Financial Institutions

Jeff Stolzfoos
Senior Advisor

Dan Iannicola Jr
Financial Education Deputy Assistant Secretary
Phone: 202-622-5770
e-mail: dan.iannicola@do.treas.gov

Mario Ugoletti
Financial Institutions Policy Director
Phone: 202-622-0715
e-mail: mario.ugoletti@do.treas.gov

Kimberly Reed
Community Development Financial Institutions Fund Director
Phone: 202-622-8381
e-mail: arthur.garcia@do.treas.gov

Jeffrey S Bragg
Terrorism Risk Insurance Program (TRIP) Executive Director

Phone: 202-622-6770
e-mail: jeffrey.bragg@do.treas.gov

Office of Critical Infrastructure Protection & Compliance Policy
Financial Institutions
1500 Pennsylvania Avenue NW
Washington, DC 20220
Phone: 202-622-0887
Fax: 202-622-2310
URL:
www.ustreas.gov/offices/domestic-finance/financial-institution/cip/
e-mail: ocip@do.treas.gov

Description: Coordinates the Department's development and implementation of policies regarding: the enforcement of statutes and regulations within the financial sector, including money laundering, terrorist financing, and identity theft; the protection of the critical infrastructure of the financial services sector; and the sharing of information among financial institutions and between private and public sectors, including the sharing of suspicious information pursuant to the Bank Secrecy Act.

Scott Parsons
Critical Infrastructure Protection & Compliance Policy Deputy Assistant Secretary
Phone: 202-622-0887
e-mail: scott.parsons@do.treas.gov

Valerie Abend
Director

Charles Klingman
Deputy Director

Alcohol & Tobacco Tax & Trade Bureau (TTB)
Department of the Treasury
1310 G Street NW
Washington, DC 20220
Phone: 202-927-5000
Fax: 202-927-5611
URL: www.ttb.gov
e-mail: ttbquestions@ttb.treas.gov

Description: To collect alcohol, tobacco, firearms, and ammunition excise taxes; to ensure that these products are labeled, advertised and marketed in accordance with the law; to administer the laws and regulations in a manner that protects the consumer and the revenue, and promotes voluntary compliance.

John J Manfreda
Administrator

Victoria I McDowell
Deputy Administrator

Theresa M Glasscock
Chief of Staff

Robert M Tobiassen
Chief Counsel

Robert J Hughes
Chief Information Officer

Susan B Stewart
Executive Liaison for Industry & State Matters

William H Foster
Assistant Administrator HQ Operations

Mary G Ryan
Assistant Administrator Field Operations

Cheri D Mitchell
CFO/Assistant Administrator Management

Roger L Bowling
National Revenue Center Director
Phone: 513-684-3334

Gail H Davis
International Trade Division Director

Deborah Pereira
Risk Mangement Staff Chief

Ronald Hancock
Tax Audit Division
Phone: 202-927-9595

Robert Angelo
Trade Investigations Division Director
Phone: 202-927-9200

Internal Revenue Service (IRS)
Department of the Treasury
500 N Capitol Street NW
Washington, DC 20221
Mailing Address: 1111 Constitution Ave NW, 20224
Phone: 202-874-6748
Phone: 800-829-1040
Fax: 202-622-5756
URL: www.irs.gov

Description: As the Treasury's largest bureau, it provides America's taxpayers service by helping them understand and meet their tax responsibilities and by applying the tax law with integrity and fairness to all. The IRS deals directly with more Americans than any other institution, public or private. It also is one of the world's most efficient tax administrators. In 2005, the IRS collected more than $2.2 trillion dollars in revenue and processed more than 228 million tax returns. It cost taxpayers 42 cents for each $100 collected by the IRS in 2006.

Kevin M Brown
Acting Commissioner
Phone: 202-622-9511

Donald L Korb
Chief Counsel
Phone: 202-622-3300

Sarah Hall Ingram
Appeals Chief

Frank Keith
Communications & Liaison
Phone: 202-622-4010

Criminal Investigation
Internal Revenue Service
1111 Constitution Avenue NW
Room 2501
Washington, DC 20224
Phone: 202-622-3200
Fax: 202-622-2703
URL: www.ustreas.gov/irs/ci/

Description: It is the law enforcement arm of the IRS and serves the American public by investigating potential criminal violations of the Internal Revenue Code and related financial crimes in a manner that fosters confidence in the tax system and compliance with the law and has developed a Compliance Strategy to assist in identifying, developing, and investigating cases. When money is derived through illegal sources, the primary concern for the criminals, which in the context of homeland security, included terrorists, is to legitimize the dollars, often using legitimate businesses, and the manipulation of numerous currency in schemes that are often international in scope. As part of criminal charges against an individual, Criminal Investigations (CI) makes effective use of the forfeiture statues, which deprive individuals and organizations of their illegally obtained cash and assets. In the case of terrorists, this may prevent a terrorist act from being planned, or even carried out.

Eileen C Mayer
Chief
Phone: 202-622-3200

John H Omhoff Jr
Deputy Chief
Phone: 202-622-6190

Patricia S Reid
Communications & Educations Division
Phone: 202-622-7796
e-mail: patti.reid@ci.irs.gov

Andre Martin
Operations, Policy & Support Division Director
Phone: 202-622-4100

Office of Small Business Development
Office of Small & Disadvantaged Business Utilization
1500 Pennsylvania Avenue NW
Washington, DC 20220
Mailing Address: MC 655 15th Street/6099
Phone: 202-622-0530
Fax: 202-622-4963
URL: www.ustreas.gov/offices/management/dcfo/osbdu
e-mail: osbd@do.treas.gov

Description: The Department of the Treasury's Office of Small Business Development (OSBD) assists, counsels, and advises small businesses of all types, including small disadvantaged business, women-owned small businesses, veteran-owned small businesses, service disabled veteran-owned small businesses, and small businesses located in historically underutilized business zones, on procedures for contracting with Treasury.

Virginia Bellamy-Graham
Director
Phone: 202-622-2826
e-mail: va.bellamy-graham@do.treas.gov

Jackie Barber
Business Analyst, JWOD, Mentor-Protege
Phone: 202-622-8213
e-mail: jackie.barber@do.treas.gov

Renee Fitzgerald
Business Analyst, Women-Owned, Veteran-Owned
Phone: 202-622-0793
e-mail: renee.fitzgerald@do.treas.gov

Pamela Wilson
Business Analyst, HUBZone
Phone: 202-622-1071
e-mail: pamela.wilson@do.treas.gov

FEDERAL

Environmental Protection Agency

Environmental Protection Agency
Headquarters
1200 Pennsylvania Avenue NW
Ariel Rios Building
Washington, DC 20460
Phone: 202-272-0167
Phone: 202-564-4700
Fax: 202-501-1450
URL: www.epa.gov

Description: The Environmental Protection Agency (EPA) protects human health and safeguards the natural environment. The EPA is responsible for ensuring that America's air, water, and food are kept clean and safe, as well as preventing pollution to our nation's ecosystems, and improving waste management. Homeland security is a critical aspect of the mission of the EPA. While much of the Agency's focus has been on combating environmental crimes, it has taken on a broader role in protecting our homeland. Their participation allows agents to respond to any threat to the nation's infrastructure including water supplies, chemical storage and manufacturing facilities, or illegal importation of hazardous substances, as well as any other incident that might require the expertise of the environmental enforcement agency. Every EPA program and region has reallocated resources to address the issues of homeland security.

Stephen L Johnson
Administrator
Phone: 202-564-4700
e-mail: johnson.stephen@epa.gov

Marcus C Peacock
Deputy Administrator
Phone: 202-564-4711
e-mail: peacock.marcus@epa.gov

Bill A Roderick
Acting Inspector General
Phone: 202-566-2391

Roger R Martella
General Counsel
Phone: 202-564-8040

Lyons Gray
Chief Financial Officer
Phone: 202-564-1151
e-mail: ocfoinfo@epa.gov

Stephanie Daigle
Associate Administrator Congressional & Intergovernmental Relations
e-mail: daigle.stephanie@epa.gov

Mary Upchurch Kruger
Homeland Security Officer
Phone: 202-564-6978
e-mail: kruger.mary@epa.gov

Rafael DeLeon
Cooperative Environmental Management
Phone: 202-233-0090
e-mail: deleon.rafael@epa.gov

Brian Mannix
Policy, Economics & Innovation
Phone: 202-564-0446
e-mail: baker.michael@epa.gov

Susan L Biro
Chief Administrative Law Judge
Phone: 202-564-6259

William H Sanders
Acting Director, Children's Health Protection
Phone: 202-564-2188
e-mail: sanders.william@epa.gov

Scott C Fulton
Judge, Environmental Appeals Board
Phone: 202-233-0122
e-mail: fulton.scott@epa.gov

Eurika Durr
Clerk, Environmental Appeals Board
Phone: 202-233-0122
e-mail: durr.eurika@epa.gov

Michael Baker
Acting Director, Environmental Education
Phone: 202-564-0446
e-mail: baker.michael@epa.gov

Vanessa Vu
Science Advisory Board Director
Phone: 202-343-9874
e-mail: vu.vanessa@epa.gov

National Response Team
National Response Center
c/o USCG, Room 2111B
2100 Second Street SW
Washington, DC 20593
Phone: 202-267-2180
Phone: 800-424-8802
Fax: 202-267-1322
URL: www.nrt.org

Description: The National Response Team is an organization of 16 federal departments and agencies responsible for technical assistance and the coordination on emergency preparedness, response and recovery to any national natural, technological or other environmental incident, of which the EPA co-chairs with the US Coast Guard. These incidents include: oil spills, hazardous substances, pollutants and contaminants, and weapons of mass destruction. The NRT is primarily a national planning, policy and coordinating body and does not respond directly to incidents. The National Response Center (number listed above) is the sole point of contact for reporting spills, gathering and distributing spill data and serves as the operations center for the NRT.

Office of Homeland Security
EPA
1200 Pennsylvania Avenue NW
Washington, DC 20460
Mailing Address: MC 1109A
Phone: 202-564-6978
Fax: 202-501-0026
URL: www.epa.gov/homelandsecurity/

Description: The Office of Homeland Security within the EPA was created in 2003 in order to coordinate security efforts along with the federal agency, ensuring that policy is carried out and that redundancies and gaps are identified and addressed.

Mary Upchurch Kruger
Director
Phone: 202-564-6978
e-mail: kruger.mary@epa.gov

Jonathan Edwards
Associate Director
Phone: 202-564-9197
e-mail: edwards.jonathan@epa.gov

Valarie Bynum
Staff Assistant
Phone: 202-564-4189
e-mail: bynum.valarie@epa.gov

Office of Small & Disadvantaged Business Utilization
EPA
1200 Pennsylvania Avenue NW
MC 1230A
Washington, DC 20460
Phone: 202-566-2075
Fax: 202-566-0266
URL: www.epa.gov/osdbu

Description: The Office of Small and Disadvantaged Business Utilization supports the protection of the environment and human health by fostering opportunities within the Environmental Protection Agency for partnerships, contracts, subagreements, and grants for small and socioeconomically disadvantaged concerns.

Jeanette L Brown
Director
Phone: 202-564-4100
e-mail: brown.jeanettel@epa.gov

Cassandra R Freeman
Deputy Director
Phone: 202-564-4100
e-mail: freeman.cassandra@epa.gov

Susan Galliher
Special Assistant to the Director
Phone: 202-564-0403
e-mail: galliher.susan@epa.gov

Kimberly Patrick
Attorney Advisor
Phone: 202-564-5386
e-mail: patrick.kimberly@epa.gov

Denean Jones
Information Management Specialist
Phone: 202-564-4142
e-mail: jones.denean@epa.gov

Lamont Norwood
Socioeconomic Program Officer
Phone: 202-564-0928
e-mail: norwood.lamont@epa.gov

Office of Air & Radiation
EPA
1200 Pennsylvania Avenue NW
Ariel Rios Building
Washington, DC 20460
Phone: 202-564-7400
Fax: 202-501-0986
URL: www.epa.gov/oar/

Description: Develops national programs, regulations and technical policies for controlling air pollution and radiation exposure. It is concerned with energy efficiency, climate change, pollution prevention, indoor and outdoor air quality, pollution from vehicles and engines, industrial air pollution, acid rain, radon, stratospheric ozone depletion and radiation protection.

Bill Wehrum
Acting Assistant Administrator
Phone: 202-564-7400
e-mail: wehrum.bill@epa.gov

Elizabeth Craig
Deputy Assistant Administrator
Phone: 202-564-7400
e-mail: craig.beth@epa.gov

Donald E Zinger
Chief of Staff
Phone: 202-564-1109
e-mail: zinger.don@epa.gov

John Beale
Senior Policy Advisor
Phone: 202-564-1176
e-mail: beale.jon@epa.gov

David Bloomgren
Acting Communications Director
Phone: 202-564-2903

Steve Page
Air Quality Planning & Standards Director
Phone: 919-541-5618

Brian J McLean
Atmospheric Programs Director
Phone: 202-564-9081

Margo T Oge
Transportation & Air Quality Director
Phone: 202-564-1682

Elizabeth Cotsworth
Radiation & Indoor Air Director
Phone: 202-343-9320

Office of Enforcement & Compliance Assurance
EPA
1200 Pennsylvania Avenue NW
Washington, DC 20460
Phone: 202-564-2440
URL: www.epa.gov/compliance

Description: The Office of Enforcement and Compliance Assurance works in partnership with EPA regional offices, state and tribal governments and other federal agencies to ensure compliance with the nation's environmental laws. Together these agencies and offices seek to maximize compliance and reduce threats to public health.

Granta Nakayama
Assistant Administrator
Phone: 202-564-2440
e-mail: nakayama.granta@epa.gov

Catherine R McCabe
Principal Deputy Assistant Administrator
Phone: 202-564-2440
e-mail: mccabe.catherine@epa.gov

Michael M Stahl
Compliance Office Director
Phone: 202-564-2280
e-mail: stahl.michael@epa.gov

Walker Smith
Civil Enforcement Office Director
Phone: 202-564-2220
e-mail: smith.walker@epa.gov

Peter J Murtha
Criminal Enforcement, Forensics & Training Office Director
Phone: 202-564-2480
e-mail: murtha.peter@epa.gov

Susan Bromm
Site Remediation & Enforcement Office Director
Phone: 202-564-5110

Barry E Hill
Environmental Justice Office Director
Phone: 202-564-2515
e-mail: environmental-justice-epa@epa.gov

David Kling
Federal Facilities Enforcement Office Director
Phone: 202-564-2510
e-mail: kling.dave@epa.gov

Anne Norton Miller
Federal Activities Office Director
Phone: 202-564-5400

Margaret Schneider
Planning, Policy Analysis & Communications Acting Director
Phone: 202-564-4666

Office of Criminal Enforcement, Forensics & Training
Office of Enforcement & Compliance Assurance
1200 Pennsylvania Avenue NW

MC 2231A
Washington, DC 20460
Phone: 202-564-2480
Fax: 202-501-0599
URL: www.epa.gov/compliance/about/offices/oceft.html

Description: The Office of Criminal Enforcement, Forensics and Training provides a board range of technical and forensic services for civil and criminal investigative support, and oversees the Environmental Protection Agency's enforcement and compliance assurance training programs for federal, state and local environmental professionals. The Office also provides direct investigative, technical and forensic support to the Department of Homeland Security, FBI and/or other law enforcement agencies to help detect, prevent and respond to homeland security-related environmental, biological and chemical incidents.

Peter J Murtha
Director
Phone: 202-564-2480
e-mail: murtha.peter@epa.gov

Ellen C Stough
Deputy Director
Phone: 202-564-2480
e-mail: stough.ellen@epa.gov

Ella R Barnes
Criminal Investigation Division Director
Phone: 202-564-2490
e-mail: barnes.becky@epa.gov

Michael R Fisher
Legal Counsel & Resource Management Division Director
Phone: 202-564-2485
e-mail: fisher.mike@epa.gov

Diana A Love
National Enforcement Investigations Center
Phone: 303-462-9001
e-mail: love.dianaa@epa.gov

Office of Solid Waste & Emergency Response
EPA
1200 Pennsylvania Avenue NW
MC5101T
Washington, DC 20460
Phone: 202-556-0200
Fax: 202-566-0207
URL: www.epa.gov/swerrims

Description: OWSER provides policy, guidance and direction for the Agency's solid waste and emergency response programs. It develops guidelines for the land disposal of hazardous waste and underground storage tanks, provides technical assistance to all levels of government in establishing safe practices in waste management, and administers the Brownfields program which supports state and local governments in redeveloping and reusing potentially contaminated sites.

Susan Parker Bodine
Assistant Administrator
Phone: 202-556-0200
e-mail: bodine.susan@epa.gov

Barry N Breen
Principal Deputy Assistant Administrator

Phone: 202-566-0200
e-mail: breen.barry@epa.gov

David Lloyd
Brownsfields Cleanup & Redevelopment Office
Phone: 202-566-2731
e-mail: lloyd.david@epa.gov

John Reeder
Federal Facilities Restoration & Reuse Office
Phone: 703-603-9089
e-mail: reeder.john@epa.gov

Marsha Minter
Innovation Partnership & Communication Office
Phone: 202-566-0205
e-mail: minter.marsha@epa.gov

Renee Wynn
Program Management Office
Phone: 202-566-1884
e-mail: wynn.renee@epa.gov

Deborah Dietrich
Emergency Management Office
Phone: 202-564-8600
e-mail: dietrich.debbie@epa.gov

Office of Emergency Management
Office of Solid Waste & Emergency Response
1200 Pennsylvania Avenue NW
Room 5104A
Washington, DC 20460
Phone: 202-564-8600
Phone: 800-424-9346
URL: www.epa.gov/emergencies/

Description: The new Office of Emergency Management consolidates emergency prevention, preparedness and response duties by joining together the Oil Program Center, Emergency
Response & Removal Center and CEPPO. It works with EPA
partners, federal agencies, state and local response agencies, and
industry to maintain superior response capabilities and prevent
health and environmental emergencies.

Deborah Dietrich
Director
Phone: 202-564-8600
e-mail: dietrich.debbie@epa.gov

Dana Tulis
Deputy Director
Phone: 202-564-7938
e-mail: tulis.dana@epa.gov

Steve Hawthorn
National Decontamination Team
Phone: 513-487-2420
e-mail: hawthorn.steve@epa.gov

Dana Stalcup
Business Operations Center
Phone: 202-564-2089
e-mail: stalcup.dana@epa.gov

Mark Mjoness
National Planning & Preparedness Division Director
Phone: 202-564-1976
e-mail: mjoness.mark@epa.gov

Kathleen Jones
Evaluation & Communications Division Director
Phone: 202-564-8353

R Craig Matthiessen
Regulation & Policy Development Division Director
Phone: 202-564-8016
e-mail: matthiessen.craig@epa.gov

Gilberto Irizarry
Program Operations & Coordination Division Director
Phone: 202-564-7982
e-mail: irizarry.gilberto@epa.gov

Office of Research & Development
EPA
1200 Pennsylvania Avenue NW
Washington, DC 20460
Mailing Address: MC 8101R
Phone: 202-564-6620
URL: www.epa.gov/ORD/

Description: The Office of Research and Development (ORD) is
the scientific arm of the EPA. The Agency relies on sound science to safeguard both human health and the environment. The
Office conducts research on ways to prevent pollution, protect
human health and reduce risk. It is organized into three national
laboratories, four national centers, and two offices located in 14
facilities in Washington, DC and around the country.

George M Gray PhD
Assistant Administrator
Phone: 202-564-6620
e-mail: gray.george@epa.gov

Michael Brown
Associate Assistant Administrator
Phone: 202-564-6766
e-mail: brown.michael@epa.gov

William Benson
Office of the Science Advisor (Acting)
Phone: 850-934-9208
e-mail: benson.william@epa.gov

Rebecca Calderon
Office of Science Policy (Acting)
Phone: 202-564-6812
e-mail: calderon.rebecca@epa.gov

National Homeland Security Research Center
Office of Research & Development
26 West Martin Luther King Drive
Cincinnati, OH 45268
Phone: 513-569-7907
Fax: 513-487-2555
URL: www.epa.gov/nhsrc/

Description: The Center manages, coordinates and supports
homeland security research and technical assistance efforts. It
develops and delivers reliable, responsive expertise and products
based on scientific research and evaluations of technology.

Andy Avel
Deputy Director Management
e-mail: avel.andy@epa.gov

Peter Jutro
Deputy Director Science & Policy
e-mail: jutro.peter@epa.gov

Nancy Adams
Decon & Consequence Management Division Director
e-mail: adams.nancy@epa.gov

Kim Fox
Water Infrastructure Protection Division Director
e-mail: fox.kim@epa.gov

Cindy Sonich-Mullin
Threat & Consequence Assessment Division Director
e-mail: sonich-mullin.cynthia@epa.gov

Office of Water
EPA
1200 Pennsylvania Avenue NW
Ariel Rios Building
Washington, DC 20460
Mailing Address: MC 4101M
Phone: 202-564-5700
URL: www.epa.gov/OW/
e-mail: OW-General@epa.gov

Description: The Clean and Safe Water goal of the EPA New
Strategic Plan includes: ensuring drinking water is safe; restore
and maintain oceans, watersheds and their aquatic ecosystems to
protect human health; support economic and recreational activities; and provide healthy habitat for fish, plants, and wildlife.

Benjamin Grumbles
Assistant Administrator
Phone: 202-564-5700
e-mail: grumbles.benjamin@epa.gov

Michael H Shapiro
Deputy Assistant Administrator
Phone: 202-564-5700
e-mail: shapiro.mike@epa.gov

Cynthia Dougherty
Ground Water & Drinking Water Office Director
Phone: 202-564-3750
e-mail: dougherty.cynthia@epa.gov

Ephraim King
Science & Technology Office Director
Phone: 202-566-0430
e-mail: king.ephraim@epa.gov

Denise Keehner
Standards & Health Protection Division Director
Phone: 202-566-1566
e-mail: keehner.denise@epa.gov

James A Hanlon
Wastewater Management Office Director
Phone: 202-564-0748
e-mail: hanlon.jim@epa.gov

Craig Hooks
Wetlands, Oceans & Watersheds Office Director
Phone: 202-566-1146
e-mail: hooks.craig@epa.gov

Office of Ground Water & Drinking Water
Office of Water
1200 Pennsylvania Avenue NW
Ariel Rios Building
Washington, DC 20460-0003
Phone: 202-564-3750
Fax: 202-564-3753
URL: www.epa.gov/safewater

Description: The Office of Ground and Drinking Water, together
with states, tribes, and other partners, protects public health by
ensuring safe drinking water and protecting ground water. Together with the EPA's regional offices it also oversees the implementation of the Safe Drinking Water Act.

Cynthia Dougherty
Director
Phone: 202-564-3750
e-mail: dougherty.cynthia@epa.gov

Nanci Gelb
Deputy Director
Phone: 202-564-3750
e-mail: gelb.nanci@epa.gov

Steve Heare
Drinking Water Protection Division
Phone: 202-564-3751
e-mail: heare.steve@epa.gov

David Travers
Water Security Division
Phone: 202-564-4638
e-mail: travers.david@epa.gov

Pamela Barr
Standards & Risk Management Division
Phone: 202-564-3752
e-mail: barr.pamela@epa.gov

Ann Codrington
Prevention Branch
Phone: 202-564-4688
e-mail: codrington.ann@epa.gov

Ronald Bergman
Protection Branch
Phone: 202-564-3823
e-mail: bergman.ronald@epa.gov

Patricia Tidwell-Shelton
Threats Analysis, Prevention & Preparedness Branch
Phone: 202-564-6319
e-mail: tidwell-shelton.patricia@epa.gov

Eric Burneson
Target & Analysis Branch
Phone: 202-564-5250
e-mail: burneson.eric@epa.gov

Office of International Affairs
EPA
1200 Pennsylvania Avenue NW
Washington, DC 20460
Mailing Address: MC 2610R
Phone: 202-564-6613
Fax: 202-565-2411
URL: www.epa.gov/oia/

Description: The Office of International Affairs manages the Agency's involvement in international policies and programs that cut across agency offices and regions. It provides leadership and coordination on behalf of the EPA and acts as the focal point on international environmental matters.

Judith E Ayres
Assistant Administrator
Phone: 202-564-6600
e-mail: ayres.judith@epa.gov

Office of Prevention, Pesticides & Toxic Substances
EPA
1200 Pennsylvania Avenue NW
Washington, DC 20460
Mailing Address: MC 7101M
Phone: 202-564-2902
URL: www.epa.gov/oppts

Description: The Office of Prevention, Pesticides and Toxic Substances develops national strategies for toxic substance control and promotes pollution prevention and the public's right to know about chemical risks.

James B Gulliford
Assistant Administrator
Phone: 202-564-2902
e-mail: gulliford.jim@epa.gov

Jim Jones
Principal Deputy Assistant Administrator
Phone: 202-564-2902

Debbie Edwards
Pesticide Programs Office Director
Phone: 703-305-7090
e-mail: edwards.debbie@epa.gov

Charles M Auer
Pollution Prevention & Toxics Office Director
Phone: 202-564-3810
e-mail: auer.charles@epa.gov

FEDERAL

Federal Communications Commission

Federal Communications Commission

Headquarters
445 12th Street SW
Washington, DC 20554
Phone: 888-225-5322
Phone: 202-418-1000
Fax: 866-418-0232
URL: www.fcc.gov
e-mail: fccinfo@fcc.gov

Description: An independent government agency, directly responsible to Congress and established by the Communications Act of 1934, it is charged with regulating interstate and international communications by radio, television, wire, satellite and cable. Communications during emergencies and crises must be available for public safety, health, defense and emergency personnel, as well as all consumers in need. Thus the FCC's goal for homeland security is to provide leadership in evaluating and strengthening the nation's communications infrastructure, to ensure rapid restoration of that infrastructure in the event of disruption and that essential public health and safety personnel have effective communications services available in an emergency situation. Their jurisdiction covers the 50 states, the District of Columbia, and US possessions. It is directed by five Commissioners appointed by the President and confirmed by the Senate for 5-year terms, except when filling an unexpired term. The President designates one of the Commissioners to serve as Chairperson. Only three Commissioners may be members of the same political party. None of them can have a financial interest in any Commission-related business.

Kevin J Martin
Chairman
Phone: 202-418-1000
e-mail: KJMWEB@fcc.gov

Michael J Copps
Commissioner
Phone: 202-418-2000
e-mail: michael.copps@fcc.gov

Jonathan S Adelstein
Commissioner
Phone: 202-418-2300
e-mail: jonathan.adelstein@fcc.gov

Robert M McDowell
Commissioner
Phone: 202-418-2200
e-mail: robert.mcdowell@fcc.gov

Deborah Taylor Tate
Commissioner
Phone: 202-418-2500
e-mail: dtaylortateweb@fcc.gov

Daniel Gonzalez
Chief of Staff
Phone: 202-418-1000
e-mail: daniel.gonzalez@fcc.gov

Marlene H Dortch
Office of the Secretary
Phone: 202-418-0300
e-mail: marlene.dortch@fcc.gov

Sam Feder
General Counsel
Phone: 202-418-2159
e-mail: sam.feder@fcc.gov

Michelle Carey
Senior Legal Advisor, Media Issues
Phone: 202-418-1000
e-mail: michelle.carey@fcc.gov

Ian Dillner
Legal Advisor, Wireless Issues
Phone: 202-418-1000
e-mail: ian.dillner@fcc.gov

Kent R Nilsson
Acting Inspector General
Phone: 202-418-0476
e-mail: kent.nilsson@fcc.gov

Catherine C Bohigian
Chief, Office of Strategic Planning & Policy Analysis
Phone: 202-418-2030
e-mail: catherine.bohigian@fcc.gov

Julius Knapp
Chief, Office of Engineering & Technology
Phone: 202-418-2470
e-mail: julius.knapp@fcc.gov

Anthony Dale
Managing Director
Phone: 202-418-1919
e-mail: anthony.dale@fcc.gov

Richard L Sippel
Chief Administrative Law Judge
Phone: 202-418-2280
e-mail: richard.sippel@fcc.gov

David Fiske
Media Relations Director
Phone: 202-418-0503
e-mail: david.fiske@fcc.gov

Enforcement Bureau
FCC
445 12th Street SW
Room 7-C723
Washington, DC 20554
Phone: 202-418-7450
Fax: 202-418-2810
URL: www.fcc.gov/eb

Description: The primary organizational unit within the Federal Communications Commission that is responsible for the enforcement of the Communications Act and the Commission's rules, orders and terms and conditions of station authorizations. The major areas of enforcement handled by the Enforcement Bureau are consumer protection enforcement; local competition enforcement; and public safety/homeland security enforcement.

Kris Monteith
Bureau Chief
Phone: 202-418-1098
e-mail: kris.monteith@fcc.gov

Ellen Engleman Connors
Senior Deputy Bureau Chief
Phone: 202-418-0137

Robert Ratcliffe
Deputy Bureau Chief
Phone: 202-418-2606
e-mail: robert.ratcliffe@fcc.gov

Susan McNeil
Deputy Bureau Chief
Phone: 202-418-7619
e-mail: sue.mcneil@fcc.gov

Gene Fullano
Acting Deputy Bureau Chief
Phone: 202-418-7332
e-mail: christopher.olsen@fcc.gov

Michael Carowitz
Associate Bureau Chief/Chief of Staff
Phone: 202-418-0026
e-mail: michael.carowitz@fcc.gov

Hillary S DeNigro
Investigations & Hearings Chief
Phone: 202-418-7334
e-mail: hillary.denigro@fcc.gov

Kathryn Berthot
Spectrum Enforcement Division Chief
Phone: 202-418-7454
e-mail: kathy.berthot@fcc.gov

Janice Wise
Media Relations Director
Phone: 202-418-8165
e-mail: janice.wise@fcc.gov

Colleen Heitkamp
Telecommunications Consumers Division Chief
Phone: 202-418-7320
e-mail: colleen.heitkamp@fcc.gov

International Bureau
FCC
445 12th Street SW
Washington, DC 20554
Phone: 202-418-0437
URL: www.fcc.gov/ib/

Description: The International Bureau strives to connect the globe through prompt authorizations, innovative spectrum management and responsible global leadership.

Helen Domenici
Bureau Chief
Phone: 202-418-0437
e-mail: helen.domenici@fcc.gov

John Giusti
Deputy Bureau Chief
Phone: 202-418-1407
e-mail: john.giusti@fcc.gov

Roderick Porter
Deputy Bureau Chief
Phone: 202-418-0437
e-mail: roderick.porter@fcc.gov

Breck Blalock
Chief of Staff/Associate Bureau Chief
Phone: 202-418-8191
e-mail: breck.blalock@fcc.gov

James L Ball
Policy Division Chief
Phone: 202-418-1460
e-mail: james.ball@fcc.gov

Robert Nelson
Satellite Division Chief
Phone: 202-418-2341
e-mail: robert.nelson@fcc.gov

Kathryn O'Brien
Strategic Analysis & Negotiations Division Chief
Phone: 202-418-0439
e-mail: kathryn.obrien@fcc.gov

Media Bureau
FCC
445 12th Street SW
Washington, DC 20554
Phone: 202-418-7200
URL: www.fcc.gov/mb
e-mail: mbinfo@fcc.gov

Description: The Media Bureau develops, recommends and administers the licensing programs and policy relating to electronic media in the US and its territories.

Monica Desai
Bureau Chief
Phone: 202-418-7200

Roy J Stewart
Senior Deputy Bureau Chief
Phone: 202-418-7200
e-mail: roy.stewart@fcc.gov

Thomas Horan
Chief of Staff
Phone: 202-418-7200
e-mail: thomas.horan@fcc.gov

Marybeth Murphy
Policy Division Chief
Phone: 202-418-2120
e-mail: marybeth.murphy@fcc.gov

Peter Doyle
Audio Division Chief
Phone: 202-418-2700
e-mail: peter.doyle@fcc.gov

Michael S Perko
Communications & Industry Information Chief
Phone: 202-418-7200
e-mail: michael.perko@fcc.gov

Barbara Kreisman
Video Division Chief
Phone: 202-418-1600

Public Safety & Homeland Security Bureau
445 12th Street SW
Washington, DC 20554
Phone: 202-418-1300
URL: www.fcc.gov/homeland
e-mail: PSHSBinfo@fcc.gov

Description: To fully and effectively carry out its role in promoting homeland security, network protection, redundancy, interoperability and reliability the FCC has established the following objectives: develop policies that promote access to effective communications services in emergency situations; evaluate and strengthen measures for protecting the nation's critical communications infrastructure; facilitate rapid restoration of such infrastructure after a disruption by any cause; coordinate with industry and other federal, state, tribal and local agencies on matters of public safety, disaster management and homeland security; act swiftly on such matters; participate in international organizations and conferences for the protection of global communications infrastructure.

Derek Poarch
Bureau Chief
Phone: 202-418-0642

Kenneth P Moran
Deputy Bureau Chief/Chief Preparedness Officer
Phone: 202-418-0802
e-mail: kenneth.moran@fcc.gov

Tim Peterson
Chief of Staff
Phone: 202-418-1575
e-mail: timothy.peterson@fcc.gov

Leon Jackler
Director, Public Safety Outreach & Coordination
Phone: 202-418-0946
e-mail: leon.jackler@fcc.gov

Jeffery Goldthorp
Communications Systems Analysis Division Chief
Phone: 202-418-1096
e-mail: jeffery.goldthorp@fcc.gov

Dana Shaffer
Policy Division Chief
Phone: 202-418-0832
e-mail: dana.shaffer@fcc.gov

Richard D Lee
Public Communications Outreach & Operations Division Chief
Phone: 202-418-1104
e-mail: richard.lee@fcc.gov

Homeland Security Policy Council
FCC
445 12th Street SW
Washington, DC 20554
Phone: 202-418-7450
Phone: 888-225-5322
URL: www.fcc.gov/hspc
e-mail: homeland@fcc.gov

Description: The Homeland Security Policy Council was formed in 2001 to assist the Commission in: evaluating and strengthening measures for protecting US telecommunications, broadcast and other communications infrastructure and facilities from further terrorist attacks; ensuring rapid restoration of US telecommunications, broadcast, and other communications infrastucture and facilities after dispruption by a terrorist threat or attack; and ensuring that public safety, public health, and other emergency and defense personnel have effective communications service available to them in the immediate aftermath of any terrorist attack.

Wireless Telecommunications Bureau (WTB)
FCC
445 12th Street SW
Washington, DC 20554
Phone: 202-418-0600
Fax: 202-418-0787
URL: http://wireless.fcc.gov

Description: Handles all FCC domestic wireless telecommunications programs and policies, except those involving satellite communications or broadcasting, including licensing, enforcement and regulatory functions. Wireless communications services include cellular telephone, personal communications services, paging, and other commercial and private radio services. The bureau is also responsible for implementing the competitive bidding authority for spectrum auctions.

Fred Campbell
Bureau Chief
Phone: 202-418-0600
e-mail: fred.campbell@fcc.gov

Lois Jones
Assistant Bureau Chief, Management
Phone: 202-418-0600
e-mail: lois.jones@fcc.gov

Roger Noel
Mobility Division Chief
Phone: 202-418-0620
e-mail: roger.noel@fcc.gov

John Branscome
Spectrum & Competitive Policy Division Chief
Phone: 202-418-1310
e-mail: john.branscome@fcc.govv

Joel Taubenblatt
Broadband Division Chief
Phone: 202-418-2487
e-mail: joel.taubenblatt@fcc.gov

Margaret Wiener
Auctions & Spectrum Access Division Chief
Phone: 202-418-0660
e-mail: margaret.wiener@fcc.gov

Office of Communications Business Opportunities
FCC
445 12th Street SW
Washington, DC 20554
Phone: 202-418-0990
Phone: 888-225-5322
Fax: 202-418-0235
URL: www.fcc.gov/ocbo
e-mail: ocboinfo@fcc.gov

Description: The Office of Communications Business Opportunities (OCBO) promotes telecommunications business opportunities for small, minority and women-owned businesses. Working with entrepreneurs, industry, public interest organizations, and individuals, it provides information about FCC policies, increases ownership and employment opportunities, fosters diverse voices and viewpoints over the airwaves, and encourages participation in FCC proceedings. The Office mails information on Commission notices and new service opportunities, co-hosts auction seminars, offers small business guides and advises the Commissioners.

Carolyn Fleming Williams
Director
Phone: 202-418-1026
e-mail: carolyn.williams@fcc.gov

Eric Malinen
Senior Legal Advisor/SBA Liaison
Phone: 202-418-0995
e-mail: eric.malinen@fcc.gov

Maura McGowan
Telecommunications Policy Analyst
Phone: 202-418-0987
e-mail: maura.mcgowan@fcc.gov

Belford V Lawson III
Attorney Advisor
Phone: 202-418-7264
e-mail: belford.lawson@fcc.gov

Karen M Beverly
Consumer & Industry Affairs Specialist/Management Assistant
Phone: 202-418-0993
e-mail: karen.beverly@fcc.gov

Office of Engineering and Technology
FCC
445 12th Street SW
Washington, DC 20554
Phone: 202-418-2470
Fax: 202-418-1944
URL: www.fcc.gov/oet/
e-mail: oetinfo@fcc.gov

Description: Advises the Commission on engineering matters and provides leadership and management in creating new opportunities for competitive technologies and services for the American public.

Julius P Knapp
Chief

Phone: 202-418-2470
e-mail: julius.knapp@fcc.gov

Geraldine Matise
Policy & Rules Division Chief
Phone: 202-418-2472

Rashmi Doshi
Laboratory Division Chief
Phone: 301-362-3000

Office of the Secretary
FCC
445 12th Street SW
Washington, DC 20554
Phone: 202-418-0300
URL: www.fcc.gov/osec

Description: The Office of the Secretary facilitates the Commission's decision-making process and administers the FCC library collection.

Marlene H Dortch
Secretary of the Commission
Phone: 202-418-0300
e-mail: marlene.dortch@fcc.gov

William F Caton
Deputy Secretary
Phone: 202-418-0304
e-mail: william.caton@fcc.gov

Sheryl A Segal
Associate Secretary Information Resources
Phone: 202-418-0234
e-mail: sheryl.segal@fcc.gov

Jacqueline R Coles
Manager Agenda & Publications Group
Phone: 202-418-2318
e-mail: jackie.coles@fcc.gov

Media Security & Reliability Council
FCC
445 12th Street SW
Washington, DC 20554
Phone: 202-418-1600
URL: www.mediasecurity.org

Description: As a federal advisory committee, the mission of the Media Security and Reliability Council is to prepare a comprehensive national strategy for securing and sustaining broadcast and multi-channel video programming (MVPD) facilities throughout the US during terrorist attacks, natural disasters and other threats or attacks nationwide. The council develops strategies that ensure the operation of broadcast and MVPD facilities before, during and after a major event and recommends how to detect, prepare for, prevent, protect against, respond to and recover from such incidents. These recommendations will assure optimal reliability of broadcast and MVPD facilities.

Barbara Kreisman
Video Division Chief, Media Bureau
Phone: 202-418-1605
e-mail: bkreisma@fcc.gov

Fred Young
Senior VP News, Hearst-Argyle Television

Phone: 212-887-6812
e-mail: fyoung@hearst.com

David Rehr
President/CEO, National Association of Broadcasters

John Lawson
President/CEO, Association of Public Television Stations

Kevin Klose
President/CEO, National Public Radio

Kyle McSlarrow
President/CEO, National Cable and Telecommunications Association

Dennis J FitzSimons
President/COO, Tribune Company

Robert C Wright
President, NBC

Michael D Eisner
CEO, Walt Disney Company

Bob Cahill
Vice Chairman, Univision Communications, Inc

Robert Decherd
President/Chairman/CEO, Belo Corp

David J Barrett
President/CEO, Hearst-Argyle Television, Inc

Jay Adrick
VP Strategic Development, Harris Broadcast Communications

Marshall Pagon
President/CEO, Pegasus Communications Corp

William F Baker
President/CEO, Thirteen/WNET

L Lowry Mays
CEO, Clear Channel Communications, Inc

Lew Dickey Jr
Chairman/CEO, Cumulus Radio

Catherine L Hughes
Chair, Radio One, Inc

Sharon Percy Rockefeller
President/CEO, WETA

Rick Sellers
President/General Manager, Sellers Broadcasting, Inc

Glenn Britt
Chairman/CEO, Time Warner Cable

Sumner Redstone
President/COO, Viacom, Inc

Brian L Roberts
President, Comcast Corporation

Jim Kennedy
Chairman/CEO, Cox Enterprises, Inc

Peter Brubaker
President/CEO, Susquehanna Communications

Jim Williams
Sr VP Global Broadcast, Associated Press

Chase Carey
CEO, The DirecTV Group

Charles Ergen
Chairman/CEO, EchoStar Communications Corp

Hugh Panero
President/CEO, XM Satellite Radio, Inc

Dean Olmstead
President/CEO, SES Americom, Inc

Joseph R Wright Jr
President/CEO, PanAmSat Corporation

Kevin Mulloy
President/COO, Intelsat Global Service Corporation

Gary Briese
Executive Director, International Association of Fire Chiefs

Harlin R McEwen
International Association of Chiefs of Police

Jim Taiclet
President/CEO, American Tower Corporation

Byron St Clair
President, National Translator Association

Kevin McGinnis
Program Advisor, National Association of State EMS Directors

Jack Gates
President/COO, National Captioning Institute

K Rupert Murdoch
Chairman/CEO, News Corp

Barbara Cochran
President, RTNDA

Rudolph Giuliani
Chairman/CEO, Giuliani Partners, LLC

Cheryl Heppner
Exec Director, N Virginia Resource Ctr for the Deaf & Hard of Hearing Persons

Charles E Allen
Assistant Secretary, Department of Homeland Security

David Donovan
President, MSTV, Inc

Melanie Brunson
Executive Director, American Council of the Blind

Network Reliability & Interoperability Council
FCC
445 12th Street SW
Washington, DC 20554
Phone: 703-592-8021
URL: www.nric.org

Description: The purpose of the Council is to provide recommendations for the FCC and the telecommunications industry to ensure that, if implemented, will assure optimal reliability, security, interoperability and interconnectivity, and accessibility to, public telecommunications networks and the Internet, including emergency communications networks. The council partners with the FCC, the communications industry and public safety to enhance emergency communications networks and homeland security. The Seventh Council (NRIC VII) held its final meeting on December 16, 2005.

FEDERAL

Nuclear Regulatory Commission

Nuclear Regulatory Commission

Headquarters
One White Flint N
11555 Rockville Pike
Rockville, MD 20852-2738
Mailing Address: NRC, Washington, DC 20555
Phone: 301-415-7000
Phone: 800-368-5642
Fax: 301-415-1672
URL: www.nrc.gov
e-mail: opa@nrc.gov

Description: Developed to protect public health and safety, and the environment from the effects of radiation from nuclear reactors, materials, and waste facilities. The Nuclear Regulatory Commission (NRC) regulates these materials and facilities to promote defense and security. NRC is not connected with defense matters or nuclear weapons, but carries out its mission by policy making, regulations, standards development, oversight, licensing and certification, research, advisory activities, inspection, enforcement, emergency and preparedness programs, international programs, state and tribal programs, and nuclear security and safeguards. NRC operates four regional offices in addition to its main headquarters: King of Prussia, PA; Lisle, IL; Atlanta, GA; Arlington, TX.

Dale E Klein
Chairman
Phone: 301-415-1750

Edward McGaffigan Jr
Commissioner
Phone: 301-415-1800
e-mail: cmrmcgaffigan@nrc.gov

Jeffrey S Merrifield
Commissioner
Phone: 301-415-1855
e-mail: cmrmerrifield@nrc.gov

Gregory B Jaczko
Commissioner
Phone: 301-415-7000

Peter B Lyons
Commissioner
Phone: 301-415-8420

Annette L Vietti-Cook
Commission Secretary
Phone: 301-415-1969

Karen Cyr
General Counsel
Phone: 301-415-1743

Luis A Reyes
Executive Director for Operations
Phone: 301-415-1700

Janice D Lee
Director International Programs
Phone: 301-415-1780

Hubert Bell
Inspector General
Phone: 301-415-5930

Rebecca L Schmidt
Director Office of Congressional Affairs
Phone: 301-415-1776

Eliot B Brenner
Director Public Affairs
Phone: 301-415-8200

William McCabe
Chief Financial Officer

John F Cordes Jr
Director for Office of Commission Appellate Adjudication

Office of the Executive Director for Operations

NRC
One White Flint N
11555 Rockville Pike
Rockville, MD 20852
Phone: 301-415-1700
URL: www.nrc.gov

Description: The Executive Director for Operations is the COO of the Commission and is in charge of the day-to-day operational and administrative functions. This includes supervising and coordinating policy development, agency operational activities, and implementation of Commission policy directives.

Luis A Reyes
Executive Director Operations
Phone: 301-415-1700

Vonna L Ordaz
Assistant for Operations
Phone: 301-415-1703

William F Kane
Deputy Executive Director Reactor and Preparedness Programs
Phone: 301-415-1713

Martin J Virgilio
Deputy Executive Director Materials, Waste, Research, State Tribal & Compliance Programs
Phone: 301-415-1705

Darren B Ash
Deputy Executive Director Information Services/CIO
Phone: 301-415-7443

Office of Nuclear Security & Incident Response

NRC
One White Flint N
11555 Rockville Pike
Rockville, MD 20852-2738
Phone: 301-415-8003
Fax: 301-415-6382
URL: www.nrc.gov/about-nrc/organization/nsirfuncdesc.html

Description: Develops overall agency policy and provides management direction for evaluation and assessment of technical issues involving security at nuclear facilities, and is the agency safeguards and security interface with the Department of Homeland Security (DHS), the intelligence and law enforcement communities, Department of Energy (DOE), and other agencies. Develops emergency preparedness policies, regulations, programs, and guidelines for both currently licensed nuclear reactors and potential new nuclear reactors. Provides technical expertise regarding emergency preparedness issues and interpretations, and conducts and directs the NRC program for response to incidents, and is the agency emergency preparedness and incident response interface with the DHS, Federal Emergency Management Agency (FEMA) and other federal agencies.

Roy P Zimmerman
Director
Phone: 301-415-8003

William M Dean
Deputy Director
Phone: 301-415-0174

Patricia Holahan
Director Security Policy Division
Phone: 301-415-6828

Michael C Layton
Material, Transportation & Waste Security Chief
Phone: 301-415-5751

Daniel Dorman
Director Security Operations Division
Phone: 301-415-6828

Melvyn Leach
Director Preparedness & Response Division
Phone: 301-415-2334

Office of Investigations

NRC
One White Flint N
11555 Rockville Pike
Rockville, MD 20852
Phone: 301-415-2373

Description: Develops policy, procedures and quality control standards for investigations; plans, coordinates, directs and executes office administrative affairs; and keeps commission principals informed of matters as they affect public health and safety matters.

Guy P Caputo
Director
Phone: 301-415-2373

James A Fitzgerald
Deputy Director
Phone: 301-415-3476

Ernest Wilson III
Region I-Investigations Field Office
Phone: 610-337-5243

Cheryl Montgomery
Region II-Investigations Field Office
Phone: 404-562-4870

Scott Langan
Region III-Investigations Field Office
Phone: 630-829-9519

Darrell White
Region IV-Investigations Field Office
Phone: 817-860-8115

Office of Nuclear Material Safety & Safeguards (ONMSS)

NRC
Gateway Bldg
7201 Wisconsin Ave, Ste 425
Bethesda, MD 20814
Phone: 301-492-3236
Phone: 800-368-5642
URL: www.nrc.gov/about-nrc/organization/nmssfuncdesc.html

Description: The Office of Nuclear Material Safety and Safeguards is responsible for the safe and secure production of nuclear fuel used in commercial nuclear reactors; the safe storage, transportation and disposal of high-level radioactive waste and spent nuclear fuel; and the transportation of radioactive materials regulated under the Atomic Energy Act.

Michael Weber
Director
Phone: 301-492-3236

Eric J Leeds
Deputy Director
Phone: 301-492-3237

Office of Enforcement

NRC
One White Flint N
11555 Rockville Pike
Rockville, MD 20852
Phone: 301-415-2741

Description: Oversees, manages and directs the development and implementation of policies and programs in order to enforce NRC requirements. This office coordinates with the Office of Investigations on issues involving wrongdoing or discrimination.

Cynthia A Carpenter
Director

James G Luehman
Deputy Director

Office of Nuclear Regulatory Research (RES)

NRC
One White Flint N
11555 Rockville Pike
Rockville, MD 20852-2738
Phone: 301-415-6641

URL: www.nrc.gov/about-nrc/organization/resfuncdesc.html

Description: Provides leadership and plans, recommends, manages and implements programs of nuclear regulatory research. Coordinates the development of concensus and voluntary standards for agency use, including appointment of RES staff to committees. Recommends regulatory actions to resolve ongoing and potential safety issues for nuclear power plants and other facilities regulated by the NRC, including those issues designated as Generic Safety Issues. Conducts research to reduce uncertainties in areas of potentially high safety or security risk or significance. Develops the technical basis for risk-informed, performance-based regulations in all areas regulated by the NRC. Leads the agency's initiative for cooperative research with external partners.

Brian W Sheron
Director
Phone: 301-415-6641

Michael Johnson
Deputy Director
Phone: 301-415-0774

Office of Nuclear Reactor Regulation (NRR)
NRC
One White Flint N
11555 Rockville Pike
Rockville, MD 20852-2738
Phone: 301-415-1471
URL: www.nrc.gov/about-nrc/organization/nrrfuncdesc.html

Description: NRR is responsible for accomplishing key components of the NRC's nuclear reactor safety mission. As such, NRR conducts a broad range of regulatory activities in the four primary program areas of rulemaking, licensing, oversight and incident response for commercial nuclear power reactors, and test and research reactors to protect the public health, safety and the environment. NRR works with the regions and other offices to accomplish its mission and contribute to the agency mission.

James E Dyer
Director
Phone: 301-415-1471

James Wiggins
Deputy Director
Phone: 301-415-1284

Office of Small Business & Civil Rights
NRC
One White Flint N
11555 Rockville Pike
Rockville, MD 20852
Phone: 301-415-7380
Phone: 800-368-5642
Fax: 301-415-5953
URL: www.nrc.gov

Description: The Office of Small Business and Civil Rights develops, implements, and manages four major programs: Affirmative Action, including the Federal Women's Program and implementing a managing diversity process; Civil Rights; Historically Black Colleges and Universities (HBCU); and Small Business. Its mission is to: facilitate equal employment opportunity for all NRC employees and applicants for employment; provide for prompt, fair and impartial process of discrimination complaints; administer grants to HBCU faculty and students; ensure that small, small disadvantaged and small women-owned businesses have full and fair opportunity to participte in NRC procurement activities.

Corenthis B Kelley
Director
Phone: 301-415-7380

Barbara D Williams
Senior Level Assistant Policy & Programs
Phone: 301-415-7388

Deloris Suto-Goldsby
Civil Rights Program Manager
Phone: 301-415-0590

Mauricio P Vera
Small Business Program Manager
Phone: 301-415-7160

Tuwanda Smith
Outreach & Compliance Program Manager
Phone: 301-415-7394

Region I: Nuclear Regulatory Commission
US NRC Region I
475 Allendale Road
King of Prussia, PA 19406-1415
Phone: 610-337-5000
Phone: 800-432-1156
Fax: 610-337-5024

Samuel J Collins
Regional Administrator

Marc Dapas
Deputy Regional Administrator

Nancy McNamara
State Liaison Officer

Marsha Gamberoni
Director Reactor Safety

Diane Screnci
Public Affairs Officer
Phone: 610-337-5330

Region II: Nuclear Regulatory Commission
Sam Nunn Atlanta Federal Ctr, 23 T85
61 Forsyth Street SW
Atlanta, GA 30303-8931
Phone: 404-562-4400
Phone: 800-577-8510
Fax: 404-562-4900

William D Travers
Regional Administrator

Victor McCree
Deputy Regional Administrator Operations

Robert Trajanowski
Regional State Liaison Officer

Joseph Shea
Director Reactor Safety

Kenneth M Clark
Senior Public Affairs Officer
Phone: 404-512-4416

Region III: Nuclear Regulatory Commission

US NRC Regional III
2443 Warrenville Road, Ste 210
Lisle, IL 60532-4352
Phone: 630-829-9500
Phone: 800-522-3025
Fax: 630-515-1078

James L Caldwell
Regional Administrator

Geoffrey Grant
Deputy Regional Administrator

Roland Lickus
State Liaison

Cynthia Pederson
Reactor Safety Division Director

R Jan Strasma
Senior Public Affairs Officer
Phone: 630-829-9663

Region IV: Nuclear Regulatory Commission

Texas Health Resources Tower
611 Ryan Plaza, Suite 400
Arlington, TX 76011-4005
Phone: 817-860-8100
Phone: 800-952-9677
Fax: 817-860-8210

Bruce S Mallet
Regional Administrator

Thomas Gwynn
Deputy Regional Administrator

William Maier
State Liaison

Dwight Chamberlain
Director Reactor Safety

Victor L Dricks
Senior Public Affairs Officer
Phone: 817-860-8128

FEDERAL

U.S. House of Representatives

US House of Representatives

Leadership
US Capitol
Washington, DC 20515
Phone: 202-224-3121
Phone: 202-225-1904
URL: www.house.gov

Nancy Pelosi
Speaker of the House
Phone: 202-225-0100

Steny Hoyer
House Majority Leader
Phone: 202-225-3130

John Boehner
House Republican Leader
Phone: 202-225-4000

James Clyburn
House Majority Whip
Phone: 202-226-3210

Roy Blunt
Republican Whip
Phone: 202-225-0197

Rahm Emanuel
Democratic Caucus Chairman
Phone: 202-225-1400

Adam Putnam
Republican Conference
Phone: 202-225-5107

Committee on Energy and Commerce

2125 Rayburn House Office Building
Washington, DC 20515
Phone: 202-225-2927
Fax: 202-225-1919
URL: energycommerce.house.gov

Description: The Committee on Energy and Commerce is the oldest legislative standing committee in the U.S. House of Representatives, and has served as the principal guide for the House in matters relating to the promotion of commerce and to the public's health and marketplace interests. In performing this historic function, the Committee has developed what is arguably the broadest (non-tax oriented) jurisdiction of any Congressional committee, extending over five Cabinet-level departments and seven independent agencies. Today, it maintains principal responsibility for legislative oversight relating to telecommunications, consumer protection, the supply and delivery of energy, food and drug safety, public health, air quality, environmental health, and interstate and foreign commerce in general.

John D Dingell Jr
D-MI Chairman

Diana DeGette
D-CO Vice Chair

Henry A Waxman
D-CA

Frederick (Rick) C Boucher
D-VA

Edolphus Towns
D-NY

Frank Pallone Jr
D-NJ

Bart Gordon
D-TN

Bobby L Rush
D-IL

Anna G Eshoo
D-CA

Bart Stupak
D-MI

Eliot L Engel
D-NY

Albert Russell Wynn
D-MD

Gene Green
D-TX

Edward J Markey
D-MA

Lois Capps
D-CA

Michael F Doyle
D-PA

Thomas H Allen
D-ME

Darlene Hooley
D-OR

Janice D Schakowsky
D-IL

Hilda L Solis
D-CA

Charles A Gonzalez
D-TX

Jay Inslee
D-WA

Tammy Baldwin
D-WI

Mike Ross
D-AR

Anthony D Weiner
D-NY

Jim Matheson
D-UT

G K Butterfield
D-NC

Charlie Melancon
D-LA

John Barron
D-GA

Baron P Hill
D-IN

Jane Harman
D-CA

Joe Barton
R-TX Ranking Member

J Dennis Hastert
R-IL

Charles W (Chip) Pickering
R-MS

Michael C Burgess
R-TX

John Sullivan
R-OK

Steve Buyer
R-IN

Mary Bono
R-CA

Marsha Blackburn
R-TN

Barbara Cubin
R-WY

Nathan Deal
R-GA

Mike Ferguson
R-NJ

Vito Fossella
R-NY

Ralph Hall
R-TX

John B Shadegg
R-AZ

George Radanovich
R-CA

Joseph R Pitts
R-PA

Michael Rogers
R-MI

Fred Upton
R-MI

Cliff Stearns
R-FL

Tim Murphy
R-PA

Heather Wilson
R-NM

John Shimkus
R-IL

Greg Walden
R-OR

Lee Terry
R-NE

Ed Whitfield
R-KY

Sue Wilkins Myrick
R-NC

Dennis Fitzgibbons
Chief of Staff

Gregg A Rothschild
Chief Counsel
Phone: 202-225-2927

Committee on Homeland Security
176 Ford House Office Building
Washington, DC 20515
Phone: 202-226-2616
Fax: 202-226-4499
URL: homeland.house.gov
e-mail: homeland@mail.house.gov

Bennie G Thompson
D-MS Chairman

Loretta Sanchez
D-CA Vice Chair

Peter A DeFazio
D-OR

Norman D Dicks
D-WA

Bob Etheridge
D-NC

Jane Harman
D-CA

Sheila Jackson Lee
D-TX

James R Langevin
D-RI

Zoe Lofgren
D-CA

Nita M Lowey
D-NY

Edward J Markey
D-MA

Eleanor Holmes Norton
D-DC

Donna M Christensen
D-USVI

Henry Cuellar
D-TX

Christopher P Carney
D-PA

Yvette D Clark
D-NY

Al Green
D-TX

Ed Permlutter
D-CO

Peter King
R-NY Ranking Member

Daniel E Lungren
R-CA

Lamar S Smith
R-TX

Charles W Dent
R-PA

Mike D Rogers
R-AL

Mark Souder
R-IN

Thomas M Davis III
R-VA

Christopher Shays
R-CT

Bobby Jindal
R-LA

David Reichert
R-WA

Michael McCaul
R-TX

Ginny Brown-Waite
R-FL

Gus M Bilirakis
R-FL

David Davis
R-TN

Kevin McCarthy
R-CA

Dena Graziano
Press Secretary
Phone: 202-226-2616

Committee on the Judiciary
2138 Rayburn House Office Building
Washington, DC 20515
Phone: 202-225-3951
Phone: 202-225-6906
URL: www.judiciary.house.gov

Description: The Committee on the Judiciary has been called the lawyer for the House of Representatives because of its jurisdiction over matters relating to the administration of justice in federal courts, administrative bodies, and law enforcement agencies. A standing Committee on the Judiciary was established by the House of Representatives on June 3, 1813 to consider legislation relating to judicial proceedings. Since then, the scope of the Committee's concern has expanded to include issues relating to espionage, terrorism, bankruptcy, constitutional amendments, immigration and naturalization, the protection of civil liberties, interstate compacts, national penitentiaries, antitrust law, and state and territorial boundary lines and patents.

John Conyers Jr
D-MI Chairman

Howard L Berman
D-CA

Frederick (Rick) C Boucher
D-VA

Jerrold Nadler
D-NY

Robert C Scott
D-VA

Melvin L Watt
D-NC

Zoe Lofgren
D-CA

Sheila Jackson Lee
D-TX

Maxine Waters
D-CA

William D Delahunt
D-MA

Robert Wexler
D-FL

Martin T Meehan
D-MA

Anthony D Weiner
D-NY

Adam B Schiff
D-CA

Linda T Sanchez
D-CA

Debbie Wasserman Schultz
D-FL

Steve Cohen
D-TN

Henry C Johnson
D-GA

Luis V Gutierrez
D-IL

Brad Sherman
D-CA

Artur Davis
D-AL

Keith Ellison
D-MN

Tammy Baldwin
D-WI

Lamar S Smith
R-TX Ranking Member

F James Sensenbrenner Jr
R-WI

Elton Gallegly
R-CA

Steve Chabot
R-OH

Chris Cannon
R-UT

Ric Keller
R-FL

Howard Coble
R-NC

Mike Pence
R-IN

J Randy Forbes
R-VA

Steve King
R-IA

Daniel E Lungren
R-CA

Tom Feeney
R-FL

Darrell E Issa
R-CA

Trent Franks
R-AZ

Louie Gohmert
R-TX

Robert W (Bob) Goodlatte
R-VA

Jim Jordan
R-OH

Jonathan Godfrey
Democratic Communications Director
Phone: 202-226-6888

Committee on Oversight & Government Reform
2157 Rayburn House Office Building
Washington, DC 20515
Phone: 202-225-5051
Phone: 202-225-5074
URL: oversight.house.gov

Description: The main investigative committee in the House, it has the jurisdiction to investigate any federal program and any matter with federal policy implications. The committee has dealt with recommendations of the September 11 Commission on emergency preparedness issues, the security of US nuclear facilites and other security topics.

Henry A Waxman
D-CA Chairman

Tom Lantos
D-CA

John F Tierney
D-MA

Edolphus Towns
D-NY

Paul E Kanjorski
D-PA

Carolyn B Maloney
D-NY

Elijah E Cummings
D-MD

Dennis J Kucinich
D-OH

Danny K Davis
D-IL

W Lacy Clay
D-MO

Diane E Watson
D-CA

Stephen F Lynch
D-MA

Chris Van Hollen
D-MD

John A Yarmuth
D-KY

Jim Cooper
D-TN

Brian Higgins
D-NY

Eleanor Holmes Norton
D-DC

Bruce L Braley
D-IA

Betty McCollum
D-MN

Paul W Hodes
D-NH

Christopher S Murphy
D-CT

John P Sarbanes
D-MD

Peter Welch
D-VT

Tom Davis
R-VA Ranking Member

Christopher Shays
R-CT

Dan L Burton
R-IN

John M McHugh
R-NY

John L Mica
R-FL

Mark E Souder
R-IN

Todd Russell Platts
R-PA

Chris Cannon
R-UT

John J Duncan Jr
R-TN

Michael R Turner
R-OH

Darrell E Issa
R-CA

Kenny Marchant
R-TX

Lynn A Westmoreland
R-GA

Patrick T McHenry
R-NC

Virginia Foxx
R-NC

Brian P Bilbray
R-CA

Bill Sali
R-ID

Jim Jordan
R-OH

Phil Barnett
Democratic Staff Director/Chief Counsel
Phone: 202-225-5051

Karen Lightfoot
Majority Senior Policy Advisor/Communications Director
Phone: 202-225-5051

David Marin
Minority Staff Director
Phone: 202-225-5074

Keith Ausbrook
Minority Chief Counsel

Committee on Science and Technology
2320 Rayburn House Office Building
Washington, DC 20515
Phone: 202-225-6375
Fax: 202-225-3895
URL: science.house.gov
e-mail: science@mail.house.gov

Description: The Committee has jurisdiction over all non-defense Federal scientific research and development of Federal agencies, some of which include: FAA, NASA, and the EPA. It also proposes ways in which research and development can help solve some the nation's most pressing problems.

Bart Gordon
D-TN Chairman

Daniel Lipinski
D-IL Vice Chairman

Darlene Hooley
D-OR

Mark Udall
D-CO

David Wu
D-OR

Michael M Honda
D-CA

Brad Miller
D-NC

Brian Baird
D-WA

James Matheson
D-UT

Charlie Melancon
D-LA

Eddie Bernice Johnson
D-TX

Jerry F Costello
D-IL

Lynn C Woolsey
D-CA

Nick Lampson
D-TX

Gabrielle Giffords
D-AZ

Jerry McNerney
D-CA

Paul E Kajorski
D-PA

Steven R Rothman
D-NJ

Mike Ross
D-AR

Ben Chandler
D-KY

Russ Carnahan
D-MO

Baron P Hill
D-IN

Harry E Mitchell
D-AZ

Charles A Wilson
D-OH

Ralph Hall
R-TX Ranking Member

Mario Diaz-Balart
R-FL

Randy Neugebauer
R-TX

Lamar S Smith
R-TX

Dana Rohrabacher
R-CA

Roscoe G Bartlett
R-MD

Vernon J Ehlers
R-MI

Frank D Lucas
R-OK

Judy Biggert
R-IL

W Todd Akin
R-MO

Josiah R Bonner
R-AL

Tom Feeney
R-FL

Robert D Inglis
R-SC

David G Reichert
R-WA

Michael McCaul
R-TX

F James Sensenbrenner Jr
R-WI

Phil Gingrey
R-GA

Brian P Bilbray
R-CA

Adrian Smith
R-NE

Charles Atkins
Democratic Staff Director
Phone: 202-225-6375

Louis Finkel
Director Policy & Outreach

Alisa Ferguson
Legislative Director

Alisha Prather
Director Communications
Phone: 202-225-6375

John Piazza
Counsel

Committee on Transportation and Infrastructure
2165 Rayburn House Office Building
Washington, DC 20515
Phone: 202-225-4472
Phone: 202-225-9446
Fax: 202-226-1270
URL: www.house.gov/transportation

Description: The Committee on Transportation and Infrastructure provides oversight and investigation on: satellite utilization; innovative transportation technologies; DHS integration with the transporation community; maintaining continued attention for non-security organizational objectives; and transportation safety, security and economic vitality.

James L Oberstar
D-MN Chairman

Nick J Rahall II
D-WV

Jerry F Costello
D-IL

Eleanor Holmes Norton
D-DC

Jerrold Nadler
D-NY

Corrine Brown
D-FL

Bob Filner
D-CA

Eddie Bernice Johnson
D-TX

Gene Taylor
D-MS

Elijah E Cummings
D-MD

Leonard L Boswell
D-IA

Tim Holden
D-PA

Brian Baird
D-WA

Rick Larsen
D-WA

Michael E Capuano
D-MA

Peter A DeFazio
D-OR

Julia Carson
D-IN

Timothy H Bishop
D-NY

Michael H Michaud
D-ME

Brian Higgins
D-NY

Russ Carnahan
D-MO

John T Salazar
D-CO

Grace F Napolitano
D-CA

Daniel Lipinski
D-IL

Doris O Matsui
D-CA

Nick Lampson
D-TX

Zachary T Space
D-OH

Mazie K Hirono
D-HI

Bruce L Braley
D-IA

Jason Altmire
D-PA

Timothy J Walz
D-MN

Heath Shuler
D-NC

Michael A Arcuri
D-NY

Harry E Mitchell
D-AZ

Christopher P Carney
D-PA

John J Hall
D-NY

Steve Kagen
D-WI

Steve Cohen
D-TN

Jerry McNerney
D-CA

John L Mica
R-FL Ranking Member

Jean Schmidt
R-OH

Howard Coble
R-NC

John J Duncan Jr
R-TN

William Shuster
R-PA

John Boozman
R-AR

Jim Gerlach
R-PA

Mario Diaz-Balart
R-FL

Charles W Dent
R-PA

Ted Poe
R-TX

David G Reichert
R-WA

Connie Mack
R-FL

John R Kuhl Jr
R-NY

Lynn A Westmoreland
R-GA

Wayne T Gilchrest
R-MD

Vernon J Ehlers
R-MI

Steven C LaTourette
R-OH

Richard H Baker
R-LA

Frank A LoBiondo
R-NJ

Jerry Moran
R-KS

Gary G Miller
R-CA

Robin Hayes
R-NC

Henry E Brown Jr
R-SC

Timothy V Johnson
R-IL

Todd R Platts
R-PA

Sam Graves
R-MO

Mary Fallin
R-OK

Vern Buchanan
R-FL

Don Young
R-AK

Shelley Moore Capito
R-WV

Candice S Miller
R-MI

Thelma D Drake
R-VA

David A Heymsfeld
Majority Chief of Staff
Phone: 202-225-4472

Ward W McCarragher
Chief Counsel
Phone: 202-225-4472

James W Coon II
Republican Chief of Staff
Phone: 202-225-9446

House Armed Services Committee

2120 Rayburn House Office Building
Washington, DC 20515
Phone: 202-225-4151
Phone: 202-225-2539
Fax: 202-225-9077
URL: http://armedservices.house.gov

Description: The House Armed Services Committee continues its oversight and assessment of threats to US national security. It regularly assesses national security threats and challenges. Its jurisdiction includes: common defense; conservation, development and use of naval petroleum and oil shale reserves; ammunition depots; selective service; military applications and nuclear energy; and the Department of Defense, including the Army, Navy, and Air Force, in general. The committee will initiate an aggressive new outreach program to seek views and perspectives of service members and their families including active duty, National Guard and reserve members in deployed locations overseas and throughout the US.

Ike Skelton
D-MO Chairman

John Spratt
D-SC

Solomon P Ortiz
D-TX

Gene Taylor
D-MS

Neil Abercrombie
D-HI

Martin T Meehan
D-MA

Silvestre Reyes
D-TX

Vic Snyder
D-AR

Mark Udall
D-CO

Adam Smith
D-WA

Loretta Sanchez
D-CA

Mike McIntyre
D-NC

Daniel Boren
D-OK

Ellen O Tauscher
D-CA

Robert A Brady
D-PA

Brad Ellsworth
D-IN

Nancy Boyda
D-KS

Susan A Davis
D-CA

Patrick Murphy
D-PA

Henry C Johnson
D-GA

Rick Larsen
D-WA

Jim Cooper
D-TN

Jim Marshall
D-GA

Kendrick B Meek
D-FL

Carol Sea-Porter
D-NH

Robert E Andrews
D-NJ

Madeleine Z Bordallo
D-Guam

Joe Courtney
D-CT

David Loebsack
D-IA

Kirsten Gillibrand
D-NY

Joe Sestak
D-PA

Gabrielle Giffords
D-AZ

Elijah Cummings
D-MD

Kathy Castor
D-FL

Duncan Hunter
R-CA Ranking Member

William Shuster
R-PA

Jim Saxton
R-NJ

John M McHugh
R-NY

Terry Everett
R-AL

Roscoe G Bartlett
R-MD

William (Mac) Thornberry
R-TX

Walter B Jones
R-NC

Robin Hayes
R-NC

Thelma Drake
R-VA

Jo Ann Davis
R-VA

W Todd Akin
R-MO

J Randy Forbes
R-VA

Jeff Miller
R-FL

Joe Wilson
R-SC

Frank A LoBiondo
R-NJ

Cathy McMorris
R-WA

Mike Conaway
R-TX

Michael Turner
R-OH

John Kline
R-MN

Candice S Miller
R-MI

Geoff Davis
R-KY

Mike Rogers
R-AL

Trent Franks
R-AR

Buck McKeon
R-CA

Rob Bishop
R-UT

Tom Cole
R-OK

Phil Gingrey
R-GA

Erin C Conaton
Staff Director
Phone: 202-225-4151

Bob DeGrasse
Deputy Staff Director
Phone: 202-225-4151

Paul Oostburg
General Counsel
Phone: 202-225-4151

Lara Battles
Press Secretary
Phone: 202-225-2539

House Permanent Select Committee on Intelligence
H-405 Capitol
Washington, DC 20515-6415
Phone: 202-225-7690
Phone: 877-858-9040
Fax: 202-226-5068
URL: http://intelligence.house.gov
e-mail: intelligence.hpsci@mail.house.gov

Description: Intelligence is the first line of defense against terrorism and providing effective homeland security, thus it is important to have an effective oversight process to ensure that intelligence resources are not misused and that intelligence activities are conducted lawfully. Ensuring that these laws are followed is a key component of the committee's oversight responsibilities and is the primary reason for the creation of such committees. Professional staff have experience in intelligence, legal and legislative matters.

Silvestre Reyes
D-TX Chairman

John Tierney
D-MA

Robert E Cramer Jr
D-AL

C A Dutch Ruppersberger
D-MD

Anna G Eshoo
D-CA

Rush D Holt
D-NJ

Alcee L Hastings
D-FL

Leonard L Boswell
D-IA

Mike Thompson
D-CA

Jan Schakowsky
D-IL

Jim Langevin
D-RI

Patrick Murphy
D-PA

Peter Hoekstra
R-MI Ranking Member

Darrell E Issa
R-CA

Terry Everett
R-AL

Heather Wilson
R-NM

Mac Thornberry
R-TX

John M McHugh
R-NY

Todd Tiahrt
R-KS

Mike Rogers
R-MI

Kira Maas
Press Secretary
Phone: 202-225-4831

Readiness Subcommittee
House Armed Services Committee
2340 Rayburn House Office Building
Washington, DC 20515-6040
Phone: 202-226-8979
Fax: 202-225-9077
URL: armedservices.house.gov/subcommittee.shtml

Description: The Readiness Subcommittee is responsible for military readiness, training, logistics, maintenance and programs. In addition, the Subcommittee is responsible for all military construction, installation and family housing issues, including the base closure process.

Solomon P Ortiz
D-TX Chairman

Gene Taylor
D-MI

Silvestre Reyes
D-TX

Robert A Brady
D-PA

Jim Marshall
D-GA

Madeleine Z Bordallo
D-Guam

Mark Udall
D-CO

Loretta Sanchez
D-CA

Daniel Boren
D-OK

Nancy Boyda
D-KS

Carol Shea-Porter
D-NH

Joe Courtney
D-CT

David Loebsack
D-IA

Gabrielle Giffords
D-AZ

Elijah Cummings
D-MD

Jo Ann Davis
R-VA Ranking Member

Walter B Jones
R-NC

J Randy Forbes
R-VA

Mike Rogers
R-AL

Cathy McMorris Rodgers
R-WA

John M McHugh
R-NY

Howard P McKeon
R-CA

Robin Hayes
R-NC

Candice S Miller
R-MI

Trent Franks
R-AZ

Frank LoBiondo
R-NJ

Tom Cole
R-OK

Rob Bishop
R-UT

Strategic Forces Subcommittee
House Armed Services Committee
2340 Rayburn House Office Building
Washington, DC 20515
Phone: 202-226-2211

URL: armedservices.house.gov/subcommittee.shtml

Description: Responsible for strategic forces (except deep strike), ballistic missile defense, space programs, and Department of Energy national security programs (except non-proliferation).

Ellen O Tauscher
D-CA Chair

Rick Larsen
D-WA

Jim Cooper
D-TN

Henry C Johnson
D-GA

David Loebsack
D-IA

Silvestre Reyes
D-TX

John M Spratt Jr
D-SC

Terry Everett
R-AL Ranking Member

William M Thornberry
R-TX

Trent Franks
R-AZ

Michael R Turner
R-OH

Mike D Rogers
R-AL

Terrorism, Unconventional Threats & Capabilities Subcommittee
House Armed Services Committee
2340 Rayburn House Office Building
Washington, DC 20515
Phone: 202-226-2843
Fax: 202-225-9077
URL: armedservices.house.gov/subcommittee.shtml

Description: The Terrorism, Unconventional Threats and Capabilities Subcommittee is responsible for Department of Defense counter proliferation and counter terrorism programs and initiatives. In addition, the Subcommittee is responsible for Special Operations Forces, the Defense Advanced Research Projects Agency, information technology policy and programs, force protection policy and oversight, and related intelligence support.

Adam Smith
D-WA Chairman

Mike McIntyre
D-NC

Robert E Andrews
D-NJ

Jim Marshall
D-GA

Jim Cooper
D-TN

Mark Udall
D-CO

Brad Ellsworth
D-IN

Kirsten Gillibrand
D-NJ

Kathy Castor
D-FL

William T Thornberry
R-TX Ranking Member

Robin Hayes
R-NC

Joe Wilson
R-SC

John Kline
R-MN

Ken Calvert
R-CA

Thelma Drake
R-VA

Michael Conway
R-TX

Jim Saxton
R-NJ

Subcommittee on Emergency Communications, Preparedness & Response
Committee on Homeland Security
176 Ford House Office Building
Washington, DC 20515
Phone: 202-226-2616
Fax: 202-226-4499

Henry Cuellar
D-TX Chairman

Nita M Lowey
D-NY

Eleanor Holmes Norton
D-DC

Donna M Christensen
D-USVI

Bob Etheridge
D-NC

Loretta Sanchez
D-CA

Norman D Hicks
D-WA

Charles Dent
R-PA Ranking Member

Lamar S Smith
R-TX

Mike Rogers
R-AL

Mark E Souder
R-IN

Bobby Jindal
R-LA

David Davis
R-TN

Subcommittee on Emerging Threats, Cyber Security and Science & Technology
Committee on Homeland Security
176 Ford House Office Building
Washington, DC 20515
Phone: 202-226-2616
Fax: 202-226-4499

James R Langevin
D-RI Chairman

Donna M Christensen
D-USVI

Zoe Lofgren
D-CA

Bob Etheridge
D-NC

Al Green
D-TX

Michael R McCaul
R-TX Ranking Member

Daniel E Lungren
R-CA

Ginny Brown Waite
R-FL

Kevin McCarthy
R-CA

Subcommittee on Intelligence, Information Sharing & Terrorism Risk Assessment
Committee on Homeland Security
176 Ford House Office Building
Washington, DC 20515
Phone: 202-226-2616
Fax: 202-226-4499

Description: Responsible for intelligence and information sharing for the purpose of preventing, preparing for, and responding to potential terrorist attacks on the US; the integration, analysis and dissemination of homeland security information to state, local and private entities; information gathering, analysis, and sharing by DHS entities; issuance of terrorism threat advisories and warnings; and liaison of the DHS with US intelligence and law enforcement agencies.

Jane Harman
D-CA Chair

Norman D Dicks
D-WA

James R Langevin
D-RI

Christopher P Carney
D-PA

Ed Permlutter
D-CO

David Reichert
R-WA Ranking Member

Christopher Shays
R-CT

Charles W Dent
R-PA

Subcommittee on Management, Investigations & Oversight
Committee on Homeland Security
176 Ford House Office Building
Washington, DC 20515
Phone: 202-226-2616
Fax: 202-226-4499

Christopher P Carney
D-PA Chairman

Ed Permlutter
D-CO

Peter A DeFazio
D-OR

Yvette D Clarke
D-NY

Mike Rogers
R-MI Ranking Member

Tom Davis
R-VA

Michael McCaul
R-TX

Subcommittee on Transportation Security & Infrastructure Protection
Committee on Homeland Security
176 Ford House Office Building
Washington, DC 20515
Phone: 202-226-2616
Fax: 202-226-4499

Sheila Jackson Lee
D-TX Chair

Edward J Markey
D-MA

Peter A DeFazio
D-OR

Eleanor Holmes Norton
D-DC

Yvette D Clarke
D-KY

Ed Permlutter
D-CO

Daniel E Lungren
R-CA Ranking Member

Ginny Brown Waite
R-FL

Gus M Bilirakis
R-FL

Kevin McCarthy
R-CA

Courts, the Internet & Intellectual Property Subcommittee
Judiciary Committee
B352 Rayburn House Office Building
Washington, DC 20515-6219
Phone: 202-225-5741
Fax: 202-225-3673

Description: Jurisdiction over the following subject matters: information technology, administration of US Courts, Federal Rules of Evidence, Civil and Appellate Procedure, judicial ethics, copyright, patent, trademark law, and other appropriate matters relevant referred to by the chairman.

Howard L Berman
D-CA Chairman

John Conyers Jr
D-MI

Martin T Meehan
D-MA

Robert Wexler
D-FL

Adam B Schiff
D-CA

Anthony D Weiner
D-NY

Frederick C Boucher
D-VA

Melvin L Watt
D-NC

Sheila Jackson Lee
D-TX

Steve Cohen
D-TN

Henry C Johnson
D-GA

Brad Sherman
D-CA

Howard Coble
R-NC Ranking Member

Elton Gallegly
R-CA

Robert W (Bob) Goodlatte
R-VA

Chris Cannon
R-UT

Ric Keller
R-FL

Darrell E Issa
R-CA

Mike Pence
R-IN

Tom Feeney
R-FL

F James Sensenbrenner Jr
R-WI

Steve Chabot
R-OH

Jonathan Godfrey
Democratic Communications Director
Phone: 202-226-6888

Crime, Terrorism, and Homeland Security Subcommittee
Judiciary Committee
B370 Rayburn House Office Building
Washington, DC 20515-6223
Phone: 202-225-5727

Description: Jurisdiction over the following subject matters: internal and homeland security; Federal Criminal Code/Rules of Criminal Procedure; prisons, drug enforcement; sentencing, parole and pardons; criminal law enforcement; and other appropriate matters and relevant oversight.

Robert C Scott
D-VA Chairman

Maxine Waters
D-CA

Martin T Meehan
D-MA

Sheila Jackson Lee
D-TX

William D Delahunt
D-MA

Anthony D Weiner
D-NY

Jerrold Nadler
D-NY

Henry C Johnson
D-GA

Artur Davis
D-AL

Tammy Baldwin
D-WI

J Randy Forbes
R-VA Ranking Member

Howard Coble
R-NC

Daniel E Lungren
R-CA

Steve Chabot
R-OH

Louie Gohmert
R-TX

F James Sensenbrenner Jr
R-WI

Immigration, Citizenship, Refugees, Border Security, and International Law Subcommittee
Judiciary Committee
517 Cannon House Office Building
Washington, DC 20515-6217
Phone: 202-225-3926

Description: Jurisdiction over the following subject matter: border security; immigration and naturalization; claims against the US; private immigration and claims bills; non-border enforcement; federal charters of incorporation; admission of refugees, treaties, conventions and international agreements; and relevant oversight.

Zoe Lofgren
D-CA Chairman

Linda T Sanchez
D-CA

Howard L Berman
D-CA

Maxine Waters
D-CA

Martin T Meehan
D-MA

Luis V Gutierrez
D-IL

Sheila Jackson Lee
D-TX

William D Delahunt
D-MA

Artur Davis
D-AL

Keith Ellison
D-MN

Steve King
R-IA Ranking Member

Louie Gohmert
R-TX

Elton Gallegly
R-CA

Robert W (Bob) Goodlatte
R-VA

Daniel E Lungren
R-CA

J Randy Forbes
R-VA

National Security and Foreign Affairs Subcommittee
Committee on Oversight & Government Reform
B371C Rayburn House Office Building
Washington, DC 20515-6149
Phone: 202-225-2548
Fax: 202-225-2382
URL: http://nationalsecurity.oversight.house.gov

John F Tierney
D-MA Chairman

Carolyn B Maloney
D-NY

Stephen F Lynch
D-MA

Brian Higgins
D-NY

John A Yarmuth
D-KY

Bruce L Braley
D-IA

Betty McCollum
D-MN

Jim Cooper
D-TN

Chris Van Hollen
D-MD

Paul W Hodes
D-NH

Peter Welch
D-VT

Tom Lantos
D-CA

Christopher Shays
R-CT Ranking Member

Dan Burton
R-IN

John M McHugh
R-NY

Todd R Platts
R-PA

John J Duncan
R-TN

Michael R Turner
R-OH

Kenny Marchant
R-TX

Lynn A Westmoreland
R-GA

Patrick T McHenry
R-NC

Virginia Foxx
R-NC

Subcommittee on Research & Science Education
Committee on Science and Technology
2320 Rayburn House Office Building
Washington, DC 20515
Phone: 202-225-6375
Fax: 202-225-3895
URL: http://science.house.gov/subcommittee/research.aspx

Description: Handles issues related to the Office of Science and Technology, all scientific research and engineering resources. It oversees the National Science Foundation (NSF), including earthquake programs.

Brian Baird
D-WA Chairman

Darlene Hooley
D-OR

Daniel Lipinski
D-IL

Eddie Bernice Johnson
D-TX

Jerry McNerney
D-CA

Russ Carnahan
D-MO

Baron P Hill
D-IN

Vernon J Ehlers
R-MI Ranking Member

Frank D Lucas
R-OK

Roscoe G Bartlett
R-MD

Randy Neigebauer
R-TX

Brian P Bilbray
R-CA

Jim Wilson
Democratic Staff Director
Phone: 202-225-2634

Elizabeth Grossman
Republican Staff Director
Phone: 202-225-7858

Coast Guard & Maritime Transportation Subcommittee
Committee on Transportation and Infrastructure
H2-507 Ford House Office Building
Washington, DC 20515-6231
Phone: 202-226-3587

Elijah E Cummings
D-MD Chairman

Gene Taylor
D-MS

Brian Higgins
D-NY

Brian Baird
D-WA

Corrine Brown
D-FL

Timothy H Bishop
D-NY

James L Oberstar
D-MN (Ex-Officio)

Steve LaTourette
R-OH Ranking Member

Howard Coble
R-NC

Wayne T Gilchrest
R-MD

Don Young
R-AK

Frank A LoBiondo
R-NJ

Ted Poe
R-TX

John L Mica
R-FL (Ex-Officio)

Economic Development, Public Buildings & Emergency Management Subcommittee
Committee on Transportation and Infrastructure
585 Ford House Office Building
Washington, DC 20515-6260
Phone: 202-225-9961
Phone: 202-225-3014

Description: The Subcommittee on Economic Development, Public Buildings and Emergency Management is responsible for programs addressing the federal management of emergencies and disasters; a variety of measures affecting homeland security including the Federal Response Plan, First Responder Grant Program and Federal Protective Service; and the authorization and oversight of Federal real estate programs.

Eleanor Holmes Norton
D-WV Chairwoman

Michael H Michaud
D-ME

James Altmire
D-PA

Michael A Arcuri
D-NY

Christopher P Carney
D-PA

Timothy J Walz
D-MN

Steve Cohen
D-TN

Sam Graves
R-MO Ranking Member

Charles W Dent
R-PA

John R Kuhl Jr
R-NY

Shelly Moore Capito
R-WV

Subcommittee on Aviation
Committee on Transportation and Infrastructure
2251 Rayburn House Office Building
Washington, DC 20515
Phone: 202-226-9161
Phone: 202-226-3220

Jerry F Costello
D-IL Chairman

Leonard L Boswell
D-IA

Peter A DeFazio
D-OR

Eleanor Holmes Norton
D-DC

Corrine Brown
D-FL

Eddie Bernice Johnson
D-TX

Ellen O Tauscher
D-CA

Tim Holden
D-PA

Rick Larsen
D-WA

Michael E Capuano
D-MA

Russ Carnahan
D-MO

John T Salazar
D-CO

Nick J Rahall II
D-WV

Bob Filner
D-CA

Doris O Matsui
D-CA

Mazie K Hirono
D-HI

Daniel Lipinski
D-IL

Nick Lampson
D-TX

Zachary T Space
D-OH

Bruce L Braley
D-IA

Harry E Mitchell
D-AZ

John J Hall
D-NY

Steve Kagen
D-WI

Steve Cohen
D-TN

James L Oberstar
D-MN (Ex-Officio)

Thomas E Petri
R-WI Ranking Member

Howard Coble
R-NC

John J Duncan Jr
R-TN

Vernon J Ehlers
R-MI

Frank A LoBiondo
R-NJ

Jerry Moran
R-KS

Robin Hayes
R-NC

Sam Graves
R-MO

John Boozman
R-AR

Jim Gerlach
R-PA

Mario Diaz-Balart
R-FL

Charles W Dent
R-PA

Ted Poe
R-TX

John R Kuhl Jr
R-NY

Lynn A Westmoreland
R-GA

Steven C LaTourette
R-OH

Shelly Moore Capito
R-WV

David G Reichert
R-WA

Connie Mack
R-FL

Mary Fallin
R-OK

Vern Buchanan
R-FL

John L Mica
R-FL (Ex-Officio)

Subcommittee on Intelligence Community Management
House Permanent Select Committee on Intelligence
H-405 Capitol
Washington, DC 20515-6415
Phone: 202-225-7690
Fax: 202-226-5068

Anna G Eshoo
D-CA Chair

Rush D Holt
D-NJ Vice Chair

C A Dutch Ruppersberger
D-MD

Mike Thompson
D-CA

Patrick Murphy
D-PA

Darrell Issa
R-CA Ranking Member

Mac Thornberry
R-TX

Todd Tiahrt
R-KS

Terrorism/HUMINT, Analysis & Counterintelligence Subcommittee
House Permanent Select Committee on Intelligence
H-405 Capitol
Washington, DC 20515-6415
Phone: 202-225-7690
Phone: 877-858-9040
Fax: 202-226-5068
e-mail: intelligence.house.gov

Mike Thompson
D-CA Chairman

Leonard L Boswell
D-IA Vice Chair

Alcee L Hastings
D-FL

Jim Langevin
D-RI

Patrick Murphy
D-PA

Mike Rogers
R-MI Ranking Member

Terry Everett
R-AL

John M McHugh
R-NY

FEDERAL

U.S. Senate

US Senate
Leadership
US Capitol
Washington, DC 20510
Phone: 202-224-3121
URL: www.senate.gov

Richard B Cheney
President of the Senate/US Vice President

Robert C Byrd
President Pro Tempore
Phone: 202-224-3954

Harry Reid
Majority Leader
Phone: 202-224-3542

Richard Durbin
Assistant Majority Leader (Democratic Whip)
Phone: 202-224-2152

Mitch McConnell
Minority Leader
Phone: 202-224-2541

Trent Lott
Assistant Minority Leader (Republican Whip)
Phone: 202-224-6253

Committee on Agriculture, Nutrition & Forestry
Russell Senate Office Building
Room SR-328A
Washington, DC 20510-6000
Phone: 202-224-2035
Phone: 202-224-2587
Fax: 202-224-1725
URL: http://agriculture.senate.gov

Description: Keeping America's food and agriculture safe.

Tom Harkin
D-IA Chairman

Max Baucus
D-MT

Sherrod Brown
D-OH

Bob Casey
D-PA

Kent Conrad
D-ND

Amy Klobuchar
D-MN

Patrick J Leahy
D-VT

Blanche Lincoln
D-AR

E Benjamin Nelson
D-NE

Ken Salazar
D-CO

Debbie Stabenow
D-MI

Saxby Chambliss
R-GA Ranking Member

Richard G Lugar
R-IN

Thad Cochran
R-MS

Mitch McConnell
R-KY

Pat Roberts
R-KS

John Thune
R-SD

Lindsey Graham
R-SC

Norm Coleman
R-MN

Mike Crapo
R-ID

Charles Grassley
R-IA

Mark B Halverson
Majority Staff Director

Martha S Poindexter
Minority Staff Director

Committee on Armed Services
228 Russell Senate Office Building
Washington, DC 20510
Phone: 202-224-3871
Fax: 202-228-0037
URL: http://armed-services.senate.gov/

Description: Committee jurisdiction includes: aeronautical and space activities primarily associated with the development of weapons systems or military operations; common defense; Department of Defense, Army, Navy, Air Force; maintenance and operation of the Panama Canal; national security aspects of nuclear energy; naval petroleum reserves (except Alaska); and strategic and critical materials necessary for common defense.

Carl Levin
D-MI Chairman

Edward (Ted) M Kennedy
D-MA

Robert C Byrd
D-WV

Joseph I Lieberman
D-CT

Jack Reed
D-RI

Daniel K Akaka
D-HI

Bill Nelson
D-FL

E Benjamin Nelson
D-NE

Mark Pryor
D-AR

Hillary Rodham Clinton
D-NY

Evan Bayh
D-IN

James Webb
D-VA

Claire McCaskill
D-MO

John McCain
R-AZ Ranking Member

John W Warner
R-VA

James M Inhofe
R-OK

Mel Martinez
R-FL

Susan M Collins
R-ME

Jeff Sessions
R-AL

John Thune
R-SD

John Ensign
R-NV

Saxby Chambliss
R-GA

Lindsey O Graham
R-SC

Elizabeth H Dole
R-NC

John Cornyn
R-TX

Richard D DeBobes
Majority Staff Director

Christine E Cowart
Chief Clerk

Peter K Levine
General Counsel

Michael V Kostiw
Minority Staff Director

David M Morriss
Minority Counsel

Committee on Commerce, Science & Transportation
508 Dirksen Senate Office Building
Washington, DC 20510-6125
Phone: 202-224-5115
URL: http://commerce.senate.gov

Daniel K Inouye
D-HI Chairman

John D Rockefeller
D-WV

John F Kerry
D-MA

Byron L Dorgan
D-ND

Barbara Boxer
D-CA

Bill Nelson
D-FL

Maria Cantwell
D-WA

Frank R Lautenberg
D-NJ

Mark Pryor
D-AR

Thomas Carper
D-DE

Claire McCaskill
D-MO

Amy Klobuchar
D-MN

Ted Stevens
R-AK Ranking Member

John McCain
R-AZ

Trent Lott
R-MS

Kay Bailey Hutchison
R-TX

Olympia Snowe
R-ME

Gordon Smith
R-OR

John Ensign
R-NV

John Thune
R-SD

John Sununu
R-NH

James DeMint
R-SC

David Vitter
R-LA

Committee on Energy & Natural Resources
304 Dirksen Senate Office Building
Washington, DC 20510
Phone: 202-224-4971
Fax: 202-224-6163
URL: http://energy.senate.gov/public

Description: Jurisdiction of the Committee on Energy and Natural Resources includes responsibility for the following: international energy affairs and emergency preparedness; National Energy Policy; territorial policy (including Antarctica); privatization of federal assets; Native Hawaiian issues and nuclear waste policy.

Jeff Bingaman
D-NM Chairman

Daniel K Akaka
D-HI

Maria Cantwell
D-WA

Byron L Dorgan
D-ND

Tim Johnson
D-SD

Mary L Landrieu
D-LA

Blanche Lincoln
D-AR

Robert Menendez
D-NJ

Ken Salazar
D-CO

Bernard Sanders
D-VT

Jon Tester
D-MT

Ron Wyden
D-OR

Pete V Domenici
R-NM Ranking Member

Larry Craig
R-ID

James DeMint
R-SC

Gordon Smith
R-OR

Richard Burr
R-NC

Jim Bunning
R-KY

Mel Martinez
R-FL

Lisa Murkowski
R-AK

Bob Corker
R-TN

Jeff Sessions
R-AL

Robert M Simon
Majority Staff Director
Phone: 202-224-9201

Alex Flint
Minority Staff Director

Committee on Foreign Relations
Dirksen Senate Office Building
Washington, DC 20510-6225
Phone: 202-224-4651
Phone: 202-224-6797
Fax: 202-224-0836
URL: http://foreign.senate.gov

Joseph R Biden Jr
D-DE Chairman

Robert Menendez
D-NJ

Christopher J Dodd
D-CT

John F Kerry
D-MA

Russell D Feingold
D-WI

Barbara Boxer
D-CA

Bill Nelson
D-FL

Barack Obama
D-IL

Benjamin Cardin
D-MD

Bob Casey
D-PA

James Webb
D-VA

Richard G Lugar
R-IN Ranking Member

Charles Hagel
R-NE

Bob Corker
R-TN

James DeMint
R-SC

Norm Coleman
R-MN

George V Voinovich
R-OH

Johnny Isakson
R-GA

John E Sununu
R-NH

Lisa Murkowski
R-AK

David Vitter
R-LA

Kenneth A Myers Jr
Majority Staff Director
Phone: 202-224-4651

Anthony J Blinken
Minority Staff Director
Phone: 202-224-3953

Committee on Homeland Security & Governmental Affairs
340 Dirksen Senate Office Building
Washington, DC 20510
Phone: 202-224-2627
Phone: 202-224-4751
URL: http://senate.gov/~govt-aff/

Joseph I Lieberman
D-CT Chairman

Daniel K Akaka
D-HI

Thomas R Carper
D-DE

Mary Landrieu
D-LA

Carl Levin
D-MI

Claire McCaskill
D-MO

Barack Obama
D-IL

Mark Pryor
D-AR

Jon Tester
D-MT

Susan M Collins
R-ME Ranking Member

Tom Coburn
R-OK

Norm Coleman
R-MN

Pete V Domenici
R-NM

Ted Stevens
R-AK

John Sununu
R-NH

George V Voinovich
R-OH

John W Warner
R-VA

Leslie Phillips
Majority Communications Director
Phone: 202-224-2627

Jen Burita
Minority Communications Director
Phone: 202-224-4751

Senate Select Committee on Intelligence
211 Hart Senate Office Building
Washington, DC 20510-6475
Phone: 202-224-1700
Fax: 202-224-1772
URL: http://intelligence.senate.gov

Description: The Senate Select Committee on Intelligence was created to: oversee and make continuing studies of the intelligence activities and programs of the United States; to submit to the Senate appropriate proposals for legislation and report to the Senate concerning such intelligence activities; to make every effort to assure that the appropriate departments and agencies of the United States provide informed and timely intelligence necessary for the executive and legislative branches to make sound decisions affecting the security and vital interests of the nation.

John D Rockefeller
D-WV Chairman

Dianne Feinstein
D-CA

Ron Wyden
D-OR

Evan Bayh
D-IN

Barbara A Mikulski
D-MD

Russell D Feingold
D-WI

Bill Nelson
D-FL

Sheldon Whitehouse
D-RI

Carl Levin
D-MI (Ex-Officio)

Harry Reid
D-NV (Ex-Officio)

Christopher S Bond
R-MO Vice Chairman

Orrin G Hatch
R-UT

John Wagner
R-NC

Olympia J Snowe
R-ME

Charles Hagel
R-NE

Saxby Chambliss
R-GA

Richard Burr
R-NC

Mitch McConnell
R-KY (Ex-Officio)

Bill Duhnke
Majority Staff Director
Phone: 202-224-1700

Wendy Morigi
Majority Communications
Phone: 202-224-6101

Melvin Dubee
Minority Staff Director
Phone: 202-224-6472

Robb Ostrander
Minority Communications
Phone: 202-224-7627

Ad Hoc Subcommittee on Domestic Recovery
Committee on Homeland Security & Governmental Affairs
340 Dirksen Senate Office Building
Washington, DC 20510
Phone: 202-224-2627

Mary Landrieu
D-LA Chair

Thomas Carper
D-DE

Mark Pryor
D-AR

Joe Lieberman
D-CT (Ex-Officio)

Ted Stevens
R-AK

Peter Domenici
R-NM

Susan Collins
R-ME (Ex-Officio)

Ad Hoc Subcommittee on State, Local & Private Sector Preparedness & Integration
Committee on Homeland Security & Governmental Affairs
340 Dirksen Senate Office Building
Washington, DC 20510
Phone: 202-224-2627

Mark Pryor
D-AR Chairman

Daniel Akaka
D-HI

Mary Landrieu
D-LA

Barack Obama
D-IL

Claire McCaskill
D-MO

Jon Tester
D-MT

Joe Lieberman
D-CT (Ex-Officio)

John Sununu
R-NH Ranking Member

George Voinovich
R-OH

Norm Coleman
R-MN

Peter Domenici
R-NM

John Warner
R-VA

Susan Collins
R-ME (Ex-Officio)

Subcommittee on Domestic and Foreign Marketing, Inspection & Plant and Animal Health
Committee on Agriculture, Nutrition & Forestry
Russell Senate Office Building
Room SR-328A
Washington, DC 20510
Phone: 202-224-2035
URL: agriculture.senate.gov/sub.htm

Max Baucus
D-MT Chairman

Conrad Kent
D-ND

Debbie Stabenow
D-MI

E Benjamin Nelson
D-NE

Ken Salazar
D-CO

Bob Casey Jr
D-PA

Lindsey Graham
R-SC Ranking Member

Mitch McConnell
R-KY

Pat Roberts
R-KS

Mike Crapo
R-ID

John Thune
R-SD

Subcommittee on Homeland Security
Appropriations Committee
US Capitol, S-131
Washington, DC 20510
Phone: 202-224-7363

Robert C Byrd
D-WV Chairman

Daniel Inouye
D-HI

Patrick J Leahy
D-VT

Barbara Mikulski
D-MD

Herbert Kohl
D-WI

Patty Murray
D-WA

Mary L Landrieu
D-LA

Frank Lautenberg
D-NJ

E Benjamin Nelson
D-NE

Thad Cochran
R-MS Ranking Member

Judd Gregg
R-NH

Ted Stevens
R-AK

Arlen Specter
R-PA

Peter Domenici
R-NM

Richard Shelby
R-AL

Larry Craig
R-ID

Lamar Alexander
R-TN

Subcommittee on Emerging Threats & Capabilities
Committee on Armed Services
228 Russell Senate Office Building
Washington, DC 20510
Phone: 202-224-3871
Fax: 202-228-0037
URL: armed-services.senate.gov/scmembrs.htm

Jack Reed
D-RI Chairman

Edward (Ted) M Kennedy
D-MA

Robert C Byrd
D-WV

Bill Nelson
D-FL

E Benjamin Nelson
D-NE

Evan Bayh
D-IN

Hillary Rodham Clinton
D-NY

Elizabeth H Dole
R-NC Ranking Member

John Cornyn
R-TX

John Warner
R-VA

Susan M Collins
R-ME

Mel Martinez
R-FL

Lindsey O Graham
R-SC

Richard W Fieldhouse
Majority Professional Staff

Lynn F Rusten
Minority Professional Staff

Subcommittee on Readiness & Management Support
Committee on Armed Services
228 Russell Senate Office Building
Washington, DC 20510
Phone: 202-224-3871

Daniel K Akaka
D-HI Chairman

Robert C Byrd
D-WV

Mark Pryor
D-AR

Claire McCaskill
D-MO

Evan Bayh
D-IN

Hillary Rodham Clinton
D-NY

Carl Levin
D-MI (Ex-Officio)

John Ensign
R-NV Ranking Member

James M Inhofe
R-OK

Elizabeth H Dole
R-NC

Jeff Sessions
R-AL

Saxby Chambliss
R-GA

John McCain
R-AZ (Ex-Officio)

Michael J McCord
Majority Professional Staff

Lucian L Niemeyer
Minority Professional Staff

Subcommittee on Strategic Forces
Committee on Armed Services
228 Russell Senate Office Building
Washington, DC 20510
Phone: 202-224-3871

Bill Nelson
D-FL Chairman

Robert C Byrd
D-WV

E Benjamin Nelson
D-NE

Mark Pryor
D-AR

Jack Reed
D-RI

Carl Levin
D-MI (Ex-Officio)

Jeff Sessions
R-AL Ranking Member

James M Inhofe
R-OK

Lindsey O Graham
R-SC

John Thune
R-SD

John McCain
R-AZ (Ex-Officio)

Madelyn R Creedon
Majority Professional Staff
Phone: 202-224-3871

Robert M Soofer
Minority Professional Staff

Subcommittee on Aviation Operations, Safety & Security
Committee on Commerce, Science & Transportation
508 Dirksen Senate Office Building
Washington, DC 20510
Phone: 202-224-9000
Phone: 202-224-5184

Jay Rockefeller
D-WV Chairman

John Kerry
D-MA

Byron Dorgan
D-ND

Barbara Boxern
D-CA

Bill Nelson
D-FL

Maria Cantwell
D-WA

Frank Lautenburg
D-NJ

Mark Pryor
D-AR

Thomas Carper
D-DE

Claire McCaskill
D-MO

Amy Klobuchar
D-MN

Trent Lott
R-MS Ranking Member

John McCain
R-AZ

Kay Hutchison
R-TX

Olympia Snowe
R-ME

Gordon Smith
R-OR

John Ensign
R-NV

John Sununu
R-NH

James DeMint
R-SC

David Vitter
R-LA

John Thune
R-SD

Subcommittee on Surface Transportation and Merchant Marine Infrastructure, Safety & Security

Committee on Commerce, Science & Transportation
508 Dirksen Senate Office Building
Washington, DC 20510
Phone: 202-224-5115

Frank Lautenburg
D-NJ Chairman

John E Rockefeller
D-WV

John Kerry
D-MA

Byron Dorgan
D-ND

Maria Cantwell
D-WA

Mark Pryor
D-AR

Thomas Carper
D-DE

Claire McCaskill
D-MO

Amy Klobuchar
D-MN

Gordon Smith
R-OR Ranking Member

John McCain
R-AZ

Trent Lott
R-MS

Kay Hutchison
R-TX

Olympia Snowe
R-ME

James DeMint
R-SC

David Vitter
R-LA

John Thune
R-SD

Subcommittee on Federal Financial Management, Government Info, Federal Svcs & International Security

Homeland Security & Governmental Affairs Committee
439 Senate Hart Office Building
Washington, DC 20510
Phone: 202-224-2441

Fax: 202-228-2190

Description: Responsible for the effectiveness and efficiency of federal financial management; the organization and management of US nuclear export policy; studying the effectiveness of present national security methods and arms proliferation; government information, including information technology; and census and collection of economic and social statistics.

Thomas R Carper
D-DE Chairman

Carl Levin
D-MI

Daniel K Akaka
D-HI

Barack Obama
D-IL

Claire McCaskill
D-MO

Jon Tester
D-MT

Joe Lieberman
D-CT (Ex-Officio)

Tom Coburn
R-OK Ranking Member

Ted Stevens
R-AK

George V Voinovich
R-OH

Peter Domenici
R-NM

John Sununu
R-NH

Susan Collins
R-ME (Ex-Officio)

Subcommittee on Oversight of the Terrorist Surveillance Program

Senate Select Committee on Intelligence
211 Hart Senate Office Building
Washington, DC 20510
Phone: 202-224-1700

John D Rockefeller
D-WV Chairman

Carl Levin
D-MI

Dianne Feinstein
D-CA

Orrin Hatch
R-UT

Christopher Bond
R-MO

STATE AGENCIES

Alabama

Alabama Main Homeland Security Office

401 Adams Avenue
Suite 560
Montgomery, AL 36130
Mailing Address: PO Box 304115
Phone: 334-956-7250
Fax: 334-223-1120
URL: www.homelandsecurity.alabama.gov/
e-mail: information@dhs.alabama.gov

Description: Alabama was the first state in the Nation to create its own Cabinet-level Department of Homeland Security. The department's organization mirrors the U.S. Department of Homeland Security and is divided into four major functional areas: Borders, Ports and Transportation; Science and Technology; Information Management and Budget; and Emergency Preparedness and Response.

Robert R Riley
Governor
Phone: 334-242-7100
e-mail: governorbobriley@governor.state.al.us

Jim Folfom
Lieutenant Governor
Phone: 334-242-7900
e-mail: info@ltgov.state.al.us

Troy King
Attorney General
Phone: 334-242-7300
e-mail: tking@governor.state.al.us

James Walker
Director Homeland Security
Phone: 334-956-7250
e-mail: director@dhs.alabama.gov

Bruce P Baughman
Assistant Director Emergency Preparedness & Response
Phone: 205-280-2201
e-mail: bruceb@ema.alabama.gov

Dennis Wright
Assistant Director, Borders & Transportation
Phone: 334-956-7255
e-mail: dennis.wright@dhs.alabama.gov

Norven Goddard
Assistant Director, Science & Technology
Phone: 256-955-3327
e-mail: norven.goddard@dhs.alabama.gov

Joe Davis
Assistant Director Management
Phone: 334-956-7253
e-mail: joe.davis@dhs.alabama.gov

Agriculture and Industries Department

1445 Federal Drive
Richard Beard Building
Montgomery, AL 36107-1100
Mailing Address: PO Box 3336, AL 36109
Phone: 334-240-7100
Fax: 334-240-7190
URL: www.agi.alabama.gov

Description: To provide timely, fair and expert regulatory control over product, business entities, movement, and application of goods and services for which applicable state and federal law exists and strive to protect and provide service to Alabama consumers. Department personnel will actively work to initiate and support economic development activities and promote domestic and internationalconsumption of Alabama products.

Ron Sparks
Commissioner
Phone: 334-240-7100
e-mail: ron.sparks@agi.alabama.gov

Douglas Rigney
Deputy Commissioner
Phone: 334-240-7100
e-mail: doug.rigney@agi.alabama.gov

Ronnie Murphy
Deputy Commissioner, Agriculture & Animal Protection Division
Phone: 334-240-7282
e-mail: ronnie.murphy@agi.alabama.gov

Teresa Smiley
Deputy Commissioner, Food Safety & Consumer Division
Phone: 334-240-7285
e-mail: teresa.smiley@agi.alabama.gov

Ray Hilburn
Deputy Commissioner
Phone: 334-240-7285
e-mail: ray.hilburn@agi.alabama.gov

Arnold Leak
Information Technology Director
Phone: 334-240-7201
e-mail: help.desk@agi.alabama.gov

Terry Guy
Petroleum Commodities Section
Phone: 334-240-7127
e-mail: terry.guy@agi.alabama.gov

Cathy Johnson
Public Relations & Farmers Bulletin
Phone: 334-240-7125
e-mail: cathy.johnson@agi.alabama.gov

Crystal Allen
State Veterinarian
Phone: 334-240-7253
e-mail: crystal.allen@agi.alabama.gov

Marie Spear
Shipping Point Inspection Director
Phone: 334-240-7231
e-mail: marie.spear@agi.alabama.gov

Lance Hester
Food Safety Section Director
Phone: 334-240-7202
e-mail: lance.hester@agi.alabama.gov

Alabama Association of Chiefs of Police
1 Retail Drive
Russell Building
Montgomery, AL 36110-3123
Mailing Address: PO Box 36121
Phone: 334-207-2712
Phone: 888-283-0966
Fax: 334-271-0071
URL: www.aacop.com
e-mail: aacop@aacop.com

Description: To improve the quality and professionalism of law enforcement in the state.

Daphne Leveson
Executive Director
Phone: 504-232-5104

Alabama National Guard
1720 Cong W L Dickinson Drive
Montgomery, AL 36109-0711
Mailing Address: PO Box 3711
Phone: 334-271-7200
Phone: 334-271-7266
Fax: 334-213-7511
URL: www.alguard.state.al.us; www.almont.ang.af.mil

Description: Comprised of both Army and Air National Guard components. Maintains properly trained and equipped units available for prompt mobilization for war, national emergency or as otherwise needed. The State mission is to provide trained and disiplined forces for domestic emergencies or otherwise required by State laws.

Major General John White
Adjutant General, Acting
Phone: 334-271-7200
e-mail: mark.bowen@us.army.mil

CSM Danny Ashley
State Command Sergeant Major
Phone: 334-271-7501

Lt Colonel Robert Horton
Public Affairs Office
Phone: 334-271-7244
e-mail: bob.horton1@us.army.mil

Colonel Charles Bonasera
State Army Aviation Officer
Phone: 334-280-2611

Department of Public Health
201 Monroe Street
RSA Tower
Montgomery, AL 36104
Mailing Address: PO Box 303017
Phone: 334-206-5300
Phone: 866-264-4073
Fax: 334-206-2008
URL: www.adph.org

Description: To provide caring, high quality and professional services for the improvement and protection of the public's health through disease prevention and the assurance of public health services to resident and transient populations of the state regardless of social circumstances or the ability to pay.

Donald Williamson
State Health Officer
Phone: 334-206-5200

John Wible
General Counsel
Phone: 334-206-5209

Reuben E Davidson
Public Health Administrative Officer
Phone: 334-206-5233

Kirksey Whatley
Radiation Control Office Director
Phone: 334-206-5391

David Turberville
Radioactive Materials Inspection
Phone: 334-206-5391

William P Allinder
Environmental Services Bureau Director
Phone: 334-206-5373

Jimmy Coles
Community Environmental Protection Division
Phone: 334-206-5373

Ron Dawsey
Food/Milk/Lodging Division
Phone: 334-206-5375

Disease Control & Prevention
Department of Public Health
201 Monroe Street
RSA Tower
Montgomery, AL 36104
Phone: 334-206-5325
Fax: 334-206-2090

Dr Charles H Woernle
Director/Assistant State Health Officer
Phone: 334-206-5325

Virginia Johns
Deputy Director
Phone: 334-206-5325

William Callan
Clinical Laboratories Director
Phone: 334-260-3400

Fred Grady
Epidemiology Division Director
Phone: 334-206-5347

Richard Holmes
Communicable Disease Electronic Surveillance Program
Phone: 334-206-5347

Neil Sass
Toxicology Program
Phone: 334-206-5973

Winkler Sims
Immunization Division Director
Phone: 334-206-5023

Jane Cheeks
HIV/AIDS Division Director
Phone: 334-206-5364

Scott Jones
TB Control Division Director
Phone: 334-206-5330

Sandra Langston
STD Division Director

Emergency Management Agency
5898 County Road 41
PO Drawer 2160
Clanton, AL 35046
Phone: 205-280-2200
Fax: 205-280-2495
URL: http://ema.alabama.gov
e-mail: info@ema.alabama.gov

Description: The Alabama Emergency Management Agency coordinates emergency state assistance to local communities when they are affected by disasters such as tornadoes, floods or hurricanes. AEMA also works with the Federal Emergency Management Agency (FEMA) to administer federal assistance during a presidential declared disaster, and with local EMAs and the media to provide information about how you and your family can protect yourselves from natural disasters. Preparedness, response, recovery and mitigation programs are exercised on a regular basis to make sure that Alabama is prepared for the next natural or technical emergency.

Bruce P Baughman
Director
Phone: 205-280-2201
e-mail: bruceb@ema.alabama.gov

John James
Assistant Director
Phone: 205-280-2277
e-mail: johnj@ema.alabama.gov

Bill Filter
Operations Division Chief
Phone: 205-280-2212
e-mail: billf@ema.alabama.gov

Debbie Peery
Hazard Mitigation Officer

Phone: 205-280-2476
e-mail: debbiep@aema.state.al.us

Charles Williams
Preparedness Division
Phone: 205-280-2222
e-mail: charlesw@ema.alabama.gov

Jerry McRay
Information Technology Division
Phone: 205-280-2237
e-mail: jerrym@ema.alabama.gov

Yasamie Richardson
Public Information Manager
Phone: 205-280-2275
e-mail: yasamier@ema.alabama.gov

Frank Price
Technological Hazards Branch Chief
Phone: 205-280-2261
e-mail: frankp@ema.alabama.gov

Kyle Eskridge
Training Officer
Phone: 205-280-2221

Emergency Response/Emergency Medical Services & Trauma
Department of Public Health
201 Monroe Street, Suite 750
RSA Tower
Montgomery, AL 36104
Phone: 334-206-5383
Fax: 334-206-5260
URL: www.adph.org/ems

Description: Responsible for protecting the health, safety and welfare of the public by assuring that emrgency medical services provided by ambulance services, emergency medical response agencies, training entities and emergency medical technicians meet or exceed established standards.

John Campbell, MD
Medical Director
Phone: 334-206-5440
e-mail: johncampbell@adph.state.al.us

Dennis Blair
Director
Phone: 334-206-5237
e-mail: dblair@adph.state.al.us

Russell Crowley
Deputy Director
Phone: 334-206-5294
e-mail: rcrowley@adph.state.al.us

Verla Thomas
Trauma/EMSC Manager
Phone: 334-206-5127
e-mail: verlathomas@adph.state.al.us

Hugh Hollon
Education/Certification Manager
Phone: 334-206-5293
e-mail: hhollon@adph.state.al.us

Environmental Management Department

1400 Coliseum Boulevard
Montgomery, AL 36110-2059
Mailing Address: PO Box 301463 Montgomery AL
36130-1463
Phone: 334-271-7700
Fax: 334-271-3043
URL: www.adem.state.al.us

Description: Responsibly adopt and fairly enforce rules and regulations consistent with the statutory authority grantes to the Alabama Environmental Management Commission and the Alabama Department of Environmental Management to tprotect and improve the quality of Alabama's environment and the health of all its citizens.

Onis Glenn III
Director
Phone: 334-271-7710

Ron Gore
Air Division Chief
Phone: 334-271-7868

Gerald Hardy
Land Division Chief
Phone: 334-271-7730

James McIndoe
Water Division Chief
Phone: 334-271-7823

Glenda Dean
Industrial/Municipal Facilities
Phone: 334-270-5602

Debi Thomas
Commission Executive Assistant
Phone: 334-271-7706

Health Planning and Development Agency

100 N Union Street
Suite 870
Montomgery, AL 36130
Mailing Address: PO Box 303025 Montgomery AL
36130-3025
Phone: 334-242-4103
Fax: 334-242-4113
URL: http://shpda.state.al.us
e-mail: info@shpda.state.al.us

Description: To ensure that quality health care facilities, services, and equipment are available and accessible to the citizens of Alabama in a manner which assures continuity of care at a reasonable cost.

Alva M Lambert
Executive Director
Phone: 334-242-4103

James E Sanders
Deputy Director
e-mail: james.sanders@shpda.alabama.gov

Swaid Swain, MD
Certificate of Need Review Chair
Phone: 334-242-4103

Judge John Rochester
Statewide Health Coordinating Council Chair
Phone: 334-242-4103

Oil & Gas Board

420 Hackberry Lane
PO Box 869999
Tuscaloosa, AL 35486-6999
Phone: 205-349-2852
Fax: 205-349-2861
URL: www.ogb.state.al.us
e-mail: info@ogb.state.al.us

Description: The Board is a regulatory agency of the State of Alabama responsible for preventing waste and promoting the conservation of oil and gas while ensuring the protection of both the environment and the correlative rights of owners.

Berry H Tew Jr
Supervisor/State Geologist
Phone: 205-247-3679
e-mail: ntew@ogb.state.al.us

Marvin Rogers
General Counsel
Phone: 205-247-3680
e-mail: mrogers@ogb.state.al.us

David E Bolin
Deputy Director
Phone: 205-247-3579
e-mail: dbolin@ogb.state.al.us

Richard Raymond
Assistant Supervisor, Technical Operations & Ground Water Protection
Phone: 205-247-3580
e-mail: rraymond@ogb.state.al.us

Doug Hall
Ground Water Protection Chief/Technical Evaluations
Phone: 205-247-3656
e-mail: dhall@ogb.state.al.us

Leigh Blake
Gathering Lines, Plants, Safety & Facilities
Phone: 251-438-4848
e-mail: lbalke@ogb.state.al.us

Protective Services Division/Capitol Police Unit
Public Safety Department

301 S Ripley Street
Montgomery, AL 36104
Mailing Address: PO Box 1151, Montgomery, AL 36102
Phone: 334-242-0700
Fax: 334-242-2757
URL: www.dps.state.al.us/public/protective_services
e-mail: info@dps.state.al.us

Description: Charged with the responsibility of preserving order, preventing crime, and protecting the citizens and property in the State Capitol complex and all state buildings and agencies within the state.

Major Robert Goodner
Chief
Phone: 334-242-0700

Public Safety Department
301 S Ripley Street
Montgomery, AL 36104
Mailing Address: PO Box 1511, 36102
Phone: 334-242-4371
Fax: 334-242-0512
URL: www.dps.state.al.us
e-mail: info@dps.state.al.us

Description: The mission of the Alabama Department of Public Safety is to protect and serve Alabama residents equally and objectively, enforce state laws and uphold the constitutions of the United States and the State of Alabama.

Colonel J Christopher Murphy
Director
Phone: 334-242-4394

Lt Colonel F A Bingham
Assistant Director
Phone: 334-242-4703

Major Charles Andrews
Administrative Division
Phone: 334-242-4394

Major Roscoe Howell
Highway Patrol Division Chief
Phone: 334-242-4393

Major Patrick Manning
Investigation Division Chief
Phone: 334-353-2201

Tpr John Reese
Public Information/Education Unit
Phone: 334-242-4445

Major Charles Andrews
Service Division Chief
Phone: 334-242-4387

Public Service Commission
100 N Union Street, RSA Union
Suite 850
Montgomery, AL 36130
Mailing Address: PO Box 304260
Phone: 334-242-5218
Fax: 334-242-0921
URL: www.psc.state.al.us

Description: Regulates the public utilities and some aspects of the transportation business industry in Alabama.

Jim Sullivan
President
Phone: 334-242-5207
e-mail: jim.sullivan@psc.alabama.gov

Jan Cook
Commissioner
Phone: 334-242-5203
e-mail: jan.cook@psc.alabama.gov

Susan D Parker
Commissioner
Phone: 334-242-5191
e-mail: susan.parker@psc.alabama.gov

Janice Hamilton
Energy Division Director
Phone: 334-242-2696

Britt Roberts
Transportation Division Director
Phone: 334-242-5980

Darrell Baker
Telecommunications Division Director
Phone: 334-242-5983

John Garner
Legal Division/Chief Administrative Law Judge
e-mail: john.garner@psc.alabama.gov

Chris Harvey
Gas Pipeline Safety Administrator
Phone: 334-242-5778

Judy McLean
Advisory Division Director
Phone: 334-242-5025

State Port Authority
250 N Water St
Mobile, AL 36602
Mailing Address: PO Box 1588 Mobile, AL 36633
Phone: 251-441-7200
Fax: 251-441-7216
URL: www.asdd.com

Description: Dedicated in 1928, the state docks have an economy of $3 billion statewide, $467 million in state taxes and generate 118,000 jobs. Imports are coal, aluminum, iron, steel, lumber, wood pulp, plywood, veneers, fence posts, roll & cut paper, and chemicals. Exports include coal, forest products, iron, steel and chemicals.

James K Lyons
Director/CEO
Phone: 251-441-7200
e-mail: jlyons@asdd.com

H S Thorne
Vice President, Operations
Phone: 251-441-7238
e-mail: sthorne@asdd.com

Herbert McCants
Port Police Chief
Phone: 251-441-7777
e-mail: hmccants@asdd.com

Jimmie Flanagan
Assistant Police Chief
Phone: 251-441-7777
e-mail: jflanagan@asdd.com

Polly Wilkins
Container Operation Supervisor
Phone: 251-441-7046
e-mail: pwilkins@asdd.com

Judith Adams
Media Relations Manager & Economic Development
Phone: 251-441-7003
e-mail: jadams@asdd.com

David K Carey
Harbormaster
Phone: 251-441-7250
e-mail: dcarey@asdd.com

Lynn Driskell
Terminal Railway Superintendent
Phone: 251-441-7301
e-mail: ldriskell@asdd.com

Hal Hudgins
Vice President, Security & Port Planning
Phone: 251-441-7237
e-mail: hhudgins@asdd.com

William Hurston
Information Technology Manager
Phone: 251-441-7017
e-mail: shurston@asdd.com

Transportation Department
1409 Coliseum Boulevard
Montgomery, AL 36110
Mailing Address: PO Box 303050
Phone: 334-242-6358
Fax: 334-262-8041
URL: www.dot.state.al.us

Description: Provides a safe, efficient, environmentall sound intermodal transportation system for all users, especially the taxpayers of Alabama.

Joe McInnes
Director
Phone: 334-242-6311

L Dan Morris
Assistant Director
Phone: 334-242-6319

Don Vaughn
Chief Engineer/Deputy Director
Phone: 334-242-6318

John Eagerton
Aeronautics Bureau Chief
e-mail: eagertonj@dot.state.al.us

Martha Hutsler
Aeronautics Specialist
e-mail: hutslerm@dot.state.al.us

Frank R Farmer
Aeronautics Manager
e-mail: farmerf@dot.state.al.us

William F Conway
Bridge Engineer
Phone: 334-242-6007
e-mail: conwayf@dot.state.al.us

Jeffery W Brown
Research & Development Engineer
Phone: 334-353-6940

Robert J Jilla
Transportation Senior Administrator
Phone: 334-353-6400

Norman Lumpkin
Public Affairs
Phone: 334-242-6640

Willie Franklin
Airport Engineer
e-mail: franklin@dot.state.al.us

STATE AGENCIES

Alaska

Alaska Main Homeland Security Office
Div. of Homeland Security & Emergency Mgmt
PO Box 5750
Fort Richardson, AK 99505-5750
Phone: 907-428-7000
Fax: 907-428-7009
URL: www.ak-prepared.com/homelandsecurity/
e-mail: dhs&em_emergency_mgmt@ak-prepared.com

Sarah Palin
Governor
Phone: 907-465-3500
e-mail: Governor@gov.state.ak.us

Sean Parnell
Lieutenant Governor
Phone: 907-465-3520
e-mail: lt_Governor@gov.state.ak.us

John Madden
Director Homeland Security & Emergency Management
Phone: 907-428-7000

David W Marquez
Attorney General
Phone: 907-465-2133
e-mail: Attorney General@law.state.ak.us

Air National Guard
5005 Raspberry Road
Anchorage, AK 95502-1982
Phone: 907-428-6075
Fax: 907-249-1467
URL: www.ak-prepared.com/dmva/akang.htm

Description: Motivated Air Guard flying unit, relevant in peace, indispensable in war, trained and ready to respond immediately.

Brigadier General Tony Hart
Commander

Alaska National Guard
PO Box 5800
Ft Richardson, AK 99505-0800
Phone: 907-428-6050
Fax: 907-428-6052
URL: www.ak-prepared.com/armyguard/

Description: Mission is to organize, equip and train quality units to conduct tactical operations and stability support operations in support of worldwide US Army requirements and State of Alaska emergency missions.

Brigadier Thomas Katkus
Commander

Alaska Public Broadcasting Commission
PO Box 200009
Anchorage, AK 99520
Phone: 907-277-6300
Fax: 907-277-6350
URL: www.alaska.net/~arcs
e-mail: apbc@admin.state.ak.us

Description: Provides leadership, vision, coordination, technical and administrative support to Alaska's local public broadcasting institutions.

James S Waste
Executive Director
Phone: 907-586-1600
e-mail: jamie@akpb.org

David L Geesin
Deputy Director
Phone: 972-776-300
e-mail: david@akpb.org

Association of Chiefs of Police
PO Box 167
Seward, AK 99664
Phone: 907-224-3338
Fax: 907-224-8480
URL: www.aacop.org
e-mail: spdchief@cityofseward.net

Description: The objectives are to, in general, advance and improve the criminal justice system, particularly law enforcement, by fostering cooperation and the exchange of information and experience among law enforcement administrators throughout Alaska.

Chief Thomas Clemons
President

Division of Agriculture
1800 Glenn Highway
Suite 12
Palmer, AK 99645
Phone: 907-745-7200
Fax: 907-745-7112
URL: www.dnr.state.ak.us/ag

Description: Promotes and encourages development of an agriculture industry in the State.

Douglas Warner
Acting Director/Marketing & Inspection
Phone: 907-761-3867
e-mail: douglas_warner@dnr.state.ak.us

Steve Trickett
Agricultural Land & Sales Management
Phone: 907-761-3863
e-mail: steve_trickett@dnr.state.ak.us

Environmental Health Division

555 Cordova Street
Anchorage, AK 99501
Phone: 907-269-7645
Fax: 907-269-7654
URL: www.dec.state.ak.us/eh

Description: The Environmental Health Division deals with the basics: safe drinking water, food and sanitray practices. The goal is to provide businesses with clear standards so that they can protect our environment and provide safe food and drinking water to Alaskans.

Kristin Ryan
Director
Phone: 907-269-7644
e-mail: kristin_ryan@dec.state.ak.us

Ron Klein
Food Safety/Sanitation Program Manager
Phone: 907-269-7583
e-mail: ron_klein@dec.state.ak.us

James Weise
Drinking Water Program Manager
Phone: 907-269-7647
e-mail: james_weise@dec.state.ak.us

Epidemiology Section

Public Health
3601 C Street
Suite 540
Anchorage, AK 99503
Mailing Address: PO Box 240249, 99524-0249
Phone: 907-269-8000
Phone: 800-478-0084
Fax: 907-562-7802
URL: www.epi.asaska.gov
e-mail: outbreak@health.state.ak.us

Joe McLaughlin
Acting Chief

Dr Beth Funk
Epidemiologist

Fire Marshal's Office

5700 E Tudor Road
Anchorage, AK 99507-1225
Phone: 907-269-5491
Fax: 907-338-4375
URL: www.dps.state.ak.us/fire/asp

Description: To prevent the loss of life and propery from fire and explosion.

David Tyler
Director
e-mail: david_tyler@dps.state.ak.us

Steven (Rusty) Belanger
Asst State Fire Marshal
e-mail: steven_belanger@dps.state.ak.us

Injury Prevention & Emergency Medical Services

Public Health
410 Willoughby Ave
Room 103
Juneau, AK 99801
Mailing Address: PO Box 110616, 99811-0616
Phone: 907-465-3027
Fax: 907-465-1733
URL: www.hss.state.ak.us/dph/ipems/; www.chems.alaska.gov

Description: Programs address access to health care and some of the major causes of disease, injury, and disabilities affecting people in Alaska.

Timothy Bundy
Section Chief
Phone: 907-465-8635
e-mail: timothy_bundy@health.state.ak.us

Deborah Hull-Jilly
Injury Prevention Unit Manager
Phone: 907-269-8078
e-mail: deborah_choromanski_hull-jilly@health.state.ak.us

Kathy McLeron
EMS Unit Manager
Phone: 907-465-2262
e-mail: kathy_mcleron@health.state.ak.us

Mike Branum
EMS Training Coordinator
Phone: 907-465-5467
e-mail: michael_branum@health.state.ak.us

Oil and Gas Conservation Commission

333 W 7th Avenue
Suite 100
Anchorage, AK 99501-3539
Phone: 907-279-1433
Fax: 907-276-7542
URL: www.aogcc.alaska.gov
e-mail: aogcc_customer_svc@admin.state.ak.us

Description: Protects the public interest in exploration and development of oil and gas resources, ensuring conservation pratices, and increasing ultimate recovery, while protecting health, safety, the environment, and property rights.

Cathy Foerster
Commissioner
Phone: 907-793-1221
e-mail: cathy_foerster@admin.state.ak.us

John Norman
Commissioner
Phone: 907-793-1221
e-mail: john_norman@admin.state.ak.us

Dan Seamount
Commissioner
Phone: 907-793-1221
e-mail: dan_seamount@admin.state.ak.us

Ports and Harbors

Transportation and Public Facilities Department
3132 Channel Drive
PO Box 112500
Juneau, AK 99811-2500

Phone: 907-465-3979
Fax: 907-465-2460
URL: www.dot.state.ak.us

Description: Provides design, technical and administrative assistance for coastal and harbor projects to federal, state and local agencies and communities.

Michael Lukshin
State Ports & Harbors Engineer
Phone: 907-465-3979

Public Health

350 Main Street
Room 508
Juneau, AK 99801
Mailing Address: PO Box 110610, 99811-0610
Phone: 907-465-3092
Fax: 907-586-1877
URL: www.hss.state.ak.us/dph/
e-mail: dph@health.state.ak.us

Description: Promotes the health an dquality of life of al Alaskans by preventing and controlling disease, birth defects, injury, disability and death resulting from interactions between people and their environment.

Jay C Butler, PhD
Director
Phone: 907-465-3092

Bernard J Jilly
Laboratories Section Chief
Phone: 907-334-2109
e-mail: bernd_jilly@health.state.ak.us

Rhonda D Richtsmeier
Nursing Chief
Phone: 907-465-3150
e-mail: rhonda_richtsmeier@health.state.ak.us

Phillip Mitchell
Vital Statistics Bureau
Phone: 907-465-3391
e-mail: phillip_mitchell@health.state.ak.us

Public Safety Department

PO Box 111200
Juneau, AK 99811-1200
Phone: 907-465-4322
Fax: 907-465-4362
URL: www.dps.state.ak.us

Description: Providing functions relative to the protection of life, property and wildlife resources.

Walt Monegan
Commissioner
Phone: 907-465-4322

John D Glass
Deputy Commissioner
Phone: 907-269-5086

Gretchen A Pence
Special Assistant
Phone: 907-465-4322
e-mail: gretchen_pence@dps.state.ak.us

Radiological Health

4500 Boniface Parkway
Anchorage, AK 99507-2107
Phone: 907-334-2107
Fax: 907-334-2161
URL:
www.hss.state.ak.us/dph/labs/radiological/radiological_health.htm

Description: Responsible for safe use of radiation sources in Alaska and for Radiation Protection, which includes the development of policies for evaluating radiation hazards, conducting surveys/investigations and training.

Clyde Pearce
Director
Phone: 907-334-2107
e-mail: clyde_pearce@health.state.ak.us

Spill Prevention and Response Division
Department of Environmental Conservation
410 Willoughby Avenue
Suite 303
Juneau, AK 99811-1800
Mailing Address: Po Box 111800
Phone: 907-465-5250
Fax: 907-465-5262
URL: www.dec.state.ak.us/spar

Description: The Spill Prevention and Response Division prevents spills of oil and hazardous substances, prepares for when a spill occurs and responds rapidly to protect human health and the environment.

Larry Dietrick
Director
e-mail: larry_dietrick@dec.state.ak.us

State Defense Force

PO Box 5800
Fort Richardson, AK 99505-9800
Phone: 907-428-6875
Fax: 907-428-6853
URL: www.ak-prepared.com/asdf/
e-mail: asdf@ak-prepared.com

Description: Maintains an organized, trained military force, capable of timely and effective response to state emergencies; and provides military assistance to civil and military authorities in the preservation of life, property, and public safety.

Brigadier General Thomas Westall
Commander

State Medical Examiner

4500 S Boniface Parkway
Anchorage, AK 99507
Phone: 907-334-2200
Fax: 907-334-2216
URL: www.hss.state.ak.us/dph/sme/default.htm

Description: Responsible for conducting the medical/legal investigative work related to unanticipated, sudden or violent deaths, as well as providing consultation to law enforcement and the courts.

Dr Franc Fallico
Acting Chief Medical Examiner

Phone: 907-334-2214
e-mail: franc_fallico@health.state.ak.us

Kathleen Hickman
Acting Lead Investigator
Phone: 907-334-2205
e-mail: kathleen_hickman@health.state.ak.us

State Troopers Division
Public Safety Department
5700 E Tudor Road
Anchorage, AK 99507-1225
Phone: 907-269-5641
Fax: 907-337-2059
URL: www.dps.state.ak.us/ast/

Description: Provides statewide law enforcement, prevention of crime, pursuit and apprehension of offenders, service of civil and criminal process, prisoner transportation, central communications, and search and rescue.

Colonel Audie Holloway
Director
Phone: 907-269-5641
e-mail: audie_holloway@dps.state.ak.us

Major Matthew Leveque
Administrative Commander
Phone: 907-269-5611
e-mail: matthew_leveque@dps.state.ak.us

Captain Keith Mallard
Alaska Bureau of Alcohol & Drug Enforcement
Phone: 907-243-8916
e-mail: keith_mallard@dps.state.ak.us

Transportation and Public Facilities Department
3132 Channel Drive
PO Box 112500
Juneau, AK 99811-2500
Phone: 907-465-3900
Fax: 907-586-8365
URL: www.dot.state.ak.us

Description: Provide for the movement of people and goods and the delivery of State services.

Leo von Scheben
Commissioner
e-mail: commissioner@dotpf@dot.state.ak.us

John MacKinnon
Deputy Commissioner Highways & Public Facilities
Phone: 907-465-6973
e-mail: john_mackinnon@dot.state.ak.us

John Torgerson
Deputy Commissioner, Aviation of Marine Operations
Phone: 907-269-0730
e-mail: john_torerson@dot.state.ak.us

Dennis L Hardy
Deputy Commissioner, Marine Transportation
Phone: 907-465-6977
e-mail: dennis_hardy@dot.state.ak.us

Mike Chambers
Chief Communications Officer

Phone: 907-465-8994
e-mail: mike_chamber@dot.state.ak.us

STATE AGENCIES

American Samoa

American Samoa Territorial Office of Homeland Security

Executive Office Building
Third Floor, Utulei
Pago Pago, 96799
American Samoa
Phone: 684-633-4116
Phone: 684-633-5221
URL: www.asg-gov.net

Togiola TA Tulafono
Governor
Phone: 684-633-5221
e-mail: governorsoffice@asg-gov.net

Ipulael A Ipulasi
Lieutenant Governor
Phone: 684-633-5221

Siatega Malaetasi Mauga Togafau
Attorney General

Leiataua Birdsall V Ala'ilima
Territorial Emergency Management Coordination/Special Assistant to the Governor
Phone: 684-633-5221
e-mail: stohs@samoatelco.com

American Samoa Territorial Emergency Management Coordination (TEMCO)

Pago Pago, 96799
American Samoa
Mailing Address: PO Box 1086
Phone: 684-699-6415
Fax: 684-699-6414

Department of Agriculture

American Samoa Government Executive Office
Building, Utulei Territory of American Samoa
Pago Pago, 96799
American Samoa
Phone: 684-699-1497
Fax: 684-699-4031
URL: www.asg-gov.net/agriculture

Description: The mission of the Department of Agriculture is to promote, direct and assist the efforts of American Samoa's farmers to attain a high level of diversified food production to supply the needs of the Territory's residents for fresh, good quality, and low cost food products, thus reducing the Territory's dependence on imported foods.

Apefa'i Taifane
Director

Department of Health

American Samoa Government
Pago Pago, 96799
American Samoa
Phone: 684-633-4606
Fax: 684-633-5379

Uto'ofili Asofa'afetai Maga, MPH/MP
Director
Phone: 684-633-2243
e-mail: asomaga@americansamoa.gov

Department of Marine and Wildlife Resources

American Samoa Government, Executive Office
Building, Utulei Territory of American Samoa
Pago Pago, 96799
American Samoa
Phone: 684-633-4456
Fax: 684-633-5590

Description: Functions for the protection and management or the territory's marine and wildlife resources to the extent intended to best benefit the people of American Samoa while ensuring the integrity of such resources for posterity. The various projects undertaken by the department are to designed to: Generate information for the formulation of policies and guidelines for conservation and management of the resources; provide direct services and technical assistance for the development of commuity and government programs compatable with the wise utilization of natural resources; prevent or minimize abusive or exploitative use of resources through conservation education and implementation of applicable federal and local regulations.

Ufagafa Ray Tulafono
Director

Department of Port Administration

American Samoa Government, Territory of
American Samoa
Pago Pago, 96799
American Samoa
Phone: 684-633-4251
Fax: 684-633-5281

Description: In part ownership with port users, Port shall provide excellent service to customers and the community and by so doing raise the standard of living of the Territory to that of a developed country in a matter that protects our environment and maintains the best of our Fa'aSamoa.

Fofo Tuitele
Acting Director

Department of Public Saftey

American Samoa Government, Territory
of American Samoa
Pago Pago, 96799
American Samoa
Phone: 684-633-1111
Fax: 684-633-7296

Description: Consistent with the values of a democratic society,
it is the mission of the department of public saftey to protect the
community from crime and disorder. To accomplish this mission,
the departments role is to fairly and impartially enforce the law
within the limits of the police, fire, and corrections athorities
while upholding the constitiutional rights of all citizens by the
preservation of public peace, maintaining law and order, protection of the rights of persons or property, prevention of crime, and
valuing our employees as our most important resource.

Tuiteleleapaga Peseta Fue Ioane
Director
Phone: 684-633-1111

Enviromental Protection Agency

American Samoa Government, Territory of
American Samoa
Pago Pago, 96799
American Samoa
Phone: 684-633-2304
Fax: 684-633-5801

Description: The territorial emergency management coordinating office of american samoa has the primary mission to protect
the lives and property of the territory's people from the adverse
affects of natural and manmade disasters.

Togipa Tausaga
Director
Phone: 684-699-6481

STATE AGENCIES

Arizona

Arizona Main Homeland Security Office

1700 W Washington
Phoeniz, AZ 85007
Phone: 602-542-7030
Fax: 602-364-1521
URL: www.azdohs.gov
e-mail: hs@azdohs.gov

Janet Napolitano
Governor
Phone: 602-542-1900

Janice K Brewer
Secretary of State
Phone: 602-542-4285
e-mail: sosadmin@sos.state.az.us

Leesa Berens Morrison
Director Homeland Security
Phone: 602-542-7030

Terry Goddard
Attorney General
Phone: 602-542-5025

Agriculture Department

1688 W Adams Street
Phoenix, AZ 85007
Phone: 602-542-4373
Fax: 602-542-5420
URL: www.azda.gov

Description: To regulate and support Arizona agriculture in a manner that encourages farming, ranching, and agribusiness while protecting consumers and natural resources.

Donald Butler
Director
Phone: 602-542-0997

Katie Decker
Public Information Officer/Legislative Liaison
Phone: 602-542-0958

John Hunt
Associate Director-Animal Services Division
Phone: 602-542-7186

Jack Peterson
Associate Director-Environmental Services Division
Phone: 602-542-3575

G John Caravetta
Associate Director-Plant Services Division
Phone: 602-542-0994

Doug Marsh
Assistant Director-State Agricultural Laboratory
Phone: 602-744-4924

Arizona Association of Chiefs of Police

620 W Washington
Tempe P.D./Ralph Tranter
Tempe, AZ 85281
Mailing Address: 120 E 5th Street
Phone: 480-350-8750
Fax: 480-350-8337

Ralph Tranter
Executive Director
e-mail: ralph_tranter@tempe.gov

Association of Contingency Planners

PO Box 67434
Phoenix, AZ 85032
Phone: 480-554-8717
URL: www.azacp.org
e-mail: info@azacp.org

Description: A non-profit mutual benefit association with membership open to anyone with interest or responsibility for the varied aspects of contingency planning. ACP is an organization for contingency planners, business continuity professionals, and emergency managers.

Beverly Deason
President

Capitol Police Division

1700 W Washington
B-15
Phoenix, AZ 85007
Phone: 602-542-0362
Fax: 602-542-0368
URL: www.azcapitolpolice.azdoa.gov
e-mail: capwebmail@azdoa.gov

Description: Provides a high quality service and reponse in the Phoenix and Tucson Capitol Complex area, while ensuring the protection of life, property, and preserving the peace.

Thomas Lane
Chief
Phone: 602-542-0362

Captain Andrew Stanbitz
Commander
Phone: 602-364-0399

Department of Fire, Building and Life Safety

1110 W Washington

Suite 100
Phoenix, AZ 85007
Phone: 602-364-1003
Fax: 602-364-1052
URL: www.dbfs.state.az.us

Description: Established to further the public interest of safety and welfare by maintaining and enforcing standards of quality and safety for manufactured homes, mobile homes, and factory-built buildings and by reducing hazards to life and property through the maintenance and enforcement of the state fire code.

Robert Barger
Director
Phone: 602-364-1003

Gary Grounds
Deputy Director, OMH

John Rowlinson
State Fire Marshal
Phone: 602-364-1003

Disease Control Research Commission

15 S 15th Avenue
Suite 103A
Phoenix, AZ 85007
Phone: 602-542-1028
Fax: 602-542-6380
URL: www.adcrc.com
e-mail: adcrc1@getnet.net

Description: Awards contracts for epidemiology and diagnosis, formulation of cures, medically accepted prevention of diseases, and projects for researching the causes.

Dawn C Schroeder
Executive Director

James Matthews
Deputy Director

Division of Emergency Management

5636 E McDowell Road
Phoenix, AZ 85008
Phone: 602-244-0504
Phone: 800-411-2336
Fax: 602-231-6231
URL: www.dem.state.az.us

Louis B Trammell
Director
Phone: 602-244-0504

Louis B Trammell
Deputy Director
Phone: 602-231-6206
e-mail: lou.trammell@azdema.gov

Charles McHugh
Response, Recovery & Mitigation Assistant Director
Phone: 602-231-6242
e-mail: chuck.mchugh@azdema.gov

Jan Kimmell
Preparedness Assistant Director
Phone: 602-231-6398

Mark Howard
Telecommunications Officer

Phone: 602-231-6201
e-mail: jay.vargo@azdema.gov

John Dirickson
Training & Exercise Director
Phone: 602-231-6262
e-mail: john.dirickson@azdema.gov

Vic Calderon
State Emergency Response Planning Officer
Phone: 602-231-6327
e-mail: vic.calderon@azdema.gov

Emergency Medical Services Bureau & Trauma System

Health Services Department
150 N 18th Avenue
Suite 540
Phoenix, AZ 85007
Phone: 602-364-3150
Phone: 800-200-8523
Fax: 602-364-3568
URL: www.azdhs.gov/bems

Description: Protect the health and safety of people recquiring emergency medical services; promote improvements in Arizona's EMS and trauma system through research and education og the public and EMS providers; and provide courteous, professional and responsible serves to the public and EMS providers.

Terri Mullins
Chief
Phone: 602-364-3150
e-mail: mullint@azdhs.gov

Bentley Bobrow, MD
Medical Director
Phone: 602-364-3154
e-mail: bobrowb@azdhs.gov

Ron Anderson
Certification & Enforcement Section Chief
Phone: 602-364-3182
e-mail: andersro@azdhs.gov

Vicki Conditt
Trauma System Section Chief
Phone: 602-364-3155
e-mail: conditv@azdhs.gov

Krista Anheluk
Air & Ground Ambulance Services Manager
Phone: 602-364-3164
e-mail: anheluk@azdhs.gov

Emergency Preparedness and Response Bureau

Health Services Department
150 N 18th Avenue
Suite 150
Phoenix, AZ 85007
Phone: 602-364-3289
Fax: 602-364-3264
URL: www.azdhs.gov/phs/edc/edrp/

Description: The Bureau of Emergency Preparedness and Response was created to detect and respond to natural or intentional disease events. Funded by the Centers for Disease Control and Prevention, it is the programs mission to ensure that the public health system of Arizona is prepared for public health emergencies. The Bureau has five separate programs areas: Preparedness and Planning; Electronic Disease Surveillance Program; Arizona Health Alert Network; Risk Communication and Public Information; and Education and Preparedness Training.

Emergency Response Commission
5636 E McDowell Road
Phoenix, AZ 85008
Phone: 602-231-6346
Fax: 602-392-7519
URL: www.dem.state.az.us/azserc/
e-mail: azserc@azdema.gov

Description: This commission oversees 15 Local Emergency Planning Committees and supports in planning, data management, release and incident reporting, public disclosure of information on hazardous chemicals, and development of training and outreach programs in the state of Arizona.

Daniel Roe
Executive Director
Phone: 602-231-6346
e-mail: roed@dem.state.az.us

Environmental Quality Department
1110 W Washington Street
Phoenix, AZ 85007
Phone: 602-771-2300
Phone: 800-234-5677
Fax: 602-771-2218
URL: www.azdeq.gov

Description: Protect and enhance public health, welfare and the environment in Arizona.

Stephen Owens
Director
Phone: 602-771-2203
e-mail: owens.stephen@azdeq.gov

Patrick J Cunningham
Deputy Director
Phone: 602-771-2204
e-mail: cunningham.patrick@azdeq.gov

Nancy C Wrona
Air Quality Division Director
Phone: 602-771-2308
e-mail: wrona.nancy@azdeq.gov

Amanda Stone
Waste Programs Division Director
Phone: 602-771-4208
e-mail: stone.amanda@azdeq.gov

Joan Card
Water Quality Division Director
Phone: 602-771-2303
e-mail: card.joan@azdeq.gov

Epidemiology and Disease Control Services Bureau
Health Services Department
150 N 18th Avenue
1st Floor
Phoenix, AZ 85007
Phone: 602-364-3860

Fax: 602-364-3266
URL: www.azdhs.gov/phs/edc/

Description: To monitor, prevent, and control diseases in Arizona.

John Herrington
Chief

Health Services Department
150 N 18th Avenue
Phoenix, AZ 85007
Phone: 602-542-1000
Fax: 602-542-0883
URL: www.adhs.gov

Susan Gerard
Director
Phone: 602-542-1027

Dona Marie Markley
Acting Deputy Director, Operations
Phone: 602-542-1027

Sarah K Allen
Deputy Director, Public Health Services
Phone: 602-542-1023

Will Humble
Assistant Director-Public Health Preparedness
Phone: 602-542-1023

Jeanett Shea-Ramirez
Assistant Director-Public Health Prevention
Phone: 602-542-1023

Michael Murphy
Public Information Officer
Phone: 602-542-1094

Richard S Porter
Public Health Statistics Bureau Chief
Phone: 602-542-7333

Victor G Waddell
State Laboratory Services Bureau Chief
Phone: 602-542-1188

National Guard
Department of Emergency & Military Affairs
5636 E McDowell
Phoenix, AZ 85008-3495
Phone: 602-267-2710
Fax: 602-267-2715
URL: www.az.ngb.army.mil; www.dem.state.az.us

Description: The Department of Emergency and Military Affairs consists of the Army and Air National Guard, the Division of Emergency Management, and the Joint Programs Division. It provides community, state and federal capabilities and services.

Major General David P Rataczak
Adjutant General
Phone: 602-267-2710

Colonel Wanda Wright
Air National Guard Chief Executive Officer
Phone: 602-267-2660
e-mail: wanda.a.wright@az.ngb.army.mil

Colonel Jeanne Blaes
Chief of Staff
Phone: 602-267-2721
e-mail: jeanne.blaes@az.ngb.army.mil

Edward Flinn
Director Joint Programs Office
Phone: 602-267-2732

Major Paul Aguirre
Public Affairs Officer
Phone: 602-267-2550
e-mail: paul.aguirre@us.army.mil

Power Authority
1810 W Adams Street
Phoenix, AZ 85007-2679
Phone: 602-542-4263
Fax: 602-253-7970
URL: www.powerauthority.org

Michael C Francis
Commissioner
Phone: 602-542-4263

Lt General John I Hudson
Commissioner
Phone: 602-542-4263

Dalton Cole
Commissioner
Phone: 602-542-4263

Delbert R Lewis
Commissioner
Phone: 602-542-4263

Richard Walden
Commissioner
Phone: 602-542-4263

Joseph W Mulholland
Executive Director
Phone: 602-542-4263

Public Safety Department
2102 W Encanto Boulevard
Phoenix, AZ 85005-6638
Mailing Address: PO Box 6638
Phone: 602-223-2000
Fax: 602-223-2917
URL: www.azdps.gov

Description: To protect human life and property by enforcing state laws, deterring criminal activity, assuring highway and public safety, and providing vital scientific, technical and operational support to other criminal justice agencies.

Roger Vanderpool
Director
Phone: 602-223-2359

Chief Mikel Longman
Criminal Investigations Division
Phone: 602-223-2812

Chief Georgene Ramming
Criminal Justice Support Division
Phone: 602-223-2080

Chief Pennie Gillette-Straoud
Agency Support Division
Phone: 602-223-2537

Chief Jack G Lane
Highway Patrol Division
Phone: 602-223-2348

Richard Fimbres
Governor's Office of Highway Safety
Phone: 602-255-3216

Debbie Henry
Operational Communications Bureau Manager
e-mail: dhenry@dps.state.az.us

Radiation Regulatory Agency
4814 S 40th Street
Phoenix, AZ 85040
Phone: 602-255-4845
Fax: 602-437-0705
URL: www.arra.state.az.us

Description: Responsible for the conduct of statewide radiological health and safety program and for the enforcement of State rules and regulations for the control of ionizing radiation.

Aubrey Godwin
Director
e-mail: agodwin@azrra.gov

John Gray
MRTBE/State Health Physicist
e-mail: jgray@azrra.gov

Toby Morales
Emergency Response Program Manager
e-mail: tmorales@azrra.govus

William A Wright
Radioactive Materials Division
e-mail: wwright@azrra.gov

Transportation Department
206 S 17th Avenue
Phoenix, AZ 85007
Phone: 602-712-7355
Fax: 602-712-6941
URL: www.dot.state.az.us

Description: Providing mobility to Arizona's residents and visitors, while promoting economic prosperity through its linkage to the global economy, and demonstrating respect for the environment and quality of life.

Victor Mendez
Director
Phone: 602-712-7227

David Jankofsky
Deputy Director
Phone: 602-712-7550

Barclay Dick
Aeronautics Division Director
Phone: 602-294-9144

Jim Dickey
Public Transportation Division Director

Phone: 602-712-8137
e-mail: jdickey@azdot.gov

Sam Elters
State Engineer
Phone: 602-712-7391

Stacey Stanton
Motor Vehicle Divisional Director
Phone: 602-712-8152

Water Resources Department
3550 N Central Avenue
Phoenix, AZ 85012
Phone: 602-771-8500
Phone: 800-352-8488
Fax: 602-771-8684
URL: http://azwater.gov

Description: Works to secure long-term dependable water supplies for Arizona's communities.

Herb Guenther
Director

Thomas Carr
Assistant Director Statewide Water Conservation & Strategic Planning

Patrick Schiffer
Chief Counsel

Darrell Jordan
Dam Safety & Flood Mitigation
e-mail: jdjordan@azwater.gov

Sandra Fabritz-Whitney
Assistant Director-Water Management Division
e-mail: wrsaf@azwater.gov

STATE AGENCIES

Arkansas

Arkansas Main Homeland Security Office
Building 9501
Camp Joe T Robinson
N Little Rock, AR 72199-9600
Phone: 501-683-6700
Fax: 501-683-7890
URL: www.adem.arkansas.gov

Mike Beebe
Governor
Phone: 501-682-2345
e-mail: mike.huckabee@arkansas.gov

Britt Harter
Lieutenant Governor
Phone: 501-682-2144

David Maxwell
Homeland Security Advisory Group/Director Emergency Management
Phone: 501-683-7834

Dustin McDaniel
Attorney General
Phone: 501-682-2007

Aeronautics Division
1 Airport Drive
3rd Floor
Little Rock, AR 72202
Phone: 501-376-6781
Fax: 501-378-0820

John K Knight
Director
Phone: 501-376-6781
e-mail: deptaero@mail.state.ar.us

Agriculture Department
1 Natural Resources Drive
Little Rock, AR 72205
Phone: 501-683-4851
Fax: 501-683-4852
URL: http://aad.ar.gov

Richard Bell
Secretary
e-mail: secretary@aad.ar.gov

Darryl Little
Director, State Plant Board
Phone: 501-225-1598

Jon Fitch
Director, Livestock & Poultry Commission

Phone: 501-907-2400
e-mail: info@arlpc.org

George Pat Badley
State Veterinarian
Phone: 501-907-2400

Arkansas Association of Chiefs of Police
813 West 3rd Street
Little Rock, AR 72201
Phone: 501-372-4600
Phone: 877-818-7428
Fax: 501-244-2333
URL: www.arkchiefs.org
e-mail: info@arkchiefs.org

Description: A non-profit organization of police chiefs and executives from all over Arkansas, who recognize the importance of having proven, effective leaders in law enforcement today.

Chief Danny E Bradley
President

Randy Martinsen
Executive Director

Arkansas State Capitol Police
State Capitol Building
Little Rock, AR 72201
Phone: 501-682-5173
Fax: 501-682-5121

Darrell Hedden
Chief of Police

Association of Contingency Planners
PO Box 17587
Little Rock, AR 72222
Phone: 501-220-6258
e-mail: capthubble@aol.com

Description: Arkansas chapter of the Association of Contingency Planners. It is an organization for contingency planners, business continuity professionals, and emergency managers.

Michael Turley
President

Civil Air Patrol
2201 Crisp Drive
Little Rock, AR 72201
Phone: 501-376-1729
Phone: 888-876-1729
Fax: 501-374-6743
URL: www.arwingcap.org

e-mail: arwingcap@sbcglobal.net

Description: The official civilian volunteer auxiliary of the United State Air Force.

Colonel Robert Britton
Wing Commander
e-mail: rbritto@sbcglobal.net

Major Joel Buckner
Wing Vice Commander
e-mail: jbuckner.05@comcast.net

Lt Colonel Jim Gilbert
Chief of Staff/Plans & Programs
e-mail: j.l.gilbert@sbcglobal.net

Major Tom Rea
Director Emergency Services
e-mail: arcapes@yahoo.com

Lt Colonel Herb Williams
Homeland Security Coordinator
e-mail: arwindoh@sbcglobal.net

Department of Emergency Management
Building 9501
Camp Joe T Robinson
N Little Rock, AR 72199-9600
Phone: 501-683-5700
URL: www.adem.arkansas.gov

David Maxwell
Director
Phone: 501-730-9780

Sandra Hensley
Chemical Stockpile Emergency Preparedness Program Manager
Phone: 501-730-9815
e-mail: sandi.hensley@adem.state.ar.us

Emily Taylor
Public Education Coordinator

Richard Griffin
Disaster Management Division Leader
Phone: 501-730-9750
e-mail: richard.griffin@adem.state.ar.us

Tina Owens
Preparedness Division Leader
Phone: 501-730-9750
e-mail: tina.owens@adem.state.ar.us

David Huddleston
Information Technology Division Leader
Phone: 501-730-9750
e-mail: david.huddleston@adem.state.ar.us

Tony Hourston
Public Relations Coordinator

Emergency Medical Services and Trauma Systems
Health Division
PO Box 1437
Slot H-38
Little Rock, AR 72203-1437
Phone: 501-661-2262

URL: www.healthyarkansas.com/ems/

Description: To promulgate and enforce rules and regulations which foster and encourage the development of quality pre-hospital Emergency Medical Services for the citizens of the state; and to develop a statewide trauma systems plan for implementation and the designation of trauma centers throughout Arkansas.

David Taylor
Director
Phone: 501-661-2178
e-mail: david.taylor@arkansas.gov

Larry New
Regulatory Administrator
Phone: 501-661-2257
e-mail: raymond.new@arkansas.gov

Norajean Miles
Certification Administrator
Phone: 501-661-2333
e-mail: norajean.miles@arkansas.gov

Brian Nation
Trauma Systems Administrator
Phone: 501-661-2744
e-mail: brian.nation@arkansas.gov

Environmental Quality Department
8001 National Drive
Little Rock, AR 72209
Mailing Address: PO Box 8913, 72219-8913
Phone: 501-682-0744
Fax: 501-682-0798
URL: www.adeq.state.ar.us

Description: Strive to protect Arkansas' priceless natural resources-its air, water and land from them threat of pollution.

Teresa Marks
Director
Phone: 501-682-0959
e-mail: marks@adeq.state.ar.us

Mary Leath
Chief Deputy Director
Phone: 501-682-0959
e-mail: leath@adeq.state.ar.us

Mike Bates
Air Division Chief
Phone: 501-682-0730
e-mail: bates@adeq.state.ar.us

Robert Gage
Computer Services Division Chief
Phone: 501-682-0672
e-mail: gage@adeq.state.ar.us

Ryan Benefield
Hazardous Waste Division Chief
Phone: 501-682-0831
e-mail: benefield@adeq.state.ar.us

Ellen Carpenter
Legal Division Chief
Phone: 501-682-0886
e-mail: carpenter@adeq.state.ar.us

Martin Maner
Water Division Chief
Phone: 501-682-0654
e-mail: maner@adeq.state.ar.us

Dean VanDerhoff
Emergency Response Section Manager
Phone: 501-682-0716
e-mail: vanderhoff@adeq.state.ar.us

Health Division
Department of Health and Human Services
4815 W Markham Street
Little Rock, AR 72205
Mailing Address: PO Box 1437, 72203
Phone: 501-661-2000
Fax: 501-671-1450
URL: www.healthyarkansas.com

Paul Halverson
Director & State Health Officer
Phone: 501-661-2111

Bruce Thomasson
Bioterrorism Hospital Preparedness
Phone: 501-280-4827

Kathy Hedrick
Bioterrorism Public Health Preparedness
Phone: 501-661-2196

Michael Spann
Emergency Communications
Phone: 501-661-2061

Dave Baldwin
Emergency Response & Nuclear Planning & Response
Phone: 501-661-2301

Shirley Louie
Environmental Epidemiology
Phone: 501-661-2833

John Senner
Health Statistics
Phone: 501-661-2497

Michael Loeffelholz
Laboratory Services
Phone: 501-661-2220

Jared Thompson
Radioactive Materials
Phone: 501-661-2301

Highway and Transportation Department
10324 Interstate 30
Little Rock, AR 72209
Mailing Address: PO Box 2261, 72203-2261
Phone: 501-569-2000
Fax: 501-569-2400
URL: www.arkansashighways.com
e-mail: info@arkansashighways.com

Description: Provide a safe, efficient, and aesthetically pleasing and environmentally sound intermodal transportation system for the user.

Dan Flowers
Director
Phone: 501-569-2211

Frank Vozel
Chief Engineer/Deputy Director
Phone: 501-569-2214

Phil Brand
Bridge Division
Phone: 501-569-2361

Allan Holmes
Assistant Chief Engineer-Operations
Phone: 501-569-2221

Bryan Stewart
Computer Services Division
Phone: 501-569-2436

Ronald D Burks
Highway Police Division
Phone: 501-569-2424

Hardin Steele
Motor Carrier Authority
Phone: 501-569-2358

Randy Ort
Public Affairs Officer
Phone: 501-569-2227

Law Enforcement Standards and Training Commission
PO Box 3106
East Camden, AR 71711
Phone: 870-574-1810
Fax: 870-574-2706
URL: www.clest.org

Terry Bolton
Director
Phone: 870-574-1810
e-mail: tlbolton@cji.net

Chief Robert Harrison
Chairman
Phone: 870-574-1810

Bob Satkowski
Standards Deputy Director
Phone: 501-682-2260
e-mail: robert.satkowski@asp.state.ar.us

Steve Farris
Training Deputy Director
Phone: 870-574-1810
e-mail: sbfarris@cji.net

Liquified Petroleum Gas Board
3800 Richards Road
N Little Rock, AR 72117-2944
Phone: 501-683-4100
Fax: 501-683-4110
URL: www.arkansaslpgasboard.com

Description: The Liquefied Petroleum Gas Board Operations for the State of Arkansas provides a staff and resources to carry out the duties of the Board in the application of laws and regulations governing the safe handling of liquefied petroleum gases.

Sharon E Coates
Director
Phone: 501-683-4100
e-mail: se.coates@sbcglobal.net

Military Department-National Guard
Camp Joseph T Robinson
N Little Rock, AR 72199-9600
Phone: 501-212-5909
Fax: 501-212-5009
URL: www.arguard.org

Major General Ronald Chastain
Adjutant General
Phone: 501-212-5100

Brigadier General Larry Haltom
Deputy Adjutant General
Phone: 501-212-5005
e-mail: larry.haltom@ar.ngb.army.mil

Brigadier Gen Riley Porter
Assistant Adjutant General Air
Phone: 501-987-3663

Colonel William Johnson
Chief Staff Army National Guard
Phone: 501-212-5007
e-mail: william.johnson@ar.ngb.army.mil

Lt Christopher Heatchscott
Public Affairs Officer
Phone: 501-212-5020
e-mail: christopher.heatchscott@ar.ngb.army.mil

Oil and Gas Commission
2215 W Hillsboro
El Dorado, AR 71731-1472
Phone: 870-862-4965
Fax: 870-862-8823
URL: www.aogc.state.ar.us
e-mail: aogc@aogc.state.ar.us

Description: The purpose of the Arkansas Oil and Gas Commission is to serve the public regarding oil and gas matters, prevent waste, encourage conservation, and protect the correlative rights and ownership associated with the production of oil, natural gas and brine, while protecting the environment during the production process, through the regulation and enforcement of the laws of the State of Arkansas.

Lawrence Bengal
Director
e-mail: larry.bengal@aogc.state.ar.us

Gary Looney
Assistant Director
e-mail: gary@aogc.state.ar.us

Jay Hansen
Commission Geologist
e-mail: jay.hansen@aogc.state.ar.us

Chris Weiser
Chairman

Chad White
Vice Chairman

Public Service Commission
1000 Center Street
Little Rock, AR 72201
Mailing Address: PO Box 400, 72203-0400
Phone: 501-682-2051
Phone: 800-482-1164
Fax: 501-682-1717
URL: www.state.ar.us/psc

Description: A proactive, solutions oriented agency that maximizes customer value and enhances the economic development of the state.

Paul Suskie
Chairman

Daryl E Bassett
Commissioner

Sandra Hochstetter
Commissioner

Diana Brenske
Electric Section Director
e-mail: electric@psc.state.ar.us

Bill Dennis
Telecommunications & Quality of Service Manager
e-mail: telephone@psc.state.ar.us

Robert Booth
Gas & Water Section Manager
e-mail: gas.water@psc.state.ar.us

Clint Stephens
Pipeline Safety Chief
e-mail: pipeline_safety@psc.state.ar.us

Science and Technology Authority
423 Main Street
Suite 200
Little Rock, AR 72201
Phone: 501-683-4400
Fax: 501-683-4420
URL: http://asta.ar.gov

Description: Created in 1983 by statute to bring the benefits of science and advanced technology to the state and people of Arkansas.

John W Ahlen PhD
President
Phone: 501-683-4400
e-mail: john.ahlen@arkansas.gov

Tovia Chan
Operations Manager
Phone: 501-683-4410
e-mail: tovia.chan@arkansas.gov

Chris Snider
Communications Manager
Phone: 501-683-4405
e-mail: chris.snider@arkansas.gov

Sue McGowan
Board Chair

State Police
1 State Police Plaza Drive

Little Rock, AR 72209
Phone: 501-618-8000
Fax: 501-618-8222
URL: www.asp.state.ar.us
e-mail: info@asp.arkansas.gov

Description: To protect human life and property in the state of Arkansas by providing the highest quality of law enforcement services to the citizens of Arkansas.

Colonel Winford E Phillips
Director

Lt Colonel Tim K'Nuckles
Deputy Director

Major Ed Wolfe
Highway Patrol Division Commander
Phone: 501-618-8800

Major Cleve Barfield
Criminal Investigation Division Commander
Phone: 501-618-8850

STATE AGENCIES

California

California Main Homeland Security Office
3650 Schriever Avenue
Mather, CA 95655
Phone: 916-845-8510
Fax: 916-845-8511
URL: www.oes.ca.gov

Arnold Schwarzenegger
Governor
Phone: 916-445-2841
e-mail: arnoldschwarzenegger@governor.ca.gov

John Garamendi
Lieutenant Governor
Phone: 916-445-8994
e-mail: lt.governor@ltgov.ca.gov

Edmund G Brown, Jr
Attorney General
Phone: 916-322-3360

Henry R Renteria
Governor's Office of Homeland Security Director
Phone: 916-845-8510

Association of Contingency Planners-Los Angeles Chapter
669 Pacific Cove Drive
Port Hueneme, CA 93041
Phone: 805-520-5071
URL: www.acp-international.com/la
e-mail: david_graves@countrywide.com

Description: Their mission is to provide contingency planners, business continuity professionals and emergency managers with an organization that excels in information exchange, building professional relationships with public and private partners, and strengthening their knowledge in emergency response and recovery trends.

David Graves
President

Lorraine Nelson
Vice President

Boating and Waterways
2000 Evergreen Street
Suite 100
Sacramento, CA 95815-3888
Phone: 916-263-1331
Phone: 888-326-2822
Fax: 916-263-0648
URL: www.dbw.ca.gov
e-mail: pubinfo@dbw.ca.gov

Description: Promotes on-the-water safety and helps develop convenient public access to waterways.

Raynor T Tsuneyoshi
Director

California Alarm Association
333 Washington Boulevard
Suite #433
Marina del Rey, CA 90292
Phone: 310-822-1411
Phone: 800-437-7658
Fax: 310-306-6026
URL: www.caaonline.org
e-mail: info@caaonline.org

Description: A state trade association comprised of licensed alarm company operators and suppliers of products and services. Nearly 200 alarm companies and 50 suppliers are members. The alarm companies represent 70% of the electronic security industry in California. Also provides a vehicle to promote growth and professionalism within the alarm industry throughout the state of California

Jon Sargent
President

Jerry Lenander
Executive Director

California Seismic Safety Commission
1755 Creekside Oaks Drive
Suite 100
Sacramento, CA 95833
Phone: 916-263-5506
URL: www.seiemic.ca.gov
e-mail: celli@stateseismic.com

Description: Provides decision makers and the general public with cost effective recommendations to reduce earthquake losses and speed recovery. The Commission investigates earthquakes, researches earthquake -related issues and reports, and recommends to the Governor and Legislature policies and programs needed to reduce earthquake risk.

Richard McCarthy
Executive Director

Karen Cogan
Administration

Emergency Medical Services Authority
1930 9th Street
Sacramento, CA 95814-7043
Phone: 916-322-4336

Fax: 916-324-2875
URL: www.emsa.ca.gov

Description: To ensure quality patient care by administering an effective, statewide system of coordinated emergency medical care, injury prevention and disaster medical response.

Dr Cesar Aristeguieta
Director
Phone: 916-322-4336
e-mail: director@esma.ca.gov

Daniel R Smiley
Chief Deputy Director
Phone: 916-322-4336

Jeffrey L Rubin
Chief Disaster Medical Services Division
Phone: 916-322-4336

Richard McSherry
Chief Paramedic Enforcement Division
Phone: 916-322-4336

Emergency Services Office
3650 Schriever Avenue
Mather, CA 95655
Phone: 916-845-8510
Fax: 916-845-8511
URL: www.oes.ca.gov

Description: To ensure the state is ready and able to mitigate against, prepare for, respond to, and recover from the effects of emergencies that threaten lives, property, and the environment.

Henry R Renteria
Director

Frank McCarton
Chief Deputy Director

Eric Lamoureux
Public Information Chief
Phone: 916-845-8400
e-mail: eric.lamourex@oes.ca.gov

Sue Plantz
Chief Technology Officer
Phone: 916-845-8546
e-mail: sue.plantz@oes.ca.gov

Paul Jacks
Response & Recovery Division Deputy Director

Grace Koch
Deputy Director, Preparedness & Training Division

Energy Commission
1516 9th Street
MS-29
Sacramento, CA 95814-2950
Phone: 916-654-4287
Phone: 800-555-7794
Fax: 916-653-3478
URL: www.energy.ca.gov

Description: To assess, advocate and act through public/private partnerships to improve energy systems that promote a strong economy and a healthy environment.

Jackalyne Pfannenstiel
Chair
Phone: 916-654-5036

James D Boyd
Vice-Chair
Phone: 916-654-3787

Arthur H Rosenfeld, Ph.D
Commissioner
Phone: 916-654-4930

John L Geesman
Commissioner
Phone: 916-654-4001

Jeffrey Bryon
Commissioner
Phone: 916-654-3992

B B Blevins
Executive Director
Phone: 916-654-4996

Scott Matthews
Chief Deputy Director
Phone: 916-654-4996
e-mail: smatthew@energy.ca.gov

Claudia Chandler
Media & Public Communications Office Assistant Director
Phone: 916-654-4989
e-mail: mediaoffice@energy.state.ca.us

Environmental Protection Agency
1001 I Street
PO Box 2815
Sacramento, CA 95812-2815
Phone: 916-445-3846
Fax: 916-445-6401
URL: www.calepa.ca.gov
e-mail: cepacomm@calepa.ca.gov

Description: The mission of the EPA is to restore, protect and enhance the environment, to ensure public health, environmental quality and economic vitality.

Linda S Adams
Secretary
Phone: 916-323-2514

Dan Skopec
Under Secretary
Phone: 916-324-3708

BreAnda Northcutt
Deputy Secretary Communications
Phone: 916-323-2516

Mary Ann Warmerdam
Pesticide Regulation Director
Phone: 916-445-4000

Maureen Gorsen
Toxic Substances Control Director
Phone: 916-322-0504

Catherine Witherspoon
Air Resources Executive Officer
Phone: 916-445-4383

Food and Agriculture Department

1220 N Street
Sacramento, CA 95814-5607
Phone: 916-654-0466
Fax: 916-657-4240
URL: www.cdfa.ca.gov
e-mail: cdfapublicaffairs@cdfa.ca.gov

A G Kawamura
Secretary
Phone: 916-654-0433

George Gomes
Undersecretary
Phone: 916-654-0433

Bob Wynn
Statewide Coordinator
Phone: 916-654-0433

Debbie Tonouye
Pest Detection
Phone: 916-654-1211

Anthony Herrera
Egg Quality Control
Phone: 916-445-2180

Richard Breitmeyer
State Veterinarian
Phone: 916-654-0433

Steve Lyle
Public Affairs Director
Phone: 916-654-0462
e-mail: slyle@cdfa.ca.gov

Health & Human Services Agency

1600 9th Street
Room 460
Sacramento, CA 95814-6414
Phone: 916-654-3454
Fax: 916-654-3343
URL: www.chhs.ca.gov

Description: CHHSA administers state and federal programs for health care, social services, public assistance and rehabilitation. Responsibility for administering major programs, which provide direct services to millions of Californians.

Kim Belshe
Secretary

Highway Patrol

PO Box 942898
Sacramento, CA 94298-0001
Phone: 916-657-7261
Fax: 916-375-2969
URL: www.chp.ca.gov

Description: To provide the highest level of safety, service, and security to the people of California.

Michael Brown
Commissioner
Phone: 916-657-7152

M J Padilla
Deputy Commissioner
Phone: 916-657-8048

K P Green
Assistant Commissioner
Phone: 916-657-8048

J A Farrow
Deputy Commissioner Executive Operations
Phone: 916-657-7207

Scott MacGregor
Chief Information Management Division
Phone: 916-657-7171

National Guard

3336 Bradshaw Road
Suite 230
Sacramento, CA 95826-9101
Mailing Address: PO Box 269101
Phone: 916-362-3411
Fax: 916-362-3707
URL: www.calguard.ca.gov

Description: Organizes, resources and trains forces with unique capabilities, serving the community, state and nation.

Major General William H Wade II
Adjutant General
Phone: 916-854-3392

Brigadier General Mary Kight
Assistant Adjutant General
Phone: 916-854-3392

Brigadier General Dennis Lucas
Air National Guard Commander
Phone: 916-854-3392

Brigadier General Louis J Amtonetti
Deputy Adjutant General, Army
Phone: 916-854-3302

Office of Environmental Health Hazard Assesment

1001 I Street
25th Floor, MS 25B
Sacramento, CA 95814-2815
Phone: 916-324-7572
Fax: 916-327-1097
URL: www.oehha.ca.gov
e-mail: answers@oehha.ca.gov

Joan E Denton
Director
Phone: 916-322-6325
e-mail: jdenton@oehha.ca.gov

Allan Hirsch
Chief Deputy Director
Phone: 916-324-2831
e-mail: ahirsch@oehha.ca.gov

Carol Monahan-Cummings
Chief Counsel
Phone: 916-322-0493
e-mail: cmonahan@oehha.ca.gov

George Alexander
Scientific Affaris Deputy Director
Phone: 510-622-3202
e-mail: galexeef@oehha.ca.gov

Melanie Marty, PhD
Air Toxicology & Epidemiology Branch Chief
Phone: 510-622-3150
e-mail: mmarty@oehha.ca.gov

David Siegel, PhD
Integrated Risk Assessment Branch Chief
Phone: 916-324-2829
e-mail: dsiegel@oehha.ca.gov

Anna Fan PhD
Pesticide & Environmental Toxicology Branch Chief
Phone: 510-622-3170
e-mail: afan@oehha.ca.gov

Lauren Zeise
Reproductive & Cancer Hazard Assessment Branch Chief
Phone: 510-622-3190
e-mail: lzeise@oehha.ca.gov

Southern California Earthquake Center

3651 Trousdale Parkway
Los Angeles, CA 90089
Phone: 213-740-5843
Fax: 213-740-0011
URL: www.scec.org
e-mail: scecinfo@usc.edu

Description: The mission of the Southern California Earthquake Center is to gather new information about earthquakes in Southern California, integrate this information into a comprehensive and predicitve understanding of earthquake phenomina and communicate this understanding to the end-users and the general public in order to increase earthquake awareness, reduce economic loss, and save lives

Thomas H Jordan
Center Director

Greg Beroza
Deputy Director

Spill Prevention and Response Division

1700 K Street
Sacramento, CA 94244-2090
Mailing Address: PO Box 944209
Phone: 916-445-9338
Fax: 916-324-8829
URL: www.dfg.ca.gov/ospr/

Lisa Curtis
Administrator
Phone: 916-445-9326

Transportation Department

1120 N Street
PO Box 942873
Sacramento, CA 94273-0001
Phone: 916-654-5266
Fax: 916-654-6608
URL: www.dot.ca.gov

Will Kempton
Director
Phone: 916-654-5267

Randall H Iwasaki
Chief Deputy Director
Phone: 916-654-2630

Jerry Knedel
Information Security/Operational Recovery

Michael Miles
Maintenance/Operations Deputy Director

Coco Briseno
Chief of Staff

Water Resources Department

1416 9th Street
Sacramento, CA 95814
Mailing Address: PO Box 942836, 94326
Phone: 916-653-5791
Fax: 916-653-4684
URL: www.dwr.water.ca.gov

Description: Manages the water resources of California in cooperation with other agencies, to benefit the State's people, and to protect, restore, and enhance the natural and human environments.

Lester A Snow
Director

Mark Cowin
Deputy Director, Regional Water Planning & Management

Susan Sims
Assistant Director, Public Affairs

STATE AGENCIES

Colorado

Colorado Main Homeland Security Office

700 Kipling Street
#1000
Denver, CO 80215
Phone: 303-239-4400
Fax: 303-239-4670
URL: www.ops.state.co.us
e-mail: ops@cdps.state.co.us

Bill Ritter
Governor
Phone: 303-866-2471
e-mail: governor.ritter@state.co.us

Barbara O'Brien
Lieutenant Governor
Phone: 303-866-2087
e-mail: ltgovernor.obrien@state.co.us

Joe Morales
Executive Director Homeland Security
Phone: 303-239-4400

John W Suthers
Attorney General
Phone: 303-866-4500
e-mail: attorney.general@state.co.us

Agriculture Department

700 Kipling Street
Suite 4000
Lakewood, CO 80215
Phone: 303-239-4100
Fax: 303-239-4125
URL: www.ag.state.co.us

Description: To strengthen and advance Colorado's agriculture industry; ensure a safe, high quality, and sustainable food supply; and protect consumers, the environment, and natural resources.

John Stulp
Commissioner
e-mail: john.stulp@ag.state.co.us

Sheldon Jones
Deputy Commissioner
e-mail: sheldon.jones@ag.state.co.us

Julie Zimmerman
Director Inspection & Consumer Services Division
e-mail: julie.zimmerman@ag.state.co.us

Keith Roehr
Animal Protection Bureau
Phone: 303-239-4161

Rob Wawrzynski
Ag Chemicals & Groundwater Protection Coordinator
Phone: 970-223-7017
e-mail: rob.wawrzynski@ag.state.co.us

Christi Lightcap
Director Communications

Jim Miller
Director Policy & Initiatives
e-mail: jim.miller@ag.state.co.us

Association of Contingency Planners

4300 Cherry Creek Drive S
Denver, CO 80246
Phone: 720-227-8185
URL: www.cmc-acp.org
e-mail: president@crmc-acp.org

Description: Members are involved in many areas of emergency management and recovery. They are professionals such as business continuity planners, loss prevention representatives, public safety officers, and volunteer emergency workers.

Sharon Bennett
President

Gerry Lockhart
Vice President

Colorado Association of Chiefs of Police

2170 S Parker Road
Suite 255
Denver, CO 80231
Phone: 303-750-9764
Fax: 303-750-0085
URL: www.colochiefs.org

Description: A professional organization committed to excellence in delivering quality service to the membership, the law enforcement community, and the citizens of Colorado.

Karen M Renshaw
Executive Director
e-mail: cacp@kareams.com

Communications Services
Division of Information Technologies
2452 West 2nd Avenue
Unit 19
Denver, CO 80223
Phone: 303-866-2341
Fax: 303-922-1811
URL: www.colorado.gov/dpa/doit/comm/

Description: The information backbone for Colorado's communications network of which a primary purpose is to carry public safety two-way voice traffic for local and state public safety agencies.

Paul Nelson
Communications Services Manager

Department of Military Affairs
6848 S Revere Parkway
Englewood, CO 80112
Phone: 720-250-1520
Fax: 750-250-1529
URL: www.dmva.state.co.us

Description: To exercise command and control responsibility for the planning and execution of mobilization of COARNG units through policy, procedures and logistical support.

Major General Mason C Whitney
Adjutant General
Phone: 720-250-1500

Brig General David A Sprenkle
Air Assistant Adjutant General

Colonel Greg Cortum
Civil Air Patrol Wing Commander
Phone: 719-282-3992
e-mail: cowgcc@hpi.net

Division of Emergency Management
Department of Local Affairs
9195 E Mineral Avenue
Suite 200
Centennial, CO 80112
Phone: 720-852-6600
Fax: 720-852-6750
URL: http://dola.state.co.us/oem

Description: Responsible fo the state's comprehensive emeregency management program which supports local and state agencies. Activities and services cover the four phases of emergency management: Preparedness, Prevention, Reponse, and Recovery for disasters like flooding, tornadoes, wildfire, hazardous materials incidents, and acts of terrorism.

David Holm
Interim Director
Phone: 720-852-6613
e-mail: david.holm@state.co.us

Randy Kennedy
Homeland Security Branch Officer
Phone: 720-852-6614
e-mail: randy.kennedy@state.co.us

Jack Cobb
Communications/Infrastructure Manager
Phone: 720-852-6603
e-mail: jack.cobb@state.co.us

Marilyn Gally
State Hazard Mitigation Officer
Phone: 720-852-6608
e-mail: marilyn.gally@state.co.us

Dick Vnuck
Chief of Operations

Phone: 720-852-6627
e-mail: dick.vnuck@state.co.us

Robyn Knappe
Training Coordinator
Phone: 720-852-6617
e-mail: robyn.knappe@state.co.us

Polly White
Public Information Officer
Phone: 720-852-6630
e-mail: polly.white@state.co.us

Natural Resources Department
1313 Sherman Street
Room 718
Denver, CO 80203
Phone: 303-866-3311
Phone: 800-536-5308
Fax: 303-866-2115
URL: http://dnr.state.co.us

Description: Created to develop, protect and enhance Colorado natural resources for the use and enjoyment of the state's present and future residents, as well as for visitior of the state.

Harris Sherman
Executive Director

Mike King
Deputy Director
Phone: 303-866-3311

Alexandria Davis
Assistant Director for Water Policy
Phone: 303-866-3311
e-mail: alex.davis@state.co.us

Brian Macke
Oli & Gas Conservation Commission Director
Phone: 303-894-2100

Public Health and Environment Department
4300 Cherry Creek Drive S
Denver, CO 80246-1530
Phone: 303-692-2000
Phone: 800-886-7689
Fax: 303-691-7702
URL: www.cdphe.state.co.us

James B Martin
Executive Director
Phone: 303-692-2011

Mark Salley
Communications Office Director
Phone: 303-692-2013

Jeff Stoll
Local Liaison Office Director
Phone: 303-692-3479

Lisa Miller
Disease Control & Environmental Epidemiology Division
Phone: 303-692-2663

Dr Ned Calonge
Chief Medical Officer
Phone: 303-692-2662

Joni Reynolds
Immunization Program Acting Manager
Phone: 303-692-2363
e-mail: joni.reynolds@state.co.us

John Schule
Acting Director Health Facilities & Emergency Medical Services Division
Phone: 303-692-2871

Bob O'Doherty
Center for Health/Environmental Information & Statistics
Phone: 303-692-2249

Gary Baughman
Hazardous Materials & Waste Management Division Director
Phone: 303-692-3338

Paul Toourangeau
Air Pollution Control Division
Phone: 303-692-3115

Steve Gunderson
Water Quality Control Division
Phone: 303-692-3500

Barbara Hruska
Consumer Protection Division
Phone: 303-692-3639

Public Safety Department
700 Kipling Street
#1000
Denver, CO 80215
Phone: 303-239-4400
Fax: 303-239-4670
URL: www.ops.state.co.us
e-mail: public.safety@cdps.state.co.us

Peter A Weir
Executive Director
Phone: 303-239-4398

Major Jim Wolfinbarger
Preparedness, Security & Fire Safety Office
Phone: 720-852-6705

Robert C Cantwell
Bureau of Investigation Director
Phone: 303-239-4300
e-mail: cbi.denver@cdps.state.co.us

Jeanne Smith
Director Criminal Justice Division
Phone: 303-239-4442
e-mail: carol.poole@cdps.state.co.us

Colonel Mark Trostel
Chief Colorado State Patrol
Phone: 303-239-4500
e-mail: mark.trostel@cdps.state.co.us

Kevin Klein
Division of Fire Safety Director
Phone: 303-239-4400

Public Utilities Commission
Department of Regulatory Agencies
1560 Broadway
Suite 250
Denver, CO 80202
Phone: 303-894-2000
Phone: 800-888-0170
Fax: 303-894-2065
URL: www.dora.state.co.us/PUC/

Description: To achieve a flexible regulatory environment that provides safe, reliable and quality services to utility customers on just and resonable terms, while managing the transition to effective competition where appropriate.

Doug Dean
Executive Director
Phone: 303-894-2007

Ron Binz
Chairman
Phone: 303-894-2004

Carl Miller
Commissioner
Phone: 303-894-2913

Polly Page
Commissioner
Phone: 303-894-2003

Geri Santos-Rach
Fixed Utilities Section Chief
Phone: 303-894-2533

Terry Willert
Transportation Section Chief
Phone: 303-894-2850

Steve Pott
Gas Pipeline Safety Section Chief
Phone: 303-894-2851

Pamela Fischhaber
Rail/Transit Section Chief
Phone: 303-894-2529

Transportation Department
4201 E Arkansas Avenue
Denver, CO 80222
Phone: 303-757-9011
Phone: 800-999-4997
Fax: 303-757-9717
URL: www.dot.state.co.us

Description: To provide the best multi-modal transportation system for Colorado that most effectively moves people, goods, and information.

Russell George
Executive Director
Phone: 303-757-9201

Travis Vallin
Aeronautics Division Director
Phone: 303-261-4418
e-mail: travis.vallin@dot.state.co.us

Jennifer Webster
Transportation Commission Secretary
Phone: 303-757-9703
e-mail: jennifer.webster@dot.state.co.us

Stacey Stegman
Public Reltions Officer
Phone: 303-757-9632

Jennifer Finch
Transportation Development Division
Phone: 303-757-9525
e-mail: jennifer.finch@dot.state.co.us

Pam Hutton
Chief Engineer
Phone: 303-757-9206

Water Resources and Power Development Authority
1580 Logan Street
Suite 620
Denver, CO 80203
Phone: 303-830-1550
Fax: 303-832-8205
URL: www.cwrpda.com
e-mail: info@cwrpda.com

Daniel L Law
Executive Director
e-mail: dlaw@cwrpda.com

STATE AGENCIES

Connecticut

Connecticut Main Homeland Security Office

25 Sigourney Street
6th Floor
Hartford, CT 06106-5042
Phone: 860-256-0800
Phone: 800-397-8876
Fax: 860-256-0815
URL: www.ct.gov/demhs/
e-mail: HLS.demhs@po.state.ct.us

M Jodi Rell
Governor
Phone: 860-566-4840
e-mail: Governor.Rell@po.state.ct.us

Kevin B Sullivan
Lieutenant Governor
Phone: 860-524-7384
e-mail: ltgovernonr.sullivan@ct.gov

James M Thomas
Commissioner Emergency Management & Homeland Security
Phone: 860-256-0800
e-mail: comm.demhs@po.state.ct.us

Richard Blumenthal
Attorney General
Phone: 860-808-5318
e-mail: attorney.general@po.state.ct.us

Bureau of Aviation and Ports
Department of Transportation
2800 Berlin Turnpike
Newington, CT 06131-7546
Phone: 860-594-2530
Fax: 860-594-2574
URL: www.ct.gov/dot/cwp

Description: To provide the most efficient, effective, convenient and safe use of State aviation, ferry, and pier facilities to users and customers.

Richard Jaworski
Bureau Chief

Chief Medical Examiner's Office

11 Shuttle Road
Farmington, CT 06032
Phone: 860-679-3980
Phone: 800-842-8820
Fax: 860-679-1257
URL: www.state.ct.us/ocme

Description: Provide accurate certification of the cause of death and to identify, document and interpret relevant forensic scien-
tific information for use i criminal and civil legal proceedings necessary in the investigation of violent, suspicious and sudden unexpected deaths, by properly trained physicians.

H Wayne Carver II MD
Chief Medical Examiner
e-mail: hwc2@ocme.org

Edward T McDonough MD
Deputy Chief Medical Examiner
e-mail: emcdonough@ocme.org

Connecticut Police Chiefs Association

342 N Main Street
West Hartford, CT 06117-2507
Phone: 860-586-7506
Fax: 860-586-7550
URL: www.cpcanet.org
e-mail: info@cpcanet.org

Pamela D Hayes
Executive Director
e-mail: phayes@cpcanet.org

Connecticut State Capitol Police

300 Capitol Avenue
Legislative Office Building, Room 1300
Hartford, CT 06106-1591
Phone: 860-240-0240
Fax: 860-240-0247
URL: www.cga.ct.gov/cop

Michael J Fallon
Chief

Department of Agriculture

165 Capitol Avenue
Hartford, CT 06106
Phone: 860-713-2569
Phone: 800-861-9939
Fax: 860-713-2514
URL: www.ct.gov/doag
e-mail: ctdeptag@po.state.ct.us

Description: To foster a healthy economic, environmental and social climate for agriculture by developing, promoting and regulating agricultural businesses; protecting agricultural and aquacultural resources; enforcing laws pertaining to domestic animals; and promoting an understanding among the state's citizens of te diversity of Connecticut agriculture, its cultural heritage and its contribution to the state's economy.

F Phillip Prelli
Commissioner

Phone: 860-713-2500
e-mail: philip.prelli@ct.gov

David H Carey
Aquaculture Bureau
Phone: 203-874-0696

Mary Jane Lis DVM
State Veterinarian
Phone: 860-713-2504

Joseph Dippel
Farmland Preservation Director
Phone: 860-713-2511
e-mail: Joseph.Dippel@ct.gov

Dr. Bruce Sherman DVM
Regulation & Inspection Bureau
Phone: 860-713-2504

Department of Public Health

410 Capitol Avenue
PO Box 340308
Hartford, CT 06106
Phone: 860-509-7101
Fax: 860-509-7286
URL: www.dph.state.ct.us
e-mail: webmaster.dph@po.state.ct.us

Dr J Robert Galvin
Commissioner
Phone: 860-509-7101

Norma Gyle
Deputy Commissioner
Phone: 860-509-7101

Catherine Kennelly
Chief Administrative Officer
Phone: 860-509-7101

Richard Edmonds
Community Health Bureau
Phone: 860-509-7797

Environmental Quality Council

79 Elm Street
Hartford, CT 06106
Phone: 860-424-4000
Fax: 860-424-4070
URL: www.ct.gov/ceq/site

Description: Monitors environmental trends in Connecticut and makes recommendations for improving state environmental policies.

Karl J Wagener
Executive Director
e-mail: karl.wagener@po.state.ct.us

Thomas F Harrison
Chairman

Epidemiology & Emerging Infections Program

410 Capitol Avenue
PO Box 340308
Hartford, CT 06134
Phone: 860-509-7994
Fax: 860-509-7910

URL: www.dph.state.ct.us/bch/infectiousdise/epidemio.htm

Matthew Carter
Program Coordinator

Infectious Diseases Division

410 Capitol Avenue
PO Box 340308
Hartford, CT 06134
Phone: 860-509-7995
Fax: 860-509-7910
URL: www.dph.state.ct.us/BCH/infectiousdise/id.htm

James L Hadler
Division Director/State Epidemiologist

Military Department-National Guard

360 Broad Street
Hartford, CT 06105-3795
Phone: 860-524-4943
Fax: 860-524-4898
URL: www.ct.gov/mil/site/default.asp

Major General Thaddeus Martin
Connecticut Adjutant General
Phone: 860-524-4953

Brigadier General Steven Scorzato
Assistant Adjutant General
Phone: 860-524-4957

Municipal Electric Energy Cooperative

30 Stott Avenue
Norwich, CT 06360
Phone: 860-889-4088
Fax: 860-889-8158
URL: www.cmeec.com
e-mail: webmaster@cmeec.org

Description: A publicly directed joint action supply agency formed by the state's municipal electric utilities in 1976 under authority of the state's General Statutes. CMEEC is responsible for the financing, acquisition and construction of generating resources and implementation of power supply contracts for the purpose of furnishing low-cost and reliable electric power to its Members and Participants.

Maurice R Scully
Executive Director

Brian E Forshaw
Energy Director

Gabriel B Stern
Planning & Project Development Director

Christine B Fischer
Power Supply Director

Office of Emergency Management
Division of Homeland Security
25 Sigourney Street
6th Floor
Hartford, CT 06106
Phone: 860-566-3180
Fax: 860-247-0664
URL: www.ct.gov/oem/site/default.asp

Kerry Flaherty
Director
e-mail: Kerry.Flaherty@po.state.ct.us

Office of Emergency Medical Services
Public Health Department
410 Capitol Avenue
MS #12EMS
Hartford, CT 06134-0308
Mailing Address: Po Box 340308
Phone: 860-509-7975
Fax: 860-509-7987
URL: www.dph.state.ct.us/EMS/index.htm

Description: Responsible for program development activities including: administering the emergency medical services equipment and local system development grant program; planning; training; public education and information programs; regional council oversight; and providing staff support to the advisory board.

Leonard Guercia Jr
Operations Branch Chief
Phone: 860-509-7975
e-mail: leonard.guercia@ct.gov

Bill Teel
Epidemiologist
Phone: 860-509-8116
e-mail: bill.teel@ct.gov

Richard Kamin
EMS Medical Director
Phone: 860-509-7975
e-mail: richard.kamin@ct.gov

Giovanni DiPaola
Special Investigator
Phone: 860-509-7611
e-mail: giovanni.dipaola@ct.gov

Albert L Geetter
Medical Director, Bioterrorism
Phone: 860-509-8100

Jon Bergeson
Training Coordinator-Bioterrorism
Phone: 860-509-8100
e-mail: jon.bergeson@ct.gov

Mary Duley
Hospital Preparedness Coordinator-Bioterrorism
Phone: 860-509-8100

Robert Kenny
EMS Field Program Coordinator-Bioterrorism
Phone: 860-509-8100
e-mail: robert.kelly@ct.gov

Joseph G Marino
National Pharmaceutical Stockpile Coordinator-Bioterrorism
Phone: 860-509-8100
e-mail: joseph.marino@ct.gov

Gary E Wiemokly
EMS Section Chief
e-mail: gary.wiemokly@ct.gov

Public Safety Department
1111 Country Club Road
Middletown, CT 06457
Phone: 860-685-8441
Fax: 860-685-8354
URL: www.ct.gov/dps
e-mail: dps.feedback@po.state.ct.us

Leonard C Boyle
Commissioner
Phone: 860-685-8000

Donald Harwood
Codes & Standards Committee Chairman
Phone: 860-685-8310

Wayne Maheu
Fire/Emergency & Building Services Director
Phone: 860-635-8300

Colonel Thomas Davoren
State Police Deputy Commissioner

Christopher R Laux
State Building Inspector

Public Utility Control Department
10 Franklin Square
New Britain, CT 06051-2655
Phone: 860-827-2801
Fax: 860-827-2613
URL: www.state.ct.us/dpuc

Description: To ensure that safe, reliable, modern, and fiarly-priced utility services are available throughout Connecticut.

Donald W Downes
Chairperson

John W Betkoski
Vice Chairperson

Anne C George
Commissioner

Anthony Palermino
Commissioner

William J Palomba
Executive Director
Phone: 860-827-2802

John G Haines
Attorney General
Phone: 860-827-2683

Beryl Lyons
Media Spokesperson
Phone: 860-827-2670
e-mail: beryl.lyons@po.state.ct.us

Nicholas Neeley
Advocacy/Regulatory Operations Director
Phone: 860-827-2625

Public Works Department
165 Capitol Avenue
Hartford, CT 06106
Phone: 860-713-5790

Fax: 860-713-7257
URL: www.ct.gov/dpw

Description: Providing quality facilities and in delivering cost-effective, responsive and timely services to state agencies in the areas of planning, design, construction, facilities management, leasing, real property disposition and security.

James T Fleming
Commissioner
Phone: 860-713-5800

Jonathan Holmes
Deputy Commissioner
Phone: 860-713-5850

Doug Moore
Chief of Staff
Phone: 860-713-5800

David O'Hearn
Deputy Commissioner
Phone: 860-713-5850

Manuel Becerra
Facilities/Maintenance Division
Phone: 860-713-5660

State Police
1111 Country Club Road
Middletown, CT 06457-9294
Phone: 860-685-8441
Phone: 888-767-7664
Fax: 860-685-8354
URL: www.ct.gov/dsp/cwp
e-mail: DPS.feedback@po.state.ct.us

Colonel Thomas Davoren
Deputy Commissioner

Lt Colonel Peter R Terenzi III
Commander Office Field Operations
Phone: 860-685-8090

Lt Colonel Cheryl Malloy
Commander Office Administration Services
Phone: 860-685-8180

Transportation Department
2800 Berlin Turnpike
Newington, CT 06131-7546
Phone: 860-594-3000
Fax: 860-594-3008
URL: www.ct.gov/dot

Ralph Carpenter
Commissioner
Phone: 860-594-3000

James Boice
Deputy Commissioner
Phone: 860-594-3000

Raeanne V Curtis
Deputy Commissioner
Phone: 860-594-3000

Michael Lonergan
Engineering/Highway Operations Bureau
Phone: 860-594-2701

Charles Barone
Policy & Planning Bureau
Phone: 860-594-2001

Gale Mattison
Finance & Administration Bureau
Phone: 860-594-2201

Peter Richter
Public Transportation Bureau

STATE AGENCIES

Delaware

Delaware Main Homeland Security Office

303 Transportation Circle
PO Box 818
Dover, DE 19903
Phone: 302-744-2680
Fax: 302-739-4874
URL: http://dshs.delaware.gov
e-mail: info@delawarepublicsafety.com

Ruth Ann Minner
Governor
Phone: 302-744-4101
e-mail: gminner@state.de.us

John C Carney Jr
Lieutenant Governor
Phone: 302-744-4333
e-mail: john.carney@state.de.us

David B Mitchell
Secretary, Safety & Homeland Security Department
Phone: 302-744-2680

Joseph R Biden, III
Attorney General
Phone: 302-577-8400
e-mail: attorney.general@state.de.us

Delaware Police Chiefs Council

400 S Queen Street
Dover, DE 19904
Phone: 302-739-5411
Fax: 302-736-7146
URL: www.delawarepolicechiefs.com

Martin W Johnson III
Coordinator
e-mail: mjohnson@doverpd.state.de.us

Delaware State Capitol Police

Safety & Homeland Security Department
150 William Penn Street
Dover, DE 19901
Mailing Address: PO Box 1401
Phone: 302-744-4380
Fax: 302-739-2869
URL: http://capitolpd.delaware.gov

William Jopp
Chief
Phone: 302-744-4390

Department of Agriculture

2320 S DuPont Highway
Dover, DE 19901
Phone: 302-698-4500
Fax: 302-697-4450
URL: www.state.de.us/deptagri

Description: To sustain and promote the viability of food, fiber, and agricultural industries in Delaware through quality services that protect and enhance the environment, health and welfare of the general public.

Michael T Scuse
Secretary
Phone: 302-698-4500

Harry D Shockley
Deputy Secretary
Phone: 302-698-4500

Sandra Ogden
Controller
Phone: 302-698-4500

Ewin Odor
Vegetarian/Food Products Administrator
Phone: 302-698-4539

John Thompson
Food Products Inspections Field Supervisor
Phone: 302-698-4542

Faith Kuehn
Plant Industries Administrator
Phone: 302-698-4587
e-mail: faith.kuehn@state.de.us

Dr Sara Bush
State Veterinarian/ Poultry & Animal Health
Phone: 302-698-4560

Emergency Management Agency

Safety & Homeland Security Department
165 Brick Store Landing Road
Smyrna, DE 19977
Phone: 302-659-3362
Phone: 877-729-3362
Fax: 302-659-6855
URL: www.state.de.us/dema/

Description: The state agency for coordination of comprehensive emergency preparedness, training, response, recovery and mitigation services in order to save lives, protect Delaware's economic base and reduce the impact of emergencies.

James E Turner III
Director
Phone: 302-659-2240

Glenn A Gillespie
Deputy Director
Phone: 302-659-2234

Rosanne Pack
Public Information Officer
Phone: 302-659-2210

Alan McClements
Logistical Support Services Administrator
Phone: 302-659-2239

Mark Claveloux
Training Administrator
Phone: 302-659-2233

Kevin Kille
Nuclear Biological Chemical Section Supervisor
Phone: 302-659-2237

Joseph Wessels
WMD Supervisor
Phone: 302-659-2248

Lloyd Stoebner
Natural Hazards Section Supervisor
Phone: 302-659-2246

National Guard
First Regiment Road
Wilmington, DE 19808
Phone: 302-326-7000
Fax: 302-323-3399
URL: www.delawarenationalguard.com

Major General Francis D Vavala
Adjutant General
Phone: 302-326-7001

Brigadier General Terry L Wiley
Assistant Adjutant General-Army
Phone: 302-326-7003

Brigadier General Hugh T Broomall
Assistant Adjutant General-Air
Phone: 302-326-7006

Colonel Terry L Greenwell
Chief of Joint Staff
Phone: 302-326-7005

Major Leonard A Gratteri
Public Affairs Officer
Phone: 302-326-7010

Natural Resources & Environmental Control Department
89 Kings Highway
Dover, DE 19901
Phone: 302-739-9902
URL: www.dnrec.state.de.us

Description: To protect and manage the state's vital natural resources, protect public health and safety, provide quality outdoor recreation and to serve and educate the citizens of the First State about the wise use, conservation and enhancement of Delaware's Environment.

John A Hughes
Secretary
Phone: 302-739-9000

David S Small
Deputy Secretary
Phone: 302-739-9000

Jennifer M Bothell
Enforcement Coordinator
Phone: 302-739-9037

James D Werner
Air & Waste Management Division Director
Phone: 302-739-9400

Ellen D Malenfant
Emergency Prevention & Response Branch Manager
Phone: 302-739-9404

Kevin C Donnelly
Water Resources Division Director
Phone: 302-739-9949
e-mail: kevin.donnelly@state.de.us

Sergio Huerta
Environmental Services Section Administrator
Phone: 302-739-9942

Stewart E Lovell
Water Supply Section Manager
Phone: 302-739-9945
e-mail: stewart.lovell@state.de.us

Office of Highway Safety
Safety & Homeland Security Department
303 Transportation Circle
Suite 201
Dover, DE 19901
Mailing Address: PO Box 1321, 19903-1321
Phone: 302-744-2740
URL: www.state.de.us/highway/default.shtml

Description: Committed to developing and implementing a comprehensive strategy aimed at saving lives and preventing injuries on the highways.

Tricia Roberts
Director
Phone: 302-744-2745

Jim Brown
Law Enforcement Liaison
Phone: 302-744-2747

Port of Wilmington
1 Hausel Road
Wilmington, DE 19801-5852
Phone: 302-472-7678
Fax: 302-472-7740
URL: www.portofwilmingtonde.com
e-mail: tkeefer@port.state.de.us

Gene Bailey
Executive Director
Phone: 302-472-7800
e-mail: gbailey@port.state.de.us

Thomas Keefer
Deputy Executive Director Marketing & Trade Development

Phone: 302-472-7820
e-mail: tkeefer@port.state.de.us

John Haroldson
Manager International Trade
Phone: 302-472-7822
e-mail: jharoldson@port.state.de.us

Frank Vignuli
Director Port Operations
Phone: 302-472-7695
e-mail: fvignuli@port.state.de.us

Inigo Thomas
Director Technology Solutions
Phone: 302-472-7846
e-mail: ithomas@port.state.de.us

Patrick Hemphill
Security Supervisor
Phone: 302-472-7817
e-mail: phemphill@port.state.de.us

Randy Horne
Senior Port Engineer/Facilities, Planning & Development
Phone: 302-472-7827
e-mail: rhorne@port.state.de.us

Public Health Division
Department of Health & Social Services
Jesse Cooper Building
417 Federal Street
Dover, DE 19901
Phone: 302-744-4700
Phone: 888-459-2943
Fax: 302-739-3008
URL: www.state.de.us/dhss/dph/index.htm
e-mail: dhssinfo@state.de.us

Jaime Rivera
Director
Phone: 302-744-4701

Herman Ellis
State Medical Director/Assoc Deputy Director Community Health Services
Phone: 302-744-4702

Steve Blessing
Emergency Medical Services Director
Phone: 302-744-5400

Ross Megargel
State EMS Medical Director
Phone: 302-744-5400

Paul R Silverman
Associate Deputy Director Health Indormation & Science
Phone: 302-744-4703

Jill Rogers
Health Promotion & Disease Prevention Section Chief
Phone: 302-741-2900

Robert Jackson
Bureau of Communicable Diseases Chief
Phone: 302-741-2920

Paula Eggers
Bureau of Infectious Disease Epidemiology
Phone: 302-744-4544

Martin Luta
Immunization Branch
Phone: 302-741-2950

Thom May
Health Systems Protection Section Chief
Phone: 302-744-4705

Frieda Fisher-Tyler
Office of Radiation Control
Phone: 302-744-4546

Edward G Hallock
Office of Drinking Water Administrator
Phone: 302-741-8630

Kae Mason
Office of Health & Risk Communication Chief
Phone: 302-744-4704

Emily Falone
Public Health Preparedness Section Chief
Phone: 302-744-5450

River & Bay Authority
Delaware Memorial Bridge Plaza
PO Box 71
New Castle, DE 19720
Phone: 302-571-6300
Phone: 302-571-6301
Fax: 302-571-6305
URL: www.drba.net
e-mail: contactus@drba.net

Description: Provide safe, efficient and modern terminals, crossings, vessels and related transportation while participating in controlled economic development opportunities supported by a technically proficient and professionally motivated work force dedicated to providing high quality customer service.

James T Johnson Jr
Chief Executive Officer
Phone: 302-571-6301

Donald Rainear
Deputy Executive Director Economic Development
Phone: 302-571-6445
e-mail: donald.ranear@drba.net

James H Walls
COO
Phone: 302-571-6315

Colonel John R McCarnan
Police Administrator
Phone: 302-571-6318
e-mail: police@drba.net

Lt Jack Cawman
Counter-Terrorism Coordinator
Phone: 302-571-6014

State Fire Marshal
Fire Prevention Commission
1537 Chestnut Grove Road
Dover, DE 19904-9610

Phone: 302-739-5665
Fax: 302-739-3696
URL: www.delawarestatefiremarshal.com

Description: To provide the citizens of the State and all who visit a Fire Safe Environment be it in the home, the workplace or wherever they pursue their varied lifestyles or interests.

Grover P Ingle
State Fire Marshal
Phone: 302-739-5665
e-mail: grover.ingle@state.de.us

John P Rossiter
FPS IV Chief, Technical Services

State Police
1441 N Dupont Highway
Dover, DE 19901
Mailing Address: PO Box 430
Phone: 302-739-5900
Phone: 302-739-5960
Fax: 302-739-5966
URL: www.state.de.us/dsp/

Description: To enhance the quality of life for all Delaware citizens and visitors by providing professional, competent and compassionate law enforcement services.

Colonel Thomas F Macleish III
Superintendent
Phone: 302-739-5911

Galen M Purcell
State Bureau of Identification
Phone: 302-739-5871

Captain Jeff Evans
Aviation Section Administrator
Phone: 302-378-5788

Captain Charles Simpson
Special Investigations Section
Phone: 302-378-5215

William D Carrow
Communications Section Chief
Phone: 302-659-2340

Lt Lewis Briggs
911 Operations Manager
Phone: 302-659-2349

Transportation Department
800 Bay Road
Dover, DE 19901
Mailing Address: PO Box 778, 19903
Phone: 302-760-2080
Phone: 800-652-5600
URL: www.deldot.net

Description: Provide a safe, efficient, and environmentally sensitive transportation network that offers a variety of convenient, and cost-effective choices for the movement of people and goods.

Carolann Wicks
Secretary
Phone: 302-760-2303

Darrel Cole
Public Relations Director
Phone: 302-760-2080

Robert Taylor
Chief Engineer & Transportation Solutions Director
Phone: 302-760-2305

Stephen Kingsberry
Delaware Transit Corporation Director
Phone: 302-760-2833

Marti Dobson
Technology/Support Services Director
Phone: 302-760-2203

STATE AGENCIES

District of Columbia

Washington DC Main Homeland Security Office
1350 Pennsylvania Avenue NW
Washington, DC 20004
Phone: 202-727-4036
Fax: 202-727-1617
URL: http://ohs.dmpsj.dc.gov
e-mail: ohs.eom@dc.gov

Adrian M Fenty
Mayor
Phone: 202-727-2980

Robert C Bobb
City Administrator
Phone: 202-727-6053

Edward D Reiskin
Deputy Mayor for Public Safety & Justice
Phone: 202-727-4036

Linda Singer
Attorney General
Phone: 202-727-3400

Department of Health
825 N Capitol Street NE
Washington, DC 20002
Phone: 202-671-5000
Fax: 202-442-4788
URL: http://doh.dc.gov
e-mail: doh@dc.gov

Description: Designs public health systems, diagnoses and investigates health threats, develops policy, provides education and disease prevention, and administers the low-income Medicaid insurance program.

Dr Gregg A Pane
Director

Beverly Pritchett
Director Emergency Health & Medical Services Adminsitration
Phone: 202-671-4222

Harold Monroe
Bureau of Food, Drug & Radiation Protection Chief
Phone: 202-535-2180

Sharon Cohen
Food Protection Division Program Manager
Phone: 202-535-2176

Gregory Talley
Radiation Protection Division Manager
Phone: 202-535-2320

Hamid Karimi
Bureau of Hazardous Materials & Toxic Substances Director
Phone: 202-535-2299

Robert Hamilton
Acting Director Hazardous Waste Division
Phone: 202-535-2270

Department of Human Services
64 New York Avenue NE
6th Floor
Washington, DC 20002
Phone: 202-671-4200
Fax: 202-671-4325
URL: http://dhs.dc.gov
e-mail: dhs@dc.gov

Description: Sets policy and provides social services for rehabilitation and self-sufficiency for DC residents including childhood development, youth services, public assistance, disability, and rehabilitation programs.

Kate Jesberg
Interim Director

Emergency Management Agency
2720 Martin Luther King Jr Ave, SE
Washington, DC 20032
Phone: 202-727-6161
Fax: 202-727-9524
URL: http://dcema.dc.gov
e-mail: ema@dc.gov

Darrell Darnell
Director
Phone: 202-727-3159

Kerry Payne
Operations Director
Phone: 202-727-3159

Jo Ellen G Contee
Public Information Officer
Phone: 202-727-6161

Christopher Voss
Plans & Training Division
Phone: 202-727-6161

Fire and Emergency Medical Services Department
1923 Vermont Avenue NW
Suite 102
Washington, DC 20001
Phone: 202-673-3331

Fax: 202-673-3188
URL: http://fems.dc.gov
e-mail: fems@dc.gov

Description: Provides fire protection and medical attention to residents and visitors in the District of Columbia. In addition, to identify potential fire hazards they conduct fire inspections in apartment buildings, businesses, hotels, schools (public and private), hospitals, nursing homes, correctional facilities, and residential care facilites.

Dennis L Rubin
Chief
Phone: 202-673-3320

Douglas Smith
Operations Assistant Fire Chief
Phone: 202-673-3320

Michael D Williams
Acting Emergency Medical Services Director
Phone: 202-673-3320

Metropolitan Police Department
300 Indiana Avenue NW
Washington, DC 20001
Phone: 202-727-4218
Fax: 202-727-9524
URL: http://mpdc.dc.gov
e-mail: mpd@dc.gov

Description: To prevent crime and the fear of crime, to build safe and healthy communities throughout the District of Columbia.

Cathy L Lanier
Chief of Police
Phone: 202-727-4218

Michael J Fitzgerald
Executive Assistant Chief of Police
Phone: 202-727-4363

Cheryl Pendergast
Training Division Commander
Phone: 202-645-0073

Traci Hughes
Executive Director Corporate Communication
Phone: 202-727-9346
e-mail: traci.hughes@dc.gov

Commander Patrick Burke
Special Operations Division Commander
Phone: 202-671-6511
e-mail: patrick.burke@dc.gov

National Guard
2001 E Capitol Street SE
Washington, DC 20003
Phone: 202-685-9790
Phone: 888-397-3105
URL: http://dcng.ngb.army.mil

Description: Additional protection for the District and federal government during civil emergencies.

Major General David F Wherley Jr
Commanding General

1st Lt Loneshia Reed
Public Affairs Officer
Phone: 202-685-9862
e-mail: paodc@dc.ngb.army.mil

Office of the Chief Medical Examiner
1910 Massachusetts Avenue SE
Building 27
Washington, DC 20003
Phone: 202-698-9000
Fax: 202-698-9100

Description: Investigates and certifies all deaths in the District of Columbia that occur as the result of violence (injury) as well as those that occur unexpectedly, without medical attention, in custody, or pose a threat to public health.

Marie Lydie Pierre-Louis
Chief Medical Examiner
Phone: 202-698-9000

Office of the Deputy Mayor for Public Safety and Justice
1350 Pennsylvania Avenue NW
John A Wilson Building, Suite 327
Washington, DC 20004
Phone: 202-727-4036
Fax: 202-727-1617
URL: http://dmpsj.dc.gov

Description: Provides oversight and support to the five District public safety and justice agencies: the Metropolitan Police Department, Fire and Emergency Medical Services Department, Department of Corrections, Emergency Management Agency, adn Office of the Chief Medical Examiner, and serves as the executive branch liaison to the federal justice agencies that provide services in the District.

Edward D Reiskin
Deputy Mayor
Phone: 202-727-4036

E Michael Latessa
Unified Communications Center Director
Phone: 202-673-3260

Public Service Commission
1333 H Street NW
Suite 200 W Tower
Washington, DC 20005-3200
Phone: 202-626-5100
Fax: 202-393-1389
URL: www.dcpsc.org
e-mail: support@psc.dc.gov

Description: Oversees the utility companies that provide natural gas, electricity and telecommunications services for the District.

Agnes A Yates
Chairperson
Phone: 202-626-5115
e-mail: ayates@psc.dc.gov

Betty Anne Kane
Commissioner

Richard E Morgan
Commissioner

Phone: 202-626-0518
e-mail: rmorgan@psc.dc.gov

Phylicia F Bowman
Executive Director

Richard Beverly
General Counsel
Phone: 202-626-5140

Washington Metropolitan Area Transit Authority

600 Fifth Street NW
Washington, DC 20001
Phone: 202-962-1234
Fax: 202-962-1133
URL: www.wmata.com

Dan Tangherlini
Interim General Manager

Polly L Hanson
Metropolitan Transit Police Chief
Phone: 202-962-2150

Captain William H Malone
District 1 Station Commander
Phone: 202-962-2696

Captain Erhart M Olson
District 2 Station Commander
Phone: 202-636-7117

Water and Sewer Authority

5000 Overlook Avenue SW
Washington, DC 20032
Phone: 202-787-2000
Fax: 202-787-2210
URL: www.dcwasa.com
e-mail: info@dcwasa.com

Description: To serve all its regional customers with superior
service by operating reliable and cost-effective water and
wastewater services in accordance with best practices.

Jerry N Johnson
General Manager
Phone: 202-787-2609

John T Dunn
Chief Engineer/Deputy General Manager

STATE AGENCIES

Florida

Florida Main Homeland Security Office
2331 Phillips Road
Tallahassee, FL 32308
Mailing Address: PO Box 1489, 32302-1489
Phone: 850-410-7000
Fax: 850-410-2189
URL: www.fdle.state.fl.us/osi/domesticsecurity
e-mail: florida.disaster@dca.state.fl.us

Charlie Crist
Governor
Phone: 850-488-7146

Jeff Kottkamp
Lieutenant Governor
Phone: 850-488-7146

Bill McCollum
Attorney General
Phone: 850-414-3300
e-mail: ag.mccollum@myfloridalegal.com

Scottie Sanderson
Homeland Security Advisor

Agriculture and Consumer Services Department
Plaza Level 10
The Capitol
Tallahassee, FL 32399-0800
Phone: 850-488-3022
Fax: 850-488-1806
URL: www.doacs.state.fl.us

Charles H Bronson
Commissioner
Phone: 850-488-3022

Craig Meyer
Deputy Commissioner
Phone: 850-488-3022

Joseph R Martelli
Inspector General
Phone: 850-245-1360
e-mail: martelj@doacs.state.fl.us

Dr Marion F Aller
Food Safety Division
Phone: 850-488-0295

Colonel Darrell Liford
Agricultural Law Enforcement
Phone: 850-245-1300

Dr Thomas J Holt
Animal Industry
Phone: 850-410-0900

Art Johnstone
Agricultural Emergency Preparedness
Phone: 850-410-6756

Alarm Association of Florida
1802 North University Drive
Plantation, FL 33322
Phone: 954-748-7779
Phone: 800-899-2099
Fax: 954-748-4749
URL: www.fla-alarms.org
e-mail: bneely@fla-alarms.org

Description: The objective of the AAF is to share common business interests and experiences in pursuit of collective goals, to provide strength and organizational solidarity within the security industry, to lobby effectively at levels of government, to implement and execute visionary projects, and to present members with exceptional opportunities to network on behalf of themselves and their business interests.

Mary Galloway
President

Bob Ireland
Vice President

Association of Contingency Planners-Mid Florida/Orlando Chapter
340 S Lakeside Drive
Satellite Beach, FL 32937
Phone: 321-544-1922
URL: mid-florida.acp-international.com
e-mail: aboutbc@cfl.rr.com

Description: A non-profit trade organization dedicated to fostering continued professional growth and development in effective Contingency & Business Resumption Planning.

Lynda Garaci
President

Eric Olsen
Treasurer

Bureau of Compliance Planning & Support
Division of Emergency Management
2555 Shumard Oak Boulevard
Tallahassee, FL 32399-2100
Phone: 850-413-9970
URL:
www.floridadisaster.org/compliance_planning/cps_home_page.htm

Description: The Bureau of Compliance Planning and Support works directly with the Bureau of Preparedness and Response, as well as all branches of state government to assist with logistics of disaster response and recovery operations to ensure efficiency. It also reviews plans to enhance first-response efforts at facilities storing hazardous materials.

Eve Rainey
Bureau Chief
Phone: 850-413-9970
e-mail: eve.rainey@dca.state.fl.us

Sheri Powers
Compliance Planning Section-Community Program Administrator
Phone: 850-413-9925
e-mail: sheri.richardson@dca.state.fl.us

Dianne Smith
Federal & State Program Grants-Planning Manager
Phone: 850-413-9966
e-mail: dianne.smith@dca.state.fl.us

Bureau of Preparedness & Response
Division of Emergency Management
2575 Shumard Oak Boulevard
Tallahassee, FL 32399-2100
Phone: 850-410-1597
Fax: 850-410-1392
URL: www.floridadisaster.org/bpr/

Description: The Bureau of Preparedness & Response is responsible for developing and maintaining Florida's ability to effectively respond to a wide variety of threats.

David Halstead
Bureau Chief
Phone: 850-410-1597
e-mail: david.halstead@dca.state.fl.us

Carla Boyce
Preparedness Section Administrator
Phone: 850-413-9895
e-mail: carla.boyce@dca.state.fl.us

Charles Hagan
Critical Infrastructure Administrator
Phone: 850-410-1263
e-mail: charles.hagan@dca.state.fl.us

Leo Lachat
Operations Unit Administrator
Phone: 850-413-9936
e-mail: leo.lachat@dca.state.fl.us

John Fleming
Communications/Technical Support Unit
Phone: 850-413-9888
e-mail: john.fleming@dca.state.fl.us

Jim Helms
Area 1 Coordinator/Field Office
Phone: 850-547-5168

Bryan Lowe
Area 2 Coordinator/Field Office
Phone: 850-414-8386

Jim Britts
Area 3 Coordinator/Field Office
Phone: 904-213-8208

Dana Winslett
Area 4 Coordinator/Field Office
Phone: 850-519-8633

Russell Manning
Area 5 Coordinator/Field Office
Phone: 407-893-3118

Brett Slocum
Area 6 Coordinator/Field Office

Al Howard
Area 7 Coordinator/Field Office
Phone: 850-519-8639

Bureau of Recovery & Mitigation
Division of Emergency Management
2555 Shumard Oak Boulevard
Tallahassee, FL 32399-2100
Phone: 850-487-1584
URL: www.floridadisaster.org/brm/

Description: The Bureau works to reduce or eliminate long-term risk to human life and property from disasters. Assistance from recovery is provided through the Hazard Mitigation Grand Program, human services assistance, and the federal infrastructure assistance.

Quinton Williams
Pre-Disaster Mitigation Program
Phone: 850-487-1584
e-mail: quinton.williams@dca.state.fl.us

Kathleen Marshall
Hazard Mitigation Grant Program
Phone: 850-922-5944
e-mail: kathleen.marshall@dca.state.fl.us

Department of Law Enforcement
2331 Phillips Road
Tallahassee, FL 32308
Mailing Address: PO Box 1489, Tallahassee, FL 32302
Phone: 850-410-7000
URL: www.fdle.state.fl.us
e-mail: info@fdle.state.fl.us

Gerald Bailey
Commissioner
Phone: 850-410-7001

Michael Ramage
General Counsel
Phone: 850-410-7676

Al Dennis
Inspector General
Phone: 850-410-7225

Mark Zadra
Assistant Commissioner-Public Safety Services

Don Ladner
Domestic Security & Intelligence

Division of Emergency Management
2555 Shumard Oak Boulevard

Tallahassee, FL 32399-2100
Phone: 850-413-9969
Phone: 800-413-9969
URL: www.floridadisaster.org
e-mail: florida.disaster@dca.state.fl.us

Description: Ensures that Florida is prepared to respond to, recover from and mitigate against emergencies. The division consists of four bureaus, some of which are listed in this section.

Craig Fugate
Director
e-mail: craig.fugate@dca.state.fl.us

Division of Emergency Medical Operations

4025 Esplanade Way
Tallahassee, FL 32399
Mailing Address: 4052 Bald Cypress Way, Tallahassee 32311
Phone: 850-245-4440
URL: www.doh.state.fl.us/demo/ems/
e-mail: demo_ems@doh.state.fl.us

John Bixler
Emergency Medical Services Bureau
Phone: 850-488-9408

Rhonda White
Public Health Preparedness
Phone: 850-245-4128
e-mail: demo_php@doh.state.fl.us

Environmental Protection Department

3900 Commonwealth Boulevard
Tallahassee, FL 32399
Phone: 850-245-2118
Fax: 850-245-2128
URL: www.dep.state.fl.us

Description: Protects, conserves and manages Florida's natural resources and enforces the State's environmental laws.

Michael W Sole
Secretary

Kelly Layman
Chief of Staff

Pinky Hall
Inspector General

Tom Beason
General Counsel

Nancy Blum
Communications

Joseph Kahn
Air Resource Management Division Director
Phone: 850-488-0114

Janet G Llewellyn
Water Resources Management Division Director

Tom Swihart
Water Policy Administrator
Phone: 850-245-8679

Michael Barrett
Beaches & Coastal System Bureau Chief
Phone: 850-488-7708

Mary Jean Yon
Waste Management Division Director
Phone: 850-245-8705
e-mail: mary.jean.yo@dep.state.fl.us

Henry E Barnet
Law Enforcement Division Director
Phone: 850-245-2851

Sarah Williams
Press Secretary
Phone: 850-245-2112
e-mail: sara.p.williams@dep.state.fl.us

Florida Capitol Police

400 S Monroe Street
Suite 213
Tallahassee, FL 32399
Phone: 850-488-1790
Fax: 850-922-3030
URL: www.fdle.state.fl.us/capitol_police/

Dean Register
Director
Phone: 850-410-7900

Florida Police Chiefs Association

924 N Gadsden Street
Tallahassee, FL 32303
Mailing Address: PO Box 14038, 32317
Phone: 850-219-3631
Phone: 800-332-8117
Fax: 850-219-3640
URL: www.fpca.com
e-mail: amercer@fpca.com

Amy Mercer
Executive Director
e-mail: amercer@fpca.com

Kay Huneidi
Executive Assistant
e-mail: khuneidi@fpca.com

Health Department

4052 Bald Cypress Way
Tallahassee, FL 32399
Phone: 850-487-2945
Fax: 850-487-3729
URL: www.doh.state.fl.us

Description: To promote and protect the health and safety of all people in Florida through the delivery of quality public health services and the promotion of health care standards.

M Rony Francois
Secretary
Phone: 850-245-4321

Nancy Humbert
Deputy Secretary & Director Public Health Nursing
Phone: 850-245-4244

Bonita J Sorensen
Deputy State Health Officer
Phone: 850-245-4242

Charles Alexander
Immunization Bureau Chief
Phone: 850-245-4342

William Passetti
Radiation Control Bureau Chief
Phone: 850-245-4266
e-mail: radiationcontrol@doh.state.fl.us

Bart Bibler
Water Programs Bureau Chief
Phone: 850-245-4240
e-mail: waterprograms@doh.state.fl.us

Dr Landis Crockett
Disease Control Division
Phone: 850-245-4418
e-mail: landis_crockett@doh.state.fl.us

Eric Grimm
Community Environmental Health Bureau Chief
Phone: 850-245-4277
e-mail: communityenvironmentalhealth@doh.state.fl.us

Doc Kokol
Communications Director
Phone: 850-245-4111
e-mail: doc_kokol@doh.state.fl.us

Gerald Briggs
Onsite Sewage Programs Bureau Chief
Phone: 850-245-4070

Steven T Wiersma
State Epidemiologist & Bureau Chief
Phone: 850-245-4411
e-mail: steven_wiersma@doh.state.fl.us

Military Affairs Department

St Francis Barracks
82 Marine Street
St. Augustine, FL 32084
Phone: 904-823-0100
Fax: 904-823-0125
URL: www.dma.state.fl.us

Major General Douglas Burnett
Adjutant General
Phone: 904-828-0100

Brigadier General Michael Fleming
Army Assistant Adjutant General
Phone: 904-823-0601

Brigadier General Joe Balkus
Air Assistant General
Phone: 904-823-0364

Colonel Jerry Vaughn
Chief of Staff
Phone: 904-823-0120

Municipal Power Agency

8553 Commodity Circle
Orlando, FL 32819-9002
Phone: 407-355-7767
Phone: 888-774-7606
Fax: 407-355-5794
URL: www.fmpa.com

e-mail: info@fmpa.com

Description: Develop economical and competitive power supply projects, to be proactive in providing member services, and to promote the image of public power, enabling its member utilities to succeed in a rapidly changing environment.

Roger A Fontes
General Manager/CEO

Frederick M Bryant
General Counsel/CFO

Richard Casey
Assistant General Manager, Power Resources

Thomas E Reedy
Assistant General Manager, Member Services and Information Systems

Northeast Florida Association of Contingency Planners

Phone: 904-281-3271
URL: www.acp-international.com/neflorida
e-mail: brian.strong@bsbsfl.com

Description: A no-profit mutual benefit assocation with membership open to anyone with interest in or responsibility for the vaired aspects of contingency planning. Contingency planning is a required element for successful businesses and government agencies. Emergency managers and business continuity planner alike address mitigation, repsonse and recovery planning issues.

Brian Strong
President

Matt Moyer
Vice President

Public Service Commission

2540 Shumard Oak Boulevard
Tallahassee, FL 32399-0850
Phone: 850-413-6100
Fax: 800-511-0809
URL: www.floridapsc.com
e-mail: contact@psc.state.fl.us

Description: Committed to making sure that Florida's consumers receive some of their most essential services-electric, natural gas, telephone, water and wasterwater-in a safe, affordable, and reliable manner.

Lisa Polak Edgar
Chair/Commissioner
Phone: 850-413-6044
e-mail: chairman@psc.state.fl.us

Nany Argenziano
Commissioner
Phone: 850-413-6038

Nathan A Skop
Commissioner
Phone: 850-413-6042

Matthew M Carter II
Commissioner
Phone: 850-413-6046

Katrina J McMurrian
Commissioner
Phone: 850-413-6040
e-mail: katrina.mcmurrian@psc.state.fl.us

Mary Andrews Bane
Executive Director
Phone: 850-413-6068

Seaport Office
605 Suwannee Street
MS 68
Tallahassee, FL 32399-0450
Phone: 850-414-4500
Fax: 850-994-4508
URL: www.dot.state.fl.us/seaport

Description: Responsible for programs relating to seaports, intermodal development, and planning for freight movement/intermodal connections.

Lorenzo Alexander
Manager
e-mail: lorenzo.alexander@dot.state.fl.us

Meredith Dahlrose
Intermodal Systems Specialist
e-mail: meredith.dahlrose@dot.state.fl.us

Catherine Kelly
Seaport Systems Specialist
e-mail: catherine.kelly@dot.state.fl.us

Transportation Department
605 Suwannee Street
Tallahassee, FL 32399-0450
Phone: 850-414-4100
Fax: 850-414-5201
URL: www.dot.state.fl.us

Description: To provide a safe transportation system that ensures the mobility of people and goods, enhances economic prosperity and preserves the quality of our environment and communities.

Stephanie C Kopelousos
Secretary
Phone: 850-414-5205

Dick Kane
Communications Director
Phone: 850-414-4590

Col David A Deese
Director, Motor Carrier Compliance
Phone: 850-245-7900

Sally Patrenos
Executive Director, Transportation Commission
Phone: 850-414-4105

Cecil Bragg
Inspector General
Phone: 850-410-5800

Ananth Prasad
Chief Engineer
Phone: 850-414-5240

Marian Scorza
Public Information Director
Phone: 813-975-6060

STATE AGENCIES

Georgia

Georgia Main Homeland Security Office
935 E Confederate Avenue
PO Box 18055
Atlanta, GA 30316
Phone: 404-635-7040
Fax: 404-635-4206
URL: www.ohs.state.ga.us

Description: To lead and direct the preparation, employment and management of state resources to safeguard Georgia and its citizens against threat or acts of terorism and the effects of natural disasters.

Sonny Perdue
Governor
Phone: 404-624-7030

Mark Taylor
Lieutenant Governor
Phone: 404-656-5030

Major General T Nesbitt
Director Homeland Security
Phone: 404-635-7000

Thurburt E Baker
Attorney General
Phone: 404-656-3300

Agriculture Department
19 Martin Luther King Jr Drive SW
Atlanta, GA 30334
Phone: 404-656-3645
Phone: 800-282-5852
Fax: 404-657-8387
URL: www.agr.state.ga.us

Description: To provide excellence in services and regulatory functions, to protect and promote agriculture and consumer interests, and to ensure an abundance of safe food and fiber for Georgia, America, and the world by using state-of-the-art technology and a professional workforce.

Tommy T Irvin
Commissioner
Phone: 404-656-3600
e-mail: tirvin@agr.state.ga.us

Arty Schronce
Public Affairs
Phone: 404-656-3689
e-mail: aschronce@agr.state.ga.us

Oscar Garrison
Assistant Commissioner, Consumer Protection

Phone: 404-656-3627
e-mail: ogarris@agr.state.ga.us

Van Harris
Agriculture Manager III
Phone: 404-656-3632

Chiefs of Police Association
3500 Duluth Park Lane
Suite 700
Duluth, GA 30096
Phone: 770-495-9650
Fax: 770-495-7872
URL: www.gachiefs.com
e-mail: gacp@gachiefs.com

Description: Dedicated to providing police services in the State of Georgia that are aimed at achieving more effective and efficient crime control, reduced fear of crime, improved quality of life, and improved police legitimacy, through a proactive reliance on community resources that seeks to minimize crime-causing conditions.

Frank V Rotondo
Executive Director

Department of Defense
PO Box 17965
Atlanta, GA 30316
Phone: 678-569-6060
URL: www.dod.state.ga.us
e-mail: doc@ga.ngb.army.mil

Major General David B Poythress
Adjutant General
Phone: 678-569-6001

Colonel Owen Ulmer
Director, Joint Operations
e-mail: owen.ulmer@ga.ngb.army.mil

Lieutenant Colonel James Driscoll
Director Communications
Phone: 678-569-6069
e-mail: jim.driscoll@ga.ngb.army.mil

BGen Michael McGuinn
Commandign General, Georgia State Defense Force

Department of Public Safety
PO Box 1456
Atlanta, GA 30371-1456
Phone: 404-624-7000
URL: http://dps.georgia.gov
e-mail: gadpsweb@gsp.net

Description: To work cooperatively with all levels of government to provide a safe environment for residents and visitors to the state.

Colonel Bill Hitchens
Commissioner
Phone: 404-624-7477

Lieutenant Colonel Arthur White
Deputy Commissioner
Phone: 404-624-7344

Major Corky Jewell
Communications Division
Phone: 404-624-7016

Dale Mann
Training Center Director
Phone: 478-993-4408

Emergency Management Agency (GEMA)

935 E Confederate Avenue SE
PO Box 18055
Atlanta, GA 30316
Phone: 404-635-7000
Phone: 800-879-4362
Fax: 404-635-7005
URL: www.gema.state.ga.us

Description: Part of the Office of the Governor, of which virtually all employees are on 24-hour call to assist local authorities in responding to emergencies.

Charley English
Emergency Management Director

Charles Dawson
Emergency Management Operations Director

Terry Lunn
Hazard Mitigation Director

Angi Ford
Public Assistance Director

Ralph Reichert
Terrorism Emergency Response Preparedness Director

Environmental Facilities Authority

233 Peachtree Street NE
Harris Tower, Suite 900
Atlanta, GA 30303
Phone: 404-584-1000
Fax: 404-584-1069
URL: www.gefa.org

Description: Administers a variety of programs and services to assist local governemts, state agencies,and nonprofits, in the areas of water and wasterwater, solid waste, land conservation, energy efficiency, recycling, and fuel storage tank removal. Our mission is to develop, market and finance prograssive energy efficiency and environmental programs utilizing the latest technology and expanding programmatic focus for all Georgians.

Chris Clark
Executive Director
Phone: 404-584-1000
e-mail: cclark@gefa.ga.gov

Highway Safety Office

34 Peachtree Street, Suite 800
One Park Tower
Atlanta, GA 30303
Phone: 404-656-6996
Phone: 888-420-0767
Fax: 404-651-9107
URL: www.gohs.state.ga.us

Description: To educate the public on traffic safety and to facilitate the implementation of programs that reduce crashes, injuries and fatalities on Georgia Roadways.

Robert Dallas
Director
Phone: 404-657-0540
e-mail: rdallas@gohs.state.ga.us

Spencer Moore
Deputy Director
Phone: 404-463-8977
e-mail: smoore@gohs.state.ga.us

Ricky Rich
Division Director, Special Operations
Phone: 404-657-9078
e-mail: rrich@gohs.state.ga.us

Jim Shuler
Public Information Officer
Phone: 404-657-9105
e-mail: jshuler@gohs.state.ga.us

Clifton Jenkins
Office Administrator
Phone: 404-656-9669
e-mail: cjenkins@gohs.state.ga.us

National Guard

Oglethorpe Armory
5019 GA Highway 42
Ellenwood, GA 30294
Phone: 678-569-5005
Fax: 678-569-5009
URL: www.gaguard.com

Major General William T Nesbitt
Commanding General
Phone: 404-675-5003

Port Authority

Administration Building
2 Main Street
Garden City, GA 31408
Mailing Address: PO Box 2406, Savannah, GA 31402
Phone: 912-964-3811
Phone: 800-342-8012
Fax: 912-964-3921
URL: www.gaports.com
e-mail: info@gaports.com

Description: To develop, maintain and operate ocean and inland river ports within Georgia; foster international trade and new industry for state and local communities; promote Georgia's agricultural, industrial and natural resources; and maintain the natural quality of the environment.

Doug J Marchand
Executive Director
Phone: 912-966-3615
e-mail: dmarchand@gaports.com

State Capitol Police
130 Memorial Drive SW
Atlanta, GA 30303
Phone: 404-656-4831
Fax: 404-657-8539

Description: Primary responsibility of protecting life and property; preventing and detecting criminal acts, and enforcing traffic regulations throughout Capitol Hill. This includes the apprehension of criminals, traffic enforcement and protection of public and building security in the Capitol Hill area.

Transportation Department
No 2 Capitol Square SW
Atlanta, GA 30334
Phone: 404-656-5267
Fax: 404-463-6336
URL: www.dot.state.ga.us

Description: Provides a safe, seamless and sustainable transportation system that supports Georgia's economy and is sensitive to tits citizens and environment.

Harold Linnenkohl
Commissioner
Phone: 404-656-5206
e-mail: harold.linnenkohl@dot.state.ga.us

Buddy Gratton
Deputy Commissioner
Phone: 404-656-5212

David Studstill
Chief Engineer
Phone: 404-656-5277

Terry Gable
State Aid Administrator
Phone: 404-656-5185

STATE AGENCIES

Guam

Guam Main Homeland Security/Civil Defense Office
221-B Chalan Palasyo
Agana Heights, 96910
Guam
Mailing Address: PO Box 2950
Phone: 671-475-9600
Phone: 671-475-9602
Fax: 671-477-3727
URL: www.guamhs.org

Felix P Camacho
Governor
Phone: 671-479-8931
e-mail: governor@mail.gov.gu

Michael W Cruz, MD
Lieutenant Governor

Major General Donald J Goldhorn
Homeland Security Advisor

Charles H Ada II
Acting Administrator Civil Defense

Environmental Protection Agency
17-3304 Mariner Avenue
Administration Building
Tiyan, 96913
Guam
Mailing Address: PO Box 22439 GMF, Barrigada, GU 96921
Phone: 671-475-1658
Phone: 671-475-1659
Fax: 671-477-9402
URL: www.guamepa.govguam.net

John MV Jocson
Acting Administrator
Phone: 671-475-1658
e-mail: john.jocson@guamepa.net

George Lai
Chairperson

Helen Kennedy
Legal Counsel
Phone: 671-475-1680
e-mail: helen.kennedy@guamepa.net

Conchita S N Taitano
Air & Land Division Chief
Phone: 671-475-1609
e-mail: conchita.taitano@guamepa.net

Walter S Leon Guerrero
DSMOA Manager

Phone: 671-475-1644
e-mail: walter.leonguerrero@guamepa.net

International Airport Authority
355 Chalan Pasaheru
Tamuning, 96931
Guam
Mailing Address: PO Box 8770
Phone: 671-646-0300
Fax: 671-646-8823
URL: www.guamairport.com

Description: To develop and promote competitive international and regional aviation services that ensure the safety and security of the travellin public and supports economic growth for the island community.

Frank F Blas
Chairman

Jesus (Jess) Q Torres
Executive Manager
e-mail: jesst@guamairport.net

Carlos H Salas
Deputy Executive Manager
e-mail: carloss@guamairport.net

Ray S Topasna
Chief Planner
e-mail: rayt@guamairport.net

John Leon Guerrero
Safety Administrator
e-mail: johnlg@guamairport.net

Pedro Lizama
Airport Rescue/Fire Chief
Phone: 671-475-5151
e-mail: petel@guamairport.net

Mark Charfauros
Chief of Airport Police
Phone: 671-646-0308
e-mail: markc@guamairport.net

Gerard Bautista
Air Terminal Manager
Phone: 671-642-4422
e-mail: gerardb@guamairport.net

Danny Cepeda
Information Systems
e-mail: danny@guamairport.net

Office of Public Health & Social Services
123 Chlan Kareta, Rte 10
Mangilao, 96932
Guam
Mailing Address: PO Box 2816, Hagatna, Guam 96932
Phone: 671-735-7399
Fax: 671-734-5910
URL: www.dphss.guam.gov

Peter John D Camacho, MPH
Acting Director

J Peter Roberto
Deputy Director

Police Department
233 Central Avenue
Tiyan, 96913
Guam
Mailing Address: PO Box 23909, GMF Barrigada, GU 96921
Phone: 671-475-8512
Fax: 671-472-4036
URL: http://gpd.guam.gov
e-mail: gpdchief@mail.gov.gu

Frankie T Ishizaki
Chief
Phone: 671-475-8508
e-mail: gpdchief@mail.gov.gu

Captain Leon Ryan
Highway Patrol Division
Phone: 671-477-0972

Sgt Michael Aguon
Executive Security
Phone: 671-472-8931

Sgt Joseph S Carbullido
Public Information Officer
Phone: 671-475-8532
e-mail: pio@guampd.com

Port Authority
1026 Cabras Highway
Suite 201
Piti, 96915
Guam
Phone: 671-477-5931
Phone: 671-472-7678
Fax: 671-477-2689
URL: www.portofguam.com

Description: The Port Authority of Guam operates the largest US deepwater port in the Western Pacific. It was established in 1975 and handles approximately 2 million tons of cargo a year.

Monte Mesa
Chairman

Joaquin P Cruz
Acting General Manager
e-mail: jpcruz@portofguam.com

Francisco G Santos
Harbor Master
e-mail: fgsantos@portofguam.com

Jose Guevara Jr
Financial Affairs Controller
e-mail: jbguevara@portofguam.com

Josette Javelosa
Marketing Program Coordinator IV
e-mail: jjjavelosa@portofguam.com

Major Doris Aguero
Chief of Port Police
e-mail: dcaguero@portofguam.com

Frank Roberto
Safety Administrator
e-mail: fcroberto@portofguam.com

John B Santos
Operations Manager
e-mail: jbsantos@portofguam.com

Waterworks Authority
578 N Marine Drive
Tamuning, 96913
Guam
Phone: 671-647-7800
Fax: 671-649-0369
URL: www.guamwaterworks.org
e-mail: pqlujan@mail.gov.gu

Simon Sanchez
Chairman, Consolidated Utilities Commission

John M Benavente, PE
General Manager
Phone: 671-647-2603

STATE AGENCIES

Hawaii

Hawaii Main Homeland Security Office
3949 Diamond Head Road
Honolulu, HI 96816
Phone: 808-733-4300
URL: www.scd.state.hi.us
e-mail: hscd@hawaii.gov

Linda Lingle
Governor
Phone: 808-586-0034
e-mail: gov@hawaii.gov

James R Aiona Jr
Lieutenant Governor
Phone: 808-586-0255
e-mail: ltgov@hawaii.gov

Major General Robert GF Lee
Director Homeland Security/Adjutant General
Phone: 808-733-4246
e-mail: robert.lee@hawaii.gov

Mark Bennett
Attorney General
Phone: 808-586-1500

Agriculture Department
1428 S King Street
Honolulu, HI 96814-2512
Phone: 808-973-9550
Fax: 808-973-9613
URL: www.hawaiiag.org/hdoa/
e-mail: hdoa.info@hawaii.gov

Sandra Lee Kunimoto
Chairperson
Phone: 808-973-9550
e-mail: sandra.kunimoto@hawaii.gov

James Foppoli
Animal Industry Division Administrator
Phone: 808-483-7111

Janelle Saneishi
Public Information Officer
Phone: 808-973-9560
e-mail: hdoa.info@hawaii.gov

Elaine Abe
Administrative Services Office
Phone: 808-973-9606
e-mail: elaine.t.abe@hawaii.gov

Dr Jason D Moniz
Livestock Disease Control Branch Manager
Phone: 808-483-7118

Earl Yamamoto
Planning & Division Office
Phone: 808-973-9466
e-mail: earl.j.yamamoto@hawaii.gov

Dr Lyle Wong
Plant Industry Division Adminstrator
Phone: 808-973-9535
e-mail: lyle.wong@hawaii.gov

Dr John Ryan
Quality Assurance Administrator
Phone: 808-832-0705
e-mail: john.m.ryan@hawaii.gov

Binh Loo
Chemist
Phone: 808-453-5922
e-mail: binh.t.loo@hawaii.gov

Airports Division
Department of Transportation
400 Rodgers Boulevard
7th Floor
Honolulu, HI 96819-1880
Phone: 808-838-8600
Fax: 808-838-8734
URL: www.hawaii.gov/dot/airports/index.htm
e-mail: airadministrator@hawaii.gov

Description: Develop, manage and maintain a safe and efficient global air transportation organization.

Rodney Haraga
Director
Phone: 808-838-8034
e-mail: rodney.haraga@hawaii.gov

Martinez Jacobs
Airport Fire Chief

Roy Sakata
Airports Operations Officer

Civil Defense Division
Defense Department
3949 Diamond Head Road
Honolulu, HI 96816-4495
Phone: 808-733-4300
Fax: 808-733-4287
URL: www.scd.state.hi.us/

Major General Robert GF Lee
Director
Phone: 808-733-4246
e-mail: robert.lee@hawaii.gov

Edward T Teixeira
Vice Director/State Coordinating Officer
Phone: 808-733-4300

Defense Department
3949 Diamond Head Road
Honolulu, HI 96816-4495
Phone: 808-733-4258
Fax: 808-733-4236
URL: www.dod.state.hi.us/

Description: The mission of the State of Hawaii Department of Defense, which includes the Hawaii National Guard (HING) and the State Civil Defense (SCD), is to assist authorities in providing for the safety, wlefare, and defense of the people of Hawaii.

Major General Robert GF Lee
Adjutant General
Phone: 808-733-4246
e-mail: robert.lee@hi.ngb.army.mil

Brigadier General Gary M Ishikawa
Deputy Adjutant General
Phone: 808-733-4244
e-mail: gary.ishikawa@hi.ngb.army.mil

Brigadier Gen Joseph J Chaves
Commander-Army

Major General Darryll MD Wong
Commander-Air

Environmental Health Administration
Department of Health
1250 Punchbowl Street
Honolulu, HI 96813
Phone: 808-586-4424
Fax: 808-586-4368
URL: www.state.hi.us/health/environmental/

Description: Entrusted to protect the health of Hawaii residents through the protection of the state's environment and through regulation of goods, services, and facilities used by the general public.

Lawrence K Lau
Deputy Director
Phone: 808-586-4424

Keith Kawaoka
Hazard Evaluation & Emergency Response Office
Phone: 808-586-4249

Janice Okubo
Communications Director
Phone: 808-586-4442

June Harrigan
Environmental Planning Office
Phone: 808-586-4337

Gayle Shida
Environmental Resources Office
Phone: 808-586-4575

Donna Maiava
Emergency Medical Services Branch
Phone: 808-733-9210

Wilfred K Nagamine, PE
Clean Air Branch Manager
Phone: 808-586-4200

Environmental Quality Control Office
235 Beretenia Street
Room 702
Honolulu, HI 96813
Phone: 808-586-4185
Fax: 808-586-4186
URL: www.state.hi.us/health/oegc/index.html

Genevieve Salmonson
Executive Director
Phone: 808-586-4185

Foreign Trade Zone
521 Ala Moana
Pier 2
Honolulu, HI 96813
Phone: 808-586-2507
Fax: 808-586-2512
URL: www.ftz9.org
e-mail: administration@ftz9.org

Description: Created throughout the United States to provide special customs procedures to US companies engaged in international trade-related activities. These procedures are aimed to offset customs advantages available to overseas producers who compete with domestic industry.

Gregory Barbour
Administrator
Phone: 808-586-2507

Harbors Division
Department of Transportation
Hale Awa Ku Moku Building
79 S Nimitz Highway
Honolulu, HI 96813
Phone: 808-587-1928
Fax: 808-587-1982
URL: http://state.hi.us/dot/harbors/index.htm

Description: To provide and effectively manage a commercial harbor system that facilitates the efficient movement of people and goods to, from and between the Hawaiian Islands, and enhances and/or preserve economic prosperity and quality of life.

Barry Fukunaga
Deputy Director
Phone: 808-587-3651

Glenn Okimoto
Harbors Administrator
Phone: 808-587-1927

Gaylord Harada
Information Manager
Phone: 808-587-1895

Erlinda Javier
Division Secretary
Phone: 808-587-1928

Hawaii State Law Enforcement
349 Kapiolani Street
Hilo, HI 96729

Phone: 808-935-3311
Fax: 808-961-2389
URL: www.hawaiipolice.com

Lawrence K Mahuna
Police Chief
Phone: 808-961-2244

Harry S Kubojiri
Deputy Chief

Health Department

1250 Punchbowl Street
PO Box 3378
Honolulu, HI 96801
Phone: 808-586-4400
Fax: 808-586-4444
URL: www.state.hi.us/health/

Chiyome Fukino MD
Director

Susan Jackson
Deputy Director
Phone: 808-586-4412

Morgan Barrett, MD
Health Resources Deputy Director
Phone: 808-586-4433

Lawrence K Lau
Environmental Health Deputy Director
Phone: 808-586-4424

Michelle R Hill
Behavioral Health Deputy Director
Phone: 808-586-4416

Janice Okubo
Communications Office
Phone: 808-586-4442

Health Resources Administration

Department of Health
1250 Punchbowl Street
Honolulu, HI 96813
Phone: 808-586-4433
Fax: 808-586-4368
URL: www.hawaii.gov/health/

Morgan Barrett, MD
Deputy Director
Phone: 808-586-4433

Donna Maiava
Emergency Medical Services Branch
Phone: 808-733-9210
e-mail: dmmaiava@camhmis.health.state.hi.us

Malama Markowitz
Immunizations Branch
Phone: 808-586-8300

Dr Paul Effler
Disease Outbreak Control Division
Phone: 808-586-8356
e-mail: pveffler@mail.health.state.hi.us

Loretta Fuddy
Family Health Services Division
Phone: 808-586-4122

Ruth Ota
Public Health Nursing Branch
Phone: 808-586-4620
e-mail: rkota@mail.health.state.hi.us

Mark Greer DMD
Dental Health Division
Phone: 808-832-5700

Barbara Yamashita
Community Health Division
Phone: 808-586-4126

Highways Division

Department of Transportation
869 Punchbowl Street
Room 513
Honolulu, HI 96813
Phone: 808-587-2220
Fax: 808-587-2340
URL: www.hawaii.gov/dot/highways/index.htm

Description: Provides a safe, and efficient and accessible highway system through the utilization of available resources in the maintenance, enhancement and support of land transportation facilities.

Glen M Yasui
Highways Administrator

Gerald Dang
Administrator Services Officer
Phone: 808-587-2218

Jamie Ho
Construction & Maintenance Engineering Program Manager
Phone: 808-587-2185

Ronald F Tsuzuki
Head Planning Branch
Phone: 808-587-1830

Alvin Takeshita
Traffic Engineering Program Manager
Phone: 808-692-7671

Land and Natural Resources Department

Kalanimoku Building
1151 Punchbowl Street
Honolulu, HI 96813
Phone: 808-587-0404
Fax: 808-587-0390
URL: www.state.hi.us/dlnr/Welcome.html
e-mail: dlnr@hawaii.gov

Allan A Smith
Acting Chairperson
Phone: 808-587-0400
e-mail: allansmith@hawaii.gov

Paul Conry
Forestry & Wildlife Administrator
Phone: 808-587-0166

Melanie Chinen
Historic Preservation Administrator
Phone: 808-692-8015

Dan Polhemus PhD
Aquatic Resources Division Administrator
Phone: 808-587-0100
e-mail: DLNR.aquatics@hawaii.gov

Ken Kawahara
Deputy Director of Water
Phone: 808-587-0240

Ed Underwood
Boating & Ocean Recreation Administrator
Phone: 808-587-1963

Gary Moniz
Conservation & Resources Enforcement Administrator
Phone: 808-587-0066

Eric Hirano
Engineering Administrator
Phone: 808-587-0230

Russell Tsuji
Land Adminstrator
Phone: 808-587-0230

Sam Lemmo
Conservation & Coastal Lands Administrator
Phone: 808-587-0378

Daniel Quinn
State Parks Administrator
Phone: 808-587-0300

Natural Energy Laboratory of Hawaii Authority
73 4460 Queen Kaahumanu Highway
101
Kailua-Kona, HI 96740
Phone: 808-329-7341
Fax: 808-326-3262
URL: www.nelha.org
e-mail: nelha@nelha.org

Description: To develop and diversify the Hawaii economy by providing resources and facilities for energy and ocean-related research, education, and commerical activities in an environmentally sound and culturally sensitive manner.

Ron Baird
Chief Executive Officer
Phone: 808-329-7341

Public Safety Department
919 Ala Moana Boulevard
4th Floor
Honolulu, HI 96814
Phone: 808-587-1350
Fax: 808-587-1421
URL: www.hawaii.gov/psd/

Description: To provide for the safety of the public and state facilities through law enforcement and correctional management.

Clayton A Frank
Interim Director

Phone: 808-587-1350
e-mail: clayton.a.frank@hawaii.gov

David F Festerling
Deputy Director Administration
Phone: 808-587-1251
e-mail: david.f.festerling@hawaii.gov

Tommy Johnson
Deputy Director Corrections
Phone: 808-587-1340
e-mail: tommy.johnson@hawaii.gov

Bryan Marciel
Executive Protection Division
Phone: 808-587-1380
e-mail: psdexecpro@hawaii.gov

Mike Mamitsuka
Management Information Systems Office
Phone: 808-587-1190
e-mail: mike.n.mamitsuka@hawaii.gov

James L Propotnick
Deputy Director Law Enforcement
Phone: 808-587-2562
e-mail: james.l.propotnick@hawaii.gov

Albert Cummings
Protective Services Division
Phone: 808-586-1355
e-mail: psdprotectivesvcsdiv@hawaii.gov

Louise Kim McCoy
Public Information Officer
Phone: 808-587-3477
e-mail: louise.k.mccoy@hawaii.gov

Public Works Division
Kalanimoku Building
1151 Punchbowl Street
Honolulu, HI 96813
Mailing Address: PO Box 119
Phone: 808-586-0526
Fax: 808-586-0521
URL: www.hawaii.gov/pwd

Ernest YW Lau
Administrator

Don Inouye
Staff Services Office Manager
Phone: 808-586-0512

Ralph Morita
Planning Branch Chief
Phone: 808-586-0500

Eric Nishimoto
Project Management Branch Chief
Phone: 808-586-0460

Clyde Kumabe
Inspection Branch Chief
Phone: 808-586-0414

Lawrence Uyehara
Quality Control Branch Chief
Phone: 808-586-0450

Ivan Nishiki
Leasing Branch
Phone: 808-586-0508

Strategic Industries Division
Department of Business, Economics Development & Tourism
No. 1 Capitol District Building
250 S Hotel Street
Honolulu, HI 96804
Mailing Address: PO Box 2359
Phone: 808-586-2423
Fax: 808-587-2790
URL: www.hawaii.gov/dbedt/info/energy/
e-mail: library@dbedt.hawaii.gov

Maurice Kaya
Chief Technology Officer
Phone: 808-587-3812

Dr John Tantlinger
Energy Planning & Policy Program Manager
Phone: 808-587-3805

Mark Want
Energy Emergency Preparedness Planner

Transportation Department
Aliiaimoku Building
869 Punchbowl Street
Honolulu, HI 96813
Phone: 808-587-2150
Fax: 808-587-2167
URL: www.state.hi.us/dot/

Description: To provide a safe, efficient, accessible, and intermodal transportation system that ensures the mobility of people and good, and enhances and/or preserves economic prosperity and the quality of life.

Barry Fukunaga
Director
Phone: 808-587-2150
e-mail: barry.fukunaga@hawaii.gov

Francis Paul Keeno
Deputy Diredctor-Staff
Phone: 808-587-2154
e-mail: francis.keeno@hawaii.gov

Glenn Soma
Statewide Transportation Planning Administrator
Phone: 808-587-1845
e-mail: glenn.soma@hawaii.gov

Robert Sequeira
Computer Systems Office
Phone: 808-587-2232
e-mail: robert.sequeira@hawaii.gov

Alexander Kaonohi
Motor Vehicle Safety Administrator
Phone: 808-692-7650
e-mail: alexander.kaonohi@hawaii.gov

Dean Yogi
Right-of-Way Branch Manager
Phone: 808-692-7325
e-mail: dean.yogi@hawaii.gov

Alvin Takeshita
Traffic Branch Engineering Program Manager
Phone: 808-692-7671
e-mail: alvin.takeshita@hawaii.gov

Glenn M Yasui
Highways Administrator
Phone: 808-587-2220
e-mail: glenn.yasui@hawaii.gov

Scott Ishikawa
Public Information Office
Phone: 808-587-2160
e-mail: scott.ishikawa@hawaii.gov

Glenn Okimoto
Harbors Administrator
Phone: 808-587-1927
e-mail: glenn.okimoto@hawaii.gov

STATE AGENCIES

Idaho

Idaho Main Homeland Security Office
Bureau of Homeland Security
4040 Guard Street, Building 600
Boise, ID 83705-5004
Phone: 208-422-3040
Phone: 208-422-3429
Fax: 208-422-3044
URL: www.bhs.idaho.gov;
www.state.id.us/government/homeland_security.html

Description: To savelife and to limit human suffering, injury to wildlife, damage to natural resources, private and public property, the environment and the economy as a result of the harmful affects of natural and man-caused disasters, from all hazards, including terrorism and the use of Weapons of Mass Destruction, in support of local governments and communities.

C L Otter
Governor
Phone: 208-334-2100

Jim Risch
Lieutenant Governor
Phone: 208-334-2200
e-mail: ltgov@lgo.idaho.gov

Major Gen Lawrence Lafrenz
Homeland Security Bureau Chief & Adjutant General
Phone: 208-422-5242

William H Bishop
State Director/Coordinator Homeland Security
Phone: 208-422-3040

Lawrence G Wasden
Attorney General
Phone: 208-334-2400

Agriculture Department
2270 Old Penitentiary Road
Boise, ID 83712
Mailing Address: PO Box 790, Boise 83701-0790
Phone: 208-332-8500
Fax: 208-334-2170
URL: www.agri.state.id.us/
e-mail: info@agri.idaho.gov

Cecila R Gould
Director
Phone: 208-332-8503
e-mail: cgould@agri.idaho.gov

Tom Schafer
Weights & Measures Bureau Manager
Phone: 208-332-8690
e-mail: tschafer@agri.idaho.gov

Fred Rios
Administrator Agricultural Resources
Phone: 208-332-8531
e-mail: frios@agri.idaho.gov

Dr. Greg Ledbetter
Administrator Animal Industries
Phone: 208-332-8540
e-mail: gledbetter@agri.idaho.gov

Marilyn Simunich, DVM
Animal Disease Surveillance & Diagnostics Manager
Phone: 208-332-8570
e-mail: msimunich@agri.idaho.gov

Tom Dayley
Administrator Plant Industries
Phone: 208-332-8620
e-mail: tdayley@agri.idaho.gov

Michael Becerra
Food Quality Assurance Laboratory Manager
Phone: 208-732-5325
e-mail: mbecerra@agri.idaho.gov

Lee Stacey
Agricultural Inspections Division Administrator
Phone: 208-332-8670
e-mail: lstacey@agri.idaho.gov

Cindy Stark
Program Manager Food Safety
Phone: 208-332-8670
e-mail: cstark@agri.idaho.gov

Environmental Quality Department
1410 N Hilton
Boise, ID 83706
Phone: 208-373-0502
Fax: 208-373-0417
URL: www.deq.idaho.gov

Description: To protect human health and preserve the quality of Idaho's air, land, and water for use and enjoyment today and in the future.

Toni Hardesty
Director

Martin Bauer
Air Quality Division Administrator
Phone: 208-373-0552
e-mail: martin.bauer@deq.idaho.gov

Barry Burnell
Water Quality Division Administrator

215

Phone: 208-373-0194
e-mail: barry.burnell@deq.idaho.gov

Kathleen Trever
INL Oversight & Radiation Control Coordinator
Phone: 208-373-0498
e-mail: kathleen.trever@deq.idaho.gov

Larry Koenig
Planning & Specials Projects Division Administrator
Phone: 208-373-0407
e-mail: larry.koenig@deq.idaho.gov

Jon Sandoval
Chief of Staff
Phone: 208-373-0240
e-mail: john.sandoval@deq.idaho.gov

Fire Management Bureau
3780 Industrial Avenue S
Coeur d'Alene, ID 83815
Phone: 208-769-1525
Fax: 208-769-1524
URL: www.idl.idaho.gov/bureau/firemgt.htm

Description: To conserve and protect six million acres of private, state and federal forest lands by preventing and/or suppressing all unwanted fire; to enhance forest management on state endowment lands by utilizing fire as a management tool; to help local communities better cope with wildfire in the wildland/urban interface.

Brian Shiplett
Bureau Chief
e-mail: bshiplett@idl.idaho.gov

Health and Welfare Department
450 W State Street
Boise, ID 83720-0036
Phone: 208-334-5500
Fax: 208-334-6558
URL: www.healthandwelfare.idaho.gov

Description: To promote and protect the health and safety of all Idahoans.

Richard Armstrong
Director
Phone: 208-334-5500

Quane Kenyon
Board Chairman
Phone: 208-376-2769

Richard Schultz
Deputy Director
Phone: 208-334-5945

Bill Walker
Deputy Director
Phone: 208-334-5500

David Butler
Deputy Direcotr Management Services
Phone: 208-334-5578

Jeanne Goodenough
Legal Services Chief
Phone: 208-334-5537

Russ Barron
Welfare Division
Phone: 208-334-5696

Michelle Britton
Family & Community Services Division
Phone: 208-334-0641

Jane Smith
Health Division
Phone: 208-334-5932

Idaho Chiefs of Police Association
112 Lake Street
Sandpoint, ID 83864
Phone: 208-263-3158
URL: www.icopa.org

Description: To combine ideas from every department to further preserve order, protect property, and enforce regulations for the citizen's of Idaho.

William Musser
President

Lands Department
954 W Jefferson
PO Box 83720
Boise, ID 83720-0050
Phone: 208-334-0200
Fax: 208-334-2339
URL: www.idl.idaho.gov

Description: Manage endowment trust lands to maximize long-term financial returns to the beneficiary institutions and provide protection to Idaho's natural resources.

George Bacon
Director/State Board Secretary
Phone: 208-334-0242
e-mail: gbacon@idl.idaho.gov

Jon Pope
Bureau Chief-Management Information Services
Phone: 208-334-0200
e-mail: jpope@idl.idaho.gov

Perry Whitaker
Bureau Chief-Real Estate
Phone: 208-334-0200
e-mail: pwhittaker@idl.idaho.gov

Ron Litz
Assistant Director-Forestry & Fire
Phone: 208-769-1525
e-mail: rlitz@idl.idaho.gov

Bob Brammer
Assistant Director-Lands, Minerals & Range
Phone: 208-334-0200
e-mail: bbrammer@idl.idaho.gov

Kathy Opp
Division Administrator-Support Services
Phone: 208-334-0200
e-mail: kopp@idl.idaho.gov

Military Division-National Guard
4040 W Guard Street

Building 600
Boise, ID 83705-5004
Phone: 208-422-5242
Fax: 208-442-6179
URL: www.idarng.com

Major Gen Lawrence F Lafrenz
Commanding General
Phone: 208-422-5242

William H Shawver
Joint Chief of Staff
Phone: 208-422-5815

Brigadier General Gary Sayler
Air Deputy Commanding General
Phone: 208-422-5470

Brig Gen Alan C Gayhart Sr
Army Deputy Commanding General
Phone: 208-422-5214

Lt Colonel Stephanie Dowling
Public Affairs Officer
Phone: 208-422-5268

State Police
PO Box 700
Meridian, ID 83680-0700
Phone: 208-884-7003
Fax: 208-884-7090
URL: www.isp.state.id.us

Description: To protect the lives, property and constitutional rights of the people of Idaho.

Colonel Jerry Russell
Director
Phone: 208-884-7003
e-mail: jerry.russell@isp.idaho.gov

Lt Colonel Kevin Johnson
Deputy Director
e-mail: kevin.johnson@isp.idaho.gov

Cpt Lamont Johnston
Manager Commercial Vehicle Safety
Phone: 208-884-7220

David Kane
Law Enforcement Programs
Phone: 208-884-7120
e-mail: dave.kane@isp.idaho.gov

Dawn A Peck
Manager Criminal Identification Bureau
Phone: 208-884-7130
e-mail: dawn.peck@isp.idaho.gov

Rick Ohnsman
Media & Public Information
Phone: 208-884-7231
e-mail: rick.ohnsman@isp.idaho.gov

Transportation Department
3311 W State Street
PO Box 7129
Boise, ID 83707-1129
Phone: 208-334-8800
Fax: 208-334-3858

URL: www.itd.idaho.gov

Description: To provide cost-effective transportation systems that are safe, reliable and responsive to the economical and efficient movement of people and products.

Pamela Lowe
Director
Phone: 208-334-8807

Matthew E Morre, MA
Administrator Transportation Planning/Programming Division
Phone: 208-334-8484

Steve Hutchinson
Chief Engineer Highway Division
Phone: 208-334-8802

John DeThomas
Administrator Aeronautics Division
Phone: 208-334-8788

Stephen Moreno
Administrator Federal Highway Administration
Phone: 208-334-1843

Larry Falkner
Administrator Public Transportation Division
Phone: 208-334-8281

Alan Frew
Administrator Motor Vehicles Division
Phone: 208-334-4443

Water Resources Department
322 E Front Street
PO Box 83720
Boise, ID 83720
Phone: 208-287-4800
Fax: 208-287-6700
URL: www.idwr.state.id.us/

David R Tuthill, J
Director
Phone: 208-287-4800

Hal Anderson
Administrator-Planning & Technical Services Division
Phone: 208-287-4800

Brian Patton
Water Planning Bureau Chief
Phone: 208-287-4837
e-mail: brian.patton@idwr.idaho.gov

Bob Hoppie
Administrator-Energy Division
Phone: 208-287-4800

Gary Spackman
Administrator-Water Management Division
Phone: 208-287-4800

STATE AGENCIES

Illinois

Illinois Main Homeland Security Office

207 State House
Springfield, IL 62706
Phone: 217-524-1423
URL: www.illinoishomelandsecurity.org

Rod R Blagojevich
Governor
Phone: 217-782-0244

Patrick Quinn
Lieutenant Governor
Phone: 217-782-7884

Jill Morgenthaler
Homeland Security Advisor
Phone: 217-524-1423

Lisa Madigan
Attorney General
Phone: 217-782-1090

Association of Contingency Planners-Greater Chicago Chapter

233 S Wacker Drive
Suite 3530
Chicago, IL 60606
Phone: 312-875-1069
URL: www.acp-international.com/chicago
e-mail: gsikich@aol.com

Description: The Greater Chicago Chapter of the ACP was founded to provide a forum for the area business community professionals to hear and exchange information from their peers in both the public and private sectors.

John Stagl
President

Paul Erling
Director of Membership

Capitol Police

110 E Adams Street
Springfield, IL 62701
Phone: 217-782-7126
URL:
www.cyberdriveillinois.com/departments/police/home.htm

Brad Demuzio
Director, Secretary of State Police

David Allen
Capitol Police
Phone: 217-524-4903

Michael Pippin
Command Center
Phone: 217-782-4100

Department of Agriculture

State Fairgrounds
PO Box 19281
Springfield, IL 62794-9281
Phone: 212-782-2172
Fax: 217-785-4505
URL: www.agr.state.il.us
e-mail: agr.pio@illinois.gov

Description: An advocate for Illinois' agricultural industry and provide the necessary regulatory functions to benefit consumers, agricultural industry, and the natural resources.

Charles A Hartke
Director

Margaret Van Dijk
General Counsel
Phone: 217-785-4507

Colleen O'Keefe
Food Safety & Animal Protection Division Manager
Phone: 217-785-5680

Mark Ernst
Animal Health & Welfare
Phone: 217-782-4944

Jared Thornley
Natural Resources Division Manager
Phone: 217-785-4233

Warren Goetsch
Environmental Programs
Phone: 217-785-2427

Steve Chard
Land/Water Resources
Phone: 217-782-6297

Emergency Management Agency

2200 S Dirksen Parkway
Springfield, IL 62703
Phone: 217-782-2700
URL: www.state.il.us/iema

Description: To protect the State of Illinois through integrated approaches of Emergency Management and Homeland Security. To prepare for, respond to, mitigate against, and recover from emergencies and disasters, or acts of terrorism.

Andrew Velasquez III
Director
Phone: 217-782-2700

Joseph G Klinger
Acting Assistant Director/Nuclear Safety Bureau Chief
Phone: 217-785-9868

Patti Thompson
Media
Phone: 217-785-0546

David L Smith
Disaster Assistance & Preparedness Bureau Chief
Phone: 217-785-9890

Kim Purcell
Information Technology Bureau Chief
Phone: 217-557-4785

Jim Watts
Operations Bureau Chief
Phone: 217-557-4794

Mike Parker
Nuclear Facility Safety Bureau Chief
Phone: 217-785-9854

Rich Allen
Environmental Safety Bureau Chief
Phone: 217-782-1322

Paul Eastvold
Radiation Safety Bureau Chief
Phone: 217-785-9918

Illinois Association of Chiefs of Police

426 S 5th Street
Suite 200
Springfield, IL 62701-1824
Phone: 217-523-3765
Fax: 217-523-8352
URL: www.ilchiefs.org

Description: To promote the professional and personal development of the members through innovative services, training and camaraderie.

Giacomo Pecoraro
Executive Director
e-mail: gapecoraro@ilchiefs.org

Laimutis A Nargelenas
Deputy Director
e-mail: lnargelenas@ilchiefs.org

Linda S Kunz
Executive Assistant & CFO
e-mail: lkunz@ilchiefs.org

Illinois Terrorism Task Force

Description: The Illinois Terrorism Task Force has the responsibility of ensuring that Illinois is ready to respond in the event of an act of terrorism.

Michael Chamness
Chairman
Phone: 217-557-5499

International Port District: Port of Chicago

3600 E 95th Street
Chicago, IL 60617-5193
Phone: 773-646-4400
Phone: 800-843-7678
Fax: 773-221-7678
URL: www.iipd.com
e-mail: iipd@iipd.com

Anthony Ianello
Executive Director

Military Affairs Department-National Guard

1301 N MacArthur Boulevard
Springfield, IL 62702-2399
Phone: 217-761-3589
Fax: 217-761-3527
URL: www.il.ngb.army.mil
e-mail: paoil@il.ngb.army.mil

Major General Randal E Thomas
Adjutant General
Phone: 217-761-3500

Brig General Harold E Keistler
Air Assistant Adjutant General
Phone: 217-761-3580

Brig General Dennis Cellette
Army Assistant Adjutant General
Phone: 217-761-3589

Brig General R Craig Nafziger
Air Chief of Staff

Lt Colonel Alicia Tate-Nadeau
Public Affairs Officer

Natural Resources Department

One Natural Resources Way
Springfield, IL 62702
Phone: 217-782-6302
URL: www.dnr.state.il.us

Description: To manage, protect and sustain Illinois' natural and cultural resources; provide resource-compatible recreational opportunities and promote natural resource-related public safety, education, and science.

Sam Flood
Acting Director
Phone: 217-785-0075

Leslie Sgro
Deputy Director
Phone: 217-558-7117

Debbie Stone
Deputy Director
Phone: 217-782-5694

Gary Clark
Water Resources Office Director
Phone: 217-782-2152

Office of the State Fire Marshal

1035 Stevenson Drive
Springfield, IL 62703-4288
Phone: 217-785-0969

Fax: 217-782-1062
URL: www.state.il.us/osfm

Description: Provides professional personnel and programs for the citizens of Illinois and is committed to protecting life and property from fire and explosions through inspection, investigation, training, education, data processing and statistical fire reports.

J t Somer
State Fire Marshal
Phone: 217-785-4143

Public Health Department
535 W Jefferson Street
Springfield, IL 62761
Phone: 217-782-4977
Fax: 217-782-3987
URL: www.idph.state.il.us
e-mail: dph.mailus@illinois.gov

Description: To promote the health of people of Illinois through prevention and control of disease and injury.

Eric E Whitaker MD
Director
Phone: 217-782-4977

Joseph Bogdan
Deputy Director Office of Health Preparedness
Phone: 312-793-7060
e-mail: jbogdan@idph.state.il.us

David Carvalho
Deputy Director Office of Policy, Planning & Statistics
Phone: 217-785-2040
e-mail: dcarvalh@idph.state.il.us

Tiefu Shen
Division of Epidemiologic Studies
Phone: 217-785-1873

Mark Flotow
Division of Health Statistics
Phone: 217-785-1064

Tom Hughes
Deputy Director Office of Health Protection
Phone: 217-782-3984

Gary Flentge
Division of Environmental Health
Phone: 217-782-5830

Craig Conover
Division of Infectious Diseases (Acting)
Phone: 217-785-7165

Thomas J Schafer
Division of Communications
Phone: 217-782-5750

State Police
125 E Monroe Street
Springfield, IL 62794-9461
Mailing Address: PO Box 19461
Phone: 217-782-7263
Fax: 217-785-2821
URL: www.isp.state.il.us

Larry G Trent
Director
Phone: 217-782-7263

Douglas W Brown
First Deputy Director
Phone: 217-782-7263

Scott Giles
Executive Protection
Phone: 217-782-2427

Rick Hector
Public Information Chief
Phone: 217-782-6637

Mark Robertson
Communications Services Bureau
Phone: 217-782-5282

Colonel Kathleen Stevens
Deputy Director Forensic Services Division
Phone: 217-785-7542

Colonel Charles Brueggemann
Deputy Director Operations Division
Phone: 217-782-1320

Colonel Kenneth Bouche
Deputy Director Information Technology Command
Phone: 217-557-6630

Kim Cochran
Police Academy Commander
Phone: 217-786-6909

Transportation Department
2300 S Dirksen Parkway
Springfield, IL 62764
Phone: 217-782-7820
Fax: 217-782-6828
URL: www.dot.il.gov

Milton R Sees
Acting Secretary
Phone: 217-782-5597

Clayton Harris
Chief of Staff
Phone: 312-793-2242

Jason Tai
Director Public/Intermodal Transportation
Phone: 312-793-2111

Dick Smith
Director Office of Planning & Programming
Phone: 217-782-6289

Jessica Baker
Information/Public Assistance Bureau Chief
Phone: 217-782-6953

Susan Shea
Director Division of Aeronautics
Phone: 217-785-8515

Milton Sees
Director Division of Highways, Chief Engineer
Phone: 217-782-2151

Michael R Stout
Director Division of Traffic Safety
Phone: 217-782-4972

STATE AGENCIES

Indiana

Indiana Main Homeland Security Office

302 W Washington Street
Room E-208
Indianapolis, IN 46204
Phone: 317-232-3980
Fax: 317-232-3895
URL: www.in.gov/dhs

Description: In 2005, all emergency management and homeland security efforts were consolidated into one department by creating the Indiana Department of Homeland Security (IDHS). The four divisions are Planning, Training, Emergency Response, and Fire & Building Safety (listed separately below).

Mitchell E Daniels
Governor
Phone: 317-232-4567

Rebecca Skillman
Lieutenant Governor
Phone: 317-232-4545
e-mail: s44@ai.org

Stephen Carter
Attorney General
Phone: 317-232-6201

J Eric Dietz PhD
Homeland Security Director
Phone: 317-232-8303

Clif Wojtalewicz
Planning Division Director
Phone: 317-234-2582

Greg Dhaene
Emergency Response Division Director
Phone: 317-232-3834

Joe Wainscott
Training Division Director
Phone: 317-232-2985
e-mail: jwainscott@dhs.in.gov

Agriculture Department

101 W Ohio Street
Suite 1200
Indianapolis, IN 46204
Phone: 317-232-8770
Fax: 317-232-1362
URL: www.in.gov/isda

Rebecca Skillman
Lt Governor/Secretary of Agriculture & Rural Development
Phone: 317-232-8770
e-mail: bskillman@lg.in.gov

Andy Miller
Director of Agriculture
Phone: 317-232-8774
e-mail: amiller@isda.in.gov

Beth Bechdol
Deputy Director
e-mail: bbechdol@isda.in.gov

Ken Klemme
Asst Director of Economic Development
e-mail: kklemme@isda.in.gov

Tammy Lawson
Asst Director, Regulatory Affairs & Soil Conservation
e-mail: tlawson@isda.in.gov

Melissa Acton
Asst Director of Operations
e-mail: macton@isda.in.gov

Deb Abbott
Asst Director of Communications & Outreach
e-mail: dabbott@isda.in.gov

Department of Environmental Management

100 N Senate Avenue
Indiana Government Center North
Indianapolis, IN 46204-2251
Mailing Address: MC 50-01
Phone: 317-232-8603
Phone: 800-451-6027
Fax: 317-233-6647
URL: www.in.gov/idem

Thomas W Easterly
Commissioner
Phone: 317-232-8611
e-mail: teasterl@idem.in.gov

Fire and Building Safety Division

Indiana Government Center S
402 W Washington St, Room E-241
Indianapolis, IN 46204-2739
Phone: 317-232-2222
Phone: 800-423-0765
Fax: 317-232-0307
URL: www.in.gov/dhs/fire/

Description: To develop, foster and promote methods of protecting the lives and property of the citizens of Indiana; provide building safety and permit coordination; and develop and maintain an effective Emergency Medical Services system.

Michael Garvey
Chief Deputy State Fire Marshal

Phone: 317-232-3983
e-mail: mgarvey@dhs.in.gov

Health Department
2 N Meridian Street
Indianapolis, IN 46204
Phone: 317-233-1325
Fax: 317-233-7387
URL: www.in.gov/isdh

Judith A Monroe MD
State Health Commissioner
Phone: 317-233-7400

Mary Hill, RN, Esq
Deputy State Health Commissioner
Phone: 317-233-7200

Robert Teclaw, DVM, MPH, PhD
State Epidemiologist
Phone: 317-233-7112

Jennifer Dunlap
Public Affairs
Phone: 317-233-7315

Brian Carnes
Legislative Liaison
Phone: 317-234-3808

Indiana Association of Chiefs of Police
10293 N Meridian Street
Suite 175
Indianapolis, IN 46290
Phone: 317-816-1619
Fax: 317-816-1633
URL: www.iacop.org
e-mail: info@iacop.org

Description: To promote professionalism, traning and networking for the law enforcement executive and to enhance public awareness of law enforcement and public safety issues.

Michael Ward
Executive Director
e-mail: mfw@wardmanage.com

Law Enforcement Academy
PO Box 313
Plainfield, IN 46168
Phone: 317-839-5191
Fax: 317-839-9741
URL: www.in.gov/ilea

Description: Indiana's center for law enforcement education. The Academy prepares law enforcement professionals for service through rigorous training based upon values and respect.

Rusty K Goodpaster
Executive Director

Michael J Lindsay
Deputy Director

Mark A Bridge
Basic Course Commander

Midwest Contingency Planner
PO Box 1632

Indianapolis, IN 46206
Phone: 307-285-4905
Fax: 317-285-7547
URL: www.drj.com/groups/mcp
e-mail: shelly.hogan@oneamerica.com

Description: A not for profit organization serving as a forum for business professionals working in the areas of business continuity, business resumption, contingency planning, disaster recovery and other related emergency recovery functions. Our membership area covers Indiana and surrounding states.

Shelly Hogan
President

Mike Alley
Vice President/Program Director

Municipal Power Agency
11610 N College Avenue
Carmel, IN 46032
Phone: 317-573-9955
Phone: 800-826-4672
Fax: 317-575-3372
URL: www.impa.com
e-mail: info@impa.com

Description: Created by a group of municipally-owned electric utilities, enabling them to share power resources and provide electricity more economically to their customers.

Rajeshwar G Rao
President
Phone: 317-573-9955

Steven Brown
Power System Coordination
e-mail: steve@impa.com

Niki Dick
Finance & Member Services
e-mail: niki@impa.com

Ports of Indiana
150 W Market Street
Suite 100
Indianapolis, IN 46204
Phone: 317-232-9200
Phone: 800-232-7678
Fax: 317-232-0137
URL: www.portsofindiana.com
e-mail: info@portsofindiana.com

Description: Dedicated to facilitating economic development in Indiana through logistics and services, maritime industrial and commercial development, development finance tools and strategic public-private partnerships.

Ken Kaczmarek
Chairman

Marvin Ferguson
Vice Chairman

Rich Cooper
Executive Director
Phone: 317-232-9200
e-mail: rcooper@portsofindiana.com

Greg Gibson
Commissioner

H C 'Bud' Farmer
Commissioner

Jody Peacock
Director of Corporate Affairs
Phone: 317-233-6225
e-mail: jpeacock@portsofindiana.com

Carolyn Hartley
Commissioner

Phil Wilzbacher
Port Director-Mount Vernon
Phone: 812-833-2166
e-mail: pwilzbacher@portsofindiana.com

Brian Nutter
Port Director-Jeffersonville
Phone: 812-283-9662
e-mail: bnutter@portsofindiana.com

Brian Sieg
Operations Manager-Jeffersonville
Phone: 812-283-9668
e-mail: bsieg@portsofindiana.com

Public Safety Training Institute
302 W Washington Street
Room E208
Indianapolis, IN 46204-2722
Phone: 317-233-0208
Fax: 317-233-0497
URL: www.state.in.us/sema/psti.html

J Eric Dietz
Executive Director
Phone: 317-232-3986

Michael Garvey
Deputy Director
Phone: 317-232-3983

Tony Pagano
Emergency Management Academy
Phone: 317-232-3985

Randall Wood
Hazardous Materials/Environmental Management Academy
Phone: 317-233-0498

State Police
100 N Senate Avenue
IGC N 340
Indianapolis, IN 46204
Phone: 317-233-8248
Phone: 317-232-8200
Fax: 317-232-0652
URL: www.in.gov/isp

Dr Paul E Whitesell
Superintendent

Transportation Department
100 N Senate Avenue
IGC-N, Rm 755
Indianapolis, IN 46204

Phone: 317-233-5533
Fax: 317-233-1481
URL: www.in.gov/dot
e-mail: indot@ai.org

Description: To build, maintain, and operate a superior transportation system enhancing safety, mobility and economic growth.

Karl B Browning
Commissioner

Corey Carr
Chief of Staff
Phone: 317-234-2780

Carl Bruhn
Business Information & Technology Systems

Jim Poturalski
Highway Management

Utility Regulatory Commission
101 W Washington Street
Suite 1500E
Indianapolis, IN 46204
Phone: 317-232-2071
Fax: 317-233-2410
URL: www.in.gov/iurc
e-mail: info@urc.in.gov

David Lott Hardy
Chairman
e-mail: dlhardy@urc.in.gov

Larry S Landis
Commissioner
e-mail: llandis@urc.in.gov

David Ziegner
Commissioner
e-mail: dziegner@urc.in.gov

Gregory Server
Commissioner
e-mail: gserver@urc.in.gov

Jerry Webb
Water & Sewer Director
e-mail: jlwebb@urc.in.gov

Bill Deivine
General Counsel
e-mail: bdevine@urc.in.gov

John McLaughlin
Communications Director
e-mail: jmclaughlin@urc.in.gov

Joseph Sutherland
Executive Director
e-mail: jsutherland@urc.in.gov

Mary Beth Fisher-Johnson
Chief External Affairs Officer
e-mail: mfisher@urc.in.gov

Wayne Remick
Information Technology Director
e-mail: wremick@urc.in.gov

Jane Steinhauer
Gas Director
e-mail: jsteinhauer@urc.in.gov

STATE AGENCIES

Iowa

Iowa Homeland Security and Emergency Management Division
Camp Dodge, Building W-4
7105 NW 70th Avenue
Johnston, IA 50131
Phone: 515-725-3231
Fax: 515-725-3260
URL: www.iowahomelandsecurity.org

Chet Culver
Governor

Patty Judge
Lieutenant Governor

David Miller
Homeland Security & Emergency Management Administrator
Phone: 515-725-3231

Tom Baumgartner
Homeland Security Coordinator
Phone: 515-725-3214

Thomas J Miller
Attorney General
Phone: 515-281-8373

Agriculture and Land Stewardship Department
Wallace State Office Building
502 E 9th Street
Des Moines, IA 50319
Phone: 515-281-5321
Fax: 515-281-6236
URL: www.agriculture.state.ia.us

Bill Northey
Secretary
Phone: 515-281-5322
e-mail: agri@idals.state.ia.us

Karey Claghorn
Deputy Secretary
Phone: 515-281-5322
e-mail: karey.claghorn@idals.state.ia.us

Dean Lemke
Water Resources Bureau Chief
Phone: 515-281-6146
e-mail: dean.lemke@idals.state.ia.us

John Whipple
Consumer Protection & Industry Services Division
Phone: 515-281-8610
e-mail: john.whipple@idals.state.ia.us

James Gillespie
Field Services Bureau Chief
Phone: 515-281-5258
e-mail: jim.gillespie@idals.state.ia.us

Kenneth R Tow
Soil Conservation Division Director
Phone: 515-281-6153
e-mail: ken.tow@idals.state.ia.us

Chuck Eckermann
Pesticide Bureau Chief
Phone: 515-281-8590
e-mail: chuck.eckermann@idals.state.ia.us

Association of Contingency Planners of Iowa
PO Box 1365
Des Moines, IA 50305
Phone: 505-246-7059
URL: www.iowacontingencyplanners.org
e-mail: banse.tom@principal.com

Description: A professional group of Contingency Planners and Emergency Management Officials from all sectors of society-business, industry, government, and volunteer agencies. Provides contingency planning and disaster recovery eductional and networking opportunities in a professional setting at little cost to the participants.

Thomas L Banse CBCP
Chairman

Stan Braden
Director

Emergency Medical Services Bureau
Department of Public Health
Lucas State Office Building
321 E 12th Street
Des Moines, IA 50319
Phone: 800-728-3367
Fax: 515-281-0488
URL: www.idph.state.ia.us/ems

Description: Lead agency responsible for the development, implementation, coordination and evaluation of Iowa's EMS system.

Kirk E Schmitt
Bureau Chief

Energy & Waste Management Division
Department of Natural Resources
Wallace State Office Building
502 E 9th Street

Des Moines, IA 50319-0034
Phone: 515-281-5918
Fax: 515-281-6794
URL: www.iowadnr.com/waste/aboutus.html

Description: Helps Iowa citizens, businesses and communities create a cleaner environment and stronger economy through the sustainable use of natural resources.

Brian Tormey
Bureau Chief
Phone: 515-281-8927
e-mail: brian.tormey@dnr.state.ia.us

Wayne Gieselman
Division Administrator
Phone: 515-281-5817
e-mail: wayne.gieselman@dnr.state.ia.us

Jill Cornell
Communications Coordinator
Phone: 515-281-0879
e-mail: jill.cornell@dnr.state.ia.us

Allan Goldberg
Energy Environmental Program Supervisor
Phone: 515-281-8912
e-mail: allan.goldberg@dnr.state.ia.us

Environmental Protection Division
Wallace State Office Building
502 E 9th Street
Des Moines, IA 50319-0034
Phone: 515-281-5918
Fax: 515-281-8895
URL: www.iowadnr.com/epc/index.html

Richard Leopold
Director
Phone: 515-281-5385

Liz Christiansen
Deputy Director
Phone: 515-281-3388

Kevin Baskins
Communications Bureau
Phone: 515-281-8395

Lisa Nissen
Directors Secretary
Phone: 515-281-5384

Ed Tormey
Legal Services Bureau
Phone: 515-281-8973

Information Technology Department
Hoover State Office Building
Level B
Des Moines, IA 50319
Phone: 515-281-5703
Phone: 800-532-1174
Fax: 515-281-6137
URL: www.das.ite.iowa.gov
e-mail: helpdesk@iowa.gov

Deb Madison-Levi
Chief Marketing/Communications Officer

Phone: 515-281-7056
e-mail: deb.madison-levi@iowa.gov

John P Gillispie
IT COO
Phone: 515-281-3462
e-mail: john.gillispie@iowa.gov

Vicki Luptowski
Administration & Customer Service Operations Supervisor
Phone: 515-242-5117
e-mail: vicki.luptowski@iowa.gov

National Guard
7105 NW 70th Avenue
Johnston, IA 50131-1834
Phone: 515-252-4582
Fax: 515-252-4656
URL: www.iowanationalguard.com
e-mail: paoia@ia.ngb.army.mil

Major General Ron Dardis
Adjutant General

CSM Doyle L Norris
Command Sgt Major, Army

Lt Colonel Gregory Hapsgood
Public Affairs Officer
Phone: 515-252-4582
e-mail: gregory.hapsgood@langb.army.mil

Public Defense Department
7700 NW Beaver Drive
STARC Armory, Camp Dodge
Johnston, IA 50131
Phone: 515-252-4000
Fax: 515-252-4787
URL: www.state.ia.us/government/dpd/index.html

Major General Ron Dardis
Adjutant General
Phone: 515-252-4211
e-mail: ron.dardis@ia.ngb.army.mil

Robert M Gates
Secretary of Defense

Allison Barber
Deputy Assistant Secretary of Defense

Colonel Robert King
Public Affairs Office
Phone: 515-252-4582

Public Health Department
321 E 12th Street
Des Moines, IA 50319-0075
Phone: 515-281-7689
Fax: 515-281-4958
URL: www.idph.state.ia.us/

Tom Newton
Public Health Director

Bonnie Mapes
Tobacco Use Prevention & Control Director
Phone: 515-281-8857

Julia Goodin
Chief State Medical Examiner
Phone: 515-725-1400

Julia McMahon
Health Promotion & Chronic Disease Director
Phone: 515-281-3104

Tom Newton
Environmental Health Division Director
Phone: 515-281-5099

Kevin Teale
Communication & Public Information

Public Safety Department

215 E 7th St
Des Moines, IA 50319-0040
Phone: 515-725-6182
Fax: 515-242-6136
URL: www.dps.state.ia.us
e-mail: dpsinfo@dps.state.ia.us

Description: In partnership with the people of Iowa, with professionalism, prode, and integrity, provide services for all people promoting public safety and enhancing the quality of life.

Eugene T Meyer
Commissioner
Phone: 515-725-6182

Michael Laski
Governor's Traffic Safety Bureau
Phone: 515-725-6120
e-mail: laski@dps.state.ia.us

Russ Porter
Intelligence Bureau
Phone: 515-281-8627

Dave Heuton
Administrative Services Division
Phone: 515-725-6251
e-mail: asdinfo@dps.state.ia.us

Steven E Bogle
Criminal Investigation Division
Phone: 515-725-6010
e-mail: dciinfo@dps.state.ia.us

Wendie Nerem
Missing Persons Clearing House
Phone: 515-281-7958

Jim Kenkel
State Fire Marshal
Phone: 515-725-6145
e-mail: fminfo@dps.state.ia.us

Ken Carter
Narcotics Enforcement Division
Phone: 515-725-6300
e-mail: dneinfo@dps.state.ia.us

Colonel Robert O Garrison
State Patrol Division
Phone: 515-725-6090
e-mail: ispinfo@dps.state.ia.us

Transportation Department

800 Lincoln Way
Ames, IA 50010
Phone: 515-239-1101
Fax: 515-239-1639
URL: www.dot.state.ia.us

Nancy Richardson
Director
Phone: 515-239-1111

Mark Schouten
Special Assistant Attorney General
Phone: 515-239-1509

Shirley Andre
Motor Vehicle Division Director
Phone: 515-237-3121

John Adam
Statewide Operations Bureau Director
Phone: 515-239-1128

Dan Franklin
Policy & Legislative Services
Phone: 515-239-1131

STATE AGENCIES

Kansas

Kansas Main Homeland Security Office
2800 SW Topeka Boulevard
Topeka, KS 66611
Phone: 785-274-1409
Fax: 785-274-1426
URL: www.kansas.gov/kdem

Kathleen Sebelius
Governor
Phone: 785-296-3232
e-mail: governor@gov.state.ks.us

Mark Parkinson
Lieutenant Governor
Phone: 785-296-2213
e-mail: lt.governor@gov.state.ks.us

Major General Tod M Bunting
Adjutant General & Director Homeland Security
Phone: 785-274-1911
e-mail: kansas.hlsc@agtop.state.ks.us

Paul J Morrison
Attorney General
Phone: 785-296-2215

Adjutant General's Department
2800 SW Topeka Boulevard
State Defense Building
Topeka, KS 66611-1287
Phone: 785-274-1000
Fax: 785-274-1522
URL: www.kansas.gov/ksadjutantgeneral/

Major General Tod M Bunting
Adjutant General
Phone: 785-274-1001

BGen Jonathan P Small
Army Assistant Adjutant General

BGen Edward McIhenny
Air Assistant Adjutant General
Phone: 785-274-1470

Joy D Moser
Public Information & Relations Director
Phone: 785-274-1192
e-mail: joy.moser@ks.ngb.army.mil

Agriculture Department
109 SW 9th Street
Topeka, KS 66612-1280
Phone: 785-296-3556
Fax: 785-296-8389
URL: www.ksda.gov

e-mail: ksag@kda.state.ks.us

Description: A regulatory agency that serves all Kansans. It is charged by law to ensure: a safe food supply; responsible and judicious use of pesticides and nutrients; the protection of Kansas' nautral and cultivated plants; integrity of weighing and measuring devices in commerce; and, that the state's waters are put to beneficial use.

Adrian Polansky
Secretary
e-mail: ajpolansky@kda.state.ks.us

Lisa Taylor
Public Information Officer
e-mail: ltaylor@kda.state.ks.us

Dan Riley
Chief Legal Counsel
Phone: 785-296-4171
e-mail: driley@kda.state.ks.us

Board of Emergency Medical Services
900 SW Jackson Street
Landon State Office Building, Room 1031
Topeka, KS 66612-1228
Phone: 785-296-7296
Fax: 785-296-6212
URL: www.ksbems.org

Description: The Board exists, primarily, to ensure that quality out-of-hospital care ia available throughout Kansas.

Robert Waller
Administrator
Phone: 785-296-7409
e-mail: robert.waller@ems.ks.gov

Steve Sutton
Deputy Administrator
Phone: 785-296-6211
e-mail: steve.sutton@ems.ks.gov

Dennis Allin
Chairman
e-mail: dallin@kumc.edu

Dave Cromwell
Operations & Vehicle Inspections
Phone: 785-291-3652
e-mail: dave.cromwell@ems.ks.gov

Jerry Cunningham
Investigations
Phone: 785-296-5168
e-mail: jerry.cunningham@ems.ks.gov

Jean Claude Kandagave
Information Technology
Phone: 785-296-3891
e-mail: jkandagaye@ems.ks.gov

Bureau of Investigation
1620 SW Tyler
Topeka, KS 66612
Phone: 785-296-8200
Phone: 800-572-7463
URL: www.accesskansas.org/kbi

Description: Dedicated to providing professional investigative and laboratory services to criminal justice agencies, and the collection and dissemination of criminal justice information to public and private agencies, for the purpose of promoting public safety and the prevention of crime in Kansas.

Robert E Blecha
Director

Center for Public Health Preparedness
Health and Environment Department
1000 SW Jackson, Ste 330
Curtis State Office Bldg
Topeka, KS 66612-1274
Phone: 785-296-8605
Fax: 785-296-2625
e-mail: bt_info@kdhe.state.ks.us

Description: The center was recently created in order to provide leadership for the department in health and medical response to all public health emergency situations. It evolved from the Bioterrorism Program, part of the Bureau of Epidemiology & Disease Prevention.

Mindee Reece
Director
Phone: 785-296-0201
e-mail: mreece@kdhe.state.ks.us

Kathy Holm
Administration Services Director
Phone: 785-296-8115
e-mail: kholm@kdhe.state.ks.us

Sandy Johnson
Operations Director
Phone: 785-291-3065
e-mail: sjohnso1@kdhe.state.ks.us

Randy Thode
Health Alert Network Coordinator
Phone: 785-296-4802
e-mail: rthode@kdhe.state.ks.us

Jerry Tenbrink
Preparedness Training Coordinator
Phone: 785-291-3241
e-mail: jtenbrink@kdhe.state.ks.us

Joe Blubaugh
Communications Director
Phone: 785-296-5795
e-mail: jblubaugh@kdhe.state.ks.us

Sue Riley
Laboratory Bioterrorism Program Manager

Phone: 785-296-6621
e-mail: sriley@kdhe.state.ks.us

Division of Emergency Management
2800 SW Topeka Boulevard
Topeka, KS 66611-1287
Phone: 785-274-1409
Phone: 785-296-3176
Fax: 785-274-1426
URL: www.kansas.gov/kdem

Description: To provide a 24-hour operation to reduce loss of life and property, protect Kansans from all hazards by providing and coordinating resources, expertise, leadership and advocacy through a comprehensive, risk-based emergency management program of mitigation, preparedness, response and recovery.

Major General Tod M Bunting
Director of Emergency Management & Homeland Security
Phone: 785-274-1911

Bill Chornyak
Emergency Management Administrator
Phone: 785-274-1401
e-mail: bchornyak@agtop.state.ks.us

Danny Hay
Operations Officer
Phone: 785-274-1406
e-mail: drhay@agtop.state.ks.us

Jessica Frye
Homeland Security/GIS Coordinator
Phone: 785-274-1610
e-mail: jpfrye@agtop.state.ks.us

Danita Simnitt
Network Administrator
Phone: 785-274-1420
e-mail: dwsimnitt@agtop.state.ks.us

Angee Morgan
Senior Plans Officer/SCO
Phone: 785-274-1403
e-mail: atmorgan@agtop.state.ks.us

Paula Phillips
Training Officer
Phone: 785-274-1413
e-mail: paphillips@agtop.state.ks.us

Terri Ploger-McCool
Homeland Security Programs Coordinator
Phone: 785-274-1404
e-mail: tdploger@agtop.state.ks.us

Environment Division
Health and Environment Department
1000 SW Jackson Street
Ste 400
Topeka, KS 66612-1367
Phone: 785-296-1535
Fax: 785-296-8464
URL: www.kdheks.gov/environment

Description: Conducts regulatory programs involving public water supplies, industrial discharges, wastewater treatment systems, solid waste landfills, hazardous waste, air emissions, radioactive materials, asbestos removal, refined petroleum storage tanks, and other sources which impact the environment.

Ron Hammerschmidt PhD
Director
Phone: 785-296-1535
e-mail: rhammers@kdhe.state.ks.us

Clark Duffy
Air/Radiation Bureau
Phone: 785-296-1593
e-mail: cduffy@kdhe.state.ks.us

Gary Blackburn
Environmental Remediation Bureau
Phone: 785-296-1660
e-mail: gblackbu@kdhe.state.ks.us

John Mitchell
Environmental Field Services Bureau
Phone: 785-296-6603
e-mail: jmitchel@kdhe.state.ks.us

Karl Mueldener
Water Bureau
Phone: 785-296-5500
e-mail: kmuelden@kdhe.state.ks.us

David Waldo
Public Water Supply Section Chief
Phone: 785-296-5503
e-mail: dwaldo@kdhe.state.ks.usus

Fire Marshal's Office
700 SW Jackson Street
Suite 600
Topeka, KS 66603
Phone: 785-296-3401
Fax: 785-296-0151
URL: www.kansas.gov/firemarshal/

Description: Dedicated to protecting the lives and property of the citizens of Kansas from the hazards of fire, explosion and hazardous materials by fostering a safe environment through inspection, enforcement, regulation, investigation, hazardous material incident mitigation, data collection, public education, and by acting as a liaion to the Kansas Fire Services.

Jack Alexander
Fire Marshal
Phone: 785-296-3401

Dan Thompson
Hazardous Materials Division Chief
Phone: 785-296-3401

Rose Rozmiarek
Fire Investigation Division Chief
Phone: 785-296-3401

Health and Environment Department
1000 SW Jackson Street
Topeka, KS 66612
Phone: 785-296-1500
Fax: 785-368-6368
URL: www.kdheks.gov
e-mail: info@kdhe.state.ks.us

Roderick Bremby
Secretary
Phone: 785-296-0461

Aaron Dunkel
Deputy Secretary
Phone: 785-296-0461
e-mail: adunkel@kdhe.state.ks.us

Susan Kang
Policy Director
Phone: 785-296-0461
e-mail: skang@kdhe.state.ks.us

Lorne Phillips
Director Center for Health & Environmental Statistics
Phone: 785-296-1415
e-mail: lphiliips@kdhe.state.ks.us

Ron Hammerschmidt, PhD
Acting Director Laboratories
Phone: 785-296-1535

William L Bider
Director Waste Management Bureau
Phone: 785-296-1600
e-mail: wbider@kdhe.state.ks.us

Health Division
Health and Environment Department
1000 SW Jackson Street
Suite 300
Topeka, KS 66612-1365
Phone: 785-296-1086
Fax: 785-296-1562
URL: www.kdheks.gov/health

Description: To promote and protect health and prevent disease an dinjury among the people of Kansas.

Howard Rodenberg
Director
Phone: 785-296-1086
e-mail: hrodenberg@kdhe.state.ks.us

Joseph Kroll
Child Care & Health Facilities Bureau
Phone: 785-296-1240
e-mail: healthfacilities@kdhe.state.ks.us

Brenda Walker
Disease Control & Prevention Director
Phone: 785-368-6427
e-mail: bwalker@kdhe.state.ks.us

Gail R Hansen
State Epidemiologist
e-mail: ghansen@kdhe.state.ks.us

Michael Runau
Immunization Program Manager
Phone: 785-296-5591

Highway Patrol
122 SW 7th Street
Topeka, KS 66603
Phone: 785-296-6800
Fax: 785-296-3049
URL: www.kansashighwaypatrol.org

e-mail: info@khp.ks.gov

Description: Devoted to providing the quality of life in the state of Kansas through spirited and dedicated services.

William R Seck
Superintendent

Kansas Association of Chiefs of Police

PO Box 780603
Wichita, KS 67278-0603
Phone: 316-733-7300
Fax: 316-733-7301
URL: www.kacp.cc
e-mail: kapc@cox.net

Doyle M King
Executive Director

Kansas State Capitol Police

915 SW Harrison Street
Docking State Office Building
Topeka, KS 66612
Phone: 785-296-3420
Fax: 785-296-0725
URL: http://members.aol.com/khpcasp/

Captain Eric Pippin
Troop Commander

Municipal Energy Agency

6330 Lamar Avenue
Suite 110
Overland Park, KS 66202-4286
Phone: 913-677-2884
Fax: 913-677-0804
URL: www.kmea.com
e-mail: kmea@kmea.com

Description: To support its members in fulfilling their responsibility to provide adequate reliable electric power to their communities at the most economical price possible, and to provide education, information and representation of its members in legislative/regulatory issues where warranted.

James Widener
General Manager
Phone: 913-660-0230
e-mail: widenerj@kmea.com

Lance Boyd
Electric Power Supply Director
Phone: 913-660-0232
e-mail: boyd@kmea.com

Paula Campbell
Energy Controller-Electric
Phone: 913-660-0236
e-mail: campbellp@kmea.com

Joni Shadonix
Energy Controller-Gas
Phone: 913-660-0238
e-mail: shadonix@kmea.com

Chris Merritt
Natural Gas Director
Phone: 913-660-0235
e-mail: merrittc@kmea.com

Transportation Department

Dwight D Eisenhower State Office Building
700 SW Harrison Street
Topeka, KS 66603-3754
Phone: 785-296-3566
Fax: 785-296-0287
URL: www.ksdot.org
e-mail: publicinfo@ksdot.org

Deb Miller
Secretary
Phone: 785-296-3461

Jerry Younger
Assistant Secretary/State Transportation Engineer
Phone: 785-296-3285

Joe Erskine
Chief Counsel
Phone: 785-296-3831

Julie Lorenz
Director Public Affairs
Phone: 785-296-3276

Steve Swartz
Bureau of Transportation Information
Phone: 785-296-3585

Ed Young
Director Aviation
Phone: 785-296-2553

Dan Scherschligt
Director Engineering & Design
Phone: 785-296-2270

Mike Crow
Director Operations
Phone: 785-296-2235

Pete Bodyk
Bureau of Traffic Safety
Phone: 785-296-3756

STATE AGENCIES

Kentucky

Kentucky Main Homeland Security Office
200 Mero Street
Frankfort, KY 40602
Phone: 502-564-2081
Fax: 502-564-7764
URL: http://homelandsecurity.ky.gov

Ernest Lee Fletcher
Governor
Phone: 502-564-2611

Stephen B Pence
Lieutenant Governor
Phone: 502-564-2611
e-mail: ltgovernor@ky.gov

Major Alecia Webb-Edgington
Director Homeland Security
Phone: 502-564-2081

Gregory D Stumbo
Attorney General
Phone: 502-696-5300
e-mail: attorney.general@ag.ky.gov

Chemical Stockpile Emergency Preparedness Program
Division of Emergency Management
100 Minuteman Parkway
Frankfort, KY 40601
Phone: 502-564-7815
Fax: 502-607-1614
URL: kyem.ky.gov/programs/csepp

Description: Established to enhance the emergency preparedness in communities surrounding the chemical stockpiles until they are eliminated.

Bill Hilling
Program Manager
Phone: 502-607-5719
e-mail: william.hilling@us.army.mil

Department of Agriculture
32 Fountain Place
Frankfort, KY 40601
Phone: 502-564-5126
Fax: 502-564-5016
URL: www.kyagr.com
e-mail: ag.web@kyagr.com

Richie Farmer
Commissioner
Phone: 502-564-5126
e-mail: richie.farmer@ky.gov

Mark Farrow
Deputy Commissioner/Chief of Staff
Phone: 502-564-4696
e-mail: mark.farrow@ky.gov

Glenn Mitchell
Executive Director, Strategic Planning/Admin
Phone: 502-564-4696
e-mail: glenn.mitchell@ky.gov

Dr Ed Hall
Animal Health Division Assistant Director
Phone: 502-564-3956
e-mail: ed.hall@ky.gov

Teresa Ulery
Division Director Food Distribution
Phone: 502-573-0282
e-mail: teresa.ulery@ky.gov

Bill Clary
Director Public Relations Division
Phone: 502-564-4696
e-mail: bill.clary@ky.gov

Dr Robert Stout
State Veterinarian
Phone: 502-564-4983
e-mail: robert.stout@ky.gov

Division of Emergency Management
100 Minuteman Parkway
Frankfort, KY 40601
Phone: 502-607-1611
Phone: 800-255-2587
URL: kyem.ky.gov

Description: Coordinates a system of mitigation, preparedness, response and recovery in order to protect the lives, environment and property of the people of Kentucky.

Maxwell C Bailey
Director Emergency Management

H Camille Crain
State Hazard Mitigation Officer
Phone: 502-607-5768
e-mail: heather.crain@ky.ngb.army.mil

Environmental & Public Protection Cabinet
Capital Plaza Tower
500 Mero Street, 5th Floor
Frankfort, KY 40601
Phone: 502-564-3350
Fax: 502-564-3354
URL: www.eppc.ky.gov

Teresa J Hill
Secretary
Phone: 502-564-3350

Susan Bush
Commissioner, Natural Resources Dept
Phone: 502-564-6940

Tim LeDonne
Commissioner, Public Protection Dept
Phone: 502-564-7760

Lloyd Cress
Deputy Secretary
Phone: 502-564-2225

Environmental Protection Department
300 Fair Oaks Lane
Frankfort, KY 40601
Phone: 502-564-2150
Fax: 502-564-4245
URL: www.dep.ky.gov

Description: To protect and enhance Kentucky's environment.

Cheryl Taylor
Commissioner
Phone: 502-564-2225

Valerie Hudson
Deputy Commissioner
Phone: 502-564-2225

David Morgan
Director, Division of Water
Phone: 502-564-3410

John Lyons II
Director, Division for Air Quality
Phone: 502-573-3382

Bruce Scott
Director, Division of Waste Management
Phone: 502-564-6716

Gleason Wheatley
Director, Division of Environmental Services
Phone: 502-564-6120

Susan Green
Director, Division of Enforcement
Phone: 502-564-2150

Aaron Keatley
Director, Division of Compliance Assistance
Phone: 502-564-0323

Kentucky Association of Chiefs of Police
167 Capri Drive
Ft Thomas, KY 41075
Phone: 859-781-1099
Fax: 859-781-6994
URL: www.kypolicechiefs.org

Michael Bischoff
Executive Director
e-mail: mwbischoff@fuse.net

Kentucky Contingency Planners Users Group
PO Box 436416

Louisville, KY 40233
Phone: 502-485-3948
URL: info@kcpisprepared.org

Description: A group of business continuity, emergency management, IT professionals and supporting vendors, from government, independent business and non-profit sectors. Advances the professionalism of its members and to educate and support each other in the efforts to protect the organizations and communities from disruptions caused by adverse events.

Joanna Wise
President

Lisa Baize
Vice President

Kentucky Vehicle Enforcement
125 Holmes Street
Frankfort, KY 40601
Phone: 502-564-3276
Phone: 800-928-2402
URL: www.kve.ky.gov
e-mail: bobbyi.clue@ky.gov

Description: Encourages and promotes a safe driving environment through education and safety awareness while enforcing State and Federal laws and regulations with emphasis on commercial vehicles.

Gregory G Howard
Commissioner

Military Affairs Department
Air National Guard
100 Minuteman Parkway
1101 Grade Ln, Louisville, 40213
Frankfort, KY 40601-6168
Phone: 502-607-1490
Fax: 502-607-1464
URL: kyang.ang.af.mil
e-mail: publicaffairs@kyloui.ang.af.mil

Major Gen Donald C Storm
Adjutant General

Brig Gen Robert Yaple
Asst Adjutant General, Air
Phone: 502-364-4741
e-mail: robert.yaple@kyloui.ang.af.mil

Brig Gen Norman Arflack
Asst Adjutant General, Army

Colonel Michael Hardin
Chief of Staff/Public Affairs
Phone: 502-607-1494
e-mail: publicaffairs@kyloui.ang.af.mil

Public Health Department
275 E Main Street
Frankfort, KY 40621
Phone: 502-564-3970
Fax: 502-564-6533
URL: chfs.ky.gov/dph/

William D Hacker
Commissioner

Steve Davis MD
Deputy Commissioner

Ruth Ann Shepherd
Adult & Child Health Improvement Director

Kraig Humbaugh MD
Epidemiology & Health Planning Director

Stephanie Mayfield MD
Laboratory Services Director

Steve Salt
Local Health Department Operations Manager

Clyde Bolton
Public Health Protection & Safety Director

Robert Brawley MD
Communicable Disease Branch Manager

Kenny Ratliff
Public Safety Branch Manager

State Police
919 Versailles Road
Frankfort, KY 40601
Phone: 502-695-6300
Fax: 502-573-1479
URL: www.kentuckystatepolice.org
e-mail: kspmedia@ky.gov

Description: Dedicated to preserving law and order for the protection of citizens.

John Adams
Commissioner

Rick Stiltner
Deputy Commissioner

Gregory S Motley
Executive Security

Capt Michael P Crawford
Facilities Strategic Planning

Major Lisa M Rudzinski
Media Relations

Technology Office
Capitol Annex
702 Capital Avenue, Suite 258
Frankfort, KY 40601
Phone: 502-564-7576
Phone: 502-564-1202
URL: www.technology.ky.gov

Description: The Commonwealth's technology organization for providing leadership and governance of all aspects of information technology to enhance government services, improve decision making, promote efficiency and eliminate waste.

Mark Rutledge
Executive Director/Commissioner/CIO

Rick Boggs
Deputy Director

Jim Barnhart
Executive Director Infrastructure Services

Rob Trimble
Enterprise Policy/Project Manager

Transportation Cabinet
200 Mero Street
Frankfort, KY 40622
Phone: 502-564-4890
Fax: 502-564-9540
URL: www.transportation.ky.gov
e-mail: kytc.comments@ky.gov

Bill Nighbert
Secretary
Phone: 502-564-4890
e-mail: kytc.cabinetsecretary@ky.gov

Marc Williams
Commissioner, Department Highways
Phone: 502-564-3730

Tim Hazlette
Chair, Highway Safety Committee
Phone: 502-564-3020

Allan Frank
Director Structural Design Div/Engineer
Phone: 502-564-4560

Debra Gabbard
Executive Director, Budget & Fiscal Mgmt
Phone: 502-564-4550

STATE AGENCIES

Louisiana

Governor's Office of Homeland Security & Emergency Preparedness
7667 Independence Boulevard
Baton Rouge, LA 70806
Phone: 225-925-7500
Fax: 225-925-7501
URL: www.ohsep.louisiana.gov

Kathleen Babineaux Blanco
Governor
Phone: 225-342-7015
e-mail: kblanco@crt.state.la.us

Mitchell J Landrieu
Lieutenant Governor
Phone: 225-342-7009
e-mail: ltgov@crt.state.la.us

Colonel Jeff Smith
Acting Director Home Security
Phone: 225-925-7344

Colonel Pat Santos
Assistant Deputy Director Emergency Management
Phone: 225-925-3506

Charles C Foti Jr
Attorney General
Phone: 225-326-6769

Agriculture & Forestry Department
PO Box 631
Baton Rouge, LA 70821-0631
Phone: 225-922-1234
Fax: 225-922-1253
URL: www.ldaf.state.la.us
e-mail: info@ldaf.state.la.us

Description: Responsible for the programs and regulations that impact every aspect of the state's agriculture and forestry.

Bob Odom
Commissioner
e-mail: bobodom@ldaf.state.la.us

Luke Theriot
Confidential Assistant
e-mail: luke@ldaf.state.la.us

Ashley Rodrigue
Press Secretary
e-mail: ashley@ldaf.state.la.us

Environmental Quality Department
602 N Fifth Street
Baton Rouge, LA 70802

Mailing Address: PO Box 4301
Phone: 225-219-3953
Fax: 225-219-3971
URL: www.deq.louisiana.gov

Mike D McDaniel PhD
Secretary

Karen Gautreaux
Deputy Secretary

Rodney Mallett
Communications Director

Jeffrey Meyers
Emergency & Radiological Services

Fire Marshal
8181 Independence Boulevard
Baton Rouge, LA 70806
Phone: 225-925-4911
Phone: 800-256-5452
Fax: 225-925-4241
URL: www.dps.state.la.us

Description: To protect life and property from the hazards of fire or explosion, to ensure the safety of our citizens in the contructed environment, to provide equal access to disabled individuals and promote the efficient use of energy in commercial buildings.

Paul Smith
State Fire Marshal
e-mail: paul.smith@dps.la.gov

Felicia Cooper
Administrator
Phone: 225-925-4911
e-mail: felicia.cooper@dps.la.gov

Henry Fry
Deputy Assistant Secretary
e-mail: henry.fry@dps.la.gov

Health & Hospitals Department
628 N 4th Street
PO Box 629
Baton Rouge, LA 70802
Phone: 225-342-9500
Fax: 225-342-5568
URL: www.dhh.state.la.us

Frederick P Cerise MD, MPH
Secretary
Phone: 225-342-9500

Roxane Townsend
Deputy Secretary
Phone: 225-342-7092

Jimmy Guidry MD
State Health Officer & Medical Director
Phone: 225-342-3417

Rosanne Prats
Emergency Preparedness Director
Phone: 225-342-5168

Ruben Tapia
Office of Public Health
Phone: 504-838-5300

Theresa Sokol
Asst State Epidemiologist/Infectious Disease
Phone: 504-219-4539

Louisiana Association of Chiefs of Police

603 Europe Street
Baton Rouge, LA 70802
Phone: 225-387-3261
Fax: 225-387-3262
URL: www.lachiefs.org
e-mail: norman@association.brcoxmail.com

Description: To advance the science and art of police administration and crime prevention, to develop and disseminate improved administrative and technical practices and promote their use in police work, to foster police cooperation and the exchange of information and experience among police administrators throughout the world, to bring about the enlistment and training in the police profession of qualified perosons, and to encourade adherence pf all police officers to high standards of conduct.

Norman C Ferachi
Executive Director

Louisiana Commission on Law Enforcement

1885 Wooddale Boulevard
Room 1230
Baton Rouge, LA 70806-1511
Phone: 225-925-4418
Fax: 225-925-1998
URL: www.lcle.state.la.us

Description: Promotes public safety by providing progressive leadership and coordination within the criminal justice community.

Michael A Ranatza
Executive Director

Judy Mouton
Deputy Director

Louisiana Emergency Preparedness Association

8550 United Plaza Boulevard
Suite 1001
Baton Rouge, LA 70809
Phone: 225-408-4757
Phone: 877-405-5372
Fax: 225-408-4422
URL: www.lepa.org
e-mail: office@pncpa.com

Description: State-wide organization of emergency preparedness and response practitioners formed in 1980.

Sharlot Edwards
President

Mike Deroche
President Elect

H Bland O'Connor Jr
Executive Director

Military Department-National Guard

Jackson Barracks
6400 St Claude Avenue
New Orleans, LA 70146-0330
Phone: 504-278-8364
Fax: 504-278-8081
URL: www.la.ngb.army.mil

Major General Bennett C Landreneau
Adjutant General
Phone: 504-278-8211

Brig Gen Hunt Downer
Asst Adjutant General, Army

Brig Gen Brod Veillon
Asst Adjutant General, Air

Colonel Louis May
Deputy Director, Administration
Phone: 504-278-8362
e-mail: louis.may@la.ngb.army.mil

Colonel John Pugh
Deputy Director, Operations
Phone: 504-278-8235
e-mail: john.pugh@la.ngb.army.mil

Colonel Stephen C Dabadie
Chief of Staff
Phone: 504-278-8213

Mississippi River Bridge Authority

2001 Mardi Gras Boulevard
PO Box 6297
Baton Rogue, LA 70114
Phone: 504-376-8100
Fax: 504-376-8189

Alan J Levasseur
Executive Director
Phone: 504-376-8100

Natural Resources Department

PO Box 94346
Baton Rouge, LA 70804
Phone: 225-342-4500
Fax: 225-342-5861
URL: www.dnr.louisiana.gov

Description: To preserve and enhance the nonrenewable natural resources of the state, consisting of land, water, oil, gas and other minerals, through conservation, regulation, and management/exploitation, to ensure that the state of Louisiana relaizes appropriate economic benefit from its asset base.

Scott Angelle
Secretary
Phone: 225-342-2710

James Hanchey
Deputy Secretary
Phone: 225-342-1375

Paula Ridgeway
Energy Division
Phone: 225-342-1399

Christopher Knotts
Coastal Engineering Division
Phone: 225-342-6871

Port of New Orleans
PO Box 60046
New Orleans, LA 70160
Phone: 504-522-2551
Fax: 504-524-4156
URL: www.portno.com

Description: The only deepwater port in the United States served by six class one railroads. This gives port users direct and economical rail service to or form anywhere in the country.

Gary P LaGrange
President/CEO
Phone: 504-522-3203
e-mail: glagrange@portno.com

Patrick J Gallwey
Chief Operating Officer
Phone: 504-522-3305
e-mail: patg@portno.com

Port of South Louisiana
171 Belle Terre Boulevard
PO Box 909
LaPlace, LA 70068-0909
Phone: 985-652-9278
Phone: 888-752-7678
Fax: 985-652-9518
URL: www.portsl.com
e-mail: info@portsl.com

Joel Chaisson
Executive Director
e-mail: jchaisson@portsl.com

Henry Sullivan Jr
Deputy Director
e-mail: hsullivan@portsl.com

Mitch Smith
Director Operations
e-mail: msmith@portsl.com

Public Facilities Authority
2237 S Acadian Thruway
Suite 650
Baton Rouge, LA 70808
Phone: 225-923-0020
Phone: 800-228-4755
Fax: 225-923-0021
URL: www.lpfa.com
e-mail: info@lpfa.com

Description: A financing authority created in 1974 as a public trust and public corporation by the Public Facilities Corporation, a Louisiana coprporation, pursuant to an indenture of trust.

James W Parks II
President/CEO
e-mail: parks@lpfa.com

Pam D Hutchinson
VP Public Affairs
e-mail: hutchinson@lpfa.com

Public Safety Services
PO Box 66614
Baton Rouge, LA 70896
Phone: 225-925-6023
Fax: 225-925-4623
URL: www.dps.louisiana.gov

Richard L Stalder
Secretary
Phone: 225-342-6741

Jill P Boudreaux
Acting Undersecretary, Management & Finance
Phone: 225-925-6032
e-mail: jill.boudreaux@dps.la.gov

James Champagne
Highway Safety Commission
Phone: 225-925-6991

Charles M Fuller
Director, LP Gas Commission
Phone: 225-924-7216
e-mail: cfuller@dps.state.la.us

State Police
7919 Independence Boulevard
Baton Rouge, LA 70806
Phone: 225-925-6006
Fax: 225-925-3742
URL: www.lsp.org

Description: To ensure the safety and security of the people in the state through enforcement, education, and providing other essential public safety services.

Colonel Henry L Whitehorn
Superintendent
Phone: 225-925-6117

Lt Col Stanley Griffin
Deputy Superintendent/Chief of Staff

Lt Col Dane Morgan
Bureau of Investigations

Lt Col Dale Hall
Operations, Planning & Training

Lt Col Mickey McMorris
Crisis Response/Special Operations

STATE AGENCIES

Maine

Maine Main Homeland Security Office
Maine Emergency Management Agency
72 State House Station
Augusta, ME 04333
Phone: 207-624-4400
Phone: 800-452-8735
Fax: 207-287-3178
URL: www.maine.gov/mema/homeland/

John E Baldacci
Governor
Phone: 207-287-3531
e-mail: governor@maine.gov

Robert P McAleer
Director Emergency Management Agency
Phone: 207-624-4400
e-mail: robert.mcaleer@maine.gov

Major General John Libby
Adjutant General
Phone: 207-626-4271
e-mail: john.libby@me.ngb.army.mil

G Steven Rowe
Attorney General
Phone: 207-626-8800
e-mail: Steven.Rowe@maine.gov

Center for Disease Control & Prevention
Health and Human Services
11 State House Station
286 Water Street
Augusta, ME 04333
Phone: 207-287-8016
Fax: 207-287-6865
URL: www.maine.gov/dhhs/boh

Description: The Agency's mission is to develop and deliver services to preserve,protect and promote the health and well being of the citizens of Maine.

Dora Anne Mills
Director & State Health Officer

Robert Burman
Special Assistant for Maine CDC Operations
Phone: 207-287-6865
e-mail: robert.burman@maine.gov

Sally-Lou Patterson
Infectious Disease Division Director
Phone: 207-287-6448
e-mail: sallylou.patterson@maine.gov

Dwane Hubert
Infectious Disease Epidemiology Program Manager
Phone: 207-287-7267
e-mail: dwane.hubert@maine.gov

Kathleen Gensheimer
State Epidemiologist/Medical Epidemiology Director
Phone: 207-287-5183
e-mail: kathleen.f.gensheimer@maine.gov

Jiancheng Huang
Immunization Program Manager
Phone: 207-287-3746
e-mail: jiancheng.huang@maine.gov

Don Lemieux
Data, Research & Vital Statistics Director
Phone: 202-287-5468
e-mail: don.lemieux@maine.gov

Donald Ward
Public Health Systems Director
Phone: 207-287-4077
e-mail: donald.ward@maine.gov

Kristine Perkins
Public Health Emergency Preparedness Director
Phone: 207-287-8104
e-mail: kristine.perkins@maine.gov

Thomas Patenaude
Hospital Bioterrorism Coordinator
Phone: 207-287-3288
e-mail: thomas.patenaude@maine.gov

W Clough Toppan
Environmental Health Division Director
Phone: 207-287-5686
e-mail: clough.toppan@maine.gov

Jay Hyland
Radiation Control Program Manager
Phone: 207-287-5677
e-mail: jay.hyland@maine.gov

Theodore Hensley
Regional Epidemiology Coordinator

Chief Medical Examiner Office
State House
Station #37
Augusta, ME 04333
Phone: 207-624-7180
Fax: 207-624-7178

Margaret S Greenwald MD
Chief Medical Examiner
e-mail: chief-medical.examiner@maine.gov

Defense, Veterans and Emergency Management Department

33 State House Station
Camp Keyes
Augusta, ME 04333-0033
Phone: 207-626-4271
Fax: 207-626-4509
URL: www.maine.gov/va/defense/dvs.htm

Description: Coordinates and administers the discharge of the state's responsibility relating to military, veterans and civil emergency preparedness. Its bureaus and agencies include the Army National Guard, Air National Guard, Emergency Management Agency and the Bureau of Veterans Services.

Major General John Libby
Commissioner & Adjutant General
Phone: 207-626-4271
e-mail: john.libby@me.ngb.army.mil

Lt Colonel James C Piggott
State Inspector General
Phone: 207-626-4440
e-mail: james.piggott@us.army.mil

Department of Agriculture, Food & Rural Resources

28 State House Station
Augusta, ME 04333-0028
Phone: 207-287-3871
Fax: 207-287-7548
URL: www.maine.gov/agriculture/

Seth H Bradstreet III
Commissioner
Phone: 207-287-3419
e-mail: agriculture.commissioner@maine.gov

Edwin Porter
Deputy Commissioner
Phone: 207-287-3871
e-mail: ned.r.porter@maine.gov

Shelley F Doak
Animal & Health Industry Division Director
Phone: 207-287-3701
e-mail: shelly.doak@maine.gov

Donald E Hoenig
State Veterinarian
Phone: 202-287-7615
e-mail: donald.e.hoenig@maine.gov

Robert Batteese
Plant Industry Division Interim Director
Phone: 202-287-3891
e-mail: robert.batteese@maine.gov

Jane Aiudi
Market & Production Development Division Director
Phone: 207-287-3491

Hal Prince
Quality Assurance & Regulation Division Director
Phone: 202-287-2161

Department of Marine Resources

2 Beech Street
21 State House Station
Augusta, ME 04333
Phone: 207-624-6550
Fax: 207-624-6024
URL: www.maine.gov/dmr/

George Lapointe
Commissioner
e-mail: george.lapointe@maine.gov

Colonel Joseph Fessenden
Marine Patrol Bureau
Phone: 207-624-6571
e-mail: joe.fessenden@maine.gov

Amy Fitzpatrick
Public Health Division Director
Phone: 207-633-9554
e-mail: amy.fitzpatrick@maine.gov

Emergency Management Agency

72 State House Station
45 Commerce Drive
Augusta, ME 04333
Phone: 207-624-4400
Phone: 800-452-8735
Fax: 207-287-3178
URL: www.maine.gov/mema/

Description: The Agency's mission is to lessen the effects of disaster on the lives and property of the people of Maine through coordination, leadership and support in all phases of emergency management: mitigation, preparedness, response and recovery.

Robert McAleer
Director
e-mail: robert.mcaleer@maine.gov

Ginnie A Ricker
Deputy Director
e-mail: ginnie.ricker@maine.gov

Lynette C Miller
Special Projects Director & Public Information Coordinator
e-mail: lynette.c.miller@maine.gov

Paul Clark
American Red Cross Liaison
e-mail: paul.w.clark@maine.gov

Graham A Fletcher
Civil Engineer I & Dam Inspector
e-mail: tony.fletcher@maine.gov

Bruce F Fitzgerald
Public Service Manager I
e-mail: bruce.fitzgerald@maine.gov

Emergency Medical Services
Department of Public Safety

152 State House Station
500 Civic Center Drive
Augusta, ME 04333
Phone: 207-626-3860
Fax: 207-287-6251
URL: www.maine.gov/dps/ems
e-mail: maine.ems@maine.gov

Jay Bradshaw
Director
e-mail: jay.bradshaw@maine.gov

Ben Woodard
Data & Preparedness Coordinator
e-mail: ben.woodard@maine.gov

Steve Diaz MD
State EMS Medical Director
e-mail: steve.diaz@mainegeneral.org

Environmental Protection Department
17 State House Station
Augusta, ME 04333-0017
Phone: 207-287-7688
Phone: 800-452-1942
URL: www.maine.gov/dep

David P Littell
Commissioner
Phone: 207-287-2812
e-mail: david.p.littell@maine.gov

Deborah Garrett
Deputy Commissioner
Phone: 207-287-2811
e-mail: deborah.n.garrett@maine.gov

Peter Carney
Enforcement & Procedures
Phone: 207-287-4305
e-mail: peter.j.carney@maine.gov

James P Brooks
Air Quality Bureau Director
Phone: 207-287-2437
e-mail: james.p.brooks@maine.gov

Brian Kavanah
Water Quality Management Division Director
Phone: 207-287-7700
e-mail: brian.w.kavanah@maine.gov

Mark Hyland
Remediation & Waste Management Bureau Director (Acting)
Phone: 207-287-2651
e-mail: mark.hyland@maine.gov

Scott Whittier
Oil & Hazardous Waste Facilities Regulation
Phone: 207-287-2651
e-mail: scott.whittier@maine.gov

Barbara Parker
Division of Response Services Director
Phone: 202-287-7752
e-mail: barbara.t.parker@maine.gov

Andrew Fisk
Land & Water Qulaity Bureau Director
Phone: 207-287-7671
e-mail: andrew.c.fisk@maine.gov

David Courtemanch
Environmental Assessment Division Director
Phone: 207-287-7789
e-mail: dave.l.courtemanch@maine.gov

Maine Chiefs of Police Association
PO Box 2431
S Portland, ME 04116
Phone: 207-799-9318
Fax: 207-767-2214
URL: www.mainechiefs.com

Robert M Schwartz
Executive Director
e-mail: rschwartz@mainechiefs.us

Port Authority
16 State House Station
Augusta, ME 04333-0016
Phone: 207-624-3564
Fax: 207-624-3251
URL: www.maineports.com

Description: To improve the global competitiveness of Maine business; and in concert with public and private organizations, the Maine Port Authority will stimulate commerce by developing marine and rail facilities in response fashion, for the intermodal movement of people and cargo.

Brian C Nutter
Executive Director
Phone: 207-624-3564
e-mail: brian.nutter@maine.gov

Public Safety Department
104 State House Station
45 Commerce Drive, Suite 1
Augusta, ME 04333-0104
Phone: 207-626-3800
Fax: 207-287-3042
URL: www.state.me.us/dps

Anne H Jordan
Commissioner
Phone: 207-626-3803
e-mail: anne.h.jordan@maine.gov

Roy E McKinney
Director Drug Enforcement Agency
Phone: 207-626-3850

Mary Lucia
Planning/Research Associate
Phone: 207-624-7006

Stephen H McCausland
Public Information Officer
Phone: 207-626-3811
e-mail: stephen.mccausland@maine.gov

Russell J Gauvin
Chief State Capitol Police
Phone: 207-287-4357

Richard E Perkins
Director Highway Safety Bureau
Phone: 207-626-3840
e-mail: richard.e.perkins@maine.gov

John Rogers
Director Criminal Justice Academy
Phone: 207-877-8000
e-mail: john.rogers@maine.gov

Public Utilities Commission
18 State House Station
242 State Street
Augusta, ME 04333-0018
Phone: 207-287-3831
Fax: 207-287-1039
URL: www.maine.gov/mpuc/
e-mail: maine.puc@maine.gov

Kurt Adams
Chairman
Phone: 207-287-3831

Sharon M Reishus
Commissioner
Phone: 207-287-3831

Al Gervenack
Emergency Services Communications Bureau Director
Phone: 208-887-8010

State Police
45 Commerce Drive
42 State House Station
Augusta, ME 04333-0042
Phone: 207-624-7200
Fax: 207-624-7088
URL: www.state.me.us/dps/msp/home.htm

Colonel Patrick J Fleming
Chief
e-mail: patrick.j.fleming@maine.gov

Lt Colonel John P Dyer
Deputy Chief
e-mail: john.p.dyer@maine.gov

Major Robert A Williams
Special Services
e-mail: robert.a.williams@maine.gov

Major Timothy S Doyle
Operations
e-mail: timothy.s.doyle@maine.gov

Lt Donald A Pomelow
Communications
Phone: 207-624-7294

Stephen McCausland
Public Information Officer
Phone: 207-626-3811
e-mail: stephen.mccausland@maine.gov

Transportation Department
16 State House Station
Child Street
Augusta, ME 04333-0016
Phone: 207-624-3000
Fax: 207-624-3001
URL: www.maine.gov/mdot/

STATE AGENCIES

Maryland

Maryland Main Homeland Security Office

State House
100 State Circle
Annapolis, MD 21401-1925
Phone: 410-974-3901
Phone: 800-811-8336
Fax: 410-974-3275
URL: www.gov.state.md.us/homelandsecurity.html
e-mail: gohs@gov.state.md.us

Martin O'Malley
Governor
Phone: 410-974-3901
e-mail: governor@gov.state.md.us

Anthony G Brown
Lieutenant Governor
Phone: 410-974-3591
e-mail: ltgovernor@gov.state.md.us

Andrew Lauland
Director Homeland Security Coordinator
Phone: 410-974-2389

Douglas F Gansler
Attorney General
Phone: 410-576-6300

Agriculture Department

50 Harry S Truman Parkway
Annapolis, MD 21401
Phone: 410-841-5700
Fax: 410-841-5914
URL: www.mda.state.md.us

Roger L Richardson
Secretary
Phone: 410-841-5880

Earl Hance
Deputy Secretary
Phone: 410-841-5881
e-mail: hanceef@mda.state.md.us

Mary Ellen Setting
Assistant Secretary, Plant Industries & Pest Management
Phone: 410-841-5870
e-mail: settingm@mda.state.md.us

Dr Guy Hohenhaus
State Veterinarian
Phone: 443-336-7346

Sue duPont
Director of Communications

Phone: 410-841-5889
e-mail: dupontsk@mda.state.md.us

S Patrick McMillan
Asst Secretary, Marketing, Animal Industries & Consumer Svs
Phone: 410-841-5782
e-mail: mcmillsp@mda.state.md.us

Doug Scott
Asst Secretary, Resource Conservation
Phone: 410-841-5865
e-mail: scottdd@mda.state.md.us

Aviation Administration

BWI Airport
Terminal Building, 3rd Floor
Baltimore, MD 21240-0766
Mailing Address: PO Box 8766
Phone: 410-859-7060
Fax: 410-850-4729
URL: www.marylandaviation.com

Description: Responsible for the Baltimore/Washington International (BWI) and Martin State airports _ fostering the vitality of aviation statewide and promoting safe and efficient operations.

Timothy Campbell
Executive Director

Louisa H Goldstein
Counsel
Phone: 410-859-7066

Stephen D Sheehan
Dep Exec Dir Operations Public & Safety Security
Phone: 410-859-7080

Al Pollard
Martin State Airport Manager
Phone: 410-682-8800

John Stewart
BWI Airport Operations Director
Phone: 410-859-7022

Emergency Management Agency

5401 Rue St Lo Drive
Camp Fretterd Military Reservation
Reisterstown, MD 21136
Phone: 410-517-3600
Phone: 877-636-2872
Fax: 410-517-3610
URL: www.mema.state.md.us
e-mail: help@mema.state.md.us

Description: The Maryland Emergency Management Agency (MEMA) is part of the Maryland Military Department and it provides infrastructure and logistical support for homeland security as well as, manages many of the federal grants involving enhanced protection from and responses to natural and man-made disasters which could threaten citizens.

John W Droneburg III
Director
Phone: 410-517-3625
e-mail: jdroneburg@mema.state.md.us

Russell Strickland
Deputy Director
Phone: 410-517-3687
e-mail: rstrickland@mema.state.md.us

Walter Mueller
Asst Director, Logistics
Phone: 410-517-5128
e-mail: wmueller@mema.state.md.us

Erin Holloway
Domestic Preparedness Administrator
Phone: 410-517-5145

Jeff Welsh
Public Information Officer
Phone: 410-517-3631
e-mail: jwelsh@mema.state.md.us

Emergency Numbers Systems Board
Division of Public Safety and Correctional Services
115 Sudbrook Lane
Suite 201
Pikesville, MD 21208
Phone: 410-585-3015
Fax: 410-764-4136
URL: www.dpscs.state.md.us/ensb

Description: Formed in 1979, the Board coordinates installation and enhancement of county 9-1-1 emergency telephone number services systems. The Board issues guidelines and determines review procedures to approve or disapprove county plans for these systems and sets criteria for reimbursing counties from the original 9-1-1 Trust Fund and from ongoing funds, and provides for audit of Trust Fund accounts.

Anthony Myers
Chairman
Phone: 410-585-3015
e-mail: amyers@psc.state.md.us

Gordon Deans
Executive Director
Phone: 410-585-3019
e-mail: gdeans@dpscs.state.md.us

Energy Administration
1623 Forest Drive
Suite 300
Annapolis, MD 21403
Phone: 410-260-7655
Phone: 800-723-6374
Fax: 410-974-2250
URL: www.energy.state.md.us
e-mail: meainfo@energy.state.md.us

Description: To maximize energy efficiency while promoting economic development, reducing reliance on foreign energy supplies, and improving the environment.

Frederick G Davis
Director
Phone: 410-260-7511
e-mail: fdavis@energy.state.md.us

Environment Department
1800 Washington Boulevard
Baltimore, MD 21230
Phone: 410-537-3000
Phone: 800-633-6101
Fax: 410-537-3888
URL: www.msa.md.gov/msa/mdmanual/14doe/html

Description: Protecting and restoring the quality of the air, water and land resources, while fostering smart growth, economic development, healthy and safe communities, and quality environmental education for the benefit of the environment, public health and future generations.

Shari T Wilson
Secretary
Phone: 410-537-3084

Robert M Summers
Deputy Secretary
Phone: 410-537-4187

Stephen L Pattison
Assistant Secretary
Phone: 410-537-3086

George (Tad) Aburn
Air & Radiation Management Administration Director
Phone: 410-537-3255

Jim Purvis
Information & Communications Systems Division
Phone: 410-537-3089

Roland G Fletcher
Radiological Health Program Manager
Phone: 410-537-3300

Michelle Barnes
Environmental Crimes Unit
Phone: 410-631-3025

Horacio Tablada
Waste Management Administration Director
Phone: 410-537-3304

Virginia Kearney
Water Management Administration Acting Director
Phone: 410-537-3567

Governor's Office of Crime Control and Prevention
300 E Joppa Road
Hampton Plaza, Suite 1105
Baltimore, MD 21286
Phone: 410-821-2828
Phone: 877-687-9004
Fax: 410-321-3116
URL: www.goccp.org
e-mail: info@goccp-state.md.org

Description: Improves public safety and services to victims of crime and the administartion of criminal and juvenile justice in order to prevent future victims of crime. The office assists in developing justice legislation, policies, programs and budgets; distributes and monitors funds to state and local agencies and organizations; identifies new funding sources; and collects information and research to distribute to the public.

Kristen M Mahoney
Executive Director
Phone: 410-321-3521

Gregory J Leyko
Deputy Director
Phone: 410-321-3521
e-mail: greg@goccp.usa.com

Health and Higher Educational Facilities Authority
401 E Pratt Street
Suite 1224
Baltimore, MD 21202
Phone: 410-837-6220
Fax: 410-685-1611
URL: www.mhhefa.org

Annette Anselmi
Executive Director
Phone: 410-837-6220
e-mail: aanselmi@mhhefa.org

Edward J Golas
Chief Operating Officer
Phone: 410-837-6220
e-mail: egolas@mhhefa.org

Health and Mental Hygiene Department
201 W Preston Street
Baltimore, MD 21201
Phone: 410-767-6500
Phone: 877-463-3464
Fax: 410-767-6489
URL: www.dhmh.state.md.us
e-mail: info@miemss.org

John M Colmers
Secretary
Phone: 410-767-6505

David R Fowler MD
Chief Medical Examiner
Phone: 410-333-3225
e-mail: dfowler@dhmh.state.md.us

Dr Michelle Gourdine MD
Deputy Secretary, Public Health Services
Phone: 410-767-5024

Richard Stringer
Acting Director, Community Health Administration
Phone: 410-767-6742
e-mail: stringerr@dhmh.state.md.us

Dr John M DeBoy
Laboratories Administration Director
Phone: 410-767-6100
e-mail: deboyj@dhmh.state.md.us

Karen R Black
Director Public Relations
Phone: 410-767-6490
e-mail: kblack@dhmh.state.md.us

Dr Matthew Minson
Preparedness and Response
Phone: 410-767-0968

Information Technology & Communication Division
6776 Reistertown Road
2nd Floor, Suite 209A
Baltimore, MD 21215-2346
Phone: 410-585-3100
Fax: 410-764-4035

Ronald Brothers
Acting Director

Wilson Parran
Chief Information Officer
Phone: 410-585-3100

Institute for Emergency Medical Services Systems
653 W Pratt Street
Baltimore, MD 21201-1536
Phone: 410-706-3666
Phone: 800-762-7157
Fax: 410-706-4768
URL: www.miemss.org
e-mail: info@miemss.org

Description: MIEMSS is built on the integration of diverse organizations and professionals striving for a single goal, to save the life of the critically injured or ill patient. Through the cooperation of prehospital care providers (both volunteer and career, fire and EMS, and police agencies), hospital administrators, physicians, nurses, government officials, and agency personnel, Maryland has developed one of the premier EMS systems in the world.

Robert R Bass MD
Executive Director

Maryland Chiefs of Police Association
6716 Alexander Bell Drive
Suite 200
Columbia, MD 21046
Phone: 401-516-9896
Fax: 401-290-1061
URL: http://mdchiefs.org

Description: Unites law enforcement executives by delivering innovative, high-quality police services.

Larry E Harmel
Executive Director
Phone: 410-516-9873
e-mail: lharmel@jhu.edu

Douglas Holland
President
Phone: 410-454-7740

Maryland Transit Administration
6 St Paul Street
Baltimore, MD 21202-1614

Phone: 410-539-5000
Phone: 866-743-3682
Fax: 410-333-3279
URL: www.mtamaryland.com

Description: Provides and supports accessible transit networks that are safe, appealing, reliable and efficient.

Lisa L Dickerson
CEO
Phone: 410-767-3943

John T Gowland
General Manager
Phone: 410-767-5717

Robert Mowry
Deputy Administrator, Operations
Phone: 410-454-7228

Richard Scher
Media & Public Information
Phone: 410-767-3931

Ronald Keele
Safety & Risk Management
Phone: 410-454-7141

Maryland Transit Administration Police Force

1040 Park Avenue
Baltimore, MD 21201
Phone: 410-454-7500
Phone: 410-454-7721
Fax: 410-454-7738
URL: www.mtamaryland.com/about/mtapoliceforce

Description: Ensures a safe and orderly environment within the transit system, safeguarding lives and property, protecting against deception, intimidation and violence.

Colonel David Franklin
Acting Chief of Police

Lt Colonel John Gavrilis
Deputy Chief
Phone: 410-454-7507

Captain William Collins
Special Opertions Bureau
Phone: 410-454-7765

Lt Burna McCollum
Director of Communications
Phone: 410-454-7748

Phil Vass
Director of Training
Phone: 410-454-1651

Mid-Atlantic Disaster Recovery Assocaition, Inc

4500 Paint Branch Parkway
College Park, MD
Phone: 301-226-9900
URL: www.madra.org
e-mail: mike_slingluff@freddiemac.com

Military Department

Fifth Regiment Armory
219 29th Division Street
Baltimore, MD 21201-2288

Phone: 410-576-6000
Fax: 410-576-6079
URL: www.mdmildep.org; www.md.ngb.army.mil

Major General Bruce F Tuxill
Adjutant General
Phone: 410-576-6097
e-mail: bruce.tuxill@us.army.mil

BGen Edward Leacock
Assistant Adjutant General, Army
Phone: 410-576-6094
e-mail: edward.leacock@md.ngb.army.mil

BGen Charles A Morgan
Assistant Adjutant General, Air
Phone: 410-234-3800
e-mail: morganc@mdang_balt.ang.af.mil

Major Charles S Kohler
Public Affairs
Phone: 410-576-6179
e-mail: charles.s.kohler@us.army.mil

Natural Resources Department

Tawes State Office Building
580 Taylor Avenue
Annapolis, MD 21401-2335
Phone: 410-260-8367
Phone: 877-620-8367
Fax: 410-260-8111
URL: www.dnr.state.md.us
e-mail: customerservice@dnr.state.md.us

Description: Preserves, protects, enhances and restores Maryland's natural resources for the wise use and enjoyment of all citizens.

C Ronald Franks
Natural Resources Secretary

Colonel Mark S Chaney
Natural Resources Police Superintendent
Phone: 410-260-8880

Pamela Lunsford
Land & Water Conservation Director
Phone: 410-260-8447

Steve Koehn
Forest Service Director
Phone: 410-260-8501

Paul Peditto
Wildlife & Heritage Director
Phone: 410-260-8549

Stephan Abel
Communications Director
Phone: 410-260-8008

Port Administration

401 E Pratt Street
World Trade Center
Baltimore, MD 21202-3041
Phone: 410-385-4444
Phone: 800-638-7519
Fax: 410-333-3402
URL: www.mpa.state.md.us

F Brooks Royster III
Executive Director

Dave Thomas
Operations Director
Phone: 410-633-1043
e-mail: dthomas@mdot.state.md.us

Richard Scher
Communications
Phone: 410-385-4480

Douglas E Matzke
Director of Engineering
Phone: 410-631-1157

Public Safety and Correctional Services Department
300 E Joppa Road
Suite 1000
Towson, MD 21286
Phone: 410-339-5000
Phone: 877-379-8636
Fax: 410-339-4240
URL: www.dpscs.state.md.us

Gary D Maynard
Secretary
Phone: 410-339-5000

David N Bezanson
Assistant Secretary Capital Programs
Phone: 410-339-5068

Mary L Livers PhD
Deputy Secretary/Chief of Staff
Phone: 410-339-5093

G Lawrence Franklin
Deputy Secretary Administrative Services
Phone: 410-339-5050

Richard Rosenblatt
Assistant Secretary Treatment Services
Phone: 410-339-5031

State Highway Administration
707 N Calvert Street
Baltimore, MD 21202-3601
Phone: 410-545-0400
Fax: 410-209-5009
URL: www.sha.state.md.us
e-mail: shaadmin@sha.state.md.us

Neil J Pedersen
Administrator
Phone: 410-545-0400

Thomas Hicks
Traffic & Safety Office Director
Phone: 410-787-5815

Joe Geckle
Office of Maintenance/Homeland Security Office
Phone: 410-582-5552

State Police Department
1201 Reisterstown Road
Pikesville, MD 21208-3899

Phone: 410-653-4200
Phone: 800-525-5555
Fax: 410-653-4269
URL: www.mdsp.org

Description: To protect the citizens of the state of Maryland from foreign and domestic security threats, to promote roadway safety and to fight crime. This is accomplished through leadership and assistance, aggressive investigation, patrol, intelligence gathering, and interdiction efforts.

Colonel Thomas E Hutchins
Secretary State Police

Lt Colonel Thomas P Coppinger
Homeland Security & Investigations Bureau Chief
Phone: 410-653-4200

Major Matt Lawrence
Homeland Security Command
Phone: 410-653-4200

Captain Thomas N McCord
Homeland Security Division, Commander
Phone: 410-653-4200

Transportation Authority
2310 Broening Highway
Suite 150
Baltimore, MD 21224
Phone: 866-713-1596
Fax: 410-537-1022
URL: www.mdta.state.md.us
e-mail: mdta@mdtransportationauthority.com

Description: Provides safe and convenient transportation facilities and in particular is responsible for constructing, managing, operating and improving the State's toll facilities.

John D Porcari
Chairman

Trent M Kittleman
Executive Secretary

Gary W McLhinney
Chief Transportation Authority Police
Phone: 410-288-8580

Transportation Department
7201 Corporate Center
Hanover, MD 21076
Phone: 410-865-1142
Phone: 888-713-1414
Fax: 410-865-1334
URL: www.mdot.state.md.us

John D Porcari
Secretary
Phone: 410-865-1000

Beverley K Swain-Staley
Deputy Secretary
Phone: 410-865-1000

Leif Dormsjo
Chief of Staff
Phone: 410-865-1000

John Gaver
Director, Office of ADA/Regulations, Risk Management &
Special Projects
Phone: 410-865-1126

Jack Cahalan
Public Affairs Office Director
Phone: 410-865-1027

STATE AGENCIES

Massachusetts

Massachusetts Main Homeland Security Office

1 Ashburton Place
Room 2133
Boston, MA 02108
Phone: 617-727-2200
URL: www.mass.gov

Deval Patrick
Governor
Phone: 617-725-4005

Timothy P Murray
Lieutenant Governor
Phone: 617-725-4005

Cindy Duggan
Homeland Security Policy Advisor
Phone: 617-727-3200

Robert C Haas
Secretary of Public Safety
Phone: 617-727-7775

Tom Reilly
Attorney General
Phone: 617-727-2200

Bureau of Communicable Disease Control

State Laboratory Institute
305 South Street
Jamaica Plain, MA 02130
Phone: 617-983-6550
Fax: 617-983-6925
URL: www.state.ma.us/dph/cdc/bcdc.htm

Description: Strives to improve quality of life through the elimination of communicable diseases.

Alfred DeMaria Jr
Assistant Commissioner

Chief Medical Examiner's Office

720 Albany Street
Boston, MA 02118
Phone: 617-267-6767
Fax: 617-266-6763

Description: Determines the cause and manner of death in cases under its jurisdiction through case investigation, performance of autopsies and laboratory studies.

Mark Flomenbaum
Chief Medical Examiner

Department of Conservation and Recreation

251 Causeway Street

Suite 600
Boston, MA 02114-2104
Phone: 617-626-1250
Fax: 617-626-1351
URL: www.mass.gov/dcr
e-mail: mass.parks@state.ma.us

Description: The Department of Environmental Management and Metropolitan District Commission have unified into one agency, the Department of Conservation and Recreation. The Water Supply Protection Division manages and protects the drinking water supply watersheds, provides technical support to other state agencies, and monitors dam safety.

Priscilla E Geigis
Acting Commissioner

Mike Gildesgame
Director, Office of Water
Phone: 617-626-1371
e-mail: mike.gildesgame@state.ma.us

Donna Nelson
Hazard Mitigation Planning Coordinator
Phone: 617-626-1386
e-mail: donna.nelson@state.ma.us

Division of Epidemiology & Immunization

State Laboratory Institute
305 South Street
Jamaica Plan, MA 02130
Phone: 617-983-6800
Fax: 617-983-6840
URL: www.state.ma.us/dph/cdc/epiimm2.htm

Description: Responsible for the investigation of outbreaks of communicable diseases, surveillance of reportable diseases and provision of educational materials and services to assist in reducing the incidence of these diseases.

Robert Goldstein MPH
Director

Bela Matyas
Director, Epidemiology

Susan Lett
Director, Immunization

Aldie Maria
Communicable Diseases

Emergency Management Agency

400 Worcester Road
Framingham, MA 01701
Phone: 508-820-2010

Fax: 508-820-2015
URL: www.state.ma.us/mema

Description: Coordinates Federal, state, local and private resources throughout the state during times of disaster and emergencies. Current goals: to make mergency management more community based; assist local communities to identify potential risks; and enhance response, warning and coordinating all agencies within the state.

Ken McBride
Acting Director
Phone: 508-820-2010
e-mail: cris.mccombs@state.ma.us

Kenneth J McBride
Chief of Staff
Phone: 508-820-1422
e-mail: ken.mcbride@state.ma.us

Mike Philbin
Planning
Phone: 508-820-2008
e-mail: mike.philbin@state.ma.us

John Tommaney
Response & Recovery Chief
Phone: 508-820-2000
e-mail: john.tommaney@state.ma.us

Steve Finks
Communications
Phone: 508-820-2000
e-mail: steve.finks@state.ma.us

Peter Judge
Public Information Officer
Phone: 508-820-2002
e-mail: peter.judge@state.ma.us

Barry Wante
Homeland Security/Services Chief
Phone: 508-820-1448
e-mail: barry.wante@state.ma.us

Environmental Protection Department
1 Winter Street
2nd Floor
Boston, MA 02108
Phone: 617-292-5500
Fax: 617-574-6880
URL: www.mass.gov/dep/

Arleen O'Donnell
Commissioner
Phone: 617-292-5856

Daniel McGillicuddy
Administrative Services Deputy Commissioner
Phone: 617-292-5564

Edward Kunce
Operations/Programs Deputy Commissioner
Phone: 617-292-5915

Eric Worrall
Chief of Staff
Phone: 617-292-5536

William Harkins
Legislative & Budgetary Affairs Director
Phone: 617-292-5906

Ed Coletta
Public Affairs Office
Phone: 617-292-5737

Myles Brown
Emergency Management Coordinator
Phone: 617-292-5789

Margaret R Stolfa
General Counsel
Phone: 617-292-5892

James Colman
Bureau of Waste Prevention, Assistant Commissioner
Phone: 617-292-5564

Glenn Haas
Bureau of Resource Protection, Assistant Commissioner
Phone: 617-292-5748

Janine Commerford
Bureau of Waste Site Cleanup, Assistant Commissioner
Phone: 617-556-1121

Fire Services Department
State Road
PO Box 1025
Stow, MA 01775
Phone: 978-567-3100
Fax: 978-567-3121
URL: www.mass.gov/dfs/index.htm

Description: Providing the people of Massachusetts the ability to create safer communities through coordinated training, education, prevention, investigation, leadership and emergency response.

Stephen D Coan
State Fire Marshal
Phone: 978-567-3111
e-mail: stephen.coan@state.ma.us

Thomas P Leonard
Deputy State Fire Marshal
Phone: 978-567-3112
e-mail: tom.leonard@state.ma.us

Jennifer Mieth
Public Information Officer & Education Manager
Phone: 978-567-3381
e-mail: jennifer.mieth@state.ma.us

Food and Agriculture Department
Department of Agricultural Resources
251 Causeway Street
Suite 500
Boston, MA 02114-2119
Phone: 617-626-1700
Fax: 617-626-1850
URL: www.mass.gov/agr/

Scott J Soares
Acting Commissioner
Phone: 617-626-1701

Kent Lage
Assistant Commissioner & Chief of Staff
Phone: 617-626-1702
e-mail: kent.lage@state.ma.us

Ken Collette
General Counsel
Phone: 617-626-1705
e-mail: ken.collette@state.ma.us

Mary J Jordan
Agricultural Development Division Director
Phone: 617-626-1750
e-mail: mary.jordan@state.ma.us

Bill Gillmeister
Economic Program Planner
Phone: 617-626-1811
e-mail: william.gillmeister@state.ma.us

Brad Mitchell
Regulatory Services Director
Phone: 617-626-1771
e-mail: brad.mitchell@state.ma.us

Health and Human Services Executive Office
1 Ashburton Place
11th Floor
Boston, MA 02108
Phone: 617-727-7600
Phone: 617-573-1600
Fax: 617-727-1396
URL: www.magnet.state.ma.us/eohhs/eohhs.htm

JudyAnn Bigby
Secretary
Phone: 617-727-7600

Courtney Sullivan
Chief of Staff
Phone: 617-727-7600

Kristen Apgar
General Counsel
Phone: 617-727-0077
e-mail: kris.apgar@state.ma.us

Fred Habib
Human Services Undesecretary
Phone: 617-727-7600

Tom Curran
Chief Information Officer
Phone: 617-727-7600

Massachusetts Chiefs of Police Association
47 Memorial Drive
Shrewsbury, MA 01545-4028
Phone: 508-842-2935
Phone: 800-322-2011
Fax: 508-842-3703
URL: www.masschiefs.org

Richard A Marchese
Executive Director
e-mail: chiefram@aol.com

John M Collins
General Counselor
e-mail: jackmcopa@aol.com

National Guard
50 Maple Street
Milford, MA 01757
Phone: 508-233-6561
Fax: 508-233-6554
URL: www.mass.gov/guard/
e-mail: ma-pao@ng.army.mil

Description: Providing information to the public, and to our soldiers, in order to enhance the positive image and visibility of the National Guard.

BGeneral Oliver J Mason
Adjutant General

BGeneral Winfield Danielson
Public Affairs Officer
Phone: 508-233-6560
e-mail: winfield.danielson@us.army.mil

NEDRIX-New England Disaster Recovery Information Exchange
PO Box 52120
Boston, MA 02205
Phone: 401-954-7547
URL: www.nedrix.com
e-mail: infomration@nedrix.com

Description: A non-profit organization that provides continuity and crisis management professionals access to the industry best practices and an opportunity to meet and share ideas and experiences with peers through conferences, symposiums, and Public/Private Sector services.

Chris Glebus
President

Anne-Marie McCaughey
Vice President

Northeast States Emergency Consortium
1 West Water Street
Suite 205
Wakefield, MA 01880
Phone: 781-224-9876
Fax: 781-224-4350
URL: www.nesec.org

Description: A not for profit all-hazards mitigation and emergency management organization. NESEC is th only multi-hazard consortium in the country and is supported and funded by the Department of Homeland Security Federal Emergency Management Agency (FEMA).

William J Hackett
Preident

Robert McAleer
Director

Port Authority
1 Harborside Drive
Suite 200 S
East Boston, MA 02128-2909

Phone: 617-568-3100
Fax: 617-568-1049
URL: www.massport.com

Description: Safely secures passengers and goods through our airports, seaports and other world-class transportation facilities that lay the foundation of individual freedom and economic prosperity for New England in today's global marketplace.

Thomas J Kinton Jr
Executive Director/CEO
Phone: 617-568-3100

Thomas J Butler
Director External Affairs
Phone: 617-568-3711

Public Health Department
250 Washington Street
Boston, MA 02108-4619
Phone: 617-624-6000
Phone: 866-627-7968
Fax: 617-624-5206
URL: www.state.ma.us/dph/dphhome.htm

Paul J Cote Jr
Commissioner
Phone: 617-624-6000

Kathy Atkinson
Policy/Planning Association Commissioner
Phone: 617-624-6000

Abdullah Rehayem
Acting Director, Emergency Medical Services
Phone: 617-753-7300

Kathy McLaughlin-Collin
Chief of Staff
Phone: 617-624-6000

Steve Huges
Community Sanitation Division
Phone: 617-624-5757

Joan Gorgg
Acting Director, Determination of Need Division
Phone: 617-753-7340

Bob Walker
Radiation Control Program
Phone: 617-242-3035

Donna Levin
General Counsel
Phone: 617-624-5220

Donna Rheaume
Media Office
Phone: 617-624-6000

Suzanne Condon
Environmental Assessment Division
Phone: 617-624-5757

Public Safety Executive Office
Public Safety Department
1 Ashburton Place
Room 2133
Boston, MA 02108

Phone: 617-727-7775
Fax: 617-727-4764
URL: www.state.ma.us/eops/index.htm
e-mail: eopsinfo@state.ma.us

Kevin M Burke
Secretary

Michael P Concannon
Undersecretary, Homeland Security & Law Enforcement

Cynthia Duggan
Director for Homeland Security Coordination

Patrick Bradley
Undersecretary, Criminal Justice Systems
Phone: 617-725-3301

Susan Prosnitz
General Counsel
Phone: 617-727-7775

Michael Coelho
Chief of Staff

Martha Powers
Director For Preparedness & Fiscal Coordination

State Police Department
470 Worcester Road
Framingham, MA 01702
Phone: 508-820-2300
Fax: 617-727-6874
URL: www.state.ma.us/msp

Colonel Mark F Delaney
Superintendent
Phone: 508-820-2300

Lieutenant Dermott Quinn
Media Relations Commander
Phone: 508-820-2623

Water Resources Authority
Charlestown Navy Yard
100 1st Avenue
Boston, MA 02129
Phone: 617-242-6000
Fax: 617-788-4894
URL: www.mwra.state.ma.us

Frederick Laskey
Executive Director
Phone: 617-788-1101

Michael Ralph
Public Affairs
Phone: 617-788-1112

Michael Hornbrook
Chief Operating Officer
Phone: 617-788-4359

STATE AGENCIES

Michigan

Michigan Main Homeland Security Office
714 S Harrison Road
East Lansing, MI 48823
Phone: 517-333-5042
Fax: 517-333-4987
URL: www.michigan.gov/homeland

Jennifer M Granholm
Governor
Phone: 517-373-3400

John D Cherry Jr
Lieutenant Governor
Phone: 517-373-6800

Colonel Peter Munoz
Director Homeland Security/Director State Police
Phone: 517-336-6158

Mike Cox
Attorney General
Phone: 517-373-1110

Agricultural Department
525 West Allegan Street
Lansing, MI 48933
Mailing Address: PO Box 30017, 48909
Phone: 517-373-1052
Phone: 800-292-3939
Fax: 517-335-1423
URL: www.michigan.gov/mda
e-mail: mda-info@michigan.gov

Mitch Irwin
Director
Phone: 517-373-1052

Phyllis Mellon
Deputy Director
Phone: 517-335-3402

Bradley Deacon
Emergency Management Coordinator
Phone: 517-241-4085

Dr Steve Halstead
Animal Industry Director/State Veterinary
Phone: 517-373-1077

Katherine Fedder
Food & Dairy
Phone: 517-373-1060

Steve Reh
Laboratory
Phone: 517-337-5040

Association for Medical Examiners
120 W Saginaw
East Lansing, MI 48823
Phone: 517-336-7599
Fax: 517-336-5797
URL: www.michiganme.org
e-mail: mame@michiganme.org

Description: Fosters the highest professional standards in the performance of the duties of the county medical examiners of Michigan. The association produces educational materials and holds scientific meetings, provides a forum for the discussion of professional and managerial issues, and provides information concerning the medical examiners to county and state administrators and legislators and to the general public.

Stephen Cohle MD
President
Phone: 734-763-6454
e-mail: remickd@umich.edu

Bureau of Epidemiology
201 Townsend Street
Lansing, MI 48913
Phone: 517-335-8900

Corrine Miller
Director

Community Health Department
Capital View Building
201 Townsend Street
Lansing, MI 48913
Phone: 517-373-3740
Fax: 517-335-3090
URL: www.michigan.gov/mdch

Janet Olszewski
Director
e-mail: norris@michigan.gov

Jean Chabut
Public Health Administration
Phone: 517-335-8024
e-mail: chabutj@michigan.gov

Kimberlydawn Wisdom
State Surgeon General
e-mail: christians@michigan.gov

David McLaury
Deputy Director/Chief Medical Executive
Phone: 517-335-8150
e-mail: larson@michigan.gov

Patrick Barrie
Dep Director, Gov't Health & Substance Abuse

Paul Reinhart
Sen Dep Director Medical Services Adminsitration
e-mail: cords@michigan.gov

T J Bucholz
Public Information Officer
e-mail: bucholztj@michigan.gov

Environmental Quality Department
525 West Allegan Street
Lansing, MI 48909-7973
Mailing Address: PO Box 30473
Phone: 517-373-7917
Fax: 517-241-7401
URL: www.michigan.gov/deq

Steven E Chester
Director
Phone: 517-241-7917

Jim Sygo
Deputy Director, Operations
Phone: 517-241-7394

Skip Pruss
Deputy Director, Programs & Regulations
Phone: 517-241-7392

Tim McGarry
Enforcement Coordinator/Litigation Specialist
Phone: 517-241-2050

Thor Strong
Low-Level Radioactive Waste Authority, Assoc Commissioner
Phone: 517-241-1252

Milton Scales
Criminal Investigations Director
Phone: 517-335-3434

G Vinson Hellwig
Air Quality Division
Phone: 517-373-7069

George Bruchmann
Waste & Hazardous Materials Division
Phone: 517-373-9523

Great Lakes Business Recovery Group
1647 Dancer Drive
Suite 102
Rochester Hill, MI 48307
Phone: 248-650-9900
URL:
www.geocities.com/greatlakesbusinessrecoverygroup/glbrg
e-mail: laural.charvat@chi.frb.org

Description: A non-profit association of Midwestern area individuals responsilbe for contingency, business continuity, emergency, and disaster recovery planning. GLBRG provides members an excellent information exchange experience and alliances with public and private partners.

Information Technology Department
George W Romney Building
111 South Capitol Ave, 8th Floor

Lansing, MI 48913
Phone: 517-335-4000
Fax: 517-373-8213
URL: www.michigan.gov/dit
e-mail: mdit@michigan.gov

Teresa Takai
Chief Information Officer/Director
Phone: 517-373-1006

Kenneth D Theis
Agency Services Deputy Director
Phone: 517-373-1006

Jack Harris
Infrastructure Services Deputy Director
Phone: 517-373-0805

Phyllis Mellon
Management Services Deputy Director
Phone: 517-373-1004

International Bridge Administration
934 Bridge Plaza
Sault Ste Marie, MI 49783
Mailing Address: PO Box 317
Phone: 906-635-5255
Fax: 906-635-0540
URL: www.michigan.gov/iba

Phillip M Becker
General Manager
Phone: 906-635-5255
e-mail: beckerp@michigan.gov

Mackinac Bridge Authority
N415 I-75
St. Ignace, MI 49781
Phone: 906-643-7600
Fax: 906-643-7668
URL: www.mackinacbridge.org

Robert J Sweeney
Executive Secretary
Phone: 906-643-7600

Michigan Association of Chiefs of Police
2133 University Park Drive
Suite 200
Okemos, MI 48864-3975
Phone: 517-349-9420
Fax: 517-349-5823
URL: www.michiganpolicechiefs.org
e-mail: info@michiganpolicechiefs.org

Thomas A Hendrickson
Executive Director
Phone: 517-349-9420
e-mail: hendri14@pilot.msu.edu

Michigan State Police State Capitol Post
530 W Allegan Street
Lansing, MI 48913
Phone: 517-373-2836
Fax: 517-335-4619

Lieutenant Joe Thomas
Post Commander

Military and Veterans Affairs Department

3411 Martin Luther King Jr Boulevard
Lansing, MI 48906
Phone: 517-481-8000
Fax: 517-481-8145
URL: www.michigan.gov/dmva
e-mail: paocmn@michigan.gov

Major General Thomas G Cutler
Adjutant General/Director
Phone: 517-481-8083

Col Jim Anderson
Army Assistant Adjutant General
Phone: 517-481-8082

BGen Richard Elliot
Air Assistant Adjutant General
Phone: 517-481-8083

Joel Wortley
State Operations Bureau/CFO
Phone: 517-335-3160

Col James Anderson
Chief of Staff
Phone: 517-483-5545

Lieutenant Colonel Dennis Hull
Military Support Division
Phone: 517-483-5619

Public Power Agency

809 Centennial Way
Lansing, MI 48917-9277
Phone: 517-323-8919
Fax: 517-323-8373
URL: www.mpower.org
e-mail: geninfo@mpower.org

Daniel Cooper
General Manager
Phone: 517-323-8919

Jim Weeks
Governmental Liaison
Phone: 517-323-8919

David Naberhius
Financial Manager
Phone: 517-323-8919

State Police

714 S Harrison Road
East Lansing, MI 48823
Phone: 517-336-6159
Phone: 517-332-2521
Fax: 517-336-6551
URL: www.michigan.gov/msp

Description: To prevent and investigate crime and enforce the law, improve traffic safety, provide homeland security and emergency preparedness and response, provide the highest quality support services, and develop and align organizational resources to meet department priorities.

Colonel Peter Munoz
Director
Phone: 517-336-6163

Lt Col Timothy Yungfer
Deputy Director
Phone: 517-336-6159

Captain Jack Shepherd
Executive Director
Phone: 517-336-6172

Shanon Akans
Public Affairs Director
Phone: 517-336-6202

Ray Beach Jr
Michigan Commission on Law Enforcement Standards (COLES)
Phone: 517-322-6525
e-mail: beachr@michigan.gov

Lt Col Thomas Miller
Uniform Services Bureau
Phone: 517-336-6163

Captain Robert Powers
Motor Carrier Division
Phone: 517-336-6195

Transportation Department

State Transportation Building
425 W Ottawa Street
Lansing, MI 48909
Mailing Address: PO Box 30050
Phone: 517-373-2090
Fax: 517-373-6457
URL: www.michigan.gov/mdot

Kirk T Steudle
Director
Phone: 517-373-2114
e-mail: steudlek@michigan.gov

Bill Shreck
Communications Director
Phone: 517-335-3084
e-mail: shreckw@michigan.gov

Larry E Tibbits
Chief Operations Officer
Phone: 517-373-4656
e-mail: tibbitsl@michigan.gov

Ronald K DeCook
Governmental Affairs Office
Phone: 517-373-3946
e-mail: decookr@michigan.gov

Tammy Kirschenbauer
Human Resources Office
Phone: 517-373-1680
e-mail: kirschenbauert1@michigan.gov

STATE AGENCIES

Minnesota

Minnesota Homeland Security & Emergency Management
444 Cedar Street
Suite 223
St. Paul, MN 55101-6223
Phone: 651-201-7400
Phone: 651-297-7372
Fax: 651-296-0459
URL: www.hsem.state.mn.us
e-mail: dps.hsem@state.mn.us

Timothy Pawlenty
Governor
Phone: 651-296-3391
e-mail: tim.pawlenty@state.mn.us

Carol L Molnau
Lieutenant Governor
Phone: 651-296-3391

Michael Campion
Commissioner Public Safety
Phone: 651-201-7160
e-mail: michael.campion@state.mn.us

Lori Swanson
Attorney General
Phone: 651-296-6196

Agriculture Department
625 Robert St North
St. Paul, MN 55155-2538
Phone: 651-201-6000
Phone: 800-967-2474
Fax: 651-201-6109
URL: www.mda.state.mn.us

Description: The Minnesota Department of Agriculture works toward a diverse industry that is both profitable and environmentally sound; ensures orderly commerce; and protects public health and safety regarding food and agricultural products.

Gene Hugoson
Commissioner
Phone: 651-201-6219
e-mail: gene.hugoson@state.mn.us

Greg Buzicky
Pesticide & Fertilizer Management Division
Phone: 651-201-6435
e-mail: greg.buzicky@state.mn.us

Doug Hartwig
Agricultural Statistics Division
Phone: 651-296-3896
e-mail: dhartwig@nass.usda.gov

Heidi Kassenborg
Acting Director Dairy/Food Inspection Division
Phone: 651-201-6453
e-mail: kevin.elfering@state.mn.us

Larry Palmer
Information Tech Division
Phone: 651-201-6347
e-mail: larry.palmer@state.mn.us

William Krueger
Laboratory Services
Phone: 651-201-6572
e-mail: william.krueger@state.mn.us

Division of Public Health Surveillance and Informatics
530 Chicago Avenue
Minneapolis, MN 55415
Phone: 612-215-6300
Fax: 612-215-6330
URL: www.cdc.gov/epo/dphsi/mecisp/MINNESOTA.htm

Andrew M Baker MD
Medical Examiner
e-mail: andrew.baker@co.hennepin.mn.us

Joan Jung
Executive Secretary, Minnesota Coroner/Medical Examiners' Association

Emergency Medical Services Regulatory Board
University Park Plaza, Ste 310
2829 University Avenue SE
Minneapolis, MN 55414-3250
Phone: 651-201-2800
Fax: 651-201-2812
URL: www.emsrb.state.mn.us
e-mail: emsrb.webmaster@state.mn.us

Description: Emergency Medical Services Regulatory Board is the lead state agency for EMS in Minnesota. It provides leadership, education and medical direction in order to optimize the quality of emergency medical care, in collaboration with local communities.

Mary Hedges
Executive Director
Phone: 651-201-2806
e-mail: mary.hedges@state.mn.us

Debra Teske
Administration Specialist
Phone: 651-201-2808
e-mail: debra.teske@state.mn.us

Karen Jacobson
EMS Data Specialist
Phone: 651-201-2805
e-mail: karen.jacobnson@state.mn.us

Robert Norlen
Field Services Supervisor
Phone: 218-834-5271
e-mail: robert.norlen@state.mn.us

Health Department
PO Box 64975
St. Paul, MN 55164-0975
Phone: 651-201-5000
Fax: 651-215-5801
URL: www.health.state.mn.us/

Dianne Mandernach
Commissioner
Phone: 651-201-5810
e-mail: commissioner@health.mn.us

Carol Woolverton
Community Health Bureau, Assistant Commissioner
Phone: 651-201-5809

Rick Kantorowicz
Facilities Operations Manager
Phone: 651-201-4632
e-mail: rick.kantorowicz@health.mn.us

Wendy Nelson
Information Systems Director
Phone: 651-201-5010

John Oswald
Director Center for Health Statistics
Phone: 651-201-5947

Debra Burns
Director Public Health Practice Office
Phone: 651-201-3873

Laurel Briske
Local Capacity Unit
Phone: 651-201-3872

John Stieger
Communications Director
Phone: 651-201-4998

Patricia Bloomgren
Environmental Health Division
Phone: 651-201-4569

Patricia Bloomgrem
Director Disease Prevention & Control Division
Phone: 651-201-5664

Aggie Leitheiser
Health Protection Bureau, Assistant Commissioner
Phone: 651-201-5711

Norman Crouch
Public Health Laboratory Division
Phone: 651-201-5063

Infectious Disease Epidemiology, Prevention and Control Division
PO Box 64975

St Paul, MN 55164
Phone: 651-201-5414
Phone: 877-676-5414
Fax: 651-201-5666
URL: www.health.state.mn.us/divs/idepc
e-mail: idepcweb@health.state.mn.us

Richard N Danila
Acute Disease Investigation & Control Division

John Clare
EPI Field Services

Military Affairs Department
20 W 12th Street
St. Paul, MN 55155
Phone: 651-282-4662
Fax: 651-282-4541
URL: www.dma.state.mn.us
e-mail: kevin.olson@mn.ngb.army.mi

Major General Larry W Shellito
Air Guard Adjutant General
Phone: 651-282-4666

Lt Colonel Kevin Gerdes
Army Division Personnel Commander
Phone: 651-282-4040
e-mail: kevin.gerdes@mn.ngb.army.mil

Colonel Mary Johnson
State Judge Advocate
Phone: 651-282-4682

Colonel Joe Kelly
Chief of Staff
Phone: 651-282-4665

Colonel Terry Heggemeier
Executive Support Staff
Phone: 651-282-4673

Kevin Olson
Public Affairs Officer
e-mail: kevin.olson@mn.ngb.army.mil

Minnesota State Patrol Capitol Security Executive Protection
B5 State Capitol Building
St Paul, MN 55155
Phone: 651-296-4770
Fax: 651-296-9495
URL: www.dps.state.mn.us/patrol/distindex

Description: A division of the Minnesota State Patrol responsible for providing safety and security to Executive, Judicial and Legislative officials, State employees and members of the capitol complex.

Captain Mary Schrader
Director
Phone: 651-296-4770

Sgt Mike Parker
Capitol Security
Phone: 651-296-0398
e-mail: mike.parker@state.mn.us

Operations Division
Natural Resources Department
500 Lafayette Road
St. Paul, MN 55155-4002
Phone: 651-259-5555
Fax: 651-296-4799

Description: Draws together the Chair, five citizens and the heads of ten state agencies that play a vital role in Minnesota's environment and development. The board develops policy, creates long-range plans and reviews proposed projects that would significantly influence the state's environment.

Laurie Martinson
Deputy Assistant Commissioner

Mike Hamm
Enforcement Division Director

Marty Vadis
Minerals Division Director

Kent Lokkesmoe
Waters Division

Port Authority
1200 Port Terminal Drive
Duluth, MN 55802
Phone: 218-727-8525
Phone: 800-232-0703
Fax: 218-727-6888
URL: www.duluthport.com
e-mail: admin@duluthport.com

Description: Builds and improves the Port of Duluth to create environmentally sound economic development opportunities while protecting and generating domestic and international commerce.

Adolph N Ojard
Executive Director
e-mail: aojard@duluthport.com

Andrew J McDonough
Business Development Director
e-mail: amcdonough@duluthport.com

Ronald L Johnson
Trade Development Director
e-mail: rjohnson@duluthport.com

James D Sharrow
Facilities Manager
e-mail: jsharrow@duluthport.com

Lisa Marciniak
Port Promotion Manager
e-mail: lmarciniak@duluthport.com

Robert C Maki
Legal Counsel
Phone: 218-726-0805
e-mail: bmaki@makiandoverom.com

Public Safety Department
Town Square
444 Cedar Street
St. Paul, MN 55101
Phone: 651-201-7000
Fax: 651-297-5728

URL: www.dps.state.mn.us

Description: Committed to protecting citizens and communities through activites that promote and support prevention, preparedness, response, recovery, education, and enforcement. These objectives are achieved through a focus on saving lives, providing efficient and effective services, maintaining public trust, and developing strong partnerships.

Michael Campion
Commissioner
Phone: 651-201-7160
e-mail: michael.campion@state.mn.us

Tim Leslie
Assistant Commissioner
Phone: 651-296-6642
e-mail: tim.leslie@state.mn.us

Barbara Cox
Legislative Affairs

Mary Ellison
Crime Victim Services
Phone: 651-201-7173
e-mail: mary.ellison@state.mn.us

Kris Eide
Homeland Security Emergency Management Division

Mike Schwab
Branch Director Homeland Security
Phone: 651-215-6934
e-mail: dan.v.johnson@state.mn.us

Jerry Rosendahl
State Fire Marshal Pipeline Safety Division

Public Utility Commission
121 7th Place E
Suite 350
St. Paul, MN 55101-2147
Phone: 651-296-0406
Fax: 651-297-7073
URL: www.puc.state.mn.us/

Description: The Minnesota Public Utility Commission creates and maintains a regulatory environment that ensures safe, reliable and efficient utility services at fair and reasonable rates.

Leroy Koppendrayer
Chairman
Phone: 651-201-2200
e-mail: leroy.koppendrayer@state.mn.us

Burl W Haar
Executive Secretary
Phone: 651-201-2222
e-mail: burl.haar@state.mn.us

Marshall Johnson
Commissioner
Phone: 651-201-2200
e-mail: marshall.johnson@state.mn.us

Tom Pugh
Commissioner
Phone: 651-201-2250
e-mail: tom.pugh@state.mn.us

Radiological Emergency Preparedness

444 Cedar Street
Suite 223
St Paul, MN 55101
Phone: 651-201-7400
Fax: 651-296-0459
URL: www.dps.state.mn.us/emermgt/rep/index.htm

Description: Ensures that the health and safety of the public is protceted in the event of a radiological incident. The program includes annual training and exercises, and emergency plan reviews.

Steven Willoughby
REP Administrator
Phone: 651-296-0458

Mark Kam
Readiological Emergency Preparedness/GIS Info Contact
Phone: 651-296-0444
e-mail: mark.kam@state.mn.us

State Patrol

444 Cedar Street
Suite 130
St. Paul, MN 55101
Phone: 651-201-7100
URL: www.dps.state.mn.us/patrol

Description: To ensure a safe environment on Minnesota's roadways.

Mark Dunaski
Chief
Phone: 651-201-7117
e-mail: mark.dunaski@state.mn.us

Transportation Department

395 John Ireland Boulevard
MS 100
St. Paul, MN 55155-1899
Phone: 651-296-3000
Fax: 651-297-3160
URL: www.dot.state.mn.us/

Carol L Molnau
Commissioner
Phone: 651-296-3391
e-mail: carol.molnau@state.mn.us

Lisa Freese
Deputy Commissioner/Chief Engineer
Phone: 651-296-8532

Kevin Z Gray
Deputy Commissioner/CFO
Phone: 651-296-7942
e-mail: kevin.gray@state.mn.us

Betsey Parker
Intergovernmental Policy
Phone: 651-296-3002

Water and Soil Resources Board

1 W Water Street
Suite 200
St. Paul, MN 55107
Phone: 651-296-3767

Fax: 651-297-5615
URL: www.bwsr.state.mn.us

Randy Kramer
Chairman
Phone: 320-563-8377

John Jafchke
Executive Director
Phone: 651-296-0878

Doug Thomas
Assistant Director
Phone: 651-297-5617
e-mail: doug.thomas@bwsr.state.mn.us

STATE AGENCIES

Mississippi

Mississippi Main Homeland Security Office

1230 Raymond Road
Box 1300
Jackson, MS 39204
Mailing Address: PO Box 958
Phone: 601-346-1499
URL: www.homelandsecurity.ms.gov
e-mail: info@homelandsecurity.ms.gov

Haley Barbour
Governor
Phone: 601-359-3150
e-mail: governor@govoff@state.ms.us

Amy Tuck
Lieutenant Governor
Phone: 601-359-3200
e-mail: ltgov@mail.senate.state.ms.us

Jim Hood
Attorney General
Phone: 601-359-3680
e-mail: msag05@ago.state.ms.us

J.W. Ledbetter
Director Homeland Security
Phone: 601-346-9999

Bureau of Emergency Medical Services

Office of Emergency Planning & Response
570 E Woodrow Wilson Drive
Annex Building, 3rd Floor
Jackson, MS 39215
Mailing Address: PO Box 1700
Phone: 601-576-7380
Fax: 601-576-7373
URL: www.ems.doh.ms.gov

Description: This office organizes, regulates and maintains a statewide program to improve emergency medical care. It is responsible for implementing and coordinating the agency's Plans & Response Team with MEMA, MDPS and MDEQ for all disasters including bioterrorism and weapons of mass destruction.

Keith Parker
Director Emergency Medical Services
Phone: 601-576-7380
e-mail: keith.parker@msdh.state.ms.us

Stan Welch
Director Licensure, Certification & Evaluation
Phone: 601-576-7380
e-mail: swelch@msdh.state.ms.us

Karey Riddle
EMS/Trauma Policy & Planning
Phone: 601-576-8145
e-mail: karey.riddle@msdh.state.ms.us

Scott Stinson
Director EMS Testing, Training & Certification
Phone: 601-576-7380
e-mail: scott.stinson@msdh.state.ms.us

Mark Allen
Director EMS Data Systems
Phone: 601-576-7353
e-mail: mark.allen@msdh.state.ms.us

Ken Seawright
Director Emergency Preparedness & Planning (Bioterrorism)
Phone: 601-576-7380
e-mail: ken.seawright@msdh.state.ms.us

Hugh Phillips
Director Emergency Preparedness
Phone: 601-576-8014
e-mail: hugh.phillips@msdh.state.ms.us

Jonathan Chaney
Director Hospital Preparedness
Phone: 601-576-7368
e-mail: jonathan.chaney@msdh.state.ms.us

Pamela Chief Nurse
Director Hospital Preparedness
Phone: 601-576-8081
e-mail: pamela.nutt@msdh.state.ms.us

Department of Agriculture & Commerce

121 N Jefferson Street
PO Box 1609
Jackson, MS 39201
Phone: 601-359-1100
Fax: 601-354-6290
URL: www.mdac.state.ms.us

Lester Spell Jr
Commissioner
Phone: 601-359-1100
e-mail: spell@mdac.state.ms.us

Mike Tagert
Director Plant Industry Bureau
Phone: 662-325-3391
e-mail: miket@mdac.state.ms.us

James Watson
Director Board of Animal Health
Phone: 601-359-1160
e-mail: jimw@mdac.state.ms.us

Richard A Benton
Director Regulatory Services Bureau
Phone: 601-359-1111
e-mail: richardb@mdac.state.ms.us

John Tillson
Director Consumer Protection Division
Phone: 601-359-1148
e-mail: johnt@mdac.state.ms.us

Richard A Benton
Meat Inspection Division
Phone: 601-359-1192

Robert Louys
Petroleum Products Division
Phone: 601-359-1101
e-mail: robert@mdac.state.ms.us

Guy Feltenstein
Director Fruits & Vegetables Division
Phone: 601-483-3451
e-mail: guyf@mdac.state.ms.us

Russel E Robbins
Director Weights/Measures Division
Phone: 601-325-1149
e-mail: rusty@mdac.state.ms.us

Department of Environmental Quality
Emergency Services
2380 Highway 80 W
Southport Center
Jackson, MS 39204
Mailing Address: PO Box 10385, Jackson 39289
Phone: 601-961-5171
Fax: 601-961-5741
URL: www.deq.state.ms.us

Charles Chisolm
Executive Director

Jerry Beasley
Air Qulaity Planning
Phone: 601-961-5134

Gaylan McGregor
Dam Safety
Phone: 601-961-5642

Jesse Thompson
Environmental Assistance Division
Phone: 601-961-5167

Russ Twitty
Hazardous Waste Compliance
Phone: 601-961-5094

Cragin Knox
Mississippi Digital Earth Model
Phone: 601-961-5502

Khairy Abu-Salah
Pollution Prevention
Phone: 601-961-5284

Mark Williams
Solid Waste Planning & Regulations
Phone: 601-961-5304

Jim Morris
Storm Water
Phone: 601-961-5151

Steve Spengler
Surface Water Protection
Phone: 601-961-5102

Robert Seyfarth
Wetlands Permitting (Water Quality Certification)
Phone: 601-961-5160

Robbie Wilbur
Public Information
Phone: 601-961-5277

Department of Public Safety
PO Box 958
Jackson, MS 39205
Phone: 601-987-1212
Fax: 601-987-1498
URL: www.dps.state.ms.us

George Phillips
Commissioner

Melvin Maxwell
Deputy Commissioner

Sam Albritton
Public Safety Planning Executive Director
Phone: 601-987-4990

Colonel Michael Berthay
Director Highway Patrol
Phone: 601-987-1212
e-mail: colonelmhp@mdps.state.ms.us

David Shaw
Mississippi Bureau of Investigation SAC
Phone: 601-987-1560
e-mail: dshaw@mdps.state.ms.us

Pat Cronin
Director Law Enforcement Officer's Training Academy
Phone: 601-933-2100

Jim Brinson
WMD Hazmat Response Coordinator
e-mail: jbrinson@mdps.state.ms.us

Emergency Management Agency
PO Box 5644
Pearl, MS 39208
Phone: 601-933-6362
Phone: 601-352-9100
Fax: 601-933-6800
URL: www.msema.org

Mike Womack
Interim Director
Phone: 601-352-9100

Bill Brown
R & R Bureau Operations Branch Chief
Phone: 601-960-9029
e-mail: bbrown@memsa.ms.gov

Charlie Smith
Assistant Operations Officer

Phone: 601-960-9032
e-mail: csmith@mema.ms.gov

Bob Boteler
Mitigation Bureau Director
Phone: 601-366-5706
e-mail: bboteler@mema.ms.gov

Dave Benway
State Radiological Emergency Planning (REP) Coordinator
e-mail: dbenway@mema.ms.gov

Rickey Pierce
REP Special Programs Officer
e-mail: rpierce@mema.ms.gov

Margaret Carter
Training Bureau Director
e-mail: mcarter@mema.ms.gov

Harrell Neal
HAZMAT Coordinator
Phone: 601-366-6957
e-mail: hneal@mema.ms.gov

Lea Stokes
Press Information
Phone: 601-352-9100
e-mail: lstokes@mema.ms.gov

Health Department
570 E Woodrow Wilson Drive
Jackson, MS 39216
Mailing Address: PO Box 1700, Jackson 39215
Phone: 601-576-7400
Phone: 866-458-4948
Fax: 601-576-7931
URL: www.msdh.state.ms.us

Brian W Amy
State Health Officer
Phone: 601-576-7634

Danny Miller
Deputy Director/Chief of Staff
Phone: 601-576-7951

Michael Scales
Information Technology
Phone: 601-576-8092

Jim Craig
Director Health Protection
Phone: 601-576-7680

Art Sharpe
Emergency Planning & Response
Phone: 601-576-7680

Mills McNeill
State Epidemiologist/Epidemiology Office
Phone: 601-576-7725

Jim Horne
State Public Health Laboratory Manager
Phone: 601-576-7582

Joy Sennett
Communicable Disease
Phone: 601-576-8012

Sam Dawkins
Health Policy & Planning
Phone: 601-576-7874

Human Services
Health Department
750 North State Street
Jackson, MS 39202
Phone: 601-359-4500
Phone: 800-345-6347
URL: www.mdhs.state.ms.us

Description: Provides services for people in need by optimizing all available resources to sustain the family unit and to encourage traditional family values thereby promoting self-sufficiency and personal responsibility for all Mississippians.

Sollie Norwood
Director Community Services
Phone: 601-576-7725

Julie Bryan
Office of Communications
Phone: 601-359-4517
e-mail: jbryan@mdhs.state.ms.us

Marion Dunn-Tutor
Aging & Adult Services
Phone: 601-576-7725

Information Technology Services Department
301 N Lamar Street
Suite 508
Jackson, MS 39201-1495
Phone: 601-359-1395
Fax: 601-354-6016
URL: www.its.state.ms.us

Description: Created to improve long-range planning coordination and establish a central point responsible for the fiscal management of data processing functions in state agencies and institutions of higher learning.

David L Litchliter
Executive Director
Phone: 601-359-1395
e-mail: litchliter@its.state.ms.us

Martha Pemberton
Information Systems Services Director
Phone: 601-359-2743
e-mail: pemberton@its.state.ms.us

Terry Bergin
Data Services Director
Phone: 601-359-2637
e-mail: bergin@its.state.ms.us

Karen Newman
Education Services Director
Phone: 601-359-2629
e-mail: newman@its.staate.ms.us

Michele Blocker
Internal Support Director
Phone: 601-359-5111
e-mail: blocker@its.state.ms.us

Claude Johnson
Strategic Services Director
Phone: 601-359-2748
e-mail: johnson@its.state.ms.us

Roger Graves
Voice Services Director
Phone: 601-359-2892
e-mail: graves@its.state.ms.us

Mississippi Association of Chiefs of Police
PO Box 2416
Oxford, MS 38655
Phone: 662-897-6227
Fax: 601-326-1987
URL: www.mschiefs.org
e-mail: kwinter@mschiefs.org

Ken Winter
Executive Director

National Guard
PO Box 5027
Jackson, MS 3926-5027
Phone: 601-313-6232
Fax: 601-313-6251
URL: www.ngms.state.ms.us

Description: The National Guard, supports and defends the Constitution of the United States. The state mission of the Mississippi National Guard is to provide trained and disciplined forces for domestic emergencies, or as otherwise required by state law.

Major General Harold A Cross
Adjutant General
Phone: 601-313-6232

Oil and Gas Board
500 Greymont Avenue
Suite E
Jackson, MS 39202
Phone: 601-354-7142
Fax: 601-354-6873
URL: www.ogb.state.ms.us

David A Scott
Chairman
Phone: 601-354-7142

Lisa Ivshin
Executive Director/Supervisor
Phone: 601-354-7112
e-mail: livshin@ogb.state.ms.us

Michael Loftin
Information Technology
Phone: 601-354-7118
e-mail: mloftin@ogb.state.ms.us

Kent Ford
Engineering & Field Inspections
Phone: 601-354-6474
e-mail: kford@ogb.state.ms.us

Port Authority
PO Box 40
Gulfport, MS 39502
Phone: 228-865-4300

Fax: 228-865-4335
URL: www.shipmspa.com

Donald R Allee
Executive Director/CEO
e-mail: dra@shipmspa.com

Bill McGhee
Deputy Director Facilities
e-mail: bmcghee@shipmspa.com

Enrique Hurtado
Deputy Director Trade Development
e-mail: ehurtado@shipmspa.com

John Webb
Deputy Director Engineering
e-mail: jwebb@shipmspa.com

Dale Waltman
Operations Manager
Phone: 228-323-0306
e-mail: dale@shipmspa.com

Public Service Commission
Woolfolk Building
501 N West Street
Jackson, MS 39201
Phone: 601-961-5434
Phone: 800-356-6429
Fax: 601-961-5469
URL: www.psc.state.ms.us

Robert G Waites
Executive Director

Nielsen Cochran
Chairman
Phone: 601-961-5430
e-mail: central.district@psc.state.ms.us

Leonard Bentz
Vice Chairman
Phone: 601-961-5440
e-mail: southern.district@psc.state.ms.us

Bo Robinson
Commissioner
Phone: 601-961-5450
e-mail: northern.district@psc.state.ms.us

State Capitol Police
501 NW Street
Woolfolk CMP, Suite 3001A
Jackson, MS 39201
Phone: 601-359-3125
Fax: 601-359-4191

Ken Dunlap
Director

Transportation Department
401 N West Street
Jackson, MS 39201
Mailing Address: PO Box 1850, Jackson 39215
Phone: 601-359-7001
Fax: 601-359-7050
URL: www.gomdot.com

Larry L Brown
Executive Director
Phone: 601-359-7002

Harry Lee James
Deputy Executive Director-Chief Engineer
Phone: 601-359-7004

Brenda Vanover Znachko
Deputy Executive Director-Administration
Phone: 601-359-7024

Thomas M Booth Jr
Aeronautics Division
Phone: 601-359-7850

Brad Lewis
Construction Division
Phone: 601-359-7301

John M Simpson
Information Systems Division
Phone: 601-359-7450

Mitch Carr
Bridge Division
Phone: 601-359-7200

Claiborne Barnwell
Environmental Division
Phone: 601-359-7920

Ray Balentine
Intermodal Planning Office
Phone: 601-359-7025

Lisa Hancock
Procurement Division
Phone: 601-359-7300

Charles R Carr
Public Transit Division
Phone: 601-359-7800

Wayne Parrish
Ports & Waterways Division
Phone: 601-359-7034

Steven Edwards
Rails Division
Phone: 601-359-7910

Jeff Pierce
Planning Division
Phone: 601-359-7685

STATE AGENCIES

Missouri

Missouri Office of Homeland Security
PO Box 749
Jefferson City, MO 65102
Phone: 573-522-3007
Fax: 573-522-6109
URL: www.dps.mo.gov/homelandsecurity/index.htm
e-mail: homelandsecurity@dps.mo.gov

Matt Blunt
Governor
Phone: 573-751-3222

Peter D Kinder
Lieutenant Governor
Phone: 573-751-4727

Paul Fennewald
Director Homeland Security
Phone: 573-522-3007

Jeremiah W (Jay) Nixon
Attorney General
Phone: 573-751-3321

Department of Agriculture
1616 Missouri Boulevard
PO Box 630
Jefferson City, MO 65102
Phone: 573-751-4211
Fax: 573-751-1784
URL: www.mda.mo.gov
e-mail: aginfo@mda.mo.gov

Katie Smith
Director
Phone: 573-751-3359

Matt Boatright
Deputy Director
Phone: 573-526-0948
e-mail: matt.boatright@mda.mo.gov

Department of Health & Senior Services
PO Box 570
Jefferson City, MO 65102
Phone: 573-751-6400
Fax: 573-751-6041
URL: www.dhss.mo.gov
e-mail: info@dhss.mo.gov

Jane Drummond
Director
Phone: 573-751-6001

Nancie McAnaugh
Deputy Director
Phone: 573-751-6002

Dr Bao Zhu
Chief, Epidemiology Office
Phone: 573-751-6128
e-mail: zhub@dhss.mo.gov

Bruce Clements
Emergency Response/Terrorism Center (CERT)
Phone: 573-526-4768

Nanci Goner
Public Information Officer
Phone: 573-751-6062
e-mail: gonden@dhss.mo.gov

Department of Natural Resources
PO Box 176
Jefferson City, MO 65102
Phone: 573-751-3443
Phone: 800-361-4827
Fax: 573-751-7627
URL: www.dnr.mo.gov
e-mail: oac@dnr.mo.gov

Description: Among other environmental resource duties, maintains a 24 hour emergency spill hotline.

Doyle Childers
Director
Phone: 573-751-4732

Floyd Gilzow
Deputy Director
Phone: 573-522-8796

Scott B Totten
Director, Water Protection & Soil Conservation
Phone: 573-751-5998

Anita Randolph
Director, Energy Center
Phone: 573-751-2254
e-mail: nrjohak@mail.dnr.state.mo.us

Department of Public Safety
Truman Building, Room 870
301 W High Street
Jefferson City, MO 65102-0749
Mailing Address: Po Box 749
Phone: 573-751-4905
Fax: 573-751-5399
URL: www.dps.mo.gov

Mark James
Director
Phone: 573-751-5432

Brian Jamison
Deputy Director
Phone: 573-751-5431

Randy Cole
Fire Marshal
Phone: 573-751-2930
e-mail: randy.cole@dfs.dps.mo.gov

Colonel Rad Talburt
Water Patrol Division, Commissioner
Phone: 573-751-3333

Department of Transportation
105 W Capitol Avenue
Jefferson City, MO 65102
Phone: 888-275-6636
Phone: 573-751-4622
Fax: 573-526-5419
URL: www.modot.org
e-mail: comments@mail.modot.state.mo.us

Peter K Rahn
Director
e-mail: pete.rahn@modot.mo.gov

Kevin Keith
Chief Engineer
e-mail: kevin.keith@modot.mo.gov

Roberta Broeker
Chief Financial Officer
e-mail: roberta.broeker@modot.mo.gov

Emergency Management Agency
2302 Militia Drive
Jefferson, MO 65101
Mailing Address: Po Box 116, 65102
Phone: 573-526-9101
Fax: 573-634-7966
URL: www.sema.dps.mo.gov

Description: Responds to two types of disasters— natural and man-made in order to protect the lives and property of all Missourians when major disasters threaten public safety. SEMA is also responsible for developing a State Emergency Operations Plan which coordinates the actions of Missouri State government departments and agencies.

Ronald M Reynolds
Director
Phone: 573-526-9101
e-mail: ron.reynolds@sema.dps.mo.gov

Duane R Nichols
Deputy Director
Phone: 573-526-9143
e-mail: duane.nichols@sema.dps.mo.gov

Chuck May
Planning, Disaster & Recovery Branch Manager
Phone: 573-526-9112
e-mail: chuck.may@sema.dps.mo.gov

Tom Mohr
Homeland Security Branch Chief
Phone: 573-526-9245
e-mail: tom.mohr@sema.dps.mo.gov

Sheila Huddleston
Hazard Mitigation Specialist
Phone: 573-526-9228
e-mail: sheila.huddleston@sema.dps.mo.gov

Environmental Health & Communicable Disease Prevention Division
Department of Health & Senior Services
PO Box 570
Jefferson City, MO 65102
Phone: 573-751-6080
Fax: 573-526-5348

Brad Hall
Administrator

Mid-America Contingency Planning Forum
PO Box 38112
St. Louis, MO 63138
Phone: 314-466-3509
URL: www.drj.com/groups.mcpf.mcpf
e-mail: robzada@erac.com

Description: Formed in 1994 to serve as a forum to facilitate the exchange and dissemination of information regarding all aspects of contingency planning in both the private and public sectors. This includes business interruption avoidance, business resumption planning, contingency operations and disaster recovery planning. MCPF offers the novice as well as the expert planner the opportunity to share and broaden their knowledge of contingency planning.

Missouri Capitol Police
301 W High Street, Room 101
Jefferson City, MO 65101
Phone: 573-751-2764
Fax: 573-526-3898
URL: www.mcp.dps.mo.gov

Captain Paul Minze
Operations Manager
e-mail: paul.minze@dps.mo.gov

Chief Todd Hurt
Chief of Police
e-mail: todd.hurt@dps.mo.gov

Missouri Police Chiefs Association
1001 E High Street
Jefferson City, MO 65101
Phone: 573-636-5444
Fax: 573-636-6634
URL: www.mopca.com

Sheldon Lineback
Executive Director
e-mail: slineback@mopca.com

Bryan Reid
Training Director
e-mail: breid@mopca.com

Chief Mike Wiegand
President

National Guard
2302 Militia Drive
Jefferson City, MO 65101-1202
Phone: 888-526-6664
Phone: 573-638-9500
Fax: 573-526-9929
URL: www.moguard.com
e-mail: informationmo@mo.ngb.army.mil

Brigadier General King E Sidwell
Adjutant General
Phone: 573-638-9710

Colonel Hal E Hunter
Army Assistant Adjutant General
Phone: 573-638-9500

Maj Gen Steven McCamy
Air Assistant Adjutant General
Phone: 573-638-9714

Colonel Dwight Lusk
Army Chief of Staff
Phone: 573-638-9616

Colonel Craig McCord
Air Chief of Staff
Phone: 573-638-9695

Office of the Chief Medical Examiner
1300 Clark Avenue
St Louis, MO 63103-2718
Phone: 314-622-4971
Fax: 314-622-4933
e-mail: grahamma@slu.edu

Description: Responsible for the investigation of all the deaths which occur as a result of unusual or suspicious circumstances as well as for certain deaths which by law falls under its jurisdiction.

Michael A Graham MD
Medical Examiner

State Highway Patrol
1510 E Elm Street
PO Box 568
Jefferson City, MO 65102
Phone: 573-751-3313
Fax: 573-751-9419
URL: www.mshp.dps.missouri.gov
e-mail: mshppied@mshp.dps.mo.gov

Colonel James F Keathley
Superintendent

Lt. Colonel Richard L Coffey
Assistant Superintendent

Major Ronald K Replogle
Criminal Investigations Bureau, Commander

Major Arthur D Penn
Field Operations Bureau, Commander

Major Robert E Bloomberg
Technical Services Bureau

STATE AGENCIES

Montana

Montana Main Homeland Security Office

Disaster & Emergency Services (DES)
1900 Williams Street
Helena, MT 59604-4789
Mailing Address: PO Box 4789
Phone: 406-841-3911
Fax: 406-841-3965
URL: dma.mt.gov/des/homelandsecurity
e-mail: mtdes@mt.gov

Description: Montana DES takes the lead in homeland security operations and coordinating comprehensive emergency management in the state.

Brian A Scweitzer
Governor
Phone: 406-444-3111

John Bohlinger
Lieutenant Governor
Phone: 406-444-3111

Dan McGowan
Homeland Security Administrator
Phone: 406-841-3911
e-mail: dmcgowan@mt.gov

Mike McGrath
Attorney General
Phone: 406-444-2026

Agriculture Department

303 N Roberts Street
PO Box 200201
Helena, MT 59620-0201
Phone: 406-444-3144
Fax: 404-444-5409
URL: http://agr.state.mt.us/
e-mail: agr@mt.gov

Description: The Department of Agriculture's mission is to protect producers and consumers and develop agriculture and allied industries.

Nancy K Peterson
Director
Phone: 406-444-3144

Tim Meloy
Attorney
Phone: 406-444-3144

Joel A Clairmont
Administrator, Agricultural Development Div.
Phone: 406-444-2402

Lee Boyer
Rural Development Bureau
Phone: 406-444-2402

Kimberly Falcon
Wheat & Barley Bureau
Phone: 406-761-7732

Craig Essebaggers
State Grain Lab Bureau
Phone: 406-452-9561

Gregory H Ames
Administrator, Agricultural Sciences Div.
Phone: 406-444-2944

Heidi Hickes
Laboratory Bureau
Phone: 406-444-3383

Daniel Sullivan
Technical Services Bureau
Phone: 406-444-5400

Disaster and Emergency Services (DES)

1900 Williams Street
PO Box 4789
Fort Harrison, MT 59636-4789
Phone: 406-841-3911
Fax: 406-841-3965
URL: http://dma.mt.gov/des/

Dan McGowan
Administrator
Phone: 406-841-3911
e-mail: dmcgowan@mt.gov

Dan Lieberg
Deputy Administrator
Phone: 406-841-3959
e-mail: dlieberg@mt.gov

Steve Knecht
Response Branch
Phone: 406-841-3961
e-mail: sknecht@mt.gov

Sheri Lanz
Homeland Security Branch Director
Phone: 406-841-3969
e-mail: sheris@mt.gov

Monique Lay
Public Information Officer
Phone: 406-841-3963
e-mail: mlay@mt.gov

Division of Criminal Investigation
303 N Roberts, 3rd Floor
PO Box 201417
Helena, MT 59620-1417
Phone: 406-444-3874
Fax: 406-444-2759
URL:
www.doj.state.mt.us/department/criminalinvestigationdivision.asp
e-mail: contactdoj@mt.gov

Description: The Division of Criminal Investigation (DCI) provides direct assistance to federal, state, and local public safety agencies.

Mike Batista
Administrator
Phone: 406-444-3874
e-mail: contactdoj@mt.gov

John Strandell
Investigations Bureau
Phone: 406-444-3874

Allen Lorenz
State Fire Marshal, Fire Prevention & Investigation
Phone: 406-444-2050

Epidemiology & Communicable Disease
Public Health and Human Services
1400 Broadway
Room C216
Helena, MT 59620
Phone: 406-444-4542
Fax: 406-444-1861
URL: www.dphhs.state.mt.us

Kathleen McCarthy
Bureau Chief, Communicable Disease Control
Phone: 406-444-4735

Dr Todd Damrow
State Epidemiologist/Section Supervisor
Phone: 406-444-3986

Highway Patrol Division
2550 Prospect Avenue
PO Box 201419
Helena, MT 59620-1419
Phone: 406-444-3780
Fax: 406-444-4169
URL: www.doj.state.mt.us/enforcement/highwaypatrol.asp
e-mail: mhphqcontact@mt.gov

Description: Responsible for managing highway traffic safety in the state.

Colonel Paul K Grimstad
Chief Administrator
Phone: 406-444-3780

Military Affairs Department
PO Box 4789
Fort Harrison, MT 59636-4789
Phone: 406-324-3000
Fax: 406-324-3205
URL: www.dma.mt.gov

Description: Oversees all activities in the Army and Air National Guard and Disaster and Emergnecy Services Division. Also plans for and coordinates state response in disaster and emergency situations.

Maj Gen Randall D Mosley
Adjutant General
Phone: 406-324-3000

Dan McGowan
Disaster & Emergency Services Division
Phone: 406-841-3953

Colonel Kevin Kepler
State Aviation Officer
Phone: 406-841-3033

Brig Gen Rex Tanberg
Air Chief of Staff

Colonel Stan R Putnam
Army Chief of Staff
Phone: 406-324-3000

John B Wheeler
Environmental Office Manager
Phone: 406-324-3080

Colonel Allan V Stricker
Facilities Management
Phone: 406-324-3101

Colonel John Christiansen
Logistics Manager
Phone: 406-324-3401

Colonel Peter Mohan
Plans/Operations/Training Officer
Phone: 406-324-3200

Lieutenant Colonel Hank Adams
Senior Army Advisor
Phone: 406-324-3385

Major Scott Smith
Public Affairs Officer
Phone: 406-324-3009

Montana Association of Chiefs of Police
PO Box 275
Great Falls, MT 59403
Phone: 406-454-9091
URL: www.macop.com
e-mail: info@macop.com

Description: A professional and philanthropic group of police administrators from across the state, providing training and peer support in an effort to maintain professional standards.

Troy McGee
President

Natural Resources and Conservation Department
1625 11th Avenue
PO Box 201601
Helena, MT 59620-1601
Phone: 406-444-2074
Fax: 406-444-2684
URL: http://dnrc.mt.gov
e-mail: dabushnell@mt.gov

Description: Ensures Montana's land and water resources provide benefits for present and future generations. The department is responsible for sustaining and improving the benefits derived from the water, soil and rangeland.

Mary Sexton
Director
Phone: 406-444-2074

Donald MacIntyre
Chief Legal Counsel
Phone: 406-444-6699

Susan Cottingham
Reserved Water Rights Compact Commission Program Manager
Phone: 406-444-6716
e-mail: scottingham@state.mt.us

Office of the Chief Medical Officer
2679 Palmer Street
Missoula, MT 59808
Phone: 406-728-4970
Fax: 406-549-1067

Gary Dale, M.D.
State Medical Examiner
e-mail: gdale@state.mt.us

Terry Bullis
Secretary/Treasurer
Phone: 406-665-1207

Oil and Gas Conservation Division
Natural Resources and Conservation Department
2535 St. John's Avenue
Billings, MT 59102
Phone: 406-656-0040
Fax: 406-655-6015
URL: http://bogc.dnrc.mt.gov/default.asp

Tom Richmond
Administrator
Phone: 406-656-0040

Public Health and Human Services
111 N Sanders
Helena, MT 59604
Mailing Address: PO Box 4210
Phone: 406-444-5622
Fax: 406-444-1970
URL: www.dphhs.mt.gov

Description: Improve and protect the health, well-being and self-reliance of all Montanans.

Joan Miles
Director
Phone: 406-444-5622

John Chappuis
Deputy Director
Phone: 406-444-4084

Gayle Shirley
Public Information Officer
Phone: 406-444-2596

Vicki Turner
Prevention Resource Center Director
Phone: 406-444-3484

Russ Cater
Chief Legal Counsel
Phone: 406-444-5626

Lou Thompson
Mental Health Services Bureau Chief
Phone: 406-444-9657

Public Service Commission
1701 Prospect Avenue, Vista Building
PO Box 202601
Helena, MT 59620-2601
Phone: 406-444-6199
Fax: 406-444-7618
URL: www.psc.state.mt.us

Greg Jergeson
Chairman
Phone: 406-444-6166
e-mail: gjergson@mt.gov

Brad Molnar
Commissioner
Phone: 406-444-6165
e-mail: bmolnar@mt.gov

Bob Raney
Commissioner
Phone: 406-444-6168
e-mail: braney@mt.gov

Ken Toole
Commissioner
Phone: 406-444-6169
e-mail: ktoole@mt.gov

Doug Mood
Vice Chairman
Phone: 404-444-6167
e-mail: dmood@mt.gov

Robin McHugh
Legal Administrator
Phone: 406-444-6376
e-mail: Rmchugh@mt.gov

Kate Whitney
Utility Division, Administrator
Phone: 406-444-3056
e-mail: kwhitney@mt.gov

Safety and Health Bureau
1805 Prospect Avenue
PO Box 1728
Helena, MT 59624-1728
Phone: 406-444-1605
URL: http://erd.dli.mt.gov/safetyhealth/sbhome.asp

Description: Aims to raise the level of awareness of Montana employers and employees about workplace safety and health through inspection, consultation, technical assistance and training.

Chris Catlett
Bureau Chief

Phone: 406-444-1605
e-mail: ccatlett@mt.gov

Ron Umscheid
Mine Safety Supervisor
Phone: 406-444-6419
e-mail: rumscheid@mt.gov

Sandra Mihalik
Occupational Safety and Health Supervisor
Phone: 406-444-6418
e-mail: smihalik@mt.gov

Transportation Department
2701 Prospect Avenue
PO Box 201001
Helena, MT 59620-1001
Phone: 406-444-6200
Fax: 406-444-7643
URL: www.mdt.mt.gov
e-mail: mdtquestion@mt.gov

Description: Providing a transportation system and services that emphasize safety, quality, cost effectiveness, economic vitality and sensitivity to the environment.

Jim Lynch
Director
Phone: 406-444-6201
e-mail: jilynch@mt.gov

Jim Currie
Deputy Director
Phone: 406-444-6201
e-mail: jcurrie@mt.gov

Charity Watts Levis
Public Information Officer
Phone: 406-444-7205
e-mail: cwattlevis@mt.gov

Tim Reardon
Legal Services
Phone: 406-444-7277
e-mail: treardon@mt.gov

Monte Brown
Administration
Phone: 406-444-6023
e-mail: mobrown@mt.gov

Debbie Alkie
Aeronautics Administrator
Phone: 406-444-7569
e-mail: dalke@mt.gov

Loran Frazier
Engineering Administrator
Phone: 406-444-6002
e-mail: lfrazier@mt.gov

Dennis Sheehy
Motor Carrier Services
Phone: 406-444-7638
e-mail: dsheehy@mt.gov

Sandra Straehl
Rail/Transit/Planning
Phone: 406-444-3423
e-mail: sstraehl@mt.gov

Priscilla Sinclair
State Hwy Traffic Safety Officer
Phone: 406-444-7417
e-mail: psinclair@mt.gov

Water Resources Division
Natural Resources and Conservation Department
1424 Ninth Avenue
PO Box 201601
Helena, MT 59620-1601
Phone: 406-444-6601
Fax: 406-444-5918
URL: http://dnrc.mt.gov/wrd/default.asp

John Tubbs
Administrator
Phone: 406-444-6601
e-mail: jtubbs@mt.gov

Terri McLaughlin
Water Rights Bureau Chief
Phone: 406-444-6631
e-mail: tmclaughlin@mt.gov

Kevin Smith
Water Projects Bureau Chief
Phone: 406-444-2932
e-mail: ksmith@mt.gov

Rich Moy
Water Management Bureau Chief
Phone: 406-444-6633
e-mail: rmoy@mt.gov

Laurence Siroky
Water Operations Bureau Chief
Phone: 406-444-6816
e-mail: lsiroky@mt.gov

STATE AGENCIES

Nebraska

Nebraska Main Homeland Security Office
PO Box 94848
Lincoln, NE 68509
Phone: 402-471-2256
Fax: 402-471-6031
URL: www.nema.ne.gov

David Heineman
Governor
Phone: 402-471-2244

Rick Sheehy
Lieutenant Governor/Director Homeland Security
Phone: 402-471-2256

Jon C Bruning
Attorney General
Phone: 402-471-2682

Aeronautics Department
3431 Aviation Road
Suite 150
Lincoln, NE 68524
Mailing Address: PO Box 82088
Phone: 402-471-2371
Fax: 402-471-2906
URL: www.aero.state.ne.us
e-mail: contact@aero.ne.gov

Description: The Aeronautics Department facilitates the advancement of aviation in Nebraska.

Stuart MacTaggart
Director
Phone: 402-471-7922

Bill Lyon
Flight Operations Manager
Phone: 402-471-2371
e-mail: blyon@mail.state.ne.us

Andre Aman
Legal Counsel
Phone: 402-471-7938
e-mail: aaman@mail.state.ne.us

Anna Lannin
Planning & Programming Division Manager
Phone: 402-471-7931
e-mail: alannin@mail.state.ne.us

Russ Gasper
Project Management Division Manager
Phone: 402-471-7700
e-mail: rgasper@mail.state.ne.us

Agriculture Department
301 Centennial Mall South
PO Box 94947
Lincoln, NE 68509-4947
Phone: 402-471-2341
Phone: 800-831-0550
Fax: 402-471-6876
URL: www.agr.state.ne.us/

Description: The safety and security of agriculture has been designated as high priority by the Nebraska Department of Agriculture, thus it is determined to be prepared to provide the necessary guidance, training and leadership to protect its number one industry. Their efforts include working with state and Federal partners to implement a State Homeland Security Plan, expanding the emergency response plan to include food and agriculture, and providing statewide training to officials and emergency manager concerning agricultural emergencies and related responces.

Greg Ibach
Director
Phone: 402-471-2341

Denis Blank
Chief Administrator
Phone: 402-471-2341
e-mail: denisnb@agr.state.ne.us

Chris Shubert
Legal Counsel
Phone: 402-471-2341

Christin Kamm
Public Information Officer
Phone: 402-471-6856

Tom Jensen
Agricultural Laboratories Division
Phone: 402-471-2176

Dan Borer
Bureau of Dairies & Foods
Phone: 402-471-2536

Susan Joy
Poultry & Egg Division Manager
Phone: 402-472-2051

Rich Reiman
Plant Industry Division Administrator
Phone: 402-471-2394

Chief Medical Officer
PO Box 95007
Lincoln, NE 68509
Phone: 402-471-8566

Dr Joann Schaefer
Chief Medical Officer
Phone: 402-471-8566

Emergency Management Agency

1300 Military Road
Lincoln, NE 68508-1090
Phone: 402-471-7430
Phone: 402-471-7421
Fax: 402-471-7433
URL: www.nema.ne.gov

Description: The agency serves as the nerve center for emergency management in the state of Nebraska. The Homeland Security initiative is designed to develop, coordinate and implement a comprehensive strategy for the protection of the citizens of Nebraska from attacks using weapons of mass destruction - chemical, biological and nuclear.

Major General Roger Lempke
Director/Adjutant General
Phone: 402-309-7100
e-mail: roger.lempke@ne.ngb.army.mil

Al Berndt
Assistant Director
Phone: 402-471-7410
e-mail: al.berndt@nema.ne.gov

Jim Bunstock
Public Information Officer
Phone: 402-471-7428
e-mail: jim.bunstock@nema.ne.gov

Bryan Cook
Radiological Emergency Preparedness Planner
Phone: 402-471-7213
e-mail: bryan.cook@nema.ne.gov

Lori Moore
Hazard Mitigation Officer
Phone: 402-471-7416
e-mail: lori.moore@nema.ne.gov

Cindy Newsham
Supervisor, Response & Recovery Division
Phone: 402-471-7415
e-mail: cindy.newsham@nema.ne.gov

Mardell Hergenrader
Supervisor, Preparedness Division
Phone: 402-471-7413
e-mail: mardell.hergenrader@nema.ne.gov

Brent Curtis
Response & Recovery Planner
Phone: 402-471-7426
e-mail: brent.curtis@nema.ne.gov

Bob Eastwood
Communications Officer
Phone: 402-471-7417
e-mail: bob.eastwood@nema.ne.gov

Emergency Medical Services Program

PO Box 95007
Lincoln, NE 68509-5007
Phone: 402-471-2133
URL: www.hhs.state.ne.us/ems/emsindex.htm

Description: To strengthen emergency care through cooperative partnerships to promote the well being of the citizens of Nebraska and those who live and work in the State.

Dean Cole
Program Administrator
Phone: 402-471-0124
e-mail: dean.cole@hhss.ne.gov

Sherri Wren
EMS Trauma Manager
Phone: 402-471-0539
e-mail: sherri.wren@hhss.ne.gov

Garry Steele
Education & Training Coordinator
Phone: 402-224-3298
e-mail: garry.steele@hhss.ne.gov

Environmental Quality Department

1200 N Street, Suite 400
PO Box 98922
Lincoln, NE 68509-8922
Phone: 402-471-2186
Fax: 402-471-2909
URL: www.deq.state.ne.us
e-mail: moreinfo@ndeq.state.ne.us

Description: Protects Nebraska's air, land and water resources.

Mike Linder
Director
Phone: 402-471-2186

Tom Lamberson
Administrative Deputy Director
Phone: 402-471-2186

Jay Ringenberg
Programs Deputy Director
Phone: 402-471-4231

Annette Kovar
Legal Services
Phone: 402-471-3585

Brian McManus
Public Information Office
Phone: 402-471-4223

Shelley Kaderly
Air Division
Phone: 402-471-0001

David Haldeman
Waste Division
Phone: 402-471-0001

Patrick Rice
Water Division
Phone: 402-471-3098

Marty Link
Water Division
Phone: 402-471-3098

Joe Francis
Environmental Assistance
Phone: 402-471-6974

Dennis Burling
Information Technology
Phone: 402-471-4214

Great Plains Contingency Planners
PO Box 34773
Omaha, NE 68134
Phone: 402-496-8280
e-mail: mowings@worldinsco.com

Description: An organization of business continuity professionals in the Midwest with a commitment to leadership and professionalism. We accomplish this by providing an organized environment for exchange of information, networking and continuing education for all professionals.

Melissa Owings
President

Health & Human Services, Epidemiology
PO Box 95007
Lincoln, NE 68509-5007
Phone: 402-471-6450
URL: www.hhs.state.ne.us/epi/epiindex.htm

Dennis Leschinsky
Health Surveillance Specialist
e-mail: dennis.leschinsky@hhss.ne.gov

Health and Human Services System
PO Box 95044
Lincoln, NE 68509-5044
Phone: 402-471-2306
Phone: 402-471-3121
Fax: 402-471-9449
URL: www.hhs.state.ne.us/

Scot Adams
Health & Human Services Director
Phone: 402-471-3121

Jackie Miller
Deputy Director Health Services
Phone: 402-471-6042

Vivian Chaumont
Director, Finance & Support
Phone: 402-471-8553

Chris Peterson
CEO
Phone: 402-471-9433

Joann Schaefer
Director, Regulation & Licensure

Bob Leopold
Interim Dep Dir Regulation & Licensure
Phone: 402-471-2541

National Guard
1300 Military Road
Lincoln, NE 68508
Phone: 402-309-7210
Fax: 402-309-7235
URL: www.neguard.com
e-mail: ngnej6webmaster@ng.army.mil

Description: Nebraska Military protection consists of members of the Nebraska Army and Air National Guard located in units across the state.

Major General Roger P Lempke
Adjutant General/ Emergency Management Director
Phone: 402-309-7100
e-mail: roger.lempke@us.army.mil

Maj Gen Mark Musick
Air Assistant Adjutant General
Phone: 402-309-7102

BGen William Kuehn
Army Assistant Adjutant General
Phone: 402-309-7101

Colonel Thomas Schuurmans
Army, Chief of Staff
Phone: 402-309-7113

BGen Randall Scott
Air Chief of Staff
Phone: 402-309-1111

Captain Kevin Hynes
Public Information Officer
Phone: 402-309-7302
e-mail: kevin.hynes@us.army.mil

Natural Resources Department
PO Box 94676
301 Centennial Mall South
Lincoln, NE 68509-4676
Phone: 402-471-2363
Fax: 402-471-2900
URL: www.dnr.ne.gov

Ann S Bleed
Director
Phone: 402-471-2366
e-mail: ableed@dnr.ne.gov

Brian Dunnigan
Dep Dir Head, Floodplain/Dam Safety Div
Phone: 402-471-3934
e-mail: bdunnigan@dnr.ne.gov

Steve Gaul
Div Head, Natural Resources Planning & Assistance
Phone: 402-471-3955
e-mail: sgaul@dnr.ne.gov

Ron Theis
Legal Counsel
Phone: 402-471-2363
e-mail: rtheis@dnr.ne.gov

Rex Gittins
Division Management Services Director
Phone: 402-471-1767
e-mail: rgittins@dnr.ne.gov

Mike Thompson
Division Manager Permits/Registrations
Phone: 402-471-0587
e-mail: mthompson@dnr.ne.gov

Oil and Gas Conservation Commission
922 Illinois Street

Sidney, NE 69162
Mailing Address: PO Box 399
Phone: 308-254-6919
Fax: 308-254-6922
URL: www.nogcc.ne.gov

Description: Fosters, encourages and promotes the development, production and utilization of natural resources of oil and gas in the state.

William H Sydow
Director
Phone: 308-254-6919

Chuck Borcher
Information Technology Infrastructure Support Technician
Phone: 308-254-6919
e-mail: cborcher@nogcc.ne.gov

Stan Belieu
Staff Petroleum Engineer
Phone: 308-254-6919
e-mail: sbelieu@nogcc.ne.gov

Reed Gilmore
Commissioner

Thomas Sonntag
Commissioner

James R Gohl
Commissioner

Power Review Board
301 Centennial Mall South
Lincoln, NE 68509-4713
Mailing Address: PO Box 94713
Phone: 402-471-2301
Fax: 402-471-3715
URL: www.nprb.state.ne.us

Description: Nebraska is the only state in the country that is served entirely by publicly owned power entities. The Power Review Board regulates the publicly owned electrical utility industry.

Timothy J Texel
Executive Director/General Counsel

Carol Behne
Business Manager

Sara Hayek
Paralegal

Public Health Association
1321 South 37th Street
Lincoln, NE 68510
Phone: 402-483-1039
Fax: 402-483-0570
URL: www.publichealthne.org
e-mail: publichealthne@cs.com

Description: Exists to protect and promote personal, community and environmental health throughout a variety of public health networks. The organization exercises leadership in public health policy development and advocacy, provides a forum for the discussion of emerging public health issues, and enhances the professional growth of members and other health professionals across the state.

Jeff Soukup
President
e-mail: jeff.soukup@hhss.ne.gov

Shirley Terry
Secretary
e-mail: shirley.terry@hhss.state.ne.us

Public Service Commission
1200 North Street, Suite 300
Lincoln, NE 68508
Phone: 402-471-3101
Phone: 800-526-0017
Fax: 402-471-0254
URL: www.psc.state.ne.us

Andy Pollock
Executive Director
e-mail: andy.pollock@psc.ne.gov

John Burvainis
Deputy Director
e-mail: john.burvainis@psc.ne.gov

Gerald Vap
Chairman/Commissioner
e-mail: jerry.vap@psc.ne.gov

Anne C Boyle
Commissioner
e-mail: anne.boyle@psc.ne.gov

Rod Johnson
Commissioner
e-mail: rod.johnson@psc.ne.gov

Frank E Landis Jr
Commissioner
e-mail: frank.landis@psc.ne.gov

M Gene Hand
Communications Director
Phone: 402-471-0244
e-mail: gene.hand@psc.ne.gov

Roads Department
PO Box 94759
Lincoln, NE 68509
Phone: 402-471-4567
Fax: 402-479-4325
URL: www.dor.state.ne.us

John L Craig
Director
Phone: 402-479-4615
e-mail: jcraig@dor.state.ne.us

Mary Jo Hall
Communications Division
Phone: 402-479-4512
e-mail: mjhall@dor.state.ne.us

Tom Sands
Operations Division Manager
Phone: 402-479-4339
e-mail: tsands@dor.state.ne.us

Ellis Tompkins
Rail & Public Transportation Division

Phone: 402-479-4785
e-mail: etompkin@dor.state.ne.us

State Fire Marshal's Office
246 S 14th Street
Lincoln, NE 68508-1804
Phone: 402-471-2027
Fax: 402-471-3118
URL: www.sfm.state.ne.us

John Falgione
State Fire Marshal
Phone: 402-471-2027

Jack Malicky
Investigations Division Chief
Phone: 402-471-9663
e-mail: jack.malicky@sfm.ne.gov

Clark Conklin
Chief of Fuels Safety Division
Phone: 402-471-9467
e-mail: clark.conklin@sfm.ne.gov

Thomas Barrett
Legal Counsel
Phone: 402-471-9477
e-mail: tom.barrett@sfm.ne.gov

Joe Hanson
Manager, Training Division
Phone: 308-385-6892
e-mail: joe.hanson@sfm.ne.gov

State Patrol
PO Box 94907
Lincoln, NE 68509-4907
Phone: 402-471-4545
URL: www.nsp.state.ne.us

Description: Nebraska's only state-wide full-service law enforcement agency, since 1937. The State Patrol works with communities to improve public safety, enforce traffic and drug laws, investigate crimes, and enforce laws and regulations related to motor carriers.

Colonel Bryan Tuma
Superintendent

Lt Colonel Darrell Fisher
Assistant Superintendent

Major Dave Sankey
Investigative Services Division

Major A K Anderson
Field Services Division

STATE AGENCIES

Nevada

Nevada Main Homeland Security Office

2478 Fairview Drive
Carson City, NV 89711
Phone: 775-687-0300
Fax: 775-687-6788
URL: www.homelandsecurity.nv.gov
e-mail: gwenhadd@dhs.nv.gov

Jim Gibbons
Governor
Phone: 775-684-5670
e-mail: governor@govl.state.nv.us

Brian Krollicki
Lieutenant Governor
Phone: 775-684-7111

Phil Galeoto
Homeland Security Director
e-mail: pgaleoto@dps.state.nv.us

Cortez Masto
Attorney General
Phone: 775-684-1100

Agriculture Department

350 Capitol Hill Avenue
Reno, NV 89502-2923
Phone: 775-688-1180
Fax: 775-688-1178
URL: http://agri.state.nv.us

Donna Rise
Director
Phone: 775-688-1180

Rick Gimlin
Deputy Director
Phone: 775-688-1182
e-mail: rgimlin@agri.state.nv.us

John O'Brien
Plant Industry Division
Phone: 775-688-1182

Steven Grabski
Weights & Measures Bureau
Phone: 775-688-1166
e-mail: sgrabski@agri.state.nv.us

Roger Works
Animal Industry Bureau/State Veterinarian
Phone: 775-688-1182

Conservation and Natural Resources Department

901 South Stewart Street
Suite 5001
Carson City, NV 89701
Phone: 775-684-2700
Fax: 775-684-2715

Allen Biaggi
Director
Phone: 775-684-2700

Kay Scherer
Assistant Director
Phone: 775-684-2700

Leo Drozdoff
Environmental Protection Division
Phone: 775-687-4670

Tracy Taylor
State Engineer
Phone: 775-684-2800

Dave Morrow
State Parks Division
Phone: 775-684-2770

Pete Anderson
State Forester, Division of Forestry
Phone: 775-684-2500

Division of Emergency Management

2478 Fairview Drive
Carson City, NV 89701
Phone: 775-687-0300
Fax: 775-687-0322
URL: www.dem.state.nv.us

Description: A division of the Department of Public Safety, it is the lead state agency for coordination of emergency and disaster response activities.

Frank Siracusa
Division Chief
Phone: 775-687-0300
e-mail: fsiracusa@dps.state.nv.us

Pete Reinschmidt
Emergency Management Operations Officer
Phone: 775-687-0305
e-mail: preinschmidt@dps.state.nv.us

Elizabeth Ashby
State Hazard Mitigations Officer

Phone: 775-687-0314
e-mail: eashby@dps.state.nv.us

Gary Derks
State Search & Rescue Coordinator
Phone: 775-687-0310
e-mail: gderks@dps.state.nv.us

Highway Patrol
555 Wright Way
Carson City, NV 89711
Phone: 775-684-4867
URL: www.nhp.nv.gov

Description: To promote safety on Nevada highways by providing law enforcement traffic services to the motoring public.

Colonel Chris Perry
Chief
Phone: 775-684-4478
e-mail: cperry@dps.state.nv.us

Major Brian Sanchez
Deputy Chief
Phone: 775-684-4936
e-mail: bsanchez@dps.state.nv.us

Trooper Dean Reynolds
Information Technology Section
Phone: 775-684-4902
e-mail: dreynolds@dps.state.nv.us

Medical Examiner's Office
1704 Pinto Lane
Las Vegas, NV 89106
Phone: 702-455-3210
Fax: 702-455-0416

P Michael Murphy
Coroner

John Fudenberg
Assistant Coroner

National Guard
2460 Fairview Drive
Carson City, NV 89701
Phone: 775-887-7390
Phone: 775-884-8434
Fax: 775-884-8443
URL: www.nv.ngb.army.mil/

Brigadier General Cindy Kirkland
Adjutant General

Brigadier General Frank Gonzales
Commander, Army Guard
e-mail: francis.gonzales@us.army.mil

CSM Stephen Sitton
State Command Sergeant Major, Army
e-mail: stephen.sitton@us.army.mil

Brigadier General Michael Gullihur
Air Guard Headquarters Staff

CMS John Ternau
State Command Chief, Air Guard

First Lt April Conway
Public Affairs Officer
Phone: 775-887-7252
e-mail: april.conway@nvreno.ang.af.mil

Nevada Sheriffs & Chiefs Association
PO Box 3247
Mesquite, NV 89024
Phone: 866-266-9870
Fax: 702-345-3565

Frank Adams
Executive Director
e-mail: fadams@cascadeaccess.com

Tony DeMeo
President
Phone: 702-649-9111

Nevada Site Office/US Department of Energy (NNSA)
PO Box 98518
Las Vegas, NV 89193-8518
Phone: 702-295-3521
Fax: 702-295-2383
URL: www.nv.doe.gov

Jay Norman
Director

Office of Emergency Medical Services
4150 Technology Way
Suite 200
Carson City, NV 89706
Phone: 775-687-7590
Fax: 775-684-7595
URL: http://health.nv.gov

Description: Promotes and supports a system that provides prompt, efficient and appropriate emergency medical care, ambulance transportation and trauma care to the people of Nevada.

Fergus Laughridge
Director
e-mail: flaughridge@health.nv.gov

Bob Heath
Education Coordinator
e-mail: bheath@health.nv.gov

Office of Epidemiology
State Health Division
505 East King Street
Room 204
Carson City, NV 89701
Phone: 775-684-4200
Fax: 775-684-5999
URL: http://health.nv.gov/

Description: Conducts disease surveillance, investigates disease outbreaks and initiates control activities. In order to carry out its mission, the office records and analyzes reportable disease information, refers individuals for medical treatment, analyzes data from disease investigations, conducts interviews with infected individuals, works in conjunction with appropriate agencies to enforce communicable disease laws and provides education and recommendations on disease prevention.

Ihsan Azzam MD, MPH
State Epidemiologist
Phone: 775-684-5934

Public Health Preparedness
State Health Division
4150 Technology Way
Ste 200
Carson City, NV 89706
Phone: 775-684-4013
Fax: 775-684-5951
URL: http://health2k.state.nv.us/php

Description: Assists Nevada's public health infrastructure through: early detection of threats to public health; response to natural and human-caused events; and prevention of disease, injury and disability.

Heidi Sakelarios
Public Health Preparedness Coordinator
Phone: 775-684-4212
e-mail: hsakelarios@nvhd.state.nv.us

Pamela Forest
Health Alert Network Coordinator

Robin Williams-Auer
Public Information Officer

Public Safety Department
555 Wright Way
Carson City, NV 89711-0900
Phone: 775-684-4808
Fax: 775-684-4809
URL: http://dps.nv.gov

Description: Provides services in support of protecting our citizens and visitors by promoting safer communities through prevention, preparedness, response, recovery, education and enforcement.

Phil Galeoto
Director
Phone: 775-684-4808
e-mail: pgaleoto@dps.state.nv.us

John H Douglas
Investigations Chief
e-mail: nding@dps.state.nv.us

Brad Valladon
Capitol Police Chief
Phone: 775-684-4542
e-mail: bvalladon@dps.state.nv.us

Chris Perry
Highway Patrol Division
Phone: 775-684-4867

Frank Siracusa
Emergency Management Division
Phone: 775-687-4240
e-mail: fsiracusa@dps.state.nv.us

Jim Wright
Fire Marshal
Phone: 775-684-7505
e-mail: jwright@dps.state.nv.us

Public Utilities Commission
1150 E William Street
Carson City, NV 89701-3109
Phone: 775-684-6101
Fax: 775-684-6110
URL: www.puc.state.nv.us

Donald L Soderberg
Chairman
Phone: 775-684-6107

Jo Ann P Kelly
Commissioner
Phone: 775-684-6107

Rebecca Wagner
Commissioner
Phone: 775-684-6107

Craig Steele
Safety & Quality Assurance Division
Phone: 775-687-6146
e-mail: csteele@puc.state.nv.us

State Health Division
4150 Technology Way
Ste 300
Carson City, NV 89706
Phone: 775-684-4200
Fax: 775-684-4211
URL: www.health.nv.gov/

Description: Guided by the State Board of Health to promote and protect the health of all Nevadans and visitors to the state through leadership and enforcement of laws and regulations pertaining to public health.

Alex Haartz
Administrator
Phone: 775-684-4200

Deborah McBride
Bureau of Community Health
Phone: 775-684-5996
e-mail: dmcbride@health.nv.gov

Stan Marshall
Bureau of Health Protection Services
Phone: 775-687-7530
e-mail: smarshall@health.nv.gov

Luana Ritch
Bureau of Health Planning & Statistics
Phone: 775-684-4242
e-mail: lritch@health.nv.gov

Lisa Jones
Bureau of Licensure & Certification
Phone: 775-687-4475
e-mail: ljones@health.nv.gov

Judith Wright
Bureau of Family Health Services
Phone: 775-684-4285
e-mail: jwright@health.nv.gov

Martha Framsted
Public Information Officer
Phone: 775-684-4014
e-mail: mframsted@health.nv.gov

John Flamm
Education & Information Officer
Phone: 775-684-4221
e-mail: jflamm@health.nv.gov

Transportation Department
1263 S Stewart Street
Carson City, NV 89712
Phone: 775-888-7000
Fax: 775-888-7115
URL: www.nevadadot.com
e-mail: info@dot.state.nv.us

Description: Responsible for the planning, construction, operation and maintenance of the nearly 1,000 bridges and 5,400 miles of highway making up the state highway system as well as travel by rail, bike, air or bus.

Susan Martinovich
Director
Phone: 775-888-7440

R Scott Rawlins
Deputy Director
Phone: 775-888-7440

Gary Phillips
Flight Operations
Phone: 775-888-7510

Joe Ward
Legal Division
Phone: 775-888-7420

Scott Magruder
Public Information Officer
Phone: 775-888-7777

Mark Elicegui
Bridge Division
Phone: 775-888-7542

Frederick Droes
Safety Engineering
Phone: 775-888-7468

STATE AGENCIES

New Hampshire

New Hampshire Main Homeland Security Office
222 Sheep Davis Rd
Concord, NH 03301
Mailing Address: 33 Hazen Drive, Concord, NH 03305
Phone: 603-271-2231
Phone: 603-271-6911
Fax: 603-223-3609
URL: www.nhoem.state.nh.us

Description: To protect the lives and environment of the people of New Hampshire from the threat or occurence of emergencies resulting from any man-made or natural disaster, including but not limited to flood, fire, epidemic, terrorism and technological incidents. The preparation for and carrying out of all emergency functions shall be accomplished through four phases of emergency management: mitigation, preparedness, response and recovery. Actvities to meet this end include training, planning, coordination, exercises, drills and financial assistance.

John H Lynch
Governor
Phone: 603-271-2121

William M Gardner
Secretary of State
Phone: 603-271-3242

Christopher M Pope
Director Homeland Security/Emergency Management
Phone: 603-271-6911

Kelly A Ayotte
Attorney General
Phone: 603-271-1202
e-mail: kelly.ayotte@doj.nh.gov

Agriculture, Markets and Food Department
25 Capitol Street, 2nd Fl
State House Annex
Concord, NH 03301
Mailing Address: PO Box 2042, 03302
Phone: 603-271-3551
Fax: 603-271-1109
URL: www.state.nh.us/agric
e-mail: spaul@agr.state.nh.us

Description: To promote agriculture in the public interest and to serve farmers and consumers in the marketplace. The department assures safe and healthy food supplies, provides accurate information on prices and availability of farm commodities and crops and develops markets for the state's farmers.

Stephen H Taylor
Commissioner
Phone: 603-271-3551
e-mail: staylor@agr.state.nh.us

Gail McWilliam Jellie
Agriculture Development Director
Phone: 603-271-3788
e-mail: gmcwilliam@agr.state.nh.us

Stephen K Crawford
Animal Industry Division/State Veterinarian
Phone: 603-271-2404
e-mail: scrawford@agr.state.nh.us

Richard B Uncles
Director, Regulatory Services Division
Phone: 603-271-3685
e-mail: runcles@agr.state.nh.us

Wendelyn Chapley
Pesticide Control Division Director
Phone: 603-271-3550
e-mail: pesticides@agr.state.nh.us

Thomas Durkis
Plant Industry Division/State Entomologist
Phone: 603-271-2561
e-mail: tdurkis@agr.state.nh.us

Richard Cote
Weights & Measures Bureau Supervisor
Phone: 603-271-3709
e-mail: rcote@agr.state.nh.us

Bureau of Emergency Medical Services
Department of Safety
33 Hazen Drive
Concord, NH 03305-0003
Phone: 603-271-4568
Fax: 603-271-4567
URL: www.state.nh.us/safety/ems

Description: To disseminate public education and information relative to Emergency Medical Services (EMS) and the Statewide Trauma System. The Bureau is responsible for managing the training, testing and licensing of EMS providers, units, instructors, training agencies, EMS dispatchers and vehicles. It is also responsible for facilitating the establishment and maintenance of a communications network that includes EMS units, local, county and state agencies and healthcare facilities.

Suzanne Prentiss
Bureau Chief
Phone: 603-271-4568
e-mail: sprentiss@safety.state.nh.us

William Wood
Preparedness Coordinator
Phone: 603-271-2661
e-mail: bwood@safety.state.nh.us

Department of Health & Human Services

129 Pleasant Street
Brown Building
Concord, NH 03301-3857
Phone: 603-271-8140
Phone: 800-852-3345
Fax: 603-271-4912
URL: www.dhhs.state.nh.us

Description: Designed to provide a comprehensive and coordinated system of services that promotes and protects the health, safety and well-being of New Hampshire citizens. Programs are directed at supporting families, strengthening communities and developing the independence and self-sufficiency of New Hampshire citizens.

John A Stephen
Commissioner
Phone: 603-271-4334

Nicholas Toumpas
Deputy Commissioner
Phone: 603-271-8835

Mary Ann Cooney
Public Health Services Director
Phone: 603-271-4501

Department of Safety

33 Hazen Drive
JH Hayes Safety Building
Concord, NH 03305
Phone: 603-271-2791
Fax: 603-271-3903
URL: www.state.nh.us/safety

John Barthelmes
Commissioner
Phone: 603-271-2791

Earl M Sweeney
Assistant Commissioner
Phone: 603-271-2559

Suzanne Prentiss
Emergency Medical Services
Phone: 603-271-4568

Richard Mason
Fire Standards & Training/Emergency Medical Standards
Phone: 603-271-2661
e-mail: rmason@safety.state.nh.us

David T Barrett
Safety Services Division
Phone: 603-293-0091

Colonel Frederick H Booth
State Police Division
Phone: 603-271-2575

Emergency Management Bureau

33 Hazen Drive
Concord, NH 03305

Phone: 603-271-2231
Phone: 800-852-3792
Fax: 603-225-7341
URL: www.nhoem.state.nh.us

Christopher M Pope
Director, Homeland Security & Emergency Mgmt
Phone: 603-271-2231
e-mail: christopher.pope@hsem.nh.gov

Kathryn E Doutt
Asst Director, Homeland Security & Emergency Mgmt
Phone: 603-271-2231
e-mail: kathryn.doutt@hsem.nh.gov

John Wynne
Section Chief, Communications
e-mail: john.wynne@hsem.nh.gov

Donald Keeler
Section Chief, Operations
e-mail: donald.keeler@hsem.nh.gov

Michael J Poirier
Section Chief, Planning
e-mail: mike.poirier@hsem.nh.gov

Michael M Nawoj
Section Chief, Technological Hazards
e-mail: mike.nawoj@hsem.nh.gov

Environmental Services Department

29 Hazen Drive
Concord, NH 03302-0095
Mailing Address: PO Box 95, 03302
Phone: 603-271-3503
Fax: 603-271-2867
URL: www.des.state.nh.us

Thomas S Burack
Commissioner
Phone: 603-271-4974

David Wunsch
State Geologist
Phone: 603-271-6482

Kimberly Donnellan
Administrative Services
Phone: 603-271-3288

Robert R Scott
Air Resources Division
Phone: 603-271-1370

Gretchen R Hamel
Enforcement Coordinator
Phone: 603-271-3503

Patricia Bickford
Laboratory Administrator
Phone: 603-271-3445

Timothy Drew
Public Information & Permitting
Phone: 603-271-2975

Vincent Perelli
Senior Planner
Phone: 603-271-3503

Anthony P Giunta
Waste Management Division
Phone: 603-271-2900

Harry Stewart
Water Division
Phone: 603-271-3503

Executive Council Office
107 N Main Street
State House, Room 207
Concord, NH 03301
Phone: 603-271-3632
Fax: 603-271-3633
URL: www.state.nh.us/council
e-mail: gcweb@nh.gov

Raymond S Burton
District l Councilor
Phone: 603-271-3632
e-mail: rburton@gov.state.nh.us

John D Shea
District 2 Councilor
Phone: 603-271-3632

Beverly A Hollingworth
District 3 Councilor
Phone: 603-271-3632

Raymond J Wieczorek
District 4 Councilor
Phone: 603-271-3632
e-mail: rwieczorek@gov.state.nh.us

Debora Pignatelli
District 5 Councilor
Phone: 603-271-3632
e-mail: debora.pignatelli@nh.gov

National Guard
4 Pembroke Road
Concord, NH 03301
Phone: 603-225-1200
Fax: 603-225-1257
URL: www.nharmyguard.com

Description: To respond as needed to state and local emergencies and add value to the communities; maintain and provide properly trained and equipped units, available for prompt mobilization for war, national emergency, or as otherwise needed.

BG Kenneth R Clark
Adjutant General

BG Stephen Burritt
Assistant Adjutant General

Port Authority
555 Market Street
PO Box 369
Portsmouth, NH 03801-0506
Phone: 603-436-8500
Fax: 603-436-2780
URL: www.portofnh.org
e-mail: p.gradi@peasedev.org

Description: Responsible for the maintenance and development of the ports, harbors and navigable tidal rivers of the state, in order to foster and stimulate commerce and the shipment of freight through the state's ports and as an agency of the state, to assist shipping, commercial and industrial interests that may depend on the sea for transport.

Geno Marconi
Ports & Harbors Director
e-mail: g.marconi@peasedev.org

Al Cumings
Operations Manager

Tracy Shattuck
Chief Harbor Master

Public Health Services Division
29 Hazen Drive
Concord, NH 03301
Phone: 603-271-4501
Phone: 800-852-3345
Fax: 603-271-4827
URL: www.dhhs.nh.gov/dhhs/dphs

Description: Responsible for providing leadership and core public health capacity for the citizens of New Hampshire. To assure the health and well being of it's communities and populations by protecting and promoting physical, mental, environmental health and preventing disease, injury and disability.

MaryAnn Cooney
Director
Phone: 603-271-4524
e-mail: mcooney@dhhs.state.nh.us

Public Utilities Commission
21 South Fruit Street
Suite 10
Concord, NH 03301-2429
Phone: 603-271-2431
Fax: 603-271-3878
URL: www.puc.state.nh.us
e-mail: puc@puc.nh.gov

Description: The Public Utilities Commission (NHPUC) has general jurisdiction over electric, telecommunications, natural gas, water and sewer utilities, for issues such as quality of service, safety, finance and rates. Composed of three Commissioners appointed by the Governor, its mission is to ensure that customers of regulated utilities receive safe, adequate and reliable service.

Thomas B Getz
Chairperson
Phone: 603-271-2442

Graham J Morrison
Commissioner
Phone: 603-271-2443

Clifton Below
Commissioner
Phone: 603-271-2290

Debra A Howland
Executive Director & Secretary
Phone: 603-271-2431

Donald M Kreis
General Counsel
Phone: 603-271-2431

Amanda O Noonan
Director Consumer Affairs Division
Phone: 603-271-2431

Kathryn M Bailey
Director, Telecommunications Division
Phone: 603-271-2431

Randall S Knepper
Director Safety Division
Phone: 603-271-2431

Tom Frantz
Director Electric Division
Phone: 603-271-2431

State Police Division
Department of Safety
33 Hazen Drive
Concord, NH 03305
Phone: 603-271-3636
Phone: 603-271-2575
Fax: 603-271-2527
URL: www.nh.gov/safety/nhsp

Description: Dedicated to providing the highest degree of law enforcement service throughout the State of New Hampshire while maintaining the traditions of fairness, professionalism and integrity.

Colonel Frederick H Booth
Director
Phone: 603-271-2450
e-mail: fbooth@safety.state.nh.us

Transportation Department
7 Hazen Drive
John O Morton Building
Concord, NH 03302-0483
Phone: 603-271-3734
Fax: 603-271-3914
URL: www.nh.gov/dot

Description: To plan, construct and maintain the best possible transportation system and State facilities in the most efficient, environmentally sensitive and economical manner, utilizing quality management tecniques consistent with mandated controls and available resources.

Charles P O'Leary Jr
Commissioner
Phone: 603-271-3734

Jeff Brillhart
Assistant Commissioner
Phone: 603-271-1484

Colleen Cook
Health/Safety Officer
Phone: 603-271-8023

Lyle Knowlton
Director of Operations
Phone: 603-271-1697

Jack Ferns
Director of Aeronautics, Rail & Transit
Phone: 603-271-1697

Marie-Helene Bailinson
Hearings Examiner
Phone: 603-271-1698

Frances Buczynski
Human Resources Administrator
Phone: 603-271-3460

William H Boynton
Public Information Officer
Phone: 603-271-6495

STATE AGENCIES

New Jersey

New Jersey Office of Homeland Security and Preparedness

PO Box 91
Trenton, NJ 08625-0091
Phone: 609-584-4000
Fax: 609-631-4914
URL: www.njohsp.gov
e-mail: ohsp@ohsp.state.nj.us

Jon S Corzine
Governor
Phone: 609-292-6000

Richard L Canas
Director Homeland Security & Preparedness/Task Force Chair

Stuart Rabner
Attorney General/Dept of Law & Public Safety
Phone: 609-292-3508

Agricultural Department

John Fitch Plaza
PO Box 330
Trenton, NJ 08625-0330
Phone: 609-292-3976
Phone: 609-633-2954
Fax: 609-292-3978
URL: www.state.nj.us/agriculture

Charles M Kuperus
Secretary
Phone: 609-292-3976

Louis A Bruni
Chief of Operations
Phone: 609-292-6931
e-mail: louis.bruni@ag.state.nj.us

Nancy Halpern
Animal Health Division Director
Phone: 609-292-3965

Carl P Schulze Jr
Plant Industry Division Director
Phone: 609-292-5441

Monique Purcell
Agriculture & Natural Resources Division Director
Phone: 609-292-5532
e-mail: monique.purcell@ag.state.nj.us

Lynne Richmond
Public Information Officer
Phone: 609-292-8896
e-mail: lynne.redmond@ag.state.nj.us

Board of Public Utilities

2 Gateway Center
Newark, NJ 07102
Phone: 973-648-2350
Phone: 800-624-0241
URL: www.state.nj.us/bpu

Description: To ensure the provision of safe, adequate and proper utility and regulated service at reasonable rates, while enhancing the quality of life for the citizens of New Jersey and performing these public duties with integrity, responsiveness and efficiency.

Jeanne M Fox
President
Phone: 973-648-2013

Noreen Giblin
Chief of Staff
Phone: 973-648-3175

Janeen Lawlor
Director Communications

Samuel A Wolfe
Chief Counsel
Phone: 973-648-7529

Michael Winka
Clean Energy Office
Phone: 609-777-3312

Wilma Hoggard
Information Technology
Phone: 973-648-3434

Department of Law & Public Safety

25 Market Street
PO Box 080
Trenton, NJ 08625
Phone: 609-292-4925
URL: www.state.nj.us/lps

Stuart Rabner
Attorney General

Major John Hunt
Emergency Management Office, Deputy State Director
Phone: 609-882-2000

Gregory Paw
Director Criminal Justice Division

Pam Fischer
Director Highway Traffic Safety Division
Phone: 609-633-9300

Environmental Protection Department
401 E State Street
7th Floor
Trenton, NJ 08625-0402
Mailing Address: PO Box 402
Phone: 609-292-2885
Phone: 609-984-1795
Fax: 609-282-7695
URL: www.state.nj.us/dep

Lisa P Jackson
Commissioner
Phone: 609-292-2885

Alyssa Wolfe
Counselor to the Commissioner
Phone: 609-292-8601

Gary Sondermeyer
Director Operations
Phone: 609-633-1123

Nancy Wittenberg
Asst Commissioner Environmental Regulations
Phone: 609-292-2795

Narinder K Ahuja
Director Water Quality
Phone: 609-292-4543

Tim O'Donovan
Director Communications
Phone: 609-777-1344

Health and Senior Services Department
John Fitch Plaza
PO Box 360
Trenton, NJ 08625-0360
Phone: 609-292-7837
Phone: 609-984-7160
Fax: 609-292-0053
URL: www.state.nj.us/health

Fred M Jacobs
Commissioner
Phone: 609-292-7837

Eddy A Bresnitz
Deputy Commissioner/State Epidemiologist, Public Health Services
Phone: 609-588-7463
e-mail: epi@doh.state.nj.us

Jay Jimenez
Chief of Staff
Phone: 609-292-7837

Matt D'Oria
Deputy Commissioner Senior Services/Health Systems
Phone: 609-633-6945

David W Gruber
Senior Asst Commissioner Health Infrastructure Preparedness & Emergency Response
Phone: 609-292-3509

Tom Slater
Acting Director, Communications
Phone: 609-984-7160

Military & Veteran Affairs Department
PO Box 340
Trenton, NJ 08625
Phone: 609-530-7088
Fax: 609-530-6963
URL: www.state.nj.us/military

Major General Glenn K Rieth
Adjutant General

Brig General Maria Falca-Dodson
Deputy Adjutant General

New Jersey Domestic Security Preparedness Task Force
25 Market Street
PO Box 80
Trenton, NJ 08625
Phone: 609-292-4925
URL: www.state.nj.us/lps/dsptf

Description: The State's cabinet-level body responsible for setting homeland security and domestic preparedness policy. The task force is a part of the Homeland Security & Preparedness Office and reports directly to the Governor. The following make up some of the membership: Attorney General, Superintendent of State Police, Adjutant General, Commissioner of Transportation, etc.

Richard L Canas
Chair
Phone: 609-292-4925

New Jersey State Association of Chiefs of Police
830 Bear Tavern Road
Suite 303
West Trenton, NJ 08628
Phone: 609-637-9300
Fax: 609-637-9337
URL: www.njsacop.org
e-mail: njsacop@att.net

Mitchell C Sklar
Executive Director

Kathleen Auchinleck
Training & Events Manager

New Jersey Transit Police
One Penn Plaza East
Newark, NJ 07105
Phone: 973-378-6565
Phone: 800-242-0236
Fax: 973-491-4098
URL: www.njtransit.com/an_police.shtml

Description: Ensures a safe and orderly environment within the transit system, safeguarding lives and property.

Joseph C Bober
Chief
Phone: 973-491-8677

Office of Emergency Medical Services
Health and Senior Services Department
50 E State Street
6th Floor
Trenton, NJ 08608-1715

Phone: 609-633-7777
Fax: 609-633-7954
URL: www.state.nj.us/health/ems

Karen Halupke
Director
Phone: 609-633-7777

Port Authority of New York & New Jersey

225 Park Avenue S
18th Floor
New York, NY 10003-1604
Phone: 212-435-7000
Fax: 212-435-6670
URL: www.panynj.gov

Description: Manages and maintains the bridges, tunnels, bus terminals, airports, PATH and seaport that are critical to bistate trade and transportation. It meets the critical needs of the bistate region's business, residents, and visitors, by providing quality, efficient transportation and port commerce facilities and services that move people and goods within the region to provide access to the rest of the nation and to the world, and to strengthen the economic competitiveness of the New York-New Jersey metropolitan region.

Anthony E Shorris
Executive Director

Anthony R Coscia
Board Chairman

Robert Van Etten
Inspector General
Phone: 973-565-4340
e-mail: inspectorgeneral@panynj.gov

Samuel S Plumeri Jr
Superintendent of Police(NJ)/Director Public Safety
Phone: 201-216-6800

John Paczkowski
Deputy Director Public Safety/Director Operations & Emergency Management
Phone: 201-216-6800

Christopher Trucillo
Chief of Police, NJ
Phone: 201-216-6800

Public Health and Environmental Laboratories Division

Health and Senior Services Department
John Finch Plaza
PO Box 360
Trenton, NJ 08625-0360
Phone: 609-292-5605
Fax: 609-292-9285
URL: www.state.nj.us/health/phel

Dennis Flynn
Assistant Commissioner
Phone: 609-984-2201

Steve Jenniss
Environmental/Chemical Laboratory Services
Phone: 609-530-3000

Dennis McDonough
Clinical Laboratory Improvement Services
Phone: 609-984-7923

Michal P Gerwel
Public Health Laboratory Services

Nelson DelGado
Bioterrorism Laboratory & Molecular Detection Services

State Police

PO Box 7068
West Trenton, NJ 08628
Phone: 609-882-2000
Fax: 609-882-6920
URL: www.njsp.org

Colonel Joseph R Fuentes
Superintendent
Phone: 609-882-2000

Major Drew Lieb
Homeland Security, Deputy Superintendent
Phone: 609-882-2000

Major John Hunt
Emergency Management Section Supervisor
Phone: 609-882-2000

Lt Colonel William P Meddis
Administration, Deputy Superintendent
Phone: 609-882-2000

Lt Colonel Juan Mattos
Operations, Deputy Superintendent
Phone: 609-882-2000

Lt Colonel Frank Rodgers
Investigations Branch, Deputy Superintendent
Phone: 609-882-2000

Major Edward O'Neil
Intelligence Section Supervisor
Phone: 609-882-2000

Transportation Department

1035 Parkway Avenue
PO Box 600
Trenton, NJ 08625
Phone: 609-530-3535
Fax: 609-530-3894
URL: www.nj.gov/transportation

Kris Kolluri
Commissioner
Phone: 609-530-3536

Stephen Dilts
Deputy Commissioner
Phone: 609-530-4314

Jennifer Godowski
Chief of Staff
Phone: 609-530-2002

S Shinkle Gardner
Asst Commissioner Government & Community Relations
Phone: 609-530-3686

James Hogan
Executive Director Statewide Traffic Operations
Phone: 609-530-3971

Jeffrey Callahan
Asst Commissioner Operations/Emergency Mgmt Coordinator
Phone: 609-530-2590

Patricia Ott
Director Traffic Engineering & Safety
Phone: 609-530-2590

Mark Stout
Asst Commissioner Planning & Development
Phone: 609-530-3855

Richard Hammer
Asst Commissioner Capital Program Management
Phone: 609-530-5704

Erin Phalon
Deputy Director Communications
Phone: 609-530-4280

STATE AGENCIES

New Mexico

New Mexico Main Homeland Security Office
PO Box 2387
Santa Fe, NM 87504
Phone: 505-476-1050
Phone: 505-476-0267
Fax: 505-476-1057
URL: www.governor.state.nm.us/homeland.php

Bill Richardson
Governor
Phone: 505-827-3000

Diane D Denish
Lieutenant Governor
Phone: 505-476-2250
e-mail: diane.denish@state.nm.us

Tim Manning
Homeland Securty Director
Phone: 505-476-1053

Patricia A Madrid
Attorney General
Phone: 505-827-6000

Robert Redden
Preparedness Bureau Chief
Phone: 505-476-9676
e-mail: rredden@dps.state.nm.us

Jeffrey Phillips
Response & Recovery Bureau Chief
Phone: 505-476-9677
e-mail: jphillips@dps.state.nm.us

Susan Walker
Emergency Management Grants & Administration Bureau
Phone: 505-476-9640
e-mail: swalker@dps.state.nm.us

Agricultural and Environmental Services Division
Agriculture Department
PO Box 30005
MSC 3AQ
Las Cruces, NM 88003-8005
Phone: 505-646-2133
Fax: 505-646-5977

Bonnie Rabe
Director
Phone: 505-646-2133
e-mail: brabe@nmda.nmsu.edu

Agriculture Department
Po Box 30005
MSC 3189
Las Cruces, NM 88003-8805
Phone: 505-646-3007
Fax: 505-646-8120
URL: www.nmda.nmsu.edu

Miley Gonzalez PhD
Director/Secretary
Phone: 505-646-3007
e-mail: nmagsec@nmda.nmsu.edu

Dr Flint Taylor
Veterinary Diagnostic Services
Phone: 505-841-2576
e-mail: ftaylor@nmda.nmsu.edu

Julie Maitland
Agricultural Programs & Resources Division
Phone: 505-646-2642
e-mail: ddapr@nmda.nmsu.edu

Edward M Avalos
Marketing & Development Division
Phone: 505-646-5055
e-mail: ddmd@nmda.nmsu.edu

Joe E Gomez
Standards & Consumer Services Division
Phone: 505-646-1616
e-mail: ddscs@nmda.nmsu.edu

Aviation Division
1550 Pacheo Street
Santa Fe, NM 87505
Mailing Address: PO Box 1149
Phone: 505-476-0930
Fax: 505-476-0942
URL: www.flynewmexico.com/aviationdivision

Tom Baca
Director

Energy, Minerals and Natural Resources Department
1220 S St Francis Drive
Santa Fe, NM 87505
Phone: 505-476-3200
Fax: 505-476-3220
URL: www.emnrd.state.nm.us

Joanna Prukop
Secretary

Reese Fullerton
Deputy Secretary

Jodi Porter
Public Information Officer

Environment Department
1190 Saint Francis Drive
Suite N4050
Santa Fe, NM 87505-4182
Mailing Address: PO Box 26110
Phone: 505-827-2855
Fax: 505-827-2836
URL: www.nmenv.state.nm.us

Ron Curry
Secretary
Phone: 505-827-2855
e-mail: ron.curry@state.nm.us

Derrith Watchman Moore
Deputy Secretary
Phone: 505-827-2987
e-mail: derrith.watchman-moore@state.nm.us

Marissa Stone
Communications Director
Phone: 505-827-0314
e-mail: marissa.stone@state.nm.us

Tracy Hughes
General Counsel
Phone: 505-827-2855
e-mail: tracy.hughes@state.nm.us

Glen Smutz
Technical Services Bureau
Phone: 505-827-2224
e-mail: glen.smutz@state.nm.us

Jim Norton
Environmental Protection Division
Phone: 505-827-2932
e-mail: jim.norton@state.nm.us

Mary Uhl
Air Quality Bureau
Phone: 505-955-8086

Cindy Padilla
Water & Waste Management Division
Phone: 505-827-2855
e-mail: cindy.padilla@state.nm.us

James Bearzi
Hazardous & Radioactive Material Bureau
Phone: 505-476-6016
e-mail: james.bearzi@state.nm.us

Marcy Leavitt
Surface Water Quality Bureau
Phone: 505-827-2795
e-mail: marcy.leavitt@state.nm.us

Firefighters Training Academy
PO Box 239
Socorro, NM 87801
Phone: 505-835-7500
Phone: 800-734-6553
Fax: 505-835-7506
URL: www.nmprc.state.nm.us/fta.htm

Reyes Romero
Acting Director
Phone: 505-835-7500
e-mail: reyes.romero02@state.nm.us

Danny Mayfield
Chief of Staff
Phone: 505-827-4433
e-mail: daniel.mayfield@state.nm.us

Jason Marks
Vice Chairman NM Public Regulation Commission-District 1
Phone: 505-827-8015
e-mail: jason.marks@state.nm.us

David W King
NM Public Regulation Commission-District 2
Phone: 505-827-4531
e-mail: david.king@state.nm.us

Ben R Lujan
Chairman NM Public Regulation Commission-District 3
Phone: 505-827-4533
e-mail: benr.lujan@state.nm.us

Carol K Sloan
NM Public Regulation Commission-District 4
Phone: 505-827-8019
e-mail: carol.sloan@state.nm.us

Sandy Jones
NM Public Regulation Commission-District 5
Phone: 505-827-8020
e-mail: sandy.jones@state.nm.us

Health Department
1190 Saint Francis Drive
Harold Runnels Building
Santa Fe, NM 87504
Phone: 505-827-2613
Fax: 505-827-2530
URL: www.health.state.nm.us

Description: To promote health and sound health policy, prevent disease and disability, improve health services systems and assure that essential public health functions and safety net services are available to New Mexicans.

Alfredo Vigil MD
Secretary
Phone: 505-827-2613

Dorothy Rodriguez
Deputy Secretary
Phone: 505-827-2555

C Mack Sewell
Epidemiologist
Phone: 505-827-0006
e-mail: macks@doh.state.nm.us

Kathy Kunkel
General Counsel
Phone: 505-827-2962

Christine Romero
General Services Bureau
Phone: 505-827-2561
e-mail: cromero@health.state.nm.us

Bob Mayer
Information Systems Bureau
Phone: 505-827-2461

Michael Browne
Training & Career Development Bureau
Phone: 505-827-0136
e-mail: mbrown@health.state.nm.us

Highway and Transportation Department

1120 Cerrillos Road
Santa Fe, NM 87504
Mailing Address: PO Box 1149, 87504
Phone: 505-827-5100
Fax: 505-827-3214
URL: www.nmshtd.state.nm.us

Rhonda Faught
Secretary

Robert Ortiz
Deputy Secretary Highway Operations
Phone: 505-827-0658
e-mail: robert.ortiz@state.nm.us

Robert Ashmore
Chief Information Officer
Phone: 505-827-3270
e-mail: robert.ashmore@state.nm.us

Ricardo Campos
Assistant Deputy Secretary Programs & Infrastructure
Phone: 505-827-0471
e-mail: ricardo.campos@state.nm.us

Tom Church
Chief of Staff
Phone: 505-827-5695
e-mail: tom.church@state.nm.us

Injury Prevention & Emergency Medical Service Bureau

2025 S Pacheco
Suite A203
Santa Fe, NM 87505
Phone: 505-476-7000

Tres Schnell
Chief
Phone: 505-476-7864
e-mail: tres.schnell@doh.state.nm.us

Marleen L Apodaca
EMS Bureau Chief
Phone: 505-476-7925
e-mail: marleen.apodaca@doh.state.nm.us

Military Affairs Department

47 Bataan Boulevard
Santa Fe, NM 87508-4695
Phone: 505-474-1200
Fax: 505-474-1355
URL: www.nm.ngb.army.mil/state/dma.htm

Brigadier General Kenny C Montoya
Adjutant General
Phone: 505-474-1210
e-mail: kenny.montoya@nm.ngb.army.mil

BGen Mark C Dow
Army Assistant Adjutant General
Phone: 505-710-3250
e-mail: mcd@bdllawfirm.com

Colonel Brian E Baca
Chief of Staff
Phone: 505-474-1203
e-mail: brian.baca@nm.ngb.army.mil

Cdr Sgt Major Kevin L Myers
State Command Sergeant Major
Phone: 505-474-1205
e-mail: kevin.l.myers1@nm.ngb.army.mil

New Mexico Association of Chiefs of Police

1229 Paseo de Peralta
Santa Fe, NM 87504
Phone: 505-982-5573
Phone: 800-432-2036
Fax: 505-984-1392
URL: www.nmml.org

Chief Beverley K Lennen
President

Chief Ron Haley
Vice President

Office of Emergency Management

PO Box 27111
Santa Fe, NM 87502
Phone: 505-476-9600
Fax: 505-476-9695
URL: www.dps.nm.org/emergency/index.htm

Marjolaine Greentree
Director
Phone: 505-476-9655

Office of the Chief Information Officer

5301 Central Ave NE
Suite 1500
Albequerque, NM 87108
Phone: 505-841-6605
Fax: 505-841-4780
URL: http://cio.state.nm.us
e-mail: cio@state.nm.us

Roy Soto
Chief Information Officer
Phone: 505-841-6605
e-mail: roy.soto@state.nm.us

Neil Meoni
Chief of Staff
Phone: 505-841-6605
e-mail: neil.meoni@state.nm.us

Victoria Garcia
General Counsel
Phone: 505-841-4742
e-mail: victoria.garcia@state.nm.us

Public Regulation Commission

1120 Paseo de Peralta
PERA Building, Room 536
Santa Fe, NM 87501

Mailing Address: PO Box 1269
Phone: 505-827-8019
Fax: 505-827-4734
URL: www.nmprc.state.nm.us

Carol K Sloan
Commissioner
Phone: 505-827-4533
e-mail: carol.sloan@state.nm.us

Sandy Jones
Commissioner
Phone: 505-827-8020
e-mail: sandy.jones@state.nm.us

John Standefer
Fire Marshal Division
Phone: 505-827-3721
e-mail: johnstandefer@state.nm.us

Public Safety Department
4491 Cerrillos Road
Santa Fe, NM 87504-1628
Mailing Address: PO Box 1628
Phone: 505-827-9000
Fax: 505-827-3434
URL: www.dps.nm.org

John Denko
Cabinet Secretary
Phone: 505-827-9131

Chief Faron Segotta
Deputy Secretary of Operations
Phone: 505-827-9005
e-mail: faron.segotta@state.nm.us

Ann Talbot
Crime Laboratory Bureau
Phone: 505-827-9136
e-mail: ann.talbot@state.nm.us

Paul Herrera
Law Enforcement Records Bureau
Phone: 505-827-9191
e-mail: paul.herrera@state.nm.us

Scientific Laboratory Division
700 Camino de Salud NE
PO Box 4700
Albuquerque, NM 87196-4700
Phone: 505-841-2500
Fax: 505-841-2543

Description: To provide analytical laboratory support services for tax-supported agencies and/or entities administering health and environmental programs for New Mexico citizens.

Dr David E Mills
Director
Phone: 505-841-2523
e-mail: david.mills@state.nm.us

Dr Debra Horensky
Biological Science Bureau
Phone: 505-841-2556
e-mail: debra.horensky@state.nm.us

Dr Phillip Adams
Chemistry Bureau
Phone: 505-841-2510
e-mail: phillip.adams@state.nm.us

Rocky Baros
Program Support Bureau
Phone: 505-841-2524
e-mail: rocky.baros@state.nm.us

Gary Oty
Quality Control Bureau
Phone: 505-841-2585
e-mail: gary.oty@state.nm.us

Dr Rong-Jen Hwang
Toxicology Bureau
Phone: 505-841-2562
e-mail: rong.hwang@state.nm.us

State Police
PO Box 1628
Santa Fe, NM 87501
Phone: 505-827-9002
Fax: 505-827-3395
URL: www.nmsp.com

Faron Segotta
Chief
Phone: 505-827-9219
e-mail: faron.segotta@state.nm.us

Lt Marcus Romero
Governors Security Bureau
Phone: 505-827-9002
e-mail: marcus.romero@state.nm.us

Herman Silva
SID Criminal Intelligence Section
Phone: 505-827-9081
e-mail: herman.silva@state.nm.us

Captain Robert Shilling
Criminal Investigations Bureau
Phone: 505-827-9066
e-mail: robert.shilling@state.nm.us

Deputy Chief Randy Bertram
Special Operations Bureau
Phone: 505-827-9100
e-mail: randy.bertram@state.nm.us

Scott Ford
Inspector, Special Operations Bureau
Phone: 505-827-9100
e-mail: scott.ford@state.nm.us

Transportation Programs Division
PO Box 1149
Santa Fe, NM 87504-1149
Phone: 505-827-0471
Fax: 505-827-0431

Ricardo Campos
Director
Phone: 505-827-0471
e-mail: ricardo.campos@nmshtd.state.nm.us

Josette Lucero
Public Transportation Bureau
Phone: 505-827-1577
e-mail: josette.lucero@nmshtd.state.nm.us

Virginia Jaramillo
Preliminary Design Bureau
Phone: 505-827-0429

STATE AGENCIES

New York

New York Main Homeland Security Office

1220 Washington Avenue
State Office Campus Building 7A
Albany, NY 12242
Mailing Address: Suite 710
Phone: 518-402-2227
Fax: 518-402-2052
URL: www.security.state.ny.us
e-mail: info@security.state.ny.us

Elliot Spitzer
Governor
Phone: 518-474-8390

David A Paterson
Lieutenant Governor
Phone: 518-474-4623

F David Sheppard
Director of Homeland Security Office
Phone: 212-867-7060

James K Kallstrom
Advisor to Governor for Counterterrorism

Andrew Cuomo
Attorney General
Phone: 518-474-7330

Agriculture and Markets Department

10B Airline Drive
Albany, NY 12235
Phone: 518-457-8876
Phone: 800-554-4501
Fax: 518-457-3087
URL: www.agmkt.state.ny.us
e-mail: info@agmkt.state.ny.us

Description: Mission is to foster a competitive food and agriculture industry hat benefit producers and consumers alike.

Patrick Hooker
Commissioner
Phone: 518-457-8876
e-mail: commissioner@agmkt.state.ny.us

Dolores Dybas
Information Systems Division
Phone: 518-457-7368
e-mail: dolores.dybas@agmkt.state.ny.us

Daniel Rice
Food Laboratory Division
Phone: 518-457-4477
e-mail: daniel.rice@agmkt.state.ny.us

Joseph Corby
Food Safety & Inspection Division
Phone: 518-457-4492
e-mail: joe.corby@agmkt.state.ny.us

Jessica Chittenden
Public Information Officer
Phone: 518-457-3136
e-mail: jessica.chittenden@agmkt.state.ny.us

Bureau of Communicable Disease Control

651 Corning Tower
Empire State Plaza
Albany, NY 12237-0627
Phone: 518-473-4439
Fax: 518-474-7381
URL:
www.health.state.ny.us/nysdoh/communicable_diseases/en/index.htm

Barbara Wallace
Director

Community Health Assessment Practice

750 Corning Tower
Empire State Plaza
Albany, NY 12237
Phone: 518-474-2543
URL: www.health.state.ny.us

Description: A New York State Department of Health initiative that works on projects to strengthen local planning, training and technical assistance through Internet-based tools.

Mike Medvesky
Project Manager
e-mail: mgm06@health.state.ny.us

Priti Irani
Project Director
e-mail: pri01@health.state.ny.us

Cate Bohn
Community Health Information Specialist
e-mail: cmb20@health.state.ny.us

Criminal Justice Services Division

4 Tower Place
10th Floor
Albany, NY 12203
Phone: 518-457-1260
Fax: 518-457-3089
URL: www.criminaljustice.state.ny.us
e-mail: infodcjs@dcjs.state.ny.us

Description: DCJS is a multi-function criminal justice support agency. It maintains and constantly updates criminal history records, runs the Office of Sex Offender Management, maintains Sex Offender Registry, collects and analyzes statewide crime data, advises the Governor on programs to improve the effectiveness of New York's justice system, oversees law enforcement training and accreditation programs, operates the DNA Databank and provides support for criminal justice-related agencies. It also operates the Missing and Exploited Children Clearinghouse and runs the Operation SAFE CHILD program.

Denise E O'Donnell
Commissioner
Phone: 518-457-1260

Sean M Byrne
Executive Deputy Commissioner
Phone: 518-457-6091

Daniel Foro
Office of Criminal Justice Operations Deputy Commissioner
Phone: 518-485-2995

Gina L Bianchi
Counsel & Deputy Commissioner
Phone: 518-457-4181

Cedrick L Alexander
Public Safety Deputy Commissioner
Phone: 518-457-6101

Donald Capone
Administration Deputy Commissioner

Terry Salo
Office of Justice Statistics Deputy Commissioner

John Bilich
Director of Operation IMPACT/Deputy Commissioner

Beth Ryan
Office of Strategic Planning Deputy Commissioner

Mark Kavaney
Office of Legal Services Deputy Commissioner

Cyber Security & Critical Infrastructure Coordination Office

30 South Pearl Street
Albany, NY 12207-3425
Phone: 518-474-0865
Fax: 518-402-3799
URL: www.cscic.state.ny.us
e-mail: info@cscic.state.ny.us

Description: Established in September of 2002 to address NY's cyber security readiness and critical infrastructure coordination.

William F Pelgrin
Director

Emergency Management Office

1220 Washington Avenue
Suite 101, Building 22
Albany, NY 12226-2251
Phone: 518-292-2200
Fax: 518-322-4982
URL: www.semo.state.ny.us
e-mail: maildrop@semo.state.ny.us

Description: Coordinates emergency management services with other federal and state agencies to support county and local governments to protect lives, property and the environment, and provides administrative and program support to the Disaster Preparedness Commission, the Governor's policy management group for the state's emergency management.

John R Gibb
Director
Phone: 518-292-2301

Andrew Feeney
Deputy Director
Phone: 518-457-9996

Thomas Fargione
Deputy Director
Phone: 518-457-8900

Health Department

Corning Tower
Empire State Plaza
Albany, NY 12237
Phone: 518-474-2011
Fax: 518-474-5450
URL: www.health.state.ny.us
e-mail: dohweb@health.state.ny.us

Richard F Daines
Commissioner
Phone: 518-474-2011

Wendy Saunders
Chief of Staff
Phone: 518-473-0458

Edward Wronski
EMS Bureau Director
Phone: 518-402-0996

MTA Bridges and Tunnels

Robert Moses Building
Randall's Island, NY 10035
Phone: 212-360-3100
Fax: 212-860-1596
URL: www.nysba.state.ny.us

David Moretti
Acting President
Phone: 212-360-3100

National Guard

330 Old Niskayuna Road
Latham, NY 12110
Phone: 518-786-4500
Fax: 518-786-4325
URL: www.dmna.state.ny.us

Major General Joseph J Taluto
Adjutant General
Phone: 518-786-4502

Major General Robert A Knauss
Deputy Adjutant General
Phone: 518-786-4503

Colonel Lawrence J Ashley
Chief of Staff
Phone: 518-786-4502

Colonel Robert Knauff
Air Guard Commander
Phone: 518-786-4317
e-mail: robert.knauff@ny.ngb.army.mil

Eric Durr
Public Affairs Office
Phone: 518-786-4518

New York City Homeland Security Office
633 Third Avenue
38th Floor
New York, NY 10017
Phone: 212-867-7060
Fax: 212-867-1725
e-mail: info@security.state.ny.us

F David Sheppard
Director

New York Metropolitan Transportation Authority
347 Madison Avenue
New York, NY 10017
Phone: 212-878-7274
Fax: 212-878-7030
URL: www.mta.nyc.ny.us

Elliot G Sander
Executive Director/CEO
Phone: 212-878-7274

Jim Henly
Deputy Executive Director/General Counsel & Secretary
Phone: 212-878-7172

New York Public Adjusters Association
299 Broadway
New York, NY 10007
Phone: 212-285-0510
URL: www.nypaa.com
e-mail: hguttmanpa@aol.com

Description: An association of licensed professional publi adjusters and affiliated legal and trade people whose goal is to share ides, increase knowledge and effectively promote our profession to the public.

Howard Guttmann
President

Scott Friedberg
Vice President

New York State Association of Chiefs of Police
2697 Hamburg Street
Schenectady, NY 12303
Phone: 518-355-3371
Fax: 518-356-5767
URL: www.nychiefs.org
e-mail: nysacop@nycap.rr.com

John Grebert
Executive Director

Richard P Carey
Executive Director

Port Authority of New York & New Jersey
225 Park Avenue S
18th Floor
New York, NY 10003-1604
Phone: 212-435-7000
Fax: 212-435-6670
URL: www.panynj.gov

Description: Manages and maintains the bridges, tunnels, airports, bus terminals, PATH and seaport that are critical to the bistate region's trade and transportation capabilities; ensuring that it is safe and efficient for all who live, work and travel.

Anthony E Shorris
Executive Director

James P Fox
Deputy Executive Director

Robert Van Etten
Inspector General
Phone: 973-565-4340
e-mail: inspectorgeneral@panynj.gov

Samuel J Plumeri Jr
Superintendent of Police, NJ
Phone: 201-216-6800

Christopher Trucillo
Chief of Port Police
Phone: 201-216-6800

Power Authority
30 South Pearl Street, 10th Floor
Albany, NY 12207
Phone: 518-433-6700
Fax: 518-433-6780
URL: www.nypa.gov/nupac.html

Frank S McCullough Jr
Chairman
Phone: 518-433-6751

Roger Kelly
President/CEO
Phone: 518-433-6719

John Hamor
Governmental Affairs Executive Director
Phone: 518-433-6741

Public Service Department
3 Empire State Plaza
Albany, NY 12223-1350
Phone: 518-474-7080
Fax: 518-474-0421
URL: www.dps.state.ny.us

Patricia Acampora
Chairman
Phone: 518-474-2523

James Gallagher
Electricity & the Environment
Phone: 518-473-7248

Peter McGowan
Acting General Counsel
Phone: 518-474-2510

Thomas G Dvorsky
Gas & Water
Phone: 518-473-6080

Chad Hume
Telecommunications Office, Acting Director
Phone: 518-474-2523

State Police
1220 Washington Avenue
Building 22
Albany, NY 12226
Phone: 518-457-6721
Phone: 800-342-4357
Fax: 518-485-7505
URL: www.troopers.state.ny.us
e-mail: piooffic@troopers.state.ny.us

Preston L Felton
Acting Superintendent
Phone: 518-457-6721

Colonel Bart Johnson
Deputy Superintendent, Field Command Division
Phone: 518-457-5936

Colonel Pedro Perez
Deputy Superintendent, Internal Affairs Division
Phone: 518-457-6554

Thruway Authority
200 Southern Boulevard
Albany, NY 12201
Mailing Address: PO Box 189
Phone: 518-436-3000
Fax: 518-471-5058
URL: www.thruway.state.ny.us

John L Buono
Chairman
Phone: 518-436-3000

Michael R Fleischer
Executive Director
Phone: 518-436-2900

Transportation Department
50 Wolf Road
Albany, NY 12232
Phone: 518-457-4422
Fax: 518-457-5583
URL: www.dot.state.ny.us

Astrid C Glynn
Commissioner
Phone: 518-457-4422

Jennifer K Post
Public Affairs Officer
Phone: 518-457-6400
e-mail: jpost@dot.state.ny.us

Peter Loomis
Legal Affairs Office
Phone: 518-457-2411

Steve Hewitt
Governmental Relations
Phone: 518-457-2345

STATE AGENCIES

North Carolina

North Carolina Main Homeland Security Office
4701 Mail Service Center
Raleigh, NC 27699
Phone: 919-733-2126
Fax: 919-715-8447
URL: www.nccrimecontrol.org; www.ncgov.com

Michael F Easley
Governor
Phone: 919-733-4240
e-mail: governor.office@ncmail.net

Beverly E Perdue
Lieutenant Governor
Phone: 919-733-7350
e-mail: ltgovernor@ncmail.net

Bryan Beatty
Director Homeland Security/Dept. of Crime Control and Public Safety
Phone: 919-733-2126

Roy Cooper
Attorney General
Phone: 919-716-6400

Agriculture and Consumer Services Department
2 West Edenton Street
Raleigh, NC 27601
Mailing Address: 1001 Mail Service Ctr (27699)
Phone: 919-733-7125
Fax: 919-733-1141
URL: www.ncagr.com

Description: To improve the state of agriculture in North Carolina by providing services to farmers and agribusinesses, and to serve the citizens of North Carolina by providing services to and enforcing laws to protect consumers.

Steve Troxler
Commissioner
Phone: 919-733-7125
e-mail: steve.troxler@ncmail.net

N David Smith
Chief Deputy Commissioner-Administration
Phone: 919-733-7314
e-mail: david.smith@ncmail.net

Howard Isley
Assistant Commissioner-Consumer Protection
e-mail: howard.isley@ncmail.net

Marty Zaluski
Emergency Programs
Phone: 919-807-4300

Joseph W Reardon
Food & Drug Protection
Phone: 919-733-7366
e-mail: joe.reardon@ncmail.net

Steve Wells
Meat & Poultry Inspection
Phone: 919-733-4136

David Marshall
Veterinary
Phone: 919-733-7601

Richard Reich
Assistant Commissioner-Agricultural Services
e-mail: richard.reich@ncmail.net

Brian Long
Public Affairs Division
Phone: 919-733-4216
e-mail: brian.long@ncmail.net

Association of Contingency Planning of the Carolinas
PO Box 32492
Charlotte, NC 28232
Phone: 704-408-8376
URL: www.cpcaccarolinas.org
e-mail: chairman@cpaccarolinas.org

Description: A professional peer group which shares information, education and resources in contingency planning in North and South Carolina. CPAC cupports proactive preparation for the resumption of business in the event of an unplanned interruption that adversely affects the operation of the organization.

Sue Simpson CBCP
Chairperson

Martin Myers MBCP
Vice-Chairman

Crime Control and Public Safety Department
4701 Mail Service Center
Raleigh, NC 27699-4701
Phone: 919-733-2126
Fax: 919-715-8477
URL: www.nccrimecontrol.org

Bryan Beatty
Secretary
Phone: 919-733-2126

Julia Jarema
Public Affairs Director
Phone: 919-733-5027

Colonel W Fletcher Clay
State Highway Patrol
Phone: 919-733-7952

Robert Brinson
Criminal Justice Information Network, Chair
Phone: 919-715-8000
e-mail: cjin@ncem.org

Mike Robertson III
Alcohol Law Enforcement Division Director
Phone: 919-733-4060

Chief Wayne Hobgood
Butner Public Safety Director
Phone: 919-575-6562

Pam Landreth-Strug
Civil Air Patrol Director
Phone: 336-570-6894

Douglas Hoell
Emergency Management Director
Phone: 919-733-3867

Neil Woodcock
Law Enforcement Support Services Director
Phone: 919-773-2823
e-mail: less@nccrimecontrol.org

David Jones
Governor's Crime Commission Director
Phone: 919-733-4564

Major Gen William E Ingram Jr
National Guard Division, Adjutant General
Phone: 919-664-6101

Yolanda Abram
Redevelopment Center
Phone: 919-733-1566

Environment & Natural Resources Department
Mailing Address: 1601 Mail Service Center
Phone: 919-733-4984
Fax: 919-715-3060
URL: www.enr.state.nc.us

William G Ross Jr
Secretary
Phone: 919-715-4102

Bill Laxton
Chief Deputy Secretary
Phone: 919-715-0183

Keith Overcash
Air Quality
Phone: 919-715-6290
e-mail: keith.overcash@ncmail.net

Coleen Sullins
Water Quality
Phone: 919-733-7015

Terry L Pierce
Environmental Health
Phone: 919-733-2352
e-mail: terry.pierce@ncmail.net

Diana Kees
Public Affairs
Phone: 919-715-4112

National Guard
4105 Reedy Creek Road
Claude Bowers Military Center
Raleigh, NC 27607
Phone: 919-664-6000
URL: www.nc.ngb.army.mil

Major Gen William E Ingram Jr
Adjutant General
Phone: 919-664-6101

BGen Iwan Clontz
Assistant Adjutant General

North Carolina Association of Chiefs of Police
PO Box 41368
Raleigh, NC 27629
Phone: 919-876-0687
Phone: 800-889-7118
Fax: 919-878-7413
URL: http://ncpolicechief.org

Elaine Christian
Executive Director
e-mail: exdir@ncpolicechief.org

North Carolina State Capitol Police
417 N Salisbury Street
Raleigh, NC 27603
Phone: 919-733-4646
Fax: 919-733-2974
URL: www.doa.state.nc.us/police/police.htm
e-mail: ncscp@ncmail.net

Description: The North Carolina State Capitol Police have the primary duty of providing security and law enforcement services to those within the State Capitol Complex and surrounding governmental facilities.

Scott Hunter
Chief

Port Authority
2202 Burnett Boulevard
PO Box 9002
Wilmington, NC 28402
Phone: 910-763-1621
Phone: 800-334-0682
Fax: 910-763-6440
URL: www.ncports.com
e-mail: busdev@ncports.com

Thomas J Eagar
Chief Executive Officer
e-mail: tom_eager@ncports.com

Jeffrey E Miles
Chief Operating Officer
e-mail: jeff_miles@ncports.com

Karen P Fox
Communications Director
e-mail: karen_fox@ncports.com

Doug Campen
Director-Safety & Security
e-mail: doug_campen@ncports.com

Public Health Division
Health & Human Services Department
Raleigh, NC 27699
Mailing Address: 1931 Mail Service Center
Phone: 919-707-5000
Fax: 919-870-4829
URL: www.ncpublichealth.com

Leah Devlin
State Health Director
e-mail: leah.devlin@ncmail.net

Jeff Engel
Chief of Epidemiology
Phone: 919-733-3421

John Butts
Chief Medical Examiner
Phone: 919-966-2253

Paul Buescher
Director State Center for Health Statistics
Phone: 919-733-4728

Leslie Wolf
Director State Laboratory
Phone: 919-733-7834

State Bureau of Investigation
3320 Garner Road
Raleigh, NC 27610-0500
Phone: 919-662-4500
URL: www.ncsbi.gov

Description: The State Bureau of Investigation (SBI) works closely with local police and sheriffs, state investigative agencies and the federal authorities, assisting with law enforcement. Since September 11, 2001, the SBI has especially worked closely with the FBI to identify potential threats and protect the public.

Robin P Pendergraft
Director

Jerry Richardson
Crime Laboratory Assistant Director

Bill Weis
Field Operations Assistant Director

Jerry Ratley
Special Operations Assistant Director

Transportation Department
One S Wilmington Street
Raleigh, NC 27611
Mailing Address: 1501 Mail Service Center, 27699
Phone: 919-733-2520
Phone: 877-368-4968
Fax: 919-733-9150
URL: www.ncdot.org

Description: Provides and supports a safe and integrated transportation system that enhances the state. Plans, constructs, maintains and operates the second largest state-maintained transportation system in the nation to include aviation, ferry, public transportation, rail and highway systems. Provides licenses and regulates the citizens and motor vehicles that utilize these transportation systems.

Lyndo Tippett
Secretary
Phone: 919-733-2520

Daniel DeVane
Chief Deputy Secretary
Phone: 919-733-2520
e-mail: ddevane@dot.state.nc.us

Ernie Seneca
Communications Director
Phone: 919-733-2522
e-mail: eseneca@dot.state.nc.us

William H Williams Jr
Aviation Director
Phone: 919-840-0112

Bill Rasser
Highways Administrator
Phone: 919-733-7384

Patrick Simmons
Rail Director
Phone: 919-733-7245
e-mail: pbsimmons@dot.state.nc.us

STATE AGENCIES

North Dakota

North Dakota Main Homeland Security Office

PO Box 5511
Bismarck, ND 58506
Phone: 701-328-8100
Fax: 701-328-8181
URL: www.state.nd.us/des/homeland

John Hoeven
Governor
Phone: 701-328-2200
e-mail: governor@nd.gov

Jack Dalrymple
Lieutenant Governor
Phone: 701-328-4222
e-mail: jdalrymple@nd.gov

Greg Wilz
Homeland Security Coordinator/Emergency Management Director
Phone: 701-328-8100

Wayne Stenehjem
Attorney General
Phone: 701-328-2210
e-mail: wstenehj@nd.gov

Agriculture Department

600 E Boulevard Avenue
Dept 602
Bismarck, ND 58505-0020
Phone: 701-328-2231
Phone: 800-242-7535
Fax: 701-328-4567
URL: www.agdepartment.com
e-mail: ndda@nd.gov

Roger Johnson
Commissioner
Phone: 701-328-2231
e-mail: rjohnson@nd.gov

Jeff Weispfenning
Deputy Commissioner
Phone: 701-328-2231
e-mail: jweispfe@nd.gov

Jeff Knudson
Agricultural Mediation Service Program Manager
Phone: 701-328-4764
e-mail: joknudson@nd.gov

David Nelson
State Entomologist
Phone: 701-328-4765
e-mail: danelson@nd.gov

Susan Keller DVM
State Veterinarian
Phone: 701-328-2657
e-mail: skeller@nd.gov

Ken Junkert
Plant Industries Program Manager
Phone: 701-328-4756
e-mail: kjunkert@nd.gov

Patrice Eblen
Policy/Communications Coordinator
Phone: 701-328-4757
e-mail: peblen@nd.gov

Ted Quanrud
Public Information Specialist
Phone: 701-328-2233
e-mail: tquanrud@nd.gov

Department of Emergency Services

PO Box 5511
Bismarck, ND 58506-5511
Phone: 701-328-8100
Fax: 701-328-8181
URL: www.state.nd.us/des/

Description: The Department of Emergency Services was formed on July 1, 2005 by combining the North Dakota Division of Emergency Management and State Radio Communications. Its two divisions are the Division of Homeland Security and the Division of State Radio Communications. This newly reorganized agency retains its mission to save lives, and protect property and the environment through its statewide communications capability and emergency management system.

Greg Wilz
Director/Homeland Security Coordinator
Phone: 701-328-8100

Amy Anton
Operations Officer
Phone: 701-328-8100

Ken Jarolimek
Training/Exercises & Local Programs Section
Phone: 701-328-8100
e-mail: kjarolim@nd.gov

Cindy Pazdernik
Administrative Officer
Phone: 701-328-8152

Division of Disease Control

600 E Boulevard Avenue
Dept 301

Bismarck, ND 58505-0200
Phone: 701-328-2378
Phone: 800-472-2180
Fax: 701-328-2499
URL: www.health.state.nd.us/disease
e-mail: disease@state.nd.us

Kirby Kruger
Director
Phone: 701-328-2694
e-mail: kkruger@state.nd.us

Environmental Health Section
Health Department
918 East Divide Ave
Bismarck, ND 58501-1947
Phone: 701-328-5150
Fax: 701-328-5200
URL: www.health.state.nd.us/ehs

David Glatt
Chief
Phone: 701-328-5150
e-mail: dglatt@nd.gov

Lyle Witham
Enforcement Office
Phone: 701-328-5151
e-mail: lwithman@nd.gov

Myra Kosse
Chemistry Division
Phone: 701-328-6145
e-mail: mkosse@nd.gov

Terry O'Clair
Air Quality Division
Phone: 701-328-5188
e-mail: toclair@nd.gov

Scott Radig
Waste Management Division
Phone: 701-328-5166
e-mail: sradig@nd.gov

Wayne Kern
Division of Municipal Facilities
Phone: 701-328-5211
e-mail: wkern@nd.gov

Dennis Fewless
Water Quality Division
Phone: 701-328-5210
e-mail: dfewless@nd.gov

Health Department
600 E Boulevard Avenue
Bismarck, ND 58505
Phone: 701-328-2372
Fax: 701-328-4727
URL: www.health.state.nd.us

Terry Dwelle
State Health Officer
Phone: 701-328-2372
e-mail: tdwelle@nd.gov

Arvy Smith
Deputy State Health Officer

Phone: 701-328-2372
e-mail: asmith@nd.gov

Craig Lambrecht
Chief, Medical Services Section
Phone: 701-328-2372
e-mail: clamb19@msn.com

Kirby Kruger
Disease Control Division
Phone: 701-328-2694
e-mail: kkruger@nd.gov

Myra Kosse
Microbiology Division
Phone: 701-328-6140
e-mail: mkosse@nd.gov

Highway Patrol
600 E Boulevard Avenue
Department 504
Bismarck, ND 58505
Phone: 701-328-2455
Fax: 701-328-1717
URL: www.state.nd.us/ndhp
e-mail: ndhpinfo@nd.gov

Description: To provide service to all citizens and to educate towards safety, voluntary compliance, and a better quality of life.

Colonel Bryan Klipfel
Superintendent
Phone: 701-328-2455
e-mail: bklipfel@state.nd.us

Lt Kelly Rodgers
Public Information Officer

Major Mark Nelson
Field Operations Commander

Information Technology Department
Security Administration
600 E Boulevard Avenue
Department 112
Bismarck, ND 58505-0100
Phone: 701-328-3190
Fax: 701-328-3000
URL: www.state.nd.us/itd
e-mail: itd@nd.gov

Curtis Wolfe
Chief Information Officer
Phone: 701-328-3190
e-mail: cwolfe@nd.gov

Nancy Walz
Information Technology Policy Planning Division
Phone: 701-328-3190
e-mail: nwalz@nd.gov

Mike J Ressler
Deputy CIO/Director ITD
Phone: 701-328-1001
e-mail: mressler@nd.gov

L Dean Glatt
Director Computer Systems Division

Phone: 701-328-3190
e-mail: ldglatt@nd.gov

Vern J Welder
Director Software Development Division
Phone: 701-328-3190
e-mail: vwelder@nd.gov

Jerry L Fossum
Director, Telecommunications Division
Phone: 701-328-3190
e-mail: jfossum@nd.gov

National Guard
Fraine Barracks
Bldg 30, Fraine Barracks Rd
Bismarck, ND 58506-5511
Mailing Address: PO Box 5511
Phone: 701-333-2000
Fax: 701-333-2017
URL: www.guard.bismarck.nd.us

Major General David A Sprynczynatyk
Adjutant General
Phone: 701-333-2001
e-mail: david.sprynczynatyk@us.army.mil

Colonel Patrick L Martin
Air Assistant Adjutant General/Chief of Joint Staff
Phone: 701-333-2020
e-mail: patrick.lee.martin@us.army.mil

Colonel Alan S Dohrmann
Land Component Commander/Deputy Adjutant General
Phone: 701-333-2300
e-mail: alan.dohrmann@us.army.mil

North Dakota Police Chiefs Association
PO Box 717
Hazen, ND 58545
Phone: 701-748-2414
Fax: 701-748-2400
URL: www.wrtc.com/hpd
e-mail: hpd@westriv.com

Chief Chuck Dahl
Chief of Police
Phone: 701-748-2414

Transportation Department
608 E Boulevard Avenue
Bismarck, ND 58505-0700
Phone: 701-328-2500
Fax: 701-328-4545
URL: www.dot.nd.gov
e-mail: dot@nd.gov

Francis G Ziegler
Director
Phone: 701-328-2581

T J Homer
Business Support Deputy Director
Phone: 701-328-2581

Grant Levi
Engineering Deputy Director
Phone: 701-328-2581

Keith Magnusson
Driver & Vehicle Services
Phone: 701-328-2581

D Rosendahl
Operations Office
Phone: 701-328-2584

Paul Seado
Legal & General Counsel
Phone: 701-328-2625
e-mail: pseado@state.nd.us

B Darr
Maintenance & Engineering Support
Phone: 701-328-2545

STATE AGENCIES

Northern Mariana Islands

Northern Mariana Islands Main Homeland Security Office
Capitol Hill
PO Box 100007
Saipan, 96950
Mariana Islands
Phone: 670-664-2341
Fax: 670-664-2349
URL: www.cnmi.net

Benigno R Fitial
Governor
Phone: 670-664-2280

Timothy P Villagomez
Lieutenant Governor
Phone: 670-664-2300

Patrick J Tenorio
Special Advisor for Homeland Security
Phone: 670-664-2280

Matthew T Gregory
Attorney General
Phone: 670-664-2341

CNMI Emergency Management Office
PO Box 100007
Saipan, 96950
Mariana Islands
Phone: 670-322-9529
Fax: 670-322-7743
URL: www.cnmiemo.gov.mp/

Description: Assists the Governor in overseeing the coordination and activities in responding to and recovering from a disaster.

Gregorio A Deleon Guerrero
Director
e-mail: gregorio.a.deleonguerrero@cnmiemo.gov.mp

Mark S Pangelinan
Deputy Director
e-mail: mspangelinan@cnmiemo.gov.mp

Anthony M Calvo
Federal Programs Coordinator
e-mail: amcalvo@cnmiemo.gov.mp

Patricio Tudela
Training Coordinator
e-mail: pftudela@cnmiemo.gov.mp

Florence S Calvo
Hazard Mitigation Coordinator
e-mail: fscalvo@cnmiemo.gov.mp

Maria B Kazuma
Communication Operations Supervisor
e-mail: mbkazuma@cnmiemo.gov.mp

Anthony C Tenorio
Response & Recovery Coordinator
e-mail: actenorio@cnmiemo.gov.mp

Department of Environmental Quality
Gualo Rai Center
PO Box 501304
Saipan, 96950
Mariana Islands
Phone: 670-664-8500
Fax: 670-664-8540
URL: www.deq.gov.mp/
e-mail: deq@saipan.com

Frank Rabauliman
Director

Pedro T Palacios
Deputy Director

Clarissa Tanaka-Bearden
Environmental Surveillance Laboratory Supervisor

Department of Public Health
Lower Navy Hill @ Middle Road
PO Box 500-409
Saipan, MP 96950-0409
Phone: 670-236-8201
Fax: 670-236-8930
URL: www.dphsaipan.com
e-mail: help@cnmidph.net

Description: The Department is composed of three main divisions: the Commonwealth Health Center; the Division of Public Health; and the Community Guidance Center.

Joseph Kevin P Villagomez
Secretary of Public Health
Phone: 670-236-8201
e-mail: dphsec@dphsaipan.com

Kate Lapierre
Director Community Guidance Center
Phone: 670-323-1950
e-mail: cgc1@dphcgc.com

Richard Brostrom
Medical Director for Public Health

Phone: 670-234-8950
e-mail: brostrom@cnmidph.net

Julian Calvo
Resident Director Rota Health Center
Phone: 670-532-9408

Rita Manglona
Resident Director Tinian Health Center
Phone: 670-433-9233

John Tagabuel
Bureau of Environmental Health Services

Ed Diaz
Bureau of Communicable Disease Control
e-mail: msablan_a@gtepacifica.net

Department of Public Safety
Capitol Hill
Saipan, 96950
Mariana Islands
Phone: 670-664-9000
Fax: 670-664-9019
URL: www.dps.gov.mp/

Rebecca Warfield
Commissioner
Phone: 670-664-9022

Ports Authority
PO Box 501055
Saipan International Airport
Saipan, 96950
Mariana Islands
Phone: 670-664-3500
Phone: 670-664-3501
Fax: 670-234-5962
URL: www.cpa.gov.mp/

Stanley C Torres
Acting Executive Director

Melvia Sablan
Acting Comptroller
Phone: 670-664-3528
e-mail: cpa.comptroller@saipan.com

Stanley C Torres
Airport Fire Chief
Phone: 670-664-3542

Antonio Torres
Operations Supervisor
Phone: 670-664-3540

Lee C Cabrera
Manager, Port of Saipan
Phone: 670-664-6550
e-mail: cpa.seaport@saipan.com

Ignacio L Perez
Manager, Tinian Ports
Phone: 670-433-9294
e-mail: cpatinian@vzpacifica.net

Thomas Manglona
Manager, Rota Ports
Phone: 670-532-9497
e-mail: rcpaben@gtepacifica.net

Juan R Sablan
Staff Engineer
Phone: 670-664-3534

Ports Police
PO Box 501055
Saipan, 96950
Mariana Islands
Phone: 670-664-3500
Fax: 670-234-5962
URL: www.cpa.gov.mp/police.asp
e-mail: cpa.secac@vzpacifica.net

Description: The Commonwealth Ports Authority Ports Police Department has the responsibility of maintaining safety and security at the airports and seaports of CNMI.

Pius M Helgen
Chief

Luis T Indalecio
Assistant Chief of Operations

STATE AGENCIES

Ohio

Ohio Main Homeland Security Office
1970 W Broad Street
Columbus, OH 43218
Phone: 614-387-6171
Fax: 614-752-2419
URL: www.homelandsecurity.ohio.gov/hls.asp
e-mail: homelandsec@dps.state.oh.us

Ted Strickland
Governor
Phone: 614-466-3555
e-mail: governor.taft@das.state.oh.us

Lee Fisher
Lieutenant Governor
Phone: 614-466-3636

William Vedra
Executive Director Homeland Security
Phone: 614-387-6171

Mark Dann
Attorney General
Phone: 614-466-3376

Agriculture Department
8995 E Main Street
Reynoldsburg, OH 43068-3399
Phone: 614-728-6200
Phone: 800-282-1955
Fax: 614-466-6124
URL: www.ohioagriculture.gov
e-mail: administration@mail.agri.state.oh.us

Description: To provide regulatory protection to producers, agri-businesses and consumers; to promote Ohio agricultural products in domestic and international markets; and to educate the citizens of Ohio about their agricultural industry.

Fred L Dailey
Director
Phone: 614-466-2732

Larry Adams
Assistant Director
Phone: 614-466-2732

Mark Anthony
Communications Division
Phone: 614-752-9817

Frank Forgione
Fiscal Officer
Phone: 614-466-4597

Edward J Cruttenden
Chief Legal Counsel
Phone: 614-782-6430

John Hix
Human Resources Administrator
Phone: 614-466-4595

Patricia Grinter
EEO Training Officer
Phone: 614-466-5339

Sam Waltz
Deputy Director
Phone: 614-728-6210

Dr R David Glauer DVM
Animal Industry Division
Phone: 614-728-6220

Dr. Ronald Jenkins
Consumer Analytical Lab
Phone: 614-728-6230

Jim Hoekstra
Enforcement Division
Phone: 614-728-6240

Paul Panico
Food Safety Division
Phone: 614-728-6250

Dr Tom Brisker
Meat Inspection Division
Phone: 614-728-6260

Lewis Jones
Dairy Division
Phone: 614-728-6250

Kevin H Elder
Large Livestock Division

Association of Contingency Planners of Ohio
PO Box 340825
Columbus, OH 43234
Phone: 330-887-6438
URL: www.cpohio.org
e-mail: info@cpohio.org

Description: An association of continuity, disaster recovery, information security, and business professionals and planners dedicated to educational and shared experiences in contingency planning. A long established association of professionals dedicated to sharing expertise, education, and experiences to improve the preparedness, response, mitigation, and recovery of businesses from disaster and emergencies, which affect their corporation, customers, and communities.

Rod Keely
President

Department of Public Safety
Charles D Shipley Building
1970 W Broad Street
Columbus, OH 43218-2081
Mailing Address: PO Box 182081
Phone: 614-466-2550
Fax: 614-466-0433
URL: www.ohiopublicsafety.com/odps.asp

Description: The Ohio Department of Public Safety serves and protects the safety and security of Ohioans through these seven divisions: Homeland Security, Highway Patrol, Bureau of Motor Vehicles, Emergency Management Agency, Emergency Medical Services, Investigative Unit and Administrative.

Henry Guzman
Director
Phone: 614-466-3383

George Maier
Assistant Director
Phone: 614-466-3383

William Vedra
Deputy Director of the Domestic Preparedness Office

Richard Rawlins
Deputy Director of the Counter-Terrorism Office

Cathy Collins-Taylor
Investigative Unit Executive Director
Phone: 614-466-2415

John Lang
Legislative Liaison
Phone: 614-752-0422

Thomas Hunter
Communications Director
Phone: 614-466-6178

Thomas Hunter
Public Safety Media Relations
Phone: 614-466-6178
e-mail: sraber@dps.state.oh.us

Ken Kreitel
Information Technology Administrator
Phone: 614-752-7692

Disaster Recovery Branch
Emergency Management Agency
2855 W Dublin Granville Road
Columbus, OH 43235
Phone: 614-889-7150
Fax: 614-889-7183
URL: www.state.oh.us/odps/division/ema/Recovery.htm

Description: Provides guidance, training and technical assistance regarding supplemental disaster assistance programs. DRB provides guidance for damage assessment activities following disasters. The branch also has the responsibilty for administering FEMA and State disaster assistance programs.

Kay Phillips
Branch Chief
e-mail: kphillips@dps.state.oh.us

Nancy Dragani
Executive Director

Emergency Management Agency
2855 W Dublin Granville Road
Columbus, OH 43235-2206
Phone: 614-889-7150
Fax: 614-889-7183
URL: www.ema.ohio.gov/ema.asp
e-mail: ohioema@dps.state.oh.us

Description: The central point of coordination within the state for response and recovery to disasters. The agency's primary focus is to ensure that the state and citizens residing in it, are prepared to respond to an emergency or disaster and to lead mitigation efforts against the effects of future disasters.

Nancy Dragani
Executive Director
Phone: 614-889-7152
e-mail: ndragani@dps.state.oh.us

Jessie Baker
Chief of Staff
Phone: 614-799-3675
e-mail: jtbaker@dps.state.oh.us

C J Couch
Public Affairs Branch Chief
Phone: 614-799-3695

Carol O'Claire
Radiological Branch Chief
Phone: 614-799-3915

Mel House
Operations Division Director
Phone: 614-889-7161

Chad Berginnis
Mitigation Branch Chief
Phone: 614-799-3539

James Dwertman
Readiness & Response Branch Chief
Phone: 614-799-3692

Emergency Medical Services Division
Department of Public Safety
1970 W Broad Street
PO Box 182073
Columbus, OH 43218-2073
Phone: 614-466-9447
Phone: 800-233-0785
Fax: 614-466-9461
URL: www.ems.ohio.gov
e-mail: dwalton@dps.state.oh.us

Richard N Rucker
Executive Director
Phone: 614-466-9447
e-mail: rnrucker@dps.state.oh.us

John Sands
Homeland Security Coordinator
Phone: 614-387-0649

Henry Guzman
Public Safety Director

Brian Pfeffer
EMT/Fire Coordinator
Phone: 614-466-9447

Tim Erskine
EMS & Trauma Data Program Director
Phone: 614-387-1951
e-mail: terskine@dps.state.oh.us

Doug Orahood
EMT/Fire Coordinator
Phone: 614-466-9447

Melissa Vermillion
Investigative Services
Phone: 614-752-3959
e-mail: mvermillion@dps.state.oh.us

Diane Walton
Office Manager
Phone: 614-466-3655
e-mail: dwalton@dps.state.oh.us

Health Department

246 N High Street
PO Box 118
Columbus, OH 43216
Phone: 614-466-2253
Fax: 614-644-8526
URL: www.odh.ohio.gov
e-mail: Director@odh.ohio.gov

Description: A high performance organization of dedicated professionals leading Ohioans to achieve optimal health.

Alvin D Jackson MD
Health Director
Phone: 614-466-2253

Deborah L Arms RN
Prevention Division Chief
Phone: 614-466-0302

Anne Harnish
Assistant Director
Phone: 614-466-0041

Tamara Malkoff
General Counsel
Phone: 614-466-4882

Steven Wagner
Environmental Health Bureau Chief
Phone: 614-466-1319

Shannon Ginther
Government Affairs Office
Phone: 614-644-8251

Barbara Bradley
Infectious Disease Control Chief
Phone: 614-466-0265

Robert Owen
Radiation Protection Bureau Chief
Phone: 614-466-2727

Drema Phelps
Health Service
Phone: 614-466-2188

National Guard

2825 W Dublin Granville Road
Columbus, OH 43235
Phone: 614-336-7000
Fax: 614-336-7410
URL: www.ohionationalguard.com
e-mail: pao.oh@tagoh.gov

Description: Support the Governor by providing trained units and equipment capable of protecting life and property and preserving peace, order and public safety. Community role: to be an active participant in domestic concerns through local, state and national programs.

Major General Gregory Wayt
Adjutant General

Major General Harry Feucht
Air Assistant Adjutant General

Major General Matthew Kambic
Army Assistant Adjutant General

Commander Christopher Muncy
State Command Chief

Commander Sgt. William Gilliam
State Command Sergeant Major

Ohio Association of Chiefs of Police

6277 Riverside Drive
Suite 2N
Dublin, OH 43017
Phone: 614-761-0330
Fax: 614-761-9509
URL: www.oacp.org
e-mail: oacp@oacp.org

Description: To cultivate professionalism among police executives to assure continued success of the law enforcement community.

Todd N Wurschmidt PhD
Executive Director

Chief Martin A Schmidt
Treasurer

Chief Gary Vest
President

State Capitol Police

State Capitol Building
Broad & High Street
Columbus, OH 43215
Phone: 614-466-0506
Fax: 614-752-3045

Doug Willard
Lieutenant

State Highway Patrol
Department of Public Safety
1970 W Broad Street
PO Box 182074
Columbus, OH 43223
Phone: 614-466-2990
Fax: 614-644-9749
URL: www.statepatrol.ohio.gov

Colonel Paul D McClellan
Highway Patrol Superintendent
Phone: 614-466-2990

Lt. Colonel Michael Finamore
Assistant Superintendent of Administration
Phone: 614-466-2992

Tony Vogel
Highway Operations Deputy Director

Lt. Colonel William Costas
Asssistant Superintendent of Operations
Phone: 614-752-2792

Major Peyton Watts
Recruitment/Training Office
Phone: 614-466-4896

Major Robert Brooks
Licensing & Commercial Standards
Phone: 614-466-4056

Major Lisa Taylor
Finance/Logistics
Phone: 614-466-2991

Major Robert Young
Human Resources Management Office
Phone: 614-466-3003

Major JP Allen
Planning Services
Phone: 614-752-4665

Major Robert Costas
Field Operations
Phone: 614-466-1180

Major Robert Booker
Criminal Investigations
Phone: 614-466-3375

Major Stephen Friday
Technological Services
Phone: 614-466-3554

Lt. Rick Zwayer
Public Information Officer
Phone: 614-752-2792

Transportation Department
1980 W Broad Street
Columbus, OH 43223
Phone: 614-466-7170
Fax: 614-644-8662
URL: www.dot.state.oh.us

Description: To provide a world-class transportation system that
links Ohio to a global economy while preserving the state's
unique character and enhancing its quality of life.

James G Beasley
Director
Phone: 614-466-2335

William Lindenbaum
Construction Management Deputy Director
Phone: 614-466-3598

David Humphrey
Highway Operations Acting Deputy Director
Phone: 614-752-5396

Catherine Perkins
Acting Chief Legal Counsel
Phone: 614-466-3664

Stu Nicholson
Rail Development Public Information Officer
Phone: 614-644-0513

Dave Holstein
Office of Traffic Engineering Administrator
Phone: 614-644-8137
e-mail: Dave.Holstein@dot.state.oh.us

Marianne Freed
Office of Transit Administrator
Phone: 614-466-7084
e-mail: marianne.freed@dot.state.oh.us

Henry Guzman
Public Safety Director
Phone: 614-466-3383

STATE AGENCIES

Oklahoma

Oklahoma Main Homeland Security Office
PO Box 11415
Oklahoma City, OK 73136
Phone: 405-425-7296
Fax: 405-425-7295
URL: www.homelandsecurity.ok.gov
e-mail: okohs@dps.state.ok.us

Brad Henry
Governor
Phone: 405-521-2342

Jerri Askins
Lieutenant Governor
Phone: 405-521-2161
e-mail: LtGovernor@ltgov.state.ok.us

Major Kerry Pettingill
Director Homeland Security
Phone: 405-425-7296

W A Drew Edmondson
Attorney General
Phone: 405-521-3921

Melissa McLawhorn Houston
Chief of Staff
Phone: 405-521-3921

Acute Disease Service
Health Department
1000 NE 10th Street
Room 609
Oklahoma City, OK 73117-1299
Phone: 405-271-4060
Fax: 405-271-1166
URL: www.health.state.ok.us/program/ad

Description: To control communicable diseases through: surveillance for infectious diseases; analysis of data to plan, implement and evaluate disease prevention and control measures; investigation of disease outbreaks; education of health care professionals and the public; dissemination of pertinent information; and bioterrorism preparedness.

Joe Mallonee
Deputy Commissioner of Disease and Prevention Services
Phone: 405-271-3272

Kristy Bradley, DVM, MPH
State Public Health Veterinarian/Deputy State Epidemiologist

Lauri Smithee, MES, MS
Acute Disease Service Chief

Jon Tillinghast, MD, MPH
Tuberculosis Control Officer

Agriculture, Food & Forestry Department
2800 N Lincoln Boulevard
Oklahoma City, OK 73105
Phone: 405-521-3864
Fax: 405-522-4912
URL: www.oda.state.ok.us
e-mail: tricia.shelton@oda.state.ok.us

Description: The department protects and educates consumers and producers by enforcing state laws that enhance the quality and value of agricultural crops, livestock and food products. The Department of Agriculture, Food & Forestry is primarily a regulatory agency but has branched out into services such as crop and marketing reports, market expansion and predator control.

Terry L Peach
Commissioner
Phone: 405-522-5719

Amber Lawles
Associate Commissioner
Phone: 405-522-5489

Sancho M Dickinson III
Consumer Protection Services Director
Phone: 405-522-5879

John Burwell
State Forester
e-mail: jburwell@oda.state.ok.us

Duane Harrel
Public Information Director
Phone: 405-522-5600

Kevin Grant
Wildlife Services Director
Phone: 405-521-4039

Stan Stromberg
Food Safety Director
Phone: 405-522-6113
e-mail: stans@oda.state.ok.us

Mike Talkington
Agricultural Laboratory
Phone: 405-522-5431

Association of Contingency Planners
PO Box 776
Tulsa, OK 74101
Phone: 918-830-7015
URL: www.acp-international.com/okla

Description: The Oklahoma Chapter of the ACP hs 40 members. Its mission is to provide professional information to these members concerning all aspects of contingency planning.

Richard Myers
President

Joe Robertson
Vice President

Communicable Disease Division
Health Department
1000 NE 10th Street
Room 605
Oklahoma City, OK 73117-1299
Phone: 405-271-4060
Fax: 405-271-6680
URL: www.health.state.ok.us/program/cdd

Description: To apply epidemiologic principles and methods to identify, control and prevent cases of certain communicable diseases in coordination with other divisions and departments for the public's health.

Laurence Burnsed
Division Director

Anthony Lee
Epidemiologist

Kimberly Mitchell
Health Alert Network Coordinator

Emergency Management Department
2401 Lincoln Boulevard
Suite C-51
Oklahoma City, OK 73105
Phone: 405-521-2481
Fax: 405-521-4053
URL: www.ok.gov/OEM/
Number of employees: 31

Description: Orginally created in 1951, the agency was renamed the Oklahoma Department of Emergency Management in 2003 and today is the central point of contact for coordination of four closely allied functions: Hazard Mitigation, Community Preparedness, Emergency Response and Disaster Recovery. Its mission is to minimize the effects of attack, technological and natural disasters upon the people of Oklahoma by preparing, implementing and excercising preparedness plans, by coordinating actual disaster response/recovery operations and assisting local government subdivisions with training for and mitigation of disasters.

Emergency Medical Services Division
1000 NE 10th Street
Room 1104
Oklahoma City, OK 73117
Phone: 405-271-4027
URL: www.health.state.ok.us/program/ems
e-mail: ems@health.ok.gov

Description: To protect and promote health in Oklahoma by fostering continued improvement for a comprehensive, coordinated arrangement of health and public safety resources that serve to provide timely and lifesaving care.

Shawn Rogers
Director

Glen Lellend
COO

Environmental Quality Department
707 N Robinson
PO Box 1677
Oklahoma City, OK 73102
Phone: 405-702-1000
Fax: 405-702-1001
URL: www.deq.state.ok.us

Description: To eliminate the effects of unintended consequences of historic development, to prevent new adverse environmental impacts and to provide significant input into national decision making, all the while enhancing both the environment and the economy of Oklahoma.

Miles Tolbert
Secretary of the Environment
Phone: 405-271-8056

Steven A Thompson
Executive Director
Phone: 405-702-7100
e-mail: steve.thompson@deq.state.ok.us

Scott Thomas
Air Quality Division
Phone: 405-702-4157
e-mail: Scott.Thomas@deq.state.ok.us

Rocky Chen
Water Quality Division
Phone: 405-702-8100

Kevin Sampson
Radiation Emergencies
Phone: 405-702-5161
e-mail: pam.bishop@deq.state.ok.us

David Freede
Emergencies/Natural Disasters
Phone: 405-702-6159
e-mail: david.freede@deq.state.ok.us

David Dyke
Emergency Response
Phone: 405-702-7129
e-mail: david.dyke@deq.state.ok.us

Michael Freeman
Criminal Investigations
Phone: 405-702-6156
e-mail: michael.freeman@deq.state.ok.us

Al Coulter
Hazardous Waste Disposal
Phone: 405-702-5189
e-mail: al.coulter@deq.state.ok.us

Health Department
1000 NE 10th Street
Oklahoma City, OK 73117
Phone: 405-271-4200
Fax: 405-271-3431
URL: www.health.state.ok.us
e-mail: cheryln@health.ok.gov

Description: To protect and promote health of the citizens of Oklahoma, to prevent disease and injury, and to assure the conditions by which our citizens can be healthy.

James Michael Crutcher MD
Secretary of Health & Commissioner of Health
Phone: 405-271-4200

Nick Slaymaker
General Counsel Director
Phone: 405-271-6017

Kevin Pipes
Office of State & Federal Policy Chief
Phone: 405-271-4200

Joe Mallonee
Deputy Commissioner of Disease & Prevention Services
Phone: 405-271-3272

Leslea Bennett-Webb
Communications Director
Phone: 405-271-5601

Hank Hartsell
Deputy Commissioner of Protective Health Services
Phone: 405-271-5288

Stephen Ronck
Deputy Commissioner of Community Health Services
Phone: 405-271-5585

Kelly Baker
Director for Center for Health Statistics
Phone: 405-271-6225

Rocky McElvany
COO
Phone: 405-271-4200

Edd Rhoades MD
Deputy Commissioner Family Health Services
Phone: 405-271-4200

Highway Patrol
Department of Public Safety
3600 N Martin Luther King Avenue
PO Box 11415
Oklahoma City, OK 73136-0415
Phone: 405-425-2424
Fax: 405-425-2337
URL: www.dps.state.ok.us/ohp/
e-mail: comment@dps.state.ok.us

Description: Working to provide a safe, secure environment for the public and assist governmental agencies during emergencies when requested.

Colonel Jerry Carson
Chief of Patrol

Trooper Greg Armstrong
Recruiting Officer
Phone: 918-423-3621
e-mail: garmstro@dps.state.ok.us

Highway Safety Office
3223 N Lincoln Blvd
Oklahoma City, OK 73105
Mailing Address: PO Box 11415
Phone: 405-523-1570
Fax: 405-523-1586
URL: www.dps.state.ok.us/ohso/
e-mail: comment@dps.state.ok.us

Description: Established in 1967 to combat the number and severity of traffic crashes by developing and supporting educational, enforcement and engineering programs. The department works closely with local government organizations, state agencies, and others to develop a state highway safety plan and programs to address highway safety issues.

Joe McDonald
Director
Phone: 405-523-1570
e-mail: jmcdonal@dps.state.ok.us

Rex Ice
Program Manager
Phone: 405-523-1582
e-mail: rice@dps.state.ok.us

National Guard
3501 Military Circle
Oklahoma City, OK 73111
Phone: 405-228-5000
Fax: 405-425-8659
URL: www.ok.ngb.army.mil./

Description: Trained and equipped forces as reserve components of the Army and Air Force and performs missions as directed by state and federal authorities. The JFHQ-State supports command and control of all assigned Army and Air National Guard forces.

Major General Harry M Wyatt III
Adjutant General

Brad Henry
Governor/Commander-in-Chief

Brig General David S Angle
Assistant AG Air Commander

Brig General Terry R Council
Assistant AG Army Commander

Oklahoma Association of Chiefs of Police
3701 SE 15th Street
Suite 100
Del City, OK 73115
Phone: 405-672-1225
Phone: 888-528-6227
Fax: 405-670-8763
URL: www.okla-chiefs.org
e-mail: oacp@okla-chiefs.org

Description: To promote excellence in law enforcement through professional development, technical support, ethical standards and communication.

Jim Cox
Executive Director
e-mail: imcox@okla-chiefs.org

Stacey Puckett
Deputy Director
e-mail: stacey@okla-chiefs.org

Public Safety Department
3600 Martin Luther King Avenue
PO Box 11415
Oklahoma City, OK 73136-0415

Phone: 405-425-2424
Fax: 405-425-2324
URL: www.dps.state.ok.us/

Description: Since 1937, the Oklahoma Department of Public Safety has grown into a multi-service safety and law enforcement organization. Its mission is to provide a safe and secure environment for the public through quality, courteous and professional services. The department is responsible for policing all state roads, highways, several thousand miles of lake and river shore lines, providing security related functions for the Governor, Lieutenant Governor, and state office buildings.

Kevin L Ward
Commissioner
Phone: 404-425-2001
e-mail: kward@dps.state.ok.us

Billy McClure
Assistant Commissioner
Phone: 405-425-2002

Wellon Poe
General Counsel

Van Guillotte
Highway Patrol Chief
Phone: 405-425-2003

Jerry Garcia
Comptroller
Phone: 405-425-2105

Kaye Stratton
Highway Safety Division
Phone: 405-523-1570

Gene Thaxton
Telecommunications Division
Phone: 405-425-2224

State Capitol Patrol
Department of Public Safety
3600 N Martin Luther King Avenue
PO Box 11415
Oklahoma City, OK 73105
Phone: 405-521-4541
Fax: 405-425-2287
URL: www.dps.state.ok.us/ohp/aboutcp.htm

Description: Consists of 44 officers, 12 supervisors, and one commanding officer. Patrolling the State Capitol Complex and the State Office Building in Tulsa, officers provide security for the complexes, employees and visitors.

Captain Rusty Rhoades
Commander

Transportation Department
200 NE 21st Street
Oklahoma City, OK 73105
Phone: 405-522-8000
URL: www.okladot.state.ok.us
e-mail: odotinfo@odot.org

Description: To provide a safe, economical, and effective transportation network for the people, commerce and communities of Oklahoma.

Phil Tomlinson
Secretary of Transportation
Phone: 405-521-2631

Gary Ridley
Director
Phone: 405-522-1800

John Fuller
Deputy Director/Chief Engineer

Norman Hill
General Counsel

Joe R Kyle Jr
Rail Programs/Safety
Phone: 405-521-4203

Kenneth LaRue
Transit Program Branch
Phone: 405-521-2584

STATE AGENCIES

Oregon

Oregon Main Homeland Security Office
400 Public Service Building
3225 State Street
Salem, OR 97309
Mailing Address: PO Box 14370
Phone: 503-378-2911
Phone: 503-378-3720
URL: www.oregon.gov/OOHS/

Theodore R Kulongoski
Governor
Phone: 503-378-3111

Bill Bradbury
Secretary of State
Phone: 503-986-1523
e-mail: oregon.sos@state.or.us

Joe O'Leary
Homeland Security Advisor
Phone: 503-378-3111

Kenneth Murphy
Director Homeland Security
Phone: 503-378-2911

Hardy Myers
Attorney General
Phone: 503-378-4400

Agriculture Department
635 Capitol Street NE
Salem, OR 97301
Phone: 503-986-4550
Fax: 503-986-4747
URL: www.oda.state.or.us/oda.html
e-mail: info@oda.state.or.us

Description: Serves the state of Oregon through a three-fold mission: food safety and consumer protection; protection of the natural resources base; developing and maintaining markets for agricultural products.

Katy Coba
Director
Phone: 503-986-4552
e-mail: kcoba@oda.state.or.us

Lauren Henderson
Assistant Director
Phone: 503-986-4588
e-mail: lhenders@oda.state.or.us

Lisa Charpilloz Hanson
Deputy Director
Phone: 503-986-4632
e-mail: lhanson@oda.state.or.us

Ronald McKay
Food Safety Division
Phone: 503-986-4727
e-mail: rmckay@oda.state.or.us

Kathleen Wickman
Laboratory Services Division
Phone: 503-872-6633

Ray Jaindl
Natural Resources Division
Phone: 503-986-4713
e-mail: rjaindl@oda.state.or.us

Don Hansen
State Veterinarian
Phone: 503-986-4760
e-mail: dhansen@oda.state.or.us

Department of Public Safety Standards and Training
4190 Aumsville Hwy
Salem, OR 97317
Phone: 503-378-2100
Phone: 503-378-3306
Fax: 503-378-3330
e-mail: oregon.dpsst@state.or.us

John Minnis
Director
Phone: 503-378-2042
e-mail: john.minnis@state.or.us

Eriks Gabliks
Deputy Director
Phone: 503-378-2332
e-mail: eriks.gabliks@state.or.us

Emergency Management
800 NE Oregon Street
Salem, OR 97309-5062
Mailing Address: PO Box 14370
Phone: 503-378-2911
Fax: 503-373-7857
URL: http://egov.oregon.gov/OOHS/OEM/

Kenneth D Murphy
Director
e-mail: kmurphy@oem.state.or.us

Emergency Management: Chemical Stockpile Emergency Preparedness Program

125 SE 1st Street
Pendleton, OR 97801
Phone: 541-966-9640
Fax: 541-966-9650
URL: http:egov.oregon.gov/OOHS/OEM/CSEPP.shtml

Description: Enhances emergency preparedness in communities surrounding chemical warfare agent storage sites through emergency planning efforts, community alert and warning system, and hazard mitigation strategies; protects the environment in the case of an accident; and ensures the area maintains acceptable environmental integrity.

Chris Brown
State CSEPP Manager
Phone: 541-966-9640
e-mail: cbrown@oem.state.or.us

Kevin Dallman
Communication Systems Coordinator
Phone: 541-966-9640
e-mail: kdallman@oem.state.or.us

Emergency Management: Technology & Response Services

3225 State Street
Salem, OR 97301
Mailing Address: PO Box 14370
Phone: 503-378-2911
Fax: 503-588-1378
URL: http://egov.oregon.gov/OOHS/OEM/tech_n_respon.shtml

Description: Provides and maintains a broad range of communication systems used by the state, general public, local government, and other agencies in order to warn the public of emergencies and general preparedness and emergency support.

Ken Keim
Director
Phone: 503-378-2911
e-mail: kkeim@oem.state.or.us

Marty McKillip
State Communications Officer
Phone: 503-378-2911

Georges Kleinbaum
Search & Rescue Coordinator
Phone: 503-378-2911
e-mail: gkleinba@oem.state.or.us

Mark Tennyson
Program Coordinator
Phone: 503-378-2911

Emergency Medical Services & Trauma Systems

800 NE Oregon Street
Suite 607
Portland, OR 97232
Phone: 971-673-0520
Phone: 971-673-0372
Fax: 971-673-0555
URL: http://oregon.gov/DHS/ph/ems/index.shtml
e-mail: ems.trauma@state.or.us

Grant Higginson
Acting Director
Phone: 971-673-0524

Environmental Quality Department

811 SW 6th Avenue
Portland, OR 97204
Phone: 503-229-5696
Phone: 800-452-4011
Fax: 503-229-6124
URL: www.deq.state.or.us
e-mail: deq.info@deq.state.or.us

Description: Regulatory agency whose job is to protect the quality of Oregon's environment. Responsible for protecting and enhancing Oregon's water and air quality, for cleaning up spills and releases of hazardous materials, and for managing the proper disposal of hazardous and solid waste.

Stephanie Hallock
Director
Phone: 503-229-5300

Dick Peterson
Deputy Director
Phone: 503-229-5078

Nina DeConcini
Public Affairs Office
Phone: 503-229-6271

Lauri Aunan
Water Quality Division
Phone: 503-229-5327

Al Kiphut
Waste Management & Cleanup Division
Phone: 503-229-6834

Wendy Wiles
Hazardous Waste Policy & Program Development Manager
Phone: 503-229-5769

Military Department

1776 Militia Way SE
Salem, OR 97309
Mailing Address: PO Box 14350
Phone: 503-584-3980
Phone: 800-452-7500
Fax: 503-584-3962
URL: www.oregon.gov/OMD/

Description: The Oregon Military Department is made up of the Oregon Army National Guard, Air National Guard and the Oregon State Defense Force.

BGen Raymond F Rees MG
Adjutant General
Phone: 503-584-3991

Capt Maurice Marshall
Air Assistant Adjutant General
Phone: 503-584-3638

Terri Kroeker
Air Guard Executive Support Specialist
Phone: 503-584-3646

Colonel Mike Caldwell
State Affairs Deputy Director

Phone: 503-584-3884
e-mail: mike.caldwell@mil.state.or.us

Office for Disease Prevention & Epidemiology
800 NE Oregon Street
Suite 730
Portland, OR 97232
Phone: 971-673-0982
Fax: 971-673-0994
URL: http://oregon.gov/DHS/odpe/index.shtml
e-mail: dhs.info@state.or.us

Description: Identifies, monitors, and seeks to control the factors that threaten the health of Oregonians.

Dr Melvin Kohn
Administrator
Phone: 503-731-4023
e-mail: melvin.a.kohn@state.or.us

Office of Public Health Services
800 NE Oregon Street
Portland, OR 97232
Phone: 503-731-4000
Fax: 503-731-4031
URL: http://oregon.gov/DHS/ph/
e-mail: health.webmaster@state.or.us

Description: To protect and promote the health of all the people of Oregon.

Susan Allan
Director
Phone: 503-947-1175
e-mail: susan.m.allan@state.or.us

Eva Kutas
Investigations & Training Director
Phone: 503-945-9491

Gail Shibley
Public Health Systems Administrator
Phone: 503-731-3441
e-mail: gail.r.shibley@state.or.us

Dr Grant Higginson
State Public Health Officer
Phone: 503-731-4000
e-mail: grant.k.higginson@state.or.us

Michael R Skeels PhD
State Public Health Laboratories
Phone: 503-229-5296
e-mail: michael.r.skeels@state.or.us

Oregon Association of Chiefs of Police
1191 Capitol Street NE
Salem, OR 97301
Phone: 503-315-1411
Phone: 800-784-2867
Fax: 503-315-1416
URL: www.policechief.org

Kevin Campbell
Executive Director
e-mail: kevin@victorygrp.com

Oregon State Defense Force
Military Department
10101 SE Clackamas Road
Camp Withycombe
Clackamas, OR 97015-9150
Phone: 503-557-5458
Fax: 503-557-5255
URL: www.mil.state.or.us/SDF
e-mail: snjr@charter.net

BGen Michael Caldwell
Commanding General
Phone: 503-584-3884
e-mail: mike.caldwell@mil.state.or.us

Oregon State Police Officers Association
3905 River Road N
Suite B
Keizer, OR 97303
Phone: 503-393-6535
Phone: 800-503-2327
Fax: 503-393-6542
URL: www.ospoa.com

Jeff Leighty
President
e-mail: leighty@ospoa.com

Public Broadcasting Service
7140 SW Macadam Avenue
Portland, OR 97219-3013
Phone: 503-244-9900
Fax: 503-293-4165
URL: www.opb.org

Steve Bass
President/CEO
Phone: 503-244-9900
e-mail: ceo@opb.org

State Police Department
255 Capitol Street, 4th Fl
Salem, OR 97310
Phone: 503-378-3720
Phone: 503-378-3725
Fax: 503-378-8282
URL: www.oregon.gov/OSP/
e-mail: ask.osp@state.or.us

Timothy Mclain
Superintendent
Phone: 503-934-0233

Greg Willeford
Deputy Superintendent
Phone: 503-934-0231

Captain Ed Mouery
Criminal Division Director
Phone: 503-934-0175

Lieutenant Gregg Hastings
Public Information Officer/Legislative Affairs
Phone: 503-731-3020

Karen Gunson MD
State Medical Examiner
Phone: 503-998-3746

Transportation Department
355 Capitol Street NE
Transportation Building, Room 135
Salem, OR 97301-3871
Phone: 888-275-6368
Fax: 503-986-3432
URL: http://egov.oregon.gov/ODOT/

Description: To promote a safe, efficient transportation system that supports economic opportunity and livable communities for Oregonians.

Stuart Foster
Transportation Commission Chairman
Phone: 503-986-3450

Matthew Garrett
Director
Phone: 503-986-3289

Joan Plank
Chief of Staff
Phone: 503-986-4214

Patrick Cooney
Communications Administrator
Phone: 503-986-3455

Troy Costales
Transportation Safety Division, Administrator
Phone: 503-986-4192

Kelly Taylor
Rail Division, Administrator
Phone: 503-986-4125

John R Johnson
Rail Safety Manager
Phone: 503-986-4094

Vacant
Public Transit Division, Administrator
Phone: 503-986-3413

Susan Johnson
Maritime Pilots Board, Administrator
Phone: 503-731-4044

Sherrin Coleman
Transportation Public Transit Planning Programs
Phone: 503-986-4305

STATE AGENCIES

Pennsylvania

Pennsylvania Main Homeland Security Office
2605 Interstate Drive
Harrisburg, PA 17110
Phone: 717-651-2715
Fax: 717-651-2040
URL: www.homelandsecurity.state.pa.us

Edward G Rendell
Governor
Phone: 717-787-2500

Catherine Baker Knoll
Lieutenant Governor
Phone: 717-787-3300
e-mail: lieutenant-governor@state.pa.us

James F Powers
Director Pennsylvania Homeland Security
Phone: 717-651-2715
e-mail: japowers@state.pa.us

Tom Corbett
Attorney General
Phone: 717-787-3391

Agriculture Department
2301 N Cameron Street
Harrisburg, PA 17110-9408
Phone: 717-787-4737
Fax: 717-783-9709
URL: www.agriculture.state.pa.us

Dennis C Wolff
Secretary
Phone: 717-772-2853
e-mail: dwolff@state.pa.us

Russell Redding
Executive Deputy Secretary
Phone: 717-783-6980
e-mail: rredding@state.pa.us

Dr Paul Knepley
Direcot, Bureau of Animal Health and Diagnostic Services
Phone: 717-772-2852

Bill L Wehry
Deputy Secretary, Agriculture/Consumer Protection
Phone: 717-783-6985
e-mail: bwehry@state.pa.us

Michael F Hydock
Chief, Food Safety Laboratory Division
Phone: 717-787-4315

Sean Crager
Chief Information Officer

Association of Contingency Planners-Liberty Valley Chapter
3925 Dartmouth Lane
Bethlehem, PA 18020
Phone: 609-267-9245
URL: www.acp-international.com/lv
e-mail: fleonetti@comcast.net

Description: The Association of Contingency Planners (ACP) is a non-profit trade association dedicated to fostering continued professional growth and development in Contingency & Business Resumption Planning.

Frank Leonetti
President

George Jones
Secretary

Bureau of Epidemiology
Department of Health
Health and Welfare Building
Room 933
Harrisburg, PA 17108
Phone: 717-783-4677
Fax: 717-772-6975
URL: www.health.state.pa.us

Stephen Ostroff MD
Director
Phone: 717-783-4677

Veronica V Urdaneta
State Epidemiologist/Infectious Disease
Phone: 717-787-3350
e-mail: vurdaneta@state.pa.us

Gene B Weinberg
Community Epidemiology
Phone: 717-783-4677
e-mail: gweinberg@state.pa.us

Capitol Police
Department of General Services
Capitol East Wing
Room 70E
Harrisburg, PA 17125
Phone: 717-787-9013
Fax: 717-787-8637

Description: To achieve a safe environment free of crime, to protect and serve employees and visitors while on state property, and to protect property and grounds throughout the Capitol Complex and at state office buildings in Philadelphia, Pittsburgh and Scranton.

Richard S Shaffer
Superintendent

Department of Health
Health and Welfare Building
7th & Forster Streets
Harrisburg, PA 17120
Phone: 717-787-6436
Phone: 877-724-3258
URL: www.health.state.pa.us

Calvin B Johnson
Secretary
Phone: 717-787-6436

Joseph Schmider
Director Emergency Medical Services
Phone: 717-787-8740

Emergency Management Agency
2605 Interstate Drive
Harrisburg, PA 17110
Phone: 717-651-2007
Fax: 717-651-2040
URL: www.pema.state.pa.us

James R Joseph
Director

Richard D Flinn Jr
Deputy Director Operations
Phone: 717-651-7071
e-mail: rflinn@state.pa.us

Mimi Myslewicz
Recovery & Mitigation Bureau
Phone: 717-651-2146
e-mail: mimyslewic@state.pas

Evalyn Fisher
Planning Bureau
Phone: 717-651-2196
e-mail: evfisher@state.pa.us

Jose E Morales
Chief Counsel
Phone: 717-651-2010
e-mail: jmorales@state.pa.us

Edward Mann
Fire Commissioner
Phone: 717-651-2201
e-mail: fire@state.pa.us

Maria A Finn
Press Secretary
Phone: 717-651-2009
e-mail: mfinn@state.pa.us

Environmental Protection Department
400 Market Street
Harrisburg, PA 17101
Phone: 717-783-2300
Fax: 717-705-4980
URL: www.dep.state.pa.us
e-mail: RA-epcontactus@state.pa.us

Kathleen Alana McGinty
Secretary

Joyce E Epps
Air Quality
Phone: 717-787-9702

Dana Aunkst
Water Standards & Facility Regulation
Phone: 717-787-5017

David J Allard
Radiation Protection Bureau
Phone: 717-787-2480

Rich Janati
Chief Nuclear Safety Division
Phone: 717-787-2163

National Guard
Department of Military and Veterans Affairs
Fort Indiantown Gap
Annville, PA 17003
URL: www.dmva.state.pa.us

Major General Jessica L Wright
Adjutant General

Major General Steven M Sischo
Air Deputy Adjutant General

Major General Robert P French
Army Deputy Adjutant General

Pennsylvania Chiefs of Police Association
3905 N Front Street
Harrisburg, PA 17110
Phone: 717-236-1059
Fax: 717-236-0226
URL: www.pachiefs.org

Chief Robert Ruxton
President

Amy K Rosenberry
Executive Director
e-mail: akcorl@pachiefs.org

Rick Stevens
Communications Coordinator
e-mail: rstevens@chiefs.org

Philadelphia Regional Port Authority
3460 N Delaware Avenue
Philadelphia, PA 19134
Phone: 215-426-2600
Fax: 215-426-6800
URL: www.philaport.com

Description: An independent agency charged with the responsibility of managing, maintaining, protecting, marketing and promoting the public port facilities along the Delaware River in Philadelphia.

Brian Preski
Chairman

James T McDermott Jr
Executive Director

Robert C Blackburn
Deputy Executive Director

State Police
1800 Elmerton Avenue
Harrisburg, PA 17110
Phone: 717-783-5558
Fax: 717-787-2948
URL: www.psp.state.pa.us

Colonal Jeffrey B Miller
State Police Commissioner
Phone: 717-783-5558

Lt Col Frank E Pawlowski
Deputy Commissioner of Operations
Phone: 717-787-7219

Lt Col Coleman J McDonough
Deputy Commissioner of Staff
Phone: 717-783-5567

Lt Col John R Brown
Deputy Commissioner of Professional Responsibility
Phone: 717-346-9122

Three Rivers Contingency Planning Association
225 North Shore Drive
Pittsburgh, PA 15212
Phone: 412-395-2577
Fax: 412-324-4853
URL: www.trcpa.org

Description: The primary purpose is to promote education and the exchange of information among its members, that they can develop and improve their skills in the fields of contingency planning, business continuity, and disaster recovery. TRCPA is a non-profit organization; its members or officers obtain no financial benefits. Membership is free to all business and individuals interested in contingency planning regardless of location.

George Matthews
Chair

Scott Beers
Vice Chair

Transportation Department
400 North Street
Keystone Building
Harrisburg, PA 17120
Phone: 717-787-2838
Fax: 717-787-1738
URL: www.dot.state.pa.us

Allen D Biehler
Secretary

Richard H Hogg
Deputy Secretary for Highway Administration

Sharon A Daboin
Deputy Secretary for Aviation

Mahendra G Patel
Chief Engineer

STATE AGENCIES

Puerto Rico

Puerto Rico Main Homeland Security Office
La Fortaleza
PO Box 9020082
San Juan, 00902-0082
Puerto Rico
Phone: 787-721-7433
Fax: 787-725-7800
URL: www.gobierno.pr

Anibal Acevedo-Vila
Governor
Phone: 787-721-7000

Nelson Espinell
Security Advisor to the Governor
Phone: 787-721-7433

Nazario Lugo Borges
Emergency Management Director
Phone: 787-721-3596
e-mail: nlugo@aemead.gobierno.pr

Agriculture Department
PO Box 10163
San Juan, PR 00908-1163
Phone: 787-722-0871
Fax: 787-723-8512

Jose O Fabre Laboy
Secretary
Phone: 787-721-0871
e-mail: jofabre@da.gobierno.pr

Department of Transportation & Public Works
PO Box 42007
San Juan, PR 00940
Phone: 787-725-7112
Fax: 787-725-1620
URL: www.dtop.gov.pr

Gabriel Alcaraz Emmanuelli
Director
Phone: 787-729-1531
e-mail: galcaraz@act.dtop.gov.pr

Emergency Management
PO Box 9066597
San Juan, PR 00906-6597
Phone: 787-721-3596
Fax: 787-725-4244

Nazario Lugo Burgos
Director
Phone: 787-721-3596
e-mail: nlugo@aemead.gobierno.pr

Environmental Quality Board
PO Box 11488
San Juan, PR 00910
Phone: 787-767-8181
Fax: 787-767-4861

Carlos W Lopez Freytes
President
Phone: 787-767-8181
e-mail: carloswlopez@jca.gobierno.pr

Health Department
PO Box 70184
San Juan, PR 00936
Puerto Rico
Phone: 787-756-0035
Fax: 787-250-6547

Rosa Perez Perdomo
Director

National Guard
PO Box 9023786
San Juan, PR 00902-3786
Phone: 787-289-1631
Fax: 787-723-6360
URL: www.pr.ngb.army.mil

General David Carrion Baralt
General Advisor
Phone: 787-289-1631
e-mail: david.carrionbaralt@ng.army.mil

Natural & Environmental Resources Department
PO Box 9023207
San Juan, PR 00906-6600
Phone: 787-724-8770
Fax: 787-724-0091
URL: www.gobierno.pr/drna/

Javier Velez Arocho
Secretary

Office for Public Security Affairs-Local SAA-HSA
PO Box 9020082
San Juan, PR 00902-0082
Phone: 787-722-8075
Fax: 787-722-8136

Julio R Gonzalez Rodriguez
Director
e-mail: jgonzalez@oasp.gobierno.pr

Port Authority

Calle Lindbergh #64
Antugua Base Naval Miramar
San Juan, PR 00907
Puerto Rico
Mailing Address: PO Box 362829, San Juan PR 00936-2829
Phone: 787-723-2260
Fax: 787-722-7867
URL: www.prpa.gobierno.pr

Fernando J Bonilla Ortiz
Executive Director
e-mail: fjbonilla@prpa.gobierno.pr

Puerto Rico Police Department

PO Box 70166
San Juan, PR 00936-8166
Phone: 787-792-0002
Fax: 787-781-0080
URL: www.policia.gobierno.pr

Pedro A Toledo Davila
Superintendent

Safety & Public Protection Commission

PO Box 70166
San Juan, PR 00936-8166
Phone: 787-792-0002
Fax: 787-781-0080

Pedro A Toledo Davila
Commissioner

STATE AGENCIES

Rhode Island

Rhode Island Main Homeland Security Office
645 New London Avenue
Cranston, RI 02920
Phone: 401-946-9996
Fax: 401-944-1891
URL: www.riema.ri.gov; www.state.ri.us

Donald L Carcieri
Governor
Phone: 401-222-2080
e-mail: rigov@gov.state.ri.us

Charles J Fogarty
Lieutenant Governor
Phone: 401-222-2371
e-mail: riltg@ltgov.state.ri.us

John Aucott
Director Homeland Security
Phone: 401-946-9996
e-mail: john.aucott@us.army.mil

Major Gen Robert Thomas Bray
Adjutant General/Director Emergency Management
Phone: 401-275-4102

Patrick C Lynch
Attorney General
Phone: 401-274-4400

Emergency Management Agency
645 New London Avenue
Cranston, RI 02920
Phone: 401-946-9996
Fax: 401-944-1891
URL: www.riema.ri.gov

Major Gen Robert Thomas Bray
Director
Phone: 401-275-4102

Robert J Warren
Executive Director
Phone: 401-946-9996

Diana L Arcand
Deputy Director
e-mail: diana.arcand1@us.armmy.mil

Brittan K Bates
Homeland Security Exercise & Evaluation Program Coordinator/Public Information Officer

Paul D'Abbraccio
Counter-Terrorism Planning

Lawrence Macedo
Hazard Mitigation/Public Assistance Officer
e-mail: lawrence.macedo@us.army.mil

James Bell
Telecommunications Officer
e-mail: james.bell31@us.army.mil

Environmental Management Department
235 Promenade Street
Providence, RI 02908-5767
Phone: 401-222-6800
Fax: 401-222-6802
URL: www.dem.ri.gov

W Michael Sullivan
Director
Phone: 401-222-2771

Bob Ballou
Chief of Staff
Phone: 401-222-2771

Terrence Maguire
Assistant Director, Policy & Administration
Phone: 401-222-4700
e-mail: terrence.maguire@dem.ri.gov

Michael Mulhare
Emergency Response Office Administrator
Phone: 401-222-4700
e-mail: michael.mulhare@dem.ri.gov

Environmental Protection Bureau
Environmental Management Department
235 Promenade Street
Providence, RI 02908
Phone: 401-222-4700
Fax: 401-222-3162
URL: www.dem.ri.gov/programs/benviron

Alicia Good
Assistant Director Water Resources
Phone: 401-222-3961
e-mail: alicia.good@dem.ri.gov

Terrence Gray
Assistant Director Air, Waste & Compliance
Phone: 401-222-4700
e-mail: terrence.gray@dem.ri.gov

Health Department
3 Capitol Hill
Providence, RI 02908
Phone: 401-222-2231

Fax: 401-222-6548
URL: www.health.state.ri.us
e-mail: website.DOH@health.ri.gov

Description: To prevent disease and to protect and promote the health and safety of the people of Rhode Island.

David R Gifford
Director
Phone: 401-222-2231

Walter S Combs Jr
Executive Director Environmental Health
Phone: 401-222-3118

Ernest Julian
Food Protection Chief
Phone: 401-222-2750
e-mail: erniej@DOH.state.ri.us

Marie Stoeckel
Occupational & Radiological Health
Phone: 401-222-2438

Robert Vanderslice
Risk Assessment
Phone: 401-222-3424

John Fulton PhD
Disease Prevention & Control Division
Phone: 401-222-1172
e-mail: johnf@doh.state.ri.us

Medical Examiners Office
48 Orms Street
Providence, RI 02904-2283
Phone: 401-222-5500
Fax: 401-222-5517
URL: www.health.ri.gov/osme

Robert O'Donnell
Administrator

Thomas Gilson
Chief Medical Examiner

National Guard
Command Readiness Center
645 New London Avenue
Cranston, RI 02920
Phone: 401-275-4100
Fax: 401-275-4338
URL: www.riguard.com

Major Gen Robert Thomas Bray
Adjutant General/State Commander

Brigadier General Brian G Goodwin
Assistant Adjutant General - Army
Phone: 401-275-4100

Brigadier General Thomas Haynes
Assistant Adjutant General - Air
Phone: 401-886-1200

Lt Colonel Michael B McNamara
Public Affairs Officer
Phone: 401-275-4193
e-mail: michael.mcnamara@ri.ngb.army.mil

Natural Resources Bureau & Agriculture Division
Environmental Management Department
235 Promenade Street
Providence, RI 02908
Phone: 401-222-4700
Fax: 401-222-3162
URL: www.dem.ri.gov/programs/bnatres

Kenneth Ayars
Agriculture Chief
Phone: 401-222-2781
e-mail: kayars@dem.state.ri.us

Steven H Hall
Law Enforcement Chief
Phone: 401-222-2284

Rhode Island Public Utilities Commission
89 Jefferson Boulevard
Warwick, RI 02888
Phone: 401-941-4500
URL: www.ripuc.org
e-mail: mary.kent@ripuc.org

Elia Germani
Chairman

Tom Ahern
Administrator

Doug Hartley
Director of Energy

Rhode Island State Capitol Police
State House
Room 8A
Providence, RI 02903
Phone: 401-222-6905
Fax: 401-222-1090

Steven Tocco
Chief

State Police
311 Danielson Pike
Scituate, RI 02857
Phone: 401-444-1000
Fax: 401-444-1105
URL: www.risp.state.ri.us

Colonel Brendan Doherty
Superintendent

Sgt James Manni
Training Academy
Phone: 401-444-1191

Transportation Department
2 Capitol Hill
Providence, RI 02903
Phone: 401-222-2481
Fax: 401-222-2574
URL: www.dot.ri.gov
e-mail: customerservice@dot.ri.gov

Jerome F Williams
Director
Phone: 401-222-2481

Dana A Nolfe
Public Affairs
Phone: 401-222-1362
e-mail: franseg@dot.ri.gov

John B Affleck
Chief Counsel/Legal Services
Phone: 401-222-6510

Edmund T Parker
Chief Engineer/Transportation Development
Phone: 401-222-2492
e-mail: etparker@dot.ri.gov

Paul R Annarummo
Traffic Management/Managing Engineer
Phone: 401-222-5826

Namvar Moghadam
Highway & Bridge Maintenance Administrator
Phone: 401-222-2378
e-mail: ddambra@dot.ri.gov

J Michael Bennett
Deputy Chief Engineer/Intermodal Planning
Phone: 401-222-2023

Janis Loiselle
Highway Traffic Safety Administrator
Phone: 401-222-3024

STATE AGENCIES

South Carolina

South Carolina Main Homeland Security Office
4400 Broad River Road
PO Box 21398
Columbia, SC 29221
Phone: 803-737-9000
Phone: 803-896-7001
Fax: 803-896-7041
URL: www.sled.state.sc.us

Mark Sanford
Governor
Phone: 803-734-2100

R Andre Bauer
Lieutenant Governor
Phone: 803-734-2080
e-mail: ltgov@scsenate.org

Robert M Stewart
Director Homeland Security/Law Enforcement Division
Phone: 803-896-7001

Henry McMaster
Attorney General
Phone: 803-734-3970
e-mail: info@scattorneygeneral.com

Agriculture Department
1200 Senate Street
PO Box 11280
Columbia, SC 29211-1280
Phone: 803-734-2210
Fax: 803-734-0659
URL: www.scda.state.sc.us

Hugh E Weathers
Commissioner
Phone: 803-734-2190

Becky Walton
Public Affairs
Phone: 803-734-2182
e-mail: bwalton@scda.sc.gov

Department of Public Safety
10311 Wilson Boulevard
PO Box 1993
Blythewood, SC 29016
URL: www.scdps.org

James K Schweitzer
Director

Colonel Anna Amos
Deputy Director, State Transport Police
Phone: 803-896-5500

Colonel Russell Roark
Deputy Director, Highway Patrol
Phone: 803-896-7920

Raymond Richburg
Protective Services Chief
Phone: 803-896-5442

Max Young
Highway Safety Director
Phone: 803-896-9950

Burke O Fitzpatrick
Justice Programs Office Administrator
Phone: 803-896-8702

Emergency Management Division
2779 Fish Hatchery Road
West Columbia, SC 29172
Phone: 803-737-8500
URL: www.scemd.org

Ronald C Osborne
Director
Phone: 803-737-8566

John Paolucci
Response & Operations Chief
Phone: 803-737-8650

Sandra Bush
State Warning Point Supervisor
Phone: 803-737-8562

Steven Batson
Regional Emergency Management Programs
Phone: 803-737-8661

Kim Stenson
Preparedness & Recovery Chief
Phone: 803-737-8651

Joseph Farmer
Public Information Director
Phone: 803-737-8569

Health & Environmental Control Department
2600 Bull Street
Columbia, SC 29201
Phone: 803-898-3300
Fax: 803-898-3323
URL: www.dhec.sc.gov

Description: Promotes and protects the health of the public and the environment.

Earl Hunter
Commissioner
Phone: 803-898-3300

Roger D Scott
Director, Environmental Health Bureau
Phone: 803-896-0646
e-mail: scottrd@dhec.sc.gov

Sandra D Craig
Food Protection Division
Phone: 803-896-0640
e-mail: craigsd@dhec.sc.gov

C P Kanwat
Food Safety Epidemiologist
e-mail: kanwatcp@dhec.sc.gov

Myra C Reece
Chief, Air Quality Bureau
Phone: 803-898-4123

Leslie Wood
Emergency Medical Services
Phone: 803-545-4204

National Guard
1 National Guard Road
Columbia, SC 29201-4752
Phone: 803-806-4200
Fax: 803-806-4499
URL: www.scguard.com

Major General Stanhope S Spears
Adjutant General
Phone: 803-806-4217

Major Gen Harry B Burchstead
Deputy Adjutant General
Phone: 803-806-4215

John A Shuler
Deputy Adjutant General for State Operations
Phone: 803-806-1413

Colonel Pete Brooks
Public Information Officer
Phone: 803-806-4200
e-mail: brookspj@tag.scmd.state.sc.us

Ports Authority
176 Concord Street
PO Box 22287
Charleston, SC 29401
Mailing Address: PO Box 22287, Charleston SC 29413
Phone: 843-577-8121
URL: www.port-of-charleston.com

Bernard S Groseclose Jr
President/CEO
Phone: 843-577-8600

Joe T Bryant
VP Terminal Development
Phone: 843-577-8611

William A McLean
VP Operations
Phone: 843-577-8603

L David Schronce
Director - Georgetown, Port Royal & Veterans
Phone: 843-527-4476

Stephen E Connor
VP Security, Risk Management & HR
Phone: 843-577-8134

Peter O Lehman
Director - Planning & Business Development
Phone: 843-577-8601

Pamela A Everitt
Director - Information Technology
Phone: 843-577-8678

South Carolina Police Chiefs Association
PO Box 61170
Columbia, SC 29260
Phone: 803-790-5042
Fax: 803-790-5043
URL: www.scpolicechiefs.org
e-mail: mail@scpolicechiefs.org

J C Rowe
Executive Director

Transportation Department
955 Park Street
PO Box 191
Columbia, SC 29202
Phone: 803-737-1302
Fax: 803-737-2038
URL: www.dot.state.sc.us

H B Limehouse Jr
Executive Director
Phone: 803-737-1302

Tony Chapman
State Highway Engineer
Phone: 803-737-7900

Glennith C Johnson
Deputy Director for Mass Transit
Phone: 803-737-0831

Terecia W Wilson
Safety Director
Phone: 803-737-0403

Ron Patton
Director for Planning & Environmental
Phone: 803-737-1444

Doug Harper
Chief Information Officer
Phone: 803-737-1003

STATE AGENCIES

South Dakota

South Dakota Main Homeland Security Office
118 W Capitol Avenue
Pierre, SD 57501
Phone: 605-773-3450
Phone: 866-466-5263
Fax: 605-773-3018
URL: www.state.sd.us/homeland
e-mail: homelandsecurity@state.sd.us

M Michael Rounds
Governor
Phone: 605-773-3212

Dennis M Daugaard
Lieutenant Governor
Phone: 605-773-3661
e-mail: dennis.daugaard@state.sd.us

John A Berheim
Director Homeland Security
Phone: 605-773-3450
e-mail: Homelandsecurity@state.sd.us

Larry Long
Attorney General
Phone: 605-773-3215
e-mail: atghelp@state.sd.us

Association of Contingency Planners
PO Box 884
Sioux Falls, SD 57101
Phone: 605-782-5020
URL: www.acp-international.com/sioux
e-mail: juliearnold@wellsfargo.com

Description: A non-profit trade association dedicated to fostering continued professional growth and development in effective Contingency & Business Resumption Planning. ACP is an international networking and information exchange organization in the business continuity industry.

Julie Schoep-Arnold
President

Mike May
Secretary

Department of Agriculture
523 E Capitol Avenue
Pierre, SD 57501
Phone: 605-773-5436
Phone: 800-228-5254
Fax: 605-773-3481
URL: www.state.sd.us/doa/
e-mail: agmail@state.sd.us

William Even
Secretary
Phone: 605-773-3375

George Williams
Deputy Secretary
Phone: 605-773-5425
e-mail: george.williams@state.sd.us

Darwin Kurtenbach
Dairy/Plant Protection Office
Phone: 605-773-4294
e-mail: darwin.kurtenbach@state.sd.us

Kevin Fridley
Agricultural Services
Phone: 605-773-3724
e-mail: kevin.fridley@state.sd.us

Joseph Lowe
Wildland Fire Supression
Phone: 605-393-8011
e-mail: joseph.lowe@state.sd.us

Department of Military & Veteran Affairs/National Guard
Soldiers & Sailors Memorial Building
425 E Capitol Avenue
Pierre, SD 57501-5070
Phone: 605-773-3269
Fax: 605-773-5380
URL: http://sdguard.ngb.army.mil/

Major General Michael A Gorman
Adjutant General

Andy Gerlach
Deputy Secretary
e-mail: andy.gerlach@state.sd.us

Department of Public Safety
118 W Capitol Avenue
Pierre, SD 57501
Phone: 605-773-3178
Fax: 605-773-3018
URL: www.state.sd.us/dps/
e-mail: DPSInfo@state.sd.us

Description: The department has a number of duties it is expected to perform: law enforcement, public safety communications, highway safety, traffic crash record keeping, driver licensing, regulatory inspection services, emergency medical licensing and certification, fire training and investigation, emergency preparedness and hazard mitigation, and most recently, homeland security.

Tom Dravland
Secretary
Phone: 605-773-3178
e-mail: dpsinfo@state.sd.us

Bob Graff
Director Emergency Medical Services
Phone: 605-773-4031
e-mail: bob.graff@state.sd.us

Allen Christie
State Fire Marshal
Phone: 605-773-3562
e-mail: fireinfo@state.sd.us

Kristi Turman
Emergency Management
Phone: 605-773-3231
e-mail: kristi.turman@state.sd.us

Sgt Dana Svendsen
Capitol Security Coordinator
Phone: 605-773-3105

Colonel Daniel C Mosteller
Highway Patrol Division, Superintendent
Phone: 605-773-3015
e-mail: dan.mosteller@state.sd.us

Roy Meyer
Highway Safety Office
Phone: 605-773-4949
e-mail: highwaysafetyinfo@state.sd.us

Tom Dravland
State Radio Dispatch
Phone: 605-773-3536
e-mail: dpsinfo@state.sd.us

Captain Pat Fahey
Motor Carrier Services
Phone: 605-773-4578

Environment and Natural Resources Department
523 E Capitol Avenue
Joe Foss Building
Pierre, SD 57501
Mailing Address: PO Box 2020
Phone: 605-773-3151
Fax: 605-773-6035
URL: www.state.sd.us/denr
e-mail: denrinternet@state.sd.us

Description: Protects the public health and environment by providing natural resources assessment, regulation, and financial assistance.

Steven M Pirner
Secretary
Phone: 605-773-3151

Brian Gustafson
Air Quality Administrator
Phone: 605-773-3151

Tim Tollesfrud
Environmental Services Director
Phone: 605-773-3153

Mark Mayer
Drinking Water Administrator
Phone: 605-773-3754
e-mail: mark.mayer@state.sd.us

Vonni Kallemeyn
Waste Management Administrtor
Phone: 605-773-3153

Health Department
600 E Capitol Avenue
Pierre, SD 57501-2536
Phone: 605-773-3361
Phone: 800-738-2301
Fax: 605-773-5683
URL: www.state.sd.us/doh
e-mail: doh.info@state.sd.us

Doneen Hollingsworth
Secretary
Phone: 605-773-3361

Mike Smith
Public Health Laboratory
Phone: 605-773-3368
e-mail: mike.smith@state.sd.us

Lon Kightlinger
State Epidemiologist
Phone: 605-280-4810

Stacy Ellwanger
Environmental Health Supervisor
Phone: 605-773-3368
e-mail: stacy.ellwanger@state.sd.us

Office of Emergency Management
Department of Public Safety
118 W Capitol Avenue
Pierre, SD 57501
Phone: 605-773-3231
Fax: 605-773-3580
URL: www.oem.sd.gov

Description: The Office of Emergency Management supports the national emergency management system by encouraging the development of comprehensive disaster preparedness and assistance plans, programs, capabilities and organizations by the State and local governments.

Kristi Turman
Director
Phone: 605-773-3231

Tina Titze
Assistant Director
Phone: 605-773-3231

Doug Hinkle
Citizen Corps
e-mail: doug.hinkle@state.sd.us

Jonathan Nesladek
Field Operations
e-mail: jon.nesladek@state.sd.us

Public Utilities Commission
500 E Capitol Avenue
Capitol Building, 1st Floor

Pierre, SD 57501-5070
Phone: 605-773-3201
Phone: 800-332-1782
Fax: 605-773-3809
URL: www.state.sd.us/puc

Description: Operates the natural gas pipeline safety program
and regulates the service quality/rates of investor-owned electric,
natural gas and telephone utilities.

Dusty Johnson
Chairman

Gary Hanson
Vice-Chairman

Steve Kolbeck
Commissioner

Patricia Van Gerpen
Executive Director
e-mail: patty.vangerpen@state.sd.us

Martin Bettmann
Pipeline Safety Program Manager
e-mail: martin.bettmann@state.sd.us

South Dakota Sheriffs Association
PO Box 130
Howard, SD 57349
Phone: 605-940-6554
URL: www.southdakotasheriffs.org

Staci Eggert
Executive Director
e-mail: admin@southdakotasheriffs.org

Transportation Department
700 E Broadway Avenue
Becker-Hansen Building
Pierre, SD 57501
Phone: 605-773-3265
Fax: 605-773-3921
URL: www.sddot.com

Darren Bergquist
Acting Secretary
Phone: 605-773-3265

Emilie Miller
Communications Manager
Phone: 605-773-3265

Loren Schaefer
Chief Engineer
Phone: 605-773-3174

Bruce Lindholm
Aeronautics & Local Government Assistance
Phone: 605-773-7045
e-mail: bruce.lindholm@state.sd.us

Darin Bergquist
Division of Operations
Phone: 605-773-3571
e-mail: darin.bergquist@state.sd.us

STATE AGENCIES

Tennessee

Tennessee Main Homeland Security Office
William R Snodgrass Tennessee Tower
25th Floor
Nashville, TN 37243
Phone: 615-532-7825
Fax: 615-253-5379
URL: http://state.tn.us/homelandsecurity

Phillip Bredesen
Governor
Phone: 615-741-2001
e-mail: phil.bredesen@state.tn.us

Ron Ramsey
Lieutenant Governor
Phone: 615-741-2368

David Mitchell
Director Homeland Security
Phone: 615-532-7825
e-mail: dave.mitchell@state.tn.us

Sgt Mike Zelnik
Critical Infrastructure State Coordinator & Safety Dept Liaison
Phone: 615-532-7825

Paul G Summers
Attorney General
Phone: 615-741-3491

Agriculture Department
Ellington Agricultural Center
PO Box 40627
Nashville, TN 37204-0627
Phone: 615-837-5103
Fax: 615-837-5333
URL: www.tennessee.gov/agriculture

Description: To serve the citizens of Tennessee by promoting wise uses of our agriculture and forest resources, developing economic opportunities, and ensuring safe and dependable food and fiber.

Ken Givens
Commissioner
Phone: 615-837-5100
e-mail: ken.giveens@state.tn.us

Terry Oliver
Deputy Commissioner
Phone: 615-837-5103
e-mail: terry.oliver@state.tn.us

Thomas Womack
Public Affairs Executive Assistant
Phone: 615-837-5103
e-mail: tom.womack@state.tn.us

Ron Wilson
State Veterinarian
Phone: 615-837-5125
e-mail: ron.wilson@state.tn.us

Steven Scott
State Forester
Phone: 615-837-5411
e-mail: steven.scott@state.tn.us

Joe Gaines
Market Development Assistant Commissioner
Phone: 615-837-5160
e-mail: joe.gaines@state.tn.us

John Sanford
Food Manufacturing Administrator
Phone: 615-837-5534
e-mail: john.sanford@state.tn.us

Jimmy Hopper
Regulatory Services Director
Phone: 615-837-5150
e-mail: jimmy.hopper@state.tn.us

Bob Williams
Standards Administrator
Phone: 615-837-5109
e-mail: robert.g.williams@state.tn.us

Association of Contingency Planners-Middle Tennessee/Nashville Chapter
PO Box 198050
Nashville, TN 37219
Phone: 615-344-6486
URL: www.midtenn.acp-international.com
e-mail: tara.verble@hcahealthcare.com

Description: The ACP is a non-profit trade association dedicated to fostering continued professional growth and development in Contingency & Business Resumption Planning. It is an international exchange organization for the business continuity industry.

Tara Verble
President

Emergency Management Agency
Military Department
3041 Sidco Drive
Nashville, TN 37204
Phone: 615-741-0001
Fax: 615-242-9635

URL: www.tnema.org

Maj General (Ret) James H Bassham
Director

Emergency Medical Services
Health Department
227 French Landing, Ste 303
Heritage Place Metro Center
Nashville, TN 37243
Phone: 615-741-2584
Phone: 800-778-4505
Fax: 615-741-4217
URL: www2.state.tn.us/health/ems/

Joe Philips
Director

Joe Holley
Medical Director

Environment and Conservation Department
401 Church Street
1st Floor
Nashville, TN 37243-0435
Phone: 615-532-0109
Fax: 615-532-1020
URL: www.tennessee.gov/environment

Jim Fyke
Commissioner
Phone: 615-532-0109

Paul Sloan
Deputy Commissioner
Phone: 615-532-0109

Tracy Carter
Air Resources Senior Director
Phone: 615-532-0127

David Draughon
Water Resources Senior Director
Phone: 615-532-0152

David Owenby
Public Affairs/Policy
Phone: 615-532-1531

Lawrence E Nanney
Radiological Health
Phone: 615-532-0364

Alan Schwendimann
Groundwater Protection
Phone: 615-532-0762

Health Department
425 5th Avenue N
Cordell Hull Building, 3rd Floor
Nashville, TN 37243
Phone: 615-741-3111
Fax: 615-741-2491
URL: http://health.state.tn.us
e-mail: tn.health@state.tn.us

Susan R Cooper
Commissioner
Phone: 615-741-3111

Ricky Frazier
Acting Deputy Commissioner
Phone: 615-741-3111

Shirley Correy
General Counsel
Phone: 615-741-1611

Allen Craig
Communicable & Environmental Disease Services Director
Phone: 615-741-7247

Highway Patrol
Safety Department
1150 Foster Avenue
Nashville, TN 37249-1000
Phone: 615-251-5175
Fax: 615-532-1051

Description: Responsible for the enforcement of all federal and state laws relating to traffic.

Colonel Mike Walker
Administration

Lt Colonel Albert Strawther
Administration

Major Tracy Trott
Administration

Military Department
3041 Sidco Drive
Houston Barracks
Nashville, TN 37204-1502
Mailing Address: PO Box 41502
Phone: 615-313-3001
Fax: 615-313-3129
URL: www.tnmilitary.org

Major General Gus L Hargett
Adjutant General
Phone: 615-313-3001

Brig General William R Cotney
Air Assistant Adjutant General
Phone: 615-313-3012

Brig General David E Greer
Army Assistant Adjutant General
Phone: 615-313-3002

Colonel Issac G Osborne Jr
Joint Chief of Staff
Phone: 615-313-3007

Colonel Terry A Ethridge
State Aviation Officer

Randy D Harris
Joint Public Affairs Director
Phone: 615-313-0633

Safety Department
1150 Foster Avenue
Nashville, TN 37243
Phone: 615-251-5166
Fax: 615-253-2091
URL: www.tennessee.gov/safety
e-mail: safety@state.tn.us

Description: Through education, regulation, and enforcement, we ensure the overall safety and welfare of the public.

Dave Mitchell
Commissioner
Phone: 615-251-5166

Greta Dajani
Deputy Commissioner
Phone: 615-251-5166

Captain Tommy Hale
Special Operations Commander
Phone: 615-741-5660
e-mail: tommy.hale@state.tn.us

Lt Richard Kelly
Capitol Police Division
Phone: 615-741-2138

George Dittfurth
Criminal Investigations Division
Phone: 615-251-5185

Captain Steve Binkley
Commercial Vehicle Enforcement Director
Phone: 615-687-2326

Sgt Edward Cherry
Bomb Squad Commander
Phone: 615-741-5660

Mike Browning
Public Information Officer
Phone: 615-251-5131

Tennessee Association of Chiefs of Police
530 Church Street
Suite 504
Nashville, TN 37219
Phone: 615-726-8227
Fax: 615-244-0057
URL: www.tacp.org

Maggi McLean Duncan
Executive Director
Phone: 615-726-8227
e-mail: maggi@tacp.org

Transportation Department
505 Deaderick Street
James K Polk Building, Suite 700
Nashville, TN 37243
Phone: 615-741-2848
Fax: 615-741-2508
URL: www.tdot.state.tn.us
e-mail: tdot.comments@state.tn.us

Gerald F Nicely
Commissioner
Phone: 615-741-2848

Paul Degges
Chief Engineer/Engineering Bureau Chief
Phone: 615-741-0791

John Reinbold
General Counsel
Phone: 615-741-2941

Bob Woods
Aeronautics Division
Phone: 615-741-3208

Judy Steele
Community Relations Director
Phone: 615-741-7736

Kendell Poole
Highway Safety Office Director
Phone: 615-741-2589

Vic Mangrum
Information Technology Director
Phone: 615-741-3576

Julie Oaks
Public Information Officer
Phone: 615-741-2331

STATE AGENCIES

Texas

Texas Main Homeland Security Office
1100 San Jacinto
Austin, TX 78701
Mailing Address: PO Box 12428, Austin TX 78711
Phone: 512-463-1953
Phone: 800-843-5789
Fax: 512-475-0876
URL: www.texashomelandsecurity.com

Richard Perry Jr
Governor
Phone: 512-463-2000

David Dewhurst
Lieutenant Governor
Phone: 512-463-0001

Steven McCraw
Director Homeland Security
Phone: 512-463-1953

Greg Abbott
Attorney General
Phone: 512-463-2191

Agriculture Department
1700 N Congress Avenue
11th Floor
Austin, TX 78701
Mailing Address: PO Box 12847, 78711
Phone: 512-463-7476
Fax: 888-223-8861
URL: www.agr.state.tx.us/
e-mail: customer.relations@agr.state.tx.us

Todd Staples
Commissioner
Phone: 512-463-4578
e-mail: commissioner@agr.state.tx.us

Drew DeBerry
Deputy Commissioner
Phone: 512-463-7567

Shannon Rusing
Chief of Staff
Phone: 512-463-7567

Jimmy Bush
Assistant Commissioner of Pesticide Programs
Phone: 512-463-7504

Fred Higgins
Assistant Commissioner of Food & Nutrition
Phone: 512-463-2434

Association of Contingency Planners
PO Box 631812
Irving, TX 75063
Phone: 817-699-4353
URL: www.acp-international.com/northtx

Description: Serves as a forum for business professionals working in the areas of business continuity, business resumption, contingency planning, disaster recovery and other related emergency recovery functions. Open to all professionals interested in the many fields of crisis management, business continuity and disaster recovery.

Jerry A Knight
President

Mia Marzullo
Vice President/Secretary

Bureau of Epidemiology & Disease Surveillance
Texas Department of State Health Services
1100 W 49th Street
Austin, TX 78756-3199
Phone: 512-458-7268
Fax: 512-458-7689
URL: www.dshs.state.tx.us/epidemiology/default.shtm
e-mail: Jeanne.Lain@dshs.state.tx.us

David Lakey
Commissioner

Martha Mcglothlin
Community Preparedness Program Director
Phone: 806-655-7151

Capital of Texas (Austin) Chapter
PO Box 13371
Austin, TX 78711
Phone: 512-463-1813
URL: capitaloftexas.acp-international.com

Description: A non profit mutual benefit association of professionals with responsibility or interest in the areas of risk management, business continuity planning, disaster recovery planning, emergency management of information systems security, ACP provides an effective forum for exchanging information , sharing experiences, and indentifying and trouble-shooting common needs and problems.

Ruth Hooks
President

Community Dynamics & Prevention Strategies
Health & Human Services Commission
Brown-Heatly Building

4900 N Lamar Boulevard, 7th Floor
Austin, TX 78751-2316
Phone: 512-424-6500
Fax: 512-491-1967
URL: www.hhsc.state.tx.us
e-mail: contact@hhsc.state.tx.us

Albert Hawkins
Executive Commissioner
Phone: 512-424-6603

Brian Flood
Inspector General
Phone: 512-491-2051

Anne Heiligenstein
Deputy Executive Commissioner of Social Services
Phone: 512-424-6609

Charles Bell MD
Deputy Executive Commissioner of Health Services
Phone: 512-424-6603

Carey Smith
General Counsel
Phone: 512-424-3397

Emergency Management Association of Texas
1305 San Antonio Street
Austin, TX 78701
Phone: 512-454-4476
e-mail: sjennings@rayassociates.com

Ed Schaefer
President

Molly McFadden
Vice President

Environmental and Consumer Health Protection
1100 W 49th Street
Austin, TX 78756
Phone: 512-458-7111
Phone: 800-735-2989
Fax: 512-458-7686
URL: www.dshs.state.tx.us

Joseph L Fuller
Associate Commissioner
Phone: 512-458-7541

Nick Fohn
General Sanitation Director
Phone: 830-278-7173
e-mail: nick.fohn@dshs.state.tx.us

Sandra Guerra-Cantu MD
Public Health Regional Director

Richard Boykin
Product Safety Director
Phone: 210-949-2148
e-mail: richard.boykin@dshs.state.tx.us

Roger Winkelmann
Radiation Control Director
Phone: 210-949-2176
e-mail: roger.winkelmann@dshs.state.tx.us

Dr Richard Farris
Meat Safety Assurance Regional Veterinarian

Dr Catherine Tull
Milk & Dairy Inspector

Governor's Emergency Management Division
Public Safety Department
5805 N Lamar Boulevard
Austin, TX 78752
Mailing Address: PO Box 4087
Phone: 512-424-2138
Fax: 512-424-2444
URL: www.txdps.state.tx.us/dem/
e-mail: mary.lenz@txdps.state.tx.us

Steven McCraw
Director
Phone: 512-463-1953

Jack Colley
Chief
Phone: 512-424-2443

Frank Cantu
State Coordinator for Response & Recovery
Phone: 512-424-2455

Mary Lenz
Public Information Officer
Phone: 512-424-2432

Gary Weeks
Terrorism Preparedness Supervisor
Phone: 512-424-5347

Health Department
State Health Services
1100 W 49th Street
Austin, TX 78756
Phone: 512-458-7111
Phone: 888-963-7111
Fax: 512-458-7750
URL: www.dshs.state.tx.us

David Lakey
Commissioner
Phone: 512-458-7375

Vincent P Fonseca MD
State Epidemiologist
Phone: 512-458-7676

Debra Stabeno
Assistant Commissioner for Prevention & Preparedness

Lisa Hernandez
General Counsel Office
Phone: 512-458-7236

Richard A Ratcliff
Radiation Control Program Director
Phone: 512-834-6688

Joe Vesowate
Assistant Commissioner for Mental Health & Substance Abuse
Phone: 512-206-5797

Dave Wanser PhD
Deputy Commissioner for Behavioral & Community Health
Phone: 512-206-7375

National Guard
2200 West 35th Street
Camp Mabry
Autin, TX 78763-5218
Mailing Address: PO Box 5218
Phone: 512-782-5001
Fax: 512-782-5578
URL: www.agd.state.tx.us

Major General Charles G Rodriguez
Adjutant General
Phone: 512-782-5006

Colonel George A Brinegar
Army Chief of Staff
Phone: 512-782-5007

Major General Allen Denhert
Assistant Adjutant General & Air National Guard Commander
Phone: 512-782-5007

Major General Christopher Powers
Texas State Guard Command General

Colonel Charles Bradley
Inspector General
Phone: 512-954-5122

Colonel Robert Cannon
Task Force Commander

Police Chiefs Association
1312 E Highway 290
Suite C
Elgin, TX 78621
Mailing Address: PO Box 819
Phone: 512-281-5400
Phone: 877-776-5423
Fax: 512-281-2240
URL: www.texaspolicechiefs.org
e-mail: ammymartin@texaspolicechiefs.org

Description: To promote the professional practice and development of law enforcement administration.

Public Safety Department
5805 N Lamar Boulevard
Austin, TX 78752-4422
Mailing Address: PO Box 4087
Phone: 512-424-2000
Fax: 512-424-5708
URL: www.txdps.state.tx.us
e-mail: ustomerservicedl@txdps.state.tx.us

Description: To provide public safety service to those people in the state of Texas by enforcing laws, administering regulatory programs, managing records, educating the public, and managing emergencies, both directly and through interaction with other agencies.

Colonel Thomas Davis Jr
Director
Phone: 512-424-7770

Lt Colonel David McEathron
Assistant Director
Phone: 512-424-7774

Ernest Angelo Jr
Chairman Public Safety Commission

David Gavin
Assistant Chief of Criminal Records Service

Jerry Newbury
Fleet Operations Manager

Texas Department of Public Safety Officer's Association
5821 Airport Boulevard
Austin, TX 78752
Phone: 512-451-0571
Phone: 800-933-7765
Fax: 512-451-0709
URL: www.dpsoa.com
e-mail: kim@dpsoa.com

Description: DPSOA offers and executes programs that benefit Texas Troopers and the communities around them. Publishes a quarterly magazine which has a circulation of approximately 3,600 copies.

Sgt Henry Brune Jr
President

Sgt Brian Hawthorne
President-Elect

Transportation Department
125 E 11th Street
Austin, TX 78701
Phone: 512-305-9509
Fax: 512-475-3072
URL: www.dot.state.tx.us

Description: To work cooperatively to provide safe, effective and efficient movement of people and goods.

Ric Williamson
Chairman
Phone: 512-305-9509

Thomas R Bohuslav
Construction Director

Carlos A Lopez
Traffic Operations Director

Michael W Behrens
Executive Director
Phone: 512-305-9501

Steven E Simmons
Deputy Executive Director
Phone: 512-305-9501

Amadeo Saenz Jr
Assistant Executive Director of Engineering Operations

Edward Serna
Assistant Executive Director for Support Operations

Eric L Gleason
Public Transportation Director

Brett Bray
Motor Vehicle Director

Ed Sims
Occupational Safety Director

Western States Vice Investigators' Association

PO Box 1764
Houston, TX 77251
Phone: 713-308-8600
Phone: 800-664-8423
Fax: 713-308-8665
URL: www.wsvia.com
e-mail: mail@wsvia.com

Description: A non-profit organization comprised of law enforcement officials and governmental personnel involved in the investigation of vice criminal activity throughout the United States and Canada. The Association accepts personnel from police departments from across the nation and Canada. Recognizing the changes occuring nationallu in the priorities by which departments initiated cases and understanding the smaller departments utilized their detectives for both vice and narcotics work.

Dan Peralas
Assistant Chief

STATE AGENCIES

Utah

Utah Main Homeland Security Office
State Office Building
Room 1110
Salt Lake City, UT 84114
Phone: 801-538-3400
Phone: 800-753-2858
Fax: 801-538-3770
URL: http://des.utah.gov

Jon Huntsman Jr
Governor
Phone: 801-538-1000

Gary R Herbert
Lieutenant Governor
Phone: 801-538-1041

Mike Kuehn
Director Homeland Security
Phone: 801-538-3400
e-mail: mkuehn@utah.gov

Mark Shurtleff
Attorney General
Phone: 801-538-9600
e-mail: uag@utah.gov

Association of Contingency Planners
PO Box 11434
Salt Lake City, UT 84147
Phone: 801-994-6620
URL: www.acputah.org
e-mail: michellejones@discoverfinancial.com

Description: A large and established organization for practitioners in the rapidly evolving field of business continuity, that serves Utah, Wyoming, Idaho and parts of New Mexico. ACP provides a forum for the exchange of experiences and information through networking.

Michelle Jones
President

Scott Jones
Vice President

Department of Agriculture and Food
350 N Redwood Road
Salt Lake City, UT 84116
Mailing Address: PO Box 146500, 84114-6500
Phone: 801-538-7100
Fax: 801-538-7126
URL: www.ag.state.ut.us
e-mail: UDAF-Information@utah.gov

Description: Protects and promotes Utah agriculture and food.

Leonard Blackham
Commissioner
Phone: 801-538-7101
e-mail: udaf-commissioner@utah.gov

Kyle Stephens
Deputy Commissioner
Phone: 801-538-7102
e-mail: kylestephens@utah.gov

Kay Brown
Fish Health
Phone: 801-538-7029
e-mail: udaf-fishhealth@utah.gov

Terry R Lenlove
Animal Industry Division Director
Phone: 801-538-7166
e-mail: udaf-statevets@utha.gov

Larry Lewis
Public Information Officer
Phone: 801-538-7104
e-mail: larrylewis@utah.gov

George Hopkin
Environment Quality Bureau Chief
Phone: 801-538-7177
e-mail: ghopkins@utah.gov

Bill Eccleston
Dairy Microbiology Lab
Phone: 801-538-7129
e-mail: beccleston@utah.gov

Seth Winterton
Marketing & Development Deputy Director
Phone: 801-538-7108
e-mail: udaf-marketing@utah.gov

Department of Environmental Quality
168 N 1950 West
PO Box 144810
Salt Lake City, UT 84114
Phone: 801-536-4402
Fax: 801-536-0061
URL: www.deq.utah.gov
e-mail: deqinfo@utah.gov

Rick Sprott
Acting Executive Director
Phone: 801-536-4404
e-mail: rsprott@utah.gov

Bill Sinclair
Deputy Director
e-mail: bsinclair@utah.gov

Brad T Johnson
Environmental Response & Remediation Director
Phone: 801-536-4170
e-mail: bjohnson@utah.gov

Leah Ann Lamb
Planning & Public Affairs Director
Phone: 801-536-4476
e-mail: llamb@utah.gov

Dane Finerfrock
Radiation Control Director
Phone: 801-536-4257
e-mail: dfinerfrock@utah.gov

Walter L Baker
Water Quality Division
Phone: 801-538-6047
e-mail: wbaker@utah.gov

Rick Sprott
Air Quality Director
Phone: 801-536-4022
e-mail: rsprott@utah.gov

Ken Bousfield
Drinking Water Division Director
Phone: 801-536-4207
e-mail: kbousfield@utah.gov

Dennis Downs
Solid & Hazardous Waste Director
Phone: 801-538-6170
e-mail: ddown@utah.gov

Department of Public Safety
4501 S 2700 West
Salt Lake City, UT 84119
Mailing Address: PO Box 141775
Phone: 801-965-4461
Phone: 800-222-0038
Fax: 801-965-4608
URL: www.publicsafety.utah.gov

Robert Flowers
Commissioner
Phone: 801-965-4463

Verdi R White II
Deputy Commissioner

Carol Groustra
Communications Bureau
Phone: 801-887-3892

Stu Smith
Crime Laboratory Bureau
Phone: 801-957-8546

Ed McConkie
Bureau of Criminal Investigations
Phone: 801-965-4571

Terry Mercer
Aeronautics Bureau
Phone: 801-244-5859

Ron Morris
State Fire Marshall
Phone: 801-284-6358
e-mail: onmorris@utah.gov

Dignitary Protection and Uniform Division
Highway Patrol
Capitol Building Complex
East Office Building, Room E 025
Salt Lake City, UT 84114
Phone: 801-538-1111
Fax: 801-538-1844
URL: www.highwaypatrol.utah.gov/contact

Epidemiology & Laboratory Services Division
Department of Health
46 N Medical Drive
Salt Lake City, UT 84113
Phone: 801-584-8400
Fax: 801-584-8586
URL: www.health.utah.gov/els/

Teresa Garrett
Division Director
Phone: 801-584-8450
e-mail: teresagarrett@utah.gov

Robert Rolfs MD
State Epidemiologist
Phone: 801-538-6191
e-mail: rrolfs@utah.gov

Barbara Jepson
Microbiology Bureau Director
Phone: 801-584-8595
e-mail: bjepson@utah.gov

Jennifer Brown
Communicable Disease Control Director
Phone: 801-538-6096
e-mail: ENNIFERBROWN@utah.gov

Gambrelli Layco
Forensic Toxicology Director
Phone: 801-584-8464
e-mail: glaycon@utah.gov

Highway Patrol
Department of Public Safety
4501 S 2700 West
PO Box 141775
Salt Lake City, UT 84114
Phone: 801-965-4518
Fax: 801-965-4716
URL: http://highwaypatrol.utah.gov

Description: Traffic law enforcement.

Colonel D Lance Davenport
Superintendent

National Guard
12953 S Minuteman Drive
Draper, UT 84020-9286
Phone: 801-523-4400
Fax: 801-523-4677
URL: www.utahguard.com /www.ut.ngb.army.mil/html

Major General Brian Tarbet
Adjutant General
Phone: 801-523-4401

Col Dwaine M Togersen
Military Support Officer
Phone: 801-523-4486

Col Paul D Harrell
Chief of Staff
Phone: 801-523-4403

Major Hank McIntire
Public Affairs Officer
Phone: 801-523-4407
e-mail: hank.mcintire@ut.ngb.army.mil

Office of the Medical Examiner
Division of Department of Health
48 Medical Drive
Salt Lake City, UT 84113
Phone: 801-584-8410
Fax: 801-584-8435
URL: www.health.utah.gov/ome/

Todd C Grey MD
Chief Medical Examiner
e-mail: toddgrey@utah.gov

Edward A Leis MD
Deputy Chief Medical Examiner
e-mail: eleis@utah.gov

Maureen J Frikke MD
Assistant Medical Examiner
e-mail: mfrikke@utah.gov

Robert L Deters MD
Assistant Medical Examiner
e-mail: rdeters@utah.gov

Transportation Department
4501 2 2700 W
MS 141200
Salt Lake City, UT 84114-1200
Phone: 801-965-4000
Phone: 801-965-4113
Fax: 801-965-4338
URL: www.udot.utah.gov
e-mail: srwebmail@utah.gov

John R Njord
Executive Director
Phone: 801-965-4113
e-mail: jnjord@utah.gov

Carlos Braceras
Deputy Director
Phone: 801-965-4030
e-mail: cbraceras@utah.gov

Robert E Hull
Traffic/Safety Division
Phone: 801-965-4273
e-mail: rhull@utah.gov

Glen Brown
Transportation Commission Chairman

Phone: 801-965-4103
e-mail: glen@utah.gov

Pat Morley
Aeronautics Operations Division
Phone: 801-715-2260
e-mail: pmorley@utah.gov

Richard Clasby
Motor Carrier Division
Phone: 801-965-4156
e-mail: rclasby@utah.gov

David Miles
Operations Division
Phone: 801-965-4895
e-mail: dmiles@utah.gov

Stan Burns
Engineering Services
Phone: 801-965-4190
e-mail: sburns@utah.gov

Utah Chiefs of Police Association
665 N Meadow Creek Way
Morgan, UT 84050
Phone: 801-626-8134
URL: www.utahchiefs.org

Description: A non-profit organization established to further law enforcement in the State of Utah and to assist Utah Chiefs of Police in the performance of their duties. Comprised of all active chiefs of police in the State of Utah and many other law enforcement executives in the state.

Mike Larsen
President
e-mail: mjlarsen@ci.orem.ut.us

Frank Budd
Executive Director
Phone: 801-626-8134
e-mail: FBUDD@weber.edu

STATE AGENCIES

Vermont

Vermont Main Homeland Security Office
103 S Main Street
Waterbury, VT 05671-2101
Phone: 802-241-5095
Fax: 802-241-5349
URL: www.dps.state.vt.us/homeland/

James H Douglas
Governor
Phone: 802-828-3333

Brian E Dubie
Lieutenant Governor
Phone: 802-828-2226

William H Sorell
Attorney General
Phone: 802-828-0269
e-mail: bsorrell@atg.state.vt.us

Captain Chris Reinfurt
Homeland Security Director
Phone: 802-241-5357
e-mail: creinfur@dps.state.vt.us

Agency of Transportation
1 National Life Drive
Montpelier, VT 05633-0001
Phone: 802-828-2657
Fax: 802-828-3522
URL: www.aot.state.vt.us

Description: Manages, maintains and monitors the Vermont state roads, airports and railways.

Neale Lunderville
Secretary
Phone: 802-828-2657

David Dill
Deputy Secretary
Phone: 802-828-2657
e-mail: david.dill@state.vt.us

John Dunleavy
Assistant Attorney General
Phone: 802-828-2831
e-mail: john.dunleavy@state.vt.us

Bonnie Rutledge
Commissioner of Motor Vehicles
Phone: 802-828-2011
e-mail: bonnie.rutledge@state.vt.us

Sam Lewis
Director Operations

Phone: 802-828-2709
e-mail: sam.lewis@state.vt.us

Melvin Adams
Director Policy & Planning
Phone: 802-828-3441
e-mail: mel.adams@state.vt.us

John Zicconi
Director Communications
Phone: 802-828-1647
e-mail: john.zicconi@state.vt.us

Dick Hosking
Manager Operations Rail Program
Phone: 802-828-1331

Rich Turner
Aviation Administrator
Phone: 802-828-2587

Kevin Marshia
Manager Roadway Traffic & Safety Program
Phone: 802-828-2664
e-mail: kevin.marshia@state.vt.us

Chuck Gallagher
Public Transit Administrator
Phone: 802-828-5750
e-mail: charles.gallagher@state.vt.us

Department of Agriculture, Food & Markets
116 State Street
Drawer 20
Montpelier, VT 05620-2901
Phone: 802-828-2416
Phone: 800-675-9873
Fax: 802-828-3831
URL: www.vermontagriculture.com

Steve Kerr
Secretary
Phone: 802-828-2430
e-mail: steve.kerr@agr.state.vt.us

Mark Bosma
Public Information Officer
Phone: 802-828-3829
e-mail: mark.bosma@state.vt.us

David Lane
Agricultural Development Deputy Commissioner
Phone: 802-828-3830
e-mail: davel@agr.state.vt.us

Carl Cushing
Food Safety & Consumer Protection Director

Phone: 802-828-2426
e-mail: carl@agr.state.vt.us

Henry Marckres
Consumer Protection Chief
Phone: 802-828-3458
e-mail: henry@agr.state.vt.us

Byron Moyer
Dairy Section Chief
Phone: 802-828-2433
e-mail: byron@agr.state.vt.us

Philip R Benedict
Agricultural Resource Management & Environmental Stewardship Director
Phone: 802-828-3472
e-mail: phil@agr.state.vt.us

Jon Turmel
Plant Industry Section Chief
Phone: 802-241-3545
e-mail: jon@agr.state.vt.us

Department of Health
108 Cherry Street
PO Box 70
Burlington, VT 05402-0070
Phone: 802-863-7200
Phone: 800-464-4343
Fax: 802-865-7754
URL: http://healthvermont.gov

Sharon Moffat
Acting Commissioner
Phone: 802-863-7281
e-mail: smoffat@vdh.state.vt.us

Dave Cote
Principal Assistant to Commissioner
Phone: 802-951-5181
e-mail: dcote@vdh.state.vt.us

Jessica Porter
Operations Chief
Phone: 802-865-7731
e-mail: jporter@vdh.state.vt.us

Linda Dorey
Communications Director
Phone: 802-863-7312
e-mail: ldorey@vdh.state.vt.us

Nancy Erickson
Communications Director
Phone: 802-863-7285
e-mail: nericks@vdh.state.vt.us

Patricia Berry
Community Public Health
Phone: 802-863-7347
e-mail: pberry@vdh.state.vt.us

Lawrence Crist
Health Protection
Phone: 802-863-7223
e-mail: lcrist@vdh.state.vt.us

William K Apao
Health Surveillance

Phone: 802-863-7494
e-mail: bapao@vdh.state.vt.us

W Dan Manz
Emergency Medical Services Director
Phone: 802-863-7310

Emergency Management
Public Safety Department
103 S Main Street
Waterbury, VT 05671-2101
Phone: 802-244-8721
Phone: 800-347-0488
Fax: 802-244-8655
URL: www.dps.state.vt.us/vem

Description: Strives to lessen the effects of disaster on the lives of the people of Vermont through leadership, coordination and support in the four phases of emergency management: mitigation, preparedness, response, and recovery.

Barbara Farr
Director
e-mail: bfarr@dps.state.vt.us

Bob Weinert
Emergency Management Coordinator
e-mail: rweinert@dps.state.vt.us

Ross Nagy
Deputy Director Preparedness & Planning
e-mail: rnagy@dps.state.vt.us

Ray Doherty
State Hazard Mitigation Officer
e-mail: rdoherty@dps.state.vt.us

Randy Bronson
Hazardous Materials Compliance Program Manager
Phone: 802-244-8721
e-mail: rbronson@dps.state.vt.us

Robert W Schell
Chief Field Operations
e-mail: rschell@dps.state.vt.us

Lew Stowell
Emergency Management Program Specialist
e-mail: lstowell@dps.state.vt.us

Tom Woodard
Emergency Management Specialist-Logistics
e-mail: twoodard@dps.state.vt.us

National Guard
789 Vermont National Guard Road
Camp Johnson
Colchester, VT 05446-3099
Phone: 802-338-3124
Phone: 800-488-2764
Fax: 802-338-3425
URL: www.vtguard.com

Major General Michael D Dubie
Adjutant General
Phone: 802-338-3124

Brig General William A Nayes
Deputy Adjutant General
Phone: 802-338-3121

Colonel Philip E Murdock
Air Guard Commander
Phone: 802-660-5212

Public Safety Department
103 S Main Street
State Complex
Waterbury, VT 05671
Phone: 802-244-8718
Fax: 802-241-1106
URL: www.dps.state.vt.us

Description: To promote the detection and prevention of crime, to participate in searches for lost and missing persons, and to assist in cases of statewide or local disasters or emergencies.

Kerry Sleeper
Commissioner
Phone: 802-244-8718
e-mail: ksleeper@dps.state.vt.us

Francis X Aumand III
Criminal Justice Services Division
Phone: 802-241-5488

Jeanne Johnson
Governor's Highway Safety
Phone: 802-244-1317
e-mail: jejohnso@dps.state.vt.us

John Wood
Division of Fire Safety Director
Phone: 802-479-7561

Colonel James Baker
State Police
Phone: 802-244-7345

Barbara Farr
Emergency Management Director
Phone: 802-244-8721
e-mail: bfarr@dps.state.vt.us

Terry LaValley
Communications Section Manager
Phone: 802-241-5215
e-mail: tlavalle@dps.state.vt.us

Eric C Buel
Forensic Laboratory
Phone: 802-244-8788
e-mail: ebuel@dps.state.vt.us

Vermont State Capitol Police
115 State Street
VT State House
Montpelier, VT 05633-5501
Mailing Address: Drawer 33
Phone: 802-828-2229
Fax: 802-828-2424

David A Janawicz
Chief

STATE AGENCIES

Virgin Islands

Virgin Islands Main Homeland Security Office
21-22 Kongens Gade
St Thomas, 00802
Virgin Islands
Phone: 340-712-7711
Phone: 340-774-0001
Fax: 340-778-4988
URL: www.ltg.gov.vi

John P deJongh, Jr
Governor
Phone: 340-774-0001

Gregory R Francis
Lieutenant Governor
Phone: 340-774-2991

Melvin Vanderpool
Adjutant General/Homeland Security
Phone: 340-712-7711

Department of Health
48 Sugar Estate
Charlotte Amalie, 00802
Virgin Islands
Phone: 340-774-0117
Phone: 340-773-6551
Fax: 340-777-4001
URL: www.usvi-doh.org

Darlene Carty
Commissioner
Phone: 340-776-8311
e-mail: commissioner@usvi-doh.org

Department of Planning & Natural Resources
Cyril E King Airport
Terminal Building, 2nd Floor
St Thomas, VI 00802
Phone: 340-774-3320
URL: www.dpnr.gov.vi

Claudette C Lewis
Acting Commissioner

Aaron Hutchins
Environmental Protection Division Director

Bevan Smith Jr
Energy Office Director
Phone: 340-773-1082
e-mail: bsmith@vienergy.org

Police Department
A Farrelly Criminal Justice Center

Charlotte Amalie
St Thomas, VI 00802
Phone: 340-774-2211
Fax: 340-715-5517
URL: www.vipd.gov.vi

Elton Lewis
Commissioner
e-mail: police.commissioner@vipd.gov.vi

Kenneth Blake
Crime Prevention Bureau Director

Kenneth L Gittins
Executive Security Unit Director

Ofari K Benjamin
Communications/Management Information Systems

Novelle E Francis Jr
Territorial Police Chief

Elvin Fahie Sr
Deputy Police Chief, St. Thomas

Angelo Hill
Deputy Police Chief, St. John
Phone: 340-693-8880

Herminio Velazquez
Deputy Police Chief, St. Croix

Barbara Jackson-McIntosh
Office of Highway Safety Administrator
Phone: 340-778-2244

Port Authority
PO Box 301707
St. Thomas, 00803-1707
Virgin Islands
Phone: 340-774-1629
Fax: 340-774-0025
URL: www.viport.com
e-mail: info@viport.com

Darlan Brin
Executive Director
e-mail: dbrin@viport.com

David W Mapp
Assistant Executive Director/Aviation, St Croix
Phone: 340-778-1012
e-mail: davemapp@islands.vi

John Payne
Marine Chief, St. Croix

Phone: 340-778-3131
e-mail: jpayne@viport.com

Dale A Gregory
Director Engineering
e-mail: dgregory@viport.com

Denise M Mills
Acting Director Property Manager
e-mail: dmills@viport.com

Maria Walters
Marine Manager, St. Thomas & St. John
Phone: 340-774-2250
e-mail: mwalters@viport.com

Ray Chesterfield Sr
Chief Law Enforcement Officer, St. Thomas/St. John
Phone: 340-774-5100
e-mail: rchesterfield@viport.com

Jose Nazario
Airport Manager, St. Thomas
Phone: 340-774-5100
e-mail: jnazario@viport.com

Kevin Hewitt
Acting Chief Law Enforcement Officer, St Croix
Phone: 340-778-1012
e-mail: khewitt@viport.com

Virgin Islands Public Television
PO Box 7879
Charlotte Amalie
St Thomas, VI 00801
Phone: 340-774-6255
Fax: 340-774-7092
URL: www.wtjxtv.org

Osbert Potter
Executive Director
Phone: 340-774-6255
e-mail: opotter@wtjxtv.org

Tanya-Marie Singh
Operations Manager, St. Croix
Phone: 340-773-3337

Virgin Islands Territorial Emergency Management
2-C Contant, A-Q Building
Virgin Islands, 00820
USVI
Phone: 340-774-2244
Phone: 340-774-1491

Harold M Baker
Director

STATE AGENCIES

Virginia

Virginia Main Homeland Security Office
Office of Commonwealth Preparedness
1111 East Broad Street, 4th Floor
Richmond, VA 23219
Mailing Address: PO Box 1475, 23218
Phone: 804-692-2595
Phone: 804-371-8015
Fax: 804-225-3882
URL: www.commonwealthpreparedness.virginia.gov

Description: The Office of Commonwealth Preparedness, Virginia's homeland security organization, is a Cabinet-rank office created by the Governor in order to promote security measures at the highest level. It serves as the single point of contact in Virginia for the DHS.

Timothy M Kaine
Governor
Phone: 804-786-2211

William T Bolling
Lieutenant Governor
Phone: 804-786-2078
e-mail: ltgov@ltgov.virginia.gov

Robert P Crouch
Assistant to the Governor for Commonwealth Preparedness
Phone: 804-692-2595

Bob McDonnell
Attorney General
Phone: 804-786-2071
e-mail: mail@oag.state.va.us

Agriculture and Consumer Services Department
102 Governor Street
Richmond, VA 23219
Phone: 804-786-2373
Fax: 804-371-2945
URL: www.vdacs.virginia.gov

Donald W Butts
Emergency Services Manager
Phone: 804-786-9600
e-mail: don.butts@vdacs.virginia.gov

Richard Wilkes
State Veterinarian
Phone: 804-692-0601
e-mail: richard.wilkes@vdacs.virginia.gov

Association of Contingency Planners
PO Box 17402
Arlington, VA 22216
Phone: 703-797-5710

URL: www.acpdc.org
e-mail: jbarnett@silosmashers.com

Description: A non-profit trade association dedicated to fostering continued professional growth and development in effective Contingency & Business Resumption Planning. ACP is an international networking and information exchange organization in the business continuity industry.

Jack Barnett
President

Jessica Heckert
Vice President

Department of Aviation
5702 Gulfstream Road
Richmond, VA 23250-2422
Phone: 804-236-3624
Fax: 804-236-3635
URL: www.doav.virginia.gov

Randall Burdette
Director
Phone: 804-236-3625
e-mail: randall.burdette@doav.virginia.gov

Rusty Harrington
Airport Services
Phone: 804-236-3632

Jeanie Carter
Flight Operations & Safety
Phone: 804-236-3639

Carolyn Toth
Communications & Education
Phone: 804-236-3637
e-mail: carolyn.toth@doav.virginia.gov

Department of Environmental Quality
629 E Main Street
Richmond, VA 23240-0009
Mailing Address: PO Box 10009, 23218
Phone: 804-698-4000
Phone: 800-592-5482
URL: www.deq.virginia.gov

Description: Aims to protect and enhance the environment for the benefit of the public.

David K Paylor
Director
Phone: 804-698-4020
e-mail: dkpaylor@deq.virginia.gov

Jim Sydnor
Air Quality Division
Phone: 804-698-4424
e-mail: jesydnor@deq.virginia.gov

Karen Sismour
Waste Division
Phone: 804-698-4145
e-mail: kjsismour@deq.virginia.gov

Ellen Gilinsky
Water Quality Division
Phone: 804-698-4375
e-mail: egilinsky@deq.virginia.gov

Michael Dowd
Enforcement
Phone: 804-698-4284
e-mail: mgdowd@deq.virginia.gov

Department of Health
109 Governor Street
Richmond, VA 23219
Mailing Address: PO Box 2448, Richmond, 23218-2448
Phone: 804-786-7009
Fax: 804-864-7022
URL: www.vdh.state.va.us

Marilyn B Tavenner
Secretary of Health/Human Resources

Robert B Stroube MD, MPH
State Health Commissioner
Phone: 804-786-7009
e-mail: rstroube@vhd.state.va.us

Diane Powers
Director Communications
Phone: 804-864-7008

Marcella Fierro MD
Chief Medical Examiner
Phone: 804-786-1034
e-mail: mfierro@vhd.state.va.us

Department of Rail & Public Transportation
1313 E Main Street
Suite 300
Richmond, VA 23219
Mailing Address: PO Box 590, Richmond 23218
Phone: 804-786-4440
Fax: 804-786-7286
URL: www.drpt.state.va.us

Matthew O Tucker
Director
Phone: 804-786-4440

Kevin B Page
Director of Rail Transportation
Phone: 804-786-3963

Charles M Badger
Director of Public Transportation
Phone: 804-786-8135

Charlene T Robey
Commuter Services
Phone: 804-786-7968

Corey W Hill
Director of Administration & Capital Projects
Phone: 804-786-4443

Amy Ettinger
Security & Emergency Preparedness Coordinator
Phone: 804-786-1056

Jennifer Pickett
Public Information Officer
Phone: 804-786-7432

Emergency Management Department
10501 Trade Court
Richmond, VA 23236-3713
Phone: 804-897-6500
Fax: 804-897-6506
URL: www.vaemergency.com
e-mail: pio@vdem.virginia.gov

Description: Protects the lives and property of Virginia's citizens from emergencies and disasters by coordinating the state's emergency preparedness, mitigation, response and recovery efforts.

Michael M Cline
State Coordinator
e-mail: michael.cline@vdem.virginia.gov

Janet L Clements
Chief Deputy State Coordinator
e-mail: janet.clements@vdem.virginia.gov

James W Keck
Deputy State Coordinator for Administration

Gordon Barwell
Director of Local Support Services Division
e-mail: gordon.barwell@vdem.virginia.gov

Brett A Burdick
Director of Technological Hazards Division
e-mail: brett.burdick@vdem.virginia.gov

Harry E Colestock III
Director of Operations
e-mail: harry.colestock@vdem.virginia.gov

Ted Costin
Director of Preparedness & Training Exercises Division
e-mail: ted.costin@vdem.virginia.gov

Deborah Mills
Director of Recovery & Mitigation Division
e-mail: deborah.mills@vdem.virginia.gov

Emergency Preparedness & Response Programs
Department of Health
109 Governor Street
Richmond, VA 23219
Phone: 804-864-7026
Fax: 804-864-7029
URL: www.vdh.state.va.us/epr
e-mail: eprquestion@vdh.state.va.us

Description: To effectively respond to any emergency impacting public health through preparation, collaboration, education and rapid intervention. The Emergency Response Programs involve state, regional and local emergency response partners working together to enhance readiness and respond to bioterrorism, infectious diseases outbreaks and other public health emergencies. Funding to support these efforts is provided through grants from the US Centers for Disease Control and Prevention, US Health Resources Services Administration and the US Department of Homeland Security.

Lisa G Kaplowitz
Deputy Commissioner
Phone: 804-864-7025
e-mail: lisa.kaplowitz@vdh.virginia.gov

Bob Mauskapf
Statewide Planning Coordinator
Phone: 804-864-7035
e-mail: bob.mauskapf@vdh.virginia.gov

Bill Berthrong
Hospital Coordinator
Phone: 804-864-7034
e-mail: bill.berthrong@vdh.virginia.gov

Steve Harrison
Assistant State Exercise & Strategic National Stockpile Coordinator
Phone: 804-864-7033
e-mail: steve.harrison@vdh.virginia.gov

National Guard
Fort Pickett
Blackstone, VA 23824
Phone: 434-298-6100
Fax: 434-298-6338
URL: www.virginiaguard.com

Major General Robert B Newman Jr
Adjutant General

Brig General Eugene Stockton
Assistant Adjutant General - Army
Phone: 804-438-6101

Brig General William S Busby
Assistant Adjutant General - Air

Colonel Robert H Simpson
Director - Joint Staff
Phone: 804-786-4400

Office of Drinking Water
109 Governor Street
6th Floor
Richmond, VA 23219
Phone: 804-864-7500
URL: www.vdh.virginia.gov/drinkingwater

Description: Committed to protecting public health by ensuring that all people in Virginia have access to an adequate supply of affordable, safe drinking water that meets federal and state drinking water standards

Wes Kleene
Director
Phone: 804-864-7500

Office of Emergency Medical Services
Department of Health
109 Governor Street
Suite UB-55
Richmond, VA 23219

Phone: 804-864-7600
Phone: 800-523-6019
Fax: 804-864-7580
URL: www.vdh.state.va.us/oems/index.asp

Gary Brown
Director
e-mail: gary.brown@vdh.virginia.gov

Scott Winston
Assistant Director
e-mail: scott.winston@vdh.virginia.gov

Jim Nogle
Emergency Operations Manager
e-mail: jim.nogle@vdh.virginia.gov

Office of Environmental Health Services
109 Governor Street
5th Floor
Richmond, VA 23219
Phone: 804-864-7466
Fax: 804-864-7475
URL: www.vdh.state.va.us/oehs/

Robert Hicks
Director
Phone: 804-864-7466

Gary Hagy
Food & General Environmental Services Division
Phone: 804-864-7466

Office of Epidemiology
Department of Health
109 Governor Street
Suite 516E
Richmond, VA 23219
Phone: 804-864-8141
Fax: 804-864-8139
URL: www.vdh.virginia.gov/epidemiology

Carl W Armstrong
Director
Phone: 804-864-7905

Diane Woolard
Surveillance & Investigation Division
Phone: 804-864-8141

Michele Monti
Environmental Epidemiology Division
Phone: 804-864-8141

Les Foldesi
Radiological Health Division
Phone: 804-864-8150

Kathy Hafford
Disease Prevention Division
Phone: 804-864-7964

James Farrell
Immunization Division
Phone: 804-864-8070

Port Authority
600 World Trade Center
Norfolk, VA 23510

Phone: 757-683-8000
Phone: 800-446-8098
Fax: 757-683-8500
URL: www.vaports.com

Description: To provide the Commonwealth of Virginia with a responsive statewide police department, independent yet supportive of other law enforcement agencies; to preserve law and order; to enforce criminal, traffic and regulatory laws; and, to provide essential public safety services efficiently and effectively to the citizens of the Commonwealth.

Jerry A Bridges
Executive Director
Phone: 757-683-2102
e-mail: jbridges@portofvirginia.com

Jeff Keever
Deputy Executive Director
e-mail: jjkeever@portofvirginia.com

Linda G Ford
Director, Port Promotion
e-mail: lford@vaports.com

Jeff Florin
Chief Engineer, Director, Port Development
e-mail: jflorin@portofvirginia.com

Norris E Merkle
Director Security

Andrew H Engermann Jr
Chief of Police
e-mail: aengemann@portofvirginia.com

Public Safety Office

1111 E Broad Street
Patrick Henry Building
Richmond, VA 23219
Mailing Address: PO Box 1475, 23218
Phone: 804-786-5351
Fax: 804-371-6381
URL: www.publicsafety.virginia.gov

John W Marshall
Secretary

Marilyn P Harris
Deputy Secretary

State Police

7700 Midlothian Turnpike
Richmond, VA 23235
Mailing Address: PO Box 27472, 23261-7472
Phone: 804-674-2000
Phone: 800-553-3144
Fax: 804-674-2267
URL: www.vsp.state.va.us
e-mail: bud.cox@vsp.state.va.us

Description: To provide the Commonwealth with a responsive, coordinated, composite statewide police department, independent yet supportive of local law enforcement agencies; to preserve law and order; to enforce traffic and regulatory laws; and, to provide security and safety services to citizens of Virginia.

Colonel W Steven Flaherty
Superintendent

Phone: 804-674-2000
e-mail: supt@vsp.virginia.gov

Lt Colonel Robert B Northern
Deputy Superintendent
Phone: 804-674-2000
e-mail: supt@vsp.virginia.gov

First Sgt Ronald M Watkins
Executive Protection Unit
Phone: 804-786-8414

Lt N E Saunders
Avaiation Unit
Phone: 804-743-2228
e-mail: aviation@vsp.virginia.gov

Lt Colonel Eugene A Stockton
Bureau of Field Operations
Phone: 804-674-2088
e-mail: bfo@vsp.virginia.gov

Captain Ronald B Saunders
Safety Division
Phone: 804-674-6774
e-mail: safetydivision@vsp.virginia.gov

Lt Colonel Terry A Bowes
Bureau of Criminal Investigations
Phone: 804-674-2088
e-mail: vspbci@vsp.virginia.gov

Transportation Department

1221 E Broad Street
Richmond, VA 23219
Phone: 804-786-2801
Fax: 804-786-6683
URL: www.virginiadot.org
e-mail: vdotinfo@vdotinfo@virginia.gov

Description: Responsible for building, maintaining and operating the state's roads, bridges and tunnels.

David S Ekern
Commissioner

Gregory A Whirley Sr
Chief Deputy Commissioner
Phone: 804-786-2702
e-mail: ga.whirley@vdot.virginia.gov

Mary L Tischer
Director, Multimodal Transportation Planning Office
e-mail: mary.tischer@vdot.virginia.gov

Richard L Walton
Chief of Policy, Planning & Environment
Phone: 804-786-2703
e-mail: richard.walton@vdot.virginia.gov

Malcolm T Kerley
Chief Engineer
Phone: 804-786-4798
e-mail: mal.kerley@vdot.virginia.gov

Constance S Sorrell
Chief of System Operations
Phone: 804-786-1476
e-mail: connie.sorrell@vdot.virginia.gov

Barbara W Reese
Chief Financial Officer
Phone: 804-786-5128
e-mail: barbara.reese@vdot.virginia.gov

Dr Gary R Allen
Chief of Technology, Research & Innovation
Phone: 434-293-1938
e-mail: gary.allen@vdot.virginia.gov

Meredith Baker
Chief of Organizational Development
Phone: 804-786-2707
e-mail: meredith.baker@vdot.virginia.gov

Virginia Association of Chiefs of Police

1606 Santa Rosa Road
Suite 134
Richmond, VA 23288
Phone: 804-285-8227
Fax: 804-285-3363
URL: www.vachiefs.org

Dana G Schrad
Executive Director
e-mail: dana@vachiefs.org

Virginia State Capitol Police

200 N 9th Street
Richmond, VA 23218
Phone: 804-786-2568
Phone: 877-449-4704
Fax: 804-371-8698
URL: www.vcp.state.va.us

Colonel Kimberly S Lettner
Chief
Phone: 804-786-5035
e-mail: klettner@vcp.state.va.us

Cpt Raymond Goodloe
Acting Deputy Chief Operations
Phone: 804-786-5035
e-mail: rgoodloe@vcp.state.va.us

Sgt Nancy L Goergner
Communications
Phone: 804-786-2568
e-mail: ngoergner@vcp.state.va.us

STATE AGENCIES

Washington

Washington Main Homeland Security Office
Emergency Management Division
Camp Murray TA-20
Tacoma, WA 98430
Mailing Address: Building 20
Phone: 253-512-8000
Fax: 253-512-8497
URL: http://emd.wa.gov

Christine Gergoire
Governor
Phone: 360-753-6780

Brad Owennberg
Lieutenant Governor
Phone: 360-786-7700
e-mail: owen_br@leg.wa.gov

James Mullen
Director Emergency Management Division
Phone: 253-512-7001
e-mail: j.mullen@emd.wa.gov

Rob McKenna
Attorney General
Phone: 360-753-6200
e-mail: robm@atg.wa.gov

Agriculture Department
1111 Washington Street SE
Olympia, WA 98504-2560
Mailing Address: PO Box 42560
Phone: 360-902-1800
Fax: 360-902-2092
URL: http://agr.wa.gov

Description: Serves the people of Washington State by supporting the agricultural community and promoting consumer and environmental protection.

Valoria Loveland
Director
Phone: 360-902-1887

Bob Gore
Deputy Director
Phone: 360-902-1810

Claudia Coles
Food Safety Program Manager
Phone: 360-902-1905

Dr Leonard Eldridge
State Veterinarian
Phone: 360-902-1878

Carl Harris
Chief Technology Officer
Phone: 360-902-2004

Jason Kelly
Communications Director
Phone: 360-902-1815

Jim Quigley
Fruit/Vegetables Inspection Program Manager
Phone: 360-902-1833

Randy Deike
Grains Inspection Program Manager
Phone: 360-902-1921

Mike Louisell
Public Information Officer
Phone: 360-902-1813

Diane Dolstad
Food Microbiological Program
Phone: 360-586-3645

Tom Wessels
Plant Services Program Manager
Phone: 360-902-1984

Emergency Management Division
Building 20, M/S: TA-20
Camp Murray, WA 98430-5122
Phone: 253-512-7000
Phone: 800-562-6108
Fax: 253-512-7200
URL: emd.wa.gov

James Mullen
Director
Phone: 253-512-7001
e-mail: j.mullen@emd.wa.gov

Arel Solie
Homeland Security Section Supervisor
Phone: 253-512-7468
e-mail: a.solie@emd.wa.gov

Don Miller
Telecommunications Section Project Manager
Phone: 253-512-7035
e-mail: d.miller@emd.wa.gov

Mark Clemens
Public Information Officer
Phone: 253-512-7006
e-mail: m.clemens@emd.wa.gov

Rob Harper
Public Information Officer
Phone: 253-512-7005
e-mail: r.harper@emd.wa.gov

Kurt Hardin
Mitigation, Response & Recovery Unit Manager
Phone: 253-512-7061
e-mail: c.hagerhjelm@emd.wa.gov

Dr Terry Egan
Plans, Exercise & Training Unit Manager
Phone: 253-512-7041
e-mail: t.egan@emd.wa.gov

Health Department
101 Isreal Road SE
Tumwater, WA 98501
Mailing Address: PO Box 47890, Olympia, WA 98504-7890
Phone: 360-236-4501
Fax: 360-586-7424
URL: www.doh.wa.gov

Description: Works to protect and improve the health of the people in Washington State.

Mary C Selecky
Secretary
Phone: 360-236-4030
e-mail: secretary@doh.wa.gov

Bill White
Deputy Secretary
Phone: 360-236-4030
e-mail: bill.white@doh.wa.gov

Maxine Hayes
State Health Officer
Phone: 360-236-4030
e-mail: maxine.hayes@doh.wa.gov

Frank M Westrum
Chief Information Officer
Phone: 360-236-3105
e-mail: Frank.Westrum@doh.wa.gov

Timothy J Church
Communications Office Director
Phone: 360-236-4077
e-mail: timothy.church@doh.wa.gov

Gregg Grunenfelder
Environmental Health Programs Assistant Secretary
Phone: 360-236-3050
e-mail: gregg.grunenfelder@doh.wa.gov

Romesh K Gautom PhD
Public Health Laboratories Director
Phone: 206-418-5400
e-mail: Romesh.Gautom@doh.wa.gov

Jude VanBuren
Epidemiology, Health Statistics & Public Health Laboratories
Phone: 360-236-4202
e-mail: jude.vanburen@doh.wa.gov

Joan M Brewster
Public Health Systems Planning & Development Director
Phone: 360-236-4085
e-mail: joan.brewster@doh.wa.gov

National Guard
Camp Murray
Buildign 1
Tacoma, WA 98430-5000
Phone: 253-512-8000
Fax: 253-512-8497
URL: www.washingtonguard.com

Major General Timothy J Lowenberg
Adjutant General
Phone: 253-512-8201
e-mail: timothy.lowenberg@wa.ngb.army.mil

Brigagier General Gordon Tony
Army Assistant Adjutant General
Phone: 253-512-8202

Brigadier General Gary T Magonigle
Air Assistant Adjutant General

Glen Woodbury
Emergency Management Division
Phone: 253-512-7001

Office of Epidemiology
Department of Health
101 Israel Road SE
PO Box 47812
Olympia, WA 98504-7812
Phone: 360-236-4243
URL: www.doh.wa.gov/ehsphl/epidemiology

Juliet Van Eenwyk
State Epidemiologist, Non-Infectious Conditions
Phone: 360-236-4250
e-mail: juliet.vaneenwyk@doh.wa.gov

Jo Hofmann
State Epidemiologist, Communicable Disease
Phone: 206-418-5500
e-mail: jo.hofmann@doh.wa.gov

State Patrol
Homeland Security Division
C/O USCG Tier 36, Bldg 7
1519 Alaskan Way S
Seattle, WA 98134
Phone: 206-389-2728
Fax: 206-389-2730
URL: www.wa.gov/wsp/
e-mail: questions@wsp.wa.gov

John Batiste
Chief
Phone: 360-753-6545

Diane C Perry
Management Services Bureau Director
Phone: 360-753-5141
e-mail: diane.perry@wsp.wa.gov

Dr Barry K Logan
Burearu Administrator, Forensic Services Lab
Phone: 360-262-6000
e-mail: barry.logan@wsp.wa.gov

Mike Matlick
State Fire Marshal

Phone: 360-753-0404
e-mail: sa.pierre@wsp.wa.gov

Transportation Department
310 Maple Park Avenue SE
Olympia, WA 98504-7300
Mailing Address: PO Box 47300
Phone: 360-705-7054
Phone: 360-705-7000
Fax: 360-705-6800
URL: www.wsdot.wa.gov

Description: Responsible for maintaining highways, bridges and tunnels, including the longest and widest of the world's first floating bridges. WSDOT is also a partner with Amtrak in providing the Amtrak Cascades passenger rail service connecting Seattle and other western Washington cities in the Vancouver BC/Portland, Oregon corridor.

Douglas B McDonald
Secretary
Phone: 360-705-7054
e-mail: macdond@wsdot.wa.gov

John Conrad
Engineering/Regional Operations
Phone: 360-705-7032
e-mail: conradj@wsdot.wa.gov

Paula Hammond
Chief of Staff
Phone: 360-705-7032

W Michael Anderson
State Ferries Executive Director
Phone: 206-515-3401

John Sibold
Director of Aviation
e-mail: siboldj@wsdot.wa.gov

Washington Association of Sheriffs & Police Chiefs
3060 Willamette Drive NE
Suite 200
Lacey, WA 98516
Phone: 360-486-2380
Fax: 360-486-2381
URL: www.waspc.org

Description: Offers support services, which enhance public safety, to law enforcement executives in the State of Washington.

Don Pierce
Executive Director
e-mail: dpierce@waspc.org

Jim LaMunyon
Deputy Director
e-mail: jlamunyon@waspc.org

Tom Corzine
Deputy Director
e-mail: tcorzine@waspc.org

Washington Electronic Disease Surveillance System (WEDSS)
Health Department
101 Israel Road SE
Olympia, WA 98504
Mailing Address: PO Box 47904
Phone: 360-236-4458
Phone: 877-889-3377
URL: www.doh.wa.gov/wedss

Description: A series of programs that standardize and automate the reporting of communicable diseases in the state, in effect, making the reporting and investigation of disease faster, simpler and more reliable. This system also assures the consistent and secure exchange of information during a public health emergency.

Michael Davisson
Project Director
Phone: 206-418-5420
e-mail: michael.davisson@doh.wa.gov

STATE AGENCIES

West Virginia

West Virginia Main Homeland Security Office

1900 Kanawha Boulevard E
Building 1, Room EB-80
Charleston, WV 25305
Phone: 304-558-5380
Fax: 304-344-4538
URL: www.wvdhsem.gov

Joe Manchin III
Governor
Phone: 888-438-2731
e-mail: governor@wvgov.org

Darrell V McGraw Jr
Attorney General
Phone: 304-558-2021

James W Spears
State Homeland Security Advisor/Secretary
Phone: 304-558-2930
e-mail: jspears@wvdmaps.gov

Jimmy Gianato
Homeland Security & Emergency Management Director
Phone: 304-558-5380
e-mail: jgianato@wvdmaps.gov

Department of Agriculture

1900 Kanawha Boulevard E
M28, Capitol Building
Charleston, WV 25305
Phone: 304-558-2201
Fax: 304-558-0451
URL: www.wvagriculture.org

Gus R Douglass
Commissioner
Phone: 304-558-3200
e-mail: douglass@ag.state.wv.us

Steve Hannah
Deputy Commissioner
Phone: 304-558-3200
e-mail: shannah@ag.state.wv.us

Janet Fisher
Deputy Commissioner
Phone: 304-558-3200
e-mail: jfisher@ag.state.wv.us

Dr Joe Starcher
Animal Health Division Director
Phone: 304-558-2214
e-mail: jstarcher@ag.state.wv.us

Christina S Kelley-Dye
Communications Division Director
Phone: 304-558-3708
e-mail: ckelley@ag.state.wv.us

Dr Warren J Charminski
Meat/Poultry Inspection Division Director
Phone: 304-558-2206
e-mail: jcharminski@ag.state.wv.us

Gary Gibson
Plant Industries Division Director
Phone: 304-558-2212
e-mail: ggibson@ag.state.wv.us

Herma Johnson
Regulatory & Environmental Affairs Division
Phone: 304-558-2208
e-mail: hjohnson@ag.state.wv.us

Lee Orr
Agricultural Health & Safety Program Coordinator
Phone: 304-558-2208

Division of Homeland Security & Emergency Management

1900 Kanawha Boulevard E
Building 1, Room EB-80
Charleston, WV 25305
Phone: 304-558-5380
Fax: 304-344-4538
URL: www.wvdhsem.gov

Description: To provide coordination to assist local emergency managers and first responders tp provide for the protection of life and property.

Jimmy Gianato
Director
Phone: 304-558-5380
e-mail: jgianato@wvdmaps.gov

Paul Howard
Director Operations
Phone: 304-558-5380
e-mail: phoward@wvdmaps.gov

Al Lisko
Director Mitigation & Recovery
Phone: 304-965-3014
e-mail: alisko@wvdmaps.gov

Rob Jelacic
Radiological Emergency Planning Manager
Phone: 304-558-5380
e-mail: rjelacic@wvdmaps.gov

Bill Wood
Communications Officer
Phone: 304-558-5380
e-mail: bwood@wvdmaps.gov

Environmental Protection Division
601 57th Street
Charleston, WV 25304
Phone: 304-926-0440
Fax: 304-926-0446
URL: www.wvdep.org

Description: Committed to protecting and improving the environmental quality of life for all of West Virginia's citizens.

Stephanie R Timmermeyer
Secretary
Phone: 304-926-0440

Randy Huffman
Deputy Secretary
Phone: 304-926-0440

Jerry Forren
Information Technology Office
Phone: 304-926-0499
e-mail: jeforren@wvdep.org

Charles J Miller
Abandoned Mine Lands & Reclamation Assistant Director
Phone: 304-926-0485
e-mail: cmiller@wvdep.org

James Martin
Oil & Gas Office Chief
Phone: 304-926-0450
e-mail: jmartin@wvdep.org

Lisa McClung
Water & Waste Management Director
Phone: 304-926-0499

Mike Zeto
Environmental Enforcement Office
Phone: 304-926-0470
e-mail: mzeto@wvdep.org

Heather Connolly
General Counsel
Phone: 304-926-0440

John A Benedict
Air Quality Division Director
Phone: 304-926-0475

Jessica Greathouse
Chief Communications Officer
Phone: 304-926-0440

Health and Human Resources Department
State Capitol Complex
Building 3, Room 206
Charleston, WV 25305
Phone: 304-558-0684
Fax: 304-558-1130
URL: www.wvdhhr.org

Martha Yeager Walker
Secretary
Phone: 304-558-0684
e-mail: wvdhhrsecretary@wvdhhr.org

Molly Jordan
Inspector General
Phone: 304-558-2278
e-mail: mollyjordan@wvdhhr.org

Dan Hill
Environmental Health
Phone: 304-558-6772
e-mail: danhill@wvdhhr.org

John D Law
Communications Director
Phone: 304-558-7899

Military Affairs and Public Safety Department
1900 Kanawha Boulevard E
Building #1, Room W400
Charleston, WV 25305-0155
Phone: 304-558-2930
Fax: 304-558-6221
URL: www.wvdmaps.gov

James W Spears
Secretary
Phone: 304-558-2930
e-mail: jspears@wvdmaps.gov

Terry L Miller
Homeland Security State Administrative Agency Director
Phone: 304-558-2930
e-mail: tmiller@wvdmaps.gov

Jimmy Gianato
Homeland Security Division & Emergency Management Director
Phone: 304-558-5830
e-mail: jgianato@wvdmaps.gov

Major General Allen Tackett
Adjutant General

Jim Rubenstein
Division of Corrections Commissioner
Phone: 304-558-2036

Norbert Federspiel
Criminal Justice Services Division Director
Phone: 304-558-8814
e-mail: nfederspiel@wvdcjs.org

Sterling Lewis Jr
State Fire Marshal
Phone: 304-558-2191

Colonel David L Lemmon
State Police Superintendent
Phone: 304-746-2111

Public Health Bureau
Health and Human Resources Department
350 Capitol Street
Room 702
Charleston, WV 25301-3712
Phone: 304-558-2971
Fax: 304-558-1035
URL: www.wvdhhr.org/bph

Description: Helps to shape the environments within which people and communities can be safe and healthy.

Nancye Bazzle
Community Health Systems Office Director
Phone: 304-558-3210
e-mail: nancyebazzle@wvdhhr.org

Susan G Chapman
Operations
Phone: 304-558-0580

Jerry Kyle
Emergency Medical Services Division Director
Phone: 304-558-3956

William Ramsey
State EMS Medical Director
Phone: 304-285-3331
e-mail: wramsey@wvdhhr.org

James A Kaplan
Chief Medical Examiner
Phone: 304-558-6920

Barbara Taylor
Environmental Health Services Office Director
Phone: 304-558-2981

Joe Barker
Epidemiology & Health Promotion Office Director
Phone: 304-558-7078
e-mail: joebarker@wvdhhr.org

State Police Division
725 Jefferson Road
S Charleston, WV 25309-1698
Phone: 304-746-2111
Fax: 304-746-2230
URL: www.wvstatepolice.com
e-mail: troopers@wvstatepolice.com

Colonel David L Lemmon
Superintendent

Lieutenant Colonel SC Tucker
Deputy Superintendent

First Lieutenant G E McCabe
Communications
Phone: 304-746-2151

Threat Preparedness Division
Public Health Bureau
505 Capitol Street
Suite 200
Charleston, WV 25301
Phone: 304-558-1218
Phone: 304-558-6900
Fax: 304-558-0464
URL: www.wvdhhr.org/healthprep/
e-mail: phthreatprep@wvdhhr.org

Description: Through collaborative leadership and coordination, ensure adequate capacity and effective systems ready to respond to natural and intentional threats to the public's health.

Cathy Slemp
Executive Director
e-mail: cathyslemp@wvdhhr.org

Jerry Rhodes
Deputy Director
e-mail: jerryrhodes@wvdhhr.org

Terry Shorr
Hospital Preparedness Coordinator
e-mail: dtshorr@wvdhhr.org

Matt Musgrave
Strategic National Stockpile Coordinator
e-mail: mattmusgrave@wvdhhr.org

Kim Coleman
Public Information Officer
e-mail: kimcoleman@wvdhhr.org

Transportation Department
1900 Kanawha Boulevard E
Building 5
Charleston, WV 25305
Phone: 304-558-0103
Fax: 304-558-9131
URL: www.wvdot.com

Description: To create and maintain for the people of West Virginia, the US and the world a multi-modal and inter-modal transportation system that supports the safe, effective and efficient movement of people, information and goods that enhances the opportunity for the people and communities to enjoy environmentally sensitive and economically sound development.

Paul Mattox Jr
Secretary/Highways Commissioner
Phone: 304-558-3505
e-mail: commissioner@dot.state.wv.us

Susie Watkins
Communications
Phone: 304-558-0103
e-mail: swatkins@dot.state.wv.us

Darrell W Allen
Contract Administration
Phone: 304-558-3304
e-mail: dwallen@dot.state.wv.us

Cindy Butler
Acting State Rail Authority
Phone: 304-538-3521
e-mail: ckbutler@dot.state.wv.us

Joseph Cicchirillo
Motor Vehicles Commissioner
Phone: 304-558-3900
e-mail: dmvcommissioner@dot.state.wv.us

Susan V Chernenko
Aeronautics Director
Phone: 304-558-3436
e-mail: schernenko@dot.state.wv.us

Greg Barr
Parkway Authority
Phone: 304-926-1900
e-mail: gregbarr@wvturnpike.com

Patrick Donovan
Public Port Authority Director
Phone: 304-558-0330
e-mail: pdonovan@dot.state.wv.us

Susan O'Connell
Public Transit Director
Phone: 304-558-0428
e-mail: soconnell@dot.state.wv.us

West Virginia State Capitol Protective Services
1900 Kanawha Boulevard E
Building 1 Room 152A
Charleston, WV 25305
Phone: 304-558-9911
Fax: 304-558-5604

Jay Smithers
Director
Phone: 204-558-5626
e-mail: jsmithers@state.wv.us

STATE AGENCIES

Wisconsin

Wisconsin Main Homeland Security Office
2400 Wright Street
Madison, WI 53704
Phone: 608-242-3232
Fax: 608-242-3247
URL: http://homelandsecurity.wi.gov
e-mail: homelandsecurity@dma.state.wi.us

James Doyle
Governor
Phone: 608-266-1212

Barbara Lawton
Lieutenant Governor
Phone: 608-266-3516
e-mail: ltgov@ltgov.state.wi.us

Major Al Wilkening
Homeland Security Advisor
Phone: 608-242-3000

Peg Lautenschlager
Attorney General
Phone: 608-266-1221

Agriculture, Trade and Consumer Protection Department
PO Box 8911
Madison, WI 53708-8911
Phone: 608-224-5012
Fax: 608-224-5045
URL: http://datcp.state.wi.us

Description: Inspects and licenses more than 100,000 business and individuals, analyzes millions of laboratory samples, conducts hundreds of hearings and investigations, educate businesses and consumers about best practices, adopts rules that have the force of law, and promotes Wisconsin agriculture at home and abroad.

Rod Nilsestuen
Sectretary
Phone: 608-224-5015
e-mail: rod.nilsestuen@datcp.state.wi.us

Robin Schmidt
Agency Liaison for Food/Ag Security
Phone: 608-224-5009
e-mail: robin.schmidt@wisconsin.gov

Steven Steinhoff
Food Safety Division
Phone: 608-224-4701
e-mail: steve.steinhoff@datcp.state.wi.us

Business Recovery Planners Association of Wisconsin
5910 Mineral Point Road
Madison, WI 53705
Phone: 608-231-7502

Paul Bergee
President

Department of Military Affairs
2400 Wright Street
Madison, WI 53701
Mailing Address: PO Box 14587
Phone: 608-242-3001
Fax: 608-242-3111
URL: http://dma.wi.gov

Description: The Wisconsin Guard currently has approximately 6,360 soldiers and airmen available to provide effective military capability on short notice anywhere is Wisconsin. The Joint Force Headquarters-Wisconsin consists of members of the Air and Army National Guard.

BGen Albert H Wilkening
Adjutant General
Phone: 608-242-3001
e-mail: al.wilkening@wi.ngb.army.mil

BGen Fred G Sloan
Air Deputy Adjutant General
Phone: 608-242-3020
e-mail: fred.sloan@wimadi.ang.af.mil

BGen Kerry G Denson
Army Deputy Adjutant General
Phone: 608-242-3010
e-mail: kerry.denson@wi.ngb.army.mil

Division of Criminal Justice
Department of Justice
PO Box 7857
Madison, WI 53707-7857
Phone: 608-266-1221
Fax: 608-267-2779
URL: www.doj.state.wi.us/dci

Description: Investigates crimes that are statewide in nature or importance. Special agents work closely with local officials in training, investigations, and prosecution.

James R Warren
Administrator

Emergency Management
2400 Wright Street

PO Box 7865
Madison, WI 53707-7865
Phone: 608-242-3232
Phone: 800-943-0003
Fax: 608-242-3247
URL: http://emergencymanagement.wi.gov

Description: Specializes in Hazard Mitigation, Warning & Communications, Emergency Police Services, Disaster Response & Recovery, Hazardous Materials & EPCRA, Radiological Emergency Preparedness, and Exercise & Training for the state of Wisconsin. Coordinates effective disaster response and recovery efforts in support of local government. Through planning, training and exercising we prepare our citizens and response personnel to minimize the loss of lives and property.

Johnnie Lee Smith
Administrator
Phone: 608-242-3210

Steve Peterson
Deputy Administrator
Phone: 608-242-3206
e-mail: steve.peterson@dma.state.wi.us

Sally Pagel
Administrative Services
Phone: 608-242-3236
e-mail: sally.pagel@dma.state.wi.us

Lori Getter
Public Information Officer
Phone: 608-242-3239
e-mail: lori.getter@dma.state.wi.us

Rob Rude
Response & Recovery Bureau Director
Phone: 608-242-3203
e-mail: rob.rude@dma.state.wi.us

Roxanne Gray
Hazard Mitigation Program
Phone: 608-242-3211
e-mail: roxanne.gray@dma.state.wi.us

Dallas Neville
Emergency Police Services
Phone: 608-444-0003
e-mail: dallas.neville@dma.state.wi.us

Keith Tveit
Emergency Fire Services
Phone: 608-220-6049
e-mail: keith.tveit@dma.state.wi.us

Kent Maclaughlin
Warning & Communications
Phone: 608-242-3250
e-mail: kent.maclaughlin@dma.state.wi.us

Steve Peterson
Planning & Preparedness Bureau Director
Phone: 608-242-3206
e-mail: steve.peterson@dma.state.wi.us

Diane Kleiboer
Natural Disasters Planning & Response
Phone: 608-242-3200
e-mail: diane.kleiboer@dma.state.wi.us

Jerry Haberl
Training & Exercise
Phone: 608-242-3213
e-mail: jerry.haberl@dma.state.wi.us

Jan Grunewald
EPCRA
Phone: 608-242-3224
e-mail: janice.grunewald@dma.state.wi.us

Bob Host
Radiological Emergency Preparedness
Phone: 608-242-3241
e-mail: bob.host@dma.state.wi.us

Bill Clare
Emergency Planning & Volunteer Program
Phone: 608-242-3220
e-mail: william.clare@dma.state.wi.us

Port of Green Bay/Brown County Port & Solid Waste Department
2561 S Broadway
Green Bay, WI 54304
Phone: 920-492-4950
Fax: 920-492-4957
URL: www.portofgreenbay.com
e-mail: bc_port@co.brown.wi.us

Description: Plan and promote harbor improvements to spur the economic development by stimulating trade and business through safe and cost-effective waterborne transportation activities while taking into consideration the needs of the community with regards to tourism and recreation.

Dean R Haen
Port Manager
e-mail: haen_dr@co.brown.wi.us

Public Health Division
PO Box 2659
Madison, WI 53701-2659
Phone: 608-266-1251
Fax: 608-267-2832
URL: www.dhfs.state.wi.us/aboutdhfs/dph/dph.htm

Description: Provides public health services and environmental and public health regulation. Programs include: environmental health, occupational health, family and community health, emergency medical services, and injury prevention, chronic disease prevention and health promotion and communicable diseases. Responsibilities also inclde: issuing birth, death, marraige and divorce certificates.

Sheri Johnson PhD
Administrator & State Health Officer
Phone: 414-227-4922
e-mail: johnssL1@dhfs.state.wi.us

Tom Sieger, MS
Deputy Administrator
Phone: 608-266-9780
e-mail: siegetl@dhfs.state.wi.us

Sandy Breitborde
Bureau Director, Bureau of Communicable Diseases and Preparedness

Phone: 608-267-9363
e-mail: breitsa@dhfs.state.wi.us

Chuck Warzecha
Bureau Director, Bureau of Environmental and Occupational Health
Phone: 608-264-9880
e-mail: warzecj@dhfs.state.wi.us

Larry Gilbertson
Bureau Director, Bureau of Local Health Support and Emergency Medical Services
Phone: 608-266-8154
e-mail: gilbelm@dhfs.state.wi.us

Patricia Guhleman
Bureau Director, Bureau of Health Information and Policy
Phone: 608-266-1347
e-mail: guhlepa@dhfs.state.wi.us

Susan Uttech
Bureau Director, Bureau of Community Health Promotion
Phone: 608-267-3561
e-mail: uttecsm@dhfs.state.wi.us

Transportation Department
PO Box 7910
4802 Sheboygan Ave
Madison, WI 53707-7910
Phone: 608-266-1113
Fax: 608-266-9912
URL: www.dot.wisconsin.gov

Frank Busalacchi
Secretary
Phone: 608-266-1114
e-mail: frank.busalacchi@dot.state.wi.us

Ruben Anthony Jr
Deputy Secretary
Phone: 608-266-1114
e-mail: ruben.anthony@dot.state.wi.us

David Collins
State Patrol Division
Phone: 608-266-0454
e-mail: david.collins@dot.state.wi.us

Peg Schmitt
Public Affairs Office
Phone: 608-266-7744
e-mail: peg.schmitt@dot.state.wi.us

Wisconsin Capitol Police
B2N State Capitol
Madison, WI 53702
Phone: 608-266-8797
Fax: 608-267-9343
URL: www.doa.state.wi.us
e-mail: doaweb@doa.state.wi.us

Description: The State Capitol Police Department is made up of seven work units - Investigative Court Services, Dignitary Services, Police & Security, Bike Unit, Horse Patrol, State Safety Office, and a Communication Unit.

Sgt Ruth Halm
Captain, Milwaukee Patrol Unit

David Heinle
Chief, Madison Unit
e-mail: david.heinle@wisconisin.gov

Wisconsin Chiefs of Police Association
River Ridge
1141 S Main Street
Shawano, WI 54166
Phone: 715-524-8283
URL: www.wichiefs.org
e-mail: info@wichiefs.org

Donald L Thaves
Executive Director
Phone: 715-524-8283
e-mail: dthaves@frontiernet.net

Daneil Vergin
President
Phone: 715-359-4202
e-mail: drvergin@mail.co.marathon.wi.us

STATE AGENCIES

Wyoming

Wyoming Main Homeland Security Office

122 W 25th Street, 1st Floor E
Herschler Building
Cheyenne, WY 82002
Phone: 307-777-4663
Fax: 307-635-6017
URL: http://wyohomelandsecurity.state.wy.us

Dave Freudenthal
Governor
Phone: 307-777-7434
e-mail: governor@missc.state.wy.us

Max Maxfield
Secretary of State
Phone: 307-777-7378

Joe Moore
Director Homeland Security
Phone: 307-777-4663

Patrick J Crank
Attorney General
Phone: 307-777-7841

Aeronautics Division

Transportation Department
200 East 8th Avenue
Cheyenne, WY 82001
Phone: 307-777-3952
Fax: 307-777-7352
URL: www.dot.state.wy.us

Description: Works in conjunction with members of the Aeronautics Commission to support aviation and publicly-owned airports in the state. The division is made up of the Airports section and the Operations section.

Shelly Reams
Administrator
Phone: 307-777-3953
e-mail: sreams@dot.state.wy.us

Tom Gould
Flight Operations Manager
Phone: 307-777-3955

Christy Wilson
Planning & Budgeting
Phone: 307-777-3956

Cheryl Bean
Engineering
Phone: 307-777-3960

Jamie Conrad
Flight Scheduling
Phone: 307-777-3951

Agriculture Department

2219 Carey Avenue
Cheyenne, WY 82002-0100
Phone: 307-777-7321
Fax: 307-777-6593
URL: http://wyagric.state.wy.us
e-mail: wda@state.wy.us

Description: To assists the citizens of Wyoming to live safe and healthy lives, promote and preserve agricultural community, be responsible stewards of natural resources, and achieve integrity in the marketplace.

John Etchepare
Director
Phone: 307-777-6569
e-mail: jetche@state.wy.us

Jason Fearnehough
Deputy Director
Phone: 307-777-6591
e-mail: jfearn@state.wy.us

Leanne Stevenson
Natural Resources Manager
Phone: 307-777-6579
e-mail: lsteve@state.wy.us

Dean Finkenbinder
Consumer Health Services Manager
Phone: 307-777-6587
e-mail: dfinke@state.wy.us

Mike Leath
Laboratory Manager/State Chemist
e-mail: mleath@wyaslab.net

Roy Reichenbach
Manager Technical Services
Phone: 307-777-6590
e-mail: rreich@state.wy.us

Division of Criminal Investigation

316 W 22nd Street
Cheyenne, WY 82002
Phone: 307-777-7181
Fax: 307-777-7252
URL: http://attorneygeneral.state.wy.us/dci
e-mail: dciwebmaster@dci.wyo.gov

Description: Created in 1973 and part of the Wyoming Attorney General, it employs 30 Special Agents.

Forrest C Bright
Director

Kebin Haller
Deputy Director, Operations
Phone: 307-777-7181

Stephen Holloway
Deputy Director, Crime Lab
Phone: 307-777-7181

Kevin R Smith
Records & Communications
Phone: 307-777-7181

Emergency Medical Services
Health Department
Hathaway Building
4th Floor
Cheyenne, WY 82002
Phone: 307-777-7955
Phone: 888-228-8996
Fax: 307-777-5639
URL: http://wdhfs.state.wy.us/ems

Jim Mayberry
Program Manager
e-mail: jmaybe@state.wy.us

Skip Johnson
Senior Trainer, State Emergency Response Commission Rep
e-mail: sjohns@state.wy.us

Carol Zorna
Emergency Medical Services for Children
e-mail: czorna@state.wy.us

Health Department
401 Hathaway Building
Cheyenne, WY 82002
Phone: 307-777-7656
Phone: 866-571-0944
Fax: 307-777-7439
URL: http://wdh.state.wy.us

Description: Promotes, protects, and enhances the health of all Wyoming citizens, as well as administers programs to maintain that health.

Dr Brent Sherard
Director/State Health Officer
Phone: 307-777-7656

Ginny Mahoney
Chief of Staff

Traci Lindsten
Information Technology

Molly Brunner
Community & Rural Health Division

Kim Deti
Public Information Officer

Highway Patrol Division
5300 Bishop Boulevard
Cheyenne, WY 82009-3340
Phone: 307-777-4301
Fax: 307-777-3877

URL: http://whp.state.wy.us
e-mail: john.townsend@dot.state.wy.us

Colonel Sam Powell
Administrator

Lt Colonel Jess Oyler
Operations Commander

Major John Butler
Field Operations Commander

National Guard
5500 Bishop Boulevard
Cheyenne, WY 82009-3320
Phone: 307-772-5253
Phone: 307-772-5229
Fax: 307-772-5010
URL: www.wy.ngb.army.mil/default.asp

Description: Composed of the Army and Air National Guard, the Oregon Trail State Veterans Cementery, and the Wyoming Veterans Commission. The Air and Army National Guard has a dual (federal and state) mission. The Governor is the Commander-in-Chief of the Wyoming Army and Air National Guard in all matters relating to the Guard's state mission. The Adjutant General of Wyoming is responsible to the Governor for carrying out the mission of the state's National Guard. Command of the National Guard is exercised by the Adjutant General through Assistant Adjutant General and the Army and Air National Guard.

Major General Edward L Wright
Adjutant General
Phone: 307-772-5234
e-mail: jamie.ciz@us.army.mil

BGen Don Haught
Assistant Adjutant General, Air
Phone: 307-772-5293
e-mail: 153.pa@wychey.ang.af.mil

BGen Olin O Oedekoeven
Assistant Adjutant General, Army
Phone: 307-772-5491

Deidre Forster
Public Information/Affairs Officer
Phone: 307-772-5253
e-mail: deidre.forster@us.army.mil

Preventative Health & Safety/Epidemiology Program
6101 Yellowstone Road
Qwest Building, Suite 510
Cheyenne, WY 82002
Phone: 307-777-7172
Phone: 888-996-9104
Fax: 307-777-5402
e-mail: lfresq2@state.wy.us

Description: The Infectious Disease Epidemiology Program oversees the surveillance and control of communicable diseases throughout the state. It provides analytical and medical consultations for the Preventative Health & Safety Division.

Tracy Murphy
State Epidemiologist
Phone: 307-777-7716
e-mail: tmurph@state.wy.us

Dr Joe Grandpre
Deputy State Epidemiologist
Phone: 307-777-8654
e-mail: jgrand@state.wy.us

Terry Creekmoore
Vectorborne Disease Surveillance Coordinator
Phone: 307-742-6638
e-mail: tcreek@state.wy.us

Public Health & Terrorism Prepardness Program
Health Department
2300 Capitol Avenue
Hathaway Building, 4th Floor
Cheyenne, WY 82002
Phone: 307-777-5778
Phone: 888-996-9104
Fax: 307-777-6345
URL: http://wdh.state.wy.us/hazards/index.asp

Description: Develop emergency ready public health departments by upgrading, integrating and evaluating state and local public health preparedness for and response to terrorism, pandemic influenza and other public health emergencies with federal, state, local and tribal governments, the private sector, and non-governmental organizations.

James McCameron
Director
e-mail: jmccam@state.wy.us

Dr Richard Harris
Public Health Laboratory

Transportation Department
5300 Bishop Boulevard
Cheyenne, WY 82009
Phone: 307-777-4375
Fax: 307-777-4289
URL: www.dot.state.wy.us

Description: The agency's major responsibilities include planning and supervising road improvement work, maintaining the roads, providing law enforcement on the highways, and supporting airports and aviation in the state.

John Cox
Director
Phone: 307-777-4484
e-mail: john.cox@dot.state.wy.us

Del McOmie
Chief Engineer
Phone: 307-777-4484
e-mail: del.mcomie@dot.state.wy.us

Bob Stauffacher
Compliance & Investigation
Phone: 307-777-3849
e-mail: bob.stauffacher@dot.state.wy.us

Pat Collins
Engineering & Planning, Asst Chief Engineer
Phone: 307-777-4484
e-mail: pat.collins@dot.state.wy.us

Matt Carlson
Highway Safety

Phone: 307-777-4450
e-mail: matt.carlson@dot.state.wy.us

Vince Garcia
Intelligent Transportation Systems
Phone: 307-777-4231
e-mail: vince.garcia@dot.state.wy.us

Richard Douglass
Local Government Coordinator
Phone: 307-777-4384
e-mail: rich.douglass@dot.state.wy.us

Richard Smith
Port of Entry
Phone: 307-777-4878
e-mail: richard.smith@dot.state.wy.us

Doug McGee
Public Affairs Manager
Phone: 307-777-4010
e-mail: doug.mcgee@dot.state.wy.us

Wyoming Sheriffs & Police Chiefs Association
PO Box 605
Gillette, WY 82717
Phone: 307-682-8949
URL: www.wascop.com

Description: This association works towards the advancement of the skills and knowledge of police executives, thus being able to strengthen the ability to meet the demands of providing quality and professional law enforcement.

Byron Oedekoven
Executive Director
e-mail: byrono@direcway.com

Listing of Homeland Security Products & Services

The following list of 753 products and services are those provided by the 3,238 companies that follow this listing. These companies are indexed in the Products & Sevices Index at the back of the book.

A

Absorbents
Access Control
Access Control: Digital Touchpad
Access Control: Locking Systems
Access Control: Optical
Access Control: Rotating Devices
Access Control: Weatherproof Digital Keypads
Accountability Services
Air Analyzers
Air Cleaning Systems
Air Support & Logistics
Air Support: Purifying Respirators
Air Support: Airline Passenger Units
Air Support: Fire Fighting Breathing Apparatus
Air Support: Self Contained Breathing Apparatus
Air Systems
Aircraft Design
Aircraft Security Systems
Alarms: Systems
Alarms: Annunciator Panel
Alarms: Door
Alarms: Environmental
Alarms: High Security
Alarms: Intrusion
Alarms: Monitoring
Alarms: Perimeter
Alarms: Personal
Alarms: Remote Monitoring
Alarms: Request to Exit
Alarms: Sealed Hold Up
Alarms: Panic Hardware
Alarms: Wireless
Alarms: Wrong Direction
Aluminum Extruded Components
Annunciators
Annunciators: Multi-zone
Annunciators: Printers
Anti-counterfeiting Devices
Anti-pilferage Seals
Area-of-rescue Systems
Armored Body Inserts

Armored Cars
Armored Door & Briefcase Inserts
Armored Door Loops
Armored Helicopter Seats
Armored Passenger Vehicles
Armored Ships
Audio Intelligence Equipment
Audio Noise Removal & Enhancements
Audio Recording Analysis
Audio Visual Door Entry Systems
Audio Visual Intercoms
Audio Visual Signaling Systems
Authentication Software
Authentication Token Cards
Automated Notification System

B

Backup Recovery Centers
Badges
Badge & Coded Card Services
Badge Holders
Ballistic-resistant Building Panels
Ballistic-resistant Clipboards
Ballistic-resistant Doors & Windows
Ballistic-resistant Lighting
Ballistic-resistant Plates
Ballistic-resistant Shields
Ballistic-resistant Vests
Bar Code Readers
Bar Codes
Barbed Wire
Base Stations
Battery Powered Microphones
Behavior & Threat Assessment
Bi-National Support Services
Bins: Confiscated Items
Biohazard Recovery
Biometric Identification Mangement
Biometric Resources
Biometric Security Systems
Biometric Verification Device
Board-up Services
Bolt & Cable Seals
Bomb Bins

Bomb Blankets
Bomb Countermeasures
Bomb Disposal Equipment
Bomb Threat Prevention
Breathalyzers
Building Automation Products
Building Control
Bulletproof Protection
Bulletproof Vehicles
Bullet-resistant Doors & Frames
Bullet-resistant Fiberglass
Bullet-resistant Materials
Bullet-resistant Systems
Bunker Gear
Business Continuity Planning
Button Memory

C

Cabinets: Narcotics
Cabinets: Security
Cabinets: Siren
Cables
Cameras: Concealed
Cameras: Fire Fighting
Cameras: ID Badge
Cameras: Microminiature
Cameras: Millimeter Wave
Cameras: Passport/Mugshot
Cameras: Simulated Video
Cameras: Vehicle Rearview
Cameras: Wireless
Card Access Systems
Card Scan Devices
Card Transmitters & Receivers
Cash Drop Boxes
Cellular Scrambling
Central Station Monitoring
Chain Closure Systems
Chemical Defense Weapons
Classroom Protection
Clean-up Kits
Clip Straps
Closed Circuit Television
Closed Circuit Video Equipment

Coded Card Systems

Command Center Design

Communications Systems

Computer Components

Computer Forensics

Computer Identification Systems

Computer Programming

Computer Security

Computer Theft Protection

Confined Space Safety Gear & Equipment

Connectors

Consulting: Anti-Fraud Training and Education

Consulting: Aircraft Security

Consulting: Bomb Awareness

Consulting: Communications

Consulting: Counterterrorism

Consulting: Economic Reform

Consulting: Engineering Services

Consulting: Environmental Services

Consulting: Fire Alarm

Consulting: Government & Public Affairs

Consulting: Information Technology

Consulting: Management

Consulting: Office Automation

Consulting: Security

Consulting: Surveillance

Containers

Containers: Blast Mitigation

Containers: Weapons Storage

Content Management

Contingency Planning

Control Devices

Counterespionage

Countersurveillance

Counterfeit Identification

Counting Systems: Body & Traffic

Courier Services

Courtroom Protection

Crash Barriers

Crime Forecasting

Crime Scene Cleanup

Crime Scene Investigation Equipment

Crisis Management

Critical Condition Monitoring Systems

Cryptographic Development Kits

Cryptographic Devices

Cylinder Guard Rings

D

Data Communication Systems

Data Recovery Services

Data Storage Architecture

Debugging Services

Decals

Detection Systems: Biological

Detection Systems: Bistatic Microwave

Detection Systems: Bugs

Detection Systems: Carbon Monoxide

Detection Systems: Chemical

Detection Systems: Contraband, Explosives & Drugs

Detection Systems: Digital Motion

Detection Systems: Flames

Detection Systems: Gas

Detection Systems: Glass Break

Detection Systems: Hazardous Gas & Water

Detection Systems: Intrusion

Detection Systems: Life Safety

Detection Systems: Metal

Detection Systems: Motion

Detection Systems: Multi-Sensor

Detection Systems: Piezoelectric

Detection Systems: Portable Mobile

Detection Systems: Proximity

Detection Systems: Radio Telemetry

Detection Systems: Smoke

Detection Systems: Tailgate

Detection Systems: Telephone Tap

Detection Systems: Trace

Detection Systems: Weapons

Detection Systems: X-Ray

Detection Systems: Video

Detection Systems: Video Motion

Detection Systems: Walkthrough

Detectors & Monitors

Detention Facility Security Systems

Deterrance Systems

Digital & Analog Recorders

Digital Emergency & Information Phones

Digital Hardware & Software

Digital Imaging

Digital Indentification Systems

Digital Intercom Systems

Digital Keypads

Digital Security Systems

Digital Video Badging

Digital Video Encoders

Digital Video Recorders

Digital Wireless Communication

Disaster Recovery Services

Disaster Response Products

Document Destruction

Document Management

Doors: Automatic Revolving

Doors: Balanced

Doors: Extra Large Revolving

Doors: Manual Revolving

Doors: Pivot/Swing

Doors: Security Revolving

Door Closers

Door Closers: Concealed

Drill Bits

Drive-up Bank Windows

Drug Testing Services

E

E-commerce Safeguards & Security

Egress Control

Egress Control: Delayed

Electric Gates

Electric Strikes

Electric Security Sytems

Electrical Safety

Electro-magnetic Shielding Systems

Electronic Asset Disposal

Electronic Countermeasures

Electronic Photo Identification Systems

Electronic Radios & Scanners

Electronic Security for Vehicles

Electronic Security Systems

Electronic Security Systems Integration

Electronic Transponders

Electronic Vibration Detection

Electronic Visitor Management Software

Electronic Wire & Cable

Elevator Signal Fixtures

E-mail Security

E-mail Threat Software

Emergency Access Phones

Emergency Assistance

Emergency Communications Systems

Emergency Evacuation Equipment

Emergency Exits & Lights

Emergency Food & Water

Emergency Medical Training Aids

Emergency Phones & Intercoms

Emergency Preparedness & Response

Listing of Homeland Security Products & Services

Emergency Pull Stations
Emergency Response Systems
Emergency Telephones
Employee Background Screening
Enclosures for Security Monitoring
Encryption: Public Key
Encryption Systems
Energy Storage Systems
Engraving Machines
Entry Control & Communications Systems
Environmental Cleanup
Environmental Monitoring
Environmental Security Products
Evacuation Systems
Event Logistics
Exit Devices
Expert Witness Services
Expert Witness Services: Firearms
Explosive Blast Containment
Explosive Handling Systems
Eye Protection

F

Face Recognition Technology
Facility Surveys
Fencing
Face Protection
Fiber Optic Cable Security Systems
Fiber Optic Phone Lines
Fiber Optic Transmission Products
Financial Investment
Fingerprint Identification
Fingerscan Readers
Fire Alarm Control Panels
Fire Alarm Peripherals
Fire Alarms Radio Controlled
Fire Alarm Printers
Fire Alarm Systems
Fire Alarms
Fire Alarm Exit Doors
Fire Extinguishers
Fire Fighting Cameras
Fire Monitoring Systems
Fire Panels
Fire Protection
Fire Protection: Hazard
Fire Safe Waste Receptacles
Fire Sprinklers
Fire Suppression

Fire Systems
Firearms Safety Devices
First Aid Health Products
Fixed Dome Surveillance Systems
Flashlights & Lanterns
Foam 3-D Humanoid Targets
Forensic Analysis Services
Forensic Analysts, Structures
Forensic Engineering

G

GPS Surveillance Equipment
Gates
Gates: Automatic
Gates: Operators
Gates: Remote Control
Gear Bags & Storage
Geographical Information Systems
Global Positioning Systems
Government Security Products
Graphic Panels
Grills
Guard Booths & Shelters
Guard Equipment & Supplies
Guard Tour Management & Verification
Guided Weapon Design

H

Hand Protection
Handwriting Examination
Hardware Security
Hardwired Loss Prevention
HazMat Products
Hearing Protection
Helmets
Hijacking Prevention
Hostage Negotiation

I

Identification Badge: Cameras
Identification Badge: Holders
Identification Badge: Systems
Identification Card: Access
Identification Card: Alien
Identification Card: Printers
Identification Card: Scanners
Identification Card: Systems
Identification Card: Transmitters & Receivers

Identification Equipment
Industrial Machine Vision Systems
Industrial Security Devices
Information & Security Awareness
Information Systems Maintenance
Information Technology Security
Infrared Application Equipment
Infrared Lighting Systems
Infrared Sensors
Infrared Tags
Infrared Thermal Imagers
Infrared Viewers
Inkless Fingerprint Systems
Instant Messaging Services
Insurance: Crime & Cargo
Insurance: Network Security
Insurance: Security
Intelligent Node Controllers
Intelligent Optical Turnstiles
Intelligent Repeaters
Intelligent Transportation Systems
Intercom Systems
Interior Communications Systems
Internet-Based Reporting Services
Internet Security Systems
Intrusion & Fire Control Panels
Investigative Services
Iris Recognition Technology

K

Key Control Equipment
Key Control: Mechanical & Mechatronic Systems
Key Control: Pads
Key Control: Switches
Key Control: Tracking Systems
Keyless Entry System
Kits: Development

L

Laminated Composites
Laminated Pouches
Lasers
Lasergrips
Law Enforcement
License Plate Reading
Lighting Control
Lighting Equipment
Lightning & Noise Protection

Lockers
Locking Magnets
Locks
Locks: Cabinets
Locks: Cam
Locks: Deadbolts
Locks: Doors
Locks: Industrial
Locks: Padlocks
Logistics Support Services
Long-range Radio Transmitters
Loss & Risk Prevention
Loudspeakers
Low Power Electronic Designs
Low Voltage Wire & Cable

M

Magnetic Contacts
Magnetic Strip Encoders & Readers
Magnets
Marketing and Design
Market Intrusions
Marking Products
Material Storage: Hazardous
Mating Receptacles
Mechanical Security Systems
Mechanical Testing & Design
Media Restoration
Message Authentification
Message Centers
Metal Marking Equipment
Microphones
Microwave Transmission Radios
Military Aircraft
Military Paper Targets
Military Products Engineering & Design
Military Systems
Mobile Communications
Mobile Data Collection & Reporting
Mobile Recovery Communication
   Systems
Motorized Dome Surveillance Systems
Mounting Systems for Audio Video

N

Network Security Protection
Night Vision Equipment
Night Vision Goggles
Noise Masking &Testing Equipment

Nonalarmed Panic Hardware
Nonlinear Junction Detectors
Nuclear Site Security
Nurse Call System
Nylon Bomber Jackets
Nylon Holsters & Belts

O

Occupational Violence Prevention
Off-site Data Storage
On-site Drug Testing Kits
Operations Management Software
Optical Devices
Optical Turnstiles
Overseas Security Services

P

Paging Switchers
Paging Systems
Paging Transmitters
Panic Devices
Panic Exit Devices
Paper Handling Equipment
Parking Control Systems
Penetration Testing
Perimeter Fencing
Perimeter Protection Systems
Perimeter Security Systems
Peripherals
Personal Defense Sprays
Personal Protection Devices
Personnel Database Integration
Personnel Placement
Phantom Powered Microphones
Photo Identification Supplies
Photo Identification Systems
Photoelectric Beams
Physical Search Equipment
Physical Security Products
Pneumatic Controls
Pocket Scopes
Police Equipment
Police Paper Targets
Polygraph Services
Portable Two-way Radios
Portable X-ray Systems
Power Failure Systems
Preventive Security
Process Equipment Control Systems

Protective Apparel
Protective Signaling Services
Proximity Cards
Proximity Readers
Psychological Profiling
Public Address & Paging Systems
Public Address Horns
Push-button Controls
Push-button Entry

Q

Quality Management Solutions

R

Radiation Safety Surveys
Radio Communications Systems
Radio Frequency Identification
   Equipment
Radio Frequency Links
Radio Frequency Sweeps
Radio Spectrum Analyzers
Razor Ribbon
Real-time Locating & Reporting
Recess Contacts
Reed Devices
Reed Switches
Relays
Releasing Control Panels
Remote Alarm Monitoring
Remote Control Lighting
Remote Site Management
Remote Video Transmission
Renewable Energy Inverters
Repeaters
Reprogrammable Keys and Tokens
Resource Management Systems
Respiratory Protection Equipment
Riot Gear
Riot Prevention
Risk Assessment
Risk Management

S

Safety Surveys
Safes: High Security
Safes: Protection
Sampling Systems
Satellites
Scales

Listing of Homeland Security Products & Services

Scanners
Scanners: Body Orifice
Scanners: Full Body
Scanners: X-Ray
Screening Devices
Screening: X-Ray
Secure Banking
Secure Communications Systems
Secure Documents
Secure Faxes
Secure Storage Facilities
Secure Telephones
Secure Voice Quality
Security Associations
Security Banking Equipment
Security Barriers
Security Boxes
Security Cameras
Security Consultants
Security Conventions
Security Design
Security Directories
Security Equipment Rental
Security Evaluations
Security Furniture Systems
Security Glass
Security Glazing
Security Hardware
Security Implementation Services
Security Information Management Software
Security Labels
Security Management Consulting
Security Management Products
Security Officers
Security Pass-through Transaction Drawers
Security Photo ID Pouches
Security Planning
Security Products: Buried
Security Products: Fence Mounted
Security Products: Structural
Security Products: Underwater
Security Programs
Security Publishing
Security Revolving Doors
Security Screens/Doors
Security Seals
Security Steel Doors
Security Surveys
Security System Integration

Security Systems
Security Systems for Aircraft
Security Systems Monitoring
Security Tapes/Seals
Security Think Tanks
Security Training
Security Uniforms
Security Window Film
Security Windows/Doors/Panels
Security Windows/Skylights/Wall Systems
Security/Safety Systems
Seismic & Fence Sensors
Self-contained Products
Self-expiring Parking Permits
Self-expiring Wristbands
Sensors: Electronic
Sensors: Fiber Optic
Sensors: Interior Intrusion
Sensors: Intrusion
Sensors: Microwave
Sensors: Motion
Sensors: Motion Door Release
Sensors: Systems
Sensors: Shock
Sensors: Toxic Vapor
Sensors: Vibration
Shielded & Secure Facilities
Signature & Photo Capture Devices
Sign-in Systems
Signs
Simulation Services & Training
Single Fiber Transmission Products
Sirens
Smart Card Readers
Smart Cards
Smart Data Repeaters
Smoke & Light Intruder Deterrent Systems
Software: Access Control
Software: Anti Virus
Software: Auditing
Software: Biometrics
Software: Computer
Software: Communication
Software: Content Security
Software: Crash Management
Software: Data Access
Software: Encryption
Software: Identification Badging
Software: Information Management

Software: Lobby Security
Software: Network Security
Software: Photo Identification
Software: Project Management
Software: Public Safety
Software: Publishing
Software: Risk Analysis
Software: Safety/Security Equipment
Software: Surveillance
Software: Training
Software: Web-based Security
Software: Work Station Security
Soil Contacts
Specification
Speech & Transcript Clarification
Speech Processors
Spill Kits
Sprinkler Systems
Status Indicators
Stored Energy Solutions
Strike & Labor Disruption Protection
Strobes
Structured Wiring Systems
Supervised Wireless Control Panels & Components
Supervised Wireless Security Systems
Surface Reeds
Surge Protection Devices
Surveillance: Audio Countermeasures
Surveillance: Audio
Surveillance: Audio Visual
Surveillance: Bulletproof Article
Surveillance: Cellular & Pager
Surveillance: Countermeasures
Surveillance: Covert Audio
Surveillance: Covert Video
Surveillance: Digital Video
Surveillance: Disease
Surveillance: Video
Surveillance: Portable & Fixed Equipment
Surveillance: Vehicles
Systems Design & Development
Systems Integration

T

Tactical Equipment
Tamper-evident Seals
Tamper-resistant Devices
Tape Recording Authentification

Telecommunications Security & Support
Telemetry Links
Telephone Access for Gates & Elevators
Telephone Analyzers
Telephone Entry Systems
Telephone Line Fault Monitors
Telephone Scramblers
Temperature Monitoring
Terrorism Prevention
Thermal & Dye-Sublimation Printers
Thermal Imaging
Threat Assessments
Threat Recordings
Time & Attendance Monitoring
Time Controllers
Time Display Products
Touch Pads
Touch Screens
Tracking & Locating Systems
Traffic Analysis
Traffic Control
Traffic Safety Devices
Training: Computer
Training: Counterterrorism
Training: Defensive Tactics
Training: Driving
Training: Executive Protection
Training: Explosives Identification
Training: Instructional Design
Training: Interviewing & Interrogation
Training: Management Systems

Training: Public Safety
Training: Security Guards
Training: Security Videos
Training: Smart Cards
Training: Workplace Violence Prevention
Transportation
Transportation: Air & Ground
Trauma Plates
Travel Security
Truth Verification Testing
Turnstiles
Two-way Radios

U

Ultraminiature Microphones
Ultrasensitive Microphones
Ultrasonic Fingerprint Scanners
Uniforms
Uninterruptible Power Systems
Universal Receivers
Universal Transmitters

V

Vandal-resistant Stations
Vehicle Hijacking Prevention
Vehicle Location Systems
Vehicle Loop Sensors
Vehicle Rearview Camera Systems
Vehicle Tracking Equipment
Vehicular Seismic Sensors

Video Communication Systems
Video Conferencing Systems
Video Compression Products
Video Imaging
Video Intercom Systems
Video Transmission Command & Control
Visitor Management
Voice Communication Services
Voice Dialers
Voice Identification
Voice Logging Recorders
Voice Scramblers
Voice-activated Recorders
Vulnerability Studies & Security
    Assessments

W

Weapons Racks
Window Film
Wireless Concealed Video Cameras
Wireless Hardwired Emergency Call Box
    Systems
Wireless Transmitters & Receivers
Workstation Security Software

X

X-ray Security Systems